Propositions

To the thesis *Rigorous Scrutiny versus Marginal*

1. International and EU asylum law require an inde   ...cial
    scrutiny comprising facts and law. National courts   ... make an independent
    determination of the disputed facts and of the credibility of a claimant. National courts
    must also be able to use investigative powers whenever they consider this necessary to
    bring further clarification to the facts. National courts may never be precluded from de-
    termining 'the central issue in dispute'.

2. Thorough national judicial investigations aimed at finding the truth have nothing to do
    with helping one of the parties, but have to do with judicial independence and impartiali-
    ty.

3. Marginal national judicial review of the credibility of asylum seekers' accounts will often
    be at variance with the full jurisdiction requirement flowing from Articles 6 ECHR and
    47 of the EU Charter, as it will preclude the national court from determining 'the central
    issue in dispute'.

4. The HRC, the ComAT and the ECtHR have the free choice to apply an intense and full
    factual scrutiny or, instead, rely on the facts as presented by the respondent State. Na-
    tional asylum courts should similarly at least have a fully free choice to apply, in the spe-
    cific cases coming before them, either full factual scrutiny or a somewhat more deferent
    approach towards the determination of the facts.

5. The standards on judicial scrutiny and evidence as applied by the ECtHR in cases con-
    cerning the expulsion of asylum seekers are, as minimum norms, binding on national asy-
    lum courts. Whenever a particular standard developed by the UNHCR, the HRC, the
    ComAT or the CJEU offers higher protection to the asylum seekers, national asylum
    courts must use the standard offering the highest protection.

6. The HRC, the ComAT, the ECtHR and the CJEU have all made clear that evidence,
    including medical evidence, presented by the applicant for asylum must be taken seriously
    and examined carefully by the national authorities, including national courts. *Singh v. Bel-
    gium* (ECtHR, 2012) is the perfect illustration of this principle.

7. Unfortunately, many views of the HRC and the ComAT offer little to no guidance to
    national asylum courts on the burden of proof, the assessment of credibility, and the ad-
    mission and evaluation of evidence. It is crucial for national asylum courts to receive
    clearer guidance from the HRC and the ComAT on those aspects of evidence. Only then
    will national asylum courts be truly able to live up to the obligations accepted by the
    States Parties to relevant treaties.

8. EU law causes a transformation in legal status of existing standards on evidence and
    judicial scrutiny contained in international asylum law by virtue of their incorporation in-
    to EU law, via Articles 18, 19, 47, 52(3) and 53 of the EU Charter of Fundamental
    Rights. This is a transformation from non-binding principles into more important rules
    which must be respected (the standards developed by the UNHCR), from intergovern-
    mental international law into binding primary supranational EU law (the standards devel-
    oped by the ECtHR) and from intergovernmental international law into important
    sources of inspiration for binding EU law (the standards developed by the HRC and the
    ComAT). National asylum courts can no longer disregard or discard these standards, as
    that would amount to a violation of the EU Charter, which is binding primary suprana-
    tional EU law.

9. The added value of EU asylum law is also that Article 6 ECHR on a fair hearing is – via Article 47 of the Charter – now fully applicable to national asylum court proceedings. Article 6 ECHR contains important specific standards on the intensity of judicial scrutiny to be applied by national courts, as well as standards on handling evidence.

10. Under international and EU asylum law, there are no procedural barriers to the admissibility of evidence.

11. Given the positions of the HRC, the ComAT, the ECtHR and the UNHCR on the required quantity of evidence, national (judicial) practices demanding evidence in corroboration of more than the core of the flight narrative are not allowed.

12. In repeat asylum cases a *nova*-test is in itself not problematic from the viewpoint of international and EU asylum law. National courts, however, should not fully or formally exclude evidence just because it should have been presented at an earlier moment, in a previous asylum procedure. In a significant number of cases dealt with by the ECtHR and the ComAT, crucial evidence was submitted for the first time in the context of repeat national asylum proceedings, and the ECtHR and the ComAT did not regard this as problematic *per se*.

13. The CJEU (*N.S. and Others*, 2011) and the ECtHR (*M.S.S. v. Belgium and Greece*, 2011) have put a firm restriction on the presumption of treaty compliance in Dublin cases. As soon as information to the contrary becomes available – either because the applicant has submitted this information or because the national authorities are familiar with it or should be familiar with it – the national authorities, including the courts, must assess whether the asylum procedure in the intermediary EU Member State affords 'sufficient guarantees' and whether living conditions are compliant with the ECHR and EU law.

14. When processing asylum appeals in fast-track national judicial proceedings, national courts must be aware that the safeguards of national judicial protection should never be sacrificed to speed. The national court must at all times remain able to perform a thorough review on the merits of the claim.

15. Under international and EU asylum law, reasonable national time limits for submitting statements and evidence will normally not be problematic. However, there must be room for national courts to be flexible when the circumstances of the case so require.

16. Under international and EU asylum law, belated presentation of evidence corroborating statements is seen as one among many other relevant factors. Belated presentation of evidence is – as a factor alone and in itself – not problematic

Rigorous Scrutiny versus Marginal Review

Standards on judicial scrutiny and evidence
in international and European asylum law

Dana Baldinger

Rigorous Scrutiny versus Marginal Review

Standards on judicial scrutiny and evidence
in international and European asylum law

Proefschrift

ter verkrijging van de graad van doctor
aan de Radboud Universiteit Nijmegen
op gezag van de rector magnificus
prof.mr. S.C.J.J. Kortmann
volgens besluit van het College van Decanen
in het openbaar te verdedigen op
dinsdag 16 april 2013
om 10.30 uur precies
door
Helena Johanna Margo Baldinger
geboren op 7 januari 1969
te Amsterdam

Promotores:
prof. dr. E. Guild
prof. mr. C.A. Groenendijk

Manuscriptcommissie:
prof. mr. A.B. Terlouw
prof. mr. R. Fernhout
prof. mr. B.E.P. Myjer (Vrije Universiteit Amsterdam)

ISBN 978-90-5850-952-9

Omslagbeeld: Suzan Baldinger, 2013

Lay-out: Hannie van de Put, CMR

Printed by: Wolf Legal Publishers

'Insufficient facts will often result in the judge having to assess the reliability of the account given by the person concerned. Bearing in mind the subjective elements which are inherent in making such an assessment, judges will to a certain extent, in an area where the most fundamental human rights are at stake, find themselves on thin ice. Given what is at stake, a conclusion that an asylum-seeker's account is not credible should therefore be based on a thorough investigation of the facts and be accompanied by adequate reasoning.'

Judge Thomassen of the European Court of Human Rights in her concurring opinion to *Said v. the Netherlands* (2005).

Preface

Two judgments of the European Court of Human Rights (ECtHR) formed the immediate reason for my embarking upon this research project. These were the judgments in the cases of *Said v. the Netherlands* (ECtHR, *Said v. the* Netherlands, 5 July 2005, Appl. No. 2345/02) and *Salah Sheekh v. the Netherlands* (ECtHR, *Salah Sheekh v. the Netherlands*, 11 January 2007, Appl. No. 1948/04). In both cases, the District Court of Amsterdam, where I had just started working as an immigration and asylum judge, functioned as the national first instance court. In both cases it approved the stance of the administration that there was no reason to grant asylum protection to the individuals concerned. The ECtHR reached the opposite conclusion and assumed in both cases that there were substantial grounds for believing that upon expulsion there was a real risk that the individuals would be subjected to torture or cruel, inhuman or degrading treatment in their country of origin and that, as a result, their expulsion would lead to a violation of Article 3 of the European Convention on Human Rights (ECHR).

There were clear signs that the ECtHR was dissatisfied with the level of judicial scrutiny offered at national level in the Netherlands. This worried and troubled me. Together with a colleague from the Amsterdam Court, I analysed a number of the ECtHR's well-known judgments in expulsion cases concerning asylum seekers to find out in a more precise way how this international Court assessed the risk. We discovered significant differences between the judicial practice applied at an international level and our own national judicial practice. First, the intensity or thoroughness of the judicial scrutiny seemed to be different. Second, issues of evidence, such as the admission and evaluation of evidence, were approached and resolved in very different ways at international and national level. This small-scale investigation made me very anxious to find out in a more precise way what lessons on both aspects – intensity of judicial scrutiny and evidence – could and should be drawn from the ECHR. I also became anxious to find out whether other relevant international treaties and EU asylum law contained concrete instructions on evidentiary issues and on judicial scrutiny. That is how the idea to embark upon this research project was born.

In 2007, I was invited to a seminar on the EU Family Reunification Directive in Nijmegen organised by the Centre for Migration Law (CMR) to speak as a national judge about the application of the Directive in national Dutch case law. It was there that I met Elspeth Guild and Kees Groenendijk, and we first spoke about my plan for a PhD project on evidence and judicial scrutiny in international and European asylum law. They reacted with great enthusiasm and felt that a book on this topic would be very welcome. It was soon after these meetings that I handed in a concrete plan to Elspeth and Kees and that we started working on the project.

I wish to express my deep gratitude to Elspeth Guild and Kees Groenendijk for supervising, coaching and inspiring me throughout the entire research process. The beginning was not easy as I was accustomed to thinking, working and writing as a judge, and academic writing was a completely new challenge for me. But our confidence grew with each new chapter I handed in. Thanks to the constructive criticism I received from Elspeth and Kees, every supervision meeting gave me great inspiration and new energy to go on and to restructure and rewrite the chapters of this book time and again. I learned so many different things during the process of writing this book, both as a PhD student and as a judge. I discovered vast bodies of case law which I had, in fact, not been very familiar with before: the case law of the Human Rights Committee, the Committee against Torture and the Court of Justice of the European Union. I learned how to work with extensive EU law data bases such as EUR-lex and PreLex. I learned a lot about the relationship between international and European asylum law and I discovered the impact of EU law on national asylum procedures and court proceedings in particular.

I want to say a sincere thank you to Carla Eradus, President of the District Court of Amsterdam, for making it possible to combine my work as a judge with writing this book, and to all my colleagues in the administrative law section and the criminal law section of the District Court of Amsterdam for expressing their interest in my research work and supporting me from beginning to end.

Marcelle Reneman, Karen Geertsema and Hannah Helmink, thank you so much for commenting on earlier versions of many chapters and for our numerous interesting meetings on procedural issues. Many thanks also go to René Bruin who critically commented on an earlier version of the chapter on the United Nations Convention against Torture, to Kees Wouters who commented on earlier versions of the Introduction and who helped me out a number of times when I could not find certain UNHCR documents on RefWorld, and to Hermine Masmeyer who commented on earlier versions of the chapter on the ECHR and the chapter on European Union asylum law.

Henja Korsten, thank you for helping me to become familiar with EUR-lex, the Legislative Observatory, PreLex and the digital public register of the Council of the European Union. I also wish to thank Beverley Slaney for her editorial work, Carolus Grütters and Aslan Zorlu for helping me to make the index and Hannie van de Put for making the layout.

I am grateful to the members of the manuscript committee, professors Ashley Terlouw, Roel Fernhout and Egbert Myjer for reviewing the manuscript and providing valuable comments.

Finally I wish to thank my beloved husband, Siros, and our dear little sons, Nour and Aziz, for loving and supporting me all the way. Without your energy I would not have been able to complete this work. Mom and sisters, special thanks also to you for your love and interest in my work. A very special thanks to my sister Suzan for making the cover illustration. Dad, you are no longer here on earth, but I hope that, in Heaven, you will be a little bit proud of my book.

Every week individuals who are in the most vulnerable and difficult circumstances, far away from their homes and home countries, appear before me as a national judge. It is these people who continually remind me that an independent, impartial, fair and thorough judicial investigation and hearing is a crucial human right, and that national judges are the primary guardians of it.

2006	2007	2008	2009	2010	2011	2012
Mexico City	Nijmegen	Amsterdam	Tun Fun	Paris	Amsterdam	Den Bosch

Table of Contents

List of abbreviations and acronyms

A-G	Advocate General
CAT	Convention against Torture and Other Cruel, Inhuman or Degrading Treatment or Punishment
CEAS	Common European Asylum System
CJEU	Court of Justice of the European Union
CMLRev	Common Market Law Review
CoE	Council of Europe
ComAT	Committee against Torture
ECHR	European Convention for the Protection of Human Rights and Fundamental Freedoms
ECtHR	European Court of Human Rights
EJIL	European Journal of International Law
EJML	European Journal of Migration and Law
ELRev	European Law Review
ETS	European Treaty Series
EU	European Union
EU Charter	Charter of Fundamental Rights of the European Union
EU Dublin Regulation	Council Regulation (EC) No 343/2003 of 18 February 2003 establishing the criteria and mechanisms for determining the Member State responsible for examining an asylum application lodged in one of the Member States by a third-country national
EU Procedures Directive	Council Directive 2005/85/EC of 1 December 2005 on minimum standards on procedures in Member States for granting and withdrawing refugee status
EU Qualification Directive	Council Directive 2004/83/EC of 29 April 2004 on minimum standards for the qualification and status of third country nationals or stateless persons as refugees or as persons who otherwise need international protection and the content of the protection granted
Directive 2011/95/EU of the European Parliament and of the Council of 13 December 2011 on standards for the qualification of third-country nationals or stateless persons as beneficiaries of international protection, for a uniform status for refugees or for persons eligible for subsidiary protection, and for the content of the protection granted.
EU Reception Conditions Directive	Council Directive 2003/9/EC of 27 January 2003 laying down minimum standards for the reception of asylum seekers

EU Temporary Protection Directive	Council Directive 2001/55 of 20 July 2001 on minimum standards for giving temporary protection in the event of a mass influx of displaced persons and on measures promoting a balance of efforts between Member States in receiving such persons and bearing the consequences thereof
EXCOM	Executive Committee of the High Commissioner's Programme
GAOR	General Assembly Official Record
HRC	Human Rights Committee
HRQ	Human Rights Quarterly
HRW	Human Rights Watch
IARLJ	International Association of Refugee Law Judges
ICCPR	International Covenant on Civil and Political Rights
ICESCR	International Covenant on Economic, Social and Cultural Rights
ICJ	International Court of Justice
IJRL	International Journal of Refugee Law
JV	Jurisprudentie Vreemdelingenrecht
LTTE	Liberation Tigers of Tamil Eelam
MoU	Memorandum of Understanding
NAV	Nieuwsbrief Asiel- en Vluchtelingenrecht
NJCM-Bulletin	Nederlands Juristen Comité voor de Mensenrechten-Bulletin
OAU	Organisation of African Unity
OJ of the EU	Official Journal of the European Union
para.	paragraph
PKK	Partiya Karkerên Kurdistan (Kurdistan Workers' Party)
RC, Refugee Convention	Convention Relating to the Status of Refugees
RP, Refugee Protocol	Protocol Relating to the Status of Refugees
Res.	Resolution
RV	Rechtspraak Vreemdelingenrecht
TEU	Treaty on the European Union
TFEU	Treaty on the Functioning of the European Union
UDHR	Universal Declaration of Human Rights
UK	United Kingdom
UN	United Nations
UNGA	United Nations General Assembly
UNHRC	United Nations High Commissioner for Refugees
UNHCR Handbook	UNHCR Handbook on Procedures and Criteria for Determining Refugee Status
UNTS	United Nations Treaty Series
Vol.	Volume
VTC	Vienna Convention on the Law of Treaties

Chapter 1: Introduction

1.1 Research context and reasons

Every judge who has worked in a court for a number of years will admit that facts and evidence play a crucial role in judicial investigations and judicial decision making. This not only goes for criminal law and civil law, but certainly also for administrative law. In individual cases before the court, judges apply legal norms to the established facts. To be able to do this, they must first obtain clarity about the facts. This is not problematic when the parties to the case do not argue about the facts. In many cases, however, the parties disagree about what actually happened. In such cases, the first step in the judicial investigative and decision making process is determination of the facts. At this stage, the judge will determine the facts, on the basis of the statements by the parties and, possibly, other available evidence.

In asylum[1] cases, determination of the facts is a particularly difficult task. The question which has to be answered is whether a risk exists that the individual will be persecuted or ill-treated in the future, upon expulsion to the country of origin. As we can never predict what will happen in the future, the assessment of a future risk is inherently a very difficult task.[2] At the same time, much is at stake in asylum cases: the expulsion of an individual who fears that, in his or her country of origin, his or her life or safety will be at risk.

There are more particularities which make determination of the facts in asylum cases an extremely difficult job. The facts, as related by the asylum seeker, have mostly happened in a country far away from decision makers and judges in the country of refuge. In addition to this, there is often not much direct evidence corroborating the statements by the asylum seeker. As a result, the reliability and credibility of the flight narrative become very important. Bearing in mind the subjective elements which are inherent in making an assessment of the credibility and reliability of an asylum seeker, judges – and, of course, administrative decision makers as well – will find themselves on thin ice, in an area where the most fundamental human rights are at stake.[3]

The immediate reason for my embarking upon this research was formed by two judgments of the ECtHR: *Said v. the Netherlands* (2005)[4] and *Salah Sheekh v. the Netherlands* (2007).[5] These two judgments clearly demonstrated that the national court and the international court (the ECtHR) are sometimes miles apart when it comes to determining the facts and assessing the risk in asylum cases. In both cases, the District Court of Amsterdam, where I had just started working as an immigration and asylum judge, functioned as the national first instance court. In both cases, this national court

---

1 By 'asylum' I mean the protection offered to a non-citizen on account of a threat abroad, by a state, within the territory of that state. See Battjes 2006, p. 6.
2 See in the same vein Wouters 2009, p. 26.
3 Concurring opinion of European Court of Human Rights Judge Thomassen to the judgment in the case of *Said v. the Netherlands*, 5 July 2005, Appl. No. 2345/02.
4 ECtHR, *Said v. the* Netherlands, 5 July 2005, Appl. No. 2345/02.
5 ECtHR, *Salah Sheekh v. the Netherlands*, 11 January 2007, Appl. No. 1948/04.

approved the stance of the administration that there was no reason to grant asylum to the individuals concerned. In both cases, the ECtHR determined the facts and assessed the risk in a completely different way and assumed that there were substantial grounds for believing that upon expulsion there was a real risk that the individuals would be subjected to torture or cruel, inhuman or degrading treatment in their country of origin, resulting in the determination that their expulsion would lead to a violation of Article 3 ECHR. The ECtHR based its ruling in both judgments on substantive grounds. At the same time, there were clear signs that the ECtHR was dissatisfied with the level of judicial scrutiny offered at national level in the Netherlands. In a concurring opinion to *Said v. the Netherlands* (2005), Judge Thomassen expressed the view that no serious investigation had been carried out by the Netherlands authorities (administrative and judicial). To illustrate this, Thomassen pointed to the fact that the District Court of Amsterdam had not investigated the identity documents presented by the claimant during the court proceedings and had refused to hear Mr. Khalifa, a witness, put forward by the claimant, as it had already found the flight narrative incredible.[6]

In *Salah Sheekh v. the Netherlands* (2007), the ECtHR declared the complaint admissible although the claimant had failed to lodge a higher appeal against the Amsterdam Court's judgment to the Council of State and had, thus, failed to exhaust national legal remedies before applying to the ECtHR, as required by Article 35, first paragraph, ECHR.[7] By declaring the complaint admissible, the ECtHR conveyed the message that further appeal to the Council of State constituted no effective national remedy. Although this conclusion rested on substantive reasons[8] the judgment in *Salah Sheekh* contained a suspiciously elaborate explanation on how the ECtHR itself determines the facts and assesses the risk of a breach of Article 3, arousing the impression that the Court wished to set an example for national courts.

This dissatisfaction with the level of judicial scrutiny offered at national level in the Netherlands deeply troubled me. Together with a colleague from the Amsterdam Court, Willem van Bennekom, I analysed a number of well-known judgments of the ECtHR in expulsion cases concerning asylum seekers to find out in a more precise way how the ECtHR assessed the risk.[9] We discovered significant differences

---

6   Concurring opinion of European Court of Human Rights Judge Thomassen to the judgment in the case of *Said v. the* Netherlands, 5 July 2005, Appl. No. 2345/02.

7   Article 35, first paragraph, ECHR stipulates: 'The Court may only deal with the matter after all domestic remedies have been exhausted, according to the generally recognised rules of international law, and within a period of six months from the date on which the final decision was taken.'

8   The ECtHR found that further appeal to the Council of State did not constitute an effective remedy as it stood virtually no prospect of success, given the constant jurisprudence of the Council of State on the individualisation requirement for assuming an Article 3-risk and on internal protection alternatives in Somalia, see ECtHR, *Salah Sheekh v. the Netherlands*, 11 January 2007, Appl. No. 1948/04, paras. 123 and 124.

9   These judgments were: *Cruz Varas and others v. Sweden*, 20 March 1991, Appl. No. 15576/89; *Vilvarajah and others v. the UK*, 30 October 1991, Appl. Nos. 13163/87, 13164/87, 13165/87, 13447/87 and 13448/87; *Chahal v. the UK*, 15 November 1996, Appl. No. 22414/93; *Ahmed v. Austria*, 17 December 1996, Appl. No. 25964/94; *Bahaddar v. the Netherlands*, 19 February 1998, Appl. No. 25894/94; *Jabari v. Turkey*, 11 July 2000, Appl. No. 40035/98; *Hilal v. the UK*, 6 March 2001, Appl. No. 45276/99; *Mamatkulov and Abdurasulovic*, 6 February 2003, Appl. Nos. 46827/99 and 46951/99;

→

between the judicial scrutiny applied at international level and our own national judicial review. First, the intensity[10] or thoroughness of the judicial scrutiny was very different. It seemed that the ECtHR, fully independently and on its own account, determined the facts and assessed the risk, whereas national asylum courts in the Netherlands had to pay deference to the position taken by the administration concerning the credibility of the past facts as stated by the asylum seeker. Second, issues of evidence, such as the admission and evaluation of evidence, were approached and resolved in very different ways at the international and the national level. The main results of this small-scale investigation conducted in early 2007 are summarised below.

Results of the analysis conducted in early 2007: differences between the judicial review at national level in the Netherlands at that time, and the judicial scrutiny performed by the ECtHR

The scrutiny conducted by the ECtHR in the cases researched in January 2007 was characterised by full, rigorous and *ex nunc* fact finding and risk assessment. This entailed, among other things, full judicial review of flight narrative credibility,[11] active use of investigative powers by the ECtHR whenever this was deemed necessary[12] and flexibility in accepting and using evidence that had not been presented earlier during the procedure in the respondent State party.[13] More in general, we discovered that the ECtHR took a highly material approach towards the evidence presented by the

---

Thampibillai v. the Netherlands, 17 February 2004, Appl. No. 61350/00; *Venkadajalasarma v. the Netherlands*, 17 February 2004, Appl. No. 58510/00; *Mamatkulov and Askarov v. Turkey*, 4 February 2005, Appl. Nos. 46827/99 and 46951/99; *Müslim v. Turkey*, 26 April 2005, Appl. No. 53566/99; *Said v. Netherlands*, 5 July 2005, Appl. No. 2345/02; *N. v. Finland*, 26 July 2005, Appl. No. 38885/02; *Bader and Kanbor v. Sweden*, 8 November 2005, Appl. No. 13284/04; *D. and others v. Turkey*, 22 June 2006, Appl. No. 24245/03; *Salah Sheekh v. the Netherlands*, 11 January 2007, Appl. No. 1948/04.

10   The intensity of judicial scrutiny relates to how thorough or rigorous the court examines a certain issue. The intensity of judicial scrutiny concerns the question whether the court pays deference to (part of) the administrative decision or, instead, carries out its own rigorous assessment.

11   This means that the Court determines whether the Court itself finds the account by the claimant credible or not. Elements of this assessment are whether the account is consistent and is in line with information about the country of origin, and with circumstantial evidence if presented or available. Part of the assessment is also the question of whether the claimant has convincingly rebutted the stance of the administration that his or her account is not credible. An assessment of flight narrative credibility was made, for example, in ECtHR, *Cruz Varas v. Sweden,* 20 March 1991, Appl. No. 15576/89; ECtHR, *Hilal v. the United Kingdom,*6 March 2001, Appl. No. 45276/99; ECtHR, *Said v. the Netherlands*, 5 July 2005, Appl. No. 2345/02; ECtHR, *N. v. Finland*, 26 July 2005, Appl. No. 38885/02.

12   An example of the use of the investigative power to hear witnesses in order to assess the credibility of the flight narrative of the claimant is ECtHR, *N. v. Finland*, 26 July 2005, Appl. No. 38885/02. In almost all the cases we examined we found that the ECtHR not only relies on information on the situation in the country of origin presented by the claimant, but also obtains information from different sources *propriomotu*. An example is ECtHR, *Salah Sheekh v. the Netherlands*, 11 January 2007, Appl. No. 1948/04, in which case the ECtHR obtained large quantities of information on the situation in Somalia.

13   A good example of the acceptance of new evidence that had not been presented earlier during the procedure in the Netherlands, is ECtHR, *Said v. the Netherlands*, 5 July 2005, Appl. No. 2345/02, see paras. 27-30 of the judgment.

parties and obtained *proprio motu*. The evidence was weighed and assessed in order to: 1) obtain a complete picture of what had happened to the claimant in the past; and 2) make a sound assessment of the risk the claimant might run upon expulsion to his or her country of origin or to another State. We did not come across any examples of judgments where evidence had been discarded, without any material consideration, on formal grounds, such as the ground that it had been presented too late, or that the evidence did not stem from an objective source (family members' witness statements).

We found that, compared to the review in Strasbourg, the national judicial review in asylum cases in the Netherlands was different in a significant number of ways. First, judges only marginally reviewed the administrative stance on flight narrative credibility as far as the related facts in the past were concerned. This doctrine had been introduced by the case law of the Administrative Litigation Division of the Council of State[14] (hereafter: Council of State).[15] This doctrine implied that, when assessing flight narrative credibility as far as the facts in the past were concerned, the yardstick was not the opinion of the judge, but the question of whether there was reason to rule that the administration could not reasonably have come to its finding on credibility of the flight narrative. Second, according to the case law of the Council of State, first instance judges were not always allowed to use the investigative powers they possessed under the General Administrative Law Act.[16] The idea behind this was that it was the task of the asylum seeker to present the facts and the evidence and it was not up to the judge to help him or her in fulfilling this task. Third, the possibilities for *ex nunc* judicial review were limited at the time when this research was embarked upon (January 2007). Article 83 of the Dutch Aliens Act 2000 stipulated that, in considering the case, the court took into account relevant facts and circumstances that arose after the administrative decision, unless by doing so the course of the proceedings would be unduly hampered or the decision in the case would be intolerably delayed. In case law, however, strict criteria had been developed for the application of Article 83. When, at the judicial review stage, the asylum seeker brought forward evidence that had not been presented earlier to the administration, this

---

14 The Administrative Litigation Division of the Council of State (Council of State) functions as the highest Court of Appeal in asylum cases. A higher appeal against judgments of the District Court can be lodged to the Council of State.

15 See, for example, the judgments of the Council of State of 3 July 2002, *AB* 2002, 242, 15 November 2002, *AB* 2003, 96, 27 January 2003, *AB* 2003, 286, 28 December 2005, *AB* 2006, 96.

16 See, for example, the judgment of the Council of State of 28 December 2005, *AB* 2006, 96. In the case underlying the judgment the flight narrative of an asylum seeker was found not credible by the administration because the alleged Sierra Leonean nationality was doubted on the basis of a linguistic report stating that the asylum seeker did not speak any Krio. On the basis of Article 8:47 of the General Administrative Law Act, the Court appointed a second linguist in order to obtain a second opinion. On appeal, the Council of State ruled that the Court had exceeded its powers and annulled this judgment. The reason for this ruling was that it is the asylum seeker who has to make his or her account plausible vis-à-vis the administration. Therefore, it is also the task of the asylum seeker to submit a second language opinion where the administration has based its findings on the opinion of a qualified language expert.

evidence needed to fulfil a number of strict criteria before the judge could take it into consideration.[17]

Fourth, we discovered that in the national judicial review procedure, evidence presented by the asylum seeker in the form of witness statements was approached first and foremost in a formal, and not material, way. The question of whether or not the information came from an objective source, and the procedural stage at which the evidence was presented, determined to a large extent whether or not the evidence would be taken into consideration by the judge.[18] Statements from family members, third private persons and certain organisations were not seen as 'evidence coming from an objective source' and were, for that reason, not considered, weighed and assessed materially, but discarded on the ground that they were not from an objective source.[19] It is interesting to mention here that in the case of *Said v. the Netherlands* (2005), the District Court of Amsterdam deemed it unnecessary to hear the witness named by Said for the reasons that the applicant's account was neither credible nor plausible.[20]

The ECtHR's judgment in *N. v. Finland* (2005)[21] provided a very clear illustration of the contrast as far as the use of investigative powers and the approach towards evidence was concerned. The ECtHR *proprio motu* decided to take oral evidence in Finland. With that purpose, a fact-finding mission was organised. Several representatives from the Finnish Government, the counsel and advisers of the applicant were

---

17 Article 83 of the Aliens Act 2000 concerns both 'facts' and 'evidence sustaining alleged facts'. In steady case law it has been ruled that this Article concerns facts or circumstances that occurred after the administrative decision. It also covers facts or circumstances that existed before the administrative decision was taken, as well as evidence sustaining those facts and evidence containing a date preceding the administrative decision that could and should not have been presented before the administrative decision was taken. This test is rarely passed, in general, it is said that the asylum seeker should have mentioned the facts or should have submitted the evidence at an earlier stage. See, for example, the judgments of the Council of State of 8 August 2003, *JV* 2003/439. Furthermore, evidence needs to meet a number of strict formal requirements: documents have to be original, for otherwise authenticity cannot be established (see, for example, the judgment of the Council of State of 19 February 2003, 200206080/1), documents have to be dated, otherwise it cannot be established that the document concerns a new fact, that is, a fact which came up after the administrative decision (see, for example, the judgment of the Council of State of 15 January 2003, *JV* 2003, 83), documents have to be translated (see, for example, the judgment of the Council of State of 30 August 2002, *JV* 2002, 357), and documents have to come from an objective source (for example, a family member is not an objective source, see judgment of the Council of State of 6 August 2003, *JV* 2003, 159). See also judgment ofthe Council of State of 2 March 2007, 200606382/1/v. In this judgment, it was ruled that the medical report from a doctor working for Amnesty International was not a 'fact' in the sense of Article 83 of the Aliens Act, because the doctor had based his medical assessment on the account of the asylum seeker. The doctor working for Amnesty International was, in other words, not an 'objective source'.

18 Survey of jurisprudence of the *Newsletter on Asylum and Refugee Law* of June 2006 (*Rechtspraakoverzicht NAV*, nr. 3 June 2006), p. 179 and further.

19 For an example of judicial appreciation of statements made by family members of the asylum seeker, see the judgment of the Council of State of 7 November 2003, nr. 200305086/1, *JV* 2004, 16; for an example of statements of third private persons, see the judgment of the Council of State of 19 February 2002, nr. 200200390/1; for an example of statements of organisations, see the judgment of the Council of State of 3 March 2006, nr. 200510175/1, *JV* 2006, 155.

20 See ECtHR, *Said v. the Netherlands*, 5 July 2005, Appl. No. 2345/02, para. 16.

21 ECtHR, *N. v. Finland*, 26 July 2005, Appl. No. 38885/02.

heard. Testimony was taken from the applicant, his common-law wife, a person who had worked for the same organisation as the applicant, and the Head of the Africa Section in the Directorate of Immigration.[22]

Fifth, we found that, in the national judicial review proceedings, country of origin information compiled by the national Dutch Ministry of Foreign Affairs was given considerably more weight than country of origin information stemming from reputable human rights organisations, such as the UNHCR, Amnesty International and Human Rights Watch. Country of origin information from the Dutch Ministry of Foreign Affairs was regarded as expert information. Because of this status, the State Secretary of Justice could, in principle, rely on this information, unless there were concrete reasons for doubting the veracity or the completeness of the country information. Such concrete reasons were not readily assumed.

The discovered significant differences between the judicial scrutiny applied at international level by the ECtHR and the national judicial review in the Netherlands seemed problematic to me. These differences seemed to run counter to the notion of subsidiarity, meaning that citizens should be able to vindicate their rights in the national courts and that, however well organised, international protection of human rights can never be as effective as a well-functioning national system of protection.[23] If national judicial proceedings offer fewer safeguards compared to the proceedings before the ECtHR, it will always make sense for individuals to apply to the ECtHR. This would clearly run counter to the subsidiary nature of the Convention system. In *Salah Sheekh v. the Netherlands* (2007), the ECtHR was particularly clear that in cases concerning expulsion or extradition involving an Article 3-claim rigorous scrutiny is needed. As the considerations in the judgment were so elaborate on this point, the judgment gave the impression that the ECtHR had specifically and critically reacted to the (partially) marginal judicial review applied by the asylum courts in the Netherlands and that the ECtHR had wanted to remind national courts of its subsidiary nature.[24]

The idea that different standards were problematic was not shared by everyone, though. At the time when this research was embarked upon, the highest national asylum court in the Netherlands, the Council of State took the position that different standards at national and international judicial level were acceptable.[25] In support of this position, it was argued that the position of national courts was different from that of the ECtHR, as national courts operated within a framework of checks and balances with the national executive and legislative powers. In discussions about this dilemma at the District Court of Amsterdam, the term 'national procedural autono-

---

22 See ECtHR, *N. v. Finland*, 26 July 2005, Appl. No. 38885/02, paras. 7-9 and 77-116.
23 Barkhuysen 1998, p. 12 and 13. See also the annual report for 2006 of the ECtHR, p. 30.
24 ECtHR, *Salah Sheekh v. the Netherlands*, 11 January 2007, Appl. No. 1948/04, para. 136; Wouters 2009, p. 339.
25 See the judgment of the Council of State of 5 June 2006, 200602132/1 and 200602135/1, para. 2.6; it was stated that the immigration judge in the Netherlands is not obliged to review the administrative stance on flight narrative credibility in the same way as the ECtHR investigates whether or not the Netherlands have violated their treaty obligation under Article 3.

my' was often used, but nobody knew exactly whether and to what extent that concept would sufficiently justify the discovered differences.

Thus, the small-scale investigation, conducted in early 2007, made me anxious to find out in a more precise way what lessons on both main aspects – intensity of judicial scrutiny and evidence – could and should be drawn from the ECHR and from other international asylum law and EU asylum law. I also wanted to find a more precise answer to the question whether the discovered differences in judicial scrutiny offered at international and at national level could or could not continue to exist. My anxiety became even stronger when I shared the results of the small-scale investigation with some of my colleagues in the International Association of Refugee Law Judges (IARLJ) and found out that it was not only in the Netherlands that national courts encountered the problems described above, but that similar issues with regard to the intensity of judicial scrutiny and evidence also existed in a number of other EU countries.[26] I realised that the problems I had encountered as a national judge in fact also occurred in other EU countries and that solutions to these problems might be of interest to national asylum judges throughout the EU. That is how the idea of embarking upon this research project was born.

1.2   Research questions

The main objective of this research is to explore what international and EU asylum law require from the national judge with regard to:
-    the required intensity of the judicial scrutiny to be applied
-    evidentiary issues, such as the standard and burden of proof, the admission and evaluation of evidence and time limits for submitting evidence.

The research questions are:
-    Which provisions of international and EU (asylum) law regulate national judicial asylum proceedings?
-    Do the provisions regulating national judicial asylum proceedings contain concrete norms about the required intensity of judicial scrutiny to be offered at national level?
-    Do these provisions contain concrete norms on evidentiary issues such as the standard and burden of proof, the admission and evaluation of evidence and time limits for submitting evidence?

---

26   First instance judges from a number of other EU countries, for example Poland and Belgium, mentioned during IARLJ meetings that they encountered (some of) the problems described.. See also Reneman 2012, p. 259. As to Belgium, however, Constitutional Court Judge Marc Bossuyt has expressed fierce criticism on the ECtHR in a number of publications (see, for example, Bossuyt 2012). To his mind, the ECtHR acts too often as a first instance asylum court with full factual jurisdiction, whereas it should play a much more subsidiary role. From ECtHR, *Hilal v. the UK*, 6 March 2001, Appl. No. 45276/99, it appears that in the past, judges in the UK experienced (some of) the problems described; this seems to have been solved by now as they apply 'the most anxious scrutiny' in cases concerning the expulsion of asylum seekers. Reference is made to chapter 7, section 7.3.4.

- What standards and principles do the international courts and treaty monitoring bodies apply concerning judicial scrutiny and evidence?
- Are these standards and principles normative or binding for national asylum courts?
- How do the found norms (inter) relate, and what should be done if there is divergence or conflict ?

To find answers to the fourth question on the standards and principles applied by the international courts and treaty monitoring bodies, eleven aspects of evidence and judicial scrutiny are used as a research tool. These aspects are mentioned below:

- Standard of proof: what is the standard or criterion used to measure whether there is a risk of *refoulement*?
- Burden of proof: who has to prove that the standard is met?
- Relevant facts and circumstances: what kind of facts and circumstances are necessary to conclude that a risk exists?
- Required degree of individual risk: to what degree must an applicant be singled out ?
- Credibility assessment: Does the international court or supervisor independently and on its own account assess the credibility? How does the international court or supervisor assess the credibility of the claimant's statements?
- Admission of evidence, sources of evidence, minimum quantity and quality of evidence: what means and sources of evidence can be brought in to substantiate a claim or to refute a claim? How much evidence is required to corroborate the applicant's statements? What quality of evidence is required?
- Appreciation and weighing of evidence: how are different types of evidence weighed and appreciated? Is there a certain hierarchy in the appreciation of evidence, in the sense that certain sources are given more value than others?
- Opportunities for presenting evidence: do both parties have the same opportunities and chances to present evidence and to react on the evidence presented to the other party?
- Judicial application of investigative powers: does the international court or supervisor apply investigative powers (of its own motion or otherwise)? In what kinds of situations does this happen?
- Time limits for the presentation of statements and evidence: at what moment in the proceedings must the claimant submit the relevant statements and corroborating evidence?
- Point in time for the risk assessment: at what point in time does the international court or supervisor assess the risk?

1.3   Sources and methodology

This research includes three global human rights treaties, established within the framework of the United Nations. These are the Convention relating to the Status of Refugees and the Protocol relating to the Status of Refugees (the Refugee Convention or RC, 1951, and the Refugee Protocol or RP, 1967), the International Covenant on Civil and Political Rights (ICCPR, 1966) and the Convention against Torture (CAT, 1984). In addition, this research embraces one regional human rights treaty, being the European Convention for the Protection of Human Rights and Fundamental Freedoms (ECHR, 1950). It also includes European Union primary legislation on asylum, comprising provisions in the Treaty on the European Union (TEU), the Treaty on the Functioning of the European Union (TFEU) and the Charter of Fundamental Rights of the European Union, and a number of secondary law instruments, such as the EU Qualification Directive[27] and the EU Procedures Directive.[28]

Literature of eminent scholars and UNHCR documentation[29] formed the main source of interpretation of the RC. For the chapter on the ECHR, the case law of the ECtHR[30] formed the prime source, and, of course, literature was used as well. The views of the Human Rights Committee (HRC) and the Committee against Torture (ComAT)[31] were the main sources of research for the chapters on the ICCPR and the CAT. Literature was used in addition to that source. Finally, for the chapter on EU asylum law, I used literature and judgments of the Court of Justice of the EU (CJEU).[32] For the analysis of the relevant provisions in secondary EU asylum law I traced the history of these provisions. For this purpose I used EUR-lex,[33] the Legislative Observatory,[34] PreLex[35] and the digital public register of the Council of the European Union,[36] which all constitute extensive EU law databases.

27　Council Directive 2004/83 on minimum standards for the qualification and status of third country nationals or stateless persons as refugees or as persons who otherwise need international protection and the content of the protection granted.

28　Council Directive 2005/85 on minimum standards on procedures in Member States for granting and withdrawing refugee status.

29　I used the list provided by Wouters 2009, pp. 601-605 and pp. 624-625, and RefWorld, the UNHCR internet database (http://www.unhcr.org/cgi-bin/texis/vtx/refworld) to find UNHCR documents containing guidelines on national judicial asylum proceedings.

30　To find case law of the ECtHR, I used the Court's database Hudoc (reachable via www.coe.int), the list of cases provided by Wouters 2009, pp. 607-613, the list provided by Mole 2008 and the UNHCR Manual on Refugee Protection and the ECHR (http://www.unhcr.org/3ead312a4.html); I also used case law I obtained in my capacity as a judge at the Court of Amsterdam.

31　To find the case law of both Committees I used the SIM database (http://sim.law.uu.nl), RefWorld (the UNHCR internet database) the lists provided by Wouters 2009, pp. 613-618 and the case law I obtained as a judge.

32　I used the CURIA database of the Court of Justice of the EU (http://curia.europa.eu) and the EUR-lex database (http://eur-lex.europa.eu) to find case law of the Court of Justice of the EU. I obtained much case law of the Court of Justice of the EU on the principle of effective judicial protection during a conference on this subject of the Academy of European Law (ERA, https://www.era.int) held in Paris in February 2010.

33　http://eur-lex.europa.eu/en/index.htm.

34　http://www.europarl.europa.eu/oeil/index.jsp.

35　http://ec.europa.eu/prelex/apcnet.cfm.

36　http://www.consilium.europa.eu/showPage.aspx?id=245&lang=en.

1.4 Methods and rules of interpretation

The treaty provisions are analysed with the aid of the general rules of interpretation laid down in Articles 31 and 32 Vienna Convention on the Law of Treaties (VTC). Article 31 stipulates:

> '1. A treaty shall be interpreted in good faith in accordance with the ordinary meaning to be given to the terms of the treaty in their context and in the light of its object and purpose.
> 2. The context for the purpose of the interpretation of a treaty shall comprise, in addition to the text, including its preamble and annexes:
> (*a*) any agreement relating to the treaty which was made between all the parties in connection with the conclusion of the treaty;
> (*b*) any instrument which was made by one or more parties in connection with the conclusion of the treaty and accepted by the other parties as an instrument related to the treaty.
> 3. There shall be taken into account, together with the context:
> (*a*) any subsequent agreement between the parties regarding the interpretation of the treaty or the application of its provisions;
> (*b*) any subsequent practice in the application of the treaty which establishes the agreement of the parties regarding its interpretation;
> (*c*) any relevant rules of international law applicable in the relations between the parties.
> 4. A special meaning shall be given to a term if it is established that the parties so intended.'

And Article 32 stipulates:

> 'Recourse may be had to supplementary means of interpretation, including the preparatory work of the treaty and the circumstances of its conclusion, in order to confirm the meaning resulting from the application of article 31, or to determine the meaning when the interpretation according to article 31:
> (*a*) leaves the meaning ambiguous or obscure; or
> (*b*) leads to a result which is manifestly absurd or unreasonable.'

For the interpretation of the relevant provisions of the ECHR, account has been taken of the relevant specific principles of interpretation developed by the ECtHR, including the principle that rights must be interpreted in such a way that they are practical and effective,[37] the notion that rights must be interpreted in a liberal way and restrictions in a narrow way,[38] the idea that the ECHR is a living instrument, to be interpreted in the light of present-day conditions,[39] the principle that treaty provisions must be interpreted in such a way that they are internally consistent and coherent,[40] and finally, the notion that treaty concepts must be interpreted autonomously.[41]

---

37 See, for example, ECtHR, *Soering v. the UK*, 7 July 1989, Appl. No. 14038/88, para. 87.
38 See, for example, ECtHR, *Stoll v. Switzerland*, 10 December 2007, Appl. No.69698/01, para. 61.
39 ECtHR, *T. and V. v. the UK*, 16 December 1999, Appl. No. 24724/94, para. 70.
40 This principle establishes that the ECHR must be read as a whole. See, for example, ECtHR, *Klass v. Germany*, 6 September 1987, Appl. No. 5029/71, para. 68.

I refer to Dembour (2006), Wouters (2009) and Rietiker (2010) for more detailed descriptions of these principles.[42] Just as the ECtHR has done in relation to the ECHR, the Human Rights Committee (HRC) has made clear that the ICCPR should be interpreted as a living instrument and the rights protected under it should be applied in context and in the light of present-day conditions.[43]

For the interpretation of EU asylum law, the methods of interpretation of the CJEU are used. This approach deviates from the rules in the VTC. The CJEU bases its interpretation of EU law on wording, context (the preamble and documents or instruments explicitly referred to) and purpose, whereby interpretation of wording and context are supplementary to the purpose of the treaty or the instrument as a whole.[44] The preparatory works (legislative history) play a role as a supplementary means of interpretation of secondary Union law.[45] According to the Court of Justice of the EU, when interpreting Union law, national courts must take into account the different language versions; the various language versions must be interpreted uniformly, and in the case of divergence, the provision in question must be interpreted by reference to the purpose and general scheme of the rules of which it forms part.[46]

In this study, the treaties and instruments investigated are approached dynamically, for the following reasons. Multilateral treaties are normally meant and concluded for a long period. When interpreting their provisions it is, therefore, not very logical to cling strictly to (only) the circumstances prevailing at the time of conclusion. Particularly human rights treaties are meant to be living instruments which are to be interpreted according to present-day conditions.[47] Article 31, third paragraph, Vienna Convention on the Law of Treaties (VTC) also offers support for a dynamic interpretation of treaty provisions as it mentions subsequent agreements and practice as instruments of treaty interpretation.[48] The ICJ also interprets treaty provisions dynamically.[49]

---

41 Under the 'autonomous concepts doctrine', it is up to the ECtHR only, and not up to the States parties to the ECHR, to define core concepts such as 'criminal charge', 'possessions', 'victim', 'home'. See, for example, ECtHR, *Engel and others v. the Netherlands*, 8 June 1976, Appl. Nos. 5100/71, 5101/71, 5102/71, 5354/72, 5370/72.

42 Dembour 2006, pp. 21-22, Jacobs & White 2006, pp. 38-55, Wouters 2009, pp. 199-202, Rietiker 2010, pp. 245-277. In the list of principles mentioned here I do not mention the proportionality principle and the doctrine on the margin of appreciation as they are not relevant for (non-medical) asylum cases.

43 HRC, *Judge v. Canada*, 13 August 2003, No. 829/1998, para. 10.3, last sentence.

44 The first clear example of a judgment in which the Court of Justice of the EU used this approach to interpretation is the judgment in the case of *Van Gend en Loos*, 5 February 1963, C-26/62, p. 3.

45 Battjes 2006, pp. 44 and 45.

46 See, for example, the judgment of the Court of Justice of the EU in the case of *Srl CILFIT and Lanificio di Gavardo SpA*, 6 October 1982, C-283/81, para. 18.

47 The 'living instrument' notion has mainly been developed in the case law of the ECtHR, see, for example, ECtHR, *Selmouni v. France*, 28 July 1999, Appl. No. 25803/94, para. 101, but is also present in the case law of the Human Rights Committee under the ICCPR, see, for example, HRC, *Judge v. Canada*, 13 August 2003, Com. No. 829/1998, para. 10.3, last sentence.

48 Article 31(3) of the VTC stipulates: 'There shall be taken into account, together with the context: (*a*) any subsequent agreement between the parties regarding the interpretation of the treaty or the application of its provisions; (*b*) any subsequent practice in the application of the treaty which estab-

→

The treaties and instruments investigated in this study are, furthermore, approached holistically. They are seen as interdependent and interrelated, in conformity with the Vienna Declaration and Programme of Action, as adopted by the United Nations World Conference on Human Rights on 25 June 1993,[50] and in conformity with Article 31, third paragraph, sub c VTC, which states, in short, that any relevant rules of international law applicable in the relations between the parties may be taken into account when clarifying a treaty.[51] An integrated approach is also called for by Article 78 TFEU, which stipulates, in short, that the secondary EU asylum instruments must be in accordance with the international treaties investigated in this study.[52] The treaties and instruments explored in this study can thus not be seen separately, but should, rather, be seen as complementary and mutually influencing each other.[53]

1.5   Structure of the book

After this introduction, five separate chapters analyse the content of the relevant provisions in international and EU law. The chapters work their way down from the universal level to the regional level and, finally, the level of the EU. Chapter 2 covers the RC, followed by the ICCPR in chapter 3 and the CAT in chapter 4. Chapter 5 is dedicated to the ECHR. Chapter 6 deals with EU asylum law. The chapters 3 (ICCPR), 4 (CAT) and 5 (ECHR) follow by and large the same structure, because these treaties have similar individual complaint mechanisms and also similar provisions on national proceedings. Chapter 7 draws the link between the international and EU law standards on evidence and judicial scrutiny and national asylum courts. It attempts to integrate the different international and EU law standards on national judicial scrutiny and on evidence. It also raises and tries to answer the question of wheth-

---

lishes the agreement of the parties regarding its interpretation; (*c*) any relevant rules of international law applicable in the relations between the parties.'

49   ICJ, Legal consequences for States of the Continued Presence of South Africa in Namibia (South West Africa) Notwithstanding Security Council Resolution 276 (1970) (Advisory Opinion), 21 June 1971, ICJ Reports 1971, p. 16 para. 53. The ICJ stated here that an international instrument has to be interpreted and applied within the entire legal system prevailing at the time of interpretation.

50   United Nations World Conference on Human Rights, Vienna Declaration and Programme of Action, 25 June 1993, ILM(32) 1993, p. 1661, para. 5, VN Doc. A/CONF.157/ 23(1993), para.5.

51   Article 31(3) of the VTC stipulates: 'There shall be taken into account, together with the context: (*a*) any subsequent agreement between the parties regarding the interpretation of the treaty or the application of its provisions; (*b*) any subsequent practice in the application of the treaty which establishes the agreement of the parties regarding its interpretation; (*c*) any relevant rules of international law applicable in the relations between the parties.'

52   Article 78, first paragraph, TFEU, states: 'The Union shall develop a common policy on asylum, subsidiary protection and temporary protection with a view to offering appropriate status to any third-country national requiring international protection and ensuring compliance with the principle of *non-refoulement*. This policy must be in accordance with the Geneva Convention of 28 July 1951 and the Protocol of 31 January 1967 relating to the status of refugees, and other relevant treaties.'

53   See for the same stance Wouters 2009, p. 526; United Nations World Conference on Human Rights, Vienna Declaration and Programme of Action, 25 June 1993, ILM(32) 1993, p. 1661, para. 5, VN Doc. A/CONF.157/23 (1993), para.5.

er the standards on evidence and judicial scrutiny as applied by the international supervisors and courts are binding on national asylum courts and whether national asylum courts can choose, from among the international supervisors, a 'best role model'. The question of what to do in case of conflicting or diverging standards is addressed as well.

Chapter 8 pays separate attention to three special types of national asylum court proceedings and the positions of the international supervisors on these proceedings. The three special types of proceedings concern Dublin cases, repeat cases and fast-track proceedings. Dublin cases concern those cases in which an asylum application was decided upon on the basis of the EU Dublin Regulation 2003/343/EC.[54] The EU Dublin Regulation provides criteria for establishing which Member State is responsible for the examination of an asylum application submitted in one of the Member States. The Regulation is based on the 'single application' principle which prohibits a person from applying for asylum in more than one country. Based on the criteria laid down in the Regulation, Member States may decide not to examine an asylum application and to refer the asylum applicant to the authorities of another Member State. Repeat cases concern those cases in which a claimant lodged a second (or third or fourth *et cetera*) asylum application after he or she received a negative decision on a first application, often with the aim of submitting new evidence corroborating the claim for protection. Fast-track proceedings are proceedings in which shorter than normal time limits (and sometimes also other special rules) apply, created with the aim of quickly and more efficiently processing asylum claims and asylum appeals.

In the Epilogue at the end of this book, the main highlights of this study are revisited and some concluding remarks are made.

1.6   Limitations of the research

This study focuses on issues of judicial scrutiny and issues of evidence in asylum court proceedings. This book is not a comprehensive analysis of the prohibitions on *refoulement* contained in the different instruments of international asylum law and EU asylum law. For such an analysis I refer to Wouters' work.[55]

Another limitation of this study is that it is very much EU focused. The problems that formed the research context and reason occurred in the Netherlands and, according to judges in the International Association of Refugee Law Judges, are also present in some other EU countries. The treaties and instruments included in this study are those that are relevant for asylum courts within the EU. As it was my intention to conduct this research mainly for judges and other legal practitioners in the

---

54   Council Regulation 2003/343/EC of 18 February 2003, establishing the criteria and mechanisms for determining the Member State responsible for examining an asylum application lodged in one of the Member States by a third country national, *OJ of the EU* L 50, 25 February 2003, pp. 1-10, last amended by *OJ of the EU* L 304, 14 November 2008, p. 83.

55   Wouters 2009.

EU, I decided not to investigate regional asylum treaties in force outside Europe, such as the Convention on Refugee Problems in Africa.[56]

Excluded from this study is the question of the suspensive effect of judicial review. Although this is a very important issue, suspensive effect, or the absence of it, is often a question of legislation and is an issue which is to be distinguished from questions of evidence and judicial scrutiny. It is a complex issue which merits separate PhD research by itself. This research has been undertaken by Rieter and I refer to her book for those interested in this specific issue.[57]

Also excluded are so-called medical asylum cases, cases in which seriously ill individuals claim asylum abroad because they fear death due to the absence of medical care facilities in their home countries. To my mind, these medical cases are so specific and differ so much from normal asylum cases that they merit separate research.

Another limitation is that there is no particular or separate focus on cases concerning the cessation of earlier granted refugee status, or the exclusion from refugee status of certain categories of individuals, such as war criminals. Additionally, in this investigation I did not search for special rules for particularly vulnerable groups of asylum seekers, such as minors. Such special categories of cases would, in my opinion, merit separate comprehensive research.

Case law and literature up to 1 January 2012 have been included in this research. Judgments of the ECtHR and the CJEU with particular relevance for this study, issued in the course of 2012, have also been included.

1.7   State of the Art

In 1995, Boeles completed his dissertation entitled 'Fair immigration proceedings in Europe'; his book with the same title was published in 1997. The central question posed in his research was what obligations international law imposes on national remedies by means of proceedings in immigration affairs.[58] Compared to Boeles' research, this work is narrower in three ways. First, it covers asylum only. Second, it focuses on the judicial work and not primarily the administrative asylum procedure. Third, Boeles' research tool or criteria used to study the norms are broader than the list of aspects of evidence and judicial scrutiny used as a research tool in this book. The aspects used in this research in fact form more elaborated aspects of the fifth criterion used by Boeles: the procedure for the establishment of the facts and the court's margin of appreciation.

In 1997, Tom Barkhuysen completed his research on Article 13 ECHR. His book entitled 'Article 13 ECHR: effective domestic legal protection against violations of human rights' was published in 1998. Barkhuysen's work constitutes an in-depth investigation into the history, scope and content of Article 13 ECHR, and the relationship between Article 13 and other provisions on proceedings and the material rights

---

56   The Organisation of African Unity (OAU) adopted this Convention in 1969. The Convention is available at the site of the OAU: http://www.africa-union.org.
57   Rieter 2010.
58   Boeles 1997, p. 3.

contained in the ECHR.[59] The current research is broader in the sense that it encompasses more legal instruments and more provisions from these instruments. It is, however, narrower in terms of subject matter: this research focuses on judicial asylum proceedings only.

In 2005, Hemme Battjes completed his research entitled 'European Asylum Law and International Law'; his book with the same title appeared in 2006. In this comprehensive work, Battjes describes and analyses the EU measures which together make up the Common European Asylum System (CEAS). Battjes focuses on the relationship between this EU body of law and international asylum law. In his work, he describes and analyses the material and procedural rights and obligations laid down in the EU measures, and compares them to those set out in the RC, and to those flowing from the prohibitions on *refoulement* contained in the CAT, the ECHR, the ICCPR and international custom and principles recognised by civilised nations.[60] Some of the research questions I attempt to answer are discussed by Battjes as well, but Battjes does not go into great detail as far as judicial handling of evidence is concerned.

In 2009, Kees Wouters completed his research entitled 'International legal standards for the protection from *refoulement*'. In this comprehensive study, Wouters analyses the exact scope and content of the *refoulement* prohibitions contained in the RC, the ICCPR, the CAT and the ECHR and compares these prohibitions with each other. Wouters' work focuses on the scope and content of the mentioned prohibitions and the responsibilities of States deriving from them. Wouters' work and this research have some overlap. In Wouters' work, however, issues of facts and evidence form minor parts of a large comprehensive study into the content of the prohibitions on *refoulement*. As this research focuses only on issues of evidence and judicial scrutiny, these issues are studied in a more detailed and profound way.

In 2012, Marcelle Reneman completed her research entitled 'EU asylum procedures and the right to an effective remedy'. Marcelle and I met in 2007 when we both had just embarked upon our research projects. We decided to meet on a regular basis to discuss procedural issues and read and review draft chapters. Our 'Procedural issues Club' was enlarged in 2008 when researchers Hannah Helmink and Karen Geertsema joined in. Reneman's work and this study have some overlap as Reneman also covers issues of evidence and issues of intensity of judicial scrutiny. However, Reneman's work is broader and covers also other aspects of asylum procedures, such as the right to remain on the territory of the EU Member States and the right to be heard on asylum motives. As opposed to Reneman's work, which also encompasses the work of the (administrative) determining authority, this study focuses on the daily work of judges and addresses only two categories of issues in detail: issues of evidence and issues of judicial scrutiny.

---

59   Barkhuysen 1998, pp. 1-16.
60   Battjes 2006, pp. 1-57.

Chapter 2: The 1951 Convention relating to the Status of Refugees (RC) and the 1967 Protocol relating to the Status of Refugees[1]

2.1 Introduction

The Convention Relating to the Status of Refugees (the Refugee Convention or RC) was signed in Geneva on 28 July 1951 and it entered into force on 22 April 1954.[2]

On 31 January 1967, a Protocol which amended and supplemented the Refugee Convention was signed in New York (the Refugee Protocol or RP). The Refugee Protocol entered into force on 4 October 1967.[3] States parties to the Refugee Protocol undertake to apply Articles 2 to 34 Refugee Convention without the temporal and optional geographical limitation contained in Article 1A(2) and Article 1B Refugee Convention. Pursuant to Article 1A of the Refugee Convention, the term refugee shall apply to any person who fulfils the criteria of the refugee definition contained in Article 1A(2), but only as a result of events occurring before 1 January 1951. This temporal limitation was based on the idea that the RC was primarily meant to alleviate pain as a result of past events, not future events, and out of fear that without such a restriction the RC would create a *carte blanche* for all future situations.[4] However, Article 1(2) of the Refugee Protocol removes this limitation;[5] a very important development because it detaches the Refugee Convention from the Second World War and the Cold War and gives it, instead, a timeless character. It can be said, therefore, that the history of the RC does not support the idea that this treaty does not suit the needs of today's world.[6] Article 1(B) Refugee Convention gives States parties the choice to understand 'events before 1 January 1951' in Article 1(A) either as events occurring in Europe or events occurring in Europe or elsewhere; Article 1(3) of the Refugee Protocol stipulates, however, that the Protocol shall be applied without any geographical limitation, without, however, affecting existing declarations

---

1 See the following literature for comprehensive general descriptions and analyses of the history and working of the RC and the refugee definition (see bibliography for full titles): Bem 2007, Van Bennekom & Van der Winden 2011, Boeles 1997, Boeles 2009, Fernhout 1990, Goodwin-Gill 1998, Goodwin-Gill & McAdam 2007, Grahl-Madsen 1963, Grahl-Madsen 1966-1972, Hathaway 2005, Spijkerboer & Vermeulen 2005, Wouters 2009. See also Zwaan 2005 for an analysis of the role of the RC and the UNHCR in EU asylum law. I also refer to the special edition on the Refugee Convention of *A&MR* (*Asylum and Migration Law*) of 2011, No. 5/6.

2 UNTS No. 2545, Vol. 189, p. 137.

3 UNTS No. 8791, Vol. 606, p. 267.

4 Van Bennekom 2011, p. 203.

5 Article 1(2) of the Refugee Protocol stipulates: 'For the purpose of the present Protocol, the term "refugee" shall, except as regards the application of paragraph 3 of this article, mean any person within the definition of article 1 of the Convention as if the words "As a result of events occurring before 1 January 1951 and..." and the words "...as a result of such events", in article 1 A (2) were omitted.'

6 Van Bennekom 2011, p. 203.

made by States parties.[7] This is also an important amendment as it has made the Refugee Convention a truly universal instrument.

At the moment of completion of this book, 141 States, including all 27 Member States of the EU,[8] had ratified both the Refugee Convention and the Refugee Protocol.[9]

2.1.1 The RC's place in international and EU asylum law

The Refugee Convention is the only universal treaty on refugee protection. It is also the cornerstone of the Common European Asylum System (CEAS) which has been developed since the entering into force on 1 May 1999 of the Treaty of Amsterdam which made the EU competent in the field of asylum and immigration (see Chapter 6). The EU Charter of Fundamental Rights stipulates in Article 18 that the right to asylum shall be guaranteed with due respect for the rules of the Refugee Convention and the Refugee Protocol. Article 78 TFEU stipulates that the EU asylum instruments must be in accordance with the Refugee Convention (as well as other relevant treaties). Many of the secondary EU asylum instruments explicitly reaffirm that the Refugee Convention is the cornerstone of the CEAS. For example, the Preamble to the EU Qualification Directive stipulates that

> 'The Geneva Convention and Protocol provide the cornerstone of the international legal regime for the protection of refugees.'[10]

And the Preamble to the EU Dublin Regulation states that

> 'The European Council, at its special meeting in Tampere on 15 and 16 October 1999, agreed to work towards establishing a Common European Asylum System, based on the full and inclusive application of the Geneva Convention relating to the Status of Refugees of 28 July 1951, as supplemented by the New York Protocol of 31 January 1967, thus ensuring that nobody is sent back to persecution, i.e. maintaining the principle of *non-refoulement* (...).'[11]

The notion that the Refugee Convention and the Refugee Protocol constitute the cornerstone of the CEAS has been explicitly reaffirmed by the Court of Justice of the

---

7   Article 1(3) of the Refugee Protocol.
8   The number of Member States mentioned here, 27, reflects the situation on 31 December 2012; see http://europa.eu/abc/european_countries/eu_members/index_nl.htm.
9   See http://www.unhcr.org/protect/PROTECTION/3b73b0d63.pdf and the UNHCR Statement on the right to an effective remedy in relation to accelerated asylum procedures, May 2010, to be found at: http://www.unhcr.org/refworld/pdfid/4bf67 fa12.pdf.
10 Preamble (3) to Directive 2004/83/EC on minimum standards for the qualification and status of third country nationals or stateless persons as refugees or as persons who otherwise need international protection on the content of the protection granted, *OJ of the EU* L 304, 30 September 2004, pp. 12-23, last amended by *OJ of the EU* L 204, 5 August 2005, p. 24.
11 Preamble (2) to Regulation 2003/343/EC of 18 February 2003, establishing the criteria and mechanisms for determining the Member State responsible for examining an asylum application lodged in one of the Member States by a third country national, *OJ of the EU* L 50, 25 February 2003, pp. 1-10, last amended by *OJ of the EU* L 304, 14 November 2008, p. 83.

EU in a number of judgments, for example, *Abdulla* (2010), *Bolbol* (2010) and *B and D* (2010).[12]

Together with the definition of refugee in Article 1 A (2), the prohibition on *refoulement* contained in Article 33 forms the core of the Refugee Convention. Under Article 1 A (2), refugees may be identified according to four characteristics:

1) they are outside the country of their nationality or the country of their former habitual residence;
2) they are unable or unwilling to avail themselves of the protection of this country or to return to it;
3) this impossibility or unwillingness is due to well-founded fear of persecution; and
4) this persecution is based on race, religion, nationality, membership of a particular social group or political opinion.[13]

According to Article 33, a refugee may not in any manner whatsoever be expelled or returned to the frontiers of territories where his or her life or freedom would be threatened on account of his or her race, religion, nationality, membership of a particular social group or political opinion. According to the second paragraph of Article 33, refugees whom there are reasonable grounds for regarding as a danger to the security of the host country or who constitute a danger to the community of that country are not protected.

This book focuses on issues of evidence and judicial scrutiny in asylum court proceedings. It is not a comprehensive analysis of the prohibitions on *refoulement* contained in international asylum law. For that reason, the different components of the refugee definition and the prohibition on *refoulement* will not be analysed any further here. Other authors have done this extensively before.[14]

2.1.2   Supervisory mechanisms

2.1.2.1   The ICJ

According to Article 38 Refugee Convention, disputes between States concerning its interpretation and application can be lodged to the International Court of Justice

---

12   CJEU, *Abdulla*, 2 March 2010, C-175/08, C-176/08, C-178/08 and C-179/08, paras. 52 and 53. The EU Court of Justice ruled that 'the Geneva Convention is the cornerstone of the international legal regime for the protection of refugees (…). Therefore, the provisions of the Qualification Directive must be interpreted in the light of the general system and the purpose of the Directive, taking into account the Geneva Convention and other relevant treaties mentioned in Article 63, para. 1, sub 1, EC. This was repeated in the judgments of the CJEU in *Bolbol*, 17 June 2010, C-31/09, para. 37 and *B and D,* 9 November 2010, C-57/09 and C-101/09), para. 77. See also Van Bennekom 2011, p. 204, and Westerveen 2011, p. 215.

13   Article 1 A (2) of the Refugee Convention.

14   See for extensive analyses of the elements of the refugee definition Grahl-Madsen 1966-1972, vol. 1, pp. 173-220, Fernhout 1990, pp. 52-124, Spijkerboer & Vermeulen 2005, pp. 23-64, Goodwin-Gill 1998, pp. 32-80, Goodwin-Gill & McAdam 2007, pp. 63-131, Wouters 2009, pp. 56-113, Van Bennekom & Van der Winden 2011, pp. 155-182. See also Bem 2007 for a thorough analysis of how the Dutch and American courts defined the refugee in the period 1975-2005.

(ICJ).[15] According to Article 34(1) of the Statute of the ICJ, only States, and not individuals, can bring cases before it. To date no case regarding the Refugee Convention has ever been brought before the ICJ.[16]

2.1.2.2 The UNHCR

The Refugee Convention does not establish a monitoring court or body of its own to which individual complaints can be brought. However, there is an international supervisory body which monitors and supervises the application of the Refugee Convention by States: the UNHCR.[17] According to the Preamble of the Refugee Convention, 'the UNHCR is charged with the task of supervising international conventions providing for the protection of refugees (…)'. In addition to the Preamble, Article 35, first paragraph, stipulates that States parties to the Convention undertake to co-operate with the Office of the UNHCR in the exercise of its functions, and shall in particular facilitate its duty of supervising the application of the provisions of the Refugee Convention.[18] The UNHCR's supervisory responsibility has also been reflected in EU primary and secondary law.[19]

The RC does not give the UNHCR the power to issue binding decisions on interpretation of its provisions. Nor does it create a mechanism by which the UNHCR can enforce adherence to the Convention by States. The absence of a possibility for the UNHCR to issue binding opinions on non-compliance with the RC by States and to receive individual complaints, make its supervisory and enforcement mechanisms rather weak.[20] As a consequence, in literature different opinions are defended on the question of how much legal weight is to be attached to the UNHCR's opinions. Battjes (2006), who refers to Spijkerboer and Vermeulen (2005), states that the UNHCR's opinions are a subsidiary means of interpretation and that their relevance depends on their quality of reasoning.[21] Wouters (2009) mentions Battjes' opinion and, just like Battjes, points out the problem that the UNHCR lacks an enforcement power or tool. According to Wouters, however, the UNHCR's opinions are authoritative, have global scope and are accepted as important sources of interpretation by

---

15   In Article IV of the Refugee Protocol the jurisdiction of the ICJ is foreseen as well.

16   Zwaan 2005, p. 37, Battjes 2006, p. 19, Wouters 2009, p. 14, Van Bennekom 2011, p. 204. See also the digital register of contentious cases of the ICJ at http://www.icj-cij.org, last visited on 31 December 2012.

17   The UNHCR was established in 1949 by the UN General Assembly. UN GA res. 319 (IV), 3 December 1949.

18   The supervisory role of the UNHCR is also laid down in Article II(1) of the Refugee Protocol and in Article 8 of the UNHCR Statute. See for a more extensive analysis of the supervisory role of the UNHCR: Takahashi 2001, Türk 2002, Zwaan 2005, pp. 4-8.

19   See, for example, Recital 15 of the EU Qualification Directive which states that consultations with the UNHCR 'may provide valuable guidance for Member States when determining refugee status according to Article 1 of the Geneva Convention' and Article 21, first paragraph, sub c, of the EU Procedures Directive which stipulates that Member States shall allow the UNHCR to 'present its views, in the exercise of its supervisory responsibilities under Article 35 of the Geneva Convention, to any competent authorities regarding individual applications for asylum at any stage of the procedure.'

20   Takahashi 2001, Türk 2002, Wouters 2009, pp. 39-44, Westerveen 2011, p. 213.

21   Battjes 2006, p. 20.

States parties.[22] Although conscious of the criticisms expressed by many over the functioning of the UNHCR, in this research its opinions are considered to be highly relevant and authoritative. First, because of the explicit recognition in the Refugee Convention and the CEAS of the UNHCR as supervisor over the application of the RC. Recognition of the UNHCR's supervisory role in the CEAS implies that EU Member States are highly conscious of, and respect, its supervisory power.[23] Second, as will be demonstrated in more detail below in Part 2 of this chapter, the ECtHR, as well as the Advocates-General of the Court of Justice of the EU, treat the UNHCR's opinions as highly relevant and authoritative.[24]

In 1979, the UNHCR issued the 'Handbook on Procedures and Criteria for de-termining Refugee Status under the 1951 Convention and the 1967 Protocol relating to the Status of Refugees' (hereafter: the UNHCR Handbook). The Handbook con-tains guidelines on how to determine who is a refugee, including a number of proce-dural guidelines with particular relevance for this research. According to paragraph V of the foreword to the Handbook, these guidelines are based on the practice of States, exchanges of views between the UNHCR and the competent authorities of Contracting States and the views of scholars. The Handbook is an important source of guidance for interpreting and applying the Refugee Convention[25] for 'government officials concerned with the determination of refugee status.'[26] Taking into account that Article 21 of the EU Procedures Directive stipulates in its first paragraph at sub c that the UNHCR is entitled 'to present its views (...) to any competent authorities regarding individual applications for asylum at any stage of the procedure',[27] it must be assumed that the guidelines issued by the UNHCR address not only first instance administrative decision makers, but certainly also the judiciary.

As well as the Handbook, the UNHCR has issued many other documents con-taining guidelines, including the so-called 'Guidelines on International Protection', *amicus curiae* briefs or advisory opinions in national and international proceedings, dis-cussion papers under the heading 'Legal and Protection Policy Research Series' and working papers under the heading 'New Issues in Refugee Research'.[28]

---

22 Wouters 2009, p. 38.
23 In the same vein: Zwaan 2005, p. 27.
24 The ECtHR speaks of the UNHCR as an organisation whose independence, reliability and objec-tivity are beyond doubt. See, for example, admissibility decision *K.R.S. v. UK*, 2 December 2008, Appl. No. 32733/08, p. 16. See for an example of a judgment in which the ECtHR attaches great weight to the opinion of the UNHCR *Jabari v. Turkey*, 11 July 2000, Appl. No. 40035/98, para. 41. See also the opinion of A-G with the CJEU Sharpston delivered on 4 March 2010 in Case C-31/09 of *Bolbol v. Bevándorlási és állampolgársági Hivatal*, para. 16, in which this A-G stated that she intended to treat the UNHCR information as an unofficial *amicus curiae* brief.
25 Hathaway 2005, pp.114-118, Battjes 2006, p. 20, Wouters 2009, p. 43.
26 *UNHCR Handbook*, Foreword, para. VII.
27 The supervisory role of the UNHCR is also laid down in a number of provisions contained in other EU asylum directives with less relevance for this research as they do not primarily concern the rela-tionship between the UNHCR and national courts. Zwaan 2005 provides a list of these provisions on pp. 84-88; see also the table in Zwaan 2005 on pp. 26-27.
28 Wouters 2009 contains a list of UNHCR documents with relevance for interpretation of the Refugee Convention on pp. 601-605.

2.1.2.3   The ExCom

In 1958 the Executive Committee of the UNHCR programme (ExCom) was established.[29] The ExCom consists of representatives of the Member States of the United Nations Organisation who meet annually in plenary sessions, with regular smaller meetings of its Standing Committee in between, to discuss, among other things, the legal activities of the UNHCR. Its findings and recommendations are laid down in so-called Conclusions. These Conclusions are not legally binding, as neither the Refugee Convention nor any other treaty has conferred law-making competence on the ExCom. The ExCom Conclusions No. 8, 65, 71, 74, 81, 82 and 103 contain recommendations on procedures and mention that 'refugee status determination procedures must be accessible, fair and efficient'. It is, however, not explained any further what is meant by this. The ExCom Conclusion No. 8, (XXVIII), 1977, para. (e) (vi) contains a 'right to appeal to either an administrative or judicial authority', but it is not further explained what kind of appeal is required.[30] As the ExCom Conclusions are rather unspecific on the subject of this study, they will not be used any further here.

2.1.2.4   The Court of Justice of the EU (CJEU)

Under Article 267 TFEU, the CJEU is fully competent to rule on the validity of the EU secondary asylum instruments and on the interpretation of primary and secondary EU law on asylum. In this way, the Court is in a position which entitles it to explain provisions of the EU Qualification Directive[31] which are in turn explanations of provisions of the Refugee Convention.[32] Although at the moment of completion of this book the number of judgments concerning asylum was still rather limited,[33] the

---

29   The ExCom was established by resolution 672 (XXV) on 30 April 1958 of the Economic and Social Council of the United Nations.

30   See ExCom Conclusion No. 8, (XXVIII), 1977, para. (e); ExCom Conclusion No. 65 (XLII), 1991, para. (o); ExCom Conclusion No. 71 (XLIV), 1993, para. (i); ExCom Conclusion No. 74 (XLV), 1994, para. (i); ExCom Conclusion No. 81 (XLVIII), 1997, para. (h); ExCom Conclusion No. 82 (XLVIII), 1997, para. (d) (iii); ExCom Conclusion No. 103 (LVI), 2005, para. (r).

31   Directive 2004/83/EC on minimum standards for the qualification and status of third country nationals or stateless persons as refugees or as persons who otherwise need international protection on the content of the protection granted, *OJ of the EU* L 304, 30 September 2004, pp. 12-23, last amended by *OJ of the EU* L 204, 5 August 2005, p. 24.

32   Westerveen 2011, p. 215.

33   The judgments issued up to 31 December 2012 by the CJEU on preliminary questions in asylum cases are: *Petrosian and others*, 29 January 2009, C-19/08, *Elgafaji*, 17 February 2009, C-465/07, *Abdulla and others*, 2 March 2010, C-175/08, C-176/08, C-178/08, C-179/08, *Bolbol*, 17 June 2010, C-31/09, *B and D,* 9 November 2010, C-57/09 and C-101/09, and *Brahim Samba Diouf*, 28 July 2011, C-69/10; *N.S. and Others*, 21 December 2011, C-411/10 and C-493/10; *Migrationsverk Sweden v. Nurije, Valdrina and Valdri Kastrati*, 3 May 2012, C-620/10; *Bundesrepublik Deutschland v. Y. and Z.*, 5 September 2012, C-71/11 and C-99/11; *M.M. v. Ireland*, 22 November 2012, C-277/11. In addition, of relevance to the field of asylum are two other judgments, being *Parliament v. Council*, 6 May 2008, C-133/06, concerning an application by the European Parliament for the annulment of Articles 29(1) and (2) and 36(3) of the EU asylum Procedures Directive, concerning safe countries of origin and safe third countries, and *European Commission v. Ireland*, 7 April 2011, C-431/10, concerning an action for failure by Ireland to implement Procedures Directive 2005/85/EC. The CJEU ruled that Ireland had failed to implement the Directive.

CJEU will be playing an increasingly important role in interpreting the Refugee Convention.[34] A more extensive analysis of the judgments of the CJEU relevant for this research is made in Chapter 6 on EU asylum law.

2.1.3 Provisions on proceedings

The Refugee Convention contains a number of provisions on national proceedings. These are Article 16 on access to courts and Article 32 on expulsion and the procedure to be followed in cases of expulsion. Article 35 on co-operation of national authorities with the UNHCR is also relevant: as we will see in section 2.5, information from the UNHCR may serve as an important source of evidence in asylum court proceedings. The content of these three provisions will be explored in this chapter.

2.1.4 Chapter outline

The next sections of this chapter discuss and analyze the RC's provisions on national proceedings – Articles 16 and 32 – and what these provisions say with regard to the required intensity of judicial scrutiny and the evidentiary issues in national asylum proceedings. The requirement of access to courts in Article 16 is discussed in section 2.2. In section 2.3, attention is paid to the procedural rights in expulsion cases under Article 32. Different views will be discussed on the applicability of both provisions to contemporary court proceedings concerning asylum. After that, the content of both provisions is addressed. In section 2.4, it will be demonstrated that these two provisions can be read and interpreted with the aid of the UNHCR's positions on the eleven aspects of evidence and judicial scrutiny in national asylum proceedings. Section 2.5 pays attention to the co-operation requirement in Article 35 and its implications for national asylum courts. Final concluding remarks are made in section 2.6.

2.2 Article 16: access to courts

2.2.1 Applicability

Article 16 stipulates:

'1. A refugee shall have free access to the courts of law on the territory of all Contracting States.

2. A refugee shall enjoy in the Contracting State in which he has his habitual residence the same treatment as a national in matters pertaining to access to the Courts, including legal assistance and exemption from *cautio judicatum solvi*.[35]

---

34 See also Zwaan 2005, p.1: 'For the first time an international court will not only be competent but also most likely requested to decide cases with direct implications for the interpretation of provisions of the Refugee Convention.' See also Van Bennekom 2011, p. 204, and Westerveen 2011, p. 215.

35 '*Cautio judicatum solvi*' is the security for costs which foreigners sometimes have to furnish for the costs of the other party in civil proceedings provided the plaintiff loses the lawsuit.

3. A refugee shall be accorded in the matters referred to in paragraph 2 in countries other than
that in which he has his habitual residence the treatment granted to a national of the country of
his habitual residence.'

Opinions differ as to the question of whether Article 16 applies to judicial review or
appeal proceedings concerning the determination of refugee status and the expulsion
of failed asylum seekers. The text of Article 16 (the French text speaks of 'libre et
facile accès devant les tribunaux') and the preparatory works do not provide an answer to this question.[36] The fact that the preparatory works do not mention refugee
status determination proceedings should be seen in the light of the circumstances
existing at the time when the Refugee Convention was drawn up. At that time, national asylum court proceedings as we know them nowadays were practically non-
existent in many States parties to the Convention. To illustrate this: in the Netherlands, no developed national procedure for refugee status determination, including a
judicial appellate system, existed before 1975; in the UK, it was in 1980 that changes
were made to the so-called Immigration Rules with the specific aim of refugee status
determination, and it was not until 1993 that a national asylum appeals system was set
up.[37] The fact that the text of the second paragraph of Article 16 mentions an exemption from *cautio judicatum solvi* indicates that the drafters (primarily) had civil proceedings in mind. The preparatory works speak of a 'right to sue and be sued' and contain
some indications that the drafters indeed had mainly civil proceedings in mind when
drawing up Article 16; examples of court proceedings mentioned in the preparatory
works are an 'action to secure a divorce' and 'actions to recover a debt'.[38]

In literature different answers are given to the question of whether or not Article
16 applies to judicial proceedings against a negative administrative decision on an
asylum request. In earlier literature, this question is not addressed explicitly; Grahl-
Madsen (1966-1972) and Swart (1987) do not raise it.[39] In more recent literature different stances are voiced. According to Fernhout (1990), it follows from Article 16
that 'a national court shall be available, also in every case in which a provision from
the Convention is to be applied'. To support his opinion, he refers to examples of the
early jurisprudence of the Dutch Council of State in which Article 16 was applied to
asylum proceedings (see section 2.2.2).[40] Spijkerboer & Vermeulen (1995) consider
Article 16 to be applicable to asylum proceedings; they do not repeat this opinion,
however, in their work of 2005.[41] Boeles (1997) considers Article 16 of paramount
importance for asylum proceedings. To support his stance, he points to the place of
Article 16 in the chapter on 'juridical status' and argues that it follows from the context of the RC that Article 16 is applicable to matters of inclusion and *refoulement*, as

---

36 Travaux Préparatoires, UN Doc. E/AC.32/2, Weis 1995, p. 131.
37 Zwaan 2003, pp. 87-89; Shah 2005, p. 2.
38 See UN Doc. E/AC.32/SR.11, at 7 and UN Doc. A/CONF.2/SR.8, at 12.
39 Grahl-Madsen 1966-1972, first volume, pp. 33-35. Grahl-Madsen discusses the historical
    background of Article 16. His second volume contains some brief pieces on procedural aspects but
    does not contain any comments on Article 16. Swart 1987does not explicitly discuss Article 16.
40 Fernhout 1990, pp. 192 and 234-240.
41 Spijkerboer & Vermeulen 1995, pp. 379-384.

such matters affect the refugee's juridical status. Boeles also points to the principle of effectiveness and argues that, if Article 16 is to lead to effective protection for refugees against *refoulement*, then that provision must also be considered to oblige the Contracting States to guarantee free access to the courts in all those cases in which the refugee status or the threat of *refoulement* is involved.[42] In addition to these two arguments, Boeles, like Fernhout, points to the jurisprudence of the national courts in Belgium and the Netherlands in which it was accepted that Article 16 applies to disputes concerning the application of the Refugee Convention. Hathaway (2005) states that 'in principle, Article 16(1) governs when refugees seek to litigate their Convention rights or any other rights before national courts' and 'the efforts of an increasing number of countries to deny access to their courts to refugees seeking review or appeal of a negative assessment of refugee status are prima facie incompatible with Article 16 RC.'[43] Wouters (2009) refers mainly to Boeles and states that Article 16 is applicable to all refugees, including refugee claimants.[44]

A different stance is taken by Battjes (2006): as Article 16 only speaks of access to courts and is silent about the type of proceedings and the kind of dispute, Battjes assumes that this provision has no implications for judicial asylum proceedings.[45]

The UNHCR Handbook does not make clear whether or not the UNHCR considers Article 16 to be applicable to appeal procedures against negative administrative decisions on asylum requests. Para. 12(ii) of the Handbook stipulates that 'the provisions of the Refugee Convention (…) that define the legal status of refugees and their rights and duties in their country of refuge (…) have no influence on the process of determination of refugee status (…)'. This leaves undecided whether or not the right to free access to a court applies in the appeal stage.

Following the majority of the scholars mentioned above, I consider it more logical to assume that Article 16 does indeed apply to contemporary judicial asylum proceedings. The argument given by Battjes is, in my view, not very convincing. Battjes says in fact that Article 16 is not applicable to proceedings and disputes which are not explicitly mentioned. As the text of Article 16 does not give any examples of proceedings and disputes, this would mean that Article 16 would never apply. Boeles' argument of the place of Article 16 in the Convention is convincing, but there are still some other good arguments in favour of assuming applicability. Multilateral treaties are normally meant and concluded for a long period. When interpreting their provisions it is, therefore, not very logical to cling strictly to (only) the circumstances prevailing at the time of conclusion. Particularly human rights treaties are living instruments which are to be interpreted according to present day conditions.[46] Article 31, third paragraph, VTC also offers support for a dynamic interpretation of treaty

---

42 Boeles 1997, pp. 71-77.

43 Hathaway 2005, pp. 644-647.

44 Wouters 2009, p. 174.

45 Battjes 2006, p. 319.

46 The 'living instrument' notion has mainly been developed in the case law of the ECtHR, see, for example, ECtHR, *Selmouni v. France*, 28 July 1999, Appl. No. 25803/94, para. 101. It is also present in the case law of the Human Rights Committee under the ICCPR. See, for example, HRC, *Judge v. Canada*, 13 August 2003, Com. No. 829/1998, para. 10.3, last sentence.

provisions as it mentions subsequent agreements and practice as instruments of treaty interpretation.[47] The ICJ also interprets treaty provisions dynamically.[48] Finally, as was pointed out in Chapter 1, it is a general principle of interpretation that human rights should be interpreted liberally in view of individual human rights protection.[49]

2.2.2 Equal treatment

It follows from the text of Article 16, the *travaux préparatoires*, early case law and literature that Article 16 is primarily a non-discrimination or equal treatment provision, meaning that it entails that refugees should not be required to meet extra, or more stringent, admissibility conditions which do not apply to nationals in similar court proceedings. Article 16 is a response to the widespread European practice during the nineteenth and early twentieth centuries of excluding foreigners from access to courts and, as a result, from judicial protection.[50] Good examples may be drawn from older jurisprudence of the Dutch Council of State in which it was inferred from Article 16 that refugees staying in the Netherlands should receive equal treatment as Dutch citizens as far as access to the Council of State was concerned, on the basis of the former Administrative Litigation Act.[51] For example, in its judgment of 10 April 1979, the Council of State ruled that Article 34, paragraph b, of the former Dutch Aliens Act was incompatible with Article 16. The national provision stipulated that there was only a right of appeal to the *Raad van State* from a negative decision of the administration on a request for reconsideration if the refugee had had his or her habitual residence in the Netherlands for one year on the date of the administrative decision, whereas this limitation did not apply to persons who wished to appeal to the Council of State, on the basis of the former Administrative Litigation Act, from other administrative decisions.[52]

Grahl-Madsen (1966-1972), Boeles (1997) and Hathaway (2005) read Article 16 in the same way: the meaning of Article 16 is to make sure that the right nationals of

---

47 Article 31, third paragraph, of the Vienna Convention on the Law of Treaties stipulates: 'There shall be taken into account, together with the context: (*a*) any subsequent agreement between the parties regarding the interpretation of the treaty or the application of its provisions; (*b*) any subsequent practice in the application of the treaty which establishes the agreement of the parties regarding its interpretation; (*c*) any relevant rules of international law applicable in the relations between the parties.'

48 ICJ, Legal consequences for States of the Continued Presence of South Africa in Namibia (South West Africa) Notwithstanding Security Council Resolution 276 (1970) (Advisory Opinion), 21 June 1971, ICJ Reports 1971, p. 16, para. 53. The ICJ stated here that an international instrument has to be interpreted and applied within the entire legal system prevailing at the time of interpretation.

49 Wouters 2009, p. 13.

50 Grahl-Madsen 1966-1972, Vol. I, pp. 33-35; Hathaway 2005, pp. 644-647.

51 Wet AROB: Wet van 1 mei 1975, *Stb.* 284, houdende regels betreffende beroep op de Raad van State tegen overheidsbeschikkingen.

52 Judgment of the Council of State of 10 April 1979, *RV* 1979, no. 3. See also the judgments of the Council of State of 20 December 1977, *RV* 1977; 13 July 1979, *RV* 1979, no. 9; and 20 December 1979, *RV* 1979, no. 13. Interestingly, in the judgment of 20 December 1977, the Council of State implicitly considered the national provision at variance with Article 16(1) of the RC, whereas in the later judgments of 1979 it was explicitly ruled that the national provision was non-compliant with Article 16(2).

a country possess to bring a case to court also works for refugees. Article 16, therefore, requires that obstacles which are particularly felt by refugees are to be removed so that they have real, and not illusive, access to courts, just like nationals. Examples of such obstacles are financial barriers and obstacles to obtaining legal aid. Grahl-Madsen also makes clear that Article 16 should be read in conjunction with Article 29, stipulating that the Contracting States shall not impose upon refugees duties, charges or taxes, of any description whatsoever, other or higher than those which are or may be levied on their nationals in similar situations.[53]

On the basis of the text and the mentioned case law and literature, it may be argued that shorter time limits for bringing an appeal against a negative administrative decision on an asylum application to court (compared to other administrative appeals) are incompatible with Article 16 Refugee Convention. Such shorter time limits are, in fact, more stringent admissibility conditions which do not apply to nationals in administrative court proceedings. Such shorter time limits for lodging an appeal exist in a number of EU Member States, for example, the Netherlands, France, Germany, the Czech Republic and Slovenia.[54] The EU Procedures Directive leaves the Member States discretion as to the determination of time limits for bringing appeals to court in Article 39, second paragraph. However, this provision does not give them leeway to set shorter time limits for asylum cases as Article 78 TFEU requires that European asylum law is in accordance with the Refugee Convention and Preamble 2 to the Procedures Directive stipulates that the asylum system of the EU is based on the full and inclusive application of the Refugee Convention.

2.3   Procedural rights in expulsion cases: Article 32

2.3.1   *Applicability*

Article 32 stipulates:

> '1. The Contracting States shall not expel a refugee lawfully in their territory save on grounds of national security or public order.
>
> 2. The expulsion of such a refugee shall be only in pursuance of a decision reached in accordance with due process of law. Except where compelling reasons of national security otherwise require, the refugee shall be allowed to submit evidence to clear himself, and to appeal to and be represented for the purpose before a competent authority or a person or persons specially designated by the competent authority.

---

53   Grahl-Madsen 1966-1972, Vol. I, p. 33; Boeles 1997, pp. 71-77, 80-81; Hathaway 2005, pp. 906-913.

54   In the Netherlands, the time limit for lodging an appeal to the court of first instance in administrative law cases is six weeks, whereas in asylum cases this time limit is only one or four weeks (Article 6:7 Algemene wet bestuursrecht (General Administrative Law Act), and Article 69, paras. 1 and 2 Vreemdelingenwet (Aliens Act)); shorter time limits also apply in many other EU countries, for example France, Germany, the Czech Republic, Slovenia (information was obtained from colleagues in the International Association of Refugee Law Judges (IARLJ)).

3. The Contracting States shall allow such a refugee a reasonable period within which to seek legal admission into another country. The Contracting States reserve the right to apply during that period such internal measures as they may deem necessary.'

The text of this provision makes clear that States parties to the Refugee Convention are limited in their right to expel a refugee lawfully in their territory on both substantive grounds (national security or public order) and procedural grounds; procedurally, expulsion can only take place after a decision has been taken in accordance with due process of law. Grahl-Madsen (1963) explains the reason for drawing up and including this provision in the Refugee Convention by referring to the habit of certain States in the early years of the twentieth century of expelling refugees and pushing those so expelled across the frontier to a neighbouring country. This practice caused hardship to the refugees, who were often pushed back and forth between two or more countries and punished each time for illegal entry. It also caused considerable inconvenience for the countries into whose territory the expelled refugees were sent. It was, therefore, natural that the expulsion of refugees became a matter of concern to the international community.[55]

Does Article 32 apply to contemporary judicial proceedings concerning refugee status determination and *refoulement*? The text of Article 32 and the preparatory works do not provide an answer to this question, which is logical as national court proceedings concerning asylum as we know them nowadays were practically non-existent in many States at the time when the RC was drafted. Literature is, again, divided over this question. Grahl-Madsen (1966-1972) does not link Article 32 to asylum court proceedings.[56] Fernhout (1990) does not discuss the meaning of Article 32 in his work. Boeles (1997), Hathaway (2005) and Wouters (2009) are of the opinion that Article 32 rights inhere in all refugees 'lawfully in a state party's territory', including those awaiting the results of their status verification inquiry.[57] Boeles and Hathaway refer to the history of negotiations on the personal scope of Article 32, which shows that the text 'lawfully in the territory' was adopted on second reading at the Conference of Plenipotentiaries immediately after attention had been drawn by the Swedish delegate to the fact that there was a discrepancy between the English language version ('lawfully *admitted*') and the French language version ('*résidant* regulièrement') and that, therefore, the personal scope of Article 32 needed clarification. It was then decided to drop the words 'admitted' and 'résidant' and, by doing so, to lessen the attachment to the country of asylum. Hathaway and Boeles infer from this that the drafters had a broad interpretation of the personal scope of Article 32 in mind.[58] To the contrary, Battjes (2006) and Goodwin-Gill & McAdam (2007) state that the benefit of Article 32 is limited to refugees who enjoy what might be called 'resident status' in the State in question. This means that Article 32 only applies to recognised refugees and that the provision is only relevant for the withdrawal of an awarded

---

55   Grahl-Madsen 1963, pp. 185-186.
56   See Grahl-Madsen 1972, second volume, pp. 344-389.
57   Boeles 1997, p. 78, Hathaway 2005, pp. 666-669, Wouters pp. 176, 177.
58   See for this change in text the *Travaux Préparatoires*, UN Doc. E/AC.32/SR.42, pp. 11-36.

asylum-related residence permit and the decision to expel a recognised refugee.[59] Battjes' argument for this line of reasoning is that considering Article 32 applicable would render Article 33 superfluous.

In my opinion, it makes more sense to consider Article 32 RC applicable to contemporary asylum court proceedings concerning status determination and *refoulement*. The argument of the history of this provision, referred to by Boeles and Hathaway, is convincing. Other arguments were mentioned above in section 2.2.1 when discussing the applicability of Article 16. Battjes' argument that considering Article 32 applicable would render Article 33 superfluous is not very convincing as both these provisions differ in many ways, so that it is difficult to see how one of them could become superfluous. To mention just a few differences, Article 33 protects from removal to territories where there is a threat to life or freedom, whereas Article 32 protects from removal to any territory, including safe countries, and Article 32 provides explicit procedural safeguards, unlike Article 33.[60]

2.3.2 *Due process of law*

'Due process of law' includes, according to the second sentence of the second paragraph, at least three rights: the right of the refugee to submit evidence to clear himself or herself, the right to appeal the decision on expulsion to a competent authority and the right to be represented before this appellate body. These three rights may be constrained to the extent required by compelling reasons of national security. We do not find any further explanation of the term 'due process of law' in the RC itself, or in the preparatory works. Weis (1995) comments that the term 'due process of law' stems from Anglo-Saxon law and that the term has a procedural and a substantial aspect. Procedurally, it means a decision reached in accordance with a procedure established by law, and containing the safeguards which the law provides for the class of cases in question, in particular equality before the law and the right to a fair hearing. Substantially, it means that the decision must be based on law, that it may not be unreasonable, arbitrary or capricious and must have a real and substantive relation to its object.[61] Boeles (1997) considers 'due process of law' to include a number of minimum requirements. These are: 1) knowledge of the decision against one; 2) an opportunity to submit evidence to rebut the decision; and 3) the right to appeal against an adverse decision before an impartial authority independent of the initial decision-making body.[62]

According to Hathaway (2005), the right to appeal does not necessarily entail an appeal to a court. Originally, there was an intention within the drafting committee to entrust all expulsion cases to the courts. In the course of the debates and negotiations it became clear, however, that most governments were unwilling to guarantee judicial oversight of refugee expulsion. According to Hathaway, the right to appeal must be understood in such a way that it provides a right to appeal to an authority of some

---

59 Battjes 2006, pp. 360-361, 462-463; Goodwin-Gill & McAdam 2007, p. 263.
60 Wouters 2009, pp. 176-177.
61 Weis 1995, p. 322.
62 Boeles 1997, p. 79.

seniority which is not connected to the body or person who took the initial decision on expulsion. This appellate authority should be explicitly empowered to take account of all the circumstances of the case so as to ensure a meaningful legal check on the powers of the administration. The right to submit evidence encompasses any evidence to clear oneself and not just evidence against the expulsion, and the person or body considering the appeal against expulsion must consider evidence relevant to, for example, a criminal conviction underpinning the expulsion order, rather than limiting itself simply to the consideration of evidence about the propriety of the expulsion order itself. The right to be represented entails a right to be represented on the review, it does not mean a right to legal counsel or to the appointment of an attorney. According to Hathaway, as well as these three rights, 'due process of law' embraces a duty to respect a range of technical, procedural requirements associated with basic fairness, such as suspension of the expulsion while the case is *sub judice*.[63] Goodwin-Gill & McAdam (2007) mention the three requirements also listed by Boeles and mention, as a fourth requirement, reasoned negative decisions.[64]

2.4 Articles 16 and 32: the UNHCR's position on evidence and judicial scrutiny

The UNHCR Handbook and many other UNHCR documents contain guidelines for the assessment of asylum applications. These guidelines are meant 'for the guidance of government officials concerned with the determination of refugee status'.[65] Among them are also specific guidelines on evidence and judicial scrutiny. Taking into account that Article 21 of the EU Procedures Directive stipulates under 1(c) that the UNHCR is entitled 'to present its views, in the exercise of its supervisory responsibilities under Article 35 of the Geneva Convention, to any competent authorities regarding individual applications for asylum at any stage of the procedure',[66] it may safely be assumed that the guidelines issued by the UNHCR address not only first instance administrative decision makers, but certainly also national asylum courts. The UNHCR has issued specific and concrete guidelines on almost all of the eleven aspects of evidence and judicial scrutiny covered by this study. Articles 16 and 32 may be interpreted with the aid of these guidelines. Such an interpretation significantly broadens the content of Article 16 and implies that Article 16 is more than just a prohibition on more stringent admissibility conditions and embraces not only the right to enter the court building and appear before a judge, but also the right to material judicial protection. Such a broader interpretation of Article 16 would be well in line

---

63 Hathaway 2005, pp. 670-677.
64 Goodwin-Gill & McAdam 2007, p. 523. In other literature, the meaning of 'due process of law' is not addressed extensively. For example, Fernhout 1990, Spijkerboer & Vermeulen 2005, Battjes 2006 and Wouters 2009 do not extensively discuss the meaning of 'due process of law'.
65 *UNHCR Handbook*, Foreword, para. VII.
66 The supervisory role of the UNHCR is also laid down in a number of provisions contained in other EU asylum directives with less relevance for this research as they do not primarily concern the relationship between the UNHCR and national courts. Zwaan 2005 provides a list of these provisions on pp. 84-88; see also the table on pp. 26-27.

with the ECtHR's case law on the requirement of access to an independent and impartial tribunal flowing from Article 6 ECHR, under which requirement the ECtHR has developed a doctrine on the required intensity of national judicial scrutiny. (See Chapter 5, sections 5.4 and 5.5.) A broad interpretation would also be in line with the fact that the European Convention on Establishment (1955),[67] which was drafted in the same period as the Refugee Convention, contains similar rules regarding access to court in Articles 7, 8 and 9, and in Article 7 explicit mention is made of 'judicial protection'.[68]

2.4.1 Standard of proof

The UNHCR takes the stance that it must be established, *to a reasonable degree* (italics by author) that, upon expulsion, the claimant's life or freedom would be threatened, in other words, that he or she would be persecuted, on account of one of the persecution grounds.[69] In its Note on Burden and Standard of Proof in Refugee Claims[70] the UNHCR has made clear that the determination of refugee status does not purport to identify refugees as a matter of certainty, but as a matter of likelihood. It is not required to prove well-foundedness conclusively beyond doubt, or even that persecution is more probable than not. To establish 'well-foundedness', persecution must be proved to be reasonably possible.[71]

2.4.2 Burden of proof

The UNHCR has stated that, in accordance with the general legal principle that the burden of proof lies on the person submitting a claim, the relevant facts have to be furnished in the first place by the applicant. While the burden of proof, in principle, rests on the applicant, the duty to ascertain and evaluate all the relevant facts is shared between the applicant and the examiner. In some cases, it may be for the examiner to use all the means at his or her disposal to produce the necessary evidence in support of the application.[72] This means that, in some cases, the examiner – whether the first

---

67 See on this Convention Boeles 1997, pp. 329-339.
68 Article 7 of the European Convention on Establishment stipulates: 'Nationals of any Contracting State shall enjoy in the territory of any other Party, under the same conditions as nationals of the latter Party, full legal and judicial protection of their persons and property and of their rights and interests. In particular, they shall have, in the same manner as the nationals of the latter Party, the right of access to the competent judicial and administrative authorities and the right to obtain the assistance of any person of their choice who is qualified by the laws of the country.' Grahl-Madsen also refers to these Articles in the European Convention on Establishment in his analysis of the meaning of Article 16 Refugee Convention. See Grahl-Madsen 1966-1972, Volume I, pp. 33-35.
69 UNHCR Handbook, paras. 42 and 51, Wouters 2009, p. 93, p. 549: there must be a 'serious possibility' that the claimant's life or freedom would be threatened on account of one of the persecution grounds.
70 *Note on Burden and Standard of Proof in Refugee Claims* of 16 December 1998, available at: http://www.unhcr.org/refworld/docid/3ae6b3338.html, last visited on 23 August 2011.
71 *Ibidem*, paras. 2 and 17.
72 Paras. 195 and 196 of the *UNHCR Handbook*; *Note on Burden and Standard of Proof in Refugee Claims* of 16 December 1998, para. 6. See also para. 19 in the Submission in the case of *Mir Isfahani v. the Netherlands*, available at: http://www.unhcr.org/refworld/docid/454f5e484.html, last visited on 23

→

instance administrative organ or the court on appeal or both – need(s) to actively search for evidence. This holds true particularly where there is not much public information available on the situation in the country of origin.[73] Importantly, the refugee claimant does not have the specific burden of proof as to the reasons for which he or she may be persecuted: it is for the examiner, when investigating the facts of the case, to ascertain the reasons for the persecution and to see whether these reasons match the grounds mentioned in the RC.[74]

A principle alleviating the burden of proof can be found in paragraph 45 of the UNHCR Handbook. This provision states that

> 'It may be assumed that a person has well-founded fear of being persecuted if he has already been the victim of persecution for one of the reasons enumerated in the 1951 Convention.'

According to this principle, persecution in the past is a serious indication of the applicant's well-founded fear of persecution in the future.

2.4.3   Relevant facts and circumstances

The UNHCR has made clear that, on the one hand, personal circumstances, and on the other hand, elements concerning the situation in the country of origin are relevant. The applicant's personal circumstances include his or her background, experiences, personality, membership of a particular racial, religious, national, social or political group and any other personal factors which could expose him or her to persecution. Important personal circumstances are, for example, whether the applicant has previously suffered persecution or other forms of mistreatment; persecution experienced by relatives or friends of the applicant; persecution experienced by those persons in the same situation as the applicant; holding and expressing opinions not tolerated by the authorities which are critical of their policies or methods; unlawful departure or unauthorized stay in another country; desertion or draft-evasion for genuine political, religious or moral convictions; associating, in the country where asylum is requested, with refugees already recognised, expressing political views in the country where asylum is requested, and whether such actions have come to the notice of the authorities.[75]

Also relevant are personal experiences, such as arrest, detention, criminal charges, communication possibilities with one's lawyer, and, in general, experiences that make a person known and/or vulnerable.[76]

The applicant's statements must be viewed in the context of the relevant background situation, meaning the situation in the country of origin.[77] Relevant elements

---

August 2011. The case of *Mir Isfahani v. the Netherlands* brought to the ECtHR ended in a decision of 31 January 2008, Appl. No. 31252/03, to strike the application out of the list as, pending the proceedings on her asylum application, she was allowed to stay in the Netherlands.

73   Hoeksma 1990, p. 72.

74   *UNHCR Handbook*, paras. 66 and 67. See also Wouters 2009, p. 97.

75   UNHCR, *Note on Burden and Standard of Proof in Refugee Claims* of 16 December 1998, para. 19, *UNHCR Handbook*, paras. 41, 43, 45, 80-82, 96, 169.

76   Wouters 2009, p. 547.

concerning the situation in the country of origin include, for example, whether or not the country in question is party to international human rights treaties, a poor human rights situation and record or even gross violations of fundamental human rights, legislation imposing penal prosecution for a Convention ground, legislation imposing penalties on unlawful departure or unauthorized stay in another country (penalties for *Republikflucht*), disproportionately severe punishment on account of a Convention ground for desertion or draft-evasion, serious racial or religious or other discrimination, absence of protection by the authorities in cases of persecution committed by the local populace, the (non-)existence of an internal protection alternative, meaning an area inside the country of origin, not being the original place of residence, which is practically, legally and safely accessible to the person concerned, where this person has no risk of being subjected to persecution.[78]

Importantly, the UNHCR has made clear that the particular facts and circumstances of the case – both individual and concerning the country of origin – have to be seen in conjunction, and not in isolation.[79] Where isolated facts are insufficient to conclude that an applicant is a refugee, all the facts seen in conjunction may well lead to the opposite conclusion.

2.4.4   *Required degree of individual risk*

The Handbook distinguishes two main kinds of situations: the situation in which refugee status is determined on an individual basis and the situation in which group determination takes place whereby each member of the group is *prima facie* regarded as a refugee, which presumption can be rebutted on specific individual grounds. The first situation – individual status determination – is envisaged in paragraph 45 of the Handbook, which stipulates that an applicant for refugee status must normally show good reason why he or she individually fears persecution.[80]

Individual status determination does not mean, however, that an applicant must show that he or she, and only he or she, is singled out. The idea that refugee status determination requires a very high degree of individual risk (this applicant and only this applicant is targeted) has no basis in the RC.[81] The literal meaning of 'well-founded fear' does not point to such a requirement. The persecution grounds of race, nationality, and social group, rather, point in the opposite direction as they imply affiliation to a certain group. The experiences of others who are related or in a similar

---

77   *UNHCR Handbook*, para. 42.
78   UNHCR, *Note on Burden and Standard of Proof in Refugee Claims* of 16 December 1998, para. 19, *UNHCR Handbook*, paras. 43, 54, 55, 57, 61, 65, 68, 72, 74, 97-100, 169; see on the (non-)existence of an internal protection alternative Wouters 2009, pp. 104-110 and 556-559.
79   See Hoeksma 1990, pp. 123 and 138. The need to approach facts and circumstances not in an isolated manner but rather in a holistic way is also expressed in the *UNHCR Handbook*, paras. 43 and 55, which state that 'all these factors, e.g. a person's character, his background, his influence, his wealth or his outspokenness, may lead to the conclusion that his fear of persecution is "well-founded"', and 'where measures of discrimination are in themselves not of a serious character, they may nevertheless give rise to a reasonable fear of persecution if they produce, in the mind of the person concerned, a feeling of apprehension and insecurity as regards his future existence.'
80   *UNHCR Handbook*, para. 45.
81   See Battjes 2011, p. 20, who refers to Spijkerboer 2005 and Durieux 2008.

position, such as family members or fellow political activists, may well indicate the existence of a risk of being persecuted for the applicant concerned.[82] In other words, the risk does not necessarily need to be based on personal experiences of the applicant demonstrating that he or she has been singled out.

The second situation – group determination – is envisaged in paragraph 44 of the Handbook, stating:

> 'While refugee status must normally be determined on an individual basis, situations have also arisen in which entire groups have been displaced under circumstances indicating that members of the group could be considered individually as refugees. In such situations, the need to provide assistance is often extremely urgent and it may not be possible for purely practical reasons to carry out individual determination of refugee status for each member of the group. Recourse has therefore been had to so-called "group determination" of refugee status, whereby each member of the group is regarded prima facie (i.e. in the absence of evidence to the contrary) as a refugee.'[83]

For individuals belonging to a group that is targeted as a whole it is not necessary to be further singled out. To put it differently, in the words of Grahl-Madsen: once a person is subjected to a measure of such gravity that we consider it 'persecution', that person is persecuted in the sense of the Convention, irrespective of how many others are subjected to the same or similar measures.[84]

The scale of violence in a country must be very grave for the UNHCR to assume that certain groups have been targeted and that group determination is the more appropriate method.[85] Some examples of situations in which it assumed that certain groups were targeted and that group determination seemed more appropriate are the armed conflicts in Iraq and Somalia. In the Eligibility Guidelines for Assessing the International Protection Needs of Iraqi Asylum-seekers of August 2007, the UNHCR stated that this armed conflict was victimising specific groups and that members of such groups did not need to be singled out or individually targeted.[86] And in the Eligibility Guidelines for Assessing the International Protection Needs of Asylum-seekers from Somalia of May 2010, the UNHCR stated that it encouraged the adoption of a group-based protection approach where individual refugee status determination would exceed local capacities.[87]

---

82 *UNHCR Handbook*, para. 43.

83 *Ibidem*, para. 44.

84 Grahl-Madsen 1966, p. 213. See also Goodwin-Gill 1998, pp. 76, 77, Wouters 2009, p. 87.

85 See, for the same conclusion, Wouters 2009, p. 88, who states that 'the UNHCR seems to think that such a situation will not easily emerge'.

86 *Eligibility Guidelines for Assessing the International Protection Needs of Iraqi Asylum-seekers* of August 2007, p. 134. These guidelines can be found at: www.unhcr.org/refworld/docid/46deb05557.html, last visited on 23 August 2011.

87 *Eligibility Guidelines for Assessing the International Protection Needs of Asylum-seekers from Somalia* of May 2010, p. 9. These guidelines can be found at: www.unhcr.org/refworld/pdfid/4be3b9142.pdf, last visited on 23 August 2011.

2.4.5   *Credibility assessment*

The UNHCR has stated that general, or overall, credibility is required. This means that the applicant's statements must generally be coherent and plausible, and must not run counter to generally known facts. Where the adjudicator considers that the applicant's story is, on the whole, coherent and plausible, any element of doubt should not prejudice the applicant's claim; that is, the applicant should be given the 'benefit of the doubt'.[88] In assessing the credibility of a claimant, consideration must be given to the fact that a person who, because of his or her experiences, is in fear of the authorities of his or her own country, may be afraid to speak freely and give a full and accurate account of his or her case to the authorities of the country in which he or she has requested asylum. Due to the intensity of past events, or due to time lapse, the applicant may not be able to remember all factual details or to recount them accurately or may confuse them; thus he or she may be vague or inaccurate in providing detailed facts. Inability to remember or provide all dates or minor details, as well as minor inconsistencies, insubstantial vagueness or incorrect statements which are not material may be taken into account in the final assessment on credibility, but should not be used as decisive factors.[89]

Absence of corroborative evidence supporting the statements of the applicant does not automatically make these statements incredible. Given the special situation of asylum seekers, they should not be required to produce evidence supporting every single statement made. Many asylum seekers have valid reasons for the absence of documents or reliance on fraudulent documents, for example, because they were forced to leave their countries without documents or they have been compelled to protect the identity of the individuals who assisted them in reaching the country of asylum. The absence of corroborative documents should not prevent the claim from being accepted if such statements are consistent with known facts and the general credibility of the applicant is good.[90]

In its Submission to the ECtHR in the case of *Mir Isfahani v. the Netherlands* (2005),[91] the UNHCR made clear that there was no justification for imposing a stricter credibility standard (stricter than the standard of general credibility) in cases where corroborating evidence was totally absent. It criticised Dutch jurisprudence, which imposed a stricter credibility standard – being that the flight narrative has to be positively persuasive – in a large majority of asylum cases where the applicant had not submitted all documents necessary for the assessment of the claim and the lack of documentation had not been attributable to him or her.[92] The UNHCR has expressed

---

88   *UNHCR Handbook*, paras. 197, 204, UNHCR, *Note on Burden and Standard of Proof in Refugee Claims* of 16 December 1998, paras. 11, 12.

89   *UNHCR Handbook*, para. 198, UNHCR, *Note on Burden and Standard of Proof in Refugee Claims* of 16 December 1998, para. 9. Submission in the case of *Mir Isfahani v. the Netherlands*, para. 21.

90   UNHCR, *Note on Burden and Standard of Proof in Refugee Claims* of 16 December 1998, para. 10.

91   See note 71 above.

92   Submission in the case of *Mir Isfahani v. the Netherlands,*paras. 25-27. In the Submission reference is made to a number of judgments of the Council of State in which this stricter credibility standard is applied, among them the judgments of 27 January 2003, 200206297/1, *JV* 2003/103 and 11 August 2003, 200304080/1, *JV* 2003/441. At the moment of completion of this book, application of the

→

deep concern over this practice in the Netherlands, which appears to be the rule rather than the exception, for two reasons. First, too much corroborative evidence is demanded from the asylum seeker. The strict application of the requirement for documentary proof of identity, nationality, travel route and reasons for leaving the country does not take sufficient account of the special situation of asylum-seekers. Second, a too strict and, therefore, incorrect credibility standard is applied when corroborative evidence on one of the four mentioned elements is absent and the asylum seeker is, as a result, deemed to be 'without documents'. The UNHCR stresses that lack of documentation does not in itself render a claim abusive and that many asylum seekers have valid reasons for the absence of documents, for example because they were forced to leave their countries without documents or they have been compelled to protect the identity of the individuals who assisted them in reaching the country of asylum. According to the UNHCR, there is no justification for imposing a higher credibility standard in such cases.[93]

The UNHCR has on numerous occasions expressed its opinion that judges dealing with asylum cases should be able to obtain a personal impression of the applicant and that appeal or review proceedings should involve points of fact and points of law.[94] It considers necessary that national courts independently and of their own account assess the credibility of the statements by the asylum seeker. Indeed, in its Submission to the ECtHR in the case of *Mir Isfahani v. the Netherlands* (2005), the UNHCR stressed that a meaningful appeal was a fundamental requirement in the context of refugee status determination, where the consequences of an erroneous decision could be particularly serious. The Submission explained that a 'formal reconsideration' as mentioned in ExCom Conclusion No. 8 implied a completely new consideration of the case on appeal, both on facts and on law, meaning full judicial review. It criticised the limitations in the scope of judicial review in the Netherlands, in particular the fact that the judicial appeal authorities did not have the authority to fully examine the credibility assessment of the asylum seeker's account made by the administrative authority (the Immigration and Naturalisation Service, IND).[95]

It is, finally, important to mention here that in September 2011, UNHCR started working on guidelines for credibility assessment under the name Credo – Improving Credibility Assessment in EU asylum procedures. Within the framework of this project UNHCR works together with the Helsinki Committee and the IARLJ. At the

---

stricter credibility standard in cases where the asylum seeker is held to be attributably without documents was still the prevailing jurisprudential line in the Netherlands. See for a more detailed description Van Bennekom & Van der Winden 2011, pp. 287-308.

93 See paras. 25-27 in the Submission in the case of *Mir Isfahani v. the Netherlands*.

94 To mention just a few examples, see UNHCR, *Global Consultations on International Protection / Third Track: Asylum Processes (Fair and Efficient Asylum Procedures)*, 31 May 2001, EC/GC/01/12, available at: www.unhcr.org/refworld/docid/3b36f2fca.html, last visited 23 August 2011, paras. 43 and 41; Submission by the UNHCR in the case of *Mir Isfahani v. the Netherlands* – Appl. No. 31252/03, May 2005, www.unhcr.org/refworld/docid/454f5e484.html, last visited 23 August 2011, paras. 31-42; UNHCR comments on the European Commission's proposal for a Directive of the European Parliament and of the Council on minimum standards on procedures in Member States for granting and withdrawing international protection (COM(2009)554, 21 October 2009), available at: http://www.unhcr.org/refworld/pdfid/4c63ebd32.pdf, last visited 23 August 2011, p. 40, 41.

95 See para. 32 in the Submission in the case of *Mir Isfahani v. the Netherlands*.

moment of completion of this study, these guidelines were not ready but expected to appear in March 2013.[96]

2.4.6 Admission of evidence, means and sources of evidence, minimum quantity and quality of evidence

2.4.6.1 Admission of evidence, means and sources of evidence

The asylum seeker should submit 'any available evidence'. The UNHCR Handbook states that the applicant should make an effort to support his or her statements by any available evidence and give a satisfactory explanation for any lack of evidence.[97] The UNHCR's Submission in the case of *Mir Isfahani v. the Netherlands* (2005) mentioned, as examples of evidence, documents or the testimony of witnesses who could support the applicant's claim for refugee status or who had expertise on relevant country conditions.[98] The principle that any available evidence should be brought in to support statements, arguably, implies, first of all, that evidence, in order to be admitted to the procedure, does not necessarily need to have a particular form. Written but also oral evidence (witness statements) must, in principle, be allowed into the procedure and examined. Secondly, it entails that evidence may not be excluded too easily from the examination on the single ground that the source is not reliable, without materially considering its content. Documentary evidence, first of all, comprises documents corroborating statements regarding identity (such as a passport, identity card, military service card) and flight narrative (for example, arrest warrants, medical reports stating that scars are the result of torture, letters from political organisations confirming membership).[99] The UNHCR is of the opinion that any documentary evidence submitted in an attempt to support statements must be examined seriously; when it is clear, however, that forged documents have been submitted, then such evidence may be discarded on the ground that it is false or forged.[100]

As well as this individual evidence, information on the country of origin plays an important role, which, logically, follows from the principle that statements must be viewed in the context of the relevant background situation, meaning the situation in the country of origin.[101] In its submissions, the UNHCR refers to country reports from a wide variety of sources. Particularly often reference is made to reports drawn up by UN bodies and organisations, including the UNHCR itself. Also used are reports by non-governmental organisations, such as Amnesty International and Human Rights Watch. Country reports issued by foreign affairs ministries are also a much used source.[102]

---

96 See http://helsinki.hu/en/credo-improving-credibility-assessment-in-eu-asylum-procedures.
97 *UNHCR Handbook*, para. 205.
98 See para. 19 in the Submission in the case of *Mir Isfahani v. the Netherlands*.
99 The examples of individual documentary evidence considered as relevant and important evidence by UNHCR are drawn from Hoeksma 1990.
100 See, for, example, the Submission of the UNHCR in Hoeksma 1990 on pp. 261-269.
101 *UNHCR Handbook*, para. 42.
102 The examples of sources of country of origin information are drawn from the UNHCR's Submissions to the ECtHR in different cases. See below notes 122-128, and from Hoeksma 1990.

2.4.6.2   Minimum quantity and quality of evidence

The UNHCR has often underlined that, as far as evidence is concerned, refugee claims are unlike criminal and civil cases. Due to the special and difficult evidentiary position of the applicant for asylum, the requirement of evidence should not be applied too strictly.[103] Due to this principle, it is not allowed to require evidence of every single statement. It must always be remembered that it is often difficult for asylum seekers to provide evidence in relation to key facts or their personal history and that they often have valid reasons for the absence of documents. This implies, first of all, that administrative decision makers and judges will always have to ask specifically why evidence is lacking. Secondly, it implies that they will often have to conclude, in a spirit of justice and understanding,[104] that the reasons for the absence of evidence are valid and that this absence may, therefore, not be held against the applicant. The complete absence of supportive evidence does not automatically mean that the claim is unmeritorious; the UNHCR has stressed that the adjudicator will often need to depend entirely on the oral statements by the applicant and make an assessment in light of the objective situation in the country of origin. Reference is made to the UNHCR's Submission in the case of *Mir Isfahani v. the Netherlands* (2005), which was described above in section 2.4.5.[105]

2.4.7   Appreciation and weighing of evidence

To the best of my knowledge the UNHCR has so far not issued any explicit position on this aspect.

2.4.8   Opportunities for presenting evidence and reacting to evidence

The UNHCR takes the stance that information used as a basis for decisions should be similarly available to the asylum seeker and his or her legal adviser or counsellor, and should, further, be subject to the scrutiny of review or appeal authorities (national courts). Information and its sources may only be withheld under clearly defined conditions, where disclosure of sources would seriously jeopardize national security or the security of the organisations or persons providing information.[106]

The UNHCR has addressed the issue of secret evidence in more detail within the context of exclusion from refugee protection on the basis of Article 1F of the RC. According to the UNHCR such exclusion should not be based on sensitive evidence that cannot be challenged by the individual concerned. It accepts, however, that ex-

---

103   *UNHCR Handbook*, paras. 196, 197, 203; Report of July 2003 'Implementation of the Aliens Act 2000 in the Netherlands, UNHCR's Observations and Recommendations'; UNHCR, *Note on Burden and Standard of Proof in Refugee Claims* of 16 December 1998, paras. 10, 20, 22. See also paras. 25-27 in the Submission in the case of *Mir Isfahani v. the Netherlands*.

104   *UNHCR Handbook*, para. 202.

105   See paras. 18-27 in the Submission in the case of *Mir Isfahani v. the Netherlands*.

106   UNHCR, *Fair and Efficient Asylum Procedures: A Non-Exhaustive Overview of Applicable International Standards*, 2 September 2005, www.unhcr.org/refworld/docid/432ae9204.html, last visited 23 August 2011, pp. 5 and 6.

ceptionally, anonymous evidence may be relied upon, but only where this is absolutely necessary to protect the safety of witnesses and the asylum seekers's ability to challenge the substance of the evidence is not substantially prejudiced. Furthermore, the UNHCR has stated that where national security interests are at stake, these may be protected by introducing procedural safeguards which also respect the asylum seeker's due process rights.[107]

2.4.9 Judicial application of investigative powers

The UNHCR has taken the position that, in some cases, it may be for the administrative and judicial examiner to use all the means at his or her disposal to produce the necessary evidence in support of the application.[108] As has been said above, the UNHCR has, on numerous occasions, expressed its opinion that judges dealing with asylum cases should be able to examine points of fact and points of law and that on appeal, a fresh consideration of the case, both on facts and on law, should take place.[109] In its document 'Improving Asylum Procedures: Comparative Analysis and Recommendations for Law and Practice – Detailed Research on Key Asylum Procedures Directive Provisions' (2010), the UNHCR explicitly recommended that the appeal body should have fact-finding competence, in order to fulfil the requirement of rigorous scrutiny established in international human rights law (see Chapter 5).[110]

2.4.10 Time limits for the presentation of statements and evidence

In the UNHCR's opinion, it is the applicant's duty to submit all available evidence supporting his or her claim as early as possible. It also stresses, however, that failure to fulfil this obligation may be for a variety of reasons. The applicant may, for example, not have been aware of the evidence, or it may not have been available to him or her. To avoid any erroneous decision, the appeal authorities should have an opportunity either to take evidence into consideration which was not submitted earlier, or to refer the case back to the first instance authority for such a review. No case should be rejected solely on the basis that the relevant information was not presented or documents were not submitted earlier. To ignore evidence which supports the essence of the claim would be in breach of the 1951 Convention and may, depending on the specific circumstances of the case, lead to a violation of the *non-refoulement* principle.[111]

---

107 UNHCR, *Guidelines on International Protection No. 5: Application of the Exclusion Clauses: Article 1F of the 1951 Convention relating to the Status of Refugees* (HCR/GIP/03/05) 4 September 2003, para. 36.
108 *UNHCR Handbook*, paras. 195, 196.
109 See note 95 above.
110 UNHCR, *Improving Asylum Procedures: Comparative Analysis and Recommendations for Law and Practice - Detailed Research on Key Asylum Procedures Directive Provisions* (2010), available at: http://www. unhcr.org/cgi-bin/texis/vtx/refworld/rwmain?docid=4bab55752, last visited 23 August 2011, pp. 89, 90.
111 See para. 41 in the Submission in the case of *Mir Isfahani v. the Netherlands*.

2.4.11   *Point in time for the risk assessment*

The UNHCR has underlined the necessity for an examination at the time of appeal of the question of whether or not expulsion breaches the prohibition on *refoulement*.[112] In other words, the risk must always be assessed *ex nunc*.[113]

2.5   The requirement of co-operation with the UNHCR

Article 35 stipulates:

> '*Article 35: Co-operation of the national authorities with the United Nations*
> 1. The Contracting States undertake to co-operate with the Office of the United Nations High Commissioner for Refugees, or any other agency of the United Nations which may succeed it, in the exercise of its functions, and shall in particular facilitate its duty of supervising the application of the provisions of this Convention.
> 2. In order to enable the Office of the High Commissioner or any other agency of the United Nations which may succeed it, to make reports to the competent organs of the United Nations, the Contracting States undertake to provide them in the appropriate form with information and statistical data requested concerning:
> (a) the condition of refugees,
> (b) the implementation of this Convention, and
> (c) laws, regulations and decrees which are, or may hereafter be, in force relating to refugees.'[114]

As the text makes clear, Article 35 is about two things: an obligation for states to co-operate with the UNHCR, and the supervisory role of the UNHCR.[115]

2.5.1   *The UNHCR and national courts*

Türk (2002), Zwaan (2005) and Bruin (2011) distinguish different models of participation by the UNHCR in national asylum proceedings:
a.   Status determination: the UNHCR makes the decision of who is a refugee.
b.   Membership of the national committee or commission responsible for status determination.
c.   Advising and consulting the national administrative and judicial authorities.

---

112 See, for example, Hoeksma 1990, p. 49; UNHCR comments on the European Commission's proposal for a Directive of the European Parliament and of the Council on minimum standards on procedures in Member States for granting and withdrawing international protection (COM(2009)554, 21 October 2009), at: http://www.unhcr.org/refworld/pdfid/4c63ebd32.pdf, p. 40, 41.
113 See also Wouters 2009, pp. 552, 553.
114 The supervisory role of the UNHCR is also laid down in Preamble para. 6 of the Refugee Convention, Article 8 of the UNHCR Statute and Article II of the Refugee Protocol.
115 Bruin 2011, p. 243.

The first two models nowadays occur only exceptionally in Europe.[116] The focus below will, therefore, be on the advisory and consulting role of the UNHCR in relation to national courts. Article 21 of the EU Procedures Directive stipulates in its first paragraph at sub c that the UNHCR is entitled 'to present its views, in the exercise of its supervisory responsibilities under Article 35 of the Geneva Convention, to any competent authorities regarding individual applications for asylum at any stage of the procedure'.[117] This provision entails that the UNHCR is entitled to make submissions to national courts in the form of *amicus curiae* briefs, statements or letters.[118] National courts cannot refuse the UNHCR leave to intervene with reference to national law. ExCom has made clear in its Note on International Protection of 2 July 2003 that it considers Article 35 RC very important and that 'amicus curiae briefs and court submissions represent valuable tools to promote the proper interpretation of national and international refugee law'.[119] Article 21 of the EU Procedures Directive cannot be seen in isolation from Articles 8, second paragraph, sub b, and 38, of that Directive, which concern the administration (not national courts) but also concern the advisory role of the UNHCR and stipulate, in short, that decision makers in asylum cases must have access to and gather accurate actual information from different sources, including the UNHCR, about the general situation in the countries of origin, and that the UNHCR information must also be taken into account in decision making concerning the revocation of refugee status.[120]

UNHCR submissions may enter the national court proceedings via different possible routes:

1. The UNHCR of its own motion approaches the court and submits a view regarding a particular aspect of a pending case, or an integral view on the question of whether or not the asylum seeker is a refugee and would, consequently, run the risk of being persecuted upon expulsion to the country of origin.

---

116 Türk 2002, p. 17, Zwaan 2005, p. 51, Bruin 2011, pp. 242, 243.

117 The supervisory role of the UNHCR is also laid down in a number of provisions contained in other EU asylum directives with less relevance for this research as they do not primarily concern the relationship between the UNHCR and national courts. Zwaan 2005 provides a list of these provisions on pp. 84-88; see also the table on pp. 26-27.

118 Türk 2002, p. 11, Zwaan 2005, p. 7, Wouters 2009, p. 41.

119 A/AC.96/975, 2 July 2003, para. 45.

120 EU Directive 2005/85 of 1 December 2005 on minimum standards on procedures in Member States for granting and withdrawing refugee status, *OJ of the EU* L 326, 13 December 2005, p. 13-34. Article 8, second paragraph, sub b, stipulates: 'Member States shall ensure that decisions by the determining authority on applications for asylum are taken after an appropriate examination. To that end, Member States shall ensure that: (b) precise and up-to-date information is obtained from various sources, such as the United Nations High Commissioner for Refugees (UNHCR), as to the general situation prevailing in the countries of origin of applicants for asylum and, where necessary, in countries through which they have transited, and that such information is made available to the personnel responsible for examining applications and taking decisions.' Article 38 stipulates in the first paragraph: 'Member States shall ensure that, where the competent authority is considering withdrawing the refugee status of a third country national or stateless person in accordance with Article 14 of Directive 2004/83/EC, the person concerned shall enjoy the following guarantees: (c) the competent authority is able to obtain precise and up-to date information from various sources, such as, where appropriate, from the UNHCR, as to the general situation prevailing in the countries of origin of the persons concerned.'

2a. One of the parties brings in general information compiled by the UNHCR, that is, information which was not specifically compiled for a particular pending case, for example, country of origin reports or UNHCR guidelines.

2b. One of the parties brings in a view by the UNHCR on the question of whether or not the asylum seeker is a refugee.

2c. (One of) the parties asks the court to invite the UNHCR to participate in court proceedings as an expert or as a witness regarding a particular aspect of the pending case.

3a. The court decides of its own motion to use general written information compiled by the UNHCR, for example, country of origin reports or UNHCR guidelines.

3b. The court decides of its own motion to invite the UNHCR to submit a view on the question of whether or not the asylum seeker is a refugee.[121]

3c. The court decides of its own motion to invite the UNHCR to submit a view on a particular aspect of a case as an expert or witness, either in writing or orally during court hearings.

In order to provide national asylum courts with concrete examples of how co-operation with the UNHCR can take place, the next section will analyse how the two international Courts in the European Union, the ECtHR and the CJEU, co-operate with the UNHCR.

2.5.2 The ECtHR and the UNHCR

Zwaan (2005) provides a list of judgments and decisions of the ECtHR in which the UNHCR is mentioned.[122] In at least the following final cases the UNHCR filed case-specific submissions to the ECtHR:[123]

- *T.I. v. the United Kingdom* (2000), a case concerning (the operation and application of) the Dublin Convention[124] (see Chapter 7);[125]

---

121 In the past, the Dutch Council of State used to invite the UNHCR representative in the Netherlands to submit its view, during a hearing open to the public, in every single asylum case coming before it. In the period between 1976 and 1994 the Raad van State functioned as the court of first instance performing judicial review in asylum cases. The old practice of inviting the UNHCR to submit its view in every asylum case was not taken up again in 2001, the year in which – after a period of absence of jurisdiction – the Council of State became the higher appeal instance in asylum cases. Hoeksma (former legal advisor of the UNHCR branch office in the Netherlands) has collected UNHCR Submissions to the Council of State in his book 'De Menselijke maat, zienswijzen in asielzaken' of 1990, see bibliography.

122 Zwaan 2005, pp. 97-146.

123 See also Westerveen 2011, p. 214.

124 At the time of this case, the predecessor of the EU Dublin Regulation (Regulation 2003/ 343/EC of 18 February 2003, establishing the criteria and mechanisms for determining the Member State responsible for examining an asylum application lodged in one of the Member States by a third country national, *OJ of the EU* L 50, 25 February 2003, pp. 1-10, last amended by *OJ of the EU* L 304, 14 November 2008, p. 83), was in force, being the Dublin Convention (Convention determining the State responsible for examining applications for asylum lodged in one of the Member States of the European Communities, 15 June 1990).

- *K.K.C. v. the Netherlands* (2001), in which the ECtHR granted leave to the UNHCR to submit a written intervention and specifically requested that its submission should address the practical and legal situation of displaced persons from Chechnya in the Russian Federation;[126]
- *Mir Isfahani v. the Netherlands* (2008), in which case the UNHCR made a submission in order to assist the ECtHR in clarifying the appropriate standard and burden of proof in asylum cases as well as the scope of judicial review, in particular in relation to credibility issues (see above 2.4.2 and 2.4.5);[127]
- *Saadi v. the United Kingdom* (2008), in which the UNHCR expressed its stance on, *inter alia*, the legal status of asylum seekers pending the processing of an asylum claim;[128]
- *Abdolkhani and Karimnia v. Turkey* (2009), discussed in more detail below;[129]
- *M.S.S. v. Belgium and Greece* (2011), a case concerning the operation and application of the EU Dublin Regulation (see Chapter 7);[130]
- *Hirsi Jamaa and others v. Italy* (2012), which submission addressed the practice and justification of 'push-back' operations, that is interception and return of asylum seekers at sea by the Italian government, the situation and legal status of asylum seekers and refugees in Libya, and the extra-territorial scope of the principle of *non-refoulement* and pursuant legal obligations concerning the rescue and interception of people at sea.[131]

The cases mentioned by Zwaan and those listed above may serve as examples to national courts in three ways. First, they illustrate what kind of information the UNHCR submitted. Second, they show how this information entered the ECtHR's proceedings and whether the initiative was taken by the UNHCR, a party to the case, or the ECtHR. In principle, the UNHCR's views may enter the proceedings before

---

125 ECtHR, *T.I. v. the UK*, admissibility decision, 7 March 2000, Appl. No. 43844/98; the UNHCR Submission can be found at: http://www.unhcr.org/refworld/pdfid/42f7737c4, last visited 23 August 2011.

126 ECtHR, *K.K.C. v. the Netherlands*, admissibility decision, 3 July 2001, Appl. No. 58964/00; the UNHCR Submission can be found at: http://www.unhcr.org/refworld/pdfid/ 42f774674.pdf, last visited 23 August 2011.

127 ECtHR, *Mir Isfahani v. the Netherlands*, 31 January 2008, Appl. No. 31252/03, decision to strike the application out of the list; the UNHCR Submission can be found at http://www.unhcr.org/refworld/docid/454f5e484.html, last visited 23 August 2011.

128 ECtHR, *Saadi v. the UK*, 29 January 2008, Appl. No. 13229/03; the UNHCR Submission can be found at: http://www.unhcr.org/refworld/pdfid/47c520722.pdf, last visited 23 August 2011.

129 ECtHR, *Abdolkhani and Karimnia v. Turkey*, 22 September 2009, Application No. 30471/08. Bruin and Reneman have extensively commented on this judgment in *NAV*, No. 6 of December 2009; the UNHCR Submission can be found at: http://www.unhcr.org/refworld/docid/4991ad9f2.html, last visited 23 August 2011.

130 ECtHR, *M.S.S. v. Belgium and Greece*, 21 January 2011, Appl. No. 30696/09. See for a detailed analysis of this case Van Bennekom & Van der Winden 2011, pp. 99-103, and Battjes 2011. The UNHCR Submission can be found at: http://www.unhcr.org/refworld/docid/4c19e7512.html, last visited 23 August 2011.

131 ECtHR, *Hirsi Jamaa and others v. Italy*, 23 February 2012, Appl. No. 27765/09. The UNHCR Submission in this case can be found at: http://www.unhcr.org/refworld/docid/4d92d2c22.html, last visited 19 December 2012.

the ECtHR via the same routes as those described above, the only difference being that the UNHCR has no right of intervention before the ECtHR but needs to be granted leave to intervene.[132] Third, these cases illustrate how the ECtHR weighed and appreciated the information submitted by the UNHCR. A good illustration of all three questions is the case of *Abdolkhani and Karimnia v. Turkey* (2009).[133] The case concerned two Iran ian applicants who were former members of the Iranian People's Mojahedin Organisation (PMOI). They were recognised as refugees by the UNHCR while they were staying in Iraq. After leaving the PMOI, they went to the Temporary Interview and Protection Facility, a camp created by the United States forces in Iraq, subsequently named the Ashraf Refugee Camp. In April 2008, the Ashraf Refugee Camp was closed down and the applicants, along with other former PMOI members, were transferred to northern Iraq. After this, on an unspecified date, the applicants arrived in Turkey, with the aim of contacting the UNHCR in Turkey and asking it to process their (resettlement) cases. The Turkish authorities arrested them and deported them back to Iraq, after which they immediately re-entered Turkey. The authorities then attempted to deport them once again, to Iran this time. The ECtHR assessed the risk the applicants would run if expelled to Iraq and the risk they would run if expelled to Iran. In this assessment, the ECtHR used three different types of UNHCR information which entered the proceedings in three different ways.

First, the ECtHR invited the UNHCR to submit a written intervention as a third party. The Chamber President gave it leave to intervene in the written procedure as a third party under Article 36(2)ECHR and Rule 44(2) of the Rules of Court.[134] The Court specifically requested that the UNHCR's submission should address a number of specific questions, *inter alia* the procedural rules and principles governing its refugee status determination in Turkey, the situation and legal status of asylum seekers and refugees in Turkey, and the relationship between the UNHCR in Turkey and the Turkish national authorities.[135]

Second, the applicants brought in UNHCR information, being a Report by the UNHCR Resettlement Service of February 2008, entitled 'Information Regarding Iranian Refugees in the Temporary Interview Protection Facility (ex-TIPF/ARC) at Al-Ashraf, Iraq'.[136] The applicants also relied on the refugee status determination made by the UNHCR while they were living in Iraq.[137] Third, the ECtHR, of its own motion, decided to bring in and use general UNHCR information: its press release

---

132 See Article 36, second paragraph, ECHR. The President of the Chamber may, in the interests of the proper administration of justice, invite, or grant leave to, any person concerned who is not the applicant, to submit written comments, or, in exceptional cases, to take part in a hearing. See also Rules 1(o), 34 paras. 4, 44 and 77 para. 3, Rules of Court. The Rules of Court do not provide a right of intervention. The invitation or grant of leave to organisations to intervene is made in the event that such an organisation can establish an interest in the outcome of the case and contribute information or argumentation of use to the Court during the consideration of the case. See Zwaan 2005, p. 39.

133 ECtHR, *Abdolkhani and Karimnia v. Turkey*, 22 September 2009, Application No. 30471/08.

134 *Ibidem*, para. 5.

135 See the Submission by the UNHCR in the case of *Abdolkhani & Karimnia v. Turkey*, 22 September 2009, Appl. No. 30471/08, p. 1.

136 ECtHR, *Abdolkhani & Karimnia v. Turkey*, 22 September 2009, Appl. No. 30471/08, para. 46.

137 *Ibidem*, paras. 66 and 67.

issued on 25 April 2008 stating: 'UNHCR deplores refugee expulsion by Turkey which resulted in four deaths'.[138]

The ECtHR used these three types of UNHCR information, as well as other sources containing country of origin information and other, more individual, evidence, to assess the risk. It gave considerable weight to the different documents submitted by or compiled by the UNHCR, considering that:

> 'The UNHCR submitted that former PMOI refugees faced further security risks in Iraq in addition to being affected by the general conditions of insecurity in the country. (…) The Court finds the UNHCR's concerns reasonable having regard, in particular, to the fact that Iraq is not a party to the 1951 Geneva Convention. (…) Given that the applicants' deportation to Iraq would be carried out in the absence of a legal framework providing adequate safeguards against risks of death or ill-treatment in Iraq and against the applicants' removal to Iran by the Iraqi authorities, the Court considers that there are substantial grounds for believing that the applicants risk a violation of their rights under Article 3 of the Convention if returned to Iraq.'[139]

Particularly interesting is the weight the ECtHR attached to information from the UNHCR in the assessment of the risk upon expulsion to Iran. It referred to information from different sources and considered that it was, in fact, unclear what consequences expulsion to Iran would have, and that, as a consequence, it could not draw firm conclusions on the risk of expulsion of the applicants to Iran.[140] The ECtHR considered it important that the UNHCR never obtained access to returned former PMOI members:

> 'Nevertheless, it is significant that there is a lack of reliable public information concerning such a large group of persons. Furthermore, the Court cannot overlook the fact that the UNHCR have not had access to the returnees in Iran, and that the Iranian Government's promise of amnesty for PMOI members has never been realised.'[141]

The Court also attached considerable weight to the refugee status determination by the UNHCR while the applicants were living in Iraq. It considered:

> 'The Court must also give due weight to the UNHCR's conclusions regarding the applicants' claims, before making its own assessment of the risk which the applicants would face if they were to be removed to Iran (see *Jabari*, cited above, § 41, and *N.A. v. the United Kingdom,* cited above, § 122). In this connection, the Court observes that, unlike the Turkish authorities, the UNHCR interviewed the applicants and had the opportunity to test the credibility of their fears and the veracity of their account of circumstances in their country of origin. Following these interviews, it found that the applicants risked being subjected to an arbitrary deprivation of life, detention and ill-treatment in their country of origin (see paragraphs 8 and 9 above).'[142]

---

138 *Ibidem*, para. 47.
139 *Ibidem*, paras. 71, 86-89.
140 *Ibidem*, paras. 78-81.
141 *Ibidem*, para. 81.
142 *Ibidem*, para. 82.

The case of *Abdolkhani and Karimnia v. Turkey* (2009) demonstrates that the ECtHR generally gives considerable weight to information submitted by the UNHCR. Other judgments confirm this. For example, in *K.R.S. v. UK* (2008), the ECtHR considered that information submitted by the UNHCR is to be regarded as independent, reliable and objective.[143] In addition to *Abdolkhani and Karimnia*, there are many other cases in which the ECtHR attached great weight to refugee status determinations by the UNHCR.[144] Information on countries of origin compiled by the UNHCR is also frequently used by the ECtHR (next to other sources) as happened in the case of *Abdolkhani and Karimnia*. The ECtHR tends to give the UNHCR's information on the countries of origin substantial value because of its access to the authorities of the country of origin as well as its ability to carry out on-site inspections and assessments in a manner which States and non-governmental organisations may not be able to do.[145] The exact evidentiary value accorded by the ECtHR to the UNHCR's country of origin information is also determined by the specific content of this information: the more the information is couched in terms of an Article 3-ECHR risk, the more weight the ECtHR tends to give to it, whereas when the UNHCR information focuses more on general socio-economic and humanitarian conditions in a particular country, the ECtHR is inclined to accord less weight to it.[146]

2.5.3   The CJEU and the UNHCR

So far, the UNHCR has had no possibility to intervene of its own accord in cases before the CJEU. According to Article 40 of the Protocol of the Statute of the CJEU,[147] the right of intervention in cases before the CJEU belongs only to Member States and institutions of the EU. The right of intervention is also open to any other person establishing an interest in the result of any cases submitted to the Court, save in cases between Member States, between EU institutions or between Member States and EU institutions. An important limitation is that an application to intervene shall be limited to supporting one of the parties. A third party wishing to intervene, therefore, has to have an interest in the case and has to support one of the parties. All of this

---

143 See, for example, the admissibility decision of the ECtHR *K.R.S. v. UK*, 2 December 2008, Appl. No. 32733/08, p. 16.

144 See, in addition to *Abdolkhani and Karimnia v. Turkey* also ECtHR, *Jabari v. Turkey*, 11 July 2000, Appl. No. 40035/98, para. 41; ECtHR, *Ayatollahi and Hosseinzadeh v. Turkey*, admissibility decision, 23 March 2010, Appl. No. 32971/98; ECtHR, *Charahili v. Turkey*, 13 April 2010, Appl. No. 46605/07, para. 59; ECtHR, *Khaydarov v. Russia*, 20 May 2010, Appl. No. 21055/09, para. 109; ECtHR, *M.B. and others v. Turkey*, 15 June 2010, Appl. No. 36009/08, paras. 14 and 33-34; ECtHR, *Dbouba v. Turkey*, 13 July 2010, Appl. No. 15916/09, paras. 42, 43.

145 See, for example, ECtHR, *N.A. v. the UK*, 17 July 2008, Appl. No. 25904/07, para. 121.

146 *Ibidem*, para. 122. See also ECtHR. *F.H. v. Sweden*, 20 January 2009, Appl. No. 32621/06, para. 92, where the ECtHR stated that where reports are focused on general socio-economic and humanitarian conditions, it has been inclined to accord less weight to them, since such conditions do not necessarily have a bearing on the question of a real risk to an individual applicant of ill-treatment within the meaning of Article 3.

147 Protocol of the Statute of the Court of Justice of the EU, 30 March 2010, OJ 2010, C 83/210, http://curia.europa.eu under Statute of the Court of Justice of the EU.

means that in a large number of cases only Member States or EU institutions can intervene.[148]

Under Article 25 of the Protocol of the Statute of the CJEU, the Court may at any time entrust any individual, body, authority, committee or other organisation it chooses with the task of giving an expert opinion. Under Article 26 of the Protocol the Court may hear witnesses. Via these routes the Court is able to invite the UNHCR to submit an expert opinion and hear it as a witness in asylum cases. Unlike the ECtHR, the CJEU has so far not used these opportunities. And unlike the ECtHR, the Court has so far not explicitly referred to UNHCR statements, position papers or other UNHCR information.[149]

However, what has actually happened and happens in asylum cases before the CJEU is that the UNHCR has in fact intervened in an informal and indirect way by making a statement or comment in the context of a case pending before the Court and issuing such a statement or comment on the internet. In fact, the UNHCR has issued such documents in the context of every asylum case before the CJEU. For example, in the context of the case of *Brahim Samba Diouf* (2011) it issued its Statement on the right to an effective remedy in relation to accelerated asylum procedures of 21 May 2010.[150] Advocates-General (A-Gs) take notice of these UNHCR statements and also of other documents issued by the UNHCR and refer to them in their opinions on the case. In this way, the UNHCR has become an informal *amicus* of the CJEU.[151] Some examples are provided below to illustrate how this works in practice.

In his opinion on the case of *M. and N. Elgafaji* (2008, discussed in Chapter 6),[152] A-G Maduro pointed out that the EU Member States had adopted very different refugee protection systems and that certain Member States had provided for a higher level of protection than that conferred under Article 3 ECHR. To illustrate this point, Maduro referred to the study by the UNHCR entitled 'Asylum in the European Union, A Study of the Implementation of the Qualification Directive' of November

---

148 Article 40 of the Protocol of the Statute of the Court of Justice of the EU stipulates: 'Member States and institutions of the Union may intervene in cases before the Court of Justice. The same right shall be open to the bodies, offices and agencies of the Union and to any other person which can establish an interest in the result of a case submitted to the Court. Natural or legal persons shall not intervene in cases between Member States, between institutions of the Union or between Member States and institutions of the Union. Without prejudice to the second paragraph, the States, other than the Member States, which are parties to the Agreement on the European Economic Area, and also the EFTA Surveillance Authority referred to in that Agreement, may intervene in cases before the Court where one of the fields of application of that Agreement is concerned.

An application to intervene shall be limited to supporting the form of order sought by one of the parties.'

See on the limited possibilities for the UNHCR to participate in proceedings before the ECtHR also Zwaan 2005, p. 50 and Pollet 2011, p. 220.

149 See for the same conclusion Bruin 2011, p. 244.

150 These statements are readily accessible on RefWorld via the query UNHCR, name of the case, under the heading 'related documents'.

151 Bruin 2011, p. 244. See on this practice also Pollet 2011, p. 220.

152 Opinion of A-G Poiares Maduro delivered on 9 September 2008 in Case C-465/07 of *M. and N. Elgafaji v. Staatssecretaris van Justitie* (reference for a preliminary ruling from the Nederlandse Raad van State).

2007.[153] Another example is the A-G's opinion in the case of *Abdulla and others* (2009).[154] A-G Mazák mentioned in his opinion on the case that the referring national court had doubts as to exactly which conditions should be met for cessation of refugee status under Article 11(e) of Directive 2004/83, and that this doubt had also been caused by the fact that the UNHCR's comments on the provisions of the RC governing cessation of refugee status were somewhat unclear. The A-G referred in note 7 to the 'UNHCR Guidelines on International Protection: Cessation of Refugee Status under Article 1(C) (5) and (6) of the RC' of 10 February 2003. These UNHCR Guidelines stipulate in points 15 and 16 that, in addition to the requirement that the fear of persecution has ceased to exist, there is a need for the existence of a functioning government and fundamental administrative structures, as evidenced by a functioning system of law and justice, as well as the existence of an adequate infrastructure to enable residents to exercise their rights, including their right to a basic livelihood. This position taken by the UNHCR clearly influenced the A-G's opinion as, in answering one of the posed questions, the A-G stated that, for refugee status to cease to exist, there had to be a lasting solution from persecution in the country of nationality. To assume this, there had to be an actor of protection which took reasonable steps to prevent persecution, *inter alia*, by operating an effective legal system for the detection, prosecution and punishment of acts constituting persecution.[155]

In her opinion on the case of *Bolbol* (2010)[156] A-G Sharpston made clear how she treated the statement issued by the UNHCR specifically in the context of the *Bolbol* case. In her opinion, she stated that:

> 'The UNHCR occasionally makes statements which have persuasive, but not binding, force. His Office has published various statements which relate to the interpretation of Article 1D of the 1951 Convention: a commentary in its Handbook (…), a note published in 2002 (and revised in 2009) and a 2009 statement (also subsequently revised) which relates expressly to Ms Bolbol's case. I intend to treat this last as an unofficial amicus curiae brief.'[157]

Bolbol concerned a stateless Palestinian who had arrived in Hungary from the Gaza Strip. The case hinged on the interpretation of Article 12(1)(a) of EU Council Directive 2004/83, a provision reflecting Article 1D RC which stipulates, in short, that the RC does not apply to persons receiving protection from UN organs or agencies other than the UNHCR. In her opinion, A-G Sharpston quoted a number of provisions from the UNHCR Handbook and from two UNHCR notes concerning the interpretation of Article 1D RC.[158] Materially, A-G Sharpston partly agreed and partly

---

153 To be found at: http://www.unhcr.org/47302b6c2.html, last visited 19 December 2012.

154 Opinion of A-G Mazák delivered on 15 September 2009 in joined Cases *C-175/08, C-176/08, C-178/08 and C-179/08 of Abdulla and others v. Bundesrepublik Deutschland.*

155 Opinion of A-G Mazák in joined Cases *C-175/08, C-176/08, C-178/08 and C-179/08 of Abdulla and others v. Bundesrepublik Deutschland*, para. 77.

156 CJEU, *Bolbol v. Bevándorlási és állampolgársági Hivatal*, 17 June 2010, C-31/09. Commented on by R. Bruin, National Officer UNHCR the Netherlands, in *JV* 2010, 338.

157 Opinion of A-G Sharpston delivered on 4 March 2010 in Case C-31/09 of *Bolbol v. Bevándorlási és állampolgársági Hivatal*, para. 16.

158 *Ibidem*, paras. 17, 18, 19.

disagreed with the UNHCR's interpretation. Importantly, she motivated her disagreement very carefully.[159] The fact that the A-G quoted the UNHCR's position and the fact that she partly agreed with it, and extensively motivated her partial disagreement implied that she regarded the UNHCR's interpretation as authoritative and attached serious weight to it.

As a final example, the opinion of A-G Mengozzi of the joined Cases of the *Federal Republic of Germany v. B and D* can be mentioned.[160] Mengozzi referred numerous times to the UNHCR's Handbook and to its Guidelines of International Protection. The case of *B. and D.* concerned Turkish nationals of Kurdish origin with a past of commitment to the right of Kurds to self-determination and of guerrilla fighting for that purpose. The case hinged on the interpretation of Article 12(2) (b) and (c) of EU Council Directive 2004/83, provisions concerning exclusion from refugee status. Mengozzi made clear that he considered it important to take account of the guidance that emerged from the various documents issued by the UNHCR.[161]

To conclude, it may be said that although the CJEU has so far not explicitly referred to UNHCR statements, position papers, guidelines or other information, the A-Gs *de facto* treat the UNHCR as an *amicus curiae* and regard UNHCR information as very authoritative. Given the approach of the A-Gs, and given the ECtHR's approach to the UNHCR, it will probably be only a matter of time before the CJEU itself will start to make direct use of the UNHCR's information by, for example, appointing it as a witness under Article 26 of the Protocol of the Court or by entrusting it, under Article 25 of the Protocol of the Court, with the task of giving an expert opinion. Such a development would be all the more logical, given the fact that Article 21, first paragraph, at sub c, of the EU Procedures Directive entitles the UNHCR to present submissions to national courts.

2.6 Concluding remarks

The Refugee Convention, which is the only universal treaty on refugee protection and the cornerstone of the CEAS, contains a number of provisions on national (judicial) proceedings. These are Article 16 on access to courts, Article 32 on expulsion on grounds of national security and public order and the procedure to be followed in cases of expulsion, and Article 35 on co-operation of national authorities with the UNHCR. In this chapter the content of these provisions has been explored.

Article 16 RC requires that refugees have free access to national courts. Article 32 requires that the decision to expel a refugee shall be taken in accordance with due process of law. In literature, different positions are taken on the question of whether these two provisions apply to contemporary judicial proceedings concerning the determination of refugee status and *refoulement*. A dynamic and liberal interpretation of Articles 16 and 32 leads to the conclusion that both provisions do apply to such

---

159 *Ibidem*, paras. 59, 72 and 76.
160 Opinion of A-G Mengozzi delivered on 1 June 2010 in joined Cases C-57/09 and C-101/09 of *Federal Republic of Germany v. B and D*.
161 *Ibidem*, paras. 42 and 43.

judicial proceedings. Article 16 RC is primarily a non-discrimination provision, meaning that it entails that refugees should not be required to meet extra, or more stringent, admissibility conditions which do not apply to nationals in similar court proceedings. In a number of EU countries, shorter time limits for lodging an appeal to the court apply in asylum cases (compared to other administrative law cases). Shorter time limits constitute a more stringent admissibility condition and are incompatible with Article 16. In section 2.4 it was argued that Articles 16 and 32 RC may be interpreted in the light of the UNHCR's position on issues of evidence and on judicial scrutiny in national judicial asylum proceedings. The investigation has demonstrated that the UNHCR has developed concrete standards and principles with regard to ten of the eleven aspects of evidence and judicial scrutiny. These standards and principles are summarised below.

The standard of proof is that persecution is reasonably possible; it is not required to prove well-foundedness conclusively beyond doubt. The burden of proof, in principle, rests on the applicant, but the duty to ascertain and evaluate all the relevant facts is shared between the applicant and the examiner (the first instance (administrative) decision maker and the court); in some cases, it may be for the examiner to use all the means at his or her disposal to produce the necessary evidence in support of the application; this means that in some cases it is necessary that the court actively applies investigative powers to bring in additional evidence.

Both personal circumstances and elements concerning the situation in the country of origin are relevant. A number of examples were provided. The particular facts and circumstances of the case – both individual and concerning the situation in the country of origin – have to be seen in conjunction and approached in a holistic way, and not in isolation.

As far as the required degree of individual risk is concerned, the UNHCR Handbook distinguishes two main kinds of situations: the normal situation in which refugee status is determined on an individual basis and the exceptional situation in which group determination takes place whereby each member of the group is *prima facie* regarded as a refugee. Neither of these two situations poses a strict requirement of being singled out as the risk does not necessarily need to be based on the personal experiences of the applicant. For individuals belonging to a group that is targeted as a whole it is not necessary to be further singled out.

Overall credibility is required, not absolute credibility of every single statement, the inability to remember or provide all dates or minor details, as well as minor inconsistencies, insubstantial vagueness or incorrect statements but should not be used as decisive factors. It is necessary that national courts independently and on their own assess the credibility of the statements of the asylum seeker.

The requirement of evidence should not be applied too strictly, and it is not allowed to require evidence of every single statement; even the complete absence of supportive evidence does not automatically mean that the claim is unmeritorious. It is not allowed to impose a stricter credibility criterion than the criterion of overall credibility in cases of complete absence of corroborating evidence.

Information used as a basis for decisions should be similarly available to the asylum seeker and his or her legal adviser/counsellor, and should, further, be subject to the scrutiny of review/appeal authorities.

It is the task of the national court to independently establish the disputed facts of the case, which includes the possibility to apply investigative powers so as to adduce additional evidential materials in order to establish the facts.

As far as time limits for the presentation of statements and evidence are concerned, the applicant should, in principle, make all the relevant statements and submit all the available corroborating evidence as early as possible; however, in order to avoid any erroneous decision, the appeal authorities should have an opportunity either to take statements and corroborating evidence, which was submitted during the appeal stage and not earlier, into consideration or to refer the case back to the first instance authority so that this authority can first look at this new evidence; no case should be rejected solely on the basis that the relevant information was not presented or documents were not submitted earlier.

The risk assessment by the national court should be *ex nunc*, that is, at the time of investigation by the national court.

Article 35 RC, in conjunction with Article 21, first paragraph, sub c, of the EU Procedures Directive, entails that the UNHCR is entitled to make submissions to national courts in individual asylum appeal cases in the form of *amicus curiae* briefs, statements or letters. UNHCR submissions may enter the national court proceedings via different avenues: on the initiative of the UNHCR, on the initiative of a party to the case or by invitation of the national court. On the basis of Articles 16 and 35, seen in conjunction, national courts may invite the UNHCR to participate in court proceedings as an expert or witness who can advise the court on a particular aspect of a case or submit its opinion on the question of whether or not the claimant is a refugee. In order to provide national asylum courts with concrete examples of how co-operation with the UNHCR can take place, it was demonstrated how the two international Courts in the European Union, the ECtHR and the CJEU, work together with the UNHCR. The ECtHR frequently takes into consideration, and attaches significant weight to, general information compiled by the UNHCR, such as country reports and guidelines, and has in some cases invited it to intervene in the case and bring in a submission on the specific merits of pending cases or a submission concerning a specific question. The case law of the ECtHR clearly illustrates what role the UNHCR and information compiled by it may play in court proceedings. This case law may serve as a source of inspiration for national courts. Generally, the ECtHR treats the UNHCR as an independent, reliable and objective source of information, and attaches significant weight to the information it submits, particularly when this information is couched in terms of Article 3 ECHR.

The CJEU has, so far, not explicitly referred to UNHCR statements, position papers, guidelines or other information. This may partly be explained by the fact that this Court has so far dealt with only a very limited number of asylum cases. Another explanation is that the UNHCR has so far had no possibility to intervene of its own accord in cases before the CJEU, as Article 40 of the Protocol of the Statute of the CJEU bars this. What has actually happened, however, is that the UNHCR has, in fact, intervened in an informal and indirect way because Advocates-General have treated its statements, position papers, guidelines or other information as information submitted by informal *amicus curiae*. It was made clear that the A-Gs at the CJEU treat the UNHCR's information as highly authoritative. Given the approach of the A-Gs and the ECtHR, and given the fact that the UNHCR is entitled to make submissions to national courts, it may be expected that, in the near future, the CJEU will start to make direct use of its positions.

Chapter 3: The 1966 International Covenant on Civil and Political Rights (ICCPR)[1]

3.1   Introduction

The ICCPR was adopted by the General Assembly of the United Nations on 16 December 1966 and it entered into force on 23 March 1976.[2] The ICCPR has been ratified by a large number of States: 167.[3] They include all 27 Member States of the European Union.[4] There are two Optional Protocols to the ICCPR. The First Optional Protocol,[5] which entered into force on the same date as the ICCPR itself, establishes an individual complaints mechanism, allowing individuals to complain to the Human Rights Committee (HRC) about violations of the ICCPR.[6] The First Optional Protocol has 113 parties, including all the EU Member States, except the UK.[7] As the UK is party to the ICCPR itself, this State is bound by it and by the interpretations of treaty provisions given by the HRC, the body created by the ICCPR to monitor the compliance of States parties with the treaty provisions. However, as a result of the fact that the UK has not ratified the First Optional Protocol, individuals in the UK, including asylum seekers, cannot bring communications to the HRC. The Second Optional Protocol[8] entered into force on 11 July1991. It commits its members to the abolition of the death penalty within their borders.[9] The Second Optional Protocol has 73 States parties, including all 27 EU Member States.

---

1   See the following literature for more comprehensive descriptions and analyses of the history and working of the ICCPR: Van Dijk (and others) 1987, Nowak 1993, McGoldrick 1996, Ghandi 1998, Hanski & Scheinin 2003, Carlson& Gisvold 2003, Conte, Davidson & Burchill 2004, Nowak 2005, Joseph, Schultz & Castan 2005, Hanski & Scheinin 2007, Steiner, Alston & Goodman 2008. For the role of the ICCPR in international asylum law, see in particular Wouters 2009, Chapter 4.

2   United Nations General Assembly Resolution 2200 A (XXI), 21 U.N. GAOR Supp. (No. 16) at 52, U.N. Doc. A/6316 (1966), 999 U.N.T.S. 171; see http://treaties.un.org under 'Status of Treaties'.

3   The number of States Parties mentioned here reflects the situation on 31 December 2012. See: http://treaties.un.org and http://en.wikipedia.org/wiki/International_Covenant_on_Civil_and_Political_Rights.

4   The number of Member States mentioned here reflects the situation on 31 December 2012; see http://europa.eu/abc/european_countries/eu_members/index_nl.htm.

5   United Nations General Assembly Resolution 2200A (XXI), 21 U.N. GAOR Supp. (No. 16) at 59, U.N. Doc. A/6316 (1966), 999 U.N.T.S. 302.

6   Article 1 of the First Optional Protocol to the ICCPR stipulates: 'A State Party to the Covenant that becomes a Party to the present Protocol recognizes the competence of the Committee to receive and consider communications from individuals subject to its jurisdiction who claim to be victims of a violation by that State Party of any of the rights set forth in the Covenant. No communication shall be received by the Committee if it concerns a State Party to the Covenant which is not a Party to the present Protocol.'

7   The number of Member States mentioned here reflects the situation on 31 July 2011; see http://treaties.un.org.

8   United Nations General Assembly Resolution 44/128, annex, 44 U.N. GAOR Supp. (No. 49) at 207, U.N. Doc. A/44/49 (1989).

9   Article 1 of the Second Optional Protocol to the ICCPR stipulates that: 'no one within the jurisdiction of a State Party to the present Protocol shall be executed and that each State Party shall take all necessary measures to abolish the death penalty within its jurisdiction.'

The ICCPR (1966) is a universal general human rights treaty which, together with the International Covenant on Economic, Social and Cultural Rights (ICESCR, 1966)[10] gives treaty status to human rights proclaimed in the Universal Declaration of Human Rights (UDHR, 1948).[11] Both these treaties form the core of the international human rights protection instruments of the United Nations, the so called 'International Bill of Human Rights'. Unlike the UDHR, the ICCPR and ICESCR are both treaties and, therefore, legally binding on the States parties to them. The International Bill of Human Rights is further supplemented by a number of specialised treaties established within the framework of the United Nations, for example, the Convention against Torture and Other Cruel, Inhuman or Degrading Treatment or Punishment (CAT), investigated in Chapter 4 of this book.

3.1.1   The ICCPR and asylum

The ICCPR does not contain a right to asylum.[12] Article 7 ICCPR stipulates that no one shall be subjected to torture or to cruel, inhuman or degrading treatment or punishment and that no one shall be subjected without his or her free consent to medical or scientific experimentation. The HRC has interpreted Article 7 in such a way that States parties must not expose individuals to the danger of torture or cruel, inhuman or degrading treatment or punishment upon return to another country by way of their extradition, expulsion or *refoulement*. The first decision on the merits of an individual complaint in which the prohibition on *refoulement* was confirmed by the HRC was *Kindler v. Canada* (1993),[13] a case concerning the extradition from Canada of a United States citizen who had been convicted in the United States of first degree murder and kidnapping. Kindler claimed that he would be put on death row upon extradition to the US. The HRC found that Kindler's extradition did not amount to a violation of Articles 6 (the right to life) and 7. It considered, in short, that Articles 6 and 7 did not prohibit the imposition of the death penalty for the most serious crimes, that Kindler had been indeed convicted of premeditated murder, a very serious crime, that Kindler was an adult, that the extradition took place after extensive proceedings in the Canadian courts, which reviewed all the evidence, that the bilateral treaty on extradition between the United States and Canada did not require Canada to refuse to extradite or to seek assurances, and, finally, that the case differed very much from the *Soering* case[14] decided upon by the ECtHR (see chapter 5, section 5.1.1).[15]

The *refoulement* prohibition elaborated in *Kindler* was expanded to the situation of the expulsion of asylum seekers in the case of *A.R.J. v. Australia* (1997).[16] A.R.J., a

---

10 United Nations General Assembly Resolution 2200A (XXI), 21 U.N. GAOR Supp. (No. 16) at 49, U.N. Doc. A/6316 (1966), 993 U.N.T.S. 3, which entered into force on 3 January 1976.

11 United Nations General Assembly Resolution 217 A (III), U.N. Doc A/810 at 71 (1948).

12 See, for example, HRC, *V.M.R.B. v. Canada*, 26 July 1988, No. 236/1987, para. 6.3.

13 HRC, *Kindler v. Canada*, 18 November 1993, No. 470/1991.

14 ECtHR, *Soering v. the UK*, 7 July 1989, Appl. No. 14038/88.

15 HRC, *Kindler v. Canada*, 18 November 1993, No. 470/1991, paras. 14.2-15.3. See also General Comment of the HRC No. 20 on Article 7 (1992), para. 9; General Comment of the HRC No. 31 (2004) on general legal obligations imposed on States parties to the Covenant, para. 12.

16 HRC, *A.R.J. v. Australia*, 11 August 1997, No. 692/1996.

crew member of a vessel of the Iranian Shipping Line, was arrested in Australia for illegal importation and possession of two kilograms of cannabis resin. While in prison, the author applied for refugee status, which was refused. Before the HRC, A.R.J. complained that his deportation to Iran would violate Articles 6 and 7 ICCPR. He stated that, because of the drug-related offence committed, he would be subject to the death penalty and would be persecuted in Iran.[17] Australia stated that it had sought independent legal advice through its embassy in Tehran, and that the advice given was that it would be very unlikely that an Iranian citizen who had already served a sentence abroad for a drug-related offence would be retried and resentenced and that, in short, in this case there was no risk of a violation of Article 7.[18] The HRC found that the author's allegations that his deportation to Iran would expose him to treatment contrary to Article 7 had been refuted by the evidence provided by the State party. This evidence had shown that the maximum sentence for trafficking the amount of cannabis the author had been convicted of in Australia would be five years in Iran, that no arrest warrant was outstanding in Iran, and that there were no precedents in which an individual in a situation similar to the author's had faced capital charges and been sentenced to death. The HRC found the risk that the author would be retried and resentenced, and, as a result, exposed to lashes, not real, as, first, there was no evidence of an actual intention on the part of the Iranian authorities to prosecute him, and second, there were no similar deportation cases in which prosecution had been initiated in Iran.[19] After *A.R.J. v. Australia* (1997), other cases concerning the expulsion of asylum seekers reached the HRC. In a limited number of these cases the HRC considered the merits.[20] In other cases, it declared the communication inadmissible, mostly for lack of substantiation.[21]

The prohibition on *refoulement* under Article 7 ICCPR is non-derogable. This means that even in times of war or other public emergencies, it is not allowed for

---

17 *Ibidem*, paras. 3.1, 3.2, 3.3.
18 *Ibidem*, paras. 4.6, 4.7.
19 *Ibidem*, paras. 6.12-6.15.
20 HRC, *C. v. Australia*, 13 November 2002, No. 900/1999 (violation Article 7); HRC, *Ahani v. Canada*, 15 June 2004, No. 1051/2002 (violation Article 13 in conjunction with Article 7); HRC, *Byaruhanga v. Denmark*, 9 December 2004, No. 1222/2003 (violation Article 7); HRC, *Alzery v. Sweden*, 10 November 2006, No. 1416/2005 (violation Article 7, read alone, and in conjunction with Article 2); HRC, *Mehrez Ben Abde Hamida v. Canada*, 18 March 2010, No. 1544/2007 (violation Article 7);HRC, *Kaba v. Canada*, 25 March 2010, No. 1465/2006 (violation Article 7); HRC, *Pillai and Joachimpillai v. Canada*, 25 March 2011, No. 1763/2008 (violation Article 7).
21 Cases concerning the expulsion of asylum seekers in which the HRC declared the communication inadmissible are HRC, *Bakhtiyari and Bakhtiyari v. Australia*, 6 November 2003, No. 1069/2002; HRC, *Daljit Singh v. Canada*, 28 April 2006, No. 1315/2004; HRC, *Dawood Khan v. Canada*, 10 August 2006, No. 1302/2004; HRC, *Jagjit SinghBhullar v. Canada*, 13 November 2006, No. 982/2001; HRC, *Hamid Reza Taghi Khadje v. the Netherlands*, 15 November 2006, No. 1438/2005; HRC, *Bianca Lilia Londoño Soto and others v. Australia*, 14 April 2008, No. 1429/2005 (deportation case, the authors had not lodged an asylum claim at national level but contended that their deportation to Colombia would violate Article 7); HRC, *Mahmoud Walid Nakrash and Liu Qifen v. Sweden*, 30 October 2008, No. 1540/2007; HRC, *A.C. v. the Netherlands*, 22 July 2008, No. 1494/2006; HRC, *Moses Solo Tarlue v. Canada*, 27 March 2009, No. 1551/2007.

States parties to take measures derogating from it.[22] It is also absolute, which means that it is not open to the respondent State to claim that its own public interest reasons for deporting the individual outweigh the risk of ill-treatment on his or her return.[23] Because of its absolute and non-derogable character, and because Article 7 is not conditioned by the five grounds of persecution contained in Article 1 A (2) RC, Article 7 ICCPR, just like Article 3 ECHR, offers broader protection than Article 33 RC.[24]

As this book focuses on issues of evidence and judicial scrutiny in asylum court proceedings, but is not a comprehensive analysis of the prohibitions on *refoulement* contained in international asylum law, the concepts of torture and inhuman or degrading treatment or punishment are not analysed further here. Other authors have done this before so I refer to them.[25]

3.1.2 *Supervisory mechanisms*

Article 28 ICCPR establishes an autonomous treaty body which monitors the application and implementation of the ICCPR: the Human Rights Committee (HRC).[26] The HRC consists of eighteen members who have to be of high moral standing with a recognised competence in the field of human rights. The members serve in their personal capacity and not as representatives of their States.[27] The HRC is not a court or tribunal, but an independent body of experts *sui generis*, with elements of judicial, quasi-judicial, administrative, investigative, inquisitorial, supervisory and conciliatory functions.[28]

The HRC has three monitoring mechanisms at its disposal to supervise compliance with the ICCPR.[29] First, it receives and examines reports from the States parties on the steps they have taken to give effect to the rights spelled out in the ICCPR. This reporting mechanism is laid down in Article 40 ICCPR.[30] The submission of

---

22 Article 4(2) ICCPR states: 'No derogation from articles 6, 7, 8 (paragraphs 1 and 2), 11, 15, 16 and 18 may be made under this provision.' General Comment No. 24 (1994), para. 8 states that 'a State may not reserve the right to engage in (…) torture, to subject persons to cruel, inhuman or degrading treatment or punishment (…)'.

23 General Comment No. 20 (1992), para. 3; General Comment No. 29 (2001), para. 7; HRC, *Ahani v. Canada*, 15 June 2004, No. 1051/2002, para. 10.10.

24 See Wouters 2009 for a much more detailed material comparison of the prohibitions on *refoulement* on pp. 525-578.

25 See, for example, Wouters 2009, pp. 377-391.

26 Article 28 para. 1 ICCPR stipulates: 'There shall be established a Human Rights Committee (hereafter referred to in the present Covenant as the Committee). It shall consist of eighteen members and shall carry out the functions hereinafter provided.' For an extensive description and analysis of the work of the HRC I refer to Dominic McGoldrick's 1996 book *The Human Rights Committee, Its Role in the Development of the International Covenant on Civil and Political Rights*.

27 Article 28, paras. 2 and 3 ICCPR.

28 McGoldrick 1996, p. 54, Wouters 2009, pp. 364-367.

29 Human Rights Fact Sheet No. 15 (Rev. 1) 'Civil and Political Rights: The Human Rights Committee'; McGoldrick 1996, pp. 50-51; Hanski & Scheinin 2003, pp. 1-24, Carlson & Gisvold 2003, pp. 1-13; Steiner, Alston & Goodman 2008, Chapter 10.

30 Article 40, para. 1 ICCPR stipulates: 'The States Parties to the present Covenant undertake to submit reports on the measures they have adopted which give effect to the rights recognized herein and on

→

country reports is mandatory for States parties to the ICCPR. The HRC examines submitted country reports and issues Concluding Observations containing guidelines for States parties on how to improve affairs that have been found to be problematic. Second, Article 41 ICCPR provides for an optional inter-State complaint mechanism.[31] This procedure has not been used so far.[32] Third, under Article 1 of the First Optional Protocol, the HRC receives and considers individual complaints, known as 'communications', submitted by individuals who claim violations of their ICCPR rights by a State party.[33] As has been said above, all the EU Member States, except the UK, have ratified the first Optional Protocol (see section 3.1 above). The HRC gives its decisions on these communications in so-called 'views.'

In addition to the mentioned monitoring functions, the HRC develops and issues so-called 'General Comments' on particular provisions of the ICCPR to assist States parties to give effect to the provisions of the ICCPR by providing greater detail regarding the substantive and procedural obligations of States parties. The legal basis of this interpretative function of the HRC may be found in Article 28 ICCPR, which states that the HRC shall carry out the functions set out in the ICCPR; it may be argued that this provision makes the HRC competent to interpret the ICCPR in so far as this is required for the performance of its functions.[34] In its case law the HRC has reaffirmed this interpretative function and stated that

'Each international treaty has a life of its own and must be interpreted in a fair and just manner, if so provided, by the body entrusted with the monitoring of its provisions.'[35]

The opinions of the HRC set out in its various documents are not legally binding as the ICCPR and the Protocol do not contain a provision like Article 46, first paragraph, ECHR, which provision stipulates, in short, that the respondent State is

---

the progress made in the enjoyment of those rights: (a) Within one year of the entry into force of the present Covenant for the States Parties concerned; (b) Thereafter whenever the Committee so requests.'

31   Article 41, para. 1, ICCPR stipulates, *inter alia*: 'A State Party to the present Covenant may at any time declare under this article that it recognizes the competence of the Committee to receive and consider communications to the effect that a State Party claims that another State Party is not fulfilling its obligations under the present Covenant. Communications under this article may be received and considered only if submitted by a State Party which has made a declaration recognizing in regard to itself the competence of the Committee. No communication shall be received by the Committee if it concerns a State Party which has not made such a declaration.'

32   Joseph, Mitchell, Gyorki & Benninger-Budel 2006, p. 44; Wouters 2009, p. 365, site HRC: http://www.ohchr.org/english/bodies/petitions/index.htm#interstate, last visited 15 May 2012.

33   Article 1 of the First Optional Protocol stipulates: 'A State Party to the Covenant that becomes a Party to the present Protocol recognizes the competence of the Committee to receive and consider communications from individuals subject to its jurisdiction who claim to be victims of a violation by that State Party of any of the rights set forth in the Covenant. No communication shall be received by the Committee if it concerns a State Party to the Covenant which is not a Party to the present Protocol.'

34   Human Rights Fact Sheet No 15 (rev 1): Civil and Political Rights: the Human Rights Committee, Office of the United Nations High Commissioner for Human Rights 2005, p. 24; Wouters 2009, p. 365.

35   See, for example, HRC, *J. and others v. Canada*, 18 July 1986, No. 118/1982, para. 6.2.

obliged to abide by the final judgment of the ECtHR. Unlike the ECHR, the ICCPR has no separate body with a practice to keep cases on its agenda until the States concerned have taken satisfactory measures.[36] The enforcement procedure under the ICCPR is weaker and works in the following way. The Rules of Procedure of the HRC stipulate in Rule 101, first paragraph, which forms part of the Rules on individual communications, that 'The Committee shall designate a Special Rapporteur for follow-up on Views adopted under article 5, paragraph 4, of the Optional Protocol, for the purpose of ascertaining the measures taken by States parties to give effect to the Committee's Views.' In addition to this mechanism, where it is established in views on an individual complaint that a State party has violated its obligations under the ICCPR, the HRC often invites the respondent State, in a separate standard consideration at the very end of the views, to inform it of the steps it has taken in accordance with the observations given in the views. The HRC bases this request on Article 2 ICCPR, which obliges the respondent State party to ensure to all individuals within its territory and subject to its jurisdiction the rights recognised in the ICCPR and to provide an effective and enforceable remedy if a violation has been established.[37]

Although they are not legally binding, the opinions of the HRC are of a high authority, for different reasons. When States ratify or accede to the ICCPR, they undertake to live up to their obligations under this instrument and to honour the decisions of the autonomous body created under it, the HRC. When they ratify the First Optional Protocol they recognise the competence of the HRC to establish in individual complaint cases whether or not there has been a violation of the ICCPR. Decisions of the HRC are mostly made by consensus,[38] which increases its credibility and authority.[39] The HRC has followed its decisions on numerous occasions, and has also explicitly stressed that it should ensure consistency and coherence in its jurisprudence.[40] In structure, the views of the HRC resemble judgments: they provide an overview of the positions taken by the parties and include a conclusion on a violation or non-violation.[41] The HRC also often recommends appropriate remedies. All of the mentioned reasons establish that States parties must normally treat HRC opinions as authoritative and important.[42] Christian Tomuschat, former HRC member, makes clear that, in the light of the reasons mentioned, it is not very relevant that the decisions of the HRC are not binding. He states:

36 Under the ECHR, the Committee of Ministers performs this function. See Chapter 5, section 5.1.
37 See, for example, HRC, *Judge v. Canada*, 13 August 2003, No. 829/1998, para. 13; HRC, *Mansour Ahani v. Canada*, 15 June 2004, No. 1051/2002, para. 13; HRC, *Byahuranga v. Denmark*, 9 December 2004, No. 1222/2003, para. 14; *Alzery v. Sweden*, 10 November 2006, No. 1416/2005, para. 14.
38 According to Rule 51 of the Rules of Procedure of the HRC, decisions shall be made by a majority vote, but a footnote to the Rules adds that the HRC shall make every effort to reach a consensus before voting.
39 Wouters 2009, p. 366.
40 See, for example, HRC, *Judge v. Canada*, 20 October 2003, No. 829/1998, para. 10.3.
41 See also Mc Goldrick 1996, who states that the HRC's views follow a judicial pattern.
42 Many eminent scholars treat the opinions of the HRC in the same way; see, for example, Boeles 1997, p. 96, McGoldrick 1996, pp. 151-152, Nowak 1993, p. XXIV, Hathaway 2005, pp. 119-123, Goodwin-Gill & McAdam 2007, pp. 305-309, Wouters 2009, p. 365.

'Legally, the views formulated by the HRC are not binding on the State party concerned which remains free to criticize them. Nonetheless, any State party will find it hard to reject such finding in so far as they are based on orderly proceedings during which the defendant party had ample opportunity to present its submissions. The views of the HRC gain their authority from their inner qualities of impartiality, objectiveness and soberness. If such requirements are met, the views of the HRC can have far-reaching impact, at least vis-à-vis such Governments which have not out rightly broken with the international community and ceased to care anymore for concern expressed by international bodies. If such a situation arose, however, even a legally binding decision would not be likely to be respected.'[43]

3.1.3   *Provisions on national proceedings*

The ICCPR contains a number of provisions dealing explicitly with national (judicial) proceedings. In this chapter the focus is on those provisions which are relevant for national judicial proceedings in asylum cases. These are Article 2, third paragraph on the right to an effective remedy; Article 7, which hosts a prohibition on *refoulement* and contains a procedural limb; Article 13 on the expulsion of aliens and the procedure to be followed in cases of expulsion; and Article 14, first paragraph, on a fair hearing.

It may seem odd to investigate Article 14 as the HRC has, so far, been ambiguous about the question of whether or not this provision applies to national proceedings concerning asylum status determination and the expulsion of asylum seekers (see section 3.4.1 below). I have, nevertheless, chosen to explore the content of Article 14, for the same reasons as those underpinning the choice made in Chapter 5 to explore Article 6 ECHR. Article 14 is the counterpart in the ICCPR of Article 6 ECHR, and of Article 47, paragraph 2, of the EU Charter of fundamental rights, which will almost always be applicable in asylum cases (see Chapter 6, section 6.1.3.2). Case law of the HRC under Article 14 ICCPR may – just like the case law of the ECtHR under Article 6 ECHR – be used as an additional tool for interpretation of Article 47 of the EU Charter. The CJEU has ruled explicitly in a number of cases that the ICCPR is one of the international instruments for the protection of human rights of which it takes account as a source of inspiration and interpretation.[44] Article 14 is, therefore, a relevant provision, which makes it worthwhile to explore its implications for the research questions.

Also explored is Article 5, second paragraph, b, of the First Optional Protocol, which requires that applicants should first exhaust effective national remedies before applying to the HRC. The reason for including this provision is that the case law under this Article – in addition to the jurisprudence on Article 2, third paragraph –

---

43   McGoldrick 1996, pp. 151, 204, with reference.

44   Examples in which the Court of Justice of the EU ruled that the ICCPR is one of the international instruments for the protection of human rights of which the Court takes account as a source of inspiration and interpretation are: *Dzodzi*, 18 October 1990, C-197/89, para. 68; *Grant*, 17 February 1998, C-249/96, para.44. See for a good example of a judgment in which the Court of Justice of the EU stressed the special character of the ECHR as a source of inspiration, but at the same time also drew on the ICCPR and the International Convention on the Rights of the Child: *European Parliament v. Council*, 27 June 2006, C-540/03, paras. 35-37, 54-57.

may help to explain when a national remedy is considered by the HRC to be (in)effective.

3.1.4   *Chapter outline*

Part 1 of this chapter deals with the ICCPR's provisions on national proceedings and what these provisions say with regard to the required intensity of national judicial scrutiny and on evidentiary issues in national asylum proceedings. The provisions on national proceedings are first briefly introduced in section 3.2, as it is necessary to have some knowledge of the basic requirements under these provisions, before turning to the context of national asylum court proceedings. After this introduction, section 3.3 discusses and analyses how these provisions work in the context of national asylum court proceedings.

The focus will then shift towards Article 14, first paragraph, and its implications for the required intensity of national judicial scrutiny and for issues of evidence in national court proceedings.

Part 2 of this chapter explores the assessment performed by the HRC in cases concerning the expulsion of asylum seekers. The analysis of this assessment in section 3.5 is made with the aid of the eleven aspects of evidence and judicial scrutiny introduced in Chapter 1. Each aspect is discussed in a separate sub-section. In section 3.6, final concluding remarks are made.

ICCPR, Part 1:

Provisions on national proceedings; issues of intensity of judicial scrutiny and evidentiary issues in national judicial proceedings

3.2 Basics: introduction to the provisions on national proceedings

3.2.1 Texts of the provisions on national proceedings

Article 2, third paragraph 3, stipulates:

> 'Each State party to the present Covenant undertakes:
> a) To ensure that any person whose rights or freedoms as herein recognized are violated shall have an effective remedy, notwithstanding that the violation has been committed by persons acting in an official capacity;
> b) To ensure that any person claiming such a remedy shall have his rights thereto determined by competent judicial, administrative or legislative authorities, or by any other competent authority provided for by the legal system of the State, and to develop the possibilities of judicial remedy;
> c) To ensure that the competent authorities shall enforce such remedies when granted.'

Article 7 stipulates:

> 'No one shall be subjected to torture or to cruel, inhuman or degrading treatment or punishment. In particular, no one shall be subjected without his free consent to medical or scientific experimentation.'

Article 13 stipulates:

> 'An alien lawfully in the territory of a State party to the present Covenant may be expelled there from only in pursuance of a decision reached in accordance with law and shall, except where compelling reasons of national security otherwise require, be allowed to submit the reasons against his expulsion and to have his case reviewed by, and be represented for the purpose before, the competent authority or a person or persons especially designated by the competent authority.'

Article 14, first paragraph, stipulates:

> 'All persons shall be equal before the courts and tribunals. In the determination of any criminal charge against him, or of his rights and obligations in a suit at law, everyone shall be entitled to a fair and public hearing by a competent, independent and impartial tribunal established by law. The press and the public may be excluded from all or part of a trial for reasons of morals, public order (ordre public) or national security in a democratic society, or when the interest of the private lives of the parties so requires, or to the extent strictly necessary in the opinion of the court in special circumstances where publicity would prejudice the interests of justice; but

any judgement rendered in a criminal case or in a suit at law shall be made public except where the interest of juvenile persons otherwise requires or the proceedings concern matrimonial disputes or the guardianship of children.'

Article 5, second paragraph, b, of the First Optional Protocol stipulates:

'2. The Committee shall not consider any communication from an individual unless it has ascertained that:
(b) The individual has exhausted all available domestic remedies. This shall not be the rule where the application of the remedies is unreasonably prolonged.'

3.2.2   *The right to an effective national remedy, the exhaustion rule*

Article 2, third paragraph, accords to individuals a means whereby they can obtain relief at national level for violations of their ICCPR rights, before having recourse to the HRC. It embodies the general principle of international law that the protection of individuals against violations of human rights is primarily a national concern and that the machinery of complaint to the HRC is subsidiary to national systems safeguarding human rights. Article 2, third paragraph accords a right to an effective remedy to any person who tenably asserts (in other words, arguably claims) that a substantive ICCPR right has been violated.[45]

The preparatory works do not shed much light on the question of what is meant by 'effective remedy'.[46] The discussions in the drafting process focused on the question of whether only judicial or also administrative and other remedies could constitute an 'effective remedy'. It is clear that the text of the provision is a compromise reached after lengthy discussions between the common law and other legal traditions.[47] From sub b it is clear, though, that effective remedies can be provided by competent judicial, administrative, legislative or other competent authorities, but that States are obliged to further develop the possibilities of judicial remedies. Judicial remedies, thus, have priority, and the HRC has made clear that both Article 2, third

---

45   Nowak 1993, p. 35, McGoldrick 1996, pp. 279-280, Nowak 2005, p. 67, Wouters 2009, p. 414, Boeles 1997, pp. 112-113.

46   See Bossuyt 1987, pp. 64-73. Bossuyt refers to UN document A/2929, Chapt. V, 14, which states: 'An opinion was expressed that there was no need to specify the obligations of States parties in the event of a violation of the covenant, since it was obvious that if the States undertook to abide by the Covenant, they would have to provide for effective remedies against infringements. It was also likely that provisions of that kind might be too broad and sweeping to be of much value. The view was accepted, however, that the proper enforcement of the provisions of the covenant depended on the guarantees of the individual's rights against abuse, which comprised the following elements: the possession of a legal remedy, the granting of this remedy by national authorities and the enforcement of the remedy by the competent authorities'.

47   See Bossuyt 1987, p. 67, Nowak 1993, pp. 31-32 and Nowak 2005, pp. 63-64. Nowak mentions that whereas the United Kingdom proposed a right to a decision by independent national tribunals analogous to that under Article 14, other States, Continental European as well as Latin American and Arab delegations sought to leave the States parties at liberty to entrust political and administrative organs with decision-making authority regarding violations of the Covenant.

paragraph, and Article 5, second paragraph, sub b, of the Optional Protocol refer in the first place to judicial remedies.[48]

In accordance with Article 5, second paragraph, of the Optional Protocol, before lodging a communication to the HRC, individuals must first exhaust available and effective national remedies.[49] As has been said, the machinery of complaint to the HRC is subsidiary to national systems safeguarding human rights and the purpose of Article 5, second paragraph, of the Optional Protocol is to afford the respondent State party the opportunity of preventing or putting right the violations alleged against it before those allegations are submitted to the HRC. The rule in Article 5, second paragraph, of the Optional Protocol is based on the assumption, reflected in Article 2, third paragraph, that there is an effective national remedy available in respect of the alleged breach of an individual's ICCPR rights. The rule of exhaustion of effective national remedies does not apply when, in short, there is no effective national remedy. The last sentence of Article 5, second paragraph includes a clause according to which inadmissibility is not applicable when national remedies are unreasonably prolonged.

Whether a national remedy is effective must be determined on the basis of concrete cases, taking into consideration all relevant circumstances, the respective national legal system and the special features of the substantive right concerned. Judicial remedies are essential in cases of allegations of serious abuse, such as torture and killing.[50] It follows from General Comment No. 31(80) (2004) that, in order to be effective, the national remedy must be accessible and effective,[51] and that allegations of covenant violations must be investigated promptly, thoroughly, and effectively through independent and impartial bodies, which must be endowed with appropriate powers.[52] The assessment of the effectiveness of national remedies under Articles 2, third paragraph and Article 5, second paragraph, sub b, of the Optional Protocol is similar to the appreciation of the effectiveness of national remedies under Article 13 ECHR.[53]

3.2.3   Article 7: prompt, impartial and full investigations

General Comment No. 20 stipulates that Article 7 should be read in conjunction with Article 2, third paragraph, and that Article 7-complaints must be investigated prompt-

---

48   See, for example, HRC, *R.T. v. France*, 30 March 1989, No. 162/87, para. 7.4; HRC, *José Vicente and others v. Colombia*, 29 July 1997, No. 612/1995, para. 5.2. See also Nowak 1993, p. 59, Boeles 1995, pp. 108-109, Nowak 2005, pp. 63-65 and Wouters 2009, p. 412. See also Boeles 1997, p. 109, Wouters 2009, p. 413.

49   See for more detailed information on the requirement of exhaustion of effective domestic remedies Nowak 1993, p. 58, McGoldrick 1996, pp. 188-197, Carlson & Gisvold 2003, pp. 15-17, Nowak 2005, pp. 62-63, Hanski & Scheinin 2003, pp. 20, 21.

50   HRC, *Vicente et al v. Colombia*, 29 July 1997, No. 612/95, para. 5.2.

51   General Comment No. 31(80) (2004), para.15. General Comments of the HRC can be found at: www.unhchr.ch/tbs/doc.nsf, and on www.ohchr.org. See 'CCPR Human Rights Committee', 'General Comments'; see also Wouters 2009, p. 413.

52   General Comment No. 31(80) (2004), para.15.

53   See Chapter 5, section 5.2.

ly and impartially by competent authorities so as to make the remedy effective.[54] In a number of cases concerning the torture and disappearance of individuals in dictatorial regimes (internal torture or disappearance cases), the HRC has constantly ruled that Article 7, seen in conjunction with Article 2, third paragraph, requires from the national authorities, including national courts, that 'full investigations', or 'full and thorough inquiries',[55] are made. In a significant number of internal torture or disappearance cases the HRC found the inquiries made at national level non-compliant and concluded that there had been a violation of Article 2, third paragraph, in conjunction with Article 7.[56]

3.2.4   Article 13: procedural safeguards for expulsion

The preparatory works on Article 13 make clear that this provision is about the protection of aliens against arbitrary expulsion and that Article 13 is based on Article 32 RC, which provision was discussed in Chapter 2 (section 2.3).[57] The drafters of the text wished to leave up to the national legislation the question of whether the competent review authority should be a judicial or an administrative body.[58] Indeed, the HRC made clear in *Maroufidou v. Sweden* (1981)[59] that Article 13 did not necessarily entail an appeal to a court, but that administrative review was compatible with Article 13.[60] In literature, different opinions are expressed on the question of whether Article 13 is applicable to contemporary appeal proceedings in asylum cases.[61] The question of applicability is triggered by the text of Article 13, which speaks of 'aliens lawfully in the territory of a State party'. The debate on this issue resembles the discussion on the relevance for asylum appeal proceedings of Article 32 RC, which provision also requires lawful presence in the territory of a Contracting State.[62] The debate may be considered highly theoretical as the HRC normally considers Article 13 applicable to cases where the lawfulness of residency is disputed, and the HRC itself has also con-

---

54 General Comment No. 20: Replaces General Comment No. 7 concerning prohibition of torture and cruel treatment or punishment (Art. 7): 10/03/92, para. 14.

55 HRC, *Irene Bleier Lewenhoff and Rosa Valino de Bleier v. Uruguay*, 29 March 1982, No. 30/1978, para. 11.1.

56 See, for example, HRC, *Alberto Grille Motta v. Uruguay*, 29 July 1980, No. 11/1977; HRC, *Delia Saldias de Lopez v. Uruguay*, 29 July 1981, No. 52/1979; HRC, *Hugo Rodriguez v. Uruguay*, 19 July 1994, No. 322/1988; HRC, *Bautista v. Colombia*, 27 October 1995, No. 563/ 1993.

57 E/CN.4/SR.106, p.12-13; E/CN.4/SR.153; E/CN.4/SR.154; E/CN.4/SR.316. See also Bossuyt 1987, pp. 267-276.

58 A/c.3/SR.959, 960. See also Bossuyt 1987, p. 270, Nowak 1993, p. 229, Nowak 2003, p. 297, Carlson & Gisvold 2003, pp. 100-101, Hathaway 2005, pp. 670-677, Joseph, Schultz & Castan 2005, p. 381.

59 HRC, *Maroufidou v. Sweden*, 9 April 1981, No. 58/79.

60 See also Nowak 1993, p. 229, Nowak 2003, p. 297, Carlson & Gisvold 2003, pp. 100-101, Hathaway 2005, pp. 670-677, Joseph, Schultz & Castan 2005, p. 381.

61 See, for example, Joseph, Schultz & Castan 2005, p. 379. They state that, due to the requirement of being lawfully in the territory of a State party, Article 13 is probably of little use to asylum seekers who illegally enter a State in search of protection. See for a different opinion Nowak 1993, p. 225 and Nowak 2005, p. 293.

62 See for this discussion Chapter 2, section 2.3.1.

sidered Article 13 applicable to cases concerning the expulsion of asylum seekers, as we will see in more detail below.[63]

The text of Article 13 mentions three procedural rights or safeguards:

- The right to submit the reasons against the expulsion (right to a hearing);
- The right to have the case reviewed by the competent authority (appeal to a higher instance);
- The right to be represented before the competent authority (right to representation, not implying the right to legal counsel).[64]

The preparatory works[65] and literature draw a link with the procedural safeguards of Article 32, paragraph 2, RC. Nowak (1993) points out that the slight change in wording from 'to submit the reasons against his expulsion' (Article 13 ICCPR) to 'to submit evidence to clear himself' (Article 32 RC) did not change the substance of the safeguards.[66] The comments on the safeguards of Article 32, second paragraph RC in Chapter 2 are, therefore, relevant for the interpretation of the safeguards in Article 13.[67]

General Comment No. 15 (27) stipulates in paragraph 10 that

'An alien must be given full facilities for pursuing his remedy against expulsion so that this right will in all the circumstances of his case be an effective one. The principles of Article 13 relating to appeal against expulsion and the entitlement to review by a competent authority may only be departed from when 'compelling reasons of national security' so require.'[68]

The procedural safeguards of Article 13 do not apply where compelling reasons of national security require otherwise. According to the case law of the HRC, States parties normally have wide discretion in the assessment of whether a case presents national security considerations, bringing the exception contained in Article 13 into play.[69] Joseph, Schultz&Castan (2005) warn that the HRC's approach severely under-

---

63   The HRC started its jurisprudential line on broad applicability of Article 13 in *Maroufidou v. Sweden*, 9 April 1981, No. 58/1979, in which a Greek woman had been granted a residency permit by the Swedish authorities for the duration of the proceedings to decide on her request for asylum; the HRC held in this case that the applicability of Article 13 was beyond dispute. See Nowak 1993, p. 225 and Nowak 2005, p. 293.

64   See on these procedural rights or safeguards also Nowak 1993, p. 228, Nowak 2003, pp. 297, 298, Carlson & Gisvold 2003, p. 100, Joseph, Schultz & Castan 2005, pp. 381-382.

65   E/CN.4/SR.106, P.12-13; E/CN.4/SR.153; E/CN.4/SR.154; E/CN.4/SR.316. See Bossuyt 1987, pp. 267-276.

66   Nowak 1993, p. 228, Nowak 2003, pp. 297, 298.

67   See Chapter 2, section 2.3.

68   General Comment No. 15 (27) of 22 July 1986 on the rights of aliens; General Comments of the Committee can be found on the internet at: www.ohchr.org, and on www.ohchr.org. See 'CCPR Human Rights Committee' and then 'General Comments'.

69   See, for example, HRC, *V.M.R.B. v. Canada*, 18 July 1988, No. 236/1987, para. 6.3; HRC, *Borzov v. Estonia*, 26 July 2004, No. 1135/2002, para. 7.3; *Mohamed Alzery v. Sweden*, 25 October 2006, No. 1416/2005, para. 11.10.

mines the protection offered by Article 13 and potentially invites States parties to defend Article 13 breaches with spurious national security claims.[70]

3.2.5 *Fair trial*

In literature the importance of Article 14 is strongly emphasised.[71] In General Comment No. 32,[72] the HRC explains the various requirements of Article 14.The first requirement flowing from Article 14 is the right to equality before courts and tribunals.[73] This encompasses equal access to the courts.[74] Equal treatment of individuals by the court also means that the law should be applied without discrimination by the judiciary.[75]

The second requirement following from Article 14 is that courts and tribunals must be competent, independent, established by law and impartial.[76] Competent and established by law means that the jurisdictional power of the court is determined by law generally, in advance and independent of the given case. Independence refers to the structural relationship between the judiciary and other government structures.[77] The functions and competences of the judiciary and, for example, the executive, should be clearly distinguishable and the latter should not be able to control or direct the former. Impartiality refers to the relationship between a judge and the matter at issue in a specific case; it implies that judges must not harbour preconceptions about the matter put before them and must not act in ways that promote the interests of one of the parties.[78]

The third requirement of Article 14 is that courts and tribunals must hold fair hearings. The most important criterion of a fair hearing is the principle of equality of arms between the parties, which means that the same procedural rights are to be provided to all the parties, unless the distinctions are based on law and can be justified on objective and reasonable grounds, not entailing actual disadvantage or other

---

70 Joseph, Schultz & Castan 2005, p. 383.
71 See, for example, McGoldrick 1996, p. 396, who speaks of 'a central feature of the rule of law'. Carlson & Gisvold qualify Article 14 as a 'foundation Covenant Article' necessary for the proper implementation of all basic substantive rights, Carlson & Gisvold 2003, p. 38; Joseph, Schultz & Castan state that the right to a fair trial and equality before the courts have historically been regarded as fundamental rules of law, Joseph, Schultz & Castan 2005, p. 390.
72 General Comment No. 32 of 24 July 2007 'Equality before the courts and the right to a fair and public hearing by an independent court established by law'. This General Comment replaces General Comment No. 13 of the HRC.
73 See General Comment No. 32, paras. 8 and 9; Nowak 1993, p. 239, Carlson & Gisvold 2003, p. 39, Nowak 2005, p. 308, Joseph, Schultz & Castan 2005, pp. 396-404.
74 See, for example, HRC, *Oló Bahamonde v. Equatorial Guinea*, 20 October 1993, No. 468/1991; HRC, *Avellanal v. Peru*, 28 October 1988, No. 202/1986.
75 See Nowak 1993, p. 239 and Nowak 2005, p. 308.
76 See General Comment No. 13, paras. 3 and 4. See on the requisite characteristics of courts Nowak 1993, pp. 245, 246, McGoldrick 1996, pp. 399-403 and 416, 417, Weissbrodt 2001, pp. 141-145, Carlson & Gisvold 2003, pp. 39-40, Joseph, Schultz & Castan 2005, pp. 404-408, Nowak 2005, pp. 319-321.
77 See General Comment No. 32, para. 19.
78 *Ibidem*, para. 21.

unfairness to the defendant.[79] In addition, a fair hearing requires respect for the principle of adversarial proceedings, meaning that each party must be given the opportunity to contest all the arguments and evidence adduced by the other party.[80] A fair hearing also entails preclusion of *reformatio in pejus* (a claimant/plaintiff should not, as a result of a suit at law, end up worse off than before starting the proceedings) and expeditious procedure.[81]

Finally, court hearings and judgments should be public. This means, first, that, in principle, hearings must be conducted orally and publicly. The text of Article 14, first paragraph, makes clear that specific circumstances allow for exceptions to the requirement of an oral public hearing. Even in cases in which the public is excluded from the trial, the judgment, including the essential findings, evidence and legal reasoning must be made public, except where the interests of juvenile persons otherwise requires, or the proceedings concern matrimonial disputes or the guardianship of children.[82] The requirement of publicity serves to make the administration of justice transparent. In other words, justice must not be secret.

3.2.6   *Mutual relationships*

Boeles (1997) and Carlson & Gisvold (2003) have promoted the idea that the different provisions on procedures in the ICCPR do not stand apart, but should be read as a whole.[83]

It has already been said above that the HRC has made clear in its General Comment No. 20 that Article 7 should be read in conjunction with Article 2, third paragraph. The procedural limb of Article 7 requires that an effective remedy is available for alleged violations of Article 7. The HRC has also made clear that, where judicial remedies exist at national level, Article 2, third paragraph, requires that these remedies are in accordance with the safeguards secured by Article 14.[84]

General Comment No. 32 states that the procedural guarantees of Article 13 incorporate the notions of due process reflected in Article 14 and, thus, should be interpreted in the light of Article 14. Insofar as national law entrusts a judicial body with the task of deciding about expulsions or deportations, the guarantee of equality of all persons before the courts and tribunals as enshrined in Article 14, first para-

---

79   See General Comment No. 32, para. 13; see also, for example, HRC, *Dudko v. Australia*, 23 July 2007, No. 1347/2005, para. 7.4.

80   See, for example, HRC, *Jansen-Gielen v. the Netherlands*, 3 April 2001, No. 846/1999, para. 8.2.

81   In the View in the case of *Morael v. France*, 28 July 1989, No. 207/1986, these aspects of a fair hearing were mentioned for the first time; since then they have been repeated in many subsequent cases. See on expeditiousness General Comment No. 32, para. 27.

82   See General Comment No. 32, para. 28, Nowak 1993, pp. 247-253, McGoldrick 1996, pp. 418, 419, Weissbrodt 2001, pp. 145, 146, Carlson & Gisvold 2003, p. 42, Nowak 2005, pp. 323-329, Joseph, Schultz & Castan 2005, pp. 422-426.

83   Boeles 1997, p. 106, Carlson & Gisvold 2003, p. 20.

84   HRC, *Singarasa v. Sri Lanka*, 21 July 2004, No. 1033/2001, para. 7.4; HRC, *Czernin v. Czech Republic*, 29 March 2005, No. 823/1998, para. 7.5.

graph, and the principles of impartiality, fairness and equality of arms implicit in this guarantee are applicable.[85]

Close affinity exists between Articles 2, third paragraph, and 5, second paragraph, sub b, of the Optional Protocol. The rule of exhaustion of national remedies does not apply when national remedies are not effective, which makes the case law under Article 5, second paragraph, sub b, Optional Protocol directly relevant to the notion of an effective remedy contained in Article 2, paragraph 3.

Finally, the HRC has made clear that, under Article 5, second paragraph, sub b, of the Optional Protocol, national remedies must be effective and available, and that this entails that procedural guarantees for a fair and public hearing by a competent, independent and impartial tribunal must be scrupulously observed.[86] To phrase it differently, an effective judicial remedy in the sense of Article 5, second paragraph, sub b, of the Optional Protocol, and in the sense of Article 2, third paragraph, is a remedy which complies with the safeguards of Article 14.

3.3 The provisions on national proceedings in the context of national asylum court proceedings

3.3.1 *Reluctance to critically review national court decisions*

Article 2, third paragraph, read in conjunction with Article 7, requires from the national authorities, including the national courts that claims for protection are considered in a thorough and fair manner.[87] However, the HRC is generally reluctant to put national proceedings to a rigorous test of compliance with this rule. Instead, it seems that the HRC almost always assumes that national proceedings are compliant. A number of cases are examined below to illustrate this reluctance.

In the case of *Daljit Singh v. Canada* (2006), the author claimed that if he were removed to India, Canada would be in violation of Article 7 ICCPR, to the extent that he would be subjected to torture, have no possibility of obtaining medical treatment, and possibly lose his life. The author claimed, furthermore, that national proceedings leading to the removal order violated, *inter alia*, Articles 2, third paragraph, and 13. He asserted that the national authorities had failed to consider carefully the evidence submitted in support of his case. According to the author, medical reports and photographs establishing that he and some of his family members had been victims of torture, affidavits from the mayors of the surrounding villages about the problems he had had with the police, and a report following an investigation from the Sikh Human Rights Group into the incidents in question, had not been considered. In addition, information from other sources on the general human rights situation in India

---

85   General Comment No. 32, para. 62. Reference is made to HRC *Ahani v. Canada*, No. 1051/2002, para. 10.9; HRC, *Everett v. Spain*, 9 July 2004, No. 961/2000, para. 6.4; HRC, *Taghi Khadje v. Netherlands*, 15 November 2006, No. 1438/2005, para. 6.3.

86   HRC, *Felicia Gilboa de Reverdito on behalf of her niece, Lucia Arzuada Gilboa, v. Uruguay*, 1 November 1985, No. 147/1983.

87   See, for example, HRC, *Dawood Khan v. Canada*, 10 August 2006, No. 1302/2004, para. 5.3.

had not been considered, including a Human Rights Watch Report, and an academic journal. The author also claimed that there was no effective judicial control of the administrative decision as applicants must first apply for leave to appeal to the Federal Court, and, if granted, the Federal Court might only review errors of law.[88]

The HRC observed in *Daljit Singh* that the author had not substantiated how the Canadian authorities' decisions had failed to consider, thoroughly and fairly, his claim that he would be at risk of violations of Articles 6 and 7 if returned to India. It considered this part of the claim inadmissible for this reason. It noted that the Refugee Division of the Immigration and Refugee Board, after thorough examination, had rejected the author's asylum application on the basis of lack of credibility of his testimony and supporting evidence and that the rejection of his Pre-Removal Risk Assessment application had been based on similar grounds.[89] The HRC further noted that in both cases applications for leave to appeal had been rejected by the Federal Court, and that the author had not shown sufficiently why these decisions were contrary to the standard set out above.[90]

We find the same reluctance to critically review national (court) proceedings in the cases of *Dawood Khan v. Canada* (2006)[91] and *A.C. v. the Netherlands* (2008). The case of *A.C.* is discussed in more detail because of the serious nature of the procedural complaints brought forward by the author. A.C. claimed that her expulsion to Armenia with her children would violate their rights under, *inter alia*, Article 7. She stated that her husband had been killed, and she had been assaulted, threatened and raped by police officers, because her husband had made protests against the diversion of foreign aid sent to Armenia after the Nagorno-Karabakh conflict. The Immigration and Naturalisation Department (IND) rejected the asylum application for lack of credibility. This position of the IND was based on a report issued by the Dutch Foreign Affairs Department and on the lack of identity papers. The first instance court rejected her appeal and the Council of State, the highest court in immigration affairs, rejected the author's higher appeal.[92] The author complained before the HRC of a violation of the procedural limb of Article 7 (and Article 14). She stated that the IND decision had been based solely on the report by the Foreign Ministry and the lack of identity papers; this had led the IND to conclude that her account was not credible and to dismiss the application without examining the merits. In additional submissions to the HRC, the author provided a summary of the Dutch ombudsman's report concerning reports by the Ministry of Foreign Affairs based on investigations conducted in the countries of origin of asylum seekers. According to the ombudsman's report, the reliability of these investigations had decreased and it was unrealistic to expect from people interrogated that they would report what they knew since they were enemies of the state in which they still lived. Based on this, the author argued that the State party's authorities should not have based their decision not to examine

---

88   HRC, *Daljit Singh v. Canada*, 30 March 2006, No. 1315/2004, paras. 3.1-3.3.

89   HRC, *Daljit Singh v. Canada*, 30 March 2006, No. 1315/2004, para. 2.4.

90   *Ibidem*, para. 2.5.

91   HRC, *Dawood Khan v. Canada*, 10 August 2006, No. 1302/2004, paras. 5.3, 5.4.

92   HRC, *A.C. v. the Netherlands*, 22 July 2008, No. 14942006, paras. 2.1-2.4.

her asylum claim on the merits of such unreliable investigations.[93] The author also pointed out that the information underpinning the report by the Ministry of Foreign Affairs and the sources of this information had been kept confidential. According to her, this had led to an unfair situation, as she could not challenge the credibility of the report.[94] With regard to the complaint that the procedural limb of Article 7 had been violated by the national authorities, the HRC responded as follows:

> 'The Committee notes that the State party challenges the admissibility of the entire communication. With regard to the author's claim under Article 7, the Committee (…) notes that the IND considered and rejected the author's asylum application for lack of credibility on two occasions, on the second occasion after having received the findings of an investigation that its authorities had undertaken in Armenia itself. It further notes that the author's appeal was considered and rejected by the Court of The Hague residing in Groningen and then subsequently rejected by the "Raad van State", the Highest Administrative Court of the Netherlands. The Committee recalls its jurisprudence that it is generally for the courts of States parties to the Covenant to evaluate facts and evidence in a particular case, unless it is found that the evaluation was clearly arbitrary or amounted to a denial of justice. It also recalls that the same jurisprudence has been applied to removal proceedings. The material before the Committee is insufficient to show that the proceedings before the authorities in the State party suffered from any such defects. The Committee accordingly considers that the author has failed to substantiate her claims under Article 7, for purposes of admissibility, and it concludes that this part of the communication is inadmissible under article 2 of the Optional Protocol.'[95]

The HRC's reluctance to overturn decisions of national courts is linked to the notion or principle of primacy for the national courts in reviewing facts, evidence and applying national law, and, correspondingly, of the subsidiary role of the HRC in this, and to the principle of national procedural autonomy. In its decision in the case of *A.C.*, and in later jurisprudence, the HRC stated that

> 'It is for the national courts to evaluate facts and evidence in a particular case.'[96]

This principle of primacy for the national authorities in the determination of the facts, and the corresponding national procedural autonomy, are deeply ingrained in the HRC's case law. They are expressed not only within the framework of the procedural limb of Article 7, but also under Article 14 (see section 3.4.2 below). Ghandi (1998), Joseph, Schultz & Castan (2005) and Kjaerum (2010) explain the HRC's position by a number of facts.[97] First, the HRC does not operate as an appellate court to

---

93   *Ibidem*, para. 7.2.
94   *Ibidem*, paras. 3.1, 3.2.
95   *Ibidem*, para. 8.2.
96   HRC, *Moses Solo Tarlue v. Canada*, 28 April 2009, No. 1551, para. 7.4. See, for exactly the same consideration under Article 14, the following cases: HRC, *Carlton Linton v. Jamaica*, 22 October 1992, No. 255/1987, paras. 3.1, 3.2, 8.3; HRC, *A.C. v. the Netherlands*, 22 July 2008, No. 14942006, para. 8.2.
97   Ghandi 1998, p. 216; Joseph, Schultz & Castan 2005, p. 381, pp. 22-23, p. 416, p.616; Kjaerum 2010, pp. 27-32.

which appeals may be taken from a State's highest national court. Second, the HRC receives only written and no oral evidence (see section 3.5.9) and is, therefore, in a worse position to determine the facts of cases than national authorities. Third, the meeting time of the HRC is very limited, which is difficult to reconcile with the time required to assess evidence and to write down an assessment of the presented evidence. The HRC convenes only three times a year for sessions of three weeks' duration, normally in March at the United Nations headquarters in New York, and in July and November at the United Nations Office in Geneva. The Working Group on Communications meets one week prior to the plenary sessions. In this very limited timeframe, decisions need to be taken in a large number of individual communications.[98]

3.3.2   'Arbitrary evaluation of evidence' or a 'denial of justice'

It appears from the HRC's case law that national judicial proceedings cannot be qualified as ICCPR-compliant if evidence was evaluated in a clearly arbitrary way or if a denial of justice occurred.[99] Within the framework of this research, no views have been found in which the HRC concluded explicitly that this had happened in the national court proceedings.

3.3.3   Insufficiently thorough investigations at national level

In one case concerning the expulsion of asylum seekers, the HRC concluded that the national proceedings had not met the requirement of a thorough and fair examination, without explicitly using the terms 'arbitrary evaluation of evidence' or 'denial of justice'. The case of *Pillai and Joachimpillai v. Canada* (2011)[100] concerned Christian Tamils from Colombo. The authors claimed that after 1999, they found themselves caught between the LTTE Tamil Tigers, on one side, and the Sri Lankan police, on the other. They were subjected to a series of threats and extortion by the Tigers. In particular, because Ms. Joachimpillai originated from Jaffna (North), the Tigers targeted her because they believed she would be likely to be sympathetic to their cause, whereas the police targeted her because they presumed she would be sympathetic to the Tigers. The authors were twice arrested by the police, on suspicion of lending support to the Tigers, in July 2001 and in February 2003. During their detention by the police, both were tortured. The authors submitted detailed statements about the ways in which they had been tortured.[101]

In the national proceedings before the Immigration and Refugee Board (IRB) the authors submitted a Diagnostic Interview Report by a psychotherapist, containing a diagnosis of post-traumatic stress disorder (PTSD) for Mr Pillai, attributed to threats by the Tigers to himself and his wife, extortion by the Tigers from himself and his

---

98   See for information on the sessions of the HRC the HRC site: http://www2.ohchr.org/english/bo-dies/hrc/sessions.htm, last visited 12 November 2011.

99   See, for example, HRC, *A.C, v. the Netherlands*, 22 July 2008, No. 14942006, para. 8.2.

100   HRC, *Pillai and Joachimpillai v. Canada*, 25 March 2010, No. 1763/2008.

101   *Ibidem*, paras. 2.1, 2.2.

wife, his own and his wife's arrest, detention and abuse. The report further noted that 'the symptoms of PTSD often mimic the behaviours that we associate with shiftiness, mendacity or lying', the differential in apparent power between the Refugee Board Commissioners and the applicant might have recalled the torturer-victim relationship for the applicant, thus 'exacerbating the already intense symptoms of anxiety and panic.' According to the report, this could provoke 'confusion due to extremely elevated autonomic arousal (and) difficulty concentrating'. The report considered it crucial that any judgements about the trustworthiness of Mr Pillai's testimony took this into account. Also filed in evidence before the Immigration and Refugee Board was a letter from the authors' doctor, which recommended that Mr Pillai's wife represent both of them before the IRB, as she was considered stronger and less traumatized than her husband.[102]

The IRB rejected the asylum claim, leave for judicial review by the Federal Court was denied, and a Pre-Removal Risk Assessment Application (PRRA) and an application for a permanent residence permit on humanitarian and compassionate grounds were refused as well.[103] In these national proceedings, the authors' protection claim was found incredible for three main reasons. First, it was doubted that Mr Pillai, as he had stated, had indeed been the owner of a communication centre between 2001 and 2003 which was at the source of the authors' problems. The only document proving ownership was a 'Certificate of Registration of an Individual Business' dated 23 January 1999. Neither of the authors had been able to give the Communication centre's address. Furthermore, conflicting testimony and evidence had been provided with respect to the dates he had travelled to India, Indonesia and the Congo in connection with his business. Finally, there were inconsistencies between the information in the Personal Information Form and the authors' testimony before the IRB.[104]

In line with its steady jurisprudence, the HRC reiterated that it must pay deference to the national authorities' evaluation of the evidence. It continued to note that in the national proceedings the authors had not been questioned at all about the alleged earlier torture, whereas it appeared from the country reports invoked by both parties that torture was widespread in Sri Lanka. The HRC did not use the terms 'clearly arbitrary' or 'denial of justice', but from the consideration quoted below it became obvious that it was clearly of the opinion that more attention should have been paid to the allegations of past torture, and that the failure of the national authorities to do so made the national proceedings defective:

'The Committee further notes that the diagnosis of Mr Pillai's post-traumatic stress disorder led the IRB to refrain from questioning him about his earlier alleged torture in detention. The Committee is accordingly of the view that the material before it suggests that insufficient weight was given to the authors' allegations of torture and the real risk they might face if deported to their country of origin, in the light of the documented prevalence of torture in Sri Lanka [19]. Notwithstanding the deference given to the immigration authorities to appreciate

---

102 *Ibidem*, para. 2.3.
103 *Ibidem*, para. 2.3.
104 *Ibidem*, paras. 7.4, 7.5, 7.6.

the evidence before them, the Committee considers that further analysis should have been carried out in this case. The Committee therefore considers that the removal order issued against the authors would constitute a violation of article 7 of the Covenant if it were enforced.'[105]

This case may indicate that the HRC has begun to steer away from deference to national procedural autonomy. So far we cannot be sure about this, however, as it is – apart from the case of *Mansour Ahani v. Canada* (2004, see next section) – the only case concerning the expulsion of asylum seekers in which the HRC explicitly concluded that the national proceedings had been defective.

3.3.4   Equality of arms, adversariality

It has been made clear in the previous section that the HRC will not easily conclude that the national proceedings did not comply with the 'thorough and fair examination' rule. The case of *Mansour Ahani v. Canada* (2004)[106] demonstrates, however, that the HRC found a lack of equality of arms and a lack of adversarial national proceedings a very serious problem, meriting the conclusion that no thorough and fair examination had taken place at national level.

In the case of *Ahani*, the author had been recognized by Canada as a refugee under the RC in 1992. On 17 June 1993, the Solicitor-General of Canada and the Minister of Employment & Immigration, having considered security intelligence reports stating that the author had been trained as an assassin by the Iranian Ministry of Intelligence and Security, both certified that they were of the opinion that he was inadmissible to Canada as there were reasonable grounds for believing that he would engage in terrorism, that he was a member of an organization that would engage in terrorism and that he had engaged in terrorism. On the same date the certificate was filed with the Federal Court, the author was served with a copy of the certificate and taken into mandatory detention, where he remained until his deportation nine years later. In 1993, the Federal Court examined the security intelligence reports *in camera* and heard other evidence presented by the Solicitor-General and the Minister, in the absence of the plaintiff. The Federal Court provided the author with a summary of the information, and offered him an opportunity to respond. Following extensive hearings, and after an unsuccessful attempt by the author to challenge the constitutionality of the proceedings before the Federal Court, this Court concluded that the national security certificate was reasonable. The evidence included information gathered by foreign intelligence agencies which had been divulged to the Federal Court *in camera* in the author's absence on national security grounds. The Federal Court also heard the author testify on his own behalf in opposition to the reasonableness of the certificate.[107]

On 12 August 1998, the Minister of Citizenship & Immigration, following representations by the author that he faced a clear risk of torture in Iran, determined, without reasons and on the basis of a memorandum attaching the author's sub-

---

105 *Ibidem*, para. 11.4.
106 HRC, *Mansour Ahani v. Canada*, 15 June 2004, No. 1051/2002.
107 *Ibidem*, paras. 2.1-2.5.

missions, other relevant documents and a legal analysis by officials, which memorandum was not provided to Ahani, that Ahani (a) constituted a danger to the security of Canada and (b) could be removed directly to Iran. In June 1999, the Federal Court rejected the author's application for judicial review of the Minister's decision, and the Court of Appeal rejected the author's appeal. In January 2001, the Supreme Court unanimously rejected the author's appeal, finding that there was ample support for the Minister to decide that the author was a danger to the security of Canada. On the constitutionality of deportation of persons at risk of harm, the Court referred to its reasoning in a companion case of *Suresh v Canada*[108] decided the same day, where it held that barring extraordinary circumstances, deportation to torture would generally violate the principles of fundamental justice. As Suresh had established a *prima facie* risk of torture, he was entitled to enhanced procedural protection, including provision of all the information and advice the Minister intended to rely on, receipt of an opportunity to address the evidence in writing and to be given written reasons by the Minister. In the author's case, however, the Supreme Court considered that Ahani had not cleared the evidentiary threshold required to make a *prima facie* case and, therefore, had no access to these procedural safeguards.[109]

Ahani claimed before the HRC to be a victim of violations of, *inter alia,* Articles 2, third paragraph, 7, and 13. He argued, *inter alia,* that both the national proceedings on the reasonableness of the national security certificate and the national proceedings concerning the planned expulsion violated the procedural requirements of the provisions invoked.

With regard to the proceedings on the reasonableness of the national security certificate, Ahani claimed that in 1993 the Federal Court had not tested the evidence which formed the basis of the allegation that he was a national security threat and had not heard independent witnesses. The HRC did not follow the author in this complaint. It observed that at the Federal Court's 'reasonableness hearing' on the security certification the author had been provided by the Court with a summary redacted for security concerns reasonably informing him of the claims made against him. The HRC noted that the Federal Court had been conscious of the heavy burden upon it to ensure through this process the author's ability appropriately to be aware of and respond to the case made against him, and he had been able to, and had, presented his own case and cross-examined witnesses. In the circumstances of national security involved, the HRC was not persuaded that this process had been unfair to him. Nor, recalling its limited role in the assessment of facts and evidence, did the HRC discern on the record any elements of bad faith, abuse of power or other arbitrariness which would vitiate the Federal Court's assessment of the reasonableness of the certificate asserting the author's involvement in a terrorist organization. (…) Accordingly, the HRC concluded that the author had not made out a violation of the requirements of the invoked provisions.[110]

---

108 Supreme Court of Canada, 11 January 2002, *Suresh v. Canada* (Minister of Citizenship and Immigration), 2002 SCC 1, [2002] 1 S.C.R. 3.
109 HRC, *Mansour Ahani v. Canada*, 15 June 2004, No. 1051/2002, paras. 2.7-2.9.
110 *Ibidem*, para. 10.5.

With regard to the author's complaint about the unfairness of the national proceedings concerning expulsion, the HRC noted that the Supreme Court had held, in the companion case of *Suresh*, that the process of the Minister's determination in that case of whether the affected individual was at risk of substantial harm and should be expelled on national security grounds had been faulty for unfairness, as Suresh had not been provided with the full materials on which the Minister had based his or her decision and an opportunity to comment in writing thereon and, further, as the Minister's decision had not been reasoned. The HRC further observed that where one of the highest values protected by the Covenant, namely the right to be free from torture, was at stake, the closest scrutiny should be applied to the fairness of the procedure applied to determine whether an individual was at substantial risk of torture. The HRC emphasised that this risk was highlighted in this case by its request for interim measures of protection. It did not see reasons why Suresh and Ahani should be treated differently, and concluded that there had been a violation of Article 13, in conjunction with Article 7.[111]

The decision in *Ahani* strongly conveys the message that, in expulsion cases, both parties to the case must have equal access to the documents in the case file. The HRC seems to be stricter in guarding adversariality and equality of arms than the ECtHR as it required in the *Ahani* decision that all the documents in the file be disclosed to the claimant, including those underpinning the allegation that Ahani constituted a threat to Canada's national security. In other words, in *Ahani* the HRC treated adversariality and equality of arms as an absolute right and did not tolerate the assumption that national security interests justified non-disclosure of part of the evidentiary materials. As will be shown in more detail in chapter 5, section 5.5.4, the ECtHR treats adversariality and equality of arms as relative rights and has ruled that non-disclosure of evidentiary materials may be justified if this is strictly necessary to preserve the fundamental rights of another individual or to safeguard an important public interest, such as the protection of national security.[112]

3.3.5 *Compliance with reasonable national procedural rules*

Article 5, second paragraph, sub b of the Optional Protocol not only requires that available national remedies must be exhausted before an applicant applies to the HRC, but also that such national remedies are exhausted in a proper way, in accordance with time limits and other procedural rules and formalities of national law. In other words, proper and full use and advantage of the remedies available under national law must be made. Failure to do so leads to inadmissibility before the HRC, due to non-exhaustion of national remedies.[113] For national courts this entails that failure to adhere to national procedural rules, in principle, absolves those courts from carrying out an investigation on the merits. The case of *Ngoc Si Truong v. Canada*

---

111 *Ibidem*, paras. 10.6-10.8.
112 See, for example, ECtHR, *Edwards and Lewis v. the UK*, 27 October 2004, Appl. Nos. 39647/98 and 40461/98, para. 46.
113 McGoldrick 1996, p. 195, Joseph, Schultz & Castan 2005, p. 113.

(2003)[114] may illustrate this. In that case, the author fled Viet Nam in 1978 illegally for fear of being drafted into the Vietnamese armed forces in the armed conflict with Cambodia. In 1980 (aged 16 years), he arrived in Canada and was granted permanent resident status. In 1985 and 1988 the author was convicted of a number of crimes (among them assault causing bodily harm) and sentenced to imprisonment. By virtue of his criminal offences, the Canadian authorities on 8 July 1992 ordered his deportation pursuant to the Immigration Act, which requires the deportation of permanent residents who have been convicted of serious criminal offences. In 1993, the author's appeal to the Appeals Division of the Immigration and Refugee Board, based on 'the existence of compassionate or humanitarian considerations', was dismissed. The author then sought leave to apply for judicial review to the Federal Court. However, his counsel at the time inadvertently failed to request written reasons for the decision from the Appeals Division within the 10-day limit provided, and as a result the Appeals Division refused to supply its reasons once requested thereafter. The Federal Court dismissed the author's application for failure to supply an application record (including the Appeals Division's reasons for the decision).[115]

The author argued before the HRC that his removal to a country where he allegedly had no legal status would amount to cruel, inhuman and degrading treatment contrary to Article 7. He submitted that, as a result of his illegal departure from Viet Nam and the loss of his Canadian permanent residency status, he had become stateless. As a result, he would, upon deportation to Viet Nam, be unable to work, reside or otherwise enjoy the rights associated with employment. He pointed out that when he travelled to Viet Nam in 1991, he had been required to obtain a visa for four months and had not been allowed to engage in employment. He submitted that he might be imprisoned in a 're-education camp' upon return as a result of his illegal departure and his father's involvement in the former South Vietnamese Government.[116]

The author also claimed before the HRC that his deportation would be arbitrary and contrary to Article 13, taken in conjunction with Article 2, third paragraph. The Appeals Division's refusal to issue written reasons for its decision denied him the opportunity to challenge the legality of his deportation order in the Federal Court.[117]

As regards the proceedings before the Canadian immigration and judicial authorities, the HRC noted that the author, aided by counsel, had had a full and independent review of the decision by the Appeals Division of the Immigration and Refugee Board to deport him. Further judicial appeal had been available under the State party's law, provided that he lodged a timely request for the full decision, and he had failed to do so. The HRC recalled its jurisprudence pursuant to which failure to adhere to procedural time limits for the filing of complaints amounted to failure to exhaust national remedies, and concluded that, as a consequence, it would be inappropriate for the author to raise on the merits his subsequent inability, due to inadvertence, to pursue an effective appeal. The HRC concluded that the author had failed to substantiate, for purposes of admissibility, his claim of a violation of Articles

114 HRC, *Ngoc Si Truong v. Canada*, 5 May 2003, No. 743/1997.
115 *Ibidem*, paras. 2.1-2.5.
116 *Ibidem*, para. 3.1.
117 *Ibidem*, para. 3.4.

2 and 13 of the Covenant. It decided that the communication was inadmissible under Article 5, second paragraph, sub b of the Optional Protocol.[118]

From the case of *Jagjit Singh Bhullar v. Canada* (2006)[119] it becomes clear that national procedural rules must be reasonable. After the rejection of the author's asylum claim in Canada, he applied to become part of the Post-Determination Refugee Claimants in Canada Class. He was found ineligible on account of late filing. After this, he filed two applications for judicial review. Both applications were filed out of time (submitted past the deadline for such applications).[120] Before the HRC, Canada disputed the admissibility of the application on the ground that national remedies had not been exhausted. The HRC agreed with Canada and stated that

> 'The Committee recalls its jurisprudence that authors are bound by procedural rules such as filing deadlines applicable to the exhaustion of domestic remedies, provided that the restrictions are reasonable. (…) The Committee notes that both applications for judicial review were filed out of time by the author and were not subsequently pursued. The author has failed to advance any reasons for these delays, nor any argument that the specified time limits in question were either unfair or unreasonable. It follows that the author has failed to pursue domestic remedies with the "requisite diligence" and the communication must be declared inadmissible for failure to exhaust domestic remedies.'[121]

The cases of *Ngoc Si Truong v. Canada* (2003) and *Jagjit Singh Bhullar v. Canada* (2006) strongly resemble the judgment of the ECtHR in *Bahaddar v. Netherlands* (1998, see chapter 5, section 5.3.2).[122] In both *Ngoc Si Truong v. Canada* and *Bahaddar v. Netherlands* the applicant's counsel inadvertently failed to take crucial steps in the national proceedings, although offered ample opportunity to take such steps, and in both cases this was attributed to the asylum seeker. In both cases, the international court or international supervisor did not find it problematic that the national court had not considered the case on the merits because of non-compliance with national procedural rules. And in both cases, the international court or supervisor declared the claim inadmissible for failure to exhaust national remedies.

In a number of older cases concerning other subject matters (not expulsion of asylum seekers), the HRC took a more lenient approach when it was established that the author or author's counsel had made an unsuccessful yet genuine attempt to comply with national procedural rules in order to exhaust national remedies. In *J.R.T. and the W.G. Party v. Canada* (1983),[123] there was ambiguity ensuing from conflicting time limits laid down in national laws. For that reason, non-compliance with the national time limits was not held against the author and did not lead to inadmissibility

---

118 *Ibidem*, para. 7.6. In a number of cases outside the asylum context the HRC reached the same conclusion. See, for example, HRC, *A.P.A. v. Spain*, 25 March 1994, No. 433/90, para. 6.3.

119 HRC, *Jagjit Singh Bhullar v. Canada*, 13 November 2006, No. 982/2001.

120 *Ibidem*, para. 2.4, para. 2.7.

121 *Ibidem*, para. 7.3.

122 ECtHR, *Bahaddar v. the Netherlands*, 19 February 1998, Appl. No. 25894/94.

123 HRC, *J.R.T. and the W.G. Party v. Canada*, 6 April 1983, No. 104/81.

for non-exhaustion of national remedies. In *Griffin v. Spain* (1995)[124] the author was excused from exhausting national remedies because his failure to do so had resulted from the negligence and incompetence of a State-provided lawyer (as opposed to privately retained counsel).

3.3.6   National remedy is bound to fail

It follows from the HRC's case law under Article 5, second paragraph, sub b, of the Optional Protocol that a national remedy is not effective when it offers virtually no prospect of success, in other words, is bound to fail. A national remedy may be bound to fail when the application of a constant jurisprudential line, developed in earlier cases by national courts, to a newly pending case, bars an individual, case-specific, factual assessment in that pending case. The HRC has ruled in a number of cases that authors are not expected to use national remedies in the face of contrary superior court precedents. For example, in *Länsman et al v. Finland* (1994), the HRC stated that:

> 'Wherever the jurisprudence of the highest domestic tribunal has decided the matter at issue, thereby eliminating any prospect of success of an appeal to the domestic courts, authors are not required to exhaust national remedies, for the purposes of the Optional Protocol.'[125]

When we contemplate this HRC case law on the effectiveness of national remedies in conjunction with the requirement of a thorough and fair examination of the claim, flowing from Article 2, third paragraph, and in conjunction with the procedural limb of Article 7, it may be argued that this requirement demands that national courts must normally make an individual case-specific factual assessment and must be careful in automatically and mechanically relying on steady jurisprudential lines.

3.3.7   The provisions on national proceedings in the asylum context: interim conclusions

Under Articles 7 and 2, third paragraph, ICCPR the national authorities are required to consider the protection claim thoroughly and fairly. So far the HRC has not specified in a detailed way what this requirement of a thorough and fair consideration means. The HRC is generally reluctant to put national asylum proceedings, including court proceedings, to a rigorous ICCPR-compliance test and does often not respond in a meaningful way to specific procedural problems raised by authors of individual communications. This reluctance is linked to the fact that it regards the determination and evaluation of facts and evidence as matters for the national courts. The HRC itself will normally not engage in that. As a consequence, it will not easily find na-

---

124 HRC, *Griffin v. Spain*, 4 April 1995, No. 493/92.

125 HRC, *Länsman et al v. Finland*, 26 October 1994, No. 511/92, para. 6.1. See also HRC, *Faurisson v. France*, 8 November 1996, No. 550/93, para. 6.1, in which case the HRC ruled that the author was not required to appeal his case to the French Court of Appeal, where his co-accused had already lost his appeal. See also HRC, *Johannes Vos v. the Netherlands*, 26 July 1999, No. 786/97, para. 6.2.

tional remedies ineffective for reasons having to do with determination of the facts. The HRC's hands-off approach may be explained by its limited investigative possibilities and by the fact that its meeting time is very limited, which is difficult to reconcile with the time required to assess evidence and to write down an assessment of the presented evidence. The case of *Pillai and Joachimpillai v. Canada* (2011),[126] in which the HRC deemed the national proceedings defective because insufficient attention had been paid to statements on past torture, may mark a turning point towards firmer monitoring of procedural ICCPR-compliance, but more jurisprudence is to be awaited to firmly draw such a conclusion.

The case of *Mansour Ahani v. Canada* (2004)[127] has shown that the HRC is incidentally prepared to give up its hands-off approach if the national authorities breached the crucial requirements of equality of arms and adversarial proceedings. The HRC found the national expulsion proceedings in *Ahani* to be defective under Article 13 as the Minister did not provide the author with all the materials – including secret information that Ahani was a danger to Canada's national security – on which the expulsion decision was based and the national courts did not correct this unfairness in the procedure.

National procedural rules will normally not render national proceedings non-compliant with the requirement of a thorough and fair examination of the claim, provided that such rules are reasonable and provided that they are not applied in an automatic and mechanical way. National courts must be careful in automatically relying on steady jurisprudential lines.

3.4 Article 14: intensity of national judicial scrutiny and issues of evidence

3.4.1 Applicability?

Article 14, first paragraph, stipulates that in the determination of any criminal charge against him, or of his rights and obligations in a suit at law, everyone shall be entitled to a fair and public hearing by a competent, independent and impartial tribunal established by law. The text of Article 14, first paragraph and the preparatory works do not explain in detail what is meant by 'a suit at law'. At the time when the ICCPR was drawn up, national asylum court proceedings as we know them nowadays were in many States parties to the Covenant practically non-existent.[128] The drafters could, therefore, not explicitly have had asylum proceedings in mind when defining the scope of Article 14. The preparatory works demonstrate that there was much debate on the question of whether Article 14 applied to judicial review of administrative ac-

---

126 HRC, *Pillai and Joachimpillai v. Canada*, 25 March 2010, No. 1763/2008.
127 HRC, *Mansour Ahani v. Canada*, 15 June 2004, No. 1051/2002.
128 Zwaan 2003, pp. 87-89; 'Providing protection, towards fair and effective asylum procedures', JUSTICE/ILPA/ARC research project into asylum procedures in Europe, Canada and Australia, p. 50. Shah 2005, p. 2.

tions and decisions, and that this question remained unresolved in the end.[129] In a number of cases, however, the HRC has outlined its view that a 'suit at law' can occur between an individual and the authorities. Accordingly it has held Article 14, first paragraph, to be applicable in a number of cases where the dispute occurred within a national setting of administrative law, between an individual and administrative authorities.[130]

The HRC has, so far, been ambiguous about the question of whether or not Article 14 applies to national proceedings concerning asylum status determination and the expulsion of asylum seekers. In *V.R.M.B. v. Canada* (1988),[131] the HRC considered that

> 'Even if immigration hearings and deportation proceedings were to be deemed as constituting "suits at law" within the meaning of article 14 (1) of the Covenant, as the author contends, a thorough examination of the communication has not revealed any facts in substantiation of the author's claim to be a victim of a violation of this article. In particular, it emerges from the author's own submissions that he was given ample opportunity, in formal proceedings including oral hearings with witness testimony, both before the Adjudicator and before the Canadian Courts, to present his case for sojourn in Canada.'

In *Williams Adu v. Canada* (1997) and *Hamid Reza Taghi Khadje v. the Netherlands* (2006), the HRC ducked the question of the applicability of Article 14 by considering that, given the circumstances, there was no need to determine whether the proceedings relating to the asylum applications fell within the scope of Article 14.[132] In a number of, mostly later, cases it explicitly ruled that proceedings related to an alien's expulsion, the guarantees in regard to which are governed by Article 13, do not fall within the ambit of a determination of rights and obligations in a suit at law, within the meaning of Article 14, first paragraph.[133] In line with this later jurisprudence, General Comment No. 32 states that the guarantee of equal access to courts does not apply to

---

129 UN Doc. E/CN.4/AC.1/24/Rev.1 (12 May 1948); UN Doc. E/CN.4/AC.1/24/Rev./Add.1 (14 May 1948); UN Doc. E/CN.4/SR.107 at 6 (31 May 1949); UN Doc. E/CN.4/SR.109 at 7 (1 June 1949); UN Doc. E/CN.4/SR.109 at 3 (1 June 1949); UN Doc. E/CN.4/SR.109 at 8 and 9 (1 June 1949). For more detailed information on the question of applicability of Article 14 to cases within the ambit of administrative law, see Boeles 1997, pp. 133-140 and Joseph, Schultz & Castan 2005, pp. 390-394.

130 See, for example, HRC, *Muñoz Hermoza v. Peru*, 4 November 1988, No. 203/1986, in which case the HRC found that the claim of a dismissed sergeant of the Guardia Civil for reinstatement in public service as such was a 'suit at law' so that Article 14, paragraph 1, was applicable; HRC, *Y.L. v. Canada*, 8 April 1986, No. 112/81, a case about an appeal to a Pension Review Board against a decision by the Pension Commission to refuse an invalidity pension after discharge from the army; HRC, *Jansen-Gielen v. the Netherlands*, 3 April 2001, No. 846/1999, in which case the HRC found that tribunal proceedings to determine the psychiatric ability of people to perform their jobs amounted to a suit at law.

131 HRC, *V.M.R.B. v. Canada*, 18 July 1988, No. 236/1987.

132 HRC, *Williams Adu v. Canada*, 18 July 1997, No. 654/1995, para. 6.3; HRC, *Hamid Reza Taghi Khadje v. the Netherlands*, 15 November 2006, No. 1438/2005, para. 6.3.

133 HRC, *Ahani v. Canada*, 15 June 2004, No. 1051/2002, para. 10.9; HRC, *P.K. v. Canada*, 3 April 2007, No. 1234/2003, para. 7.5; HRC, *A.C. v. the Netherlands*, 22 July 2008, No. 14942006, para. 8.4; HRC, *Moses Solo Tarlue v. Canada*, 28 April 2009, No. 1551/2007, para. 7.8

extradition, expulsion and deportation procedures.[134] This General Comment also makes clear, however, that many of the guarantees of Article 14 form part of Article 13 as well and are, as such, applicable:

> 'The procedural guarantees of Article 13 incorporate notions of due process also reflected in Article 14 (…) and thus should be interpreted in the light of this latter provision. Insofar as domestic law entrusts a judicial body with the task of deciding about expulsions or deportations, the guarantee of equality of all persons before the courts and tribunals as enshrined in Article 14, paragraph 1, and the principles of impartiality, fairness and equality of arms implicit in this guarantee are applicable.'[135]

The more recent jurisprudence and General Comment No. 32 justify the conclusion that Article 14 is, in principle, not applicable to national proceedings concerning asylum and expulsion. However, in *Dranichnikov v. Australia* (2007)[136] the HRC ruled differently. The author in this case claimed that the Australian asylum court proceedings she went through had not offered her a fair hearing as the Review Tribunal was not an independent court and this Tribunal was deliberately delaying the determination of her husband's refugee claim. The HRC found the complaint that the national tribunal was not an independent court lacking in substantiation and, therefore, inadmissible. It considered the complaint about the delay on the merits, considering that it was concerned about the delay in the determination of the author's husband's refugee claim, but also that this delay was caused by the totality of the proceedings and not just by the Refugee Review Tribunal. As the HRC examined at least one aspect of the Article 14-complaint on the merits, it did consider Article 14 to be applicable to the national asylum court proceedings the author went through.[137] Based on the case law discussed above, the only conclusion we can draw is that the HRC has, so far, been ambiguous and inconsistent about the question of whether or not Article 14, first paragraph, is applicable to national asylum court proceedings. The case of *Dranichnikov* may indicate that the HRC has begun to steer another course. So far we cannot be completely sure about this, however, as it has so far not repeated the position taken in *Dranichnikov* in other cases.

3.4.2 *National procedural autonomy*

General Comment No. 32 states in paragraph 26 that

---

134 General Comment No. 32, para. 17.

135 *Ibidem*, para. 62.

136 HRC, *Dranichnikov v. Australia*, 16 January 2007, No. 1291/2004.

137 A number of authors consider Article 14 to be applicable to national asylum court proceedings. See Boeles 1995, p. 140 and Hathaway 2005, pp. 647-649. Hathaway writes that 'it would be difficult to conceive a reason to exclude a determination of entitlement to claim refugee rights from the ambit of Article 14(1) scrutiny'. See also Wouters 2009, pp. 417-419. He concludes that the basis for the procedural safeguards in cases involving *refoulement* is found in Article 2, paragraph 3, and in Article 13, and that moreover important principles of impartiality, fairness and equality as developed under Article 14, paragraph 1, are also applicable in *refoulement* cases.

'Article 14 guarantees procedural equality and fairness only and cannot be interpreted as ensuring the absence of error on the part of the competent tribunal. (...) It is generally for the courts of States parties to the Covenant to review facts and evidence, or the application of domestic legislation, in a particular case, unless it can be shown that such evaluation or application was clearly arbitrary or amounted to a manifest error or denial of justice, or that the court otherwise violated its obligation of independence and impartiality.'[138]

The quoted paragraph from General Comment No. 32 clarifies the division of tasks in offering protection of human rights between the HRC and national courts. According to the HRC, it is generally the task of national courts – and not the task of the HRC – to review facts, evidence and the application of national law. This is in line with the subsidiary role of the HRC, as reflected in Article 2, third paragraph, and Article 5, second paragraph, of the Optional Protocol. The task of the HRC is to determine whether in a specific case before it ICCPR rights were violated, not to establish the facts or to apply national law. It follows from this that the HRC will normally allow national courts considerable leeway in this area. From the description of the task of national courts given in General Comment No. 32 – review facts, evidence and the application of national legislation – we may infer that, in the opinion of the HRC, national courts must have jurisdiction on points of fact and points of law. However, unlike the ECtHR, the HRC has (so far) not developed a full jurisdiction doctrine (see chapter 5, section 5.4.1). No views of the HRC have been found in which – either under Article 14 or under another provision – it was explicitly stated that national courts must have, in principle, full jurisdiction on points of fact and points of law and that under particular circumstances less intense forms of judicial scrutiny are permitted.

In a number of views the HRC has made clear that the procedural practice applied by national courts in order to establish the relevant facts is a matter for those courts to determine in the interests of justice. In the case of *Anni Äärelä and Jouni Näkkäläjärvi v. Finland* (2001),[139] the authors, reindeer breeders of Sami ethnic origin and members of a reindeer herding co-operative, claimed a violation of Article 27 ICCPR[140] because logging and road construction was allowed on the best winter lands of the co-operative. In the proceedings before the HRC, the authors claimed a violation of Article 14, first paragraph, contending that the Appeal Court had violated the principle of equality of arms in allowing oral hearings, while denying an on-site inspection. The HRC did not follow the authors in this complaint. It ruled:

'As to the authors' claims under Article 14 that the procedure applied by the Court of Appeal was unfair in that an oral hearing was granted and an on-site inspection was denied, the Committee considers that, as a general rule, the procedural practice applied by domestic courts is a

---

138 HRC, General Comment No. 32, para. 26.
139 HRC, *Anni Äärelä and Jouni Näkkäläjärvi v. Finland*, 7 November 2001, No. 779/1997.
140 Article 27 ICCPR is about the protection of minorities and states: 'In those States in which ethnic, religious or linguistic minorities exist, persons belonging to such minorities shall not be denied the right, in community with the other members of their group, to enjoy their own culture, to profess and practise their own religion, or to use their own language.'

matter for the courts to determine in the interests of justice. The onus is on the authors to show that a particular practice has given rise to unfairness in the particular proceedings. In the present case, an oral hearing was granted as the Court found it necessary to determine the reliability and weight to be accorded to oral testimony. The authors have not shown that this decision was manifestly arbitrary or otherwise amounted to a denial of justice. As to the decision not to pursue an on-site inspection, the Committee considers that the authors have failed to show that the Court of Appeal's decision to rely on the District Court's inspection of the area and the records of those proceedings injected unfairness into the hearing or demonstrably altered the outcome of the case. Accordingly, the Committee is unable to find a violation of Article 14 in the procedure applied by the Court of Appeal in these respects.'[141]

The HRC has reiterated this principle of national procedural autonomy in many other decisions.[142] As was made clear above in section 3.3.1, this principle is also applied within the context and framework of Article 7.

General Comment No. 32, and the HRC's case law in other areas (not asylum) make clear that exceptions to the hands-off approach are made where national courts evaluated evidence or applied national law in a clearly arbitrary way, made a manifest error or denied justice, or where the national court otherwise violated its obligations of independence and impartiality.[143] As the cases discussed in the next section will demonstrate, the HRC finds a lack of equality of arms and a lack of adversariality in the national proceedings a serious problem, meriting the conclusion that no fair proceedings in the sense of Article 14 have taken place. This jurisprudential line mirrors the HRC's stance on Articles 7 and 13 in the case of *Mansour Ahani v. Canada* (2004),[144] discussed above in section 3.3.4.

3.4.3   Equality of arms and adversariality

The case of *Sandra Fei v. Colombia* (1995)[145] concerned national proceedings over the custody of children after the divorce of their parents. The author alleged before the HRC that the national proceedings had been unfair, in violation of Article 14, first paragraph. The HRC agreed with the author. The national court proceedings were considered unfair for a number of reasons. One reason was that the national courts had not guaranteed equality of arms and had not offered adversarial proceedings:

'Finally, it is noteworthy that in the proceedings under article 86 of the Colombian Constitution instituted on behalf of the author's daughters in December 1993, the hearing took place, and judgement was given, on 16 December 1993, that is, before the expiration of the deadline for the submission of the author's defence statement. The State party has failed to address this

---

141 HRC, *Anni Äärelä and Jouni Näkkäläjärvi v. Finland*, 7 November 2001, No. 779/1997, para. 7.3.
142 See, for example, HRC, *R.M. v. Finland*, 27 March 1989, No. 301/1988 para. 6.4; HRC, *Carlton Linton v. Jamaica*, 22 October 1992, No. 255/1987, paras. 3.1, 3.2, 8.3; HRC, *Errol Sims v. Jamaica*, 3 April 1995, No. 541/1993, para. 6.2.
143 General Comment No. 32, para. 26.
144 HRC, *Mansour Ahani v. Canada*, 15 June 2004, No. 1051/2002.
145 HRC, *Sandra Fei v. Colombia*, 26 April 1995, No. 514/1992.

point, and the author's version is thus uncontested. In the Committee's opinion, the impossibility for Mrs Fei to present her arguments before judgement was given was incompatible with the principle of adversary proceedings, and thus contrary to article 14, paragraph 1, of the Covenant.'[146]

The case of *Jansen-Gielen v. the Netherlands* (2001)[147] provides another example in which the HRC concluded that there had been a violation of Article 14, first paragraph for reasons of non-compliance with the principles of equality of arms and adversarial proceedings. The author, a primary school teacher, was declared disabled for work by 80% by the Director of the General Civil Pension Scheme. The decision rested on a psychiatrist's report. She contested this decision in administrative and then judicial proceedings. In the proceedings before the Central Appeals Tribunal (Centrale Raad van Beroep), the highest court, the author changed counsels. Her new counsel submitted to the Tribunal a psychological report, refuting the conclusions of the first expert report. This new report was submitted by letter on 26 September 1994 and the hearing of the Central Appeals Tribunal took place, as scheduled, on 29 September 1994. In its judgment of 20 October 1994, the Central Appeals Tribunal dismissed the author's appeal. It considered that it could not take into account the expert report submitted by the author because of its late presentation. It appears from the judgment that the Tribunal considered that the defending party would have been unreasonably hindered in its defence if the document had been allowed. In reaching its decision the Tribunal also referred to the provisions of Article 8:58 of the (new) General Administrative Law. The author argued before the HRC that the Tribunal's failure to take the expert report into account violated her right to provide evidence, since it had prevented her from refuting the other party's arguments as to her ability to work. She claimed that this constituted a violation of Article 14, since she had not received a fair hearing.[148] The HRC agreed with the author and considered:

'The author has claimed that the failure of the Central Appeals Tribunal to append the psychological report, submitted by her counsel, to the case file two days before the hearing, constitutes a violation of her right to a fair hearing. The Committee has noted the State party's argument that the Court found that admission of the report two days before the hearing would have unreasonably obstructed the other party in the conduct of the case. However, the Committee notes that the procedural law applicable to the hearing of the case did not provide for a time limit for the submission of documents. Consequently, it was the duty of the Court of Appeal, which was not constrained by any prescribed time limit to ensure that each party could challenge the documentary evidence which the other filed or wished to file and, if need be, to adjourn proceedings. In the absence of the guarantee of equality of arms between the parties in the production of evidence for the purposes of the hearing, the Committee finds a violation of article 14, paragraph 1 of the Covenant.'[149]

---

146 *Ibidem*, para. 8.6.
147 HRC, *Jansen-Gielen v. the Netherlands*, 14 May 2001, No. 846/1999.
148 *Ibidem*, paras. 2.1-3.1.
149 *Ibidem*, para. 8.2.

In the case of *Anni Äärelä and Jouni Näkkäläjärvi v. Finland* (2001, see above 3.4.2)[150] the HRC agreed with the authors that Article 14, first paragraph, had been violated as the Appeal Court had violated the principle of equality of arms in taking into account material information without providing an opportunity to the other party to comment.[151]

The case of *Fuenzalida v. Ecuador* (1996)[152] shows that in certain cases and under specific circumstances, national courts are required to apply investigative powers, for the sake of guaranteeing full equality of arms and fully adversarial proceedings. The author in this case complained before the HRC that his national trial, at which he had been convicted of rape, had been unfair. The victim in this case had submitted to the national court a laboratory report on samples (blood and semen) taken from her and samples of blood and hair taken from the author against his will, showing the existence of an enzyme which the author did not have in his blood. The author requested the national court to order an examination of his own blood and semen, but the court denied this request.[153] The HRC agreed with the author and found that the national court's refusal to order expert testimony of crucial importance to the case constituted a violation of Article 14.[154] The HRC's consideration is very brief, which can probably be explained by the fact that the respondent State party did not provide much information concerning this aspect of the national court proceedings. It is, however, interesting to point out that the HRC found the national court's refusal to order an expert investigation incompatible with Article 14, third paragraph, sub e, which provision applies specifically to criminal proceedings and embodies the principles of equality of arms and adversarial proceedings, stating that 'in the determination of any criminal charge against him, everyone shall be entitled to the following minimum guarantees, in full equality (…)(e) to examine, or have examined, the witnesses against him and to obtain the attendance and examination of witnesses on his behalf under the same conditions as witnesses against him'. Thus, the HRC found the national court's refusal to order the requested expert investigation incompatible with the principles of equality of arms and adversarial proceedings.

3.4.4   Article 14: interim conclusions

Within the framework of Article 14, the procedural practice applied by national courts to determine the facts and to admit, exclude, weigh and evaluate evidence is a matter for those courts to determine. Unlike the ECtHR (see chapter 5, section 5.4.1), the HRC has (so far) not developed a doctrine regarding the required intensity of national judicial scrutiny in administrative law cases. In a number of cases not concerning the expulsion of asylum seekers, the HRC concluded that there had been a breach by national courts of the principles of equality of arms and adversarial proceedings. In those cases, the HRC relinquished its deference to national procedural

---

150 HRC, *Anni Äärelä and Jouni Näkkäläjärvi v. Finland*, 7 November 2001, No. 779/1997.
151 *Ibidem*, para. 7.4.
152 HRC, *Fuenzalida v. Ecuador*, 15 August 1996, No. 480/1991.
153 *Ibidem*, paras. 3.4, 3.5.
154 *Ibidem*, para. 9.5.

autonomy and overtly criticised the national court proceedings for being unfair. It is obvious from these cases that the HRC regards equality of arms and adversarial proceedings as the very essence of fair proceedings. The principles developed by the HRC within the framework of Article 14 strongly mirror those developed within the context of Articles 7 and 13, discussed in section 3.3 and summarised in 3.3.7.

ICCPR, Part 2:

The assessment performed by the HRC in cases on the expulsion of asylum seekers

3.5 **The assessment performed by the HRC in cases on expulsion of asylum seekers**

The HRC has dealt with the merits in only a limited number of cases concerning the expulsion of asylum seekers.[155] Furthermore, in a limited number of cases, it has declared the communication inadmissible.[156] Below, a step by step analysis is made of the examination performed by the HRC in these cases, with the aid of the eleven aspects of evidence and judicial scrutiny introduced in Chapter 1. As the number of cases concerning the expulsion of asylum seekers is limited, which makes it difficult to discern clear jurisprudential lines, I also examined a number of internal torture cases: cases in which the author alleged before the HRC that he had been tortured in his own country, being the respondent State party. In addition to that category of cases, I examined a number of cases concerning extradition, in which Article 7 was invoked.

3.5.1 Standard of proof

General Comment No. 31 (2004) states:

> 'Moreover, the Article 2 obligation requiring that States Parties respect and ensure the Covenant rights for all persons in their territory and all persons under their control entails an obligation not to extradite, deport, expel or otherwise remove a person from their territory, where there are substantial grounds for believing that there is a real risk of irreparable harm, such as that contemplated by Articles 6 and 7 of the Covenant, either in the country to which removal is to be effected or in any country to which the person may subsequently be removed. The relevant judicial and administrative authorities should be made aware of the need to ensure compliance with the Covenant obligations in such matters.'[157]

It follows from this that the standard of proof applied by the HRC in expulsion cases is that there are substantial grounds for believing that there is a real risk of a violation of Article 7. This standard has been further explained by the HRC in a number of cases. In the first two *refoulement* cases concerning extradition to the USA, *Kindler v. Canada* (1993)[158] and *Chitat Ng v. Canada* (1994),[159] the HRC defined the real risk as the necessary and foreseeable consequence of the extradition. It also considered in

---

155 See note 20 in section 3.1.1 above.
156 See note 21 in section 3.1.1 above.
157 General Comment No. 31 (2004), para. 12.
158 HRC, *Kindler v. Canada*, 18 November 1993, No. 470/1991.
159 HRC, *Chitat Ng v. Canada*, 7 January 1994, No. 469/1991.

both cases that treatment contrary to the ICCPR was 'certain'. In both cases, the following consideration was used:

> 'However, if a State party takes a decision relating to a person within its jurisdiction, and the necessary and foreseeable consequence is that that person's rights under the Covenant will be violated in another jurisdiction, the State party itself may be in violation of the Covenant. That follows from the fact that a State party's duty under article 2 of the Covenant would be negated by the handing over of a person to another State (whether a State party to the Covenant or not) where treatment contrary to the Covenant is certain or is the very purpose of the handing over.'[160]

In the next *refoulement* case concerning extradition, *Cox v. Canada* (1994),[161] the HRC again defined the real risk as the necessary and foreseeable consequence, but did not repeat the 'certainty' requirement. Wouters (2009) points out that it may seem strange to define the risk criterion as a certain consequence of extradition, but that from a contextual point of view it may be understandable as extradition cases involve transparent criminal proceedings so that it is by and large known what will happen to the authors after their extradition.[162] Cases involving the expulsion of asylum seekers differ from extradition cases in that it is often much less certain what will happen to the author after expulsion. Nevertheless, in the first case about the expulsion of an asylum seeker, *A.R.J. v. Australia* (1997, see section 3.1.1), the HRC once again explained that a real risk means that it is a necessary and foreseeable consequence of the expulsion that Article 7 will be violated.[163] In following cases concerning expulsion, the HRC has been fairly consistent in reiterating the necessary and foreseeable consequence criterion, although the criterion is not explicitly mentioned in all the cases.[164]

The 'necessary and foreseeable consequence' criterion clearly indicates a high threshold which is not easily met. This threshold seems to be higher than under Article 3 ECHR, where the level of risk required is a real (not fictional), personal (relates to the individual), and foreseeable risk exceeding the mere possibility of being subjected to proscribed ill-treatment, but where the risk does not need to be certain (necessary) or highly probable.[165]

---

160 HRC, *Kindler v. Canada*, 18 November 1993, No. 470/1991, para. 6.2, HRC, *Chitat Ng v. Canada*, 7 January 1994, No. 469/1991, para. 6.2.
161 HRC, *Cox v. Canada*, 9 December 1994, No. 539/1993, para. 16.1.
162 Wouters 2009, p. 393.
163 HRC, *A.R.J.v. Australia*, 11 August 1997, No. 692/1996, para. 6.8.
164 Examples of cases in which the HRC explicitly referred to the criterion of a necessary and foreseeable consequence are: HRC, *G.T. v. Australia*, 4 December 1997, No. 706/1996, para. 8.1; HRC, *Byaruhanga v. Denmark*, 9 December 2004, No. 1222/2003, para. 11.2; HRC, *Daljit Singh v. Canada*, 28 April 2006, No. 1315/2004, para. 6.3; HRC, *Dawood Khan v Canada*, 10 August 2006, No. 1302/2004, para. 5.4; HRC, *Mehrez Ben Abde Hamida v. Canada*, 18 March 2010, No. 1544/2007, para. 8.7. Examples of cases in which the HRC did not explicitly mention this criterion are: HRC, *C. v. Australia*, 13 November 2002, No. 900/1999; HRC, *Ahani v. Canada*, 15 June 2004, No. 1051/2002; HRC, *Alzery v. Sweden*, 10 November 2006, No. 1416/2005; HRC, *Moses SoloTarlue v. Canada*, 27 March 2009, No. 1551/2007. See on the standard of proof also Wouters 2009, pp. 391-396.
165 See Chapter 5.

3.5.2   Burden of proof

It is constant case law of the HRC that in Article 7-cases, the burden of proof is shared between the author and the authorities of the State party. A consideration which is reiterated in many views in internal torture cases is that

> 'With regard to the burden of proof, this cannot rest alone on the author of the communication, especially considering that the author and the State party do not always have equal access to the evidence and that frequently the State party alone has access to relevant information. It is implicit in article 4 (2) of the Optional Protocol that the State party has the duty to investigate in good faith all allegations of violation of the Covenant made against it and its authorities, especially when such allegations are corroborated by evidence submitted by the author of the communication, and to furnish to the Committee the information available to it. In cases where the author has submitted to the Committee allegations supported by witness testimony, as in this case, and where further clarification of the case depends on information exclusively in the hands of the State party, the Committee may consider such allegations as substantiated in the absence of satisfactory evidence and explanations to the contrary submitted by the State party.'[166]

It follows from this consideration that the burden of proof is shared: there is an initial burden of assertion, and, preferably, also some corroboration, on the author. After that, an investigative burden on the authorities of the State party emerges. The authorities must investigate 'in good faith' the alleged violation. In some cases the HRC has stated that 'a State party must investigate thoroughly, in good faith and within the imparted deadlines' the alleged violation.[167]

The term 'especially' (in the middle of the quote above) makes clear that, the more detailed and the more corroborated the author's statements are, the more detailed the investigation by the authorities of the respondent State party needs to be. For example, in the case of *Joaquin Herrera Rubio v. Colombia* (1987),[168] the author of the communication to the HRC submitted detailed allegations of torture inflicted upon him in a military camp in an attempt to extract from him information about a guerrilla movement. The author mentioned specific names of military officers who allegedly tortured him. The HRC requested the respondent State party to provide information on the investigations undertaken with regard to the military officers named specifically by the author.[169] In reply, Colombia forwarded copies of various documents relating to the investigation of the author's case, but did not provide specific answers to the questions posed by the HRC. The HRC considered that

---

166 For examples of internal cases concerning torture, see HRC, *Irene Bleier Lewenhoff and Rosa Valino de Bleier v. Uruguay*, 29 March 1982, No. 30/1978, para. 13.3, HRC; *Ilda Thomas on behalf of her brother, Hiber Conteris, v. Uruguay*, 17 July 1985, No. 139/1983.

167 See, for example, the internal disappearance case HRC, *Basilio Laureano Atachahua v. Peru*, 16 April 1996, No. 540/1993.

168 HRC, *Joaquin Herrera Rubio v. Colombia*, 2 November 1987, No. 161/1983.

169 *Ibidem*, para. 8.2.

'It is implicit in article 4, paragraph 2, of the Optional Protocol that the State party has the duty to investigate in good faith all allegations of violation of the Covenant made against it and its authorities, and to furnish to the Committee the information available to it. In no circumstances should a State party fail to investigate fully allegations of ill-treatment when the person or persons allegedly responsible for the ill-treatment are identified by the author of a communication. The State party has in this matter provided no precise information and reports, inter alia, on the questioning of military officials accused of maltreatment of prisoners, or on the questioning of their superiors.'[170]

The same principle – the more detailed and the more corroborated the author's statements are, the more detailed the investigation by the authorities of the respondent State party needs to be – is applied in other internal torture cases as well.[171] So far the HRC has not used its standard consideration on the shared burden of proof in cases concerning the expulsion of asylum seekers.

3.5.3   *Relevant facts and circumstances*

In the case of *Alzery v. Sweden* (2006),[172] the HRC made clear that

'In determining the risk (…) the Committee must consider all relevant elements, including the general situation of human rights in a State.'[173]

The relevant facts and circumstances can be divided into two categories. First, personal circumstances, such as background, gender, ethnicity, age, sexual orientation, beliefs, activities, personal profile, experiences are relevant. Second, as is clear from the quote above, the general human rights situation in the country of origin is relevant. Some examples are provided below of relevant personal facts, and relevant facts and circumstances concerning the country of origin. The description is illustrative, but is by no means exhaustive.

3.5.3.1   *Personal facts and circumstances*

The case law of the HRC demonstrates that it attaches great significance to recognition as a refugee by a State party, in combination with (largely) unchanged circumstances in the country of origin. This is – explicitly or implicitly – considered to be an important indication of a real Article 7-risk. The case of *C. v. Australia* (2002)[174] concerned an Iranian Assyrian Christian who had been granted refugee status in Australia in 1995 on account of his experiences in Iran as an Assyrian Christian, along with the

---

170 *Ibidem*, para. 10.5.
171 See, for example, HRC, *Mukong v. Cameroon*, 10 August 1994, No. 458/1991, paras. 9.1 and 9.2; HRC, *Almeida de Quinteros v. Uruguay*, 21 July 1983, No. 107/1981, paras. 11, 12.1, 12.2; HRC, *Nina Muteba on behalf of Tshitenge Muteba v. Zaire*, 24 July 1984, No. 124/1982, para. 11; HRC, *Agnès N'Goya, v. Zaire*, 16 April 1996, No. 542/1993.
172 HRC, *Alzery v. Sweden*, 10 November 2006, No. 1416/2005.
173 *Ibidem*, para. 11.3.
174 HRC, *C. v. Australia*, 13 November 2002, No. 900/1999.

deteriorating situation of that religious minority in Iran, and also because of his bad psychiatric status over a protracted period of detention and a diagnosis of delusional disorder, paranoid psychosis and depression requiring pharmaceutical and psycho-therapeutic intervention. After a conviction and sentence for aggravated burglary and threats to kill, a deportation order was brought against him in 1997, which he appeal-ed against in different national proceedings, without success. In the proceedings be-fore the HRC, the author described the situation of Assyrian Christians as very bad. He relied on a report compiled by expert Dr. Rubinstein, Senior Lecturer in Middle East Politics of the Monash University, on the human rights situation in Iran.[175] By contrast, the respondent State party, referring to various sources, contended that the human rights situation in Iran, and the position of Assyrian Christians there, had much improved in recent years.[176]

The HRC found the recognition as a refugee highly important. It ruled:

> 'As to the author's arguments that his deportation would amount to a violation of article 7, the Committee attaches weight to the fact that the author was originally granted refugee status on the basis of a well-founded fear of persecution as an Assyrian Christian, coupled with the likely consequences of a return of his illness. In the Committee's view, the State party has not estab-lished that the current circumstances in the receiving State are such that the grant of refugee status no longer holds validity.'[177]

Byahuranga v. Denmark (2004)[178] was a case concerning a Ugandan army officer who had served under Idi Amin, fled Uganda in 1981 and was granted asylum in Denmark on 4 September 1986. In 2002, he was convicted of drug-related offences, sentenced to two years and six months' imprisonment and ordered to be expelled from Den-mark. In the expulsion order, it was indicated that there was no risk that he would be ill-treated in Uganda. The HRC, nevertheless, assumed a real Article 7-risk. In this case, it did not state explicitly that recognition as a refugee in Denmark had played a role, but it is hard to imagine that this fact had not played a role.

Other important personal facts and circumstances are engagement in opposi-tional political or other activities and the level, type and scale of these activities, as well as past experiences of torture, ill-treatment, persecution or other serious human rights violations. In the case of *Mehrez Ben Abde Hamida v. Canada* (2010),[179] both op-positional activities and past experiences of ill-treatment played an important role. The author, a police officer of the Political Security Directorate in Tunisia, claimed refugee status in Canada, alleging that he had a well-founded fear of persecution in Tunisia on account of his political opinions. As a guard of political detainees, he had fed hungry young prisoners, for which act he had been disarmed, interrogated, ac-cused of sympathizing with political prisoners and placed under arrest for five months before being dismissed. After his release in August 1996, the author attempt-

---

175 *Ibidem*, para. 4.14 and notes 22 and 44.
176 *Ibidem*, paras. 4.14, 4.15, 4.16.
177 *Ibidem*, para. 8.5.
178 HRC, *Byahuranga v. Denmark*, 9 December 2004, No. 1222/2003.
179 HRC, *Mehrez Ben Abde Hamida v. Canada*, 18 March 2010, No. 1544/2007.

ed to leave Tunisia, but was stopped at the airport because he had no exit visa from the Director of the Security Services. He was then placed in detention for one month. On leaving prison he was subjected to very strict administrative surveillance, which required him to present himself twice a day to the security service to sign a surveillance register. The author managed to leave Tunisia three years later by bribing an employee of the Ministry of the Interior to issue him with a new passport.[180] At national level, the claim for protection was found incredible due to certain inconsistencies concerning the question of whether or not the author had been able to work after detention. The HRC, however, assumed a real Article 7-risk in this case.[181]

Oppositional political activities carried out in the country of refuge are also relevant, as the case of *Byahuranga v. Denmark* (2004)[182] demonstrates. In this case, the HRC attached great importance to the oppositional activities carried out in Denmark by the author, a former Ugandan army officer, and to the fact that it was very likely that the Ugandan authorities were aware of these activities.[183]

3.5.3.2   *Facts and circumstances concerning the situation in the country of origin*

Relevant circumstances concerning the country of origin are the general human rights situation, the plight of refugees, the level of violence in the country and control thereof by the authorities, the practice of torture in prisons and other conditions in detention, changes in government or policies, the existence of a peace process or an agreed ceasefire, and the repatriation of refugees under the supervision of the UNHCR. Reference is made, again, to *Mehrez Ben Abde Hamida v. Canada* (2010),[184] where the HRC considered that, according to a variety of sources, torture was known to be practised in Tunisia.[185]

Diplomatic assurances guaranteeing that the expelled (or extradited) applicant will not be subjected to treatment proscribed by Article 7 play an important role in a number of cases. An example is *Alzery v. Sweden* (2006).[186] The HRC considered in that case that

> 'The existence of diplomatic assurances, their content and the existence and implementation of enforcement mechanisms are all factual elements relevant to the overall determination of whether, in fact, a real risk of proscribed ill-treatment exists.'[187]

In the case of *G.T. v. Australia* (1997),[188] the author had been convicted in Australia for drug-related offences. He faced deportation to Malaysia. He feared the death penalty and up to nine years' detention on death row. He also feared being caned.

---

180   *Ibidem*, paras. 2.1, 22.
181   *Ibidem*, para. 8.7.
182   HRC, *Byahuranga v. Denmark*, 9 December 2004, No. 1222/2003.
183   *Ibidem*, paras. 11.2, 11.3, 11.4.
184   HRC, *Mehrez Ben Abde Hamida v. Canada*, 18 March 2010, No. 1544/2007.
185   *Ibidem*, para. 8.7.
186   HRC, *Alzery v. Sweden*, 10 November 2006, No. 1416/2005.
187   *Ibidem*, para. 11.3.
188   HRC, *G.T. v. Australia*, 4 December 1997, No. 706/1996.

Malaysia had provided diplomatic assurances that the author would not be prose-cuted for his offences committed overseas.[189] In addition, the Australian authorities had investigated the possibility of the imposition of the death sentence on the author and had concluded that in similar cases no prosecution had occurred.[190] Based on this and on the fact that Malaysia had not requested the author's return, the HRC concluded that there was no real risk.[191]

However, two HRC members, Klein and Kretzmer, pointed out in a separate dissenting opinion that the diplomatic assurances also stated that 'a Malaysian na-tional may be charged by the Malaysian authorities due to other offences that he might have committed in Malaysia'.[192] Klein and Kretzmer stressed that the death sentence was mandatory in Malaysia for the drug-related offence committed by the author: importing 240 grams of heroin from Malaysia to Australia; obviously, these HRC members assumed that the Malaysian authorities would not see this offence as having been committed overseas, but as an offence committed in Malaysia.

3.5.4 *Required degree of individual risk*

In chapter 5 on the ECHR we will distinguish three categories of cases: 1) cases of extreme general violence, where an Article 3-risk is assumed for everyone returning to the particular country; 2) cases of group violence; and 3) individual risk cases. In the third category, it is required that an individual risk is established. So far the HRC has not developed its position on the question of the required degree of individual risk in the same way as the ECtHR has done. Nevertheless, case law of the HRC gives good reasons to assume that it has taken significant steps towards incorporating the lines of theory developed by the ECtHR on situations of group violence.[193] In the case of *Kaba v. Canada* (2010),[194] the HRC assumed that expulsion of the Guinean author and her daughter, Fatoumata, to Guinea would entail a real Article 7-risk, as it was foreseeable that Fatoumata would be subjected to female genital mutilation. The HRC considered as follows:

'(…) nor is there any question that women in Guinea traditionally have been subjected to geni-tal mutilation and to a certain extent are still subjected to it. At issue is whether the author's daughter runs a real and personal risk of being subjected to such treatment if she returns to Guinea. The Committee notes that in Guinea female genital mutilation is prohibited by law. However, this legal prohibition is not complied with. The following points should be noted: (a) genital mutilation is a common and widespread practice in the country, particularly among women of the Malinke ethnic group; (b) those who practise female genital mutilation do so with impunity; (c) in the case of Fatoumata Kaba, her mother appears to be the only person opposed to this practice being carried out, unlike the family of Fatoumata's father, given the

---

189 *Ibidem*, para. 8.4.
190 *Ibidem*, paras 5.12 and 8.4.
191 *Ibidem*, para 8.4.
192 *Ibidem*, para. 4.2 and dissenting opinion of HRC members Klein and Kretzmer, para. 2.
193 Kjaerum 2010, p. 28.
194 HRC, *Kaba v. Canada*, 25 March 2010, No. 1465/2006.

context of a strictly patriarchal society; (d) the documentation presented by the author, which has not been disputed by the State party, reveals a high incidence of female genital mutilation in Guinea; (e) the girl is only 15 years old at the time the Committee is making its decision. Although the risk of excision decreases with age, the Committee is of the view that the context and particular circumstances of the case at hand demonstrate a real risk of Fatoumata Kaba being subjected to genital mutilation if she was returned to Guinea.'[195]

These considerations clearly demonstrate that the HRC, in fact, accepted that all Guinean girls of a certain age risked being subjected to the practice of FGM, thereby running a real Article 7-risk.

The same approach is found in the case of *Pillai and Joachimpillai v. Canada* (2011, see section 3.3.3 above).[196] Although the reasoning is extremely brief, it does become clear that the HRC assumed that individuals such as the authors, with the same ethnic background, from the same part of the country, ran a risk of being subjected to treatment prohibited by Article 7 (from both the police and the LTTE).

The relaxation of the individualisation requirement in the HRC's case law may be qualified as a significant step forward in the protection of individuals at risk, both in relation to the substantive scope of protection (the individual does not always need to be personally singled out) and the possibility to prove that a threat exists.[197] In situations where serious group violence may be assumed to exist, less individual evidence of a personal risk is needed.

3.5.5 Credibility assessment

As has already been pointed out, the HRC frequently emphasises its subsidiary role in the determination of the facts, including the credibility assessment and the assessment of evidence. The State party has a central role in assessing the facts and the HRC allows itself only a limited role in the determination of the relevant facts and the assessment of evidence.[198] Limited investigative powers (see below section 3.5.9) and limited meeting time may explain this. The HRC's case law on expulsion features eight cases in which, at national level, the claim for protection was found incredible, for example, because of contradictory statements.[199]

In the majority (five) of these cases, the HRC did not, or at least not in an explicit and detailed manner, make a fresh and new credibility assessment of its own. In one

---

195 *Ibidem*, paras. 10.1 and 10.2.
196 HRC, *Pillai and Joachimpillai v. Canada*, 25 March 2011, No. 1763/2008.
197 Kjaerum 2010, pp. 28-29.
198 For the same conclusion see Wouters 2009, pp. 397, 398; Kjaerum 2010, pp. 28-29.
199 The number of cases mentioned here represent the cases I have been able to trace up to 1 January 2012. The cases where, at national level, the claim for protection had been found incredible, are: HRC, *Daljit Singh v. Canada*, 28 April 2006, No. 1315/2004; *Dawood Khan v. Canada*, 10 August 2006, No. 1302/200; HRC, *Hamid Reza Taghi Khadje v. the Netherlands*, 15 November 2006, No. 1438/2005; HRC, *A.C. v. the Netherlands*, 22 July 2008, No. 1494/2006; 4; HRC, *Mahmoud Walid Nakrash and Liu Qifen v. Sweden*, 30 October 2008, No. 1540/2007; HRC, *Mehrez Ben Abde Hamida v. Canada*, 18 March 2010, No. 1544/2007; *Pillai and Joachimpillai v. Canada*, 25 March 2011, No. 1763/2008; HRC, *Kaba v. Canada*, 25 March 2010, No. 1465/2006.

of these five cases, it considered that deportation was not imminent and for that reason the communication was declared inadmissible as insufficiently substantiated.[200] In the other four of these five cases the HRC considered that the claim for protection had been thoroughly considered by the national authorities and had been found incredible at national level.[201] In two of the five cases, the HRC added that, furthermore, the author had not adduced sufficient evidence to support an Article 7-claim.[202] And in two of the five cases, the HRC considered that 'It is generally for the courts of States parties to evaluate facts and evidence in a particular case, unless it is found that the evaluation was clearly arbitrary or amounted to a denial of justice'.[203]

However, in the three remaining cases of the eight, the HRC made a fresh and independent credibility assessment of its own.[204] It did so without giving specific reasons for choosing this approach. The question remains on what grounds and under what circumstances the HRC chooses one of these two approaches: reliance on the respondent State's credibility assessment or an independent assessment of credibility on its own account? It has, so far, not developed an elaborate doctrinal position on this issue. It is interesting to note that all three cases in which the HRC made a fresh and independent credibility assessment are views of 2010 and 2011. This, perhaps, indicates that the HRC is intensifying its international supervisory scrutiny. In all three cases, in its conclusions on the merits (under the heading 'issues before the Committee') the HRC did not discuss at all the debate between the parties concerning the credibility of the account. Neither did it explain explicitly why it found certain statements credible or not. The conclusions on the merits are mostly extremely brief and not very explicit. What can be inferred from these conclusions, however, is that in assessing the credibility of the claim and the claimant, the HRC focuses on those statements which are not in dispute, examines whether these statements are couched in terms of Article 7 (for example, statements on past torture), then examines whether these statements are consistent with country information, and, finally, verifies whether there is serious corroborative evidence.

In the case of *Mehrez Ben Abde Hamida v. Canada* (2010), the core of the flight narrative – dissent in the Tunisian police, the six-month police detention, the strict administrative surveillance to which the author had been subjected – had not been contested at national level, or in the proceedings before the HRC. The core part of the

---

200 HRC, *Hamid Reza Taghi Khadje v. the Netherlands*, 15 November 2006, No. 1438/2005, para. 6.3.

201 HRC, *Daljit Singh v. Canada*, 28 April 2006, No. 1315/2004, para. 6.3; *Dawood Khan v. Canada*, 10 August 2006, No. 1302/200, para. 5.4; HRC, *A.C. v. the Netherlands*, 22 July 2008, No. 1494/2006, para. 8.2; HRC, *Mahmoud Walid Nakrash and Liu Qifen v. Sweden*, 30 October 2008, No. 1540/2007, para. 7.3

202 HRC, *Daljit Singh v. Canada*, 28 April 2006, No. 1315/2004, para. 6.3; *Dawood Khan v. Canada*, 10 August 2006, No. 1302/200, para. 5.4; HRC, *Mahmoud Walid Nakrash and Liu Qifen v. Sweden*, 30 October 2008, No. 1540/2007, para. 7.3 (only in relation to the female author, Liu Qifen, did the HRC state that she had not provided sufficientevidence to the effect that she would be subjected to treatment contrary to Article 7.)

203 HRC, *A.C. v. the Netherlands*, 22 July 2008, No. 1494/ 2006, para. 8.2; HRC, *Mahmoud Walid Nakrash and Liu Qifen v. Sweden*, 30 October 2008, No. 1540/ 2007, para. 7.3.

204 These are the following cases: HRC, *Mehrez Ben Abde Hamida v. Canada*, 18 March 2010, No. 1544/ 2007; HRC, *Kaba v. Canada*, 25 March 2010, No. 1465/2006; HRC, *Pillai and Joachimpillai v. Canada*, 25 March 2010, No. 1763/2008.

claim was supported by different types of serious evidence, including a wanted notice and summons to his mother, and was consistent with country information. For those reasons, the HRC found this core of the account credible. It did not explicitly state this, but it assumed an Article 7-risk on the basis of it.[205]

The HRC applied the same approach in the case of *Kaba v. Canada* (2010). Just like in *Mehrez Ben Abde Hamida v. Canada* (2010), the HRC did not discuss the contradictions and implausibility pointed out by the respondent State party. Neither did it discuss the problems raised by the State party concerning the reliability of the evidence presented by the author. Instead, it focused on the high incidence of FGM in Guinea appearing from the different country reports relied on by the parties, and on the fact that Guinean society was strictly patriarchal. Next, it considered that Fatoumata's mother seemed to be the only person opposed to the practice of FGM. From these three circumstances the HRC inferred a real Article 7-risk.[206] It is important to note that, just as in the case of *Mehrez Ben Abde Hamida v. Canada* (2010), in the *Kaba* case a significant amount of evidentiary materials were submitted in support of the protection claim, including different country reports and reports on the practice of FGM in Guinea from UNICEF and other sources, a medical certificate attesting to the fact that Fatoumata had not been excised, and different letters from family members.[207]

The case of *Pillai and Joachimpillai v. Canada* (2011, see section 3.3.3 above) is a third example of this approach. Again, the HRC did not discuss at all the contradictions and inconsistencies in the protection claim mentioned by the State party. It only noted that in the national proceedings the authors had not been questioned at all about the alleged earlier torture, whereas it appeared from the country reports invoked by both parties that torture was widespread in Sri Lanka.[208] The HRC's conclusion in this case was strikingly short. The linkage between the facts – defective national proceedings in which insufficient attention had been paid to allegations of past torture – and the conclusion that expulsion would lead to a violation of Article 7 was not clearly spelt out by the HRC.[209] The brief reasoning resulted in a lack of clarity and legal precision as to exactly how the HRC had arrived at its findings that the author's statements were credible and that that there was a real Article 7-risk.

The three cases discussed above make clear that the HRC is of the opinion that incredibility of peripheral aspects does not necessarily lead to incredibility of the entire claim. This mirrors the ECtHR's approach (see chapter 5, section 5.6.5). The core part or basic story as to why an Article 7-risk is feared must be credible, though. Although the HRC does not make clear in an explicit way how the credibility of the core part of the claim is assessed, it may be inferred from the conclusions drawn in the three cases discussed above that credibility is assessed by examining whether the basic story (the core part) was and is in dispute between the parties, whether it is con-

---

205 HRC, *Mehrez Ben Abde Hamida v. Canada*, 18 March 2010, No. 1544/2007, para. 8.7.
206 HRC, *Diene Kaba, on her own behalf and on behalf of her daughter, Fatoumata Kaba, v. Canada*, 25 March 2010, No. 1465/2006, para. 10.2.
207 *Ibidem*, paras. 2.2, 2.3, 2.5.
208 HRC, *Pillai and Joachimpillai v. Canada*, 25 March 2010, No. 1763/2008, para. 11.4.
209 McGoldrick 1996, p. 151, points to the same problem in relation to early views.

sistent with country information, and whether there is serious corroborative evidence in support of it.

3.5.6 Admission of evidence, means and sources of evidence, minimum quantity and quality of evidence

3.5.6.1 Means and sources of evidence

In all the cases concerning the expulsion of asylum seekers in which the HRC decided on the merits, it considered that

> 'The Committee has considered the present communication in the light of all the information received, in accordance with Article 5, paragraph 1, of the Optional Protocol.'[210]

This means that it is open to the HRC to consider evidence from whatever source and then decide as to its relevance and probative value. The system of admission of evidence is open, flexible and liberal, and the HRC's approach in this respect is the same as the one applied by the UNHCR (see chapter 2, section 2.4.6.1), the ComAT (see chapter 4, section 4.5.6.1) and the ECtHR (see chapter 5, section 5.6.6.1).[211] Two examples are given to illustrate this. In the case of *Mehrez Ben Abde Hamida v. Canada* (2010),[212] the author submitted as evidence corroborating his statements that he would be at risk of ill-treatment in Tunisia a wanted notice from the Tunisian police, a summons addressed to his mother, a letter from his family, letters of support from Amnesty International, the Association for Human Rights in the Maghreb, the Quebec League of Rights and Liberties, a member of Parliament and Radhia Nasraoui, a Tunisian lawyer. All this evidence was considered admissible and was materially considered by the HRC.[213] The same happened in the case of *Kaba v. Canada* (2010),[214] a case in which the author alleged fear of the female genital mutilation (FGM) of her daughter Fatoumata in Guinea. The author presented many different types of documents from different sources, including country reports from different sources, including UNICEF, a medical certificate attesting to the fact that Fatoumata had not been excised, letters from family members, a decision on the divorce of the author and her husband, and counsel's explanation that, according to the Guinean Civil Code, custody of a child aged over seven years was automatically granted to the

---

210 See, for some examples, HRC, *C. v. Australia*, 13 November 2002, No. 900/1999, para. 8.1; HRC, *Byahuranga v. Denmark*, 9 December 2004, No. 1222/2003; HRC, *Mehrez Ben Abde Hamida v. Canada*, 18 March 2010, No. 1544/2007, para. 8.1; HRC, *Kaba v. Canada*, 25 March 2010, No. 1465/2006, para. 9.1; HRC, *Pillai and Joachimpillai v. Canada*, 25 March 2011, No. 1763/2008.
211 McGoldrick 1996, p. 143. McGoldrick states that the HRC's approach accords with the general practice of international tribunals in the admission of evidence of adopting the liberal system of procedure of civil law countries.
212 HRC, *Mehrez Ben Abde Hamida v. Canada*, 18 March 2010, No. 1544/2007.
213 *Ibidem*, paras. 5.1, 8.3.
214 HRC, *Kaba v. Canada*, 25 March 2010, No. 1465/2006.

father. All the evidence was admitted to the proceedings and was considered materially by the HRC.[215]

3.5.6.2   *Minimum quantity and quality of evidence*

It is clear from the case law of the HRC that allegations that expulsion will expose the individual to a real Article 7-risk must be substantiated, meaning that the individual has to put forward more than simple allegations. If the individual has submitted only simple allegations, and has not responded to contentions made by the State party, the HRC declares the communication inadmissible for failure to substantiate statements. This is what happened in the case of *Ngoc Si Truong v. Canada* (2003, see section 3.3.5).[216]

From the HRC's case law, it seems that 'substantiate' can mean more than one thing. It can mean submitting more or further details to earlier statements, in response to the reaction of the other party. It can also mean submitting evidentiary materials corroborating statements. And it can mean a combination of the two. An example of the first category – the claim was found substantiated because the author's statements were detailed and uncontested or insufficiently contested – is the internal torture case of *Thomas v. Jamaica* (1993).[217] The author of the communication was a Jamaican citizen awaiting execution in prison. He claimed to have been maltreated by soldiers and prison warders while in detention. His statements were very detailed. Specifically, he mentioned the prison warders by name and stated that he had been severely beaten with rifle butts, that he had sustained injuries to his chest, his back, left hip and lower abdomen, that one of the soldiers had wounded him in the neck with a bayonet and had torn his clothes. In the proceedings before the HRC, the respondent State party confined itself to issues of admissibility and did not address the merits of the case. The HRC, therefore, first remarked that the author's allegations were uncontested. In addition, it stated that the author's claims 'have been substantiated'. As no mention whatsoever was made of corroborating evidence, it must be assumed that there was no such evidence in this case, and that the HRC found the claim substantiated and, therefore, admissible because the author's statements were detailed and uncontested (or not seriously contested).[218]

A case in which the HRC makes clear that the author corroborated his account with evidence and the account was found substantiated for that reason is *Isidore Kanana Tshiongo a Minanga v. Zaire* (1993), again an internal torture case. The respon-

---

215   See also McGoldrick 1996, p. 143, who provides a list of particular sources of evidence the HRC has taken into consideration in different types of cases. He mentions testimonies from authors and alleged victims, testimonies of alleged witnesses of violations, medical reports, psychiatric reports, legal judgments, legislative, executive and administrative acts, statements by a representative of the State party in proceedings before another United Nations body, the submissions from the respondent State party.

216   HRC, *Ngoc Si Truong v. Canada*, 5 May 2003, No. 743/1997.

217   HRC, *Maurice Thomas v. Jamaica*, 19 October 1993, No. 321/1988.

218   The same happened in HRC, *Dwayne Hylton v. Jamaica*, 21 July 1994, No. 407/1990. Here too, the HRC found statements substantiated because they were detailed, whereas the State party had provided very limited information. Substantiated here means detailed and not sufficiently contested.

dent State party did not provide any information concerning the merits of the case. The author of the communication provided to the HRC photographic evidence of the consequences of the torture inflicted upon him. On the basis of this material, the HRC concluded that the author had substantiated his claim.[219] It is obvious that the HRC treated the photos provided by the author as serious evidence, and as sufficient corroboration of the statements of past torture.

There have been a number of cases in which, in the national proceedings and in the proceedings before the HRC, the author has submitted various evidentiary materials in support of his protection claim, but the HRC has, nevertheless, declared the Article 7-claim inadmissible for failure of substantiation.[220] At the other end of the spectrum there are cases in which, apart from detailed statements, no evidence at all seems to have been submitted (at least evidence was not mentioned by the HRC), but the HRC considered the Article 7-claim to be substantiated and concluded that there had been a violation of Article 7.[221] Combined with the fact that the reasoning in the HRC's conclusions on the merits is often extremely brief, it is very difficult to infer from the jurisprudence clear guidelines concerning the required minimum quantity and quality of the evidence. However, in the three cases concerning the expulsion of asylum seekers, discussed in the previous section on credibility assessment,[222] a significant amount of evidentiary materials from different sources was submitted to both the national authorities and to the HRC. In these cases, the HRC deemed the basic story of the claimant credible and assumed the existence of an Article 7-risk. These cases make clear that the HRC is more willing to consider the merits of the case and conclude that expulsion entails an Article 7-risk when a substantial amount of strong and persuasive evidentiary materials is submitted in support of the claim.

It is not only important to submit evidence corroborating the individual account. Equally important is evidence about the human rights situation in the country of origin. No judgments or decisions have been found in which the HRC explicitly explained which of the parties – the applicant or the State party's authorities – was responsible for submitting recent information about the general human rights situation in the country of origin. It may be argued that, although the burden of proof remains a shared one, in the case of an arguable claim particular responsibility for shaping clarity on the general human rights situation in the country of origin lies with the administrative and judicial authorities of the State. This follows from the fact that, where the claimant has provided a basic level of substantiation of his or her claim, an investigative burden on the authorities of the State party emerges: the authorities must investigate thoroughly and in good faith the alleged violation.[223] The national authorities, thus, have an active role not only in verifying information put forward by the

---

219 HRC, *Isidore Kanana Tshiongo a Minanga v. Zaire*, 8 November 1993, No. 366/1989, para. 5.3.
220 Examples are HRC, *Daljit Singh v. Canada*, 30 March 2006, No. 1315/2004, HRC, *G.T. v. Australia*, 4 December 1997, No. 706/1996, HRC, *Moses Solo Tarlue v. Canada*, 27 March 2009, No. 1551/2007.
221 See note 219.
222 HRC, *Mehrez Ben Abde Hamida v. Canada*, 18 March 2010, No. 1544/2007; HRC, *Kaba v. Canada*, 25 March 2010, No. 1465/2006; HRC, *Pillai and Joachimpillai v. Canada*, 25 March 2011, No. 1763/2008.
223 See, for example, the internal disappearance case HRC, *Basilio Laureano Atachahua v. Peru*, 16 April 1996, No. 540/1993.

complainant, but also in collecting and presenting evidence regarding the general human rights situation in the country of origin. With regard to the particular responsibility resting on the national authorities for shaping clarity on the situation in the country of origin, reference is also made to chapter 6 on EU asylum law, section 6.4.4.

3.5.7 Appreciation and weighing of evidence

The HRC adheres to a free evaluation of all the evidence presented by the parties. There are no pre-determined rules for the weighing of evidence.[224] In the paragraphs below, an attempt is made to discover factors determining the probative value and persuasiveness of evidence. After that, we will look in more detail at four particular categories of evidence, being reports containing the result of inquiries conducted by embassies or missions, witness statements by family members, medico-legal reports and reports about the human rights situation in the country of origin.

3.5.7.1 Factors determining the probative value of evidence

It is not an easy task to distinguish in the case law of the HRC the exact factors determining the probative value and persuasiveness of the evidence presented. The reasons are that the HRC's conclusions on the merits are often very brief and it is often completely silent on the issue of evaluation of the evidence. In *Daljit Singh v. Canada* (2006),[225] the author invoked a Human Rights Watch Report and an academic journal in support of his statements and fear. The HRC remained completely silent about this evidence and declared the communication inadmissible for failure of substantiation. Another striking example is *G.T. v. Australia* (1997),[226] in which the author, who was to be deported to Malaysia, feared the death penalty and up to nine years' detention on death row, as well as being caned, and submitted, in corroboration of these statements, a letter from the Australian Office of Amnesty International (AI). In this letter, AI opposed the forcible return of the author as it believed that, as a result of the conviction in Australia, the death penalty would be imposed on the author in Malaysia. The HRC did not say a word about this letter.[227] As it did not say anything at all about the evidence presented by the authors of the mentioned cases, while at the same time declaring the communications inadmissible, it may be inferred

---

224 McGoldrick 1996, p. 143. McGoldrick states that the HRC's approach accords with the general practice of international tribunals in the admission of evidence of adopting the liberal system of procedure of civil law countries.

225 HRC, *Daljit Singh v. Canada*, 30 March 2006, No. 1315/2004.

226 HRC, *G.T. v. Australia*, 4 December 1997, No. 706/1996.

227 Another example in which the HRC remained completely silent about evidence presented by the author is HRC, *Moses Solo Tarluo v. Canada*, 28 April 2009, No. 1551/2007. In that case, the author submitted, in the national proceedings, three letters signed by one Senator Mobutu Vlah Nyenpan of the Liberian Senate Committee on Human Rights and Petition, stating that there was no record of his being involved in war crimes during the civil war in Liberia, and also stating that the author's life would be in danger if he was deported to Liberia due to the war crime allegations made against him by Canada. The HRC declared the communication inadmissible as insufficiently substantiated, remaining completely silent about the mentioned three letters.

that it did not attach great weight to the evidence presented. The reasons for this low appreciation remain unclear, however.

However, from other decisions of the HRC, we may deduce that the specificity, comprehensiveness and consistency of the information, and the independence, reliability and objectiveness of the source, are relevant factors in determining the probative value and persuasiveness of the evidence presented.[228] In *Byahuranga v. Denmark* (2004), a case concerning a Ugandan army officer who had served under Idi Amin, had fled Uganda in 1981 and was granted asylum in Denmark in 1986, the HRC attached significant weight to a letter from the former chairman of the Schiller Institute in Denmark (a human rights institute). This chairman confirmed that the author participated in conferences of the Institute in his capacity as chairman of the Ugandan Union in Denmark. The letter also stated that the author's participation in a September 1997 conference, during which Ugandan President Museveni's alleged links with the Rwandan Patriotic Front were criticized, had been documented in an article published in the Executive Intelligence Review on 10 October 1997, as well as in a German-language newspaper. The letter expressed concern that the Ugandan Embassy in Copenhagen may have registered Ugandan citizens who participated in the Schiller Institute's conferences. Based on this letter – which contained detailed and specific information on the author's activities and very specific reasons for assuming that the Ugandan authorities were aware of these activities – and based on different country reports, the HRC followed the author's statements that the Ugandan authorities were aware of his oppositional activities in Denmark, and assumed an Article 7-risk.[229]

3.5.7.2 *Reports of inquiries conducted by embassies or missions*

In a number of cases, the HRC attached strong evidentiary value to reports submitted by States parties, containing the result of inquiries conducted by embassies or missions in the country to which the particular individual was planned to be expelled. The HRC generally regards such information as reliable and relies on it. Reference is made to the case of *A.R.J. v. Australia* (1997), discussed above in section 3.1.1).[230]

By contrast, the HRC did not attach much value to information from the Australian Mission in Iran in the case of *C. v. Australia* (2002), discussed above in section

---

228 These factors are also important in the opinion of the ECtHR; reference is made to chapter 5, section 5.6.7. See, for example,ECtHR, *Bader and Kanbor v. Sweden*, 8 November 2005, Appl. No. 13284/04, para. 44, ECtHR, *Saadi v. Italy*, 28 February 2008, Appl. No. 37201/06, para. 143, ECtHR, *NA v. the UK*, 17 July 2008, Appl. No. 25904/07, para. 120. See also Wouters 2009, p. 271.

229 HRC, *Byahuranga v. Denmark*, 9 December 2004, No. 1222/2003, paras. 8, 11.2, 11.3, 11.4.

230 HRC, *A.R.J.v. Australia*, 11 August 1997, No. 692/1996. See also HRC, *G.T. v. Australia*, 4 December 1997, No. 706/1996. The State party relied on the result of inquiries made by its mission in Kuala Lumpur, Malaysia, which stated that 'The Royal Malaysian Police have orally confirmed to us that they do not institute criminal proceedings for trafficking in drugs against a person returned to Malaysia – that is for exporting narcotics – and to our knowledge this has never occurred nor do any of our interlocutors consider it ever likely to occur. We have no reason to doubt that Malaysia will continue to abide by the principles governing double jeopardy as it has in the past.' The HRC concluded that no real risk of a violation of Article 7 existed, see para. 5.7.

3.5.3.1.[231] Unfortunately, the decision in this case did not contain explicit considerations on the weighing and evaluation of the different evidentiary materials brought in by the parties to the case. The HRC did not explain why it attached decisive value to the evidence presented by the author and why it was not persuaded by the evidence relied on by the State party, including the information from the Australian Mission in Iran.

3.5.7.3 *Witness statements by family members*

The cases of *Mehrez Ben Abde Hamida v. Canada* (2010)[232] and *Kaba v. Canada* (2010)[233] make clear that the HRC may accord significant probative value to statements made by family members. In *Mehrez Ben Abde Hamida v. Canada* (2010), the author submitted as evidence corroborating his statements that he would be at risk of ill-treatment in Tunisia, a letter from his family (as well as other evidence, such as a wanted notice from the Tunisian police, a summons addressed to his mother, letters of support from various NGOs, including Amnesty International). Whereas the respondent State party contended in the proceedings before the HRC that the letter from the author's family did not constitute independent, objective evidence and was, therefore, of little probative value,[234] the HRC, by contrast, considered that it gave due weight to the author's allegations regarding the pressure put on his family in Tunisia, which indicated that it attached strong probative value to the letter from the author's family.[235]

In *Kaba*,[236] the author submitted different letters from family members (her ex-husband, brother, uncle) in corroboration of her fear of the excision of her daughter. The State party raised various problems in relation to this evidence, *inter alia*, that the author's uncle was not an objective and independent source.[237] Although the HRC did not explicitly discuss the debate between the parties concerning the reliability of the presented evidence, it did consider explicitly that the author seemed to be the only person opposed to the excision of Fatoumata.[238] This meant that the HRC – albeit implicitly – accorded significant probative value to the letters from family members who expressed that Fatoumata would be seriously at risk of excision upon return to Guinea.

3.5.7.4 *Medico-legal reports*

In the case of *Pillai and Joachimpillai v. Canada* (2011, see section 3.3.3)[239] the authors submitted in the national proceedings before the Immigration and Refugee Board

---

231 HRC, *C. v. Australia*, 13 November 2002, No. 900/1999.
232 HRC, *Mehrez Ben Abde Hamida v. Canada*, 18 March 2010, No. 1544/2007.
233 HRC, *Kaba v. Canada*, 25 March 2010, No. 1465/2006.
234 HRC, *Mehrez Ben Abde Hamida v. Canada*, 18 March 2010, No. 1544/2007, para. 6.2.
235 *Ibidem*, paras. 5.1, 8.3.
236 HRC, *Kaba v. Canada*, 25 March 2010, No. 1465/2006.
237 *Ibidem*, para. 4.9.
238 *Ibidem*, para. 10.2.
239 HRC, *Pillai and Joachimpillai v. Canada*, 25 March 2010, No. 1763/2008.

(IRB) a Diagnostic Interview Report by a psychotherapist, containing a diagnosis of post-traumatic stress disorder (PTSD) for Mr Pillai. Also filed in evidence before the IRB was a letter from the authors' doctor, which recommended that Mr Pillai's wife represent both of them before the IRB, as she was considered stronger and less traumatized than her husband.[240] The HRC expressed fierce criticism of the fact that in the national proceedings the authors had not been questioned at all about the alleged earlier torture, whereas it appeared from the country reports invoked by both parties that torture was widespread in Sri Lanka.[241] The HRC considered the medical evidence submitted by the authors to corroborate their allegations of past torture to be reliable and objective and attached serious probative value to it. It must be noted that the authors in this case also submitted country information making clear that torture was endemic in Sri Lanka. Thus, the statements on the past torture of the authors found confirmation in both the medical evidence and this country information.

3.5.7.5   *Reports on the human rights situation in the country of origin*

Many views of the HRC demonstrate that information on the situation in the countries of origin plays a very important role. This is a logical consequence of the fact that the assessment of whether there are substantial grounds for believing that the applicant faces a real Article 7-risk inevitably requires that the HRC assesses the conditions in the receiving country.

Three sources of country of origin information used by the HRC can be distinguished:

- Information compiled by agencies of the United Nations;[242]
- Information compiled by States (whether respondent in a particular case or any other Contracting or non-Contracting State, such as the US);[243]
- Information from independent international human-rights protection organisations.[244]

There seems to be no hierarchy of sources and it seems that the precise probative value accorded to country of origin information is determined primarily by its specific content. Again, it is difficult to draw firm conclusions here as the HRC's conclusions on the merits are brief and do not contain explicit reasons for according certain probative value to reports on the situation in the country of origin.

---

240 *Ibidem*, para. 2.3.
241 *Ibidem*, para. 11.4.
242 See, for example, HRC, *Kaba v. Canada*, 25 March 2010, No. 1465/2006, in which case reports compiled by UNICEF on the practice of FGM in Guinea played an important role.
243 See, for example, HRC, *A.R.J.v. Australia*, 11 August 1997, No. 692/1996; HRC, *G.T. v. Australia*, 4 December 1997, No. 706/1996. In both cases, the result of inquiries conducted by the embassy or mission of the respondent State party in the country of origin of the author played a decisive role. See also HRC, *Kaba v. Canada*, 25 March 2010, No. 1465/2006, in which case a report on FGM in Guinea compiled by the United States Department of State played an important role.
244 See, for example, HRC, *Byahuranga v. Denmark*, 9 December 2004, No. 1222/2003, in which case a letter from the former chairman of the Schiller Institute in Denmark (a human rights institute) played an important role.

3.5.8 *Opportunities for presenting evidence and reacting to evidence*

In its proceedings, the HRC adheres to the principle of adversarial proceedings. In Rule 97 of its Rules of Procedure,[245] it is stipulated that, as soon as possible after the communication has been received, it is transmitted to the State party. The State party is then requested to submit a written reply, relating both to the admissibility and the merits of the complaint, within six months. A complaint may not be declared admissible unless the State party concerned has received its text and has been given an opportunity to furnish information or observations as provided in the first paragraph of this rule. The State party or the complainant may request to be afforded an opportunity to comment on any submission received from the other party. The Committee sets a time limit for submitting such additional comments.[246] Rule 99 stipulates that, when the Committee has decided that a complaint is admissible, the Committee shall transmit to the State party the text of its decision together with any submission received from the author of the communication not already transmitted to the State party under rule 97, first paragraph. The Committee shall also inform the complainant, through the Secretary-General, of its decision. Within the period established by the Committee, the State party concerned shall then submit to the Committee written explanations or statements clarifying the case under consideration and the measures, if any, that may have been taken by it. These explanations or statements submitted by a State party are then transmitted to the complainant who may submit any additional written information or observations within such time limit as the Committee shall decide.[247]

In a number of views, the HRC has also explicitly pointed out that it adheres strictly to the principle of adversarial proceedings. The HRC uses the Latin term *audiatur et altera pars*. The views in which this principle is stressed concern mainly internal torture or disappearance cases in which the respondent State party did not reply to requests made by the HRC to furnish information, and the HRC, as a consequence, fully relied on the author's allegations. This, in turn, provoked criticism on the part of the respondent State party, which stated that the HRC had displayed legal ignorance. The HRC emphasised in these cases that it had offered the respondent State party every opportunity to furnish information to refute the evidence presented by the author.[248]

In a number of cases, authors have raised new statements or submitted new evidence for the first time before the HRC, which statements and evidence have not been presented earlier to the national authorities in the national proceedings. The HRC normally does not tolerate this: it does not consider such statements and

---

245 Rules of Procedure of the Human Rights Committee of 13 January 2011. They may be found at: http://www.ohchr.org/english/bodies/hrc
246 Rule 97 of the Rules of Procedure of the Human Rights Committee, para. 1, 2, 4 and 6.
247 Rule 99 of the Rules of Procedure of the Human Rights Committee, paras. 1, 2, 3.
248 See, for example, HRC, *Irene Bleier Lewenhoff and Rosa Valino de Bleier v. Uruguay*, 29 March 1982, No. 30/1978, para. 13.1; HRC, *Almeida de Quinteros v. Uruguay*, 21 July 1983, No. 107/1981, para. 11. See on the principle of equality of arms of the proceedings conducted by the HRC also Hanski & Scheinin 2003 and 2007, p. 13.

evidence on the merits, but instead refers authors back to the national proceedings. It considers, in such cases, that applicants are required to submit statements and evidentiary materials in the national proceedings before the national authorities. This, then, leads it to the conclusion that national remedies have not been exhausted. In the case of *A.C. v. the Netherlands* (2008),[249] the author submitted to the HRC medical evidence from a doctor and a psychologist.[250] The HRC noted that in the national proceedings no medical evidence had been submitted and no statements had been made that expulsion would lead to a violation of Article 7 for medical reasons, such as the absence of treatment. For that reason, it found this part of the communication inadmissible for non-exhaustion of national remedies.[251] The HRC took exactly the same approach in the case of *Dawood Khan v. Canada* (2006): it noted that it could not take medical reports into account, as they had not been presented in the national proceedings.[252]

A different approach was taken in *Kaba v. Canada* (2010).[253] This may be explained by the fact that, in the proceedings before the HRC, the respondent State party not only stated that part of the evidence had been presented too late (which would have led to inadmissibility of the claim due to non-exhaustion of domestic remedies) but, in fact, had also responded to the evidence in a material way, pleading that this new evidence was not credible. Given the fact that, in the proceedings before the HRC, the State party had also materially considered the new evidence, the HRC did not find it problematic to take this evidence into account and use it for its conclusions.[254]

3.5.9 *Application of investigative powers by the HRC*

Pursuant to Article 5, paragraph 1, of the Optional Protocol,[255] and Rule 94 of the Rules of Procedure of the HRC,[256] the HRC considers communications and formulates its views on the basis of all written information made available to it by the individual and the State party concerned. The HRC holds no oral hearings.[257] It follows from this system that the HRC has at its disposal and applies only a limited number of investigative powers. It can request a party to a pending case to submit certain specific information in writing which it deems necessary for taking a decision. Under Rule 91 of the Rules of Procedure of the HRC, the HRC may request the State party concerned or the author of the communication to submit additional written infor-

---

249 HRC, *A.C. v. the Netherlands*, 22 July 2008, No. 1494/2006.

250 *Ibidem*, paras. 2.1-2.4.

251 *Ibidem*, para. 8.3.

252 HRC, *Daewood Khan v. Canada*, 10 August 2006, No. 1302/2004, para. 5.5.

253 HRC, *Kaba v. Canada*, 25 March 2010, No. 1465/2006.

254 *Ibidem*, para.6.5.

255 Article 5, para. 1, of the Optional Protocol states: 'The Committee shall consider communications received under the present Protocol in the light of all written information made available to it by the individual and by the State Party concerned.'

256 Rule 94 of the Rules of Procedure of the HRC stipulates: 'If the communication is admissible, the Committee shall consider it in the light of all written information made available to it by the individuals and by the State party concerned and shall formulate its views thereon.'

257 Hanski & Scheinin 2003 and 2007, p. 13.

mation or observations relevant to the question of the admissibility of the communication.[258] From its case law, it follows that the HRC has the same power to request the State party or the author to submit additional written information relevant to the merits. This power has been used in numerous internal torture or disappearance cases.[259]

It also follows from this system that, unlike the ECtHR, the HRC cannot – upon party request or *proprio motu* – hear witnesses. And, again unlike the ECtHR, the HRC cannot hold fact finding missions.[260] The case of *Oló Bahamonde v. Equatorial Guinea* (1993) concerned allegations of discrimination, intimidation and persecution of individuals opposing the ruling political party. The respondent State party, Equatorial Guinea, invited the HRC to investigate the author's allegations in Equatorial Guinea, in other words, to hold a fact finding mission in the respondent State. The HRC made clear that it lacked the power to organise such a mission:

> 'As to the State party's suggestion that the Committee should investigate the author's allegations in Equatorial Guinea, the Committee recalls that pursuant to article 5, paragraph 1, of the Optional Protocol, it considers communications "on the basis of all written information made available to it by the individual and by the State party concerned". The Committee has no choice but to confine itself to formulating its Views in the present case on the basis of the written information received.'[261]

The limited possession and application of investigative powers of the HRC explains to a certain extent its restricted role in the assessment of facts and evidence which has been stressed in literature.[262]

3.5.10   Time limits for the presentation of statements and evidence

It was pointed out above in 3.5.8 that the HRC normally does not tolerate authors raising new statements or submitting new evidence for the first time before it.

There is some HRC case law on the problem of presenting evidence at a late moment in the national proceedings. In the case of *Byahuranga v. Denmark* (2004, see section 3.5.7.1 above),[263] the applicant submitted crucial evidence in support of the alleged Article 7-risk at a late moment in the national proceedings, namely after sever-

---

258 Rule 91 of the Rules of Procedure of the HRC stipulates: 'The Committee or a working group established under rule 89, paragraph 1, or a special rapporteur designated under rule 89, paragraph 3, may request the State party concerned or the author of the communication to submit additional written information or observations relevant to the question of the admissibility of the communication. To avoid undue delays, a time-limit for the submission of such information or observations shall be indicated.'

259 See, for example, HRC, *Violeta Setelich on behalf of her husband Raul Sendic Antonaccio v. Uruguay*, 28 October 1981, No. 63/1979, para. 19; HRC, *Irene Bleier Lewenhoff and Rosa Valino de Bleier v. Uruguay*, 29 March 1982, No. 30/1978, para. 7.

260 See for the investigative powers of the ECtHR Chapter 5, Part 2.

261 HRC, *Oló Bahamonde v. Equatorial Guinea*, 10 November 1993, No. 468/1991, para. 8.2.

262 McGoldrick 1996, p. 144. He points to the closed hearings of the HRC which make it impossible to hear, in the setting of a public hearing, witnesses or experts. See also Wouters 2009, p. 397.

263 HRC, *Byahuranga v. Denmark*, 9 December 2004, No. 1222/2003.

al risk assessments had been made, during proceedings before the Danish Refugee Board (an appeal authority) after the last risk assessment made by the Immigration Service. The HRC clearly attached great weight to the author's statement that the Ugandan authorities were aware of his oppositional activities in Denmark and to the letter from the Schiller Institute which he had submitted to corroborate this statement. The HRC criticised the dismissal of this letter by the Refugee Board because of late submission. It ruled as follows:

> 'In particular, the Board merely dismissed, because of late submission, the author's claim that his political activities in Denmark were known to the Ugandan authorities, thereby placing him at a particular risk of being subjected to ill-treatment upon return to Uganda. (…) the Committee finds that due weight must be given to his detailed account of the existence of a risk of treatment contrary to Article 7. Consequently, the Committee is of the view that the expulsion order against the author would, if implemented by returning him to Uganda, constitute a violation of article 7 of the Covenant.[264]

We see a similar approach in the case of *Mehrez Ben Abde Hamida v. Canada* (2010). In this case, crucial evidence corroborating the author's allegations of a real Article 7-risk upon expulsion to Tunisia was presented at a very late moment in the national proceedings in Canada. The crucial piece of evidence was a wanted notice issued against him by the Ministry of the Interior which mentioned his escape from administrative surveillance.[265] It was presented four years after its issuance, because, according to the author, it had taken him that long to obtain the document.[266] The State party explained in the proceedings before the HRC that the author had presented his evidence, including the warrant, at a very late moment, namely only with the most recent PRRA request submitted in December 2006 (this was the second PRRA request). The HRC considered that a violation of Article 7 would be the necessary and foreseeable consequence of the author's expulsion. In arriving at this conclusion, it specifically mentioned the wanted notice as important evidence.[267] It is obvious from these cases that the HRC does not see the late presentation of crucial evidence in the national proceedings as problematic. The same approach was followed by the HRC under Article 14 in the case of *Jansen-Gielen v. the Netherlands* (2001, see section 3.4.3).

Taking into account the case law discussed above, it may be concluded that the HRC requires that evidence regarding the substance of the claim must be taken into account, even if such evidence was not presented earlier in the national proceedings, for example, during previous administrative proceedings. If evidence is presented at a moment close to the actual court hearing, the national court may adjourn proceedings in order to allow the other party more time to examine the newly presented evidence.

---

264 *Ibidem*, paras. 11.2, 11.3, 11.4.
265 HRC, *Mehrez Ben Abde Hamida v. Canada*, 18 March 2010, No. 1544/2007, paras. 5.1, 8.7.
266 *Ibidem*, para. 5.1.
267 *Ibidem*, para. 8.7.

3.5.11   *Point in time for the risk assessment*

In the case of *Bakhtiyari and Bakhtiyari v. Australia* (2003), the HRC considered

> 'that as the authors have not been removed from Australia, the issue before the Committee is whether such removal if implemented at the present time would entail a real risk of treatment contrary to article 7 as a consequence.'[268]

It follows from this that the HRC assesses the existence of the alleged Article 7-risk on an *ex nunc* basis. In other words, the material point in time is the moment at which it examines the case. The assessment needs to focus on the necessary and foreseeable consequences of the removal. The HRC has, so far, adopted no guidelines for situations where the removal has already taken place.[269]

3.6   Final concluding remarks

The ICCPR is an important universal general human rights treaty which has been ratified by all the EU Member States. It is also an important instrument in international and EU asylum law. The ICCPR does not contain a right to asylum, but the HRC has interpreted Article 7 in such a way that States parties must not expose individuals to the danger of torture or cruel, inhuman or degrading treatment or punishment upon return to another country by way of their extradition, expulsion or *refoulement*. As a result, the (intended) expulsion of a failed asylum seeker is in breach of Article 7 and, therefore, unlawful where substantial grounds have been shown for believing that upon expulsion there is a real risk of treatment contrary to Article 7.

In Part 1 it was shown that the ICCPR's provisions on national proceedings impose a number of obligations on national courts examining asylum cases. Under Articles 2, third paragraph, and 7, ICCPR the national authorities are required to consider the claim thoroughly and fairly. The HRC is generally reluctant to put national asylum court proceedings to a rigorous test of compliance with this criterion. It does not often respond in a meaningful way to specific procedural problems raised by authors of individual communications. The HRC's reluctance to put national (court) proceedings to a rigorous test is linked to the fact that it regards the determination and evaluation of facts and evidence as matters for the national courts. The HRC itself will normally not engage in that. As a consequence, it will not easily find national remedies ineffective for reasons having to do with determination of the facts. The HRC's hands-off approach may be explained by its limited investigative possibilities and by the fact that its meeting time is very limited, which is difficult to reconcile with the time required to assess evidence and to write down an assessment of the presented evidence. The case of *Pillai and Joachimpillai v. Canada* (2011) – in which the HRC deemed the national proceedings defective because the national authorities did not seriously investigate allegations and evidence of past torture – may mark a turning

---

268 HRC, *Bakhtiyari and Bakhtiyari v. Australia*, 6 November 2003, No. 1069/2002, para. 8.4.
269 Wouters 2009, p. 397.

point towards firmer monitoring of procedural ICCPR-compliance, but more juris-prudence is required to firmly draw such a conclusion. The case of *Mansour Ahani v. Canada* (2004) has shown that the HRC is prepared to give up its hands-off approach if the national authorities breach the key principles of equality of arms and adversarial proceedings. The HRC found the national expulsion proceedings in *Ahani* to be defective under Article 13 as the Minister had not provided the author with all the materials – including secret information that Ahani was a danger to Canada's national security – on which the expulsion decision had been based and the national courts had not corrected this unfairness in the procedure. National procedural rules will nor-mally not render national proceedings non-compliant with the requirement of a thor-ough and fair examination of the claim, provided that such rules are reasonable and provided that they are not applied in an automatic and mechanical way. National courts must also be careful of automatically relying on steady jurisprudential lines.

In Part 2, the assessment performed by the HRC in cases concerning the expulsion of asylum seekers was analysed with the help of the eleven aspects of evidence and judi-cial scrutiny. The investigation demonstrated that the HRC has developed concrete standards and principles with regard to seven of the eleven aspects of evidence and judicial scrutiny. With regard to four aspects – the required degree of individual risk, the credibility assessment, the admission of evidence and the appreciation and weigh-ing of evidence – the HRC has, so far, not explicitly developed standards and princi-ples, but certain approaches by the HRC follow implicitly from the conclusions ar-rived at. The standards, principles and approaches developed by the HRC are sum-marised below.

The standard of proof applied by the HRC in expulsion cases is that there are substantial grounds for believing that there is a real risk of a violation of Article 7. A real risk means that it is a necessary and foreseeable consequence of the expulsion that Article 7 will be violated. The 'necessary and foreseeable consequence' criterion indicates a high threshold which is not easily met. The threshold seems to be higher than under Article 3 ECHR.

The burden of proof is shared: there is an initial burden of assertion, and, pref-erably, also some corroboration, on the author. After that, the authorities must inves-tigate 'in good faith' the alleged violation. The more detailed and the more corro-borated the author's statements are, the more detailed the investigation by the author-ities of the respondent State party needs to be.

Relevant facts and circumstances are all possible personal circumstances, and, also, the general human rights situation in the country of origin. Many concrete ex-amples of such circumstances were given above. The personal facts must be assessed in the light of the general situation in the country of origin, and it is normally a combination of facts and circumstances, and not a single fact, which establish that there are substantial grounds for assuming a real Article 7-risk.

So far the HRC has not elaborated its position on the question of the required degree of individual risk in the same way as the ECtHR. Nevertheless, the cases of *Kaba v. Canada* (2010) and *Pillai and Joachimpillai v. Canada* (2011) have demonstrated that there are good reasons for assuming that the HRC has made significant steps towards incorporating the lines of theory developed by the ECtHR on situations of extreme general violence and on group violence (see chapter 5, section 5.6.4).

The HRC often stresses its subsidiary role with regard to the credibility assessment. This is a logical consequence of the fact that it considers the determination of the facts as primarily a matter for the authorities of the States parties. It made a fresh and independent credibility assessment in three cases and concluded that expulsion would lead to a real Article 7-risk. The HRC is of the opinion that incredibility of peripheral aspects does not necessarily lead to incredibility of the entire claim. The core part or basic story as to why an Article 7-risk is feared must be credible, though. Although the HRC does not make clear in an explicit way how the credibility of the core part of the claim is assessed, it may be inferred from its conclusions that the credibility of this core part is assessed by examining whether this core part was and is in dispute between the parties, whether it is consistent with country information, and whether there is serious corroborative evidence to support it.

The system of admission of evidence is open, flexible and liberal. It is clear from the HRC's case law that allegations that expulsion will expose the individual to a real Article 7-risk must be substantiated, but it is not very clear from the case law what exactly is meant by the term 'substantiated', which makes it difficult to infer from the HRC's jurisprudence clear guidelines concerning the required minimum quantity and quality of evidence. In the cases concerning the expulsion of asylum seekers in which an Article 7-risk was assumed, a significant amount of evidentiary materials from different sources was submitted to both the national authorities and to the HRC. These cases make clear that the HRC is more willing to consider the merits of the case and conclude that expulsion entails an Article 7-risk when a substantial amount of serious evidentiary materials is submitted in support of the claim. It is not easy to distinguish the exact factors determining the probative value and persuasiveness of the evidence presented, as the HRC is often completely silent on the issue of evaluation of the evidence. Four categories of evidence were looked at in more detail. From this examination, it became clear that strong evidentiary value is often attached to reports containing the result of inquiries conducted by embassies or missions in the country to which the particular individual is planned to be expelled. Witness statements by family members and medical reports are also accorded significant probative value. The HRC uses country reports from different sources, and it seems that the particular source and the specific content of the country report determine their probative value.

The HRC adheres to the principle of adversarial proceedings. The relevant Rules of Procedure stipulate that, at both the admissibility stage and the merits stage, both parties to the case are allowed to submit their observations and evidence and to react to the observations and evidence lodged by the other party. In a number of views, the HRC has also strongly emphasised that it adheres to the principles of adversariality and equality of arms. It normally does not allow the complainant or the respondent State to submit new statements and evidence which were not presented in the national proceedings. An exception to this rule is made when the other party materially responds to the newly presented statements and evidence.

The HRC possesses and applies only a limited number of investigative powers. It bases its views on written information made available to it by the individual and by the State party concerned. It holds no oral hearings. The HRC can request a party to a pending case to submit certain specific information in writing which it deems necessary for taking a decision. It may also request the State party concerned or the author of the communication to submit additional written information or observations relevant to the question of the admissibility of the communication or to the merits. The HRC cannot – upon party request or *proprio motu* – hear witnesses or experts, nor can it hold fact finding missions.

As far as time limits for the presentation of statements and evidence are concerned, the investigation has made clear that the HRC does not see the late presentation of crucial evidence in the national proceedings as problematic. Examples of this flexible approach are the cases of *Byahuranga v. Denmark* (2004) and *Mehrez Ben Abde Hamida v. Canada* (2010).

The HRC requires that evidence regarding the substance of the claim, which is submitted to national courts, must be taken into account by these national courts, even when such evidence was not presented earlier, for example, during previous administrative proceedings. If evidence is presented at a date close to the actual court hearing, the national court may adjourn the proceedings in order to allow the other party more time to examine the newly presented evidence. With regard to the eleventh aspect, the point in time for the risk assessment, it was concluded that the HRC assesses the existence of the alleged Article 7-risk on an *ex nunc* basis: the material point in time is the moment at which it examines the case.

Chapter 4: The 1984 Convention against Torture and other Cruel, Inhuman or Degrading Treatment or Punishment (CAT)[1]

4.1 Introduction

The CAT was adopted by the General Assembly of the United Nations on 10 December 1984 and it entered into force on 26 June 1987.[2] The CAT has been ratified in 149 States,[3] including all 27 Member States of the European Union.[4] It is a specialised human rights treaty, created as a response to the widespread and systematic practice of torture in different regions of the world, in an attempt to make more effective the struggle against torture and other cruel, inhuman or degrading treatment or punishment throughout the world.[5] According to the Committee against Torture (the Committee or ComAT), the main aim of the CAT is the prevention of torture, and not to redress torture once it has occurred.[6] The CAT establishes three different types of measures to achieve this aim: 1) repression against individual perpetrators of torture by means of national criminal law and the principle of universal jurisdiction; 2) recognition of the right of victims of torture to a remedy and adequate reparation; and 3) comprehensive obligations on States parties to prevent torture and cruel, inhuman or degrading treatment or punishment.

4.1.1 The CAT and asylum

Just like the ICCPR and, as we will see in Chapter 5, the ECHR, the CAT does not contain a right to asylum.[7] It does contain an explicit prohibition on *refoulement*, however. Article 3, first paragraph, stipulates:

---

1   See the following literature for more comprehensive descriptions and analyses of the history and working of the CAT: Burgers & Danelius 1988, Boulesbaa 1999, Joseph, Mitchell, Gyorki & Benninger-Budel 2006, Nowak & McArthur 2008, Office of the United Nations High Commissioner for Human Rights: Human Rights Fact Sheet No 4 (rev 1): Combating Torture, Human Rights Fact Sheet No 17: The Committee against Torture. For the role of CAT in international asylum law see in particular Nowak 1996, Gorlick 1999 and Wouters 2009, Chapter 5.

2   United Nations General Assembly Resolution 39/46, Doc. A/Res/39/46. See http://treaties.un.org under 'Status of Treaties'.

3   The number of States parties mentioned here reflects the situation on 31 December 2012, see: http://europa.eu/abc/european_countries/eu_members/index_nl.htm under 'Status of Treaties'. See also http://en.wikipedia.org/wiki/United_Nations_Convention_Against_Torture#Signatories_of_CAT. Both sites were visited last on 31 December 2012.

4   The number of Member States mentioned here reflects the situation on 31 December 2012; see http://europa.eu/abc/european_countries/eu_members/index_nl.htm.

5   Nowak & McArthur 2008, p. 8, Preamble to the CAT, para. 5.

6   ComAT, *Alan v. Switzerland*, 8 May 1996, No. 021/1995, para. 11.5.

7   See, for example, ComAT, *Omer v. Greece*, 28 April 1997, No. 040/1996, para. 11.2: 'the Committee cannot determine whether or not the claimant is entitled to asylum under the national laws of a country, or can invoke the protection of the 1951 Convention relating to the Status of Refugees'; ComAT, *Aemei v. Switzerland*, 29 May 1997, No. 34/1995, para.11: 'finding a violation of Article 3 in no way affects the decision(s) of the competent national authorities concerning the granting or

$\rightarrow$

'No State Party shall expel, return (*refouler*) or extradite a person to another State where there
are substantial grounds for believing that he would be in danger of being subjected to torture.'

The adoption of this explicit prohibition on *refoulement* was inspired by the case law
under Article 3 ECHR.[8]

The large majority (80%) of individual complaints under the CAT have concerned alleged violations of Article 3. Interestingly, of these complaints the large majority
were lodged by asylum seekers who had unsuccessfully claimed asylum in one of the
States parties.[9] The first decision in an Article 3-claim lodged by an asylum seeker was
issued in 1993 in the case of *Mutombo v. Switzerland* (1993).[10] This case concerned a
member of the Zairian Armed Forces who had become a member of the political
movement *Union pour la démocratie et le progrès social* (UDPS) and had participated in
several demonstrations and attended illegal meetings. The author had been arrested,
detained and severely tortured by members of the *Division Spéciale Présidentielle*. After
his provisional release from detention, a friend helped him to obtain a visa for Italy
and from that country he entered Switzerland, where he applied for recognition as a
refugee.[11] The Swiss authorities rejected his application and ordered his removal from
Switzerland. It considered that there were several contradictions in his testimony, that
the principal document, the provisional release order, had no legal value, that the
medical certificates were not persuasive and that, in general, the author's allegations
were not reliable. The authorities were, furthermore, of the opinion that the situation
in Zaire was not one of systematic violence.[12] By contrast, the Committee assumed
substantial grounds for believing that the author would be in danger of being subjected to torture upon expulsion. The Committee took into account the author's ethnic
background, his alleged political affiliation, his detention history, the fact that he had
deserted from the army and had left Zaire in a clandestine manner, the fact that,
when formulating an application for asylum, he had adduced defamatory arguments
against Zaire, and the existence in Zaire of a consistent pattern of gross, flagrant or
mass violations of human rights. The Committee finally took into consideration that
Zaire was not a party to the CAT, so that the author would be in danger, in the event
of expulsion to Zaire, not only of being subjected to torture but of no longer having
the legal possibility of applying to the Committee for protection.[13]

Many other cases followed *Mutombo*. The Committee has now developed a vast
body of case law concerning the expulsion of asylum seekers. Not everyone has wel-
comed this as a positive development. There has been fierce criticism from a number
of States that, since *Mutombo*, the Committee has been acting as a kind of fourth in-

---

refusal of asylum (…) Consequently, the State party is not required to modify its decision(s) concerning the granting of asylum.'

8   Burgers & Danelius 1988, p. 35, Wouters 2009, p. 425.
9   Joseph, Mitchell, Gyorki & Benninger-Budel 2006, p. 217; Nowak & McArthur 2008, pp. 158-159.
10   ComAT, *Mutombo v. Switzerland*, 27 April 1994, No. 13/1993. This View has been extensively com-
     mented on by eminent scholars, see, for example, Nowak 1996, Ingelse 1999, pp. 246-267, Gorlick
     1999.
11   ComAT, *Mutombo v. Switzerland*, 27 April 1994, No. 13/1993, paras. 2.1, 2.2, 2.3.
12   *Ibidem*, paras. 2.4, 2.5, 6.1.
13   *Ibidem*, paras. 9.4-9.6.

stance in asylum proceedings in the North, instead of concentrating its efforts on denouncing torture in those States in which it is actually practised.[14] Be that as it may, the huge body of case law makes the CAT an important treaty in international asylum law and distinguishes it from the ICCPR, as the HRC has, so far, dealt with only a limited number of asylum cases under Article 7 ICCPR.[15]

Just like Articles 3 ECHR and 7 ICCPR, Article 3 CAT is absolute and non-derogable.[16] Absolute means that it is not open to the respondent State to claim that its own public interest reasons for deporting the individual outweigh the risk of ill-treatment on his or her return; non-derogable means that even in times of war or other public emergencies, it is not allowed for States parties to take measures derogating from it. Because of its absolute and non-derogable character, and because Article 3 CAT is not conditioned by the five grounds of persecution contained in Article 1 A (2) RC, Article 3 CAT (like Articles 3 ECHR and 7 ICCPR) offers broader protection than Article 33 RC. Its protection is narrower than the protection under Article 3 ECHR and Article 7 ICCPR, however, as these latter provisions include protection against subjection to cruel, inhuman or degrading treatment or punishment.[17]

As this book focuses on issues of evidence and judicial scrutiny in asylum court proceedings, but is not a comprehensive analysis of the prohibitions on *refoulement* contained in international asylum law, the concept of torture is not analysed further here. Other authors have done this before.[18]

4.1.2 Supervisory mechanisms

Article 17 CAT establishes an autonomous treaty body which monitors the application and implementation of the CAT: the UN Committee against Torture (Committee or ComAT).[19] It consists of ten members who have to be of high moral standing

---

14 See Nowak & McArthur 2008, p. 128, Burns 2001.

15 See Ingelse 1999, p. 260 and Joseph, Mitchell, Gyorki & Benninger-Budel 2006, p. 221. They write that there are numerous asylum cases before the Committee against Torture and only few before the Human Rights Committee. See also Nowak & McArthur 2008, pp. 127 and 194, para. 170.

16 See, for example, ComAT, *Paez v. Sweden*, 28 April 1997, No. 039/1996, para. 14.5; ComAT, *V.X.N. and H.N. v. Sweden*, 2 September 2000, Nos. 130 and 131/1999, para. 13.4; ComAT, *Tebourski v. France*, 1 May 2007, No. 300/2006, para. 8.3. See on the non-derogable nature of Article 3, Article 2, second paragraph, CAT, which states that no exceptional circumstances whatsoever, whether a state of war or a threat of war, internal political instability or any other public emergency, may be invoked as a justification for torture, and General Comment No. 2, 23 September 2007, CAT/C/GC/2, para. 5: 'Article 2, paragraph 2, provides that the prohibition against torture is absolute and non-derogable. It emphasizes that *no exceptional circumstances whatsoever* may be invoked by a State Party to justify acts of torture in any territory under its jurisdiction. (…)'.

17 See Wouters 2009 for a much more detailed comparison of the prohibitions on *refoulement* on pp. 525-578.

18 See, for example, Wouters 2009, pp. 439-458.

19 Article 17, para. 1, CAT. See the following literature for a more extensive description and more profound analysis of the Committee against Torture's functioning and work: Burgers & Danelius 1988, pp. 150-168; Byrnes 1992; Gorlick 1999; Boulesbaa 1999, pp. 237-294; Ingelse 1999, pp. 79-173; Ingelse 2000; Burns 2001; Joseph, Mitchell, Gyorki & Benninger-Budel 2006, pp. 46-48; Nowak & McArthur 2008, pp. 577-815; Wouters 2009, pp. 429-433; Office of the United Nations High Commissioner for Human Rights: Human Rights Fact Sheet No 17: The Committee against Torture.

with a recognised competence in the field of human rights. The members serve in their personal capacity and not as representatives of their States.[20] The Committee has six monitoring mechanisms at its disposal to supervise compliance with the CAT. These are the examination of State reports,[21] the consideration of individual complaints,[22] the consideration of interstate complaints,[23] the issuance of general comments,[24] special *ex officio* inquiries in cases of systematic practices of torture in a State party[25] and, finally, under the Optional Protocol (OPCAT), carrying out missions to States parties and preventive visits to places of detention.[26]

The competence of the Committee to examine inter-State and individual complaints, as well as the competence to start *ex officio* enquiries, is optional. This means that at the time of ratifying or acceding to the CAT, a State party can choose either to recognise or not to recognise this competence of the Committee. While 147 States

---

20 Article 17, para. 1, CAT.

21 Article 19, para. 1, CAT stipulates: 'The States Parties shall submit to the Committee, through the Secretary-General of the United Nations, reports on the measures they have taken to give effect to their undertakings under this Convention, within one year after the entry into force of this Convention for the State Party concerned. Thereafter the States Parties shall submit supplementary reports every four years on any new measures taken, and such other reports as the Committee may request.'

22 See Article 22, para. 1, CAT, which stipulates: 'A State Party to this Convention may at any time declare under this article that it recognizes the competence of the Committee to receive and consider communications from or on behalf of individuals subject to its jurisdiction who claim to be victims of a violation by a State Party of the provisions of the Convention. No communication shall be received by the Committee if it concerns a State Party to the Convention which has not made such a declaration.'

23 See Article 21, para. 1, CAT, which stipulates: 'A State Party to this Convention may at any time declare under this article 3 that it recognizes the competence of the Committee to receive and consider communications to the effect that a State Party claims that another State Party is not fulfilling its obligations under this Convention. Such communications may be received and considered according to the procedures laid down in this article only if submitted by a State Party which has made a declaration recognizing in regard to itself the competence of the Committee. No communication shall be dealt with by the Committee under this article if it concerns a State Party which has not made such a declaration.'

24 Rule 74, para. 1, of the Rules of Procedure of the Committee stipulates. 'The Committee may prepare and adopt general comments on the provisions of the Convention with a view to promoting its further implementation or to assisting States parties in fulfilling their obligations.'

25 Article 20 CAT, paras. 1-3 stipulate: 'If the Committee receives reliable information which appears to it to contain well-founded indications that torture is being systematically practised in the territory of a State Party, the Committee shall invite that State Party to co-operate in the examination of the information and to this end to submit observations with regard to the information concerned. Taking into account any observations which may have been submitted by the State Party concerned as well as any other relevant information available to it, the Committee may, if it decides that this is warranted, designate one or more of its members to make a confidential inquiry and to report to the Committee urgently. If an inquiry is made in accordance with paragraph 2, the Committee shall seek the co-operation of the State Party concerned. In agreement with that State Party, such an inquiry may include a visit to its territory.'

26 The OPCAT was adopted on 18 December 2002 and entered into force on 22 June 2006. The OPCAT establishes a Subcommittee on Prevention with the task of carrying out missions to States parties and preventive visits to places of detention. OPCAT also envisages that parties will establish independent national preventive mechanisms with the task of regularly visiting and inspecting all places of detention. Many States in all regions of the world are presently in the process of ratifying OPCAT. See Nowak & McArthur 2008, vii.

are formally parties to the CAT, only 65 States parties have recognised the competence of the Committee to hear individual complaints under Article 22 CAT. All the EU Member States have recognised the competence of the Committee to receive individual communications under Article 22, with the exception of Estonia, Latvia, Lithuania, Romania and the UK.[27] As these countries are parties to the CAT itself, they are bound by it and by the interpretations of treaty provisions given by the Committee. However, as a result of the fact that they have not made declarations in which they recognise the competence of the Committee to receive individual communications, individuals in these countries, including asylum seekers, cannot bring complaints to the Committee.

The Committee is not a court or tribunal, but an independent body of experts *sui generis*, with elements of judicial, quasi-judicial, administrative, investigative, inquisitorial, supervisory and conciliatory functions.[28] According to the Committee itself, it is not an appellate, quasi-judicial or administrative body, but rather a monitoring body created by the States parties themselves with declaratory powers only.[29] The opinions of the Committee set out in its various documents are not legally binding, as the CAT does not contain a provision like Article 46, first paragraph, ECHR, which provision stipulates, in short, that the respondent State is obliged to abide by the final judgment of the ECtHR.[30] Unlike the ECHR, the CAT also lacks a separate body with a practice to keep cases on its agenda until the States concerned have taken satisfactory measures.[31] The enforcement procedure under the CAT is weaker and consists of the following measures. Under Rule 118, fifth paragraph of the Rules of Procedure of the Committee,[32] the Committee will normally invite the State party concerned to inform the Committee within a specific time period of the action it has taken in conformity with the Committee's decisions. According to Rule 120, the Committee may designate one or more Rapporteur(s) for follow-up on decisions adopted under Article 22 of the Convention, for the purpose of ascertaining the measures taken by States parties to give effect to the Committee's findings. Although they are not legally binding, the opinions of the CAT are of a high authority. The reasons for this are the

---

27 This reflects the situation on 21 September 2012. See Nowak & McArthur 2008, p. 159, note 129, http://treaties.un.org, under 'Status of Treaties', and the List of States Parties Accepting Article 22 CAT in the Bayefsky.com database, http://www.bayefsky.com/complain/cat_statesparties.php. Bayefsky.com is a database designed for the purpose of enhancing the implementation of the human rights legal standards of the United Nations. It contains a range of data concerning the application of the UN human rights treaty system by its monitoring treaty bodies.

28 The term independent body of experts *sui generis* is used in relation to the HRC by McGoldrick 1996, p. 54, but it also fits the Committee against Torture as this Committee resembles the HRC in many ways. Both Committees are autonomous treaty bodies, consisting of independent experts (not only from the legal profession), with many similar monitoring mechanisms at their disposal, including receiving individual communications and issuing non-binding views on these communications. See Wouters 2009, pp. 429-434.

29 Committee, General Comment No. 1, para. 9.

30 Boulesbaa 1999, p. 63, Wouters 2009, p. 431.

31 Under the ECHR, the Committee of Ministers performs this function, see Chapter 5.

32 The Rules of Procedure of the Committee of 21 February 2011 may be found at: http://www2.ohchr.org/english/bodies/cat/ under 'Rules of Procedure'.

same as those mentioned in relation to the views of the HRC. Reference is made to chapter 3, section 3.1.2.

4.1.3   Provisions on proceedings

This chapter examines: the procedural limb of Article 3, containing the prohibition on *refoulement*; Articles 12 and 13, containing the obligation of States parties to investigate in a prompt and impartial manner every potential case of torture and ill-treatment that has occurred in its territory, either *ex officio* (Article 12) or on the basis of an allegation (Article 13); Article 15, which prohibits the use of statements made as a result of torture as evidence in any proceedings, except in criminal proceedings against a person accused of torture as evidence of the very fact that this statement was made; and Article 22, fifth paragraph, second part, which requires that applicants should first exhaust effective national remedies before applying to the Committee. The reason for including the latter provision is that the case law under it may help to explain when a national remedy is considered by the Committee to be (in)effective.

It may seem odd to investigate Articles 12 and 13 as these provisions pertain to acts of torture committed in the territory of the State party and, therefore, to internal situations. Articles 12 and 13 do not relate to situations of the expulsion of asylum seekers to their countries of origin, where the (past act(s) of persecution and) fear of persecution is connected not to the State party itself, but to another country (often not a State party to the CAT). Nevertheless, it is interesting to examine these provisions. First, the CAT constitutes a system; as the different provisions contained in it form part of this system, it is difficult to see them as completely separate stipulations. In that way, it is logical to see the procedural limb of Article 3 as a phenomenon which is related to the procedural provisions of Articles 12 and 13. Second, as we will see in more detail in sections 4.2 and 4.3 below, Article 3 requires an opportunity for effective, independent and impartial review of the decision on expulsion and Articles 12 and 13 require an impartial investigation. The requirement of impartiality thus follows from both Article 3 and Articles 12 and 13. As there is so far not much jurisprudence on this requirement of impartiality in Article 3-cases,[33] it is worthwhile examining the case law under Articles 12 and 13. Third, asylum seekers or recognised refugees sometimes start an Article 12 or Article 13 procedure, after having fled to a State party to the CAT, against their countries of origin, in order to get the country of origin condemned for not having investigated acts of torture impartially and promptly.[34] These cases create a link with the asylum context. For all these reasons it is relevant and worthwhile to examine Articles 12 and 13.

4.1.4   Chapter outline

Part 1 deals with the CAT's provisions on national proceedings and what these provisions say concerning the required intensity of national judicial scrutiny and eviden-

---

[33]   So far the only case found in which the requirement of impartiality explicitly plays a role is ComAT, *Sogi v. Canada*, 16 November 2007, No. 297/2006, discussed below in 4.2.2.6.

[34]   For example, ComAT, *M'Barek v. Tunisia*, 10 November 1999, No. 060/1996.

tiary issues in national asylum proceedings. In section 4.2, the provisions on national proceedings are first briefly introduced. After that, we will see how these provisions work in the asylum context, and what kinds of obligations they impose on national courts. The case law of the Committee is extensively discussed here, with a particular focus on how, according to the Committee, national courts should perform their review. The requirement of impartiality flowing from Articles 12 and 13 is discussed in section 4.3. It will be shown that this requirement of impartiality calls for intense judicial scrutiny at national level. Section 4.4 pays attention to the prohibition on using evidence obtained under torture, laid down in Article 15.

Part 2 focuses on the assessment performed by the Committee in cases concerning the expulsion of asylum seekers. The assessment is analysed with the aid of the eleven aspects of evidence and judicial scrutiny introduced in Chapter 1. Each aspect is dealt with in a separate sub-section. In section 4.6 final concluding remarks are made.

CAT, Part 1:

Provisions on national proceedings; issues of intensity of judicial scrutiny and evidentiary issues in national judicial proceedings

4.2 The CAT's provisions on national proceedings: introduction and asylum context

4.2.1 Texts of the provisions on national proceedings

Article 3 stipulates:

> '1. No State Party shall expel, return (refouler) or extradite a person to another State where there are substantial grounds for believing that he would be in danger of being subjected to torture.
> 2. For the purpose of determining whether there are such grounds, the competent authorities shall take into account all relevant considerations including, where applicable, the existence in the State concerned of a consistent pattern of gross, flagrant or mass violations of human rights.'

Article 12 of the CAT stipulates:

> 'Each State Party shall ensure that its competent authorities proceed to a prompt and impartial investigation, wherever there is reasonable ground to believe that an act of torture has been committed in any territory under its jurisdiction.'

Article 13 of the CAT stipulates:

> 'Each State Party shall ensure that any individual who alleges he has been subjected to torture in any territory under its jurisdiction has the right to complain to, and to have his case promptly and impartially examined by, its competent authorities. Steps shall be taken to ensure that the complainant and witnesses are protected against all ill-treatment or intimidation as a consequence of his complaint or any evidence given.'

Article 15 stipulates:

> 'Each State Party shall ensure that any statement which is established to have been made as a result of torture shall not be invoked as evidence in any proceedings, except against a person accused of torture as evidence that the statement was made.'

Article 22, fifth paragraph, second part, stipulates:

> 'The Committee shall not consider any communication from an individual under this article unless it has ascertained that:

The individual has exhausted all available domestic remedies; this shall not be the rule where the application of the remedies is unreasonably prolonged or is unlikely to bring effective relief to the person who is the victim of the violation of this Convention.'

4.2.2 The right to an effective remedy at national level

4.2.2.1 Derivation from Article 3 itself

The Committee derived the right to an effective remedy at national level in cases concerning *refoulement* from Article 3 itself in the case of *Agiza v. Sweden* (2003).[35] In this decision the Committee stated:

> 'The Committee observes that the right to an effective remedy for a breach of the Convention underpins the entire Convention, for otherwise the protections afforded by the Convention would be rendered largely illusory. (...) The prohibition on *refoulement* contained in Article 3 should be interpreted (...) to encompass a remedy for its breach (...). The Committee observes that in the case of an allegation of torture or cruel, inhuman or degrading treatment having occurred, the right to remedy requires, after the event, an effective, independent and impartial investigation of such allegations. The nature of *refoulement* is such, however, that an allegation of breach of that article relates to a future expulsion or removal; accordingly, the right to an effective remedy contained in Article 3 requires, in this context, an opportunity for effective, independent and impartial review of the decision to expel or remove, once that decision is made, when there is a plausible allegation that article 3 issues arise.'[36]

Sweden considered Agiza a serious threat to the national security and decided to expel him to Egypt, his country of origin, for this reason. Agiza did not have an opportunity to lodge an appeal against this decision prior to his expulsion. According to the Committee, that practice constituted a violation of Article 3.[37] It follows from the decision in the case of *Agiza* that Article 3 requires an opportunity for effective, independent and impartial review of the decision on expulsion, prior to the expulsion itself. The Committee reiterated this position in subsequent decisions.[38]

As follows from the last sentence of the above quotation from *Agiza*, the requirement of an effective, independent and impartial review of the decision on expulsion arises only where there is a plausible allegation that an issue under Article 3 arises. The Committee has not explained any further when a claim is plausible; it may be argued that a plausible claim is the same as an arguable claim under Article 13 ECHR, meaning that the claim is supported by demonstrable facts and not manifestly

---

35   ComAT, *Agiza v. Sweden*, 20 May 2005, No. 233/2003. See on this decision also Boeles 2008.

36   ComAT, *Agiza v. Sweden*, 20 May 2005, No. 233/2003, paras. 13.6 and 13.7.

37   *Ibidem*, para. 13.8.

38   See, for example, ComAT, *Brada v. France*, 24 May 2005, No. 195/2002, paras. 13.3, 13.4; ComAT, *Nirmal Singh v. Canada*, 30 May 2011, No. 319/2007, para. 7.3.

lacking in any ground in law.[39] The threshold for plausibility should not be set too high.[40]

4.2.2.2 *Reluctance to critically review national court decisions*

In order to find out when the Committee finds national remedies compliant or non-compliant with the requirement of effective, independent and impartial review, it is useful to look at those decisions in which the claim was declared inadmissible under Article 22, fifth paragraph, second part, for failure to exhaust national remedies.[41] Analysis of this case law demonstrates that the Committee, just like the HRC (see Chapter 3, section 3.3.1), is generally reluctant to submit national proceedings to a rigorous test of compliance with the requirement of an effective, independent and impartial review.[42] Just like the HRC, the Committee normally assumes that national proceedings are CAT-compliant. Some examples are discussed now to illustrate this. In the case of *M.A. v. Canada* (1995),[43] the Committee considered:

> 'In the present case, the author has invoked this exception (exception of non-exhaustion of do-mestic remedies), arguing that the chances of success are almost non-existent, in view of the prior jurisprudence by the Courts and the process governing the reasonableness hearing. How-ever (…) in principle, it is not within the scope of the Committee's competence to evaluate the prospects of success of domestic remedies, but only whether they are proper remedies for the determination of the author's claims.'[44]

It does not appear from the decision in *M.A. v. Canada* that the Committee made a true inquiry into the characteristics of the national jurisprudence and the national proceedings governing the reasonableness hearing.

In a number of decisions on the merits, the Committee, reacting to party sub-missions with regard to the (un)fairness of the national refugee claim determination proceedings, observed that it is not called upon to review the prevailing system in the State party in general, but only to examine whether in the present case the State party complied with its obligations under the Convention. An example of this line is *Khan v. Canada* (1994).[45] In the proceedings before the Committee, counsel complained ex-tensively about the Canadian asylum procedure. In particular, he complained that the Canadian system did not allow for a judicial appeal on the merits, but only for an ap-peal with leave on matters of law. Furthermore, he complained about the incom-

---

39   See, for example, ECtHR, *Kudla v. Poland*, 26 October 2000, Appl. No. 30210/96, para. 157.
40   Wouters 2009, p. 517.
41   In the case law of the Committee under Article 3, non-exhaustion of national remedies is the num-ber one ground for inadmissibility; on 1 January 2009 in 23 cases out of a total of 45 inadmissible cases under Article 3, the Committee established that national remedies had not been exhausted.
42   The same conclusion is drawn by Joseph, Mitchell, Gyorki & Benninger-Budel 2006, p. 221; see also Nowak & McArthur 2008, p.193.
43   ComAT, *M.A. v. Canada*, 3 May 1995, No. 22/1995.
44   ComAT, 3 May 1995, *M.A. v. Canada*, No. 22/1995, para. 4.
45   ComAT, *Khan v. Canada*, 15 November 1994, No. 15/1994. See on this decision also Nowak 1996 and Tiemersma 2006.

petence of members of the Appeal Board, about constant interruptions during the presentation of the case at the hearing of the Appeal Board, a focus on contradictions instead of a search for the truth and some other aspects of the asylum procedure. The Committee responded as follows:

> 'The Committee notes that both parties have made considerable submissions with regard to the fairness of the refugee claim determination system and the post-claim risk-assessment procedures. The Committee observes that it is not called upon to review the prevailing system in Canada in general, but only to examine whether in the present case Canada complied with its obligations under the Convention. (…).'[46]

In Chapter 3 on the ICCPR, it was noted that the HRC regards the determination and evaluation of facts and evidence as matters for the national courts and that the HRC itself will normally not engage in that (see section 3.3.1.). Exactly the same approach is found in a significant number of decisions of the ComAT. The Committee leaves the authorities of States, including national courts, much leeway in the determination of the facts and the proceedings applied for this aim. General Comment No. 1[47] stipulates in paragraph 9a that 'considerable weight will be given, in exercising the Committee's jurisdiction pursuant to Article 3, to findings of fact that are made by organs of the State party concerned'. The principle of primacy for the national authorities in the determination of the facts, and the corresponding national procedural autonomy, has been reiterated in many decisions of the Committee.[48]

The general reluctance of the Committee to engage in the determination of the facts and the evaluation of evidence when this has already been done at national level has also been emphasised in literature.[49] Various explanations are given for this, which are, in fact, the same as those mentioned in relation to the HRC (see Chapter 3, section 3.1.1). First, the Committee does not operate as an appellate court to which appeals may be taken from a State's highest national court, but is a treaty monitoring body with declaratory powers only. Second, the meeting time of the Committee is very limited, which is difficult to reconcile with the time required to assess evidence and to write down an assessment of the presented evidence. The Committee meets in

---

46   *Ibidem*, para. 12.1.
47   General Comment No. 1: Implementation of Article 3 of the Convention in the context of Article 22, adopted on 21 November 1997: A/53/44 Annex IX, CAT. This document was adopted following the high number of individual complaints relating to Article 3, in order to confirm and summarize the case law of the Committee. See Nowak&McArthur 2008, p. 156.
48   To mention a few examples: ComAT, *A.R. v. Netherlands*, 14 November 2003, No. 203/2002. The Committee considered: 'The Committee recalls its jurisprudence to the effect that it is not an appellate, quasi-judicial or administrative body. Consistent with its General Comment, whilst the Committee has the power of free assessment of the facts arising in the circumstances of each case, it must give considerable weight to findings of fact made by the organs of the State party.'; ComAT, *Rios v. Canada*, 23 November 2004, No. 133/1999. The Committee stated: 'The Committee has had due regard for its established practice according to which it is not the Committee's place to question the evaluation of evidence by the domestic courts unless the evaluation amounts to a denial of justice.'
49   See, for example, Wouters 2009, p. 490, Kjaerum 2010, pp. 28-29.

Geneva and normally holds two sessions per year consisting of a four-week session in April/May and another four-week session in November.[50]

4.2.2.3   *Arbitrary evaluation of evidence or denial of justice at national level*

National judicial proceedings cannot be qualified as CAT-compliant – that is, effective, independent and impartial – if the evidence was evaluated in a clearly arbitrary way, if a denial of justice occurred, or if the national officers clearly violated their obligations of impartiality.[51] This very much resembles the approach developed by the HRC (see sections 3.3.2 and 3.4.2). Within the framework of this research, no decisions have been found in which the Committee concluded explicitly that national courts had acted in a clearly arbitrary way or denied justice.

4.2.2.4   *Insufficiently thorough investigations at national level*

There are a number of decisions in which the Committee – without using the mentioned terminology – did reproach the national authorities for conducting insufficiently thorough investigations. An example is the case of *A.S. v. Sweden* (2000).[52] The female Iranian applicant alleged in the national proceedings and, subsequently, in the proceedings before the Committee, that she was the widow of a high-ranking officer in the Iranian Air Force who had been declared a martyr, that she had been forced into a so-called *sighe* marriage[53] with a high-ranking Ayatollah, that she had a Christian lover, that this had been discovered at a certain point in time, that she had been arrested for this reason and that she and her lover had been sentenced to death by stoning by a Revolutionary Court.[54] In the national proceedings the authorities noted that the author had failed to submit verifiable information, such as the telephone number on which she contacted her Christian lover, addresses (her own address and the address of her Christian lover) and names of her Christian friend's family members.[55] The Committee noted that the claimant had indeed provided a number of details that could have been verified by the national authorities, and that the claim fitted well with information about the stoning of women in Iran for adultery. It explicitly reproached the national authorities for failure to conduct more thorough investigations into the details that had been provided by the claimant:

> 'The Committee notes the State party's position that the author has not fulfilled her obligation to submit the verifiable information that would enable her to enjoy the benefit of the doubt.

---

50   See for information on the sessions of the Committee the site of this treaty body: http://www2. ohchr.org/english/bodies/cat, last visited 30 December 2011.

51   See, for example, ComAT, *S.P.A. v. Canada*, 7 November 2006, No. 282/2005, para. 7.6.

52   ComAT, *A.S. v. Sweden*, 24 November 2000, No. 149/1999.

53   A short-term marriage recognised legally only by Shia Muslims in order to create a situation wherein the spouses are not obliged to live together but the wife is obliged to be at the husband's disposal for sexual services whenever required, see ComAT, *A.S. v. Sweden*, 24 November 2000, No. 149/1999, para. 2.3.

54   ComAT, *A.S. v. Sweden*, 24 November 2000, No. 149/1999, paras. 2.1-2.8.

55   *Ibidem*, paras. 4.6, 4.8, 4.13.

However, the Committee is of the view that the author has submitted sufficient details regarding her sighe or mutah marriage and alleged arrest, such as names of persons, their positions, dates, addresses, name of police station, etc., that could have, and to a certain extent have been, verified by the Swedish immigration authorities, to shift the burden of proof. In this context the Committee is of the view that the State party has not made sufficient efforts to determine whether there are substantial grounds for believing that the author would be in danger of being subjected to torture.'[56]

4.2.2.5   *States parties must provide for judicial review of the merits*

In a number of decisions, the Committee has made clear that, in order to qualify as effective, judicial remedies must be more than a mere formality or reasonableness-test and must make it possible to look at the substance, the merits, of the case. The first decision in which the Committee gave expression to this new line was *Aung v. Canada*[57] (2006). It considered that

'In the view of the Committee, the decisions of the Federal Court support the contention that applications for leave and judicial review are not mere formalities, but that the Federal Court may, in appropriate cases, look at the substance of a case.'[58]

In the decision of *Nirmal Singh v. Canada* (2011),[59] the Committee concluded that the judicial review offered by the Federal Court of Canada did not constitute an effective national remedy. Two years earlier, in *Yassin v. Canada* (2009),[60] the Committee had reached the opposite conclusion at the admissibility stage. The different outcome may well be explained by the fact that Yassin had not challenged the effectiveness of the judicial review by the Federal Court of Canada.[61] In *Nirmal Singh v. Canada* (2011), the complainant stated explicitly in the proceedings before the Committee that he had not had an effective remedy to challenge the decision on expulsion. Nirmal Singh specifically pointed to the narrow character of the judicial review and to the fact that, when the Immigration Board decided that a refugee claimant was not credible, the Federal Court did not subject this decision to rigorous scrutiny.[62]

The Committee ruled in *Nirmal Singh* that the judicial review offered by the Federal Court did not constitute an effective remedy. It articulated in a very clear way

---

56   *Ibidem*, paras. 8.6, 8.7.
57   ComAT, *Aung v. Canada*, 15 May 2006, No. 273/2005.
58   *Ibidem*, para. 6.3.
59   ComAT, *Nirmal Singh v. Canada*, 30 May 2011, No. 319/2007.
60   ComAT, *Yassin v. Canada*, 4 November 2009, No. 307/2006.
61   In *Yassin v. Canada*, the complainant did not request leave to apply to the Federal Court for judicial review of the negative Pre-Removal Risk Assessment (PRRA) decision. As a result of this, in the proceedings before the Committee the respondent State party challenged the admissibility of the complaint for non-exhaustion of domestic remedies. It is important to note that, in the proceedings before the Committee, the complainant did not challenge the effectiveness of the remedy of judicial review by the Federal Court. Logically, the Committee followed the State party in its position and declared the communication inadmissible for non-exhaustion of domestic remedies. See paras. 2.11, 4.1, 6.1, 9.3.
62   ComAT, *Nirmal Singh v. Canada*, 30 May 2011, No. 319/2007, paras. 3.4 and 5.2.

that States parties to the CAT are obliged to provide for judicial review of the merits, rather than merely of the reasonableness, of decisions on expulsion:

> 'The complainant states that he did not have an effective remedy to challenge the decision on deportation and that the judicial review of the Immigration Board decision, denying him Convention refugee status, was not an appeal on the merits, but rather a very narrow review for gross errors of law. The State party in response submits that the Board's decision was subject to judicial review by the Federal Court. The Committee notes that according to Section 18.1(4) of the Canadian Federal Courts Act, the Federal Court may quash a decision of the Immigration Refugee Board if satisfied that: the tribunal acted without jurisdiction; failed to observe a principle of natural justice or procedural fairness; erred in law in making a decision; based its decision on an erroneous finding of fact; acted, or failed to act, by reason of fraud or perjured evidence; or acted in any other way that was contrary to law. *The Committee observes that none of the grounds above include a review on the merits of the complainant's claim that he would be tortured if returned to India* (emphasis added). With regard to the PRPA procedure of risk analysis, to which the complainant also subjected his claim, the Committee notes that according to the State party's submission, PRRA submissions may only include new evidence that arose after the rejection of the refugee protection claim; further, the PRRA decisions are subject to a discretionary leave to appeal, which was denied in the case of the complainant. The Committee refers to its Concluding observations (CAT/C/CR/34/CAN of 7 July 2005, para 5 (c)), *that the State party should provide for judicial review of the merits, rather than merely of the reasonableness, of decisions to expel an individual where there are substantial grounds for believing that the person faces a risk of torture* (emphasis added). The Committee accordingly concludes that in the instant case the complainant did not have access to an effective remedy against his deportation to India, in violation of article 22 of the Convention against Torture.'[63]

The Committee has, so far, not clarified any further what a 'review on the merits' exactly entails, and how intense the judicial scrutiny should exactly be. What is clear, though, is that a review on the merits is more than just a reasonableness test. It is regrettable that in *Nirmal Singh* the Committee did not explain why an 'erroneous finding of fact', which is one of the statutory grounds on which the Federal Court can quash the decision of the Immigration Refugee Board, cannot be qualified as a review on the merits of the claim. In my opinion, the ground 'erroneous finding of fact' would make a review on the merits possible. It seems that, in fact, the Committee did not find this statutory ground problematic, but that it was convinced by the complainant's argument, supported by case law, that, in practice, the Federal Court tested only the reasonableness of decisions, although it had the statutory possibilities to review cases in a more independent and rigorous way.

---

63   *Ibidem*, paras. 8.8., 8.9, 9.

4.2.2.6   *Equality of arms, adversariality*

The most explicit case on this issue in the Committee's case law is *Sogi v. Canada* (2007).[64] The complainant in this case had applied for asylum in Canada. He stated that he and his family had been falsely accused of being Sikh militants and on the basis of that allegation had been arrested and tortured several times in India. In August 2002, the Canadian Security and Intelligence Service (CSIS) issued a report stating that there were reasonable grounds to believe that the complainant was a member of the Babbar Khalsa International (BKI) terrorist group, an alleged Sikh terrorist organization whose objective was to establish an independent Sikh state called Khalistan, taking in the Indian province of Punjab. Based on this report, a warrant was issued for his arrest as he was deemed a threat to Canada's national security. While it was recognised that there was a risk of torture in the event of deportation, the complainant was refused asylum and a removal decision was taken as he was seen as a threat to Canada's national security. The information underpinning the national security rating was 'secret' and not disclosed to the complainant. The complainant applied for judicial review of the removal decision. The Federal Court concluded that the hearing officer had not erred in determining that certain information was relevant, but could not be disclosed to the complainant for reasons of national security. The Federal Court considered it relevant that this secret information could, nevertheless, be taken into account by the Court, so that a counterbalance was created. This ruling was upheld on appeal in a Federal Court of Appeal judgment.[65]

The Committee ruled that the non-disclosure of this relevant evidence to the complainant resulted in a violation of the requirement of a fair hearing. It considered as follows:

> 'As for the Canadian authorities' use of evidence that for security reasons was not divulged to the complainant, the Committee notes the State party's argument that this practice is authorized by the Immigration and Refugee Protection Act, and that in any event such evidence did not serve as a basis for the decision by the Minister's delegate, as she did not consider the threat the complainant posed to Canadian security in her assessment of the risks. However, the Committee notes that, in both her decisions, the delegate considered the threat to national security. On the basis of the above, the Committee considers that the complainant did not enjoy the necessary guarantees in the pre-removal procedure. The State party is obliged, in determining whether there is a risk of torture under Article 3, to give a fair hearing to persons subject to expulsion orders.'[66]

This case and the conclusion drawn by the Committee strongly resemble the case of *Mansour Ahani v. Canada* (2004)[67] of the HRC (see Chapter 3, section 3.3.4.)

The decision in *Sogi v. Canada* strongly conveys the message that in expulsion cases both parties to the case must have equal access to the documents in the case

---

64   ComAT, *Sogi v. Canada*, 16 November 2007, No. 297/2006.

65   *Ibidem*, paras. 2.1-2.11.

66   *Ibidem*, paras. 10.4, 10.5.

67   HRC, *Mansour Ahani v. Canada*, 15 June 2004, No. 1051/2002.

file. The Committee seems to be stricter in guarding adversariality and equality of arms than the ECtHR as it required in the *Sogi* decision that all the documents in the file be disclosed to the claimant, including those underpinning the allegation that Sogi constituted a threat to Canada's national security. In other words, in *Sogi* the Committee treated adversariality and equality of arms as an absolute right and did not tolerate that national security interests justified non-disclosure of part of the evidentiary materials. The ECtHR, however, treats these rights as relative rights and has ruled that non-disclosure of evidentiary materials may be justified if this is strictly necessary to preserve the fundamental rights of another individual or to safeguard an important public interest, such as the protection of national security.[68] For a more detailed analysis of the ECtHR's position, reference is made to chapter 5, section 5.5.4.

4.2.2.7   *Effective national remedy: interim conclusions*

Article 3 and Article 22, fifth paragraph, second part require an opportunity for effective, independent and impartial review of the decision on expulsion, prior to expulsion. Just like the HRC, the Committee has for a long time been generally reluctant to submit national proceedings to a rigorous CAT compliance test. However, in a number of decisions the Committee has made clear that – in order to qualify as an effective, independent and impartial national remedy as required by Article 3 – national judicial remedies must make it possible to look at the substance, the merits, of the case, and must guarantee equality of arms and adversarial proceedings.

4.3   Impartial investigation under Articles 12 and 13 CAT[69]

4.3.1   *Impartiality: active search for the truth by applying investigative powers*

In the case of *M'Barek v. Tunisia* (1999) the complainant was a Tunisian national residing in France where he enjoyed refugee status. He submitted the case on behalf of a friend, the late Faisal Baraket. Mr Baraket had been arrested on 8 October 1991 by members of the Criminal Investigation Brigade of the Nabeul National Guard. Mr Baraket was an activist in the Tunisian General Students' Union and a member of Al Nahdha, an unofficial political party. He knew that the police were looking for him and had, therefore, gone into hiding. After his arrest, during which he was beaten, he was brought to the headquarters of the Brigade where he was taken to the office of Ladib, the officer in charge. In the presence of the captain and police officers, Baraket was tortured. Some of the officers later threw him out into the corridor after bringing another detainee into the office. It was noted that Baraket was seriously

---

68   See, for example, ECtHR, *Edwards and Lewis v. the UK*, 27 October 2004, Appl. Nos. 39647/98 and 40461/98, para. 46.

69   Literature on these provisions of the CAT is scarce, and there is not very much jurisprudence either so far. See Burgers & Danelius 1988, pp. 144-146, Ingelse 1999, pp. 297-299, Joseph, Mitchell, Gyorki & Benninger-Budel 2006, pp. 231-233, Nowak & McArthur 2008, pp. 413-451.

injured and seemed to be dying. The officers prevented the other detainees present, including his own brother, from giving him assistance. After a further half hour it was discovered that he was dead.[70]

In October 1991, the father, Hedi Baraket, was informed that his son had died in a car accident. He was asked to identify the body and he noted that the face was disfigured and difficult to recognise. He was also not permitted to see the rest of the body. He was made to sign a statement acknowledging that his son had been killed in an accident. An autopsy report was drawn up by doctors at the Nabeul hospital. It mentioned, among other things, that death appeared to have resulted from acute respiratory insufficiency related to extensive pulmonary congestion.[71]

The author M'Barek (friend of deceased Baraket) visited the two principal witnesses to Baraket's death some months after the incident. They said that Baraket had died in their arms at the Brigade's headquarters. The author was then arrested on 15 May 1992 by the same Brigade and was detained at the same location as the victim. He was sentenced to five months' imprisonment. His detention gave him the opportunity to meet witnesses to Baraket's death.

These witnesses corroborated what the first witnesses had said, namely that Baraket had died under torture. After his release, while he was still under house arrest, the author left Tunisia and was granted asylum in France.[72] Through Amnesty International a report was drawn up in 1992 by Mr Pounder, Professor of Forensic Medicine at the University of Dundee (United Kingdom). That report, which was prepared on the basis of the autopsy report, indicated, *inter alia,* that the pattern of injuries described in the autopsy report was inconsistent with the deceased having died in a road traffic accident as a pedestrian, pedal cyclist, motor cyclist or vehicle occupant. The report also stated that the entire pattern of injury was that of a systematic physical assault, which corroborated the allegation of ill-treatment and torture that had been made.[73]

On 11 December 1991, the author sent an anonymous letter to the Prosecutor of the Republic in the town of Grombalia in which he reported the crime, identified the victim and the police officers responsible and specified the circumstances in which the victim had died. He also wrote to the Minister of Justice, his deputies and the national and international media. However, the death of Faisal Baraket was never investigated. From October 1991 onwards, Amnesty International, the World Organization against Torture, Action of Christians for the Abolition of Torture (France) and the Association for the Prevention of Torture (Switzerland) also requested the Tunisian Government to investigate the death of Faisal Baraket. The Tunisian Government, however, kept maintaining to the Committee that his death had resulted from a road accident.[74] On 13 July 1992, a report prepared by the Higher Committee for Human Rights and Fundamental Freedoms, an official Tunisian body, considered Faisal Baraket's death to be suspicious and suggested that an inquiry should be started

---

70   ComAT, *M'Barek v. Tunisia*, 10 November 1999, No. 060/1996, paras. 2.1-2.3.
71   *Ibidem*, paras. 2.4, 2.5.
72   *Ibidem*, para. 2.7.
73   *Ibidem*, para. 2.6.
74   *Ibidem*, paras. 2.9, 2.10.

under Article 36 of the Code of Criminal Procedure. On 22 September 1992, an inquiry was ordered into these allegations of torture. The examining magistrate ordered a new medical evaluation which found it impossible to determine the origins or mechanism of the injuries on the victim and dismissed the case. Assigned the case for a second time, the magistrate examined the same persons who had denied any knowledge of the alleged events, and so again dismissed the case.[75]

The Committee concluded in this case that the magistrate, in failing to investigate the case more thoroughly, had committed a breach of the duty of impartiality imposed on him by his obligation to give equal weight to both accusation and defence during the investigation. Thus, Tunisia had breached its obligations under Articles 12 and 13 CAT. The Committee was very explicit in its findings as to what other investigative activities the magistrate could and should have used: checking prison records, hearing witnesses, and even exhumation of the body:

'The Committee considers that, among other things, the examining magistrate had at his disposal the results of other important investigations which are customarily conducted in such matters, but made no use of them:

First, notwithstanding the statements made by the witnesses mentioned, and in particular bearing in mind the possibility of incomplete recall, the magistrate could have checked in the records of the detention centres referred to whether there was any trace of the presence of Faisal Baraket during the period in question, as well as that, in the same detention centre and at the same time, of the two persons mentioned by the author of the communication as having been present when Faisal Baraket died. It is not without relevance to note in this regard that in pursuance of principle 12 of the Body of Principles for the Protection of All Persons under Any Form of Detention or Imprisonment, adopted on 9 December 1988, as well as article 13 *bis* of the Tunisian Code of Penal Procedure, a record must be left of every person detained.

Next, the magistrate might have sought to identify the accused officials, examine them and arrange a confrontation between them and the witnesses mentioned as well as the complainant.

Lastly, in view of the major disparities in the findings of the forensic officials as to the causes of some of the lesions observed on the victim, the Committee considers that it would have been wise to order the exhumation of the body in order at least to confirm whether the victim had suffered fractures to the pelvis (confirming the accident hypothesis) or whether he had not (confirming the hypothesis that a foreign object had been introduced into his anus); this should have been done, as far as possible, in the presence of non-Tunisian experts, and more particularly those who have had occasion to express a view on this matter.'[76]

This case of *M'Barek* is important. It makes clear that, in cases of allegations or suspicions of torture, the requirement of impartiality enshrined in Articles 12 and 13 obliges the national judge to reconstruct as meticulously as possible what actually happened and to use his or her investigative powers to that end. Impartiality of courts and tribunals generally refers to the relationship between a judge and the matter at issue in a specific case; it implies that judges must not harbour preconceptions about

---

75   *Ibidem*, paras. 8.8, 11.8.
76   *Ibidem*, paras. 11.9, 11.10, 12.

the matter put before them and must not act in ways that promote the interests of one of the parties.[77] In *M'Barek*, the Committee gave this requirement of impartiality a new dimension. It explained that, if parties strongly disagreed about what had actually happened, the judge must make his or her own independent, thorough search for the truth. In the case of *M'Barek*, the author had stuck to allegations of torture inflicted upon his friend and the respondent government had kept on denying these allegations. Both parties referred to extensive materials to support their positions. In such situations, according to the Committee, the judge must make his or her own, thorough, independent attempt to come as close to the truth as possible by using all investigative powers at his or her disposal.

A very similar case in which the Committee concluded that there had been a violation of Articles 12 and 13, due to insufficiently effective and thorough – and therefore not impartial – investigations by the national authorities, including the national judiciary, is *Ristic v. Yugoslavia* (2001).[78] The author of the communication, Radivoje Ristic, a citizen of the former Yugoslavia, claimed that an act of torture resulting in the death of his son, Milan Ristic, had been committed by the police and that the authorities had failed to carry out a prompt and impartial investigation.[79] In this case, the Committee explicitly reproached the investigating judge for not ordering an exhumation of the body, in spite of the differences and inconsistencies between the various medical reports, the differences between statements made by the three police officers, the fact that the doctor who carried out the autopsy had admitted in a statement that he was not a specialist in forensic medicine and the fact that the police had not informed the investigating judge on duty of the incident in order for him to oversee the on-site investigation in accordance with national law. Noting these elements, the Committee considered that the investigation conducted by the State party's authorities had been neither effective nor thorough. A proper investigation would have entailed an exhumation and a new autopsy, which would in turn have allowed the cause of death to be medically established with a satisfactory degree of certainty.[80]

4.3.2   Articles 12 and 13: interim conclusions

Articles 12 and 13 CAT contain the obligation of States parties to investigate in a prompt and impartial manner every potential case of torture and, by virtue of Article 16 CAT, every potential case of ill-treatment.[81] Both provisions pertain to situations

---

77   See, for example, HRC, General Comment No. 32 on Article 14 ICCPR, para. 21.

78   ComAT, *Ristic v. Yugoslavia*, 11 May 2001, No. 113/1998.

79   *Ibidem*, para. 1.

80   *Ibidem*, paras. 9.4-9.8.

81   Article 16 CAT stipulates: 'Each State Party shall undertake to prevent in any territory under its jurisdiction other acts of cruel, inhuman or degrading treatment or punishment which do not amount to torture as defined in article 1, when such acts are committed by or at the instigation of or with the consent or acquiescence of a public official or other person acting in an official capacity. In particular, the obligations contained in articles 10, 11, 12 and 13 shall apply with the substitution for references to torture or references to other forms of cruel, inhuman or degrading treatment or punishment.'

occurring within the territory of a State party – internal situations – in which individuals become victims of torture and ill-treatment, for example in prisons and detention centres, the army, or at police stations during interrogations. They do not relate directly to national asylum proceedings where (the past act(s) of torture or ill-treatment and) the fear of torture or ill-treatment is connected not to the State party itself, but to another country. Articles 12 and 13 are, nevertheless, relevant for this research as they impose – just like the procedural limb of Article 3 – a requirement of impartiality.

In cases of allegations or suspicion of internal torture, the requirement of impartiality enshrined in Articles 12 and 13 obliges the national judge to reconstruct as meticulously as possible what actually happened and to use his or her investigative powers to that end. Impartiality under Article 3 may be interpreted as meaning the same thing as impartiality under Articles 12 and 13. That would mean that national asylum courts must act impartially and must, therefore, make their own independent, thorough search for the truth and apply investigative powers to that end. So far, we cannot be entirely sure that this interpretation of impartiality under Article 3 is correct, as the Committee has, so far, not clarified any further what a 'judicial review on the merits' exactly entails, and exactly how intense the judicial scrutiny should be (see section 4.2.2.5).

4.4 Article 15: the prohibition on using evidence obtained under torture

Article 15 prohibits the use of statements made as a result of torture as evidence in any proceedings, except in criminal proceedings against a person accused of torture as evidence of the very fact that this statement was made. The prohibition is based on two different considerations. First of all, it is clear that a statement made under torture is often unreliable, and it could, therefore, be contrary to the principle of 'fair trial' to invoke such a statement as evidence before a court. Even in countries whose court proceedings are based on free evaluation of all evidence, it is hardly acceptable that a statement made under torture should be allowed to play any part in court proceedings. In the second place, torture is often aimed at ensuring evidence in court proceedings. Consequently, if a statement made under torture cannot be invoked as evidence, an important reason for using torture is removed. The prohibition on the use of such statements can, therefore, have the indirect effect of preventing torture.[82] Article 15 only speaks of statements made as a result of torture, but due to the case law of the Committee, the provision also extends to ill-treatment.[83] The Committee has, so far, not dealt with Article 15 in the context of asylum. In *P.E. v. France* (2001) and *G.K. v. Switzerland* (2002), concerning extradition and involving allegations of torture by the Spanish authorities against female ETA suspects, the Committee consid-

---

[82] Literature on Article 15 is rather scarce and there is not much case law so far either. See Burgers & Danelius 1988, pp.147-148, Ingelse 1999, pp. 317-320, Boeles 1997, p. 174, Joseph, Mitchell, Gyorki & Benninger-Budel 2006, pp. 235-236, Nowak & McArthur 2008, pp. 503-537. Wouters 2009 has not written on Article 15.

[83] ComAT, *Halimi-Nedyibi v. Austria*, 30 November 1993, No. 9/1991.

ered Article 15 applicable to extradition proceedings.[84] Interestingly, Boeles (1997) notes that Article 15 may play a role in asylum proceedings where the facts of the claim to refugee status by someone who has been tortured in his or her own country are disputed. To the extent that statements made under pressure of torture are used against a victim of torture, in order to discredit his or her story, these statements may not be used as evidence.[85] One may think here of a case in which persuasive medical reports confirming past torture are presented and in which statements made under pressure of this torture contain discrepancies and contradictions. In such a case, such statements may not be held against the individual as evidence discrediting the claim for protection.

---

84 ComAT, *P.E. v. France*, 19 December 2002, No. 193/2001; ComAT, *G.K. v. Switzerland*, 12 May 2003, No. 219/2002. In both cases no violation of Article 15 was assumed.
85 Boeles 1997, p. 174.

CAT, Part 2:

The assessment performed by the Committee against Torture in cases on expulsion of asylum seekers

4.5   The assessment performed by the Committee against Torture

A step by step analysis of the examination performed by the Committee in its decisions concerning the expulsion of asylum seekers is made below. The eleven aspects of evidence and judicial scrutiny introduced in Chapter 1 are used as a tool for this analysis.

4.5.1   Standard of proof[86]

The standard of proof follows directly from Article 3, first paragraph CAT. This provision stipulates that there must be 'substantial grounds for believing that the claimant would be in danger of being subjected to torture.' This standard is explicitly referred to in all the decisions of the Committee concerning the expulsion of asylum seekers, from the very first case, *Mutombo v. Switzerland* (1994),[87] to the last decision included in this research, *Bakatu-Bia v. Sweden* (2011).[88] The text of Article 3 CAT and the Committee do not speak of a 'real risk', which term is used by the HRC and the ECtHR, but of a 'danger'.

In case law and in General Comment No.1,[89] the Committee has further explained what is meant by 'danger' and what level of risk is required. In *Mutombo v. Switzerland* (1994), the Committee considered that

> 'In the present circumstances, his return to Zaire would have the foreseeable and necessary consequence of exposing him to a real risk of being detained and tortured.'[90]

This 'necessary and foreseeable consequence' criterion copies the risk criterion developed by the HRC (see Chapter 3, section 3.5.1). It clearly indicates a high threshold which is not easily met. However, this criterion was never repeated by the Committee in subsequent case law: since *Mutombo*, the Committee has never again used the term 'necessary'.[91] Instead, it explains that 'danger' means that there must be more than a mere possibility of torture, more than mere theory or suspicion, but that torture does not need to be highly likely or highly probable to occur. For example, in *E.A. v. Switzerland* (1997), the Committee considered:

---

86   See for an analysis of the standard of proof, the burden of proof and the required level of individualisation also Bruin 1998 and Wouters 2009, pp. 458-487.
87   ComAT, *Mutombo v. Switzerland*, 27 April 1994, No. 13/1993, para. 9.3.
88   ComAT, *Bakatu-Bia v. Sweden*, 3 June 2011, No. 379/2009, paras. 10.2, 10.3.
89   ComAT, General Comment No. 1, 21 November 1997, A/53/44, annex IX.
90   ComAT, *Mutombo v. Switzerland*, 27 April 1994, No. 13/1993, para. 9.4
91   See also Wouters 2009, p. 460.

'The Committee has noted the State party's argument that the danger to an individual must be serious ("substantial") in the sense of being highly likely to occur. The Committee does not accept this interpretation and is of the view that 'substantial grounds' in article 3 require more than a mere possibility of torture but do not need to be highly likely to occur to satisfy that provision's conditions.'[92]

And General Comment No. 1 stipulates in paragraph 6:

'Bearing in mind that the State party and the Committee are obliged to assess whether there are substantial grounds for believing that the author would be in danger of being subjected to torture were he/she to be expelled, returned or extradited, the risk of torture must be assessed on grounds that go beyond mere theory or suspicion. However, the risk does not have to meet the test of being highly probable.'[93]

The principle that the risk does not have to meet the test of being highly probable has been reiterated in many early and more recent decisions of the Committee.[94] Furthermore, it has made clear that the risk must be foreseeable, real, personal and present.[95]

Wouters (2009) points out that the Committee has not always been consistent regarding the applicable level of risk.[96] In *Dadar v. Canada* (2005) and *El Rgeig v. Switzerland* (2007),[97] phrases are used at the end of the Committee's considerations which imply the adoption of a lower level of risk. In *Dadar*, the Committee concluded that the complainant 'might indeed be tortured upon his return'. And in *El Rgeig* the Committee considered that 'the State party has not presented to it sufficiently convincing arguments to demonstrate a complete absence of risk'.[98] However, I subscribe to Wouters' opinion that it must be assumed that it was not the Committee's intention to change the standard of proof, as in both decisions it explicitly mentioned its commonly used standard that the risk must go beyond mere theory and suspicion, but does not have to meet the test of being highly probable.[99]

To conclude, the standard of proof developed by the Committee is that there must be a real, personal, present and foreseeable risk of torture in the country to

---

92   ComAT, *E.A. v. Switzerland*, 10 November 1997, No. 028/1995, para. 11.3.

93   ComAT, General Comment No. 1, 21 November 1997, A/53/44, annex IX, para. 6.

94   See, for example,ComAT, *Haydin v. Sweden*, 20 November 1998, No. 101/1997; para. 6.5; ComAT, *S.M.R. and M.M.R. v. Sweden*, 5 May 1999, No. 103/1998, para. 9.4; ComAT, *S.G. v. the Netherlands*, 12 May 2004, No. 135/1999, para. 6.3; ComAT, *Falcon Rios v. Canada*, 23 November 2004, No. 133/1999, para. 8.2; ComAT, *Jahani v. Switzerland*, 23 May 2011, No. 357/2008, 9.3.

95   See, for example, ComAT, *Haydin v. Sweden*, 20 November 1998, No. 101/1997, para. 6.5 ('the individual concerned must face aforeseeable, real and personal risk'); see also ComAT, General Comment No. 1, 21 November 1997, A/53/44, annex IX, para. 7 ('the author must establish (…) that such danger is personal and present').

96   Wouters 2009, p. 460.

97   ComAT, *El Rgeig v. Switzerland*, 22 January 2007, No. 280/2005.

98   ComAT, *El Rgeig v. Switzerland*, 22 January 2007, No. 280/2005, para. 7.4.

99   ComAT, *Dadar v. Canada*, 5 December 2005, No. 258/2004, para. 8.4; ComAT, *El Rgeig v. Switzerland*, 22 January 2007, No. 280/2005, para. 7.3.

which the claimant is returned. Torture must not be certain or highly probable or likely, but there must be more than mere theory or suspicion.

4.5.2   Burden of proof

General Comment No. 1[100] contains a number of stipulations on the burden of proof. Paragraph 5 states:

> 'The burden is upon the author to present an arguable case. This means that there must be a factual basis for the author's position sufficient to require a response from the State party.'

Paragraph 7 stipulates:

> 'The author must establish that he/she would be in danger of being tortured and that the grounds for so believing are substantial in the way described, and that such danger is personal and present. (…)'

And paragraph 6 states:

> '(…) the State party and the Committee are obliged to assess whether there are substantial grounds for believing that the author would be in danger of being subjected to torture were he/she to be expelled (…).'

It follows from this that the burden of proof in Article 3 claims is initially on the claimant. He or she must present an arguable case, a sufficient factual basis. The Committee has confirmed this principle in several decisions.[101] It has not explained any further when a claim is arguable. The term arguable may be interpreted with the aid of the admissibility requirement under Rule 107 (b) of the Committee's Rules of Procedure that the claim must rise to a basic level of substantiation.[102] It must contain a certain number of verifiable details and must be supported by some (documentary) evidence to reach this level. The consideration of this in *K.A., on her own behalf and on behalf of her husband, R.A., and their children, v. Sweden* (2007) is illustrative and, therefore, quoted here:

> 'The Committee recalls that for a claim to be admissible under article 22 of the Convention and Rule 107 (b) of its rules of procedure, it must rise to the basic level of substantiation re-

---

100 ComAT, General Comment No. 1, 21 November 1997, A/53/44, annex IX.
101 See, for example, ComAT, *E.V.I. v. Sweden*, 1 May 2007, No. 296/2006; ComAT, *M.J.A.M.O., on his own behalf and on behalf of his wife, R.S.N., and his daughter, T.X.M.S., v. Canada*, 9 May 2008, No. 293/2006,para. 10.4: 'As to the burden of proof, the Committee recalls its general comment and its jurisprudence, which establishes that the burden is generally upon the complainant to present an arguable case (…)'; ComAT, *C.A.R.M. v. Canada*, 18 May 2007, No. 298/2006, para. 8.10; ComAT, *A.M. v. France*, 5 May 2010, No. 302/2006, para. 13.4.
102 Rule 107 (b) of the Committee's Rules of Procedure stipulate that: 'With a view to reaching a decision on the admissibility of a complaint, the Committee, its Working Group or a rapporteur designated under rules 98 or 106, paragraph 3, shall ascertain that the complaint is not (…) manifestly unfounded.'

quired for purposes of admissibility. It notes that the complainant has provided no documentary evidence in support of her account of events in Azerbaijan prior to her and R. A.'s departure for Sweden. Specifically, she claimed that in July 2001 her husband was beaten and tortured during military service in the Azerbaijani military due to his mother being Armenian. However, beyond the mere claim, she and R. A. have failed to provide any detailed account of these incidents or any medical evidence which would corroborate this claim, including a proof of possible after-effects of such ill-treatment.'[103]

It was stated above that Article 3, first paragraph, CAT was modelled on the prohibition on *refoulement* developed by the ECtHR under Article 3 ECHR. This being so, there is no reason to assume that the term 'arguable' under Article 3 CAT denotes another kind of threshold than the arguable claim under Article 13 ECHR, meaning that the claim is supported by demonstrable facts and not manifestly lacking in any ground in law.[104]

When an arguable claim is provided by the claimant, a response by the State party is required. This means that a shift of the burden takes place and an obligation arises for the State party to make sufficient efforts to determine whether there are substantial grounds for believing that the claimant would be in danger of being subjected to torture. It follows from the text of Article 3, first and second paragraphs, that the authorities have an active role in verifying information put forward by the complainant and collecting and presenting evidence. According to the first paragraph, substantial grounds must *exist* (emphasis added). It does not say that substantial grounds must be shown by the applicant. The second paragraph states that for the purpose of determining whether there are such grounds, the competent authorities shall take into account all relevant considerations.[105] The burden of proof is, thus, a shared one. The idea of a shared burden also clearly follows from the preparatory works on Article 3, first paragraph: there was consensus among the drafters that 'the burden of proof should not fall solely upon the person concerned'.[106]

Reference is made to section 4.2.2.4 in which the case of *A.S. v. Sweden* (2000)[107] was discussed. This case perfectly illustrates when a claim may be considered arguable and, as a consequence, a shift of the burden towards the authorities takes place. It follows from this case that, to be arguable, the claim must reach a basic level of substantiation, meaning that the claim must contain a certain number – not necessarily a very high number – of verifiable details and must be supported by some – not necessarily a very large amount of – evidence. Where the author has provided a basic level of

---

103 ComAT, *K.A., on her own behalf and on behalf of her husband, R.A., and their children, v. Sweden*, 16 November 2007, No. 308/2006, para. 7.2. In a substantial number of other decisions the Committee considered that the basic level of substantiation had not been reached and declared the complaint inadmissible for that reason. See, for example, ComAT, *S.A. v. Sweden*, 7 May 2004, No. 243/2004; ComAT, *R.T. v. Switzerland*, 30 November 2005, No. 242/2004; ComAT, *A.T.A. v. Switzerland*, 14 November 2003, No. 236/2003; ComAT, *H.S.V. v. Sweden*, 17 May 2004, No. 229/2003; ComAT, *H.I.A. v. Sweden*, 8 May 2003, No. 216/2002.
104 See, for example, ECtHR, *Kudla v. Poland*, 26 October 2000, Appl. No. 30210/96, para. 157.
105 See in the same vein Wouters 2009, p. 485.
106 E/CN.4/WG.1/WP.1.
107 ComAT, *A.S. v. Sweden*, 15 February 2001, No 149/1999.

substantiation the burden of proof shifts to the national authorities. It also follows from the decision in *A.S. v. Sweden* (2000) that the author must be able to explain why certain details and certain corroborative evidence have not been submitted, if this is seen as problematic by the national authorities. Where sound reasons are provided, the absence of certain details and certain evidence is not necessarily problematic.

In a number of subsequent decisions, the Committee placed a stricter burden upon the claimant than in *A.S. v. Sweden* (2000). Bruin and Reneman (2006) explain this by referring to the fact that for a number of years, States have been pushing the Committee to abstain from evaluating facts and evidence in full and to take a more reserved stand.[108] A striking example of the Committee's stricter approach is *S.L. v. Sweden* (2001),[109] in which it considered that the author had not provided it with sufficient evidence, although very detailed information had been provided, including names, an authentic verdict concerning a conviction and sentence and several medical certificates pointing to a post-traumatic stress disorder and strongly supporting the author's statements of past torture.[110] It is hard to imagine what other evidence the author should have submitted to make his claim arguable and it is difficult to reconcile this approach with the Committee's approach in *A.S. v. Sweden* (2000). Another example of this stricter approach is *F.F.Z. v. Denmark* (2002),[111] in which a report by Amnesty International's medical group was submitted stating that the physical symptoms found on the applicant were consistent with the alleged torture. The Committee concluded in this case that the complainant 'has not proved his claim', which indicated that the burden of proof rested entirely on the applicant.[112] Similarly, in *A.A.C. v. Sweden* (2006), the Committee used terminology indicating that the burden of proof rested entirely with the applicant, considering not only that it was for the complainant 'to present an arguable case', but also that it was for the complainant 'to establish that he would be in danger of being tortured and that the grounds for so believing are substantial in the way described and that such danger is personal and present'.[113]

To conclude, it may be said that the burden of proof is shared between the individual and the national authorities. In a number of cases, though, the ComAT placed the burden of proof entirely on the applicant. It is rather difficult to determine in general the exact division of responsibilities and the exact moment at which the shift of the burden takes place, as this is decided by the Committee on a case by case basis. It may be helpful to apply the guideline of the gradual scale mentioned in literature, based on the early case law of the Committee, such as *A.S. v. Sweden* (2000), that there is an inversely proportional relationship between the onus on the claimant and the general human rights situation in the country of origin. The poorer this situation, the sooner it is assumed that the claimant runs a risk, the less the claimant has to 'prove' and the sooner the onus shifts to the State party. If the human rights situation is not

---

108 Bruin & Reneman 2006, p. 90.
109 ComAT, *S.L. v. Sweden*, 11 May 2001, No. 150/1999.
110 *Ibidem*, para. 6.4.
111 ComAT, *F.F.Z. v. Denmark*, 24 May 2002, No. 180/2001.
112 *Ibidem*, para. 12. Both examples mentioned here are also noted by Wouters 2009, p. 487.
113 ComAT, *A.A.C. v. Sweden*, 16 November 2006, No. 227/2003, para. 8.5.

obviously poor, the onus shifts more towards the claimant, which means that more evidence is expected.[114]

4.5.3   Relevant facts and circumstances

Article 3, second paragraph, stipulates that the national authorities shall take into account 'all relevant considerations, including the existence in the State concerned of a consistent pattern of gross, flagrant or mass violations of human rights'. It is clear from this text that the human rights situation in the countries of origin is a 'relevant consideration'. Apart from this, however, the term 'relevant consideration' is not explained any further in the CAT. The preparatory work on the second paragraph shows that the original draft of Article 3 did not contain a provision of this kind. In 1979, the Soviet Union proposed an additional paragraph according to which, in considering whether a danger of torture existed in a given case, special regard should be had to the existence of a situation 'characterized by flagrant and massive violations of human rights brought about when *apartheid*, racial discrimination or genocide, the suppression of national liberation movements, aggression or the occupation of foreign territory are made State policy'.[115] A number of delegations were firmly opposed to an enumeration of this kind, whereas others considered that the enumeration should be further extended by also referring to State policies of colonialism or neo-colonialism. Eventually a compromise was reached which consisted of deleting the enumeration of specific situations while maintaining a reference to situations characterized by a consistent pattern of gross, flagrant or mass violations of human rights.[116]

The term 'all relevant considerations' is not confined to considerations relating to the situation in the country of origin, but also includes information relating to the individual applicant and his or her personal risk.[117] In General Comment No. 1,[118] the term 'all relevant considerations' is explained somewhat further, although slightly different terminology is used. Paragraph 7 stipulates that 'all pertinent information may be introduced by either party to bear on this matter.' Paragraph 8 gives examples of such 'pertinent information'. It stipulates:

---

114 This principle is reflected in a number of decisions of the Committee. See, for example, ComAT, *Hayden v. Sweden*, 16 December 1998, No. 97/1997, in which the Committee considered: 'The Committee is aware of the serious human rights situation in Turkey. Reports from reliable sources suggest that persons suspected of having links with the PKK are frequently tortured in the course of interrogations by law enforcement officers and that this practice is not limited to particular areas of the country. In this context, the Committee further notes that the Government has stated that it shares the view of UNHCR, i.e. that no place of refuge is available within the country for persons who risk being suspected of being active in or sympathizers of the PKK.' See also Ingelse 1999, p. 252, Nowak & McArthur 2008, pp. 190-193, particularly para. 164, and p. 224. See also Wouters 2009, p. 473, who states that the graver the general human rights situation in the country of return as regards a particular group, for example, a specific clan in Somalia or Kurds in Turkey, the more significant the general human rights situation will be in assessing the individual risk.
115 E/CN.4/WG.1/WP.2.
116 Burgers & Danelius 1988, pp. 51, 93-94 and 128 and Nowak & McArthur 2008, pp. 131-146.
117 Nowak & McArthur 2008, p. 228.
118 Committee, General Comment No. 1, 21 November 1997, A/53/44, Annex XI.

'The following information, while not exhaustive, would be pertinent:

(a) Is the State concerned one in which there is evidence of a consistent pattern of gross, flagrant or mass violations of human rights (see art. 3, para. 2)?

(b) Has the author been tortured or maltreated by or at the instigation of or with the consent or acquiescence of a public official or other person acting in an official capacity in the past? If so, was this the recent past?

(c) Is there medical or other independent evidence to support a claim by the author that he/she has been tortured or maltreated in the past? Has the torture had after-effects?

(d) Has the situation referred to in (a) above changed? Has the internal situation in respect of human rights altered?

(e) Has the author engaged in political or other activity within or outside the State concerned which would appear to make him/her particularly vulnerable to the risk of being placed in danger of torture were he/she to be expelled, returned or extradited to the State in question?

(f) Is there any evidence as to the credibility of the author?

(g) Are there factual inconsistencies in the claim of the author? If so, are they relevant?'

4.5.3.1   *Personal facts*

Based on this enumeration, and on the case law of the Committee, a number of relevant personal circumstances of substance may be identified. The focus here is on the facts and circumstances of substance; in separate sections below, attention will be paid to particular issues of credibility and evidence. The list provided below is only illustrative and by no means exhaustive.[119]

A history of detention is a relevant personal fact. So is ethnic background. Both circumstances played an important role in the first decision of the Committee concerning the expulsion of an asylum seeker, *Mutombo v. Switzerland* (1994). Ethnic background also played a major role in a number of cases concerning Turkish Kurds, for example, *Alan v. Switzerland* (1996).[120] Next, a history of torture is of relevance, as appears from numerous decisions.[121] However, in accordance with paragraph 8 of General Comment No. 1, the Committee also critically examines whether the torture took place in the recent past, or in the more remote past. Where a number of years have passed since the torture, it is easily assumed by the Committee that there is no present real, personal and foreseeable risk of torture,[122] sometimes even without

---

119 See for relevant facts and circumstances also Nowak & McArthur 2008, pp. 171-177, and Wouters 2009, pp. 462-475.

120 ComAT, *Mutombo v. Switzerland*, 27 April 1994, No. 013/1993, para. 9.4; ComAT, *Alan v. Switzerland*, 8 May 1996, No. 021/1995, para. 11.3.

121 See, for example, the following early decisions: ComAT, *Khan v. Canada*, 15 November 1994, No. 015/1994, para. 12.3; *Alan v. Switzerland*, 8 May 1996, No. 021/1995, para. 11.3; *Kisoki v. Sweden*, 8 May 1996, No. 041/1996, para. 9.3.

122 See, for example, ComAT, *T.M. v. Sweden*, 18 November 2003, No. 228/2003, para. 7.3. In this case, the Committee also took into account that a change in the situation in the country of origin, Bangladesh, had taken place, being that the complainant's political party now participated in the government. See also ComAT, *S.G. v. the Netherlands*, 12 May 2004, No. 135/1999, para. 6.4. The Committee found it relevant that since the past torture of the Turkish applicant, nine years had passed.

→

providing a reason (for example, by referring to an improved human rights situation in the country of origin) why the past torture can no longer indicate a risk of future subjection to torture. For example, in *H.A.D. v. Switzerland* (2000), the Committee only noted that, in view of the fact that fifteen years had passed since the author's detention and ill-treatment, there was no current risk to the author, without explicitly discussing the present situation in Turkey and the question of whether, and why, the past torture could or could no longer indicate a risk of future subjection to torture.[123]

Political or other activity making the claimant vulnerable is an important personal fact. In particular, the level, type and scale of these activities are taken into account. For example, in *Khan v. Canada* (1994), the Committee found it important that the claimant was the local leader of the Baltistan Student Federation.[124] Such activities may include *sur place* activities (activities against the regime in the country of origin, performed in the country of refuge). In *Kisoki v. Sweden* (1996), a combination of political activities in the country of origin and *sur place* activities played an important role: the claimant had been an active member of the opposition party UDPS in the Democratic Republic of the Congo (DRC, then Zaire) and continued her activities for the UDPS in Sweden. Another example of a case in which *sur place* activities played an important role is *Aemei v. Switzerland* (1997); in this case, too, a combination of political oppositional activities in Iran and Switzerland played an important role.[125] Also relevant is whether or not it is plausible that the authorities in the country of origin have knowledge of *sur place* activities. In *S.G. v. the Netherlands* (2004), the Committee noted that it had not been established that the Turkish authorities were aware of the author's participation in the occupation of the Greek ambassador's residence in The Hague in 1999. Based on this, and on the fact that the author's problems in Turkey had occurred a long time previously (nine years), the Committee concluded that there was no Article 3-danger.[126] To the contrary, in *Jahani v. Switzerland* (2011), the Committee noted that the Iranian complainant had participated in demonstrations organised by the Democratic Association for Refugees and in radio broadcasts where he had expressed his political opinions against the Iranian regime, and that he had written several articles published in Kanoun magazine, in which his name and telephone number had been published. Under these circumstances, the Committee considered that the complainant's name could have been identified by the Iranian authorities.[127]

Desertion from the army is another relevant personal circumstance.[128] The fact that the author is, or is not, being sought by the authorities in the country of origin is also an important personal factor. For example, in *X. v. the Netherlands* (1996), the

---

Another example is ComAT, *Ruben David v. Sweden*, 2 May 2005, No. 220/2002, in which the Committee noted that seven years had passed since the torture took place.

123 ComAT, *H.A.D. v. Switzerland*, 10 May 2000, No. 126/1999, paras. 8.5, 8.6.

124 ComAT, *Khan v. Canada*, 15 November 1994, No. 015/1994, para. 12.3.

125 ComAT, *Kisoki v. Sweden*, 8 May 1996, No. 041/1996, para. 9.4; ComAT, *Aemei v. Switzerland*, 9 May 1997, No. 034/1995, paras. 9.6 and 9.7. See for another example in which *sur place* activities played an important role also ComAT, *A.F. v. Sweden*, 8 May 1998, No. 089/1997, paras. 2.7, 6.5.

126 ComAT, *S.G. v. the Netherlands*, 12 May 2004, No. 135/1999, para. 6.4.

127 ComAT, *Jahani v. Switzerland*, 23 May 2011, No. 357/2008, para. 9.9.

128 See, for example, ComAT, *Mutombo v. Switzerland*, 27 April 1994, No. 013/1993, para. 9.4.

Committee noted that the author had been detained twice and that he had been maltreated during his first detention; however, as the periods of detention had been short, the author had not claimed to be an active political opponent and there were no indications that he was currently being sought by the authorities, the Committee concluded that there was no Article 3-risk.[129] To the contrary, in *Iya v. Switzerland* (2007), the case of a journalist who had published articles on human rights violations in the DRC, the Committee based its conclusion that an Article 3-risk existed on the fact that the complainant was being sought, in combination with his political activities and his recent detention in the DRC.[130]

Recognition as a refugee by a State party is another example of a relevant personal fact. In *Pelit v. Azerbaijan* (2007), the Committee attached importance to the fact that the Turkish Kurdish complainant had been granted refugee status in Germany in 1998 and that this status was still valid when Azerbaijan extradited her to Turkey.[131]

In some cases the author's family background plays an important role. In the case of *A.F. v. Sweden* (1998), the Iranian claimant belonged to a politically active family. His father had become a local leader for the Tudeh party in 1963 and had been imprisoned and persecuted for his political activities. Based on this and on the personal oppositional political activities of the author himself, his history of detention and torture, the Committee concluded that expulsion would expose him to a danger of torture.[132]

From the Committee's case law, it is clear that it is generally a combination of personal circumstances which, in the light of the general human rights situation in the country of origin, leads the Committee to the conclusion that expulsion would amount to a violation of Article 3. For example, in *Uttam Mondal v. Sweden* (2011), it was the combination of the complainant's political activities in the past, the findings in submitted medical reports confirming past torture, his religion and his homosexuality, seen in the light of the general deterioration of the human rights situation in Bangladesh that made the Committee assume an Article 3-danger.[133]

4.5.3.2   *Facts and circumstances concerning the situation in country of origin*

The second paragraph of Article 3 stipulates that for the purpose of determining whether there are grounds for believing that there is an Article 3-danger, the competent authorities shall take into account all relevant considerations, including, where applicable, the existence in the country of origin of a consistent pattern of gross, flagrant or mass violations of human rights. In line with this, General Comment No. 1 lists as relevant considerations in paragraph 8:

> '(a) Is the State concerned one in which there is evidence of a consistent pattern of gross, flagrant or mass violations of human rights (see art. 3, para. 2)?

---

129 ComAT, *X. v. the Netherlands*, 8 May 1996, No. 036/1995, para. 8.
130 ComAT, *Iya v. Switzerland*, 16 November 2007, No. 299/2006, paras. 2.5, 6.5, 6.8.
131 ComAT, *Pelit v. Azerbaijan*, 1 May 2007, No. 281/2005, para. 11.
132 ComAT, *A.F. v. Sweden*, 8 May 1998, No. 089/1997, paras. 2.1-2.5, para. 6.5.
133 ComAT, *Uttam Mondal v. Sweden*, 23 May 2011, No. 338/2008, paras. 7.2, 7.3, 7.7.

(d) Has the situation referred to in (a) above changed? Has the internal situation in respect of human rights altered?

The general human rights situation is supplementary to the personal facts and circumstances.[134] Even the existence of a consistent pattern of gross, flagrant or mass violations of human rights in a country cannot as such constitute a sufficient ground for determining that a person would be in danger of being subjected to torture upon return.[135]

Logically, developments and changes in the human rights situation in the country of origin are relevant. In a number of cases, concerning mainly Sri Lankan and Bangladeshi complainants, the Committee has attached much weight to information about the on-going peace process (and, in the Sri Lankan cases, to the return of large numbers of Tamils).[136]

Another relevant factor concerning the situation in the country of origin is the risk of expulsion to a third country: indirect *refoulement*. In *Korban v. Sweden* (1998), the Swedish authorities ordered the author's expulsion to Jordan. Based on information from the UNHCR and other sources, submitted by the parties, the Committee determined that it could not be excluded that the author would be deported to Iraq from Jordan. It found that substantial grounds existed for believing that the author would be in danger of being subjected to torture if returned to Iraq.[137]

A final example of a relevant fact is whether the country of origin is or is not a State party to the CAT. Where the country of origin is not a State party, there is no legal possibility of applying to the Committee for protection.[138] However, the fact that a State is party to the CAT does not always work to the detriment of the claimant: in *Alan v. Switzerland* (1996) the Committee concluded that there had been an Article 3-risk, in spite of Turkey being a party to the CAT; it noted that the practice of torture was still systematic in Turkey.[139] Again, the list of circumstances concerning the country of origin provided here is only illustrative and by no means exhaustive.[140]

---

134 Wouters 2009.

135 This is a standard consideration in the case law of the Committee, featuring in the very first case, *Mutombo v. Switzerland*, 27 April 1994, No. 013/1993, para. 9.3, and in almost all the subsequent decisions under Article 3 concerning the expulsion of asylum seekers. The Committee has a number of times concluded that there is a consistent pattern of gross, flagrant or mass violations of human rights in countries of origin. See ComAT, *Mutombo v. Switzerland*, 27 April 1994, No. 13/1993, para. 9.5 (Zaire, nowadays the Democratic Republic of the Congo); ComAT, *Elmi v. Australia,* 25 May 1999, No. 120/1998, para. 6.6 (Somalia); ComAT, *A.S. v. Sweden,*15 February 2001, No. 149/1999, para. 8.7 (Iran).

136 See, for example, ComAT, *U.S. v. Finland*, 1 May 2003, No. 197/2002, para. 7.7 (a Sri Lankan case); ComAT, *T.M. v. Sweden*, 18 November 2003, No. 228/2003, para. 7.3; ComAT, *M.N. v. Switzerland*, 17 November 2006, No. 259/2004 (a Bangladeshi case).

137 ComAT, *Korban v. Sweden*, 16 November 1998, No. 088/1997, paras. 6.4, 6.5.

138 This consideration is used in many decisions. To mention just afew examples: ComAT, *Mutombo v. Switzerland*, 27 April 1994, No. 13/1993, para. 9.6; ComAT, *Khan v. Canada*, 15 November 1994, No. 015/199, para. 12.5.

139 ComAT, *Alan v. Switzerland*, 8 May 1996, No. 021/1995, para. 11.5.

140 See, again, Nowak & McArthur 2008, pp. 171-177, Wouters 2009, pp. 469-472.

The personal facts are generally assessed in the light of the general human rights situation in the country of origin. The general human rights situation is of supplementary importance, strengthening or weakening the individual claim for protection: the graver the general human rights situation in the country of origin, the more significant this situation will be in assessing the risk.[141]

4.5.4   Required degree of individual risk

It is a constant consideration in the case law of the Committee that

> 'The aim of the determination (...) is to establish whether the individual concerned would be personally at risk of being subjected to torture in the country to which he would return. It follows that the existence of a consistent pattern of gross, flagrant or mass violations of human rights in a country does not as such constitute a sufficient ground for determining that a person would be in danger of being subjected to torture upon his return to that country; additional grounds must exist that indicate that the individual concerned would be personally at risk. Similarly, the absence of a consistent pattern of gross violations of human rights does not mean that a person cannot be considered to be in danger of being subjected to torture in his specific circumstances.'[142]

This general consideration stresses twice that a personal risk needs to be established, indicating that the Committee strictly requires that an applicant is singled out.

In Chapter 5 on the ECHR we will see that the ECtHR distinguishes between three categories of cases: 1) cases of extreme general violence, where an Article 3-risk is assumed for everyone returning to the particular country; 2) cases of group violence; and 3) individual risk cases. In the third category it is required that an individual risk is established, in other words, that the individual concerned has been singled out. So far the Committee has not developed its position on the question of the required degree of individual risk in the same way as the ECtHR has done. Nevertheless, there are good reasons for assuming that the Committee, just like the HRC (see chapter 3, section 3.5.4), has taken significant steps towards incorporating the

---

141   This principle is reflected in a number of decisions of the Committee. See, for example, ComAT, *Hayden v. Sweden*, 16 December 1998, No. 97/1997, in which the Committee considered: 'The Committee is aware of the serious human rights situation in Turkey. Reports from reliable sources suggest that persons suspected of having links with the PKK are frequently tortured in the course of interrogations by law enforcement officers and that this practice is not limited to particular areas of the country. In this context, the Committee further notes that the Government has stated that it shares the view of UNHCR, i.e. that no place of refuge is available within the country for persons who risk being suspected of being active in or sympathizers of the PKK.' See also Ingelse 1999, p. 252, Nowak & McArthur 2008, pp. 190-193, particularly para. 164, and p. 224, Wouters 2009, p. 473.

142   This consideration is included in almost all the Committee's decisions under Article 3 concerning the expulsion of asylum seekers, from the very first case of *Mutombo v. Switzerland*, 27 April 1994, No. 13/1993, para. 9.3, up to and including the most recent decisions of the Committee included in this research, *Uttam Mondal v. Sweden*, 23 May 2011, No. 338/2008, para. 7.3, and *Bakatu-Bia v. Sweden*, 3 June 2011, No. 379/2009, para. 10.3.

lines of theory developed by the ECtHR on situations of group violence.[143] This relaxation of the individualisation requirement started perhaps with the case of *Elmi v. Australia* (1999), in which the Committee based the risk assessment primarily on the human rights situation in Somalia and the fact that the claimant belonged to the small unprotected clan of the Shikal, so that the assessment came close to acceptance of the claim based on membership of a 'high risk' group. However, two personal facts also played a role in this case, being that the complainant's family had been targeted and the wide publicity surrounding the case.[144] In the case of *S.S. and S.A. v. the Netherlands* (2001), the Committee considered that

> 'The likelihood of torture of Tamils in Colombo who belong to a high risk group is not so great that the group as a whole runs a substantial risk of being so exposed.'[145]

It emerges from this decision that the Committee deemed it possible, in theory, that a claim could be based solely on the fact of belonging to a 'high risk group'. In *Njamba v. Sweden* (2010),[146] the Committee prohibited Sweden from returning a woman to the Democratic Republic of the Congo (DRC) due to the general high threat of (sexual) violence against women in that country. It noted that a number of factual issues of the case were in dispute between the parties, but it left this dispute aside, focusing instead on the future risk and pointing to the extremely high rate of violence against women across the country. In other words, the Committee left the complainant's individual account of past events for what is was, and focused instead on the general risk to women. It considered as follows:

> 'The Committee notes that the State party itself acknowledges that sexual violence occurs in Equateur Province, to a larger extent in rural villages (para. 9.2). It notes that since the State party's last response of 19 March 2010, relating to the general human rights situation in the Democratic Republic of the Congo, a second joint report from seven United Nations experts on the situation in the Democratic Republic of the Congo was published, which refers to alarming levels of violence against women across the country and concludes that, "Violence against women, in particular rape and gang rape committed by men with guns and civilians, remains a serious concern, including in areas not affected by armed conflict." In addition, a second report of the United Nations High Commissioner for Human Rights on the situation of human rights and the activities of her Office in the Democratic Republic of the Congo as well as other UN reports, also refers to the alarming number of cases of sexual violence throughout the country, confirming that these cases are not limited to areas of armed conflict but are happening throughout the country. (…) In reviewing this information, the Committee is reminded of its General Comment no. 2 on article 2, in which it recalled that the failure, "to exercise due diligence to intervene to stop, sanction and provide remedies to victims of torture facilitates and enables non-State actors to commit acts impermissible under the Convention with impunity…". Thus, in light of all of the abovementioned information, the Committee considers

---

143 Kjaerum 2010, pp. 28-29.
144 ComAT, *Elmi v. Australia*, 25 May 1999, No. 120/1998, paras. 6.6 and 6.7.
145 ComAT, *S.S. and S.A. v. the Netherlands*, 11 May 2001, No. 142/1999, para. 6.6.
146 ComAT, *Njamba v. Sweden*, 14 May 2010, No. 322/2007.

that the conflict situation in the Democratic Republic of the Congo, as attested to in all recent United Nation reports, makes it impossible for the Committee to identify particular areas of the country which could be considered safe for the complainants in their current and evolving situation. Accordingly, the Committee finds that, on a balance of all of the factors in this particular case and assessing the legal consequences aligned to these factors, substantial grounds exist for believing that the complainants are in danger of being subjected to torture if returned to the Democratic Republic of the Congo.'[147]

The Committee adopted the same approach in the case of *Bakatu-Bia v. Sweden* (2011).[148] Both cases concerned complainants from the Democratic Republic of the Congo (DRC). Just as in *Njamba v. Sweden* (2010), in *Bakatu-Bia v. Sweden* (2011), there was a dispute between the parties about the past facts stated by the complainant. Again, the Committee left this dispute for what it was, and focused instead on the extremely high rate of violence against women across the country.[149] Kjaerum (2010) calls this relaxation of the individualisation requirement in the Committee's case law a big step forward in the protection of individuals at risk, both in relation to the substantive scope of protection and the possibility to prove that a threat exists.[150] At the end of this section, it is useful to refer once again to the principle of the gradual scale (see above section 4.5.2). According to this principle, the graver the general human rights situation in the country of origin, the more significant this situation will be in assessing the risk and the sooner it is assumed that the claimant runs a risk. In such situations, the less the claimant has to 'prove', the sooner the onus shifts to the State party. If the human rights situation is not obviously poor, the onus shifts more towards the claimant, which means that more individual circumstances and more individual evidence are expected.[151] In line with this principle, it may be argued that the more a certain group or category of persons is targeted, the less individual facts and circumstances, including evidence thereof, are required.

4.5.5 Credibility assessment

General Comment No. 1 stipulates in paragraph 9:

'Bearing in mind that the Committee against Torture is not an appellate, a quasi-judicial or an administrative body, but rather a monitoring body created by the States parties themselves with declaratory powers only, it follows that:

(a) Considerable weight will be given, in exercising the Committee's jurisdiction pursuant to article 3 of the Convention, to findings of fact that are made by organs of the State party concerned; but

---

147 *Ibidem*, paras. 9.5 and 9.6.
148 ComAT, *Bakatu-Bia v. Sweden*, 3 June 2011, No. 379/2009.
149 *Ibidem*, paras. 10.6 – 10.8.
150 Kjaerum 2010, pp. 27-29
151 Ingelse 1999, p. 252, Nowak & McArthur 2008, pp. 190-193, particularly para. 164, and p. 224. See also Wouters 2009, p. 473, who states that the graver the general human rights situation in the country of return as regards a particular group, for example, a specific clan in Somalia or Kurds in Turkey, the more significant the general human rights situation will be in assessing the individual risk.

(b) The Committee is not bound by such findings and instead has the power, provided by article 22, paragraph 4, of the Convention, of free assessment of the facts based upon the full set of circumstances in every case.'

It follows from this paragraph that, depending on the particular case before it, the Committee has the possibility and freedom to choose either of two approaches: reliance on the respondent State party's determination of the facts, including the credibility assessment, or an independent determination of the facts and evaluation of the evidence on its own account. The Committee's case law demonstrates, however, that, more than the ECtHR does, the Committee stresses its subsidiary role and considers that the determination of the facts and the assessment of evidence, including the assessment of credibility, is primarily a matter for the authorities of the States parties. In this respect the Committee strongly resembles the HRC (see Chapter 3, section 3.3.1). In a number of decisions, the Committee clearly expressed this preference for reliance on the respondent State party's determination of the facts. For example, in *A.R. v. Netherlands* (2003) it considered as follows:

'The Committee recalls its jurisprudence to the effect that it is not an appellate, quasi-judicial or administrative body. Consistent with its General Comment, whilst the Committee has the power of free assessment of the facts arising in the circumstances of each case, it must give considerable weight to findings of fact made by the organs of the State party.'[152]

The reasons for the Committee's reluctance to engage in determination of the facts and evaluation of the presented evidence were mentioned above in section 4.2.2.2.

In several other – early and later – cases, the Committee made a fully independent assessment of the facts, including the claimant's credibility, on its own account. An early example is *Khan v. Canada* (1994), in which the Committee accepted as credible the facts and evidence adduced by the claimant, and considered that even if there were some doubts about the facts, it should ensure that the complainant's security was not endangered.[153] A more recent example is *Heidar v. Sweden* (2002), in which case the Committee found the author's statements incredible on the basis of numerous inconsistencies, late and vague statements about past torture, and, finally, the fact that the presented medical evidence did not state the presence of a post-traumatic stress disorder.[154] Another example is *Dadar v. Canada* (2005), in which the Committee made the following relevant consideration:

The Committee notes that the complainant's arguments and his evidence to support them have been considered by the State party's authorities. It also notes the State party's observation that the Committee is not a fourth instance. While the Committee gives considerable weight to findings of fact made by the organs of the State party, it has the power of free assessment of the facts arising in the circumstances of each case. In the present case, it notes that the

---

152   ComAT, *A.R. v. Netherlands*, 21 November 2003, No. 203/2002, para. 7.6. For a similar consideration, see ComAT, *N.Z.S. v. Sweden*, 29 November 2006, No. 277/2005, para. 8.6.
153   ComAT, *Khan v. Canada*, 15 November 1994, No. 015/1994, paras. 12.3-12.6.
154   ComAT, *Heidar v. Sweden*, 19 November 2002, No. 204/2002, para.6.3.

Canadian authorities made an assessment of the risks that the complainant might face if he was returned and concluded that he would be of limited interest to the Iranian authorities. However, the same authorities did not exclude that their assessment proved to be incorrect and that the complainant might indeed be tortured. In that case, they concluded that their finding regarding the fact that the complainant presented a danger to the Canadian citizens should prevail over the risk of torture and that the complainant should be expelled from Canada. The Committee recalls that the prohibition enshrined in article 3 of the Convention is an absolute one. Accordingly, the argument submitted by the State party that the Committee is not a fourth instance cannot prevail, and the Committee cannot conclude that the State party's review of the case was fully satisfactory from the perspective of the Convention.[155]

The remaining question is when the Committee chooses one of the two approaches: reliance on the respondent State's credibility assessment or independent assessment of the facts, including the claimant's credibility, on its own account? In *J.A.M.O. et al v. Canada* (2008), the Committee explained to a certain extent when it considered it necessary to make an independent determination of the facts and evaluation of the evidence on its own account:

'The Committee (…) recalls its general comment, which states that considerable weight will be given to findings of fact that are made by organs of the State party; however, the Committee is not bound by such findings and instead has the power, provided by article 22, paragraph 4, of the Convention, of free assessment of the facts based upon the full set of circumstances in every case. In particular, the Committee must assess the facts and evidence in a given case, once it has been ascertained that the manner in which the evidence was evaluated was clearly arbitrary or amounted to a denial of justice, and that domestic courts clearly violated their obligations of impartiality. In the case under consideration, the evidence before the Committee does not show the examination by the State party of the allegations of the complainant to have been marred by any such irregularities.'[156]

No case law has been found in which the Committee, under Article 3, further explains what is meant by a 'clearly arbitrary evaluation of evidence', a 'denial of justice', or a 'clear violation of obligations of impartiality'. Nor has any case law under Article 3 been found in which the Committee explicitly concluded that one of these three things, or a combination thereof, had occurred (see also section 4.2.2.3). Finally, no decisions have been found in which the Committee explains in a more detailed way why it has opted, in a particular case, for a marginal or, instead, intense scrutiny. What is worse, the Committee's assessment is in some decisions truly confusing as far as the intensity of scrutiny is concerned. In its decision in *S.S. and S.A. v. the Netherlands* (2001), the Committee marginally assessed the claim for protection based on the complainants' Tamil ethnicity, whereas it conducted a full examination of the individual facts and circumstances.[157] To conclude, just like the HRC, the Committee has,

---

155 ComAT, *Dadar v. Canada*, 5 December 2005, No. 258/2004, para. 8.8.

156 ComAT, *J.A.M.O. et al v. Canada*, 15 May 2008, No. 293/2006, para. 10.5

157 ComAT, *S.S. and S.A. v. the Netherlands*, 11 May 2001, No. 1421999, paras. 6.6 and 6.7.

so far, not developed an elaborate doctrinal position on the issue of the intensity of the scrutiny it applies as an international treaty supervisor.

From the cases in which the Committee did make a fully independent assessment of the facts, including the claimant's credibility, we may infer that two circumstances in particular trigger the Committee to proceed to an independent determination of the facts, including the credibility of the claimant's statements. A first trigger is that in the national proceedings the absolute nature of Article 3 CAT was not respected, and, instead, a weighing of national security considerations against the Article 3-danger occurred.[158] This happened in *Dadar v. Canada* (2005): the primary stance of the State party's authorities was that the account was incredible; their secondary position was that, if the stated facts were assumed to be true, national security considerations outweighed the alleged Article 3-risk.[159]

A second trigger is that the State party's authorities have not taken into consideration important facts or evidence. This happened in *C.T. and K.M. v. Sweden* (2007). In this case, the Committee considered that the State party's authorities had in fact not taken into account statements on past torture and corroborating medical evidence. It then proceeded to its own independent determination of the facts.[160]

When it is decided that the Committee proceeds to an independent fresh assessment of the credibility, how does it go about this and which principles does it follow?

In a significant number of (mainly early) decisions, the Committee laid down the important principle that some doubts as to the stated facts do not necessarily prevent it from establishing that an Article 3-danger exists. In this respect, it has repeatedly considered as follows (sometimes with a slight change in terminology, see note):

> 'Even if there could be some doubts about the facts as adduced by the author, it must ensure that his security is not endangered.'[161]

Furthermore, the Committee has made clear that 'general veracity' is required.[162] To assume 'general veracity', a number of requirements must be met.

First, the claim must be sufficiently detailed.[163] Second, the claim must be accurate. General veracity does not require complete accuracy and consistency of every

---

158 See for the same conclusion about the reasons for the Committee to proceed to an independent determination of the facts: Wouters 2009, p. 492.

159 ComAT, *Dadar v. Canada*, 5 December 2005, No. 258/2004; see para. 8.8.

160 ComAT, *C.T. and K.M.v. Sweden*, 22 January 2007, No. 279/2005.

161 ComAT, *Mutombo v. Switzerland*, 15 November 1994, No. 015/1994, para. 9.2; ComAT, *Khan v. Canada*, 15 November 1994, No. 015/1994, para. 12.3; *Aemei v. Switzerland,* 9 May 1997, No. 034/1995, para. 9.6; ComAT, *H.D. v. Switzerland*, 30 April 1999, No. 112/1998, para. 6.4, where the Committee used different words and stated that 'even in the presence of lingering doubts as to the truthfulness of the facts presented by the author of a communication, it must satisfy itself that the applicant's security will not be jeopardized'; ComAT, *M.S.P. v. Australia,*30 April 2002, No. 138/1999, para. 7.3.

162 The term 'general veracity' features in a number of decisions. See, for example, ComAT, *Alan v. Switzerland*, 8 May 1996, No. 021/1995, para. 11.3; ComAT, *Kisoki v. Sweden*, 8 May 1996, No. 041/1996, para. 9.3; ComAT, *Tala v. Sweden*, 15 November 1996, No. 043/1996, para. 10.3; ComAT, *Haydin v. Sweden*, 20 November 1998, No. 101/1997, para. 6.7.

163 See, for example, ComAT, *A.S. v. Sweden*, 15 February 2001, No. 149/1999, para. 8.6.

single aspect and detail of the claim, but requires the core of the story, the basic story, to be plausible. The Committee decides on a case by case basis when contradictions and inconsistencies undermine the 'general veracity'. Much depends on whether good explanations for the inconsistencies are given. An important explanation for inconsistencies is sound and conclusive medical evidence confirming past torture and stating that the author suffers from post-traumatic stress disorder as a result. In a significant number of (mostly early) decisions, the Committee explained and excused inconsistencies by referring to this past torture. For example, in *I.A.O. v. Sweden* (1998), it stated that

> 'It has noted the medical evidence provided by the author and, on that basis, is of the opinion
> that there is a firm reason to believe that the author has been tortured in the past. In this con-
> text, the Committee observes that the author suffers from a post-traumatic stress disorder, and
> that this has to be taken into account when assessing the author's presentation of the facts.
> The Committee is therefore of the opinion that the inconsistencies as exist in the author's
> story do not raise doubts as to the general veracity of his claim that he was detained and tor-
> tured.'[164]

In similar vein, the Committee has made clear that, where past torture of the claimant may be assumed on the basis of medical evidence, gaps or vague points do not necessarily affect the veracity of the claim.[165] The Committee has, however, not always been consistent in applying this principle. In a number of cases – for unknown reasons and contrary to its earlier developed line – it did not accept presented medical evidence to explain away inconsistencies. More will be said about this in the separate section on the appreciation and weighing of evidence (section 4.5.7 below).

Other explanations for inconsistencies can be difficulties in translation, certain procedural circumstances, and the fact that much time has passed by between the application for protection and the time of the assessment.[166]

Third, the Committee has made clear that, to assume general veracity of the claim, the claim, particularly its core aspects, must be corroborated by evidence other than the complainant's statements. The absence of corroborative evidence supporting the core aspects of the claim may negatively affect the veracity of the claim. This is particularly true where there are also inconsistencies in the claim.[167] At the same time, though, the Committee has made clear that not all the stated facts have to be corroborated by supporting evidence:

---

164 ComAT, *I.A.O. v. Sweden*, 6 May 1998, No. 065/1997, para. 14.3.
165 ComAT, *Falcon Rios v. Canada*, 23 November 2004, No. 133/1999, para. 8.5.
166 See, for example, ComAT, *V.X.N. and H.N. v. Sweden*, 2 September 2000, Nos. 130 and 131/1999, paras. 9.4-9.6.
167 See, for example, ComAT, *G.T. v. Switzerland*, 2 May 2000, No. 137/1999, paras. 6.5-6.8; ComAT, *N.M. v. Switzerland*, 9 May 2000, No. 116/1998, paras. 6.5, 6.6, 6.7.

'It is not necessary that all the facts invoked by the author should be proved; it is sufficient that the Committee should consider them to be sufficiently substantiated and reliable.'[168]

Fourth, the claim must be consistent with country information.[169]

Fifth, the claim must be consistent throughout the proceedings; serious changes in statements in the course of the proceedings may make these statements incredible.[170] However, in a number of early cases the Committee accepted significant changes in the complainant's statements, referring to the complainant's 'logical explanations of reasons' for having made such changes. For example, in the case of *Ayas v. Sweden* (1998),[171] the author stated in the first national asylum proceedings that his family and friends had been involved in the activities of the PKK. He did not mention that he himself had been an active PKK member. After the dismissal of his first application, he lodged a fresh application and disclosed for the first time that he himself had actively supported the PKK. He explained that his relatives had strongly advised him not to reveal any personal connection with it because of the risk of being considered a 'terrorist' by the Swedish authorities. In these second asylum proceedings, the author also submitted the verdict of a military court which showed that in 1993 he had been sentenced *in absentia* to five years' imprisonment for his activities and affiliation with the PKK.[172] In third asylum proceedings, he submitted medical evidence in support of statements of past torture.[173] Accepting the change, the Committee considered as follows:

'It is not in dispute that the author comes from a politically active family. Moreover, the Committee considers the explanations regarding his own political activities as credible and consistent with the findings of the medical reports according to which he suffers from post-traumatic stress syndrome and his scars are in conformity with the alleged causes. Although the author changed his first version of the facts he gave a logical explanation of his reasons for having done so. Hence, the Committee has not found inconsistencies that would challenge the general veracity of his claim.'[174]

In the case of *A. v. the Netherlands* (1998), the Committee accepted even more striking changes in the author's statements, including lies about identity and nationality in the first asylum procedure. Persuasive medical evidence, the failure to have a physician

---

168 ComAT, *Aemei v. Switzerland*, 9 May 1997, No. 34/1995, para. 9.6; ComAT, *H.D. v. Switzerland*, 30 April 1999, No. 112/1998, para. 6.4; ComAT, *M.S.P. v. Australia*, 30 April 2002, No. 138/1999, para. 7.3. This case is also discussed by Ingelse in his work of 1999, Chapter 10, pp. 246-267.

169 See, for example, ComAT, *Kisoki v. Sweden*, 8 May 1996, No. 041/1996, para. 9.5; ComAT, *Tala v. Sweden*, 15 November 1996, No. 043/1996, para. 10.4; ComAT, *A.S. v. Sweden*, 15 February 2001, No. 149/1999, para. 8.7; ComAT, *Falcon Rios v. Canada*, 23 November 2004, No. 133/1999, para. 8.3; ComAT, *Njamba v. Sweden*, 14 May 2010, No. 322/2007, para. 9.5; ComAT, *Chahin v. Sweden*, 30 May 2011, No. 310/2007, para. 9.4.

170 ComAT, General Comment No. 1, para. 8, sub f and sub g.

171 ComAT, *Ayas v. Sweden*, 12 November 1998, No. 097/1997.

172 *Ibidem*, paras. 2.1 and 2.6.

173 *Ibidem*, para. 2.8.

174 *Ibidem, Ayas v. Sweden*, 12 November 1998, No. 097/1997, para. 6.5.

examine the author during the national proceedings, and the very poor human rights situation in Tunisia, in particular the difficult position of persons associated with the Al-Nahdha movement, all seem to have played an important role in the Committee's conclusions in this case.[175]

Sixth, all facts and evidence must be brought forward as early as possible. Late submission of statements and late presentation of evidence – for example, after an asylum application has been rejected, or in the course of repeat proceedings –may negatively affect the general veracity of the claim, particularly when no sound reasons for this are given.[176] It seems that in the earlier case law the Committee followed a more lenient line in this respect and did not perceive the late presentation of certain facts and supportive evidence as fatal to the veracity of the claim.[177] More about this will be said below in section 4.5.10 on time limits for the presentation of statements and evidence. The list of factors mentioned here as determining credibility is by no means as exhaustive. It does, however, provide an impression of the factors taken into account by the Committee when assessing the credibility of the claimant's story.[178]

4.5.6 *Admission of evidence, possible types and sources of evidence, minimum quantity and quality of evidence*

4.5.6.1 *Admission of evidence*

General Comment No. 1 states in paragraph 7 that the parties to the case may introduce all pertinent information to bear on the question of whether there are substantial grounds for believing that there is a personal and present danger of torture.[179] It is a standard consideration in the Committee's decisions under Article 3 that

'The Committee must decide, pursuant to paragraph 1 of Article 3, whether there are substantial grounds for believing that the complainant would be in danger of being subject to torture. In reaching this conclusion, the Committee must take into account all relevant considerations, pursuant to paragraph 2 of Article 3, including the existence of a consistent pattern of gross, flagrant or mass violations of human rights.'[180]

---

175 See, for example, ComAT, *A. v. Netherlands*, 13 November 1998, No. 91/1997; this case is also discussed by Tiemersma in her article 'Medical information in the asylum procedure', *NAV* 2006, No. 1.

176 See, for example, ComAT, *X.Y. v. Switzerland*, 15 May 2001, No. 128/1999, para. 8.5.

177 Examples of early cases in which the Committee did not find late presentation of statements or evidence problematic are ComAT, *Khan v. Canada*, 15 November 1994, No. 015/1994 (presentation of statements and evidence after refusal of asylum claim and commencement of deportation proceedings, the Committee notes that this behaviour is not uncommon for torture victims); ComAT, *Kisoki v. Sweden*, 8 May 1996, No. 041/1996 (evidence submitted during second national asylum application); ComAT, *Tala v. Sweden*, 15 November 1996, No. 043/1996 (statements on past torture during national appeal stage, the Committee does not say anything about this and obviously does not see this as problematic).

178 See on the Committee's credibility assessment also Wouters 2009, pp. 475-480.

179 ComAT, General Comment No. 1, 21 November 1997, A/53/44, Annex XI, para. 7.

180 This standard consideration features in all the Committee's decisions on the merits, from the first case of ComAT, *Mutombo v. Switzerland*, 27 April 1994, No. 13/1993, up to and including the last

$\rightarrow$

Article 118, paragraph 1, of the Rules of Procedure, states that

> 'The Committee shall consider the complaint in the light of all information made available to it by or on behalf of the complainant and by the State party concerned and shall formulate its findings thereon.'[181]

The Committee has reiterated this principle in a number of decisions:

> 'The Committee has considered the communication in the light of all the information made available to it by the parties concerned, in accordance with Article 22, paragraph 4, of the Convention.'[182]

The terminology used indicates that it is open to the Committee to consider evidence from whatever source and then decide as to its relevance and probative value. The system of admission of evidence is open, flexible and liberal. The Committee's approach in this respect is the same as the one applied by the UNHCR (see chapter 2, section 2.4.6.1), the HRC (see chapter 3, section 3.5.6) and the ECtHR (see chapter 5, section 5.6.6.1).[183]

4.5.6.2   *Means and sources of evidence*

To give an impression of what kind of materials can be submitted by the parties as evidence, some examples of evidentiary materials admitted by the Committee are briefly mentioned here. A very prominent feature of the Committee's case law, particularly the earlier decisions, is the significance attached to medical reports corroborating statements on past torture and the effects of past torture.[184] Medical evidence is also explicitly mentioned in General Comment No. 1, paragraph 8, which qualifies as 'pertinent information' medical evidence to support a claim by the author that he or she has been tortured or maltreated in the past.[185] Other examples of evidentiary materials are statements made by family members[186] or other persons or

---

decision included in this research, ComAT, *Bakatu-Bia v. Sweden*, 3 June 2011, No. 379/2009, para. 10.3.

181 Article 18, para. 1, of the Rules of Procedure of the Committee against Torture, 21 February 2011. The Rules of Procedure may be found at: un.org/doc/UNDOC/GEN/G11/411/40/PDF/ G1141140/pdf, last visited 15 January 2012.

182 See, for example, ComAT, *Bakatu-Bia v. Sweden*, 3 June 2011, No. 379/2009, para. 10.1.

183 See on the open and flexible system of admission of evidence also McGoldrick 1996, p. 143, who points to the liberal practice of international treaty monitoring bodies and tribunals in the admission of evidence.

184 Examples are ComAT, *Alan v. Switzerland*, 8 May 1996, No. 021/1995, para. 11.3; ComAT, *I.A.O. v. Sweden*, 6 May 1998, No. 065/1997, para. 14.3; ComAT, *Kisoki v. Sweden*, 8 May 1996, No. 041/1996, para. 9.3; ComAT, *Tala v. Sweden*, 15 November 1996, No. 043/1996, para. 10.3; ComAT, *Haydin v. Sweden*, 20 November 1998, No. 101/1997, para. 6.7; ComAT, *E.T.B. v. Denmark*, 30 April 2002, No. 146/1999, para. 10; ComAT, *Karoui v.Sweden*, 8 May 2002, No. 185/2001, para. 10.

185 ComAT, General Comment No. 1, para. 8, 21 November 1997, A/53/44, Annex XI.

186 See, for example, ComAT, *T.A. v. Sweden*, 6 May 2005, No. 226/2003, paras. 5.5 and 7.3, and ComAT, *A.S. v. Sweden*, 15 February 2001, No. 149/1999, para. 84. These cases are discussed in more detail in the next section on appreciation of evidence.

organisations[187] that the claimant is still being sought or is wanted by the authorities of the country of origin. Another important category of evidence is reports drawn up in individual cases by the respondent State's mission or embassy in the particular country of origin.[188] Of course, of special significance are also reports from various sources containing country of origin information, as the individual claim needs to be assessed in the light of the situation in the country of origin. In section 4.5.7 below, more detailed attention will be paid to a number of specific categories of evidentiary materials, being medico-legal reports, embassy reports submitted by the respondent State, statements from family members, and country of origin information.

4.5.6.3   *Minimum quantity and quality of evidence*

How much evidence can reasonably be expected from a claimant is decided on a case by case basis and very much depends on the particularities of the personal account and the other individual features of the case, as well as on the situation in the country of origin. The Committee has not developed hard and fast rules for assessing the sufficiency of the presented evidence. Its case law features a number of decisions in which, apart from the statements of the claimant, no supporting evidence, or only very limited evidentiary materials, were submitted. This led the Committee either to the conclusion that the claim failed to rise to the basic level of substantiation for the purposes of admissibility,[189] or to the conclusion on the merits that an Article 3-risk had not been established.[190] It follows from these cases that it is generally fatal to the case when no corroborative evidence at all is submitted in support of the claim.

The Committee has also made clear that not all the stated facts have to be corroborated by supporting evidence:

> 'It is not necessary that all the facts invoked by the author should be proved; it is sufficient that the Committee should consider them to be sufficiently substantiated and reliable.'[191]

It appears from the case law that 'sufficiently substantiated' still means that all the core aspects or central aspects of the claim are supported by evidence other than the

---

187   See, for example, ComAT, *Karoui v. Sweden*, 25 May 2002, No. 185/2001, in which case the complainant relied on, *inter alia*, a support letter from Amnesty International, Sweden, and an attestation from the chairman of the Al-Nahdha organisation. See also ComAT, *Dadar v. Canada*, 23 November 2005, No. 258/2004, paras. 2.7 and 8.6, in which the Iranian complainant relied on letters from the Military Office of the Shah and the Secretariat of Reza Pahlavi referring to his activities as a member of the monarchist opposition group. The Committee attached much weight to these letters.

188   See, for example, ComAT, *H.D. v. Switzerland*, 30 April 1999, No. 112/1998, paras. 4.3, 6.5; ComAT, *Y.S. v. Switzerland*, 14 November 2000, No. 147/1999, para. 6.6; *S.S.H. v. Switzerland*, 15 November 2005, No. 254/2004, para. 6.5.

189   See, for example, ComAT, *R.T v. Germany*, 24 November 2005, No. 242/2003.

190   See, for example, ComAT, *K.T. v. Switzerland*, 19 November 1999, No. 118/1998, paras. 6.4 and 6.5; ComAT, *G.T. v. Switzerland*, 2 May 2000, No. 137/1999, para. 6.7.

191   See, for example, ComAT, *Aemei v. Switzerland*, 9 May 1997, No. 34/1995, para. 9.6; ComAT, *H.D. v. Switzerland*, 30 April 1999, No. 112/1998, para. 6.4; ComAT, *M.S.P. v. Australia*, 30 April 2002, No. 138/1999, para. 7.3; this case is also discussed by Ingelse in his work of 1999, Chapter 10, pp. 246-267.

complainant's statements. Just like the HRC, the Committee is strict on this, requiring substantial evidence of the basic story: it truly needs a strongly corroborated case to obtain a decision from the Committee in which a violation of Article 3 is established.[192] To illustrate its strict approach, three cases are discussed below in more detail.

In *G.T. v. Switzerland* (2000), the author stated that he had been a very active supporter of the Youth Union of Kurdistan, the youth branch of the PKK, and that as such he had taken part in demonstrations, meetings, the distribution of pamphlets, and that he had also collected money for the cause and helped to recruit new supporters. The Committee found it problematic that the author had not provided any evidence of his membership of, or his activities in, the PKK or the youth branch of the PKK. The absence of such evidence, together with inconsistencies in his claim and the fact that much time had elapsed since his departure from Turkey, led the Committee to the conclusion that no Article 3-risk had been established.[193] In *N.M. v. Switzerland* (2000), the Congolese complainant stated that he had worked in Kinshasa for five years as an employee of the Hyochade Company, which had belonged to Mr Kongolo Mobutu, the son of former president Mobutu. This company had been a cover for plundering the wealth of the country in various ways. Acting on behalf of the regime, the company had also carried out propaganda activities and kept track of members of the political opposition in order to keep them under control. The author's responsibilities had included collecting information on members of the opposition within a particular geographical area and denouncing any subversive activities. He had reported to his supervisors at least every two months and had been generously paid. In addition to his salary, he had received a bonus when he denounced someone and he had enjoyed a range of other privileges. After the rebellion led by Mr Kabila reached Kinshasa in May 1997, soldiers had first arrested the author's father and then the author himself. In the Kokolo military camp he had been accused of treason, extortion and complicity in murder. He had received beatings for denying the charges.[194] In the proceedings before the Committee, the respondent State party expressed serious doubts about the author's professional activities and about the very existence of the Hyochade company, since the author had never been able to produce any documents relating to his work for that company, even though he had been able to obtain a number of other documents and his family on the spot could have helped him find the papers he wanted.[195] Although the Committee did not spend many words on it, it did state that the author had not provided enough evidence to conclude that he would run a real Article 3-risk. Obviously, the Committee agreed with the State party that the author should have presented evidence in support of his work for the Hyochade Company, a central aspect of his account.[196]

---

192 See also Wouters 2009, pp. 480-484, and p. 492, where he states that it requires a strong case to get a decision of the State overruled by the Committee.
193 ComAT, *G.T. v. Switzerland*, 2 May 2000, No. 137/1999, paras. 6.5-6.8.
194 ComAT, *N.M. v. Switzerland*, 9 May 2000, No. 116/1998, paras. 2.1-2.7.
195 *Ibidem*, para. 4.8.
196 *Ibidem*, para. 6.7.

In *M.A.K. v. Germany* (2004), a central aspect of the Turkish Kurdish complainant's account was that he had been an active member of the PKK and that he had participated in a Dutch PKK military training camp. The Committee found it problematic that the author had not submitted evidence corroborating these statements and regarded as insufficient the presented affidavit, as it corroborated only that the complainant had been introduced as a guerrilla candidate, but not his membership of the PKK or his participation in the Dutch PKK training camp.[197] From this, a basic principle as to the quality of evidence emerges; being that evidence must be specific and precise and must cover the central aspects of the account.

A central aspect of the claim in many cases is that the complainant was tortured in the past in his or her home country. The Committee generally requires that such statements on past torture are supported by evidence, preferably medical reports. Such medical reports must be drawn up by medical specialists and must conclusively identify a causal link between the individual's bodily or mental injuries and the alleged past torture.[198] If statements on past torture are not supported by such evidence, this works to the detriment of the complainant and the Committee then generally finds the claim insufficiently substantiated (or incredible due to inconsistencies and inaccuracies in combination with the absence of medical evidence corroborating statements on past torture).[199]

It is not only important to submit evidence corroborating the individual account. Equally important is evidence about the human rights situation in the country of origin. No decisions have been found in which the Committee explicitly explained which of the parties – the complainant or the State party's authorities – is responsible for submitting recent information about the general human rights situation in the country of origin. It may be argued that, although the burden of proof remains a shared one, in the case of an arguable claim particular responsibility for shaping clarity on the general human rights situation in the country of origin lies with the administrative and judicial authorities of the State. This follows from the fact that paragraph 2 of Article 3 states that for the purpose of determining whether there are substantial grounds for assuming an Article 3-risk, *the competent authorities shall take into account all relevant considerations* (emphasis added). It follows from this text of Article 3, paragraph 2, that the authorities have an active role not only in verifying information put forward by the complainant, but also in collecting and presenting evidence, including evidence regarding the general human rights situation in the country of origin. With regard to the particular responsibility resting on the national authorities for shaping clarity on the situation in the country of origin, reference is also made to chapter 6 on EU asylum law, section 6.4.4.

---

197 ComAT, *M.A.K. v. Germany*, 17 May 2004, No. 214/2002, para. 13.5.
198 This terminology is used by the Committee in several cases. See, for example, ComAT, *El Rgeig v. Switzerland*, 15 November 2006, No. 280/2005, para. 7.4. See also Wouters 2009, p. 481.
199 See, for example, ComAT, *A.L.N. v. Switzerland*, 19 May 1998, No. 90/1997; this case is commented on by Tiemersma in her article 'Medical information in the asylum procedure', *NAV* 2006, No. 1; ComAT, *M.S. v. Switzerland*, 13 November 2001, No. 156/2000; ComAT, *S.N.A.W. v. Switzerland*, 29 November 2005, No. 231/2003; ComAT, *E.V.I. v. Sweden*, 2 May 2007, No. 296/2003; ComAT, *E.R.K. and Y.K. v. Sweden*, 2 May 2007, Nos. 270 & 271/2005; ComAT, *M.S. v. Switzerland*, 13 November 2001, No. 156/2000, para. 6.7. See, for the same conclusion, Bruin & Reneman 2006, p. 96.

The case law of the Committee discussed above gives some indication as to the minimum quantity and quality of evidence, but it remains very difficult to distinguish further criteria or guidelines. The reasons are that the Committee's reasoning on the merits is often extremely brief, consisting to a large extent of standard considerations on the standard of proof and some brief remarks on the individual case.[200] What is worse, in a number of cases the Committee is completely silent about the evidence presented by the complainant and does not make clear why this evidence does not support the case and is considered insufficient. More will be said about this in the next section on the appreciation of evidence. For now, as far as the minimum quantity and quality of evidence are concerned, the conclusion can be drawn that it requires a significant amount of precise, comprehensive, persuasive and conclusive evidentiary materials to win a case before the Committee.

4.5.7 *Appreciation and weighing of evidence*

Just like the HRC, the Committee adheres to a free evaluation of all the evidence presented by the parties. It is open to the Committee to consider evidence from whatever source and then to decide on its relevance and probative value. There are no pre-determined rules for the weighing of evidence. In the paragraphs below, an attempt is made to discover factors determining the probative value and persuasiveness of evidence. After that, I will look in more detail at four particular categories of evidence, being reports containing the result of inquiries conducted by embassies or missions of respondent States parties, witness statements by family members, medico-legal reports and reports about the human rights situation in the country of origin.

4.5.7.1 *Factors determining the probative value and persuasiveness of evidence*

It is not an easy task to distinguish in the case law of the Committee the exact factors determining the probative value and persuasiveness of the evidence. The reasons are that the conclusions on the merits are often very brief, consisting of a number of standard considerations on the standard and the burden of proof, followed by just one or two considerations on the merits of the individual case. In these brief conclusions, the Committee does not explicitly mention factors determining the probative value of the presented evidence.

Just like the HRC (see Chapter 3, section 3.5.7), the Committee is, in a significant number of cases, even completely silent about the evidence presented by the complainant and does not make clear how it weighed or evaluated that evidence. A truly striking example is the case of *S.L. v. Sweden* (2001).[201] In this case the Iranian complainant presented to the Swedish authorities the verdict by which he had been convicted and sentenced for cheque fraud. The Swedish embassy in Tehran concluded

---

200 See also Wouters 2009, p. 433, who states that the Committee's considerations are often brief and poorly reasoned.
201 ComAT, *S.L. v. Sweden*, 11 May 2001, No. 150/1999.

that this verdict was authentic.[202] In the proceedings before the Committee, several medical certificates were submitted, including one from the Centre for Torture and Trauma Survivors in Stockholm, stating that the author suffered from a post-traumatic stress disorder and that both medical and psychological evidence indicated that he had been subjected to torture with typical psychological effects as a result. In addition, a certificate from a psychiatrist was submitted to the Committee, stating that the circumstances, together with the author's whole attitude and general appearance, indicated very strongly that he had been subjected to severe abuse and torture for a long time and that he was considered to be completely trustworthy.[203] In its *ultra*-brief considerations on the merits and conclusions, the Committee did not mention at all or discuss the evidence presented by the author. It did not make clear why this evidence did not (sufficiently) support the complainant's claim. It only stated the following:

> 'The Committee has taken note of the arguments presented by the author and the State party and is of the opinion that it has not been given enough evidence by the author to conclude that the latter would run a personal, real and foreseeable risk of being tortured if returned to his country of origin.'[204]

As the Committee did not say anything at all about the evidence presented by the complainant and concluded that an Article 3-risk was absent, it may be inferred that it did not attach great weight to the evidence presented. The reasons for this low evaluation remain unclear, however.[205]

4.5.7.1.a Authenticity of documents

In a significant number of cases, the Committee did not attach probative value to documents submitted by the complainant because it had been established, as a result of investigations by the State party, that these documents were fakes or forged or contained false information. For example, in *Mehdi Zare v. Sweden* (2006)[206] the Committee considered as follows:

---

202 *Ibidem*, paras. 2.3, 2.5, 2.7, 4.6.
203 *Ibidem*, para. 3.2.
204 ComAT, *S.L. v. Sweden*, 11 May 2001, No. 150/1999, para. 6.4.
205 Examples of other cases in which the Committee remained completely silent about presented evidence are: ComAT, *K.S.Y. v. the Netherlands*, 15 May 2003, No. 190/2001, in which the Committee did not say anything about the presented strong medical evidence stating severe post-traumatic stress disorder and a serious restriction in the right shoulder of the complainant because he had been hanged by one arm for prolonged periods; ComAT, *A.A. v. Switzerland*, 17 November 2006, No. 251/2004; in this decision the Committee did not say anything in its considerations on the merits about the medical evidence presented which stated that the author suffered from a dissociative, trance-like condition, as a result of being subjected to sexual abuse during childhood, exacerbated by the fact that he had been ill-treated and had spent two years in prison.This report also mentioned that the author was severely traumatised; ComAT, *C.A.R.M. v. Canada*, 18 May 2007, No. 298/2006 (the complainant presented medico-legal reports mentioning post-traumatic stress disorder; the Committee did not say anything about this evidence in its considerations on the merits.
206 ComAT, *Mehdi Zare v. Sweden*, 17 May 2006, No. 256/2004.

'In assessing the risk of torture in the present case, the Committee has noted the complainant's contention that there is a foreseeable risk that he would be tortured if returned to Iran, on the basis of his alleged previous political involvement, and that the alleged sentence against him of 140 whiplashes would be carried out. (…) The Committee notes that the complainant has adduced three documents, which he purports to validate the existence of the sentence against him. He has adduced what he alleges are two summonses to attend the Public Court of Shiraz, on 31 July 2004 and 25 August 2004. He had originally alleged that these documents were originals but, in his comments on the State party's submission, confirmed that they were copies. The Committee notes that the State party has provided extensive reasons, based on expert evidence obtained by its consular services in Tehran, why it questioned the authenticity of each of the documents. In reply the complainant argues that, apparently, the criminal procedure was not applied in this case. The Committee considers that the complainant has failed to disprove the State party's findings in this regard, and to validate the authenticity of any of the documents in question. It recalls its jurisprudence that it is for the complainant to collect and present evidence in support of his or her account of events.'[207]

Another illustrative case is *E.R.K. and Y.K. v. Sweden* (2007).[208] In this case, the complainants claimed a danger of torture upon return to Azerbaijan, due to their brother's alleged previous political activities on the basis of which they claimed to have been previously mistreated by the Azerbaijani authorities. In support of their claim, they presented to the Swedish authorities a number of documents which they alleged to be judgments. The Swedish authorities conducted investigations through the embassy in Ankara[209] to find out whether the documents were authentic. As a result it was established that the authenticity was questionable. The Committee stated that the Swedish authorities had the right to investigate the authenticity of the documents and that the complainants had failed to disprove the State party's findings and to validate the authenticity of the documents presented.[210] There are numerous other cases in which the Committee found that forged documents seriously discredited the claim for protection.[211]

4.5.7.1.b Specificity and comprehensiveness of information contained in evidentiary materials
As well as authenticity, the Committee requires that evidence is specific, that is, relates specifically to the complainant and supports the claim that it is the complainant who runs a risk. In addition, the evidence must also be comprehensive, that is, prove the core aspects of the claim. When the information contained in evidentiary

---

207 *Ibidem*, paras. 9.4, 9.5.
208 ComAT, *E.R.K. and Y.K. v. Sweden*, 2 May 2007, Nos. 270 & 271/2005.
209 The ComAT's decision in *E.R.K. and Y.K. v. Sweden* mentions the embassy in Ankara, Turkey, although the applicants came from Azerbaijan and they presented documents from that country; a possible explanation is that there is no Swedish embassy (only a consulate) in Azerbaijan.
210 *Ibidem*, paras. 7.4, 7.5.
211 See, for example, ComAT, *N.Z.S. v. Sweden*, 29 November 2006, No. 277/2005; ComAT, *E.V.I. v. Sweden*, 1 May 2007, No. 296/2006; ComAT, *T.A. v. Sweden*, 22 November 2007, No. 303/2006; ComAT, *A.M. v. France*, 5 May 2010, No. 302/2006. See also Wouters 2009, p. 482, who states that it goes without saying that faked or forged documents seriously undermine the credibility of the claim.

materials does not specifically relate to the complainant, little or no evidentiary value is accorded to it. The Committee's approach is strict. In the case of *A.A. v. Switzerland* (2007), the complainant had never been tortured in the past, but claimed to fear torture during pre-trial detention in Pakistan. He submitted various documents in support of his claim, including an annual report by the Human Rights Commission of Pakistan on conditions in Pakistani prisons, and a note from a certain Mr Asif, a member of the National Assembly of Pakistan, stating that, if the complainant returned to Pakistan he would be arrested and imprisoned for political reasons because of an offence that he had not committed, and that the conditions of detention in Pakistani prisons were such that imprisonment constituted torture or at least inhuman treatment.[212]

The Committee considered that the report on detention conditions in Pakistan was of a general nature and did not, therefore, sufficiently relate to the individual complainant; as to the note from Mr Asif, the Committee found that it related mainly to Mr Asif's detention and did not, therefore, sufficiently support a future danger for the complainant.[213] In *M.A.K. v. Germany* (2004),[214] the presented evidence was deemed insufficiently comprehensive as it did not sufficiently prove the core aspects of the claim. One of the core aspects of the complainant's account was his alleged participation in a PKK training camp in the Netherlands in 1994. He did not submit evidence which supported this participation. The evidence he did submit was an affidavit from a certain F.S., which stated that the complainant had been introduced as a 'guerrilla candidate' at the Halim-Dener-Festival, and a letter from the International Association for Human Rights of the Kurds, which stated that it was not implausible that the complainant had been temporarily exempted from military PKK training in Turkey. The Committee stated that this evidence fell short of proving the complainant's alleged participation in the PKK training camp in the Netherlands in 1994.[215]

4.5.7.2   Reports containing the result of inquiries conducted by embassies or missions of respondent States parties

Just like the HRC, the Committee generally attaches strong evidentiary value to reports submitted by States parties containing the result of inquiries conducted by embassies or missions in the complainant's country of origin. In a significant number of cases from, mainly, Switzerland and Sweden, the national authorities have requested the embassy or mission in the country of origin to investigate whether the complainant was being sought by the authorities in his or her country of origin. Such an investigation was also carried out by the Swiss Embassy in Ankara in the case of *H.D. v. Switzerland* (1999).[216] The Turkish Kurdish complainant in this case stated that he had provided food and clothing to friends involved with the PKK. In 1991, one of his cousins, an active PKK member, came to live with the complainant after deten-

---

212 ComAT, *A.A. v. Switzerland*, 1 May 2007, No. 268/2005, paras. 7.1, 7.2.
213 *Ibidem*, para. 8.5.
214 ComAT, *M.A.K. v. Germany*, 12 May 2004, No. 214/2002.
215 *Ibidem*, para. 13.5.
216 ComAT, *H.D. v. Switzerland*, 30 April 1999, No. 112/1998.

tion. The security forces came to search for this cousin, but not having found this cousin, arrested the complainant. The complainant was then detained and tortured. Upon release, he learned that his cousin had been killed by the security forces. He saw his cousin's disfigured and mutilated body. He was told that the security forces were aware of his support for the PKK. He was threatened with death if he refused to co-operate with the information service. The complainant then decided to leave the country and travelled to Istanbul. Persons in civilian clothes came to his home, insulted and slapped his wife and asked her where he was. His wife then joined the complainant in Istanbul and together they travelled to Switzerland where they applied for asylum.[217]

In the proceedings before the Committee, the State party held that the author's statements contained inconsistencies and contradictions. Furthermore, the State party relied on information obtained by the Swiss embassy in Ankara that the author was not wanted by the police and was not forbidden to hold a passport.[218]

The Committee noted that the complainant's problems in Turkey dated back to 1991, a long time previously, that the question of a prosecution against him on specific charges had never arisen and that there was nothing to suggest that he or his family members had been sought or intimidated by the Turkish authorities.[219] It is obvious that the Committee attached significant weight to the embassy report, although it did not re-mention it in its own considerations on the merits under the heading 'views'. Similar decisions were taken in *K.M. v. Switzerland* (1999),[220] *H.A.D. v. Switzerland* (2000)[221] and *Y.S. v. Switzerland* (2000).[222] Just as in *H.D. v. Switzerland* (1999), in these three cases concerning Turkish Kurdish complainants the State party relied on information obtained from the Swiss embassy in Ankara. The Committee based its conclusion on the absence of an Article 3-danger on, mainly, lapse of time since the problems had occurred and information from the Swiss embassy in Turkey that the complainant was not being sought.[223]

In other cases, the national authorities requested the embassy or mission in the country of origin to investigate the truthfulness of aspects of the complainant's personal account. This was done, for example, in *M.M. et al. v. Sweden* (2008).[224] In this case, the complainant from Azerbaijan stated that he feared he would be tortured upon return to Azerbaijan on account of his past political activities for the Musavat party. He also stated that he had been tortured in the past for these activities.[225]

---

217 *Ibidem*, paras. 2.1-2.3.
218 *Ibidem*, para. 4.3.
219 *Ibidem*, para. 6.5.
220 ComAT, *K.M. v. Switzerland*, 16 November 1999, No. 107/1998.
221 ComAT, *H.A.D. v. Switzerland*, 10 May 2000, No. 126/1999.
222 ComAT, *Y.S. v. Switzerland*, 14 November 2000, No. 147/1999.
223 The Committee mentioned the information from the Swiss embassy in Ankara explicitly in its considerations on the merits in ComAT, *K.M. v. Switzerland*, 16 November 1999, No. 107/1998, para. 6.6. In ComAT, *H.A.D. v. Switzerland*, 10 May 2000, No. 126/1999, the Committee did not refer, in its considerations on the merits, to the information obtained from the Swiss Embassy. In ComAT, *Y.S. v. Switzerland*, 14 November 2000, No. 147/1999, explicit reference was made in para. 6.6 to the embassy report.
224 ComAT, *M.M. et al. v. Sweden*, 1 December 2008, No. 332/2007.
225 *Ibidem*, paras. 2.1-2.8.

However, according to the results of an investigation carried out by the Swedish consulate in Baku, the complainant had never been a member of the Musavat party and had never worked for it.[226] The Committee relied on this information, on contradictions in the complainant's flight narrative and, finally, on the fact that the medical reports were not definitive and did not coincide in their diagnosis, and concluded that there was no Article 3-danger.[227]

In another group of cases, investigations into the authenticity of documents submitted by complainants were carried out via embassies or missions in the countries of origin. This happened, for example, in *N.Z.S. v. Sweden* (2006),[228] *Y.K. and E.R.K. v. Sweden* (2007)[229] and *T.A. v. Sweden* (2007).[230] In all these cases, the State party questioned the authenticity of presented documents on the basis of inquiries made by or via the Swedish embassy or consulate in, respectively, Iran and Azerbaijan. In all three cases the Committee attached great value to the results of these investigations and based its negative decision to a large extent on these results.[231]

In a number of cases, the complainants objected to the use of the information provided by the embassy or mission in the country of origin. For example, in *H.A.D. v. Switzerland* (2000), the complainant pointed out that the information collected by the Swiss embassy in Ankara was suspect as the Turkish Government was under no obligation to provide such information to the State party.[232] In *M.M. et al. v. Sweden* (2008), the complainant pointed out that the report requested by the Swedish consulate in Baku contained several inaccuracies, did not describe how the work had been carried out and was extremely short.[233] In *Y.K and E.R.K. v. Sweden* (2007), the complainants stated that the Swedish embassy's report was based on anonymous sources and precluded the possibility of challenging the information it contained. The Committee generally does not respond to such complaints, or only responds in a very brief way. For example, in *Y.K and E.R.K. v. Sweden* (2007) it responded that

> 'The complainants challenge the decision to request information of the Embassy in Ankara, which they claim risked revealing their identities to the Azerbaijani authorities. The Committee notes that the State party denies that the complainants were identified, but in any event considers the means by which the State party conducted its investigations irrelevant for the purposes of establishing whether the complainants would be subjected to torture upon return to Azerbaijan. Having presented the State party with documents which were alleged to corroborate the complainants' claims, it was up to the State party to attempt to establish the authenticity of those documents. The Committee also notes that the only other arguments made by the complainants with respect to the information in the Embassy's report, were that the dis-

---

226 *Ibidem*, para. 4.3.
227 *Ibidem*, paras.7.4-7.6.
228 ComAT, *N.Z.S. v. Sweden*, 22 November 2006, No. 277/2005.
229 ComAT, *Y.K. and E.R.K. v. Sweden*, 30 April 2007, Nos. 270 & 271/2005.
230 ComAT, *T.A. v. Sweden*, 22 November 2007, No. 303/2006.
231 ComAT, *N.Z.S. v. Sweden*, 22 November 2006, No. 277/2005, para. 8.6; ComAT, *Y.K. and E.R.K. v. Sweden*, 30 April 2007, Nos. 270 & 271/2005, para. 7.5; ComAT, *T.A. v. Sweden*, 22 November 2007, No. 303/2006, para. 8.7.
232 ComAT, *H.A.D. v. Switzerland*, 10 May 2000, No. 126/1999, para. 5.9.
233 ComAT, *M.M. et al. v. Sweden*, 1 December 2008, No. 332/2007, para. 5.4.

crepancies in the documents were merely "alleged formal errors" and that they lack the means and necessary legal expertise to make any further comments. The Committee considers that the complainants have failed to disprove the State party's findings in this regard, and to validate the authenticity of any of the documents in question. It recalls its jurisprudence that it is for the complainants to collect and present evidence in support of his or her account of events.'[234]

We may infer from this that the Committee generally regards information obtained via embassies and missions in the countries of origin as highly reliable, and that very persuasive counter-evidence is necessary to refute such information.

4.5.7.3   *Witness statements by family members*

It follows from the Committee's case law that statements made by the complainant's family members are treated with caution, but may be accorded probative value if they corroborate, in a specific and comprehensive way, the complainant's account. Illustrative is the case of *A.S. v. Sweden* (2001). For the facts of this case reference is made to section 4.2.2.4 above. Having taken note of the submissions made by both the author and the State party regarding the merits of the case, the Committee requested further information from both parties.[235] It requested the author to submit information about the author's older son, who had tried to seek asylum in Sweden from Denmark in March 2000, including records of the asylum interview.[236] The Committee accorded significant weight to information from the asylum interview records of the author's son:

> 'From the information submitted by the author, the Committee notes that she is the widow of a martyr and as such supported and supervised by the Bonyad-e Shahid Committee of Martyrs. It is also noted that the author claims that she was forced into a sighe or mutah marriage and to have committed and been sentenced to stoning for adultery. Although treating the recent testimony of the author's son, seeking asylum in Denmark, with utmost caution, the Committee is nevertheless of the view that the information given further corroborates the account given by the author.'[237]

Unlike the national authorities, the Committee concluded in this case that there was a danger of torture in case of expulsion. The Committee based its decision on the complainant's account, the identity papers and the documentation showing that the complainant was the widow of a martyr, the statements made by the author's son, and information on the human rights situation in Iran.[238]

---

234   ComAT, *Y.K. and E.R.K. v. Sweden*, 30 April 2007, Nos. 270 & 271/2005, para. 7.5
235   ComAT, *A.S. v. Sweden*, 15 February 2001, No 149/1999, para. 7.2.
236   *Ibidem*, paras. 7.6, 7.7.
237   *Ibidem*, para. 8.4.
238   *Ibidem*, paras. 8.4-9.

Another case in which the Committee accorded significant weight to information provided by the complainant's family members is *T.A. v. Sweden* (2005).[239] In this case, the complainant stated that she feared torture upon expulsion to Bangladesh due to her and her husband's political activities for the Jatiya Party. She stated that she was being sought by the authorities; the complainant's sister visited Bangladesh from December 2002 to February 2003, where she learned that the police was still looking for the complainant.[240] The Committee, relying on this information, assumed that the complainant was indeed still being sought by the Bangladeshi authorities, and concluded that an Article 3-risk was imminent.[241]

4.5.7.4 Medico-legal reports[242]

General Comment No. 1 states in paragraph 8:

> 'The following information, while not exhaustive, would be pertinent:
> (c) Is there medical or other independent evidence to support a claim by the author that he/she has been tortured or maltreated in the past? Has the torture had after-effects?'

Medico-legal reports play a prominent role in the case law of the Committee, more so than in the case law of the HRC and the ECtHR. In many individual communications the complainants submitted medico-legal reports to support their claims. Medico-legal reports are often brought in with different functions, namely as corroboration of statements on experiences of torture in the past, but also as an explanation for inconsistencies and for belated statements or tardy presentation of evidence. Each of these reasons receives separate attention below.

4.5.7.4.a Medico-legal reports to explain inconsistencies in the personal account

As pointed out above in section 4.5.5 on the credibility assessment, in a significant number of – mostly early – decisions, the Committee explained and excused inconsistencies or gaps and vague points in the complainant's account by referring to past torture as evidenced by medico-legal reports. A commonly used consideration in these decisions is that

> 'The State party has pointed to contradictions and inconsistencies in the author's story, but the Committee considers that complete accuracy is seldom to be expected by victims of torture and that such inconsistencies as may exist in the author's presentation of the facts are not material and do not raise doubts about the general veracity of the author's claims.'[243]

---

239 ComAT, *T.A. v. Sweden*, 6 May 2005, No. 226/2003.
240 *Ibidem*, para. 5.5.
241 *Ibidem*, paras. 7.3, 7.4.
242 See on the role of medico-legal reports in the case law of the Committee against Torture also Bruin & Reneman 2006.
243 See, for example, ComAT, *Alan v. Switzerland*, 8 May 1996, No. 021/1995, para. 11.3; ComAT, *Kisoki v. Sweden*, 8 May 1996, No. 041/1996, para. 9.3; ComAT, *Tala v. Sweden*, 15 November 1996, No. 043/1996, para. 10.3; ComAT, *Haydin v. Sweden*, 20 November 1998, No. 101/1997, para. 6.7; ComAT, *E.T.B. v. Denmark*, 30 April 2002, No. 146/1999, para. 10: 'the Committee recalls its juris-
→

In a number of these cases, for example, *Alan v. Switzerland* (1996)[244] and *Kisoki v. Sweden* (1996),[245] the medical evidence presented by the complainant during the national proceedings and to the Committee was only mentioned under the heading 'facts as submitted by the complainant'. The Committee did not explicitly mention this medical evidence in its own conclusion under the heading 'issues and proceedings before the Committee'. It is, however, obvious that it attached significant weight to this evidence when determining the facts of the case as it concluded on the basis of this evidence that the complainant had been tortured in the past. In other cases, the Committee explicitly mentioned the medical evidence in its own considerations and conclusions as a reason to lower the threshold of accuracy and explain away inaccuracies in the flight narrative. An example of this more elaborate approach is *I.A.O. v. Sweden* (1998), where it considered:

> 'It has noted the medical evidence provided by the author and, on that basis, is of the opinion that there is a firm reason to believe that the author has been tortured in the past. In this context, the Committee observes that the author suffers from a post-traumatic stress disorder, and that this has to be taken into account when assessing the author's presentation of the facts. The Committee is therefore of the opinion that the inconsistencies as exist in the author's story do not raise doubts as to the general veracity of his claim that he was detained and tortured.'[246]

4.5.7.4.b Medico-legal reports to explain tardy presentation of statements and evidence
In a number of early cases, the Committee did not perceive belated presentation of facts and evidence in the national proceedings as problematic. In many of these cases, medico-legal reports confirming past torture and stating post-traumatic stress disorder or other mental disturbances or disorders were submitted. Although the Committee does not always explicitly mention such medical evidence in its considerations on the merits, it does seem to have played a role in its decision to accept the tardy presentation of statements and evidence. For example, in *Khan v. Canada* (1994),[247] the author was first interviewed by immigration officials on 9 August 1990. It was only during a so-called post-claim procedure, in 1994, that the author alleged past torture and that he submitted medico-legal reports in support of these statements. In the proceedings before the Committee, the State party contended that it doubted the veracity of the author's statements. One of the reasons for this was that he had not

---

prudence that torture victims cannot be expected to recall entirely consistent facts relating to events of extreme trauma. But they must be prepared to advance such evidence as there is in support of a claim'; ComAT, *Karoui v.Sweden*, 8 May 2002, No. 185/2001, para. 10; ComAT, *C.T. and K.M. v. Sweden*, 17 November 2006, No. 279/2005, para. 7.6; ComAT, *Falcon Rios v. Canada*, 23 November 2004, No. 133/1999, para. 8.5 (gaps and vague points are explained away by referring to medical evidence.

244 ComAT, *Alan v. Switzerland*, 8 May 1996, No. 021/1995.
245 ComAT, *Kisoki v. Sweden*, 8 May 1996, No. 041/1996.
246 ComAT, *I.A.O. v. Sweden*, 6 May 1998, No. 065/1997, para. 14.3. Other examples of this more elaborate approach are ComAT, *Haydin v. Sweden*, 20 November 1998, No. 101/1997, para. 6.7; ComAT, *Karoui v.Sweden*, 8 May 2002, No. 185/2001, para. 10.
247 ComAT, *Khan v. Canada*, 15 November 1994, No. 15/1994.

mentioned past torture and had not presented medical evidence earlier in the national proceedings.[248] Importantly, the author had not explained why he had alleged past torture so late in the national proceedings. As an explanation for the late presentation of medical evidence, he referred only to the fact that he had been detained and that he had been medically examined after detention.[249] The Committee did not find the tardy mention of torture and the late presentation of evidence in support of this problematic:

> 'The Committee notes that some of the author's claims and corroborating evidence have been submitted only after his refugee claim had been refused by the Refugee Board and deportation procedures had been initiated; the Committee, however, also notes that this behaviour is not uncommon for victims of torture. The Committee, however, considers that, even if there could be some doubts about the facts as adduced by the author, it must ensure that his security is not endangered. The Committee notes that evidence exists that torture is widely practised in Pakistan against political dissenters as well as against common detainees.'[250]

In *Kisoki v. Sweden* (1996),[251] crucial evidence was submitted in support of a third asylum application. The Committee did not say anything in its considerations about the fact that important evidence had been submitted only in support of a third application and not earlier on. It is obvious from its considerations that it saw the author as a torture victim, obviously on the basis of the medico-legal reports presented in support of the author's third asylum application. The case of *A.F. v. Sweden* (1998) is another example.[252] This case is striking, as it was only in support of a fourth asylum application that the author had corroborated his allegations about past torture in the Iranian Evin prison with medical evidence from the Centre for Torture and Trauma Survivors in Stockholm.[253] It is obvious from the Committee's considerations that it did not see the late presentation of this crucial evidence as problematic. It took the evidence into account and concluded that the author had a history of detention and torture.[254]

4.5.7.4.c Medico-legal reports as corroboration of experiences of torture and ill-treatment
In order to be considered as evidence with strong probative force in support of statements about past torture, medico-legal reports must be drawn up by medical specialists and must conclusively identify a causal link between the individual's bodily or mental injuries and the alleged past torture. For example, in *El Rgeig v. Switzerland* (2006), the Committee considered as follows:

---

248 *Ibidem*, para. 8.5.
249 *Ibidem*, para. 9.6.
250 *Ibidem*, para. 12.3.
251 ComAT, *Kisoki v. Sweden*, 8 May 1996, No. 041/1996.
252 ComAT, *A.F. v. Sweden*, 8 May 1998, No. 089/1997.
253 *Ibidem*, para. 2.6.
254 *Ibidem*, para. 6.5.

'Lastly, he has submitted a copy of a medical certificate dated 24 April 2006 *in which a specialist in post-traumatic disorders from a Geneva hospital identified a causal link between the complainant's bodily injuries, his psychological state and the ill-treatment he described at the time of his medical examination.* (Emphasis added.) According to this doctor, in his present psychological state, the complainant does not appear capable of coping with a forcible return to the Libyan Arab Jamahiriya, and such coercive action would entail a definite risk to his health. The State party has made no comments in this regard. In the specific circumstance of this case, and in particular in the light of the findings in the above-mentioned medical report on the presence of serious after-effects of the acts of torture inflicted on the complainant, his political activities subsequent to his departure from the Libyan Arab Jamahiriya (as described in paragraphs 2.4 and 5.3 above), and the persistent reports concerning the treatment generally meted out to such activists when they are forcibly returned to the Libyan Arab Jamahiriya, the Committee considers that the State party has not presented to it sufficiently convincing arguments to demonstrate a complete absence of risk that the complainant would be exposed to torture if he were to be forcibly returned to the Libyan Arab Jamahiriya.'[255]

In a number of cases, the Committee explicitly stated that it found the presented medical evidence insufficiently conclusive in identifying the required causal link between the bodily or mental injuries and the alleged past torture. The case of *X. v. Switzerland*(1997)[256] provides an example of this. In this case, counsel submitted to the Committee a medical report showing that, for a number of years, the author had been receiving treatment for psychiatric and physical problems and that the treatment had to be continued for some weeks. This report did not say anything about the cause of these problems, however. The Committee, therefore, did not attach much weight to it and did not regard it as evidence of past torture:

'The Committee notes that the author does not claim that he has been tortured by the police or security forces in Sudan, and that no medical evidence exists that he suffers from the consequences of torture, either physically or mentally. The Committee therefore concludes that the inconsistencies in the author's story cannot be explained by the effects of a post-traumatic stress disorder, as in the case of many torture victims.'

In *M.O. v. Denmark* (2003),[257] the complainant claimed that he had been tortured in the past by the Algerian authorities and presented medical evidence which was, according to the Committee, consistent with the claim, but did not discount other possible causes for his injuries. Obviously, for the Committee the medical evidence was not sufficiently conclusive in establishing the required causal link between the statements of past torture and the found harm on the complainant. Similarly, in the cases of *M.N. v. Switzerland* (2004)[258] and *R.K. and others v. Sweden*(2006),[259] the medical

---

255 ComAT, *El Rgeig v. Switzerland*, 15 November 2006, No. 280/2005, para. 7.4. See also Wouters 2009, p. 481.
256 ComAT, *X. v. Switzerland*, 9 May 1997, No. 38/1995.
257 ComAT, *M.O. v. Denmark*, 17 November 2003, No. 209/2002.
258 ComAT, *M.N.v. Switzerland*, 22 November 2006, No. 259/2004.
259 ComAT, *R.K. and others v. Sweden*, 19 May 2008, No. 309/2006.

evidence was considered insufficiently specific about the cause of scars/signs on the complainant's body.

It is important to mention here that no matter how strong and conclusive the medical evidence is in identifying a causal link between the individual's bodily or mental injuries and the alleged past torture, this does not automatically mean a violation of Article 3. Past torture does not automatically mean that a risk of torture exists upon return to the country of origin. It needs more factors to draw this conclusion.[260] It seems that over the years, the Committee has become stricter in requiring other factors, as well as past torture, to assume an Article 3-danger. In *A. v. the Netherlands* (1999), it considered that 'past torture is a major element to be taken into account when examining a case such as this'.[261] Six years later, in *M.S.H. v. Sweden* (2005), it considered that 'previous experience of torture is but one consideration in determining whether a person faces a personal risk of torture upon return to his country of origin'.[262]

4.5.7.4.d Medico-legal reports: less probative value in more recent decisions?

The Committee has not always been consistent in applying the approach outlined above in which decisive probative value is attached to conclusive medical evidence of past torture. In a number of cases the Committee – for unknown reasons and contrary to its line – was not prepared to accept past torture on the basis of persuasive and conclusive medical evidence. For example, in the case of *F.F.Z. v. Denmark* (2002),[263] a case concerning a Libyan complainant who alleged to have been detained and tortured due to activities for the Al Jama'a movement, a report prepared by Amnesty International's medical team was submitted. It stated that the symptoms identified in the author were often seen in people who had been subjected to extreme stress, such as acts of war, detention or torture, and that these symptoms were consistent with the consequences of alleged torture. The report did not identify physical symptoms of torture.[264] In its considerations on the merits, the Committee only repeated how the respondent State party had evaluated the medical report, remarking that 'the Amnesty International medical report provides no objective indication that he was subjected to gross outrages'.[265] In a number of subsequent cases, the Committee did not say anything about the presented medical evidence in its considerations on the merits, so we cannot know what the Committee made of it. For example, in the case of *K.S.Y. v. the Netherlands* (2003), medical reports were submitted stating that the complainant suffered from post-traumatic stress disorder and that his right shoulder

---

260 See, for example, ComAT, *A.D. v. Netherlands*, 24 January 2000, No. 96/1997; ComAT, *K.K. v. Switzerland*, 28 November 2003, No. 186/2001; ComAT, *S.S. v. Netherlands*, 19 May 2003, No. 191/2001; ComAT, *M.M.K. v. Sweden*, 18 May 2005, No. 221/2002; ComAT, *S.S.S. v. Canada*, 5 December 2005, No. 245/2004; ComAT, *N.Z.S. v. Sweden*, 29 November 2006, No. 277/2005; ComAT, *T.A. v. Sweden*, 22 November 2007, No. 303/2006.

261 ComAT, *A. v. the Netherlands*, 12 May 1999, No. 124/1999.

262 ComAT, *M.S.H. v. Sweden*, 14 December 2005, No. 235/2003, para. 6.5.

263 ComAT, *F.F.Z. v. Denmark*, 30 April 2002, No. 180/2001.

264 *Ibidem*, para. 2.12.

265 ComAT, *F.F.Z. v. Denmark*, 30 April 2002, No. 180/2001, para. 11.

was restricted because he had been hanged by one arm for prolonged periods.[266] The Committee did not say anything about this medical evidence, but only considered that

'Concerning the alleged difficulties faced by the complainant because of his sexual orientation, the Committee notes a number of contradictions and inconsistencies in his account of past abuses at the hands of the Iranian authorities, as well as the fact that that part of his account has not been adequately substantiated or lacks credibility.'[267]

Another striking case in which the Committee did not say anything about the conclusive medical evidence presented by the complainant is *S.P.A. v. Canada* (2006).[268] The complainant in this case, a hospital nurse and university lecturer from Iran, claimed to have been detained and tortured by the Iranian authorities after she had discovered that human bones and cadavers she received at the university for teaching purposes had been taken from 'anti-revolutionary groups' and by raiding Armenian and Baha'i cemeteries. In the national Canadian proceedings and before the Committee, counsel submitted a medical certificate based on the complainant's Personal Information Form and a clinical interview and examination. This medical certificate concluded that there was evidence of multiple scars on the applicant's body. Significant wounds were on her face and scalp, and were consistent with blunt trauma, as described by her. The irregular depressed scar on the top of her head was said to be consistent with her description of a lesion that had been left open and sutured at a later date. The scars on her arms and legs were more non-specific but were consistent with blunt trauma. The bilateral toenail onycholysis was found typical for post-traumatic nail injury and could certainly have resulted from being stepped on repeatedly as the applicant had described. The medical report concluded that her psychological history was consistent with chronic post-traumatic stress disorder. In the national proceedings and before the Committee, the Canadian authorities maintained that they doubted the veracity of the claim for a number of reasons, among them material inaccuracies. The complainant contended before the Committee that the medical evidence corroborated her claim and that, as she was a victim of torture, complete accuracy could not have been expected. In her opinion, the national authorities had not given enough weight to the medical evidence. The Committee upheld the stance taken by the national authorities. Nothing was said in its considerations about the medical evidence. It is clear from the Committee's reasoning that it found the flight narrative so doubtful that it was highly questionable whether the scars had been caused by torture inflicted by the authorities. Significant weight was attached to the fact that the applicant had travelled through seven countries before applying for

---

266 ComAT, *K.S.Y. v. the Netherlands*, 15 May 2003, No. 190/2001, para. 3.2.

267 *Ibidem*, para. 7.3. A similar case is ComAT, *S.L. v. Sweden,* 11 May 2001, No. 150/1999. In this case, too, the Committee did not say anything about very compelling medical evidence confirming past torture and stating the presence of post-traumatic stress disorder. The Committee concluded that not enough evidence had been given, although the author had provided a genuine judgment of a sentence, in addition to the medical evidence. See also ComAT, *S.U.A. v. Sweden*, 22 November 2004, No. 223/2002, paras. 6.4. and 6.5. In this case the Committee did not say anything about the presented conclusive medical evidence either.

268 ComAT, *S.P.A. v. Canada*, 6 December 2006, No. 282/2005.

asylum in Canada.[269] However, in the light of the jurisprudential line developed in earlier cases, according to which past torture is assumed when conclusive medical evidence is presented and complete accuracy is then not needed, it remains remarkable that the Committee did not make explicit its thoughts about the medical evidence presented.

From the analysis of the Committee's case law, it is obvious that in its early jurisprudence (up to 2000), the Committee rather easily assumed past torture on the basis of conclusive medical reports and also rather easily explained away inaccuracies and late presentation of statements and evidence by making reference to the presented medical evidence. It seems that the Committee started to draw stricter lines after 2000. Cases were discussed above in which the Committee did not even mention the presented medical evidence in its own considerations and concluded that there was no Article 3-risk. It seems that the Committee has become more critical in testing the conclusiveness of medical evidence. It also seems to have become stricter in requiring other factors in addition to past torture to assume an Article 3-danger.[270] My impression is, therefore, that the Committee has generally become stricter in determining the value of medical evidence and is generally inclined to attach less value to it than in its early jurisprudence. It may probably be argued that, although still prominent, medical evidence has been downgraded from decisive evidence to supportive evidence. Bruin and Reneman (2006) explain this by referring to the fact that, for a number of years, States have been pushing the Committee to abstain from evaluating facts and evidence in full and to take a more reserved stand.[271] Still, medical evidence remains important as supportive evidence. The Committee has shown dissatisfaction over the fact that in national proceedings in the Netherlands, medico-legal reports are not normally taken into account as evidence. In its Conclusions and Recommendations regarding the Netherlands of 3 August 2007 it stated:

> 'The Committee notes with concern that medical reports are not taken into account on a regular basis in the Dutch asylum procedures and that the application of the Istanbul protocol is not encouraged. The State party should reconsider its position on the role of medical investigations and integrate medical reports as part of its asylum procedures. The Committee also encourages the application of the Istanbul Protocol in the asylum procedures and the provision of training.'[272]

---

269 *Ibidem*, paras. 7.5-7.7.
270 Compare ComAT, *A. v. the Netherlands*, 12 May 1999, No. 124/1999, in which the Committee stated that 'past torture is a major element to be taken into account when examining a case such as this', and ComAT, *M.S.H. v. Sweden*, 14 December 2005, No. 235/2003, para. 6.5, in which the Committee stated that 'previous experience of torture is but one consideration in determining whether a person faces a personal risk of torture upon return to his country of origin'.
271 Bruin & Reneman 2006, p. 90.
272 ComAT, Conclusions and Recommendations regarding the Netherlands, 3 August 2007, CAT/C/NET/CO/4, para. 8.

4.5.7.5   Reports on the situation in the country of origin

The second paragraph of Article 3 stipulates that for the purpose of determining whether there are grounds for believing that there is an Article 3-risk, the competent authorities shall take into account all relevant considerations, including, where applicable, the existence in the country of origin of a consistent pattern of gross, flagrant or mass violations of human rights.[273] In line with this, General Comment No. 1 lists as relevant considerations in paragraph 8:

> '(a) Is the State concerned one in which there is evidence of a consistent pattern of gross, flagrant or mass violations of human rights (see art. 3, para. 2)?
>
> (d) Has the situation referred to in (a) above changed? Has the internal situation in respect of human rights altered?'

It follows from these rules that information on the situation in the country of origin is of vital importance. Logically, reports containing such information are a very important category of evidentiary materials. The Committee makes use of reports stemming from a variety of sources. In a significant number of decisions, however, it only mentions that it is aware of the human rights situation in the country of origin, without specifying the sources it has used and the reasons why it has considered the information reliable.[274]

The Committee makes use of reports it has drawn up as a result of *ex officio* inquiries under the Article 20 inquiry procedure.[275] An example of a case in which it explicitly made use of such a report, as well as reports from other sources, is *Falcon Ríos v. Canada* (2004).[276] The Committee also uses reports resulting from the Article

---

273 The Committee has in a number of views concluded that there is a consistent pattern of gross, flagrant or mass violations of human rights in the countries of origin. See ComAT, *Mutombo v. Switzerland*, 27 April 1994, No. 13/1993 (Zaire, nowadays the Democratic Republic of the Congo), ComAT, *Elmi v. Australia*, 25 May 1999, No. 120/1998 (Somalia); ComAT, *A.S. v. Sweden*, 15 February 2001, No. 149/1999 (Iran); ComAT, *H.M.H.I. v. Australia*, 1 May 2002, No. 177/2001 (Somalia).

274 See, for example, ComAT, *A. v. the Netherlands*, 13 November 1998, No. 091/1997, para. 6.4: 'Reports from reliable sources have over the years documented cases suggesting that a pattern of detention, imprisonment, torture and ill-treatment of persons accused of political opposition activities, including links with the Al-Nahda movement, exist in Tunisia.' See also ComAT, *El Rgeig v. Switzerland*, 15 November 2006, No. 280/2005, para. 7.4, in which the Committee mentioned 'persistent reports concerning the treatment generally meted out to such activists when they are forcibly returned to the Libyan Arab Jamahiriya'. See also Wouters 2009, p. 483.

275 Article 20 CAT, paras. 1-3 stipulate: 'If the Committee receives reliable information which appears to it to contain well-founded indications that torture is being systematically practised in the territory of a State Party, the Committee shall invite that State Party to co-operate in the examination of the information and to this end to submit observations with regard to the information concerned. Taking into account any observations which may have been submitted by the State Party concerned as well as any other relevant information available to it, the Committee may, if it decides that this is warranted, designate one or more of its members to make a confidential inquiry and to report to the Committee urgently. If an inquiry is made in accordance with paragraph 2, the Committee shall seek the co-operation of the State Party concerned. In agreement with that State Party, such an inquiry may include a visit to its territory.'

276 ComAT, *Falcon Ríos v. Canada*, 17 December 2004, No. 133/1999, para. 8.3.

19 reporting mechanism;[277] examples are the cases of *Karoui v. Sweden* (2002)[278] and *G.K. v. Switzerland* (2003).[279] Reports drawn up by other United Nations organisations and agencies are also frequently used by the Committee. A particularly important source within this category is reports drawn up by the UNHCR. An example is the case of *U.S. v. Finland* (2003)[280] concerning a Sri Lankan complainant, in which the Committee attached significant weight to information from the UNHCR according to which a large number of Tamil refugees had returned to Sri Lanka in 2001 and 2002.[281]

In a number of cases the Committee made use of information from non-governmental organisations, including Amnesty International.[282] In other cases, it referred to information from non-governmental organisations without further mentioning these organisations.[283]

As has been made clear above in section 4.5.7.2, the Committee generally attaches strong evidentiary value to reports submitted by States parties containing the result of inquiries conducted by embassies or missions in the complainant's country of origin.[284]

With regard to the country of origin information, it is, finally, important to note that, on the basis of Rules 63, and 118, paragraph 2, of the Committee's Rules of Procedure, the Committee can *proprio motu* obtain information from a variety of sources, including the entire United Nations system, intergovernmental organisations, national human rights institutions, non-governmental organisations, and other relevant civil society organisations.[285]

---

277 Article 19, para. 1, CAT stipulates: 'The States Parties shall submit to the Committee, through the Secretary-General of the United Nations, reports on the measures they have taken to give effect to their undertakings under this Convention, within one year after the entry into force of this Convention for the State Party concerned. Thereafter the States Parties shall submit supplementary reports every four years on any new measures taken, and such other reports as the Committee may request.'

278 ComAT, *Karoui v. Sweden*, 25 May 2002, No. 185/2001, para. 9.

279 ComAT, *G.K. v. Switzerland*, 12 May 2003, No. 219/2002, para. 6.3.

280 ComAT, *U.S. v. Finland*, 1 May 2003, No. 197/2002.

281 ComAT, *U.S. v. Finland*, 1 May 2003, No. 197/2002, para. 7.7. Another example is *Kisoki v. Sweden*, 8 May 1996, No. 41/1996, para. 9.5: 'the Committee has noted the position of the United Nations High Commissioner for Refugees, according to whom deportees who are discovered to have sought asylum abroad undergo interrogation upon arrival at Kinshasa airport, following which those who are believed to have a political profile are at risk of detention and consequently ill-treatment'. UNHCR information also played a significant role in ComAT, *X.Y. and Z. v. Sweden*, 6 May 1998, No. 61/1996, para. 11.5; ComAT, *Korban v. Sweden*,16 November 1998, No. 88/1997, para. 6.5; ComAT, *Haydin v. Sweden*, 16 December 1998, No. 101/1997, para. 6.4.

282 Examples of cases in which the Committee used information from Amnesty International are ComAT, *H.B.H. et al v. Switzerland*, 16 May 2003, No. 192/2001, para. 6.9 and ComAT, *S.S. v. the Netherlands*,19 May 2003, No. 191/2001, para. 6.3, footnote 8.

283 An example is ComAT, *G.K. v. Switzerland*, 12 May 2003, No. 219/2002, para. 6.3.

284 Examples are ComAT, *H.D. v. Switzerland*, 30 April 1999, No. 112/1998; ComAT, *K.M. v. Switzerland*, 16 November 1999, No. 107/1998; ComAT, *H.A.D. v. Switzerland*, 10 May 2000, No. 126/1999; ComAT, *Y.S. v. Switzerland*, 14 November 2000, No. 147/1999.

285 Rule 63, para. 1, of the Rules of Procedure of the Committee against Torture of 11 February 2011 stipulates that 'The Committee may invite the Secretariat, specialized agencies, United Nations bodies concerned, Special Procedures of the Human Rights Council, intergovernmental organiza-

→

4.5.8 *Opportunities for presenting evidence and reacting to evidence*

In its proceedings, the Committee adheres to the principle of adversarial proceedings. In Rule 115 of its Rules of Procedure, it is stipulated that, as soon as possible after the complaint has been registered, it is transmitted to the State party. The State party is then requested to submit a written reply, relating both to the admissibility and the merits of the complaint, within six months. A complaint may not be declared admissible unless the State party concerned has received its text and has been given an opportunity to furnish information or observations, as provided in paragraph 1 of this rule. The State party or the complainant may request to be afforded an opportunity to comment on any submission received from the other party. The Committee sets a time limit for submitting such additional comments.[286]

Rule 117 stipulates that, when the Committee has decided that a complaint is admissible, it shall transmit to the State party the text of its decision together with any submission received from the author of the communication not already transmitted to the State party under Rule 115, paragraph 1. The Committee shall also inform the complainant, through the Secretary-General, of its decision. Within the period established by the Committee, the State party concerned shall then submit to the Committee written explanations or statements clarifying the case under consideration and the measures, if any, that may have been taken by it. These explanations or statements submitted by a State party are then transmitted to the complainant who may submit any additional written information or observations within such time limit as the Committee shall decide. The Committee may invite the complainant or his or her representative and representatives of the State party to be present at specified closed meetings of the Committee in order to provide further clarifications or to answer questions on the merits of the complaint. Whenever one party is so invited, the other party shall be informed and invited to attend and make appropriate submissions. The non-appearance of a party will not prejudice the consideration of the case. The Committee may revoke its decision that a complaint is admissible in the light of any explanations or statements thereafter submitted by the State party pursuant to this rule. However, before the Committee considers revoking that decision, the explanations or statements concerned must be transmitted to the complainant so that he or she may submit additional information or observations within a time limit set by the Committee.[287]

The structure of the decisions of the Committee generally reflects the principle of adversariality and the resulting debating rounds between the parties. Most decisions

---

tions, National Human Rights Institutions, non-governmental organizations, and other relevant civil society organizations, to submit to it information, documentation and written statements, as appropriate, relevant to the Committee's activities under the Convention.' Rule 118, para. 2, stipulates: 'The Committee, the Working Group, or the Rapporteur may at any time in the course of the examination obtain any document from United Nations bodies, specialized agencies, or other sources that may assist in the consideration of the complaint.'

286 Rule 115 of the Rules of Procedure of the Committee against Torture, paras. 1, 2, 8 and 10.
287 Rule 117 of the Rules of Procedure of the Committee against Torture, paras. 1-5.

contain a section entitled 'author's submissions, followed by a number of sections under the headings 'State party's observations', and 'author's submissions'.

In the proceedings before the Committee, a party is not allowed, in principle, to submit new statements and evidence which were not presented in the national proceedings. In a number of cases, the complainant submitted new statements or evidence for the first time before the Committee, which statements and evidence had not been presented earlier to the national authorities in the national proceedings.[288] Similarly, in certain cases, in the proceedings before the Committee, States parties have relied on new evidence resulting from investigations conducted after the termination of the national proceedings.[289] Just like the HRC, the Committee generally does not tolerate this and does not take into account statements and evidence produced for the first time in the proceedings before it. In such a situation, the Committee will normally examine whether there is a national remedy in which such new statements and new evidence can be brought forward and considered. It does not materially consider such statements and evidence itself, but instead refers complainants back to the national remedy, and concludes that national remedies have not been exhausted.[290] In *E.J. et al v. Sweden* (2008) the State party submitted to the Committee new evidence which had not been presented in the national proceedings. The Committee did not accept this.[291]

The case of *E.J. et al v. Sweden* (2008) is interesting for yet another reason. In the proceedings before the Committee, the State party relied on a report drawn up by its embassy in Ankara. This report was based on an investigation conducted by an anonymous source. The Committee noted that the author had had no opportunity to challenge the investigator whose name had not been revealed before the national authorities. It clearly found this problematic as it stated that this was one of the reasons why the State party should not have relied on the report in the proceedings before it.

4.5.9 *Application of investigative powers by the Committee*

In the section on the credibility assessment (section 4.5.5 above), it was made clear that by virtue of General Comment No. 1, paragraph 9,[292] the Committee has the

---

288 See, for example, ComAT, *M.X. v. Switzerland*, 7 May 2008, No. 311/2007, para. 9.4 (detention and sexual assault were not mentioned before the national Swiss asylum authorities, but were submitted only within theframework of the communication to the Committee against Torture); ComAT, *F.M-M. v. Switzerland*, 26 May 2011, No. 399/2009, para. 6.5 (new evidence submitted for the first time in the proceedings before the Committee).

289 ComAT, *E.J. et al v. Sweden*, 14 November 2008, No. 306/3006, para. 8.4.

290 See, for example, ComAT, *K.K.H. v. Canada*, 22 November 1995, No. 35/1995, para. 5.

291 ComAT, *E.J. et al v. Sweden*, 14 November 2008, No. 306/2006, para. 8.4.

292 General Comment No. 1, para. 9, states: 'Bearing in mind that the Committee against Torture is not an appellate, a quasi-judicial or an administrative body, but rather a monitoring body created by the States parties themselves with declaratory powers only, it follows that:
(a) Considerable weight will be given, in exercising the Committee's jurisdiction pursuant to article 3 of the Convention, to findings of fact that are made by organs of the State party concerned; but
(b) The Committee is not bound by such findings and instead has the power, provided by article 22, paragraph 4, of the Convention, of free assessment of the facts based upon the full set of circumstances in every case.'

possibility and freedom to choose, in each case before it, one of two approaches: reliance on the respondent State party's determination of the facts, or an independent determination of the facts on its own account. It was also made clear that the Committee's case law demonstrates that the Committee stresses its subsidiary role and considers that the determination of the facts is primarily a matter for the authorities of the States parties. In this respect the Committee strongly resembles the HRC. However, in a number of cases it has made its own fully independent assessment of the facts.[293] Two circumstances in particular seem to trigger it to proceed to an independent determination of the facts. A first trigger is that in the national proceedings, the absolute nature of Article 3 CAT was not respected and a weighing of national security considerations against the Article 3-danger took place.[294] This happened in *Dadar v. Canada* (2005): the primary stance of the State party's authorities was that the account was incredible; their subsidiary position was that, if the stated facts were assumed to be true, national security considerations outweighed the alleged Article 3-risk.[295]

A second trigger is that the State party's authorities did not take into consideration important facts or evidence. This happened in *C.T. and K.M. v. Sweden* (2007). In this case, the Committee considered that the State party's authorities had, in fact, not taken into account statements on past torture and corroborating medical evidence. It then proceeded to its own independent determination of the facts.[296]

The Committee has at its disposal a number of investigative powers which may help to obtain clarity on the facts of the case. On the basis of Rules 63, and 118, paragraph 2, of the Committee's Rules of Procedure, the Committee can *proprio motu* obtain information from a variety of sources, including the entire United Nations system, intergovernmental organisations, national human rights institutions, non-governmental organisations, and other relevant civil society organisations.[297] By applying this power, the Committee can obtain reports from various sources on the situation in the countries of origin. Applying this investigative power, the Committee has obtained and used reports drawn up by itself as a result of *ex officio* inquiries under the Article 20-inquiry procedure;[298] reports resulting from the Article 19-State reporting mecha-

293 See, for example, ComAT, *Khan v. Canada*, 15 November 1994, No. 015/1994, paras. 12.3-12.6; ComAT, *Heidar v. Sweden*, 19 November 2002, No. 204/2002, para.6.3; ComAT, *Dadar v. Canada*, 5 December 2005, No. 258/2004, para. 8.8.
294 See for the same conclusion about the reasons for the Committee to proceed to an independent determination of the facts: Wouters 2009, p. 492.
295 ComAT, *Dadar v. Canada*, 5 December 2005, No. 258/2004; see para. 8.8.
296 ComAT, *C.T. and K.M.v. Sweden*, 22 January 2007, No. 279/2005.
297 Rule 63, para. 1, of the Rules of Procedure of the Committee against Torture of 11 February 2011 stipulates that 'The Committee may invite the Secretariat, specialized agencies, United Nations bodies concerned, Special Procedures of the Human Rights Council, intergovernmental organizations, National Human Rights Institutions, non-governmental organizations, and other relevant civil society organizations, to submit to it information, documentation and written statements, as appropriate, relevant to the Committee's activities under the Convention.' Rule 118, para. 2, stipulates: 'The Committee, the Working Group, or the Rapporteur may at any time in the course of the examination obtain any document from United Nations bodies, specialized agencies, or other sources that may assist in the consideration of the complaint.'
298 See, for example, ComAT, *Falcon Ríos v. Canada*, 17 December 2004, No. 133/1999, para. 8.3.

nism;[299] reports drawn up by other United Nations organisations and agencies, such as the UNHCR,[300] and reports from non-governmental organisations, including Amnesty International.[301]

On the basis of Rule 115 of the Committee's Rules of Procedure, the Committee may request the State party concerned or the complainant to submit additional written information, clarification or observations relevant to the question of admissibility or merits.[302] Rule 117 further specifies that when the Committee requests the respondent State party to submit written explanations or statements clarifying the case, it may indicate the specific type of information it wishes to receive.[303] An example of a case in which the Committee used this investigative power is *A.S. v. Sweden* (2001).[304] After taking note of the submissions made by both the author and the State party regarding the merits of the case, the Committee requested further information from both parties.[305] It specifically requested the author to submit information about the author's older son, who had tried to seek asylum in Sweden from Denmark in March 2000, including records of his asylum interview.[306] In addition to the investigative powers mentioned above, the Committee also has the possibility to invite the complainant, or his or her representative and representatives of the State party concerned, to be present at specified closed meetings of the Committee in order to provide further clarification or to answer questions on the merits of the complaint.[307] This investigative power of questioning the parties on the merits at oral hearings distinguishes the Committee from the HRC, which does not have this power and does not hold oral hearings.[308]

Unfortunately, the Committee does not often make clear in its decisions how it obtained the information used to take a decision and whether it used the mentioned investigative powers.

---

299 See, for example, ComAT, *G.K. v. Switzerland*, 12 May 2003, No. 219/2002, para. 6.3.
300 See, for example, ComAT, *U.S. v. Finland*, 1 May 2003, No. 197/2002, para. 7.7.
301 Examples of cases in which the Committee used information from Amnesty International are ComAT, *H.B.H. et al v. Switzerland*, 16 May 2003, No. 192/2001, para. 6.9 and ComAT, *S.S. v. the Netherlands*, 19 May 2003, No. 191/2001, para. 6.3, footnote 8.
302 Rule 115, para. 5, of the Rules of Procedure of the Committee against Torture stipulates: 'The Committee or the Working Group established under rule 112 or Rapporteur(s) designated under rule 112, paragraph 3, may request, through the Secretary-General, the State party concerned or the complainant to submit additional written information, clarifications or observations relevant to the question of admissibility or merits.'
303 Rule 117, para. 2, of the Rules of Procedure of the Committee against Torture stipulates: 'Within the period established by the Committee, the State party concerned shall submit to the Committee written explanations or statements clarifying the case under consideration and the measures, if any, that may have been taken by it. The Committee may indicate, if it deems it necessary, the type of information it wishes to receive from the State party concerned.'
304 ComAT, *A.S. v. Sweden*, 15 February 2001, No. 149/1999.
305 *Ibidem*, para. 7.2.
306 *Ibidem*, paras. 7.6, 7.7.
307 Rule 117, para. 4, of the Rules of Procedure of the Committee against Torture stipulates: 'The Committee may invite the complainant or his/her representative and representatives of the State party concerned to be present at specified closed meetings of the Committee in order to provide further clarifications or to answer questions on the merits of the complaint. Whenever one party is so invited, the other party shall be informed and invited to attend and make appropriate submissions.'
308 See Chapter 3, section 3.5.9.

4.5.10   Time limits for presentation of statements and evidence

It has been pointed out above in section 4.5.8 that in the proceedings before the Committee, a party is not allowed, in principle, to submit new statements and evidence which were not presented in the national proceedings.

As was made clear above in section 4.5.5 on the credibility assessment, all the relevant facts and evidence must, in principle, be brought forward as early as possible. On the issue of presentation of statements and evidence at a late stage in the national proceedings– later than the initial interview(s) in the national asylum proceedings – the Committee's case law is not entirely consistent and seems to have become stricter in the course of time. In a number of early cases, the Committee did not perceive late presentation of facts and evidence in the national proceedings as problematic. In the case of *Khan v. Canada* (1994),[309] the author was first interviewed by immigration officials on 9 August 1990. In its decision, dated 14 January 1992, the Refugee Division had determined that the author was not a refugee and that his oral testimony had been fabricated. The author's leave to appeal had been dismissed by the Federal Court of Appeal on 22 April 1992. After having been informed that the author had submitted a communication to the Committee, the State party arranged for a review of the author's case by a post-claim determination officer. It was only during this post-claim procedure, in 1994, that the author had alleged past torture and that he had submitted medical evidence in support of these statements. In the proceedings before the Committee, the State party contended that it doubted the veracity of the author's statements. One of the reasons for this was that he had not mentioned past torture and had not presented medical evidence earlier in the national proceedings.[310] Importantly, the author had not explained why he had alleged past torture so late in the national proceedings. As an explanation for the late presentation of medical evidence he had referred only to the fact that he had been detained and that he had been medically examined after detention.[311] The Committee did not find the tardy mention of torture and the late presentation of evidence in support of this problematic:

'The Committee notes that some of the author's claims and corroborating evidence have been submitted only after his refugee claim had been refused by the Refugee Board and deportation procedures had been initiated; the Committee, however, also notes that this behaviour is not uncommon for victims of torture. The Committee, however, considers that, even if there could be some doubts about the facts as adduced by the author, it must ensure that his security is not endangered. The Committee notes that evidence exists that torture is widely practised in Pakistan against political dissenters as well as against common detainees.'[312]

In *Kisoki v. Sweden* (1996),[313] crucial evidence was submitted in support of a third asylum application. After refusal of a first and second application, the author had sub-

---

309   ComAT, *Khan v. Canada*, 15 November 1994, No. 15/1994.
310   *Ibidem*, para. 8.5.
311   *Ibidem*, para. 9.6.
312   *Ibidem*, para. 12.3.
313   ComAT, *Kisoki v. Sweden*, 8 May 1996, No. 041/1996.

mitted a new application to the Swedish Aliens Appeal Board, on the basis of new forensic medical evidence, prepared by the Centre for Torture and Trauma Survivors in Stockholm. The Aliens Appeal Board had rejected the author's application, judging that the information now submitted could easily have been submitted earlier, thereby decreasing the trustworthiness of the claim. The Committee did not say anything in its considerations about the fact that important evidence had been submitted only in support of a third application and not earlier. It is obvious from its considerations that it saw the author as a torture victim, obviously on the basis of the medical evidence presented in support of the author's third asylum application. We may infer from this that the Committee did not find the late presentation of crucial evidence problematic. Another example of this flexible approach is *Tala v. Sweden* (1996), in which case statements on past torture were presented after an asylum application had been rejected at the appeal stage. As the Committee did not say anything about this and accepted as true the stated facts on past torture, it obviously did not see the late presentation of the statements on past torture as problematic.[314] A final example of the Committee's early flexible approach is the case of *A.F. v. Sweden* (1998).[315] This case is striking, as it was only in support of a fourth asylum application that the author had corroborated his allegations about past torture in the Iranian Evin prison with medical evidence from the Centre for Torture and Trauma Survivors in Stockholm.[316] It is obvious from the Committee's considerations that it did not see the late presentation of this crucial evidence as problematic. It took the evidence into account and concluded that the author had a history of detention and torture.[317]

The above cases show that, in its early case law, the Committee approached the problem of late presentation of statements and evidence in a flexible way and did not specifically require good explanations from the author as to why statements and evidence had not been submitted earlier. Over the years, however, the Committee's approach towards late presentation of statements and evidence seems to have become stricter in the sense that the author must provide very good explanations for tardy presentations of statements and evidence. In a number of decisions taken after 2000, late submission of statements and late presentation of evidence were seen as negatively affecting the general veracity of the claim. In *X.Y. v. Switzerland* (2001), the claimant had mentioned past torture and presented evidence in corroboration of these statements only after his initial request for asylum had been rejected (in second asylum proceedings). The State party had clearly found this problematic.[318] Importantly, the author had not given a personal explanation as to why he had omitted to mention past torture earlier; instead, he referred to the Committee's flexible approach described above:

---

314 ComAT, *Tala v. Sweden*, 15 November 1996, No. 043/1996.
315 ComAT, *A.F. v. Sweden*, 8 May 1998, No. 089/1997.
316 *Ibidem*, para. 2.6.
317 *Ibidem*, para. 6.5.
318 ComAT, *X.Y. v. Switzerland*, 15 May 2001, No. 128/1999, paras. 6.7 and 6.8.

'With regard to the delay in making the allegation of torture, the author claims that the Committee itself has repeatedly emphasized that it is quite understandable for a torture victim initially to remain silent about his sufferings.'[319]

Without explicitly explaining the change, the Committee saw fit not to follow its flexible approach in this case, but, instead, applied a stricter approach:

'The Committee expresses doubts about the credibility of the author's presentation of the facts, since he did not invoke his allegations of torture or the medical certificate attesting to the possibility of his having been tortured until after his initial application for political asylum had been rejected.'[320]

Two years later, in *H.B. and others v. Switzerland* (2003), the Committee made clear that, in cases of late presentation of statements and tardy presentation of evidence, the author had to have good reasons for the delay. In relation to new evidence corroborating statements on membership of the Yekiti political party, an arrest warrant and a copy of a judgment sentencing the author to three years' imprisonment, presented after rejection of the initial asylum applications, the Committee considered as follows:

'The Committee considers that the above-mentioned documents were produced by the complainants only in response to decisions by the Swiss authorities to reject their application for asylum, and that the complainants have failed to offer any coherent explanation of the delay in making submissions.'[321]

The case of *V.L. v. Switzerland* (2006)[322] demonstrates, however, that tardy presentation of important facts and evidence is not always fatal to the case at hand. If sound explanations are provided by the author as to why he or she did not mention important matters and submit evidence earlier on, tardy statements and evidence are not problematic. The case of *V.L.* is an interesting example of how the Committee dealt with a situation in which a female asylum seeker came forward with a flight narrative based on sexual abuse at a very late stage in the national asylum proceedings. The complainant, together with her husband, applied for asylum in Switzerland on 19 December 2002. Both based their claims on the alleged political persecution of the

---

319 *Ibidem*, para. 7.3.
320 *Ibidem*, para.8.5.
321 ComAT, *H.B. and others. v. Switzerland*, 16 May 2003, No. 192/2001, para. 6.8. See, for the same approach – statements and evidence presented belatedly in the national proceedings are not taken into consideration by the Committee as no consistent and convincing explanation has been offered for their tardy production – ComAT, *Zubair Elahi v. Switzerland*, 20 May 2005, No. 222/2002, para.6.7, in this decision the Committee also attached importance to the fact that the author had had legal assistance throughout the national proceedings; and ComAT, *Z.K. v. Sweden*, 16 May 2008, No. 301/2006, para. 8.4.
322 ComAT, *V.L. v. Switzerland*, 20 November 2006, 262/2005. See on this case also Boeles in his article 'Case reports of the European Court of Human Rights, the Human Rights Committee, and the Committee against Torture' in: European Journal of Migration and Law 10 (2008). See also Wouters 2009, p. 477.

husband by the Belorussian authorities. These claims were not considered credible by the Swiss Federal Office for Refugees (BFF), which considered that the documents submitted by the claimants were not genuine. Consequently, the applications had been rejected on 14 August 2003 and the complainant and her husband had been ordered to leave the country by 9 October 2003. On 11 September 2003, the complainant and her husband appealed to the Swiss Asylum Review Board (ARK). The ARK rejected the appeal on 15 September 2004. The complainant requested a revision of this judicial decision on 11 October 2004, in which she mentioned for the first time that she had been sexually abused by police officers. She urged the Swiss authorities to reconsider her asylum application in its own right, rather than as part of her husband's claims, explaining that they now lived separately. The complainant claimed that her failure to mention the rape in her initial interview with the BFF had been due to the fact that she had considered it humiliating and an affront to her personal dignity. Furthermore, the psychological pressure from her husband had prevented her from mentioning the sexual abuse. She explained that her husband had disappeared in October 2004 and that his whereabouts were unknown to her. Now that he had left the country, she was, however, willing to provide details about the events described above and a medical certificate. In its decision of 1 December 2004, the Asylum Review Board acknowledged that, in principle, rape was a relevant factor to be considered in the asylum procedure, even when reported belatedly, and that there might be psychological reasons for victims not mentioning it in the first interview. However, the complainant's claims did not seem plausible, since she had neither substantiated nor proven psychological obstacles to at least mentioning the rape in the initial interview. The Committee considered as follows:

'The State party has argued that the complainant is not credible because the allegations of sexual abuse and the medical report supporting these allegations were submitted late in the domestic proceedings. The Committee finds, to the contrary, that the complainant's allegations are credible. The complainant's explanation of the delay in mentioning the rapes to the national authorities is totally reasonable. It is well-known that the loss of privacy and prospect of humiliation based on revelation alone of the acts concerned may cause both women and men to withhold the fact that they have been subject to rape and/or other forms of sexual abuse until it appears absolutely necessary. Particularly for women, there is the additional fear of shaming and rejection by their partner or family members. Here the complainant's allegation that her husband reacted to the complainant's admission of rape by humiliating her and forbidding her to mention it in their asylum proceedings adds credibility to her claim. The Committee notes that as soon as her husband left her, the complainant who was then freed from his influence immediately mentioned the rapes to the national authorities in her request for revision of 11 October 2004. Further evidence of her psychological state or psychological "obstacles," as called for by the State party, is unnecessary. The State party's assertion that the complainant should have raised and substantiated the issue of sexual abuse earlier in the revision proceedings is insufficient basis upon which to find that her allegations of sexual abuse lack credibility, particularly in view of the fact that she was not represented in the proceedings.'[323]

---

[323] *Ibidem*, para. 8.8.

The Committee found the explanation for the delay in mentioning the rapes 'totally reasonable', so that there was no obstacle to taking the rapes into account. Also important in this case was that the applicant had not been represented by legal counsel in the national proceedings.[324]

To conclude, the case law discussed above shows that it is expected from the claimant that he or she presents all the relevant statements and corroborating evidence as soon as possible. When statements and evidence are presented later on in the national proceedings, convincing explanations have to be given for this. In general, it seems that the Committee has become somewhat stricter in testing whether convincing explanations for tardy production of statements and evidence exist. Nevertheless, in a significant number of early and also later cases, the Committee did not see the tardy presentation of relevant statements and evidence as problematic and rather easily accepted that good reasons had been brought forward for the belated presentation of statements and evidence.

4.5.11   Point in time for the risk assessment

In cases where the complainant has not yet been expelled from the respondent State at the moment of examination by the Committee, the Committee assesses the existence of the alleged Article 3-danger on an *ex nunc* basis, which means that the material point in time is the moment at which it examines the case. The assessment of the danger is made on the basis of all the information available at the moment of consideration of the case by the Committee.[325]

The Committee's case law is not entirely consistent in cases where deportation from the respondent State has already been effectuated. In a number of cases, it has stated that the point in time for its risk assessment remains the moment of the removal: the question remains as to what is real and foreseeable at the moment of removal. Facts and circumstances which become known after the removal are relevant only in that they may confirm or refute what the State party knew or ought to have

---

324 Two more examples which make clear that tardy presentation of evidence is not always fatal to the case at hand are ComAT, *Iya v. Switzerland*, 16 November 2007, No. 299/2006, in which the author submitted identity documents during the appeal stage in the national proceedings, and ComAT, *Chahin v. Sweden*, 30 May 2011, No. 310/2007, in which the author brought forward statements on past torture and evidence thereof only in the proceedings following a second request for revocation of an expulsion order.

325 See, for example, ComAT, *A.D. v. the Netherlands*, 24 January 2000, No. 96/1997, para. 7.4 : 'The Committee is aware of the human rights situation in Sri Lanka but considers that, given the shift in political authority *and the present circumstances*, the author has not substantiated his claim that he will personally be at risk of being subjected to torture if returned to Sri Lanka *at present.*' (Emphasis added.) See also ComAT, *Attiav. Sweden*, 24 November 2003, No. 199/2002, para. 12.1: 'The issue before the Committee is whether removal of the complainant to Egypt would violate the State party's obligation under article 3 of the Convention not to expel or to return a person to another State where there are substantial grounds for believing that he or she would be in danger of being subjected by the Egyptian authorities to torture. In so doing, the Committee refers to its consistent practice of deciding this question as presented at the time of its consideration of the complaint, rather than as presented at the time of submission of the complaint. It follows that intervening events transpiring between submission of a complainant and its consideration by the Committee may be of material relevance for the Committee's determination of any issue arising under Article 3.'

known at the time of removal. In *Agiza v. Sweden* (2005), the Committee considered that

> 'Subsequent events are relevant to the assessment of the State party's knowledge, actual or constructive, at the time of the removal.'[326]

And in *Tebourski v. France* (2007), it considered:

> 'The Committee must determine whether, in deporting the complainant to Tunisia, the State party violated its obligation under article 3 of the Convention not to expel, return ("refouler") or extradite a person to another State where there are substantial grounds for believing that he would be in danger of being subjected to torture. The Committee stresses that it must take a decision on the question in the light of the information which the authorities of the State party had or should have had in their possession at the time of the expulsion. Subsequent events are useful only for assessing the information which the State party actually had or could have deduced at the time of expulsion.'[327]

However, in neither of these decisions did the Committee explicitly take into consideration subsequent events. In *Agiza v. Sweden* (2005), it stated (emphasis added) that 'the natural conclusion from the facts and circumstances *known at the time of the expulsion* was that a real risk existed'.[328] However, Wouters (2009) convincingly points out that it is very likely that the Committee did take into account the large number of subsequent events put forward by both parties, albeit indirectly or explicitly.[329] The subsequent events related mainly to safety guarantees, and the Committee considered that the safety guarantees did not suffice to protect against this manifest risk; by using the past tense the Committee indicated that it took subsequent events into account. Another indication that subsequent events were taken into account is that the Committee addressed the differences between its considerations in the *Agiza* case and the case of his wife, *Attia v. Sweden* (2003).[330] One of the differences between these cases was the breach by Egypt of the element of assurances relating to guaranteeing a fair trial. This breach came to light after the removal of Agiza.[331]

In *T.P.S. v. Canada* (2000), however, the Committee explicitly took subsequent facts and circumstances into consideration, making in fact an *ex nunc* risk assessment. In this case, the complainant had been removed to India more than two and a half years before the Committee decided the complaint. It took into account the fact that after the expulsion the complainant had had no serious problems in India and concluded that

---

326 ComAT, *Agiza v. Sweden*, 20 May 2005, No. 233/2003, para. 13.2.
327 ComAT, *Tebourski v. France*, 11 May 2007, No. 300/2006, para. 8.1. See on the point in time for the risk assessment also Wouters 2009, pp. 487-490.
328 See ComAT, *Agiza v. Sweden*, 20 May 2005, No. 233/2003, para. 13.3.
329 Wouters 2009, p. 489.
330 ComAT, *Attia v. Sweden*, 24 November 2003, No. 199/2002.
331 ComAT, *Agiza v. Sweden*, 20 May 2005, No. 233/2003, para. 13.5.

'It is unlikely that the author is still at risk of being subjected to acts of torture'.[332]

4.6   Final concluding remarks

The CAT is a specialised human rights treaty with a strong focus on combating the widespread and systematic practice of torture in different regions of the world. It has been ratified by all the EU Member States. The CAT does not contain a right to asylum, but it does contain an explicit prohibition on *refoulement* in Article 3, first paragraph, which stipulates that no State Party shall expel, return (*refouler*) or extradite a person to another State where there are substantial grounds for believing that he would be in danger of being subjected to torture. The Committee against Torture has developed a vast body of case law under Article 3 and the majority of the cases concern the expulsion of asylum seekers, which makes the CAT an important instrument in international asylum law.

In the first part of this chapter, the CAT's provisions on national provisions were explored. Article 3 and Article 22, fifth paragraph, second part CAT require an opportunity for effective, independent and impartial review of the decision on expulsion, prior to the expulsion itself. Just like the HRC, the Committee against Torture has for a long time been generally reluctant to submit national remedies and proceedings to a rigorous CAT compliance test. However, in more recent jurisprudence, the Committee has made clear that in order to qualify as an effective, independent and impartial national remedy as required by Article 3, national judicial remedies must make it possible to look at the substance, the merits of the case, and must guarantee equality of arms and adversarial proceedings. In the case of *Sogi v. Canada* (2007), the Committee required that all the documents in the file be disclosed to the claimant, including those underpinning the allegation that Sogi constituted a threat to Canada's national security. In other words, in *Sogi* the Committee treated adversariality and equality of arms as an absolute right and did not tolerate that national security interests justified the non-disclosure of part of the evidentiary materials.

In cases of allegations or suspicions of internal torture, the requirement of impartiality enshrined in Articles 12 and 13 obliges the national judge to reconstruct as meticulously as possible what actually happened and to use his or her investigative powers to that end. Impartiality under Article 3 may be interpreted as meaning the same thing as impartiality under Articles 12 and 13. That would mean that the national asylum judge must act impartially and must, therefore, make his or her own independent, thorough search for the truth and apply investigative powers to that end.

Article 15 CAT prohibits the use of statements made as a result of torture as evidence in any proceedings, except in criminal proceedings against a person accused of torture as evidence of the very fact that this statement was made. The Committee has, to date, not dealt with Article 15 in the context of asylum.

In the second part of this chapter, it was analysed, with the aid of the eleven aspects of evidence and judicial scrutiny, how the Committee against Torture assesses

---

332 ComAT, *T.P.S. v. Canada*, 4 September 2000, No. 99/1997, paras. 15.4 and 15.5.

claims under Article 3. The standard of proof follows directly from Article 3, first paragraph CAT. This provision stipulates that there must be 'substantial grounds for believing that the claimant would be in danger of being subjected to torture.' This means that there must be a real, personal, present and foreseeable risk of torture in the country to which the claimant is returned. Torture need not be certain or highly probable or likely, but there must be more than mere theory or suspicion.

The burden of proof in Article 3-claims is initially on the claimant; the claimant must generally present an arguable case. Where an arguable claim is provided by the claimant, a shift of the burden takes place and an obligation arises for the State party to make sufficient efforts to determine whether there are substantial grounds for believing that he or she would be in danger of being subjected to torture. There is an inversely proportional relationship between the onus on the claimant and the general human rights situation in the country of origin. The poorer this situation, the sooner it is assumed that the claimant runs a risk, the less he or she has to 'prove' and the sooner the onus shifts to the State party. If the human rights situation is not obviously poor, the onus shifts more towards the claimant, which means that more evidence is expected. It seems that with time, the Committee has become stricter and has placed a heavier burden on the applicant, requiring more detailed information and more evidence to shift the burden towards the national authorities.

Relevant facts and circumstances are all possible personal circumstances, and, as well as these, the general human rights situation in the country of origin are relevant. Many concrete examples of such circumstances were given above. The personal facts must be assessed in the light of the general situation in the country of origin. From the Committee's case law it becomes clear that it is normally a combination of facts and circumstances, and not a single fact, which indicate that there are substantial grounds for assuming a real Article 3-danger.

As to the required level of individual risk, the general consideration used in almost all the Committee's decisions stresses that a personal risk needs to be established, suggesting that it strictly requires an applicant to be singled out. However, recent case law – in particular the decisions in the cases of *Njamba v. Sweden* (2010) and *Bakatu-Bia v. Sweden* (2011) – has made clear that, just like the HRC, the Committee has relaxed this requirement of individualisation. In both cases, the Committee prohibited Sweden from returning women to the Democratic Republic of the Congo (DRC) due to the general high threat of (sexual) violence against women in that country.

As to the assessment of credibility, it follows from General Comment No. 1 that, depending on the particular case before it, the Committee has the possibility and freedom to choose one of two approaches: reliance on the respondent State party's determination of the facts, including the credibility assessment, or an independent determination of the facts and evaluation of the evidence on its own account. The Committee generally does not explain why it chooses one of the two avenues. It generally stresses its subsidiary role and considers that the determination of the facts and the assessment of evidence, including the assessment of credibility, is primarily a matter for the authorities of the States parties. In this respect the Committee strongly resembles the HRC. Just like the HRC, it has, so far, not developed an elaborate doctrinal position on the issue of the intensity of its scrutiny as an international treaty supervisor. It seems that two triggers in particular make the Committee proceed towards an independent determination of the facts. A first trigger is that in the national proceedings the absolute nature of Article 3 CAT was not respected. A second trigger is that the State party's authorities have not taken into consideration important facts or evidence (*C.T. and K.M. v. Sweden*, 2007). In assessing the credibility of the claimant's statements the Committee examines the 'general veracity'. This means that the statements made by the asylum seeker may contain some incredible or not entirely credible aspects, but that the core aspects – the basic story – must be credible, that is, sufficiently detailed, consistent with country information, consistent throughout the (national and international) proceedings, brought forward in a timely manner and corroborated by (some) evidence.

The Committee generally admits to the proceedings every possible form of evidence corroborating an alleged Article 3-danger.It generally requires the core aspects or central aspects of the claim to be supported by evidence other than the complainant's statements. The Committee is strict on this, requiring substantial evidence of the basic story; it needs a strongly corroborated case to obtain a positive decision from the Committee. It is not only important to submit evidence corroborating the individual account. Equally important is evidence about the human rights situation in the country of origin.

It is not easy to distinguish in the Committee's case law the exact factors determining the probative value and persuasiveness of evidence. The conclusions on the merits are often very brief, and it does not explicitly mention factors determining the probative value of the presented evidence. In a number of cases it is even completely silent about the evidence presented by the complainant and does not make clear how it has weighed or evaluated that evidence. However, from other cases it may be inferred that the authenticity of documents and the specificity and comprehensiveness of the information contained in evidentiary materials are important factors. Four categories of evidence were looked at in more detail. Strong probative value is often attached to reports submitted by States parties, containing the result of inquiries conducted by embassies or missions in the country to which the particular individual is planned to be expelled. Witness statements by family members may also be accorded significant probative value. A very prominent position in the case law of the Committee is taken by medico-legal reports, submitted as corroboration of alleged past torture and to explain inconsistencies or belated statements and evidence. In order to be considered as evidence with strong probative force in support of statements about past torture, medico-legal reports must be drawn up by medical specialists and must conclusively identify a causal link between the individual's bodily or mental injuries and the alleged past torture. In the Committee's early case law, such medico-legal reports often played a decisive role. With time, the Committee has come to approach medico-legal reports in a stricter way, and it seems that conclusive medico-legal reports have been downgraded from decisive to supportive. Just like the ECtHR and the HRC, the Committee uses country reports from different sources, often without specifically mentioning these sources and without explaining the reasons for giving them probative value.

The Committee regards the principles of equality of arms and adversarial proceedings as important and crucial for fairness of its own proceedings. The relevant

Rules of Procedure stipulate that, at both the admissibility stage and the merits stage, both parties to the case are allowed to submit their observations and evidence and to react to the observations and evidence lodged by the other party. The Committee does not normally allow the complainant or the respondent State to submit new statements and evidence which were not presented in the national proceedings.

The Committee has at its disposal a number of investigative powers which may help to obtain clarity on the facts of the case. It can *proprio motu* obtain information from the entire United Nations system, intergovernmental organisations, national human rights institutions, non-governmental organisations, and other relevant civil society organisations. It may also request the State party concerned or the complainant to submit additional written information, clarification or observations relevant to the question of admissibility or merits. In addition, it also has the possibility to invite the complainant, or his or her representative and representatives of the State party concerned, to be present at specified closed meetings in order to provide further clarification or to answer questions on the merits of the complaint. Unfortunately, the Committee does not often mention in its decisions how it obtained the information used to take a decision and whether it used the mentioned investigative powers.

As far as time limits for the presentation of statements and evidence are concerned, the Committee, as has been said, does not normally permit complainants to raise new statements or submit new evidence for the first time before it. As far as the national proceedings are concerned, it has been a basic, unchanged, principle that the claimant is expected to present all the relevant statements and corroborating evidence as soon as possible. When statements and evidence are presented later on in the national proceedings, convincing explanations have to be given for this. In general it seems that the Committee has become stricter in testing whether convincing explanations for tardy production of statements and evidence exist.

With regard to the eleventh aspect, the point in time for the risk assessment, it was concluded that the main rule, applying inin cases where the applicant has not yet been expelled at the moment of examination by the Committee, is that the Committee assesses the existence of the alleged Article 3-risk on an *ex nunc* basis. In cases where deportation from the respondent State has already been effectuated, the point in time for the consideration by the Committee is still the moment of expulsion. Facts and circumstances which become known after the removal are relevant only in that they may confirm or refute what the State party knew or ought to have known at the time of removal.

Chapter 5: The 1950 European Convention for the Protection of Human Rights and Fundamental Freedoms (ECHR)[1]

5.1 Introduction

The ECHR was drafted within the Council of Europe, an international organisation formed after the Second World War in an attempt to unify Europe, as a reaction to the serious human rights violations that Europe had witnessed during the war.[2] The ECHR was adopted in 1950 and it entered into force in 1953. All 47 Member States of the Council of Europe, including the 27 EU Member States, are party to the ECHR.[3] The rights in the Convention have been supplemented by further rights in a number of Protocols to the Convention that are binding upon those States that have ratified them (the First,[4] Fourth,[5] Sixth,[6] Seventh,[7] Twelfth[8] and Thirteenth[9] Protocols). In addition to these material Protocols, there are Protocols which have strengthened the judicial character and efficiency of the enforcement machinery. These procedural Protocols are the Eleventh Protocol,[10] which introduced fundamental reforms to the enforcement machinery of the Convention as of 1998. The Commission of Human Rights was abolished and a new European Court of Human Rights (ECtHR), composed of full-time judges, was introduced. The Fourteenth Protocol,[11] which entered into force on 1 June 2010,[12] is aimed at further improving the efficien-

---

1   See the following literature for more comprehensive general descriptions and analyses of the history and working of the ECHR: (see bibliography for full titles): Barkhuijsen 1998, Blake 2004, Dembour 2006, Harris, O'Boyle, Bates & Buckley 2009, Kempees 1996-2000, Lawson 1999, Lawson 2006, Myjer & Lawson 2000, Ovey & White 2006, Robertson 1975-1985, Van Dijk et al. 2006. For the implications of the ECHR for asylum see Battjes 2006, Mole 2007, Spijkerboer & Vermeulen 2005, Wouters 2009, Van Bennekom & Van der Winden 2011.
2   Van Dijk et al. 2006, pp. 2-4.
3   All the European states, except for Belarus and the Vatican City, which are not Council of Europe members. See for this general information on the history, the adoption and the entry into force of the ECHR, as well as the States parties to it, the first chapter of Harris and others 2009, as well as the website of the Council of Europe: http://www.coe.int.
4   213 UNTS 262; ETS 9. Adopted 1952, in force 1954, 45 parties: all Convention parties except Monaco and Switzerland.
5   1469 UNTS 263; ETS 46. Adopted 1963, in force 1968, 40 parties: all Convention parties except Andorra, Greece, Spain, Switzerland, Turkey and the UK.
6   ETS 114. Adopted 1983, in force 1985, 46 parties: all Convention parties except Russia.
7   ETS 117. Adopted 1984, in force 1988. 41 parties, all Convention parties except Belgium, Germany, the Netherlands, Spain, Turkey, and the UK.
8   ETS 177; 8 IHRR 300 (2000). Adopted 2000, in force 2005, 17 parties: Albania, Andorra, Armenia, Bosnia and Herzegovina, Croatia, Cyprus, Finland, Georgia, Luxembourg, Montenegro, the Netherlands, Romania, San Marino, Serbia, Spain, FYRM, and Ukraine.
9   ETS 187; 9 IHRR 884 (2002). Adopted 2002, in force 2003, 40 parties: all Convention parties except Armenia, Azerbaijan, Italy, Latvia, Poland, Russia and Spain.
10 ETS 155;1-3 IHRR 206 (1994). Adopted 1994. In force 1998. Ratified by all Convention parties.
11 ETS 194; 9 IHRR 884 (2002). Adopted 2004. In force 2010.
12 Ratification by all the States parties to the Convention is necessary. Russia ratified on 4 February 2010, after lengthy and problematic discussions in parliament.

cy of the enforcement machinery. The large number of States parties to the ECHR, the long history and the impressive body of binding case law of the ECtHR) make the ECHR a very important human rights treaty in Europe.

5.1.1   The ECHR and asylum

The ECHR does not contain a right to political asylum.[13] However, Article 3, which provides that no one shall be subjected to torture or to inhuman or degrading treatment or punishment, contains an implicit prohibition on *refoulement*. The first case in which the ECtHR derived this prohibition on *refoulement* from Article 3 was *Soering v. the UK* (1989).[14] This was not an asylum case but a case concerning the extradition of a German national from the United Kingdom to the United States, where he faced capital murder charges in connection with the accusation of killing the parents of his girlfriend. In *Soering*, the ECtHR developed the rule that it would be a breach of Article 3 for a State party to the ECHR to send an individual to another State where substantial grounds had been shown for believing that the individual concerned, if extradited, faced a real risk of being subjected to torture or to inhuman or degrading treatment or punishment in the requesting country. The Court unanimously decided that the extradition of Soering would indeed be in breach of Article 3 as there was a real risk that he would be exposed to the death row phenomenon. Given the very long period of time spent on death row in extreme conditions, with the ever present and mounting anguish of awaiting execution of the death penalty, and given the age and the mental state of the applicant at the time of the offence, the Court concluded that extradition would indeed subject Soering to treatment contrary to Article 3.[15]

The *refoulement* prohibition developed in *Soering* was expanded to the situation of the expulsion of asylum seekers in *Cruz Varas and others v. Sweden* (1991).[16] In this case, the first applicant, Hector Cruz Varas, who had applied for asylum in Sweden together with his wife and son, stated that he had taken part in various clandestine and subversive political activities in Chile in collaboration with the Frente Patriótico Manuel Rodriguez (FPMR), a radical organisation that had tried to kill General Pinochet. As a result, he had been arrested on various occasions and tortured by the Chilean police. He claimed that because of his previous activities, his expulsion exposed him to the risk that he would be arrested and tortured once more on his return to Chile, where torture was still prevalent.[17] In the national proceedings, the Swedish

---

13   See, for example, ECtHR, *Vilvarajah and others v. the UK*, 30 October 1991, Appl. Nos. 13163/87, 13164/87, 13165/87, 13447/87 and 13448/87, para, 102, ECtHR, *Mamatkulov and Abdurasulovic v. Turkey*, 6 February 2003, Appl. Nos. 46827/99, 46951/99, para. 65, ECtHR, *Abdolkhani and Karimnia v. Turkey*, 22 September 2009, Appl. No. 30471/08, para. 72, ECtHR, *Sufi and Elmi v. the UK*, 28 June 2011, Appl. Nos. 8319/07 and 11449/07, para. 212. See also Van Bennekom and Van der Winden 2011, p. 211.

14   ECtHR, *Soering v. the UK*,7 July 1989, Appl. No. 14038/88.

15   *Ibidem*, paras. 91 and 111.

16   ECtHR, *Cruz Varas and others v. Sweden*, 20 March 1991, Appl. No. 15576/89, para. 70: 'Although the present case concerns expulsion as opposed to a decision to extradite, the Court considers that the above principle also applies to expulsion decisions and a fortiori to cases of actual expulsion.'

17   *Ibidem*, para. 72.

authorities rejected the claim on the ground that the applicant had made contradictory statements and had radically changed his story. The applicant and the claim were found incredible for these reasons.[18]

The ECtHR followed the reasoning of the Swedish Government. The Court found that the available medical evidence did support the claim that the applicant had been subjected to ill-treatment in the past, but not that the Chilean police had been behind this. Like the Swedish authorities, the Court seriously doubted the credibility of the applicant's story, due to his complete silence as to his alleged clandestine activities and torture by the Chilean police until more than eighteen months after his first interrogation, the numerous changes in his story and the fact that no evidence corroborating his clandestine activities had been presented.[19] The Court also noted that a democratic evolution was in the process of taking place in Chile, which had led to improvements in the political situation and to the voluntary return of refugees from Sweden and elsewhere.[20] The Court, finally, attached importance to the fact that the Swedish authorities had particular knowledge and experience in evaluating asylum claims lodged by Chilean asylum seekers, and that the final decision to expel the applicant had been taken after thorough examinations of his case. The Court concluded that no substantial grounds had been shown for believing that the first applicant's expulsion would expose him to a real risk of being subjected to torture or inhuman or degrading treatment on his return to Chile in October 1989 and that, accordingly, there had been no breach of Article 3.[21]

A significant number of other judgments and admissibility decisions concerning the expulsion of (failed) asylum seekers followed the case of *Cruz Varas and others v. Sweden* (1991) so that a vast body of case law concerning the expulsion of asylum seekers is now available. As a result, Article 3 has become a very important prohibition on *refoulement,* which is frequently invoked in national asylum proceedings. Article 3 offers absolute protection, which means that it is not open to the respondent State party to claim that its own public interest reasons for expelling the individual outweigh the risk of ill-treatment on his or her return.[22] Article 3 also contains a non-derogable right,[23] meaning that even in times of war or other public emergencies threatening the life of the nation, it is not allowed for States parties to take measures dero-

---

18 *Ibidem*, para. 25.
19 *Ibidem*, paras. 77 – 79.
20 *Ibidem*, para. 80.
21 *Ibidem*, paras. 81, 82.
22 Some examples of judgments concerning expulsion in which the absolute nature of Article 3 was stressed are ECtHR, *Saadi v. Italy* 28 February 2008, Appl. No. 37201/06, paras. 137-141; ECtHR, *Dbouba v. Turkey*, 13 July 2010, Appl. No. 15916/09, para. 40; ECtHR, *A. v. the Netherlands*, 20 July 2010, Appl. No. 4900/06, paras. 142-143; ECtHR, *Charahili v. Turkey*, 13 April 2010, Appl. No. 46605/07, para. 58; ECtHR, *Sufi and Elmi v. the UK*, 28 June 2011, Appl. Nos. 8319/07 and 11449/07, para. 212. See also Van Bennekom & Van der Winden 2011, p. 211.
23 Article 15 (derogation in time of emergency) stipulates in para. 1 that: 'in time of war or other public emergency threatening the life of the nation any High Contracting Party may take measures derogating from its obligations under this Convention to the extent strictly required by the exigencies of the situation, provided that such measures are not inconsistent with its other obligations under international law'. Para. 2 stipulates that: 'no derogation from Article 2, except in respect of deaths resulting from lawful acts of war, or from Articles 3, 4 (paragraph 1) and 7 shall be made under this provision'.

gating from their obligations under Article 3. Because of its absolute and non-dero-gable character, and because Article 3 is not conditioned by the five grounds of per-secution contained in Article 1 A (2) RC, Article 3 in this respect offers broader pro-tection than Article 33 RC.[24]

As this book focuses on issues of evidence and judicial scrutiny in asylum court proceedings, but is not a comprehensive analysis of the prohibitions on *refoulement* contained in international asylum law, the concepts of torture and inhuman or de-grading treatment or punishment are not analysed further here. Other authors have done this before.[25]

5.1.2 *Supervisory mechanisms*

Compared to most other international human rights treaties, the ECHR has very strong enforcement mechanisms. Three international monitoring institutions can be distinguished, being the ECtHR, the Committee of Ministers and the Secretary Gen-eral of the Council of Europe.

States[26] and individuals[27] are entitled to lodge complaints to the ECtHR, which is a permanent judicial body composed of full-time judges, established under the ECHR to ensure the observance of the obligations undertaken by the States parties.[28]

Unlike the ICCPR and the CAT, where the right of individual complaint is op-tional – that is, only applicable as against those parties that have made a declaration accepting it – under the ECHR, the right of individual complaint has been compul-sory since the Eleventh Protocol entered into force in 1998.[29] The ECtHR consists of a number of judges equal to the number of States parties[30] who have to be of high moral character and who either possess the qualifications required for appointment to high judicial office or are jurisconsults of recognised competence. The judges serve in their own personal capacity and do not represent their respective governments.[31]

It follows from Article 46, first paragraph, which stipulates that the Contracting Parties 'undertake to abide by the final judgment of the Court in any case to which

---

24 See Wouters 2009 for a much more detailed material comparison of the prohibitions on *refoulement* on pp. 525-578. See also Westerveen 2011 for an asylum-focused comparison of the RC and the ECHR.

25 See, for example, Wouters 2009, pp. 221-244 and Van Dijk et al. 2006, pp. 406-418.

26 Article 33 ECHR stipulates: 'Any High Contracting Party may refer to the Court any alleged breach of the provisions of the Convention and the Protocols thereto by another High Contracting Party.'

27 Article 34 ECHR stipulates: 'The Court may receive applications from any person, non-government-al organisation or group of individuals claiming to be the victim of a violation by one of the High Contracting Parties of the rights set forth in the Convention or the Protocols thereto. The High Contracting Parties undertake not to hinder in any way the effective exercise of this right.'

28 See Article 19 ECHR.

29 Protocol No. 11 (ETS 155;1-3 IHRR 206 (1994), adopted 1994, in force 1998, ratified by all Con-vention parties) introduced in its Article 1 a new Article 34, which stipulates: 'The Court may receive applications from any person, non-governmental organisation or group of individuals claiming to be the victim of a violation by one of the High Contracting Parties of the rights set forth in the Convention or the protocols thereto. The High Contracting Parties undertake not to hinder in any way the effective exercise of this right.'

30 See Article 20 ECHR.

31 See Article 21 ECHR.

they are parties', that the judgments of the ECtHR have binding force.[32] This feature clearly distinguishes the ECHR from the ICCPR and the CAT, which have weaker monitoring bodies in the shape of Committees issuing non-binding views. Even though it follows from the text of Article 46, first paragraph, that in a particular case only the respondent State is obliged to abide by the final judgment of the ECtHR, the judgment is of significant importance to States parties not involved in that particular case. The ECtHR has also ruled in this respect that

> 'The Court's judgments in fact serve not only to decide those cases brought before the Court, but, more generally, to elucidate, safeguard and develop the rules instituted by the Convention, thereby contributing to the observance by the States of the engagements undertaken by them as Contracting Parties (…)'.[33]

According to Article 46, second paragraph, once the Court's final judgment has been transmitted to the Committee of Ministers, the latter invites the respondent State to inform it of the steps taken to pay the amounts awarded by the Court in respect of just satisfaction, and, where appropriate, of the individual and general measures taken to abide by the judgment.[34] It is the Committee of Ministers' practice to keep cases on its agenda until the States concerned have taken satisfactory measures.[35] The ICCPR and the CAT also lack this strong supervision mechanism of Article 46, second paragraph. The Secretary General of the Council of Europe may, under Article 52 ECHR, request any State party to furnish an explanation of the manner in which its internal law ensures the effective implementation of the ECHR.[36]

5.1.3   Provisions on national proceedings

The ECHR and a number of its Protocols contain provisions regulating national proceedings. In this chapter, the focus is on provisions with immediate relevance for national judicial proceedings in asylum cases. These are Article 6, first paragraph, on the right to a fair trial, Article 13 on the right to an effective national remedy, Article 3, which contains a procedural limb imposing certain requirements on national judicial proceedings, and Article 35, first paragraph, which requires that applicants should first exhaust effective national remedies before applying to the ECtHR. The case law

---

32 See also Van Dijk et al. 2006, pp. 291-321.
33 ECtHR, *Ireland v. the United Kingdom*, 18 January 1978, Appl. No. 5310/71, para. 154. This notion of binding force towards all States parties to the ECHR was reaffirmed in *Opuz v. Turkey*, 9 June 2009, Appl. No. 33401/02.
34 See the Rules of the Committee of Ministers for the application of Article 46, second paragraph, of the Convention; http://www.coe.int/T/E/Human_rights/execution.
35 Rule 4(a) of the Rules of the Committee of Ministers provides that, until the State concerned has provided information on the payment of the just satisfaction awarded by the Court or concerning possible individual measures, the case will be placed on the agenda of each human rights meeting of the Committee of Ministers, unless the Committee decides otherwise. See for more detailed information on the supervision of the execution of the Court's judgments by the Committee of Ministers: Sitaropoulos 2008, Wouters 2009, pp. 196-198.
36 See for more information on this power of the Secretary General of the Council of Europe, Schokkenbroek 2006.

under Article 35, first paragraph, may help to explain when a national remedy is considered (in)effective, in addition to the jurisprudence on Article 13.

The choice to investigate Article 6, first paragraph may seem odd, as it is standard case law of the ECtHR that Article 6 is not applicable in asylum cases.[37] For the purpose of this research it is, nevertheless, useful to examine this provision. Since its judgment in *Kudla v. Poland* (2000),[38] the ECtHR has held that the requirements of Article 13 should be considered as 'reinforcing' those of Article 6, first paragraph.[39] It may be inferred from this that the requirements developed under Article 6, first paragraph, also form part of the more general and broader Article 13. For a good understanding of Article 13 it is, therefore, necessary to have knowledge of the requirements of Article 6, first paragraph. Second, the case law of the ECtHR under Article 6, first paragraph, defines to a large extent the content of Article 47, second paragraph, of the Charter of Fundamental Rights of the European Union,[40] containing the right to a fair hearing, which provision will normally be applicable to asylum court proceedings. Reference is made to Chapter 6 on EU asylum law, section 6.3, for a more detailed analysis of this incorporation of Article 6 ECHR into EU law via Article 47 of the EU Charter.

Article 5, fourth paragraph, ECHR, containing the right to a speedy trial in cases of detention, and Article 1 of Protocol No. 7 to the ECHR on the expulsion of aliens and the procedure to be followed in cases of expulsion, are not extensively explored in this chapter. The reasons are that the detention of asylum seekers is not covered by this research and that Article 1 of Protocol 7 has, so far, not yielded jurisprudence of interest to the questions of this research.[41]

---

37 The first judgment in which the ECtHR ruled that Article 6 is not applicable to cases concerning the expulsion of a non-citizen is ECtHR, *Maaouia v. France*, 5 October 2000, Appl. No. 39652/98, paras. 33-41; it was repeated in a number of later judgments, for example ECtHR, *Mamatkulov and Abdurasulovic v. Turkey*, 4 February 2005, Appl. Nos. 46827/99 and 46951/99, paras. 80, 81. The idea was that cases concerning expulsion did not involve either a civil right or a criminal charge. In literature, criticism has been voiced about this approach; see, for example, Wouters 2009, pp. 344-345.

38 ECtHR,*Kudla v. Poland*, 26 October 2000, Appl. No. 30210/96.

39 *Ibidem*, para. 152. Van Dijk 2006 describes a change in the caselaw of the ECtHR as the Court in pre-*Kudla* case law tended to rule that the requirements of Article 13 were less strict than, and susceptible to absorption by, those of Article 6, first paragraph.In *Kudla,* the ECtHR made a crucial departure from this case law by ruling that the requirements of Article 13 reinforced those of Article 6(1) rather than being absorbed by the requirements of Article 6, paragraph 1. See Van Dijk et al., pp. 1017-1021. The *Kudla*approach was followed in later cases, see, for example, *Romashov v. Ukraine*27 July 2004, Appl. No. 67534/01, paras. 42-47.

40 *OJ of the EU* 2000, C-364/1. Certain parts of this version of the Charter were amended subsequently. The version now in force can be found in *OJ of the EU* 2010, C-83/02. See Chapter 6 for a more detailed analysis of the (history of the) Charter.

41 Article 1 of Protocol No. 7 stipulates:
'1. An alien lawfully resident in the territory of a State shall not be expelled therefrom except in pursuance of a decision reached in accordance with law and shall be allowed:
a. to submit reasons against his expulsion,
b. to have his case reviewed, and
c. to be represented for these purposes before the competent authority or a person or persons designated by that authority.

$\rightarrow$

5.1.4   *Chapter outline*

The content of this chapter is divided into two parts. Part 1 covers the ECHR's provisions on national proceedings. The central question in Part 1 is what these provisions say about the required intensity of national judicial scrutiny and what they say about evidentiary issues in national asylum court proceedings. The provisions on national proceedings are first briefly introduced in section 5.2. Many readers will be familiar with these basics, but some knowledge of them is indispensable before we focus on the asylum context. Section 5.3 discusses how the provisions on national proceedings work in the asylum context and, more in particular, what the provisions require from national asylum courts with regard to the intensity of judicial scrutiny and with regard to issues of evidence.

In section 5.4 we will look at the question of the required intensity of judicial scrutiny under Article 6, first paragraph. The Zumtobel doctrine, and its implications for national asylum courts, is discussed here. Section 5.5 examines the implications of Article 6, first paragraph, for issues of evidence in national proceedings. Special attention will be paid to the acceptability of the use of secret evidence in national proceedings.

In Part 2, the assessment performed by the ECtHR itself in cases concerning the expulsion of asylum seekers is analysed with the aid of the eleven aspects of evidence and judicial scrutiny introduced in Chapter 1. In section 5.7, final concluding remarks are made.

---

2. An alien may be expelled before the exercise of his rights under paragraph 1.a, b and c of this Article, when such expulsion is necessary in the interests of public order or is grounded on reasons of national security.'

Article 1 of Protocol 7 very much resembles Article 32 RC (discussed in Chapter 2) and Article 13 ICCPR (discussed in Chapter 3). It contains exactly the same procedural rights in cases of expulsion, being the right to submit reasons against the expulsion, the right to review and the right to be represented before the competent review authority. Compared to Article 32 RC and Article 13 ICCPR, Article 1 of Protocol 7 to the ECHR is broader in the sense that it allows expulsion before the exercise of these rights on both grounds of public order and national security whereas Articles 32 RC and 13 ICCPR only allow such expulsions when national securityso requires. From the Explanatory Report on Protocol 7 (to be found at:) it follows, however, that persons who are waiting for a decision on a request for a residence permit are explicitly excluded from the scope of Article 1 of Protocol No. 7 and that the right of review contained in paragraph 1 of Article 1 of Protocol No. 7 does not pertain to judicial appeal proceedings. This is also stressed in literature. See Boeles 1997, pp. 286-288, Van Dijk et al. 2006, pp. 953-957 and 965-969, Wouters 2009, pp. 342-344. This restricted personal scope is also stressed in the limited jurisprudence of the Court under this provision.See ECtHR, *Sejdovic and Sulejmanovic*, admissibility decision,14 March 2002,Appl. No. 57575/00, ECtHR, *Sulejmanovic and Sultanovic v. Italy*, admissibility decision, 14 March 2002, Appl. No. 57574/00, *Bolat v. Russia*, 5 October 2006, Appl. No. 14139/03 and *Shchukin and others v. Cyprus*, 29 July 2010, Appl. No. 14030/03. It is in this respect – the personal scope – that Article 1 of Protocol No. 7 differs clearly from Articles 32 RC and 13 ICCPR. Because of the limited personal scope and because the provision does not pertain to judicial review or appeal proceedings, the relevance for this research is minimal. See also Boeles 1997, p. 288, who qualifies Article 1 of Protocol 7 as taking a subordinate position within the total web of the other provisions on proceedings within the ECHR.

ECHR, Part 1:

Provisions on national proceedings;
Issues of intensity of judicial scrutiny and evidentiary issues in national judicial proceedings

5.2   Basics: introduction to the provisions on national proceedings

5.2.1   Texts of the provisions on national proceedings

Article 3 stipulates:

'No one shall be subjected to torture or to cruel, inhuman or degrading treatment or punishment.'

Article 6, first paragraph, stipulates:

'In the determination of his civil rights and obligations or of any criminal charge against him, everyone is entitled to a fair and public hearing within a reasonable time by an independent and impartial tribunal established by law. Judgment shall be pronounced publicly but the press and public may be excluded from all or part of the trial in the interest of morals, public order or national security in a democratic society, where the interests of juveniles or the protection of the private life of the parties so require, or to the extent strictly necessary in the opinion of the court in special circumstances where publicity would prejudice the interests of justice.'

Article 13 stipulates:

'Everyone whose rights and freedoms as set forth in the Convention are violated shall have an effective remedy before a national authority notwithstanding that the violation has been committed by persons acting in an official capacity.'

Article 35, first paragraph, stipulates:

'The Court may only deal with the matter after all national remedies have been exhausted, according to the generally recognised rules of international law, and within a period of six months from the date on which the final decision was taken.'

5.2.2   The procedural limb of Article 3

According to the ECtHR's case law, Article 3 contains an important procedural obligation: where an individual raises an arguable claim that Article 3 has been violated (or threatens to be violated), Article 3 requires an independent, effective and thorough official investigation, aimed at securing all the available evidence concerning the incident, which should be a prompt response and reasonable expedition and which guarantees a sufficient element of public scrutiny.[42]

5.2.3 Article 6, first paragraph: the right to a fair hearing

Article 6, first paragraph, grants the right of access to court[43] and requires that national judicial proceedings are fair,[44] take place before an independent and impartial tribunal established by law,[45] hearings and judgments should be public[46] and judgment is to be rendered within a reasonable time.[47] Independence of courts and tribunals refers to the structural relationship between the judiciary and other government structures. The functions and competences of the judiciary and, for example, the executive, should be clearly distinguishable and the latter should not be able to control or direct the former.[48] Impartiality of courts and tribunals refers to the relationship between a judge and the matter at issue in a specific case; it implies that judges must not harbour preconceptions about the matter put before them and must not act in ways that promote the interests of one of the parties.[49]

'Fair' in Article 6, first paragraph, means that the parties to the case have equal arms, meaning that each party is afforded a reasonable opportunity to present his or her case, including his or her evidence, under conditions that do not place him or her at a substantial disadvantage vis-à-vis the other side.[50] 'Fair' also means that proceedings are adversarial: parties must have knowledge of and must be able to comment on the observations filed or evidence adduced by the other party.[51] Other components of 'fairness' are that the decision or judgment is reasoned[52] and that individuals have the right to attend proceedings and participate effectively in them.[53]

---

42 See, for example, ECtHR, *Slimani v. France*, 27 July 2004, Appl. No. 57671/00, paras. 30-32. See also Van Dijk et al. 2006, p. 410, Harris, O'Boyle, Bates & Buckley 2009, pp. 108, 110.

43 See for an extensive explanation of the right of access to court Harris et al. 2009, pp. 235-246, Van Dijk et al. 2006, pp. 557-559, Ovey & White 2006, pp. 170-174.

44 See for a detailed description of the right to a fair hearing and its different aspects: Harris, O'Boyle, Bates & Buckley 2009, pp. 246-271, Van Dijk et al. 2006, pp. 578-596, Ovey & White 2006, pp. 175-181.

45 For an extensive description of the requirements of independence and impartiality, I refer to Harris, O'Boyle, Bates & Buckley 2009, pp. 284-298, Van Dijk et al. 2006, pp. 612-623, Ovey & White 2006, pp. 181-185.

46 See for a detailed discussion of the requirement of publicity Harris et al. 2009, pp. 271-278, Ovey & White 2006, pp. 185-189.

47 For an extensive discussion of the reasonable time requirement, see Harris, O'Boyle, Bates & Buckley 2009, pp. 278-284, Ovey & White 2006, pp. 187-188, Van Dijk et al. 2006, pp. 602-612.

48 For example, ECtHR, *Ringeisen v. Austria*, 16 July 1971, Appl. No. 2614/65, para. 95.

49 For example, ECtHR, *Tierce and Others v. San Marino*, 25 July 2000, Appl. Nos 24954/94, 24971/94, 24972/94, paras. 78-81.

50 See, for example, ECtHR, *Dombo Beheer B.V. v. the Netherlands*, 27 October 1993, Appl. No. 14448/88, para. 33.

51 See, for example, ECtHR, *Kress v. France*, 7 June 2001, Appl. No.39594/98, para. 65.

52 See, for example, ECtHR, *Van de Hurk v. the Netherlands*, 19 April 1994, Appl. No. 16034/90, para. 61.

53 An example of a criminal case is ECtHR, *Kremzow v. Austria*, 21 September 1993, Appl. No. 12350/86, para. 67; an example of a civil case is ECtHR, *Salomonsson v. Sweden*, 12 November 2002, Appl.

$\rightarrow$

5.2.4   Article 13: the right to an effective remedy

Article 13 accords to individuals a means whereby they can obtain relief at national level for violations of their ECHR rights, before having recourse to the Strasbourg system.[54] The machinery of complaint to the ECtHR is, thus, subsidiary to national systems safeguarding human rights. To make Article 13 applicable, there must be an arguable claim that an ECHR right has been violated. This means that the claim is supported by demonstrable facts and is not manifestly lacking in any ground in law.[55]

The scope of obligations flowing from Article 13 depends on the nature of the complaint.[56] The Court has accepted that the context in which an alleged violation occurs (for example, national security considerations) may entail inherent limitations on the conceivable remedy.[57] In the case of alleged violations of fundamental rights of a non-derogable nature, such as the right contained in Article 3, the obligations flowing from Article 13 are more stringent.[58] To be effective, the remedy must be truly usable and personally accessible[59] and the national authority must take a decision within a reasonable time.[60] Furthermore, the national remedy must make it possible to enforce the substance of the Convention rights and freedoms and the decision taken by the national authority must be binding.[61] Although no single national remedy may itself entirely satisfy the requirements of Article 13, the aggregate of remedies provided for under national law can do so.[62]

No. 38978/97, paras. 36-40. See also Harris et al. 2009, pp. 250-251, Ovey & White 2006, pp. 180-181.

54   Collected edition of the *Travaux Préparatoires* of the ECHR, Vol. II, p. 485-490, and Vol. III, p. 651. See also ECtHR, *Kudla v. Poland*, 26 October 2000, Appl. No. 30210/96, para. 152. See for a recent judgment concerning asylum in which the subsidiary nature of the ECtHR was stressed once again: ECtHR, *M.S.S. v. Belgium and Greece*, 21 January 2011, Appl. No. 30696/09, para. 287.

55   See, for example, ECtHR, *Kudla v. Poland*, 26 October 2000, Appl. No. 30210/96, para. 157 and ECtHR, *Hirsi Jamaa and others v. Italy*, 23 February 2012, Appl. No. 27765/09, para. 197. For a more detailed discussion of the arguability test, see Van Dijk et al. 2006, pp. 1000-1006, Wouters 2009, pp. 333-336.

56   See, for example, ECtHR, *Hirsi Jamaa and others v. Italy*, 23 February 2012, Appl. No. 27765/09, para. 197.

57   See, for example, ECtHR, *Leander v. Sweden*, 26 March 1987, Application No. 9248/81, para. 84; ECtHR, *Kudla v. Poland*, 26 October 2000, Appl. No. 30210/96, para. 151. Harris, O'Boyle, Bates & Buckley 2009 give an interesting overview and analysis of Article 13 decisions with national security connotations, see pp. 568-570.

58   ECtHR, *Klass and others v. Germany*, 6 September 1978, Appl. No. 5029/71, para. 69; ECtHR, *Chahal v. the UK*, 15 November 1996, Appl. No. 22414/93, paras. 150, 151; Barkhuysen 1998, p. 123, Van Dijk et al. 2006, p. 999, Harris, O'Boyle, Bates & Buckley 2009, p. 559.

59   See ECtHR, *Akdivar v. Turkey* 16 September 1996, Appl. No. 21893/93, paras. 93-97, where the ECtHR concluded that there was a remedy on paper, but too many practical obstacles to using it, so that the remedy could not be regarded as effective.

60   See, for example, ECtHR, *Plaksin v. Russia*, 29 April 2004, Appl. No. 14949/02, para. 35.

61   See, for example, ECtHR, *Chahal v. the UK*, 15 November 1996, Appl. No. 22414/93, para. 154. This case concerned the deportation of an alleged terrorist on national security grounds. The Court was critical of the fact that the advisory panel, which reviewed the deportation order, reached decisions which were not binding.

62   In the case of *Klass and others v. Germany*, 6 September 1987, Appl. No. 5029/71, para. 68, the Court applied the 'aggregation approach' for the first time. In that case, the Court ruled that the aggregate of remedies fulfilled the conditions of Article 13. In *Chahal v. the UK*, 15 November 1996, Appl. No.

→

The 'authority' referred to in Article 13 does not *per se* require a judicial authority.[63] When, however, national judicial review proceedings are available at national level, they, in principle, constitute an effective remedy within the meaning of Article 13, provided that the national court or courts can effectively review the legality of executive discretion on substantive and procedural grounds and quash decisions as appropriate.[64] No effective remedy exists where this national judicial review is so weak that it is unable to properly address the key elements of whether there has been a violation of the ECHR.[65]

5.2.5   Article 35, first paragraph: the obligation to exhaust national remedies

Article 35, first paragraph, requires that applicants should first exhaust national remedies before applying to the ECtHR. The machinery of complaint to the ECtHR is, thus, subsidiary to national systems safeguarding human rights: the purpose of Article 35, first paragraph, is to afford the States parties to the ECHR the opportunity of preventing or putting right the violations alleged against them before those allegations are submitted to the ECtHR.[66] The rule in Article 35, first paragraph, is based on the assumption, reflected in Article 13, that there is an effective national remedy available in respect of the alleged breach of an individual's Convention rights; the rule of exhaustion of effective remedies does not apply when, in short, there is no effective national remedy.[67]

22414/93, para. 145, the aggregate of national remedies was found insufficient and, therefore, incompliant with Article 13. In *M.S.S. v. Belgium and Greece*, 21 January 2011, Appl. No. 30696/09, the Court reiterated the 'aggregation doctrine' in para. 289. In para. 321, the Court concluded that there had been a violation of Article 13 by Greece because the aggregate of national remedies was not effective. In para. 396, the Court concluded that there had been a violation of Article 13 by Belgium because the appeal stage had not been effective; with regard to Belgium the aggregation doctrine was, therefore, not applied *in concreto*. Barkhuysen and Harris, O'Boyle, Bates & Buckley criticise the 'aggregation doctrine' as the ECtHR, when applying this approach, does not make clear how different national remedies reinforce each other. See Barkhuysen 1998, pp.146-150 and Harris, O'Boyle, Bates & Buckley 2009, pp. 566-567. See also Boeles pp. 1997, p. 272, 273, 277 and Wouters 2009, p. 332.

63   See, for example, ECtHR, *Hirsi Jamaa and others v. Italy*, 23 February 2012, Appl. No. 27765/09, para. 197.

64   See, for example, ECtHR, *Slivenko v. Latvia*, 9 October 2003, Appl. No. 48321/99, para. 99; ECtHR, *Baysakov v. Ukraine*, 1 June 2010, Appl. No. 29031/04, para. 75. See also Van Bennekom & Van der Winden 2011, p. 28.

65   On this basis, the Court found violations of Article 13 in conjunction with Article 8 in *Smith and Grady v. the UK*, 27 September 1999, Appl. Nos. 33985/96 and 33986/96, paras. 135-139 and in *Hatton v. the UK*, 8 July 2003, Appl. No. 36022/97, paras. 137-142.

66   See, for a non-expulsion case, ECtHR, *Kudla v. Poland*, 26 October 2000, Appl. No. 30210/96, para. 152. See for examples of cases concerning the expulsion of asylum seekers ECtHR, *Salah Sheekh v. the Netherlands*, 11 January 2007, Appl. No. 1948/04, para. 121 and ECtHR, *Diallo v. the Czech Republic*, 23 June 2011, Appl. No. 20493/07, para. 53.

67   ECtHR, *Salah Sheekh v. the Netherlands*, 11 January 2007, Appl. No. 1948/04, para. 121.

5.2.6   *Mutual relationships*

There is close affinity between the provisions on national proceedings briefly introduced above. The ECtHR has repeatedly emphasized that once an individual makes out an arguable claim under Article 3, the notion of effectiveness under Article 13 entails the institutional, investigative and procedural elements parallel to those established under Article 3. This means that the effective investigation requirements flowing from Article 3 (see section 5.2.2 above) are also requirements which determine whether a national remedy is effective.[68]

The same kind of close affinity exists between Articles 13 and 35, first paragraph: as the rule of exhaustion of national remedies does not apply where national remedies are not effective, the case law under Article 35, first paragraph, is relevant to the notion of an effective remedy contained in Article 13. The ECtHR has emphasized a number of times that the concept of an effective remedy as required under Article 35, first paragraph, corresponds to the nature of obligations under Article 13.[69]

As has been said above, the requirements of Article 13 should be considered as reinforcing those of Article 6, first paragraph.[70] This implies that the principles and requirements developed under Article 6, first paragraph, in fact also form part of Article 13. Indeed, the Court has concluded in a number of judgments that there has been a violation of both provisions for exactly the same reasons, whereby it first concluded that there had been a violation of Article 6 and then established a breach of Article 13.[71]

5.3   The provisions on national proceedings in the asylum context

5.3.1   *The requirement of an independent and rigorous scrutiny*

National judicial review proceedings constitute, in principle, an effective remedy within the meaning of Article 13, provided that the national court can effectively review the legality of executive discretion on substantive and procedural grounds and quash decisions as appropriate.[72] This general principle has been reiterated in a num-

---

68   See, for example,ECtHR, *Yüksel v. Turkey* 20 July 2004, Appl. No.40154/98,para. 36.

69   See, for example, ECtHR, *Kudla v. Poland*, 26 October 2000, Appl. No. 30210/96, para. 152. The judgments in *Doganv. Turkey*, 29 June 2004, Appl. Nos. 8803/02, 8804/02, 8805/02 and *Rachevi v. Bulgaria* 23 September 2004, Appl. No. 47877/99, also clearly illustrate the closely intertwined relationship between issues of exhaustion of national remedies under Article 35(1) and the requirement to safeguard an effective remedy under Article 13. In both cases, the ECtHR concluded at the admissibility stage that national remedies had not been exhausted but it did not hold this against the applicant because the remedies were considered ineffective. Logically, at the merits stage, the Court concluded that there had been a violation of Article 13. See also Harris, O'Boyle, Bates & Buckley 2009, p. 561.

70   ECtHR, *Kudla v. Poland*, 26 October 2000, Appl. No. 30210/96, para. 152. See also Van Dijk et al. 2006, p. 1019.

71   See, forexample, ECtHR, *Romashov v. Ukraine*, 27 July 2004, Appl. No. 67534/01, paras. 42-47.

72   See, for example, ECtHR, *Slivenko v. Latvia*, 9 October 2003, Appl. No. 48321/99, para. 99.

ber of cases concerning the expulsion of asylum seekers.[73] In a number of judgments concerning expulsion, the ECtHR has further clarified what kind of scrutiny is required from the national court (or review authority) by virtue of the procedural limb of Article 3, and Article 13. *Chahal v. the UK* (1996) was the first judgment in which the Court considered as follows:

> 'in such cases, given the irreversible nature of the harm that might occur if the risk of ill-treat-ment materialised, and the importance the Court attaches to Article 3, the notion of an effec-tive remedy under Article 13 requires independent scrutiny of the claim that there exist sub-stantial grounds for fearing a real risk of treatment contrary to Article 3'.[74]

In *Jabari v. Turkey* (2000), the Court added the term 'rigorous' to this: it considered that the national appeal authority or court should perform an 'independent and rigor-ous scrutiny' of a claim that there were substantial grounds for believing that there was a real risk of treatment contrary to Article 3.[75] The ECtHR has reiterated in nu-merous subsequent judgments concerning the expulsion of asylum seekers that the notion of 'effective remedy' within the meaning of Article 13 taken together with Ar-ticle 3 requires independent and rigorous scrutiny of the complaint.[76] The Court has not formulated any further general rules but decides on a case-by-case basis whether or not an independent and rigorous scrutiny has occurred.[77] Nevertheless, from the Court's case law certain categories of non-compliant cases do emerge. This makes it possible to define in a more precise way what an independent and rigorous scrutiny entails. Four categories of non-compliant cases are discussed below, with a particular focus on how the national court operated in the asylum court proceedings.[78]

5.3.2 No material investigation by national courts (mostly due to failure to comply with national procedural rules)

The first category of non-compliant cases consists of cases in which the national authorities, and in particular the national court, did not conduct any material investi-

---

73 See, for example, ECtHR, *Baysakov v. Ukraine*, 1 June 2010, Appl. No. 29031/04, para. 75; ECtHR, *Abdulazhon Isakov v. Russia*, 8 July 2010, Appl. No. 14049/08, para. 137; ECtHR, *A. v. the Netherlands*, 20 July 2010, Appl. No. 4900/06, para. 158.
74 ECtHR, *Chahal v. the UK*, 15 November 1996, Appl. No. 22414/93, para. 151.
75 ECtHR, *Jabari v. Turkey*, 11 July 2000, Appl. No. 40035/98, para.50.
76 See, for some more recent examples, ECtHR, *Muminov v. Russia*, 11 December 2008, Appl. No. 42502/06, para. 101; ECtHR, *Abdolkhani and Karimnia v. Turkey*, 22 September 2009, Appl. No. 30471/08, para. 108; ECtHR, *Hirsi Jamaa and others v. Italy*, 23 February 2012, Appl. No. 27765/09, para. 198.
77 Boeles 1997, p. 278, Wouters 2009, p. 332.
78 As this research focuses on court proceedings, I specifically searched for cases in which the ECtHR expressed itself about the quality of national court proceedings. For a broader test of the entire asylum procedure (not only the court proceedings) against the requirements of Articles 3 and 13, see the case of ECtHR, *M.S.S. v. Belgium and Greece*, 21 January 2011, Appl. No. 30696/09, paras. 301-315. In this case the Court pointed out many different deficiencies in the asylum procedure, such as defective access to the asylum procedure, due to absence of information and of communication between the asylum seeker and the decision maker, inavailability of interpreters and legal aid, and ill-trained staff.

gation whatsoever into the alleged Article 3-risk, because national procedural rules barred this. This does not always lead the ECtHR to the conclusion that no independent and rigorous scrutiny was applied. Two cases in which the Court reached opposite conclusions may illustrate this.

In *Bahaddar v. the Netherlands* (1998), a case concerning a Bangladeshi asylum seeker, the ECtHR considered that

> 'even in cases of expulsion to a country where there is an alleged risk of ill-treatment contrary to Article 3, the formal requirements and time-limits laid down in national law should normally be complied with (...). Whether there are special circumstances which absolve an applicant from the obligation to comply with such rules will depend on the facts of each case. It should be borne in mind in this regard that in applications for recognition of refugee status it may be difficult, if not impossible, for the person concerned to supply evidence within a short time, especially if – as in the present case – such evidence must be obtained from the country from which he or she claims to have fled. Accordingly, time-limits should not be so short, or applied so inflexibly, as to deny an applicant for recognition of refugee status a realistic opportunity to prove his or her claim.'[79]

In *Bahaddar*, the ECtHR held, under the old Article 26 ECHR, now Article 35, first paragraph, that it could not consider the merits of the case because national legal remedies had not been exhausted. This finding was based to a large extent on the fact that the applicant's lawyer had not stated any grounds when lodging her client's appeal against the decision of the Deputy Minister of Justice to the Judicial Division of the Council of State, although she had been offered the opportunity and a significant period of time – nearly four months – to cure this failing and although it would have been possible for the lawyer to request an extension of this time-limit. The applicant's lawyer submitted grounds of appeal nearly three months after the time-limit had expired, and without explaining the delay, which led the Council of State to declare the appeal inadmissible.[80]

In *Jabari v. Turkey* (2000), a case concerning an Iranian woman who had fled to Turkey in fear of inhuman punishment for adultery in Iran, the Ankara administrative court only established that the asylum claim had not been lodged within the statutory time frame of five days after arrival in the country. It did not investigate the merits of the claim. The ECtHR concluded that there had been a violation of both the procedural limb of Article 3 and Article 13. It ruled as follows:

> 'the Court concludes that the automatic and mechanical application of such a short time-limit for submitting an asylum application must be considered at variance with the protection of the fundamental value embodied in Article 3 of the Convention.'[81]

---

79 ECtHR, *Bahaddar v. the Netherlands*, 19 February 1998, Appl. No. 25894/94, para. 45.
80 *Ibidem*, paras. 45-49.
81 ECtHR, *Jabari v. Turkey*, 11 July 2000, Appl. No. 40035/98, para. 40.

'The Ankara Administrative Court considered that the applicant's deportation was fully in line with domestic law requirements. It would appear that, having reached that conclusion, the court felt it unnecessary to address the substance of the applicant's complaint, even though it was arguable on the merits in view of the UNHCR's decision to recognise her as a refugee within the meaning of the Geneva Convention. In the Court's opinion, given the irreversible nature of the harm that might occur if the risk of torture or ill-treatment alleged materialised and the importance which it attaches to Article 3, the notion of an effective remedy under Article 13 requires independent and rigorous scrutiny of a claim that there exist substantial grounds for fearing a real risk of treatment contrary to Article 3 and the possibility of suspending the implementation of the measure impugned. Since the Ankara Administrative Court failed in the circumstances to provide any of these safeguards, the Court is led to conclude that the judicial review proceedings (…) did not satisfy the requirements of Article 13. Accordingly, there has been a violation of Article 13 of the Convention.'[82]

From *Bahaddar v. the Netherlands* (1998) and *Jabari v. Turkey* (2000), we may conclude that applicants for asylum must normally comply with national procedural rules. At the same time, the automatic and mechanical application of procedural rules, barring an examination by the national court of the merits of the asylum claim, is at variance with the requirement to conduct an independent and rigorous scrutiny of the claim. This is particularly true for short time limits. Regard must be had to the reasons for non-compliance and other particular circumstances of the case. In addition, the question of whether the particular procedural rule is not too strict, given the difficult evidentiary position of asylum seekers, must be posed. If ample opportunities have been given to the applicant to bring forward the merits of the case, but the applicant or legal counsel has chosen not to use these opportunities, the bar to a material consideration of the case by the national court is imputed to the asylum seeker and does not make the national remedy ineffective.

Abdolkhani and Karimnia v. Turkey (2009), a case discussed in Chapter 2, is another example of a case in which no material investigation whatsoever was conducted by the national court.[83] A final example of the first category worthwhile mentioning is the case of *Hirsi Jamaa and others v. Italy* (2012).[84] The case concerned interception and push back operations on the high seas by Italian military personnel, conducted in accordance with bilateral Italian-Libyan agreements aimed at combating illegal immigration. The applicants in this case were Somali and Eritrean nationals who formed

---

82 *Ibidem*, paras. 49 and 50. Another example of a case in which the national court did not conduct a material examination because national procedural rules (time limits for filing the application and rules on court fees) were not adhered to, is the case of *Charahili v. Turkey*, 13 April 2010, Appl. No. 46605/07, para. 57. The ECtHR noted that no material examination had taken place, but did not explicitly conclude that there had been a violation of the procedural limb of Article 3. Nor did the ECtHR rule on the applicant's complaint under Article 13. The Court stated that, by establishing a violation of Article 3 (and Article 5(1)), it had considered the main legal questions so that there was no need to give a separate ruling on the remaining complaints.

83 See section 2.5.2. ECtHR, *Abdolkhani and Karimnia v. Turkey*, 22 September 2009, Appl. No. 30471/08, paras. 107-117. See also the very similar cases of *Tehrani and others v. Turkey*, 13 April 2010, Appl. Nos. 32940/08, 41626/08, 43616/08 and *Charahili v. Turkey*, 13 April 2010, Appl. No. 46605/07.

84 ECtHR, *Hirsi Jamaa and others v. Italy*, 23 February 2012, Appl. No. 27765/09.

part of a group of about two hundred individuals who left Libya aboard three vessels with the aim of reaching the Italian coast. When the vessels were near Lampedusa, they were intercepted by three ships from the Italian Revenue Police and the Coast-guard. The occupants of the intercepted vessels were transferred onto Italian military ships and returned to Tripoli. On arrival in the Port of Tripoli, after a ten-hour voyage, the migrants were handed over to the Libyan authorities. They objected to this, but were forced to leave the Italian ships. According to the applicants, during the voyage the Italian authorities did not inform them of their real destination and took no steps to identify them.[85] According to the applicants' representatives, two of the applicants died in unknown circumstances after the events in question.[86] Relying on Article 13, the applicants complained that they had not been afforded an effective remedy under Italian law by which to lodge their complaints under Article 3 and under Article 4 of Protocol No. 4, which prohibits collective expulsions.[87]

The ECtHR determined that the transfer of the applicants to Libya had been carried out without any form of examination of each applicant's individual situation. The Italian authorities had restricted themselves to embarking the intercepted migrants onto military ships and disembarking them on Libyan soil. The personnel aboard the military ships were not trained to conduct individual interviews and were not assisted by interpreters or legal advisers.[88]

The Court concluded that there had been a violation of Article 13 taken together with Article 3 (and Article 4 of Protocol No. 4 prohibiting collective expulsions), as the applicants had been deprived of any remedy which would have enabled them to lodge their complaints under Article 3 with a competent authority and to obtain a thorough and rigorous assessment of their requests before the removal measure was enforced.[89]

Interestingly, the Court did not follow the Italian Government's argument that the applicants should have availed themselves of the opportunity of applying to the Italian criminal courts upon their arrival in Libya to complain about violations of national and international law by the Italian military personnel involved in their removal. The Court doubted whether such a remedy would have been accessible in practice, and pointed out that such a remedy was not compliant with Article 13 anyway for lack of suspensive effect.[90] The proposed remedy was, therefore, not effective in the sense of Article 13 and Article 35, first paragraph, so that non-exhaustion of it was not held against the applicants.[91]

---

85   *Ibidem*, paras. 9-14.
86   *Ibidem*, para.15.
87   *Ibidem*, para. 187.
88   *Ibidem*, para.185.
89   *Ibidem*, para.205.
90   *Ibidem*, paras. 60-62, para. 206.
91   *Ibidem*, paras. 60-62.

5.3.3 Insufficiently thorough national court proceedings

A second category comprises cases in which the national courts did investigate the Article 3-risk in a material way, but did not do this in a sufficiently serious or thorough manner. In *Klein v. Russia* (2010)[92] and *Khodzhayev v. Russia* (2010),[93] the ECtHR concluded that there had been a breach of the procedural limb of Article 3 because of a very limited investigation into the alleged Article 3-risk by the national courts. The Court saw no reason to make a separate examination under Article 13. *Klein v. Russia* (2010) concerned an Israeli applicant who had been convicted in Colombia for training terrorists. In 2007, Klein was arrested at an airport in Moscow and detained with the aim of extraditing him to Colombia. In the proceedings before the ECtHR, Klein alleged that the Russian authorities had not conducted a serious investigation into possible ill-treatment in Colombia. The ECtHR agreed with the applicant and considered as follows:

> 'Lastly, the Court will examine the applicant's argument that the Russian authorities did not conduct a serious investigation into possible ill-treatment in the receiving country. It notes in this respect that the applicant informed the Russian courts about the poor human rights situation in Colombia referring to the fact that there had been a lengthy internal armed conflict between State forces and paramilitaries and citing the UN General Assembly's Resolution and the materials of the meeting of the Human Rights Committee (see paragraph 18 above). Furthermore, the applicant brought to the authorities' attention the fact that the Colombian Vice-President had threatened "to have him rot in jail". The Supreme Court of Russia limited its assessment of the alleged individualised risk of ill-treatment deriving from Vice-President Santos's statement to a mere observation that the Colombian judiciary were independent from the executive branch of power and thus could not be affected by the statement in question (…). The Court is therefore unable to conclude that the Russian authorities duly addressed the applicant's concerns with regard to Article 3 in the national extradition proceedings.'[94]

It appears from the case that the Russian courts were provided with reports on the situation in Colombia in general and in Colombian prisons in particular. However, in their judgments the national courts did not say anything about the information in these reports and the question whether this information made it likely or not likely that the applicant would run an Article 3-risk upon extradition.

Khodzhayev v. Russia (2010)[95] concerned a Tajik applicant who had fled from Tajikistan to Russia in 2001 in fear of persecution on political and religious grounds. In 2002, Tajikistan requested his extradition. In 2008 an asylum request was rejected by the Russian authorities. In the summer of 2008 the extradition request was granted. In the proceedings before the ECtHR, the applicant alleged that the Russian authorities had not conducted a serious investigation into possible ill-treatment following his extradition to Tajikistan. The ECtHR ruled that the Moscow City Court and the

---

92   ECtHR, *Klein v. Russia*, 1 April 2010, Appl. No. 24268/08.
93   ECtHR, *Khodzhayev v. Russia*, 12 May 2010, Appl. No. 52466/08.
94   ECtHR, *Klein v. Russia*, 1 April 2010, Appl. No. 24268/08, para. 56.
95   ECtHR, *Khodzhayev v. Russia*, 12 May 2010, Appl. No. 52466/08.

Supreme Court of Russia had not duly investigated the applicant's concerns with regard to Article 3 when examining the appeals against the extradition order. These
national courts had merely stated that the applicant's request for asylum had been
rejected and that his allegations of persecution on religious grounds in Tajikistan had
been unsubstantiated. The national courts had failed to conduct any independent investigation into the alleged risk, in breach of the procedural limb of Article 3. The
Court also ruled that, given the findings under Article 3, it was not necessary for the
Court to carry out a separate investigation under Article 13.[96]

A similar judgment is *Soldatenko v. Ukraine* (2008).[97] This case concerned the extradition of the applicant from Ukraine to Turkmenistan. In *Soldatenko*, the ECtHR
concluded that under the Ukrainian Code of Administrative Justice the administrative
courts could potentially review a decision to extradite in the light of a complaint of a
risk of ill-treatment, but that the Ukrainian Government had failed to give any indication of the powers of the courts in such matters or to submit any examples of cases
in which an extradition decision had been reviewed on the merits by a national administrative court, while the applicant had submitted court decisions to the contrary.[98] The ECtHR ruled, under Article 35, first paragraph, that the remedy offered
by the national administrative courts was not effective and that, as a consequence, it
could not be held against the applicant that he had not used this national remedy before applying to the ECtHR. It follows from *Soldatenko* that a national court must independently consider the alleged Article 3-risk on the merits and must possess the
powers to truly do so.

A particularly interesting example is the case of *R.C. v. Sweden* (2010).[99] This case
concerned an Iranian man who had applied for asylum in Sweden in October 2003.
He stated that he had been threatened since 1997 for expressing criticism against the
regime. After participating in a demonstration in July 2001, he was arrested and spent
two years in prison, where he was tortured a number of times. Every three months,
his detention was prolonged by a so-called revolutionary court. In June 2003, while
attending such a court hearing on the prolongation of the detention, he managed to
escape with the assistance of friends. In the national proceedings before the Swedish

---

96   *Ibidem*, paras. 104, 151. See also ECtHR, *Khaydarov v. Russia*, 20 May 2010, Appl. No. 21055/09 about
    a very similar case. As in *Khodzhayev*, in *Khaydarov*, the Court concluded that there had been a breach
    of the procedural limb of Article 3 as well as a material violation of Article 3 because the Moscow
    City Court and the Supreme Court had failed to study carefully the documents produced in the ap-
    plicant's extradition case. Both the City Court and the Supreme Court had limited their analysis of
    the alleged Article 3-risk to assurances given by the Tajik Prosecutor's General Office, which they
    had interpreted as assurances that the applicant would not be ill-treated in Tajikistan, whereas it was
    clear, according to the ECtHR, from the text of the letters that no such assurances had been given.
    A similar case, also concerning extradition to Tajikistan, is *Gaforov v. Russia*, 21 October 2010, Appl.
    No. 25404/09, paras. 124-127. In this case, the ECtHR found it problematic that the City Court and
    the Supreme Court had not given any consideration on the situation in Tajikistan
    from various independent NGOs, and that, instead, the national courts had chosen to rely solely on
    scant information contained in a letter from the Russian Ministry of Foreign Affairs.
97   ECtHR, *Soldatenko v. Ukraine*, 23 October 2008, Appl. No. 2440/07.
98   *Ibidem*, para. 49.
99   ECtHR, *R.C. v. Sweden*, 9 March 2010, Appl. No. 41827/07. See for a detailed analysis of this case
    and the Court's reasoning Geertsema 2010.

authorities the applicant stated that he suffered from medical and psychiatric problems. He submitted to the Swedish Migration Board (the administrative decision maker in asylum cases) a medical certificate issued by a physician at a local health care centre. The certificate stated that the applicant had scars around both ankles, scars on the outside of both kneecaps and two lateral scars on his left thigh. He also had a reddish area stretching from his neck down to his chest and when he yawned there was a loud clicking sound from the left side of his jaw. In the physician's opinion, these injuries could very well have originated from the torture to which the applicant claimed that he had been subjected in Iran.[100] The Migration Board rejected the asylum request as incredible. The Board considered that the applicant had never been a member of a political party and had not fulfilled a leading role in the demonstrations. It also found the escape to be incredible. It furthermore noted that corroborating evidence was absent and that the medical certificate did not prove that the applicant had been tortured even if the injuries documented could very well have originated from the torture described.[101] On appeal to the Aliens Appeals Board, and, after transfer of the case to the Migration Court, the applicant stated a number of new grounds for his flight and submitted four new medical certificates. The Migration Court rejected the appeal. It considered that the applicant appeared to have expanded his grounds for asylum, that he had not been a member of a party or an organisation which was critical of the regime so that it was unlikely that he would be of any interest to the authorities in his home country if he returned, that the account of how he had escaped was incredible, and that he had failed to show that he had been tortured in Iran.[102]

The ECtHR expressed fierce criticism of the investigation conducted by the national Swedish administrative and judicial authorities. It found that either the administrative or the judicial authorities ought to have directed that an expert medical opinion be obtained as to the probable cause of the applicant's scars. The Court ruled as follows:

> 'Firstly, the Court notes that the applicant initially produced a medical certificate before the Migration Board as evidence of his having been tortured (…). Although the certificate was not written by an expert specialising in the assessment of torture injuries, the Court considers that it, nevertheless, gave a rather strong indication to the authorities that the applicant's scars and injuries may have been caused by ill-treatment or torture. In such circumstances, it was for the Migration Board to dispel any doubts that might have persisted as to the cause of such scarring (…). In the Court's view, the Migration Board ought to have directed that an expert opinion be obtained as to the probable cause of the applicant's scars in circumstances where he had made out a prima facie case as to their origin. It did not do so and *neither did the appellate courts* (italics author). While the burden of proof, in principle, rests on the applicant, the Court disagrees with the Government's view that it was incumbent upon him to produce such expert opinion. In cases such as the present one, the State has a duty to ascertain all relevant facts, particularly

---

100 *Ibidem*, para.11.
101 *Ibidem*, para. 12.
102 *Ibidem*, para. 16.

in circumstances where there is a strong indication that an applicant's injuries may have been caused by torture.[103]

To illustrate the second category of cases, it is also useful to mention the case of *Said v. the Netherlands* (2005), concerning an Eritrean deserter.[104] Just like the case of *R.C. v. Sweden*, this case illustrates the need for national courts to seriously investigate presented evidence and, if necessary for further clarification of the facts, apply investigative powers. Although the ECtHR concluded that there had been a material (and not procedural) violation of Article 3 and did not explicitly express concerns about the national judicial proceedings, Judge Thomassen did so in her concurring opinion to the judgment.[105] Separate opinions do not form part of the judgments to which they are annexed, but as they represent the opinions of the highest judges of the European continent, they do constitute authoritative statements. On the investigation conducted at national court level, Thomassen stated:

'In my view, no serious investigation was carried out in the present case. In the first decision on the applicant's request for asylum, it was held against him that he had failed to provide documentary evidence of his identity. Yet, when he subsequently submitted a number of identity documents in the appeal proceedings before the Regional Court, the relevance of these for the assessment of the credibility of his account remained unaddressed. (…) For me, the lack of rigorous scrutiny justifies the Court's decision not to follow the national courts' assessment.'

During the appeal proceedings before the District Court of Amsterdam, the applicant submitted a written statement by a certain Mr. Khalifa, to the effect that Mr. Khalifa's son had been executed in Eritrea in October 2000 after he had been staying with his mother for three months without having obtained prior permission from his army commanders. The applicant requested the court of Amsterdam to hear Mr. Khalifa as a witness. The court refused this request and dismissed the appeal. The Council of State dismissed the higher appeal and ruled that, as the Amsterdam court had concluded that the Deputy Minister had not been wrong in describing the applicant's account as not credible, the Court had been entitled to decide not to hear evidence from Mr. Khalifa as a witness.[106] The unwillingness of the national court to use its power to hear witnesses, along with the arguments stated explicitly in the concurrent opinion, may have contributed to the conclusion that no rigorous scrutiny at national level had taken place.[107]

---

103 *Ibidem*, para. 53.
104 ECtHR, *Said v. Netherlands*, 5 July 2005, Appl. No. 2345/02.
105 Para. 2 of Rule 74 of the Rules of Court stipulates: 'Any judge who has taken part in the consideration of the case shall be entitled to annex to the judgment either a separate opinion, concurring with or dissenting from that judgment, or a bare statement of dissent.' See also Harris, O'Boyle, Bates & Buckley 2009, p. 835.
106 ECtHR, *Said v. Netherlands*, 5 July 2005, Appl. No. 2345/02, paras. 16, 18.
107 See also the interview with Judge Thomassen published in *NJCM Bulletin* 31 (2006), nr. 1, pp. 6-28. In this interview, she states that 'when the Articles 2 and 3 are at stake, the Court performs a very thorough investigation of the case and if necessary, establishes the facts as if it were a first instance court. The message is that in order to safeguard the most fundamental human rights, the right to life

→

The case of *Auad v. Bulgaria* (2011)[108] forms another interesting illustration of cases in which the national authorities, including the courts, did not meaningfully investigate the applicant's concern with regard to Article 3 ECHR. The Bulgarian State Agency for National Security proposed to expel the applicant, a stateless person of Palestinian origin, from Bulgaria on national security grounds, less than three weeks after the State Refugees Agency had granted him humanitarian protection. The Palestinian refugee camp to which he would be returned, were under control of various Palestinian armed factions and the camp from which he fled, appeared to be one of the more chaotic and violent camps.[109] The Bulgarian administrative authorities and courts did not try to make any assessment of the risk the applicant would run if returned. The ECtHR concluded to a procedural and a material breach of Article 3 ECHR.[110]

In the case of *M.S.S. v. Belgium and Greece* (2011),[111] the ECtHR established that the national Belgian court (the Aliens Appeals Board) did not always take into consideration materials submitted by the asylum seeker after the initial interview, and found this practice to be at variance with Article 13.[112] The case of M.S.S. is discussed in more detail in Chapter 8, section 8.2.

A final – highly illustrative – example of a case in which the national authorities, including the national courts, did not conduct a sufficiently thorough examination is *Singh and Others v. Belgium* (2012).[113] The case concerned a family of asylum seekers who claimed to belong to the Sikh minority in Afghanistan. They complained in particular that their removal from Belgium to Moscow entailed a risk of *refoulement* to their country of origin, Afghanistan, where they would face ill-treatment. They told the Belgian authorities that they were Afghan nationals, members of the Sikh minority, and that they had fled Afghanistan for India in 1992 because of the civil war and the attacks and kidnappings endured by the Sikh and Hindu communities there at that time. They had later taken refuge in Moscow. In 2009 the applicants had apparently returned to Kabul. As they had not felt safe there they had fled to Belgium.[114]

The Office of the Commissioner General for Refugees and Stateless Persons ('CGRA') rejected their applications on the grounds that they had not provided evidence of their Afghan nationality. They had been travelling with false passports and the wife of the principal applicant, Mrs Kaur, had an insufficient knowledge of Afghanistan and the Pashto language.[115]

The applicants appealed against this decision to the Aliens Disputes Board ('CCE'). On appeal, they produced new evidence corroborating their Afghan nationality and their flight narrative. This new evidence included e-mail messages between

---

and the prohibition of torture, undue formalism and marginal review must yield under certain circumstances.'
108 ECtHR, *Auad v. Bulgaria*, 11 October 2011, Appl. No. 46390/10.
109 *Ibidem*, para. 103.
110 *Ibidem*, paras. 104, 108.
111 ECtHR, *M.S.S. v. Belgium and Greece*, 21 January 2011, Appl. No. 30696/09.
112 *Ibidem*, para. 389.
113 ECtHR, *Singh and Others v. Belgium*, 2 October 2012, Appl. No. 33210/11.
114 *Ibidem*, para. 12.
115 *Ibidem*, para. 13.

their lawyer and a representative of the Belgian Committee for Aid to Refugees, an operational partner of the Office of the United Nations High Commissioner for Refugees (UNHCR) in Belgium. It also included attestations that the applicants had been registered as refugees under the protection of the UNHCR; finally, the new evidence contained a reference to an application for Indian naturalisation, lodged by Mrs Kaur in 2009, and to the fact that she had a valid Afghan passport delivered by the Afghan Embassy in New Delhi.

The Aliens Disputes Board dismissed the applicants' appeals. It was of the opinion that the applicants had been unable to prove their Afghan nationality or the veracity of the protection granted to them by the UNHCR. The CCE took the view that the UNHCR documents were easy to falsify and that without the originals those documents had no probative value. For the CCE, the only part of the applicants' story that was not in dispute was the fact that they had lived in India and so their fear of persecution had to be examined *vis-à-vis* India, not Afghanistan. It took the view that their decision to leave India had been based merely on social and economic grounds.[116]

The ECtHR found that the applicants' fear that the Russian authorities might send them back to their State of origin was not manifestly ill-founded. It noted that the applicants had arrived at the Belgian border with identity documents and copies of pages of two Afghan passports and that copies of UNHCR attestations had subsequently been submitted. Taking this into consideration, and in the light of a number of reports about discrimination and violence against the Sikh minority in Afghanistan, the ECtHR found that the applicants' complaints under Article 3 were arguable.[117]

The ECtHR ruled that in this case, no close and rigorous scrutiny as required by Article 13 ECHR, taken together with Article 3 ECHR, had been applied by the national authorities. The administrative decision maker, the CGRA, had not made any additional enquiries, for example to authenticate the identity documents presented. The reviewing authority, the CCE, had not made up for that omission, whereas the documents presented to it by the applicants had been capable of dispelling the doubts expressed by the CGRA as to their identities and previous movements. The CCE had given no weight to those documents on the grounds that they were easy to falsify and the applicants were not able to supply the originals. The ECtHR considered that the documents presented to the CCE had not given rise to any investigation, whereas enquiries could readily have been made, for example, at the offices of the UNHCR in New Delhi. The fact that both the administrative decision making authority, and the reviewing authority, had dismissed documents which were pertinent for the protection request, finding them to have no probative value because they were only copies and could easily have been falsified, and without verifying their authenticity as they could easily have done by contacting the UNHCR, was at odds

---

116 *Ibidem*, paras. 14, 15.
117 *Ibidem*, paras. 78-88.

with the close and rigorous scrutiny required under Article 13 taken together with Article 3 ECHR.[118]

5.3.4   National courts apply incorrect evidentiary standards

A third category comprises cases in which the national court did investigate the Article 3-risk, but applied incorrect evidentiary criteria in doing so, for example, an incorrect standard of proof (see Part 2). An example is *M.S.S. v. Belgium and Greece* (2011).[119] The ECtHR concluded in this case that the Belgian national procedure for applying for a stay of execution with the Aliens Appeals Board did not constitute an effective remedy in the sense of Article 13 as, *inter alia*, the Aliens Appeals Board had limited its examination to verifying whether the persons concerned had 'produced concrete proof of the irreparable nature of the damage that might result from the alleged potential violation of Article 3.' This standard of proof was much higher than the standard developed by the ECtHR of substantial grounds for assuming a real Article 3-risk. According to the ECtHR, this incorrect standard of proof had hindered examination on the merits of the alleged risk of a violation of Article 3. For this reason, the Court concluded that there had been a violation of Article 13.[120]

Another example is the case of *Salah Sheekh v. the Netherlands* (2007). In that case, the ECtHR did not hold non-exhaustion of national remedies against the applicant. It found that a higher appeal was bound to fail anyway, as the Council of State applied a constant jurisprudential line which incorporated a too strict requirement of individualisation. Even in cases where it was obvious that applicants belonged to a group of persons systematically exposed to a practice of ill-treatment, the Council of State still required such applicants to establish, in addition to their belonging to such a group, special personal features (special distinguishing features).[121]

5.3.5   The provisions on national proceedings in the asylum context: interim conclusions

In cases concerning the expulsion of asylum seekers, a national judicial remedy is compliant with Articles 3, 13 and 35, first paragraph, if it is able to comprise both substantive and procedural points and is able to quash the administrative decision upholding refusal of a protection claim. The procedural limb of Article 3, Article 13, and Article 35, first paragraph, ECHR require the national authorities, including the national courts, to conduct an adequate examination of the claim for protection.[122] In assessing whether national proceedings are adequate, the ECtHR takes into consideration whether an applicant was heard (several times), whether he or she was assisted by appointed counsel, whether the national authorities had the benefit of seeing,

---

118 *Ibidem*, paras. 100-105.
119 ECtHR, *M.S.S. v. Belgium and Greece*, 21 January 2011, Appl. No. 30696/09.
120 *Ibidem*, para. 389, 390.
121 ECtHR, *Salah Sheekh v. the Netherlands*, 11 January 2007, Appl. No. 1948/04, paras. 123, 136, 148 (trigger 1: insufficient national proceedings and trigger 3: a too strict standard of individualisation), paras. 52-84, 94-95, 101, 105-113 (trigger 2: new developments).
122 See, for example, ECtHR, *Husseini v. Sweden*, 13 October 2011, Appl. No. 10611/09.

hearing and questioning the applicant in person, and of assessing directly the information and documents submitted by him or her, before deciding the case. The ECtHR also takes into account whether the assessment of the national authorities was sufficiently supported by both national materials as well as materials originating from other reliable and objective sources.[123]

The cases of *R.C. v. Sweden* (2010) and *Singh and Others v. Belgium* (2012) have clearly illustrated that the national authorities, including the reviewing courts, must carefully and seriously examine evidence submitted by applicants. When and if such evidence leaves questions unanswered, the national authorities, including the reviewing courts, must try to find answers by applying investigative powers in order to further clarify the facts. This is particularly necessary when it is rather easy to make further inquiries, as was the case in *Singh and Others v. Belgium*, where the national authorities could easily have made inquiries with the UNHCR. In sum, decisive is the thoroughness of the investigations undertaken at national level, including the investigations of the involved national court(s).[124]

Constant national jurisprudential lines may not normally bar an individual, case-specific and factual examination on the merits. It follows from *Bahaddar v. the Netherlands* (1998)[125] and *Jabari v. Turkey* (2000)[126] that time limits and other procedural rules laid down in national law – although they must normally be adhered to – should not be so short, or applied so mechanically or inflexibly, as to deny an applicant for asylum a realistic opportunity of proving his or her claim.

Finally, independent and rigorous scrutiny also means that the correct evidentiary standards and principles are to be applied by the national court in assessing the Article 3-risk. As was shown above, it follows from *M.S.S. v. Belgium and Greece* (2011) that the national court is not allowed to apply, for example, a stricter standard of proof than the one applied by the ECtHR. For national courts to comply with the requirement of independent and rigorous scrutiny it is, therefore, essential to know exactly what these evidentiary standards are. Part 2 of this chapter explores the evidentiary standards applied by the ECtHR.

5.4 Issues of intensity of judicial scrutiny under Article 6, first paragraph

5.4.1 The Zumtobel doctrine

Under Article 6, first paragraph, as part of the requirement of 'access to an independent and impartial tribunal', the ECtHR has gradually developed the doctrine of sufficiency of jurisdiction of national courts in administrative law cases.[127] *Albert and Le*

---

123 ECtHR, *Husseini v. Sweden*, 13 October 2011, Appl. No. 10611/09, paras. 82, 83.
124 ECtHR, *Husseini v. Sweden*, 13 October 2011, Appl. No. 10611/09, paras. 82, 86.
125 ECtHR, *Bahaddar v. the Netherlands*, 19 February 1998, Appl. No. 25894/94, paras. 45-49.
126 ECtHR, *Jabari v. Turkey*, 11 July 2000, Appl. No. 40035/98, para. 40.
127 See for a clear and detailed analysis of this doctrine the separate opinion of Judge Martens to the judgment of *Fischer v. Austria*, 26 April 1995, Appl. No. 16922/90, and also Harris, O'Boyle, Bates & Buckley 2009, pp. 228-235.

Compte v. Belgium (1983)[128] is the first case in which the Court explicitly dealt with the question of sufficiency of jurisdiction of national courts. The applicant doctors, accused by the professional medical association of having issued spurious certificates of unfitness for work, wished to challenge disciplinary decisions (suspension of the right to practice medicine and, for applicant Le Compte, finally a complete bar from practicing medicine) against them on their merits. The decisions were taken by a professional association, with a right of appeal to another such body, the Appeals Council, and finally to the Belgian Court of Cassation. The Appeals Council did not sit in public, so one of the requirements of Article 6, first paragraph, was not met. In the opinion of the ECtHR, the public character of the subsequent cassation proceedings before the Court of Cassation did not suffice to remedy this defect, because the Court of Cassation did not take cognisance of the merits of the case. This meant that many aspects in dispute, including review of the facts and assessment of the proportionality between fault and sanction, fell outside its jurisdiction. The ECtHR ruled as follows:

> 'To sum up, the cases were not heard publicly by a tribunal competent to determine all the aspects of the matter and pronouncing judgment publicly. In this respect, there was a breach of Article 6(1).'[129]

It follows from this judgment that a national court should normally be competent to determine 'all the aspects of the matter', in other words, have full jurisdiction. This means that the national court must be able to take cognisance of and decide on the merits of the case. In a number of later judgments, the Court clarified what is meant by 'all the aspects of the matter'. In *Terra Woningen B.V. v. the Netherlands* (1996, discussed below in more detail) and in the case of *Druzstevni Zálozna Pria and others v. The Czech Republic* (2008) the ECtHR ruled that

> 'For the determination of civil rights and obligations by a "tribunal" to satisfy Article 6(1), it is required that the "tribunal" in question have jurisdiction to examine all questions of fact and law relevant to the dispute before it'.[130]

And in *Veeber v. Estonia* (2002) and *Chevrol v. France* (2003), the Court, while using the same terminology, strongly emphasised that full jurisdiction on points of fact and points of law is indeed the general rule:

> 'only an institution that has full jurisdiction, including the power to quash in all respects, on questions of fact and law, the challenged decision, merits the description "tribunal" within the meaning of Article 6(1)'.[131]

---

128 ECtHR, *Albert and Le Compte v. Belgium*, 10 February 1983, Appl. Nos. 7299/75 and 7496/76.
129 *Ibidem*, para. 37.
130 ECtHR, *Terra Woningen B.V. v. the Netherlands*, 28 November 1996, Appl. No. 49/1995/555/64, paras. 46 and 51-55; ECtHR, *Druzstevni Zálozna Pria and others v. The Czech Republic*, 31 July 2008, Appl. No. 72034/01, para. 107.See also ECtHR, *Koskinas v. Greece*, 20 June 2002, Appl. No. 47760/99, for the same consideration in para. 29.

The precise meaning of this requirement of full jurisdiction on points of fact and points of law, and the boundaries of this requirement, were elaborated further in a number of other judgments.

From *W. v. the UK* (1987)[132] it becomes clear that the requirement of full judicial jurisdiction on points of fact and points of law is not an absolute right under Article 6, first paragraph. The case concerned parental access to a child in public care. The parents wished to challenge on the facts a local authority parental rights decision on the placement of their youngest child with foster parents on a long-term basis with a view to adoption. They could challenge the impugned decision in two ways: judicial review or the institution of wardship proceedings. The ECtHR ruled that both these national judicial remedies were not compliant with Article 6, first paragraph, as they were not competent to examine the merits of the case.[133] As the ECtHR spoke of a 'case of the present kind', we can infer from this judgment that there are certain types of cases which do, and certain cases which do not, require full national judicial review. However, the ECtHR did not clarify in this case which cases required full national judicial jurisdiction on the merits and which cases justified a less intense form of judicial scrutiny.

In *Zumtobel v. Austria* (1993),[134] the ECtHR gave further clarification. The case concerned expropriation proceedings instituted with a view to the construction of a provincial highway, affecting the land of the Zumtobel Company. The applicant repeatedly but unsuccessfully requested to be allowed to study various documents in the file resting with the provincial authorities. In February 1986, the Office of the Provincial Government dismissed two requests by the applicant, one for full details of the planning procedure for the projected road, and the other for the appointment of an independent road traffic expert to assess whether the planned road was necessary. The Office considered the first request to be irrelevant to the case; as to the second, it stated that the official expert had not shown any bias in favour of the authorities and had submitted a convincing report. Zumtobel thereupon applied to the Constitutional Court, claiming that the expropriation proceedings had violated its right of access to a court with full jurisdiction, guaranteed by Article 6, first paragraph. It was also alleged that there had been a breach of the principle of equality of arms, as the provincial Office had heard its own experts but had refused to consult independent ones. The Constitutional Court decided not to examine the application. One of the reasons for rejection was that, in view of its jurisprudence on Article 6 of the ECHR, and the authorities' discretion in determining the routes of highways, the application did not have sufficient prospects of success. The applicant then challenged the expropriation order in the Administrative Court. Relying on substantially the same arguments as in the Constitutional Court, Zumtobel now complained of

---

131 ECtHR, *Veeber v. Estonia*, 8 November 2002, Appl. No. 37571/97, para. 70; ECtHR, *Chevrol v. France*, 13 February 2003, Appl. No. 49636/99, para. 76.
132 ECtHR, *W. v. the UK*, 8 July 1987, Appl. No. 9749/82.
133 *Ibidem*, paras. 81-83.
134 ECtHR, *Zumtobel v. Austria*, 21 September 1993, Appl. No. 12235/86.

breaches of procedural and substantive law; it also asked for an expert to be appointed.[135] The Administrative Court dismissed the appeal, considering that

'In the context of the power of review conferred on it by Article 41 of the Administrative Court Law, the Administrative Court cannot hold to be unlawful the fact that the respondent authority had regard to road traffic requirements and based its decision principally on the consideration that no other more appropriate solution was possible'.[136]

The Administrative Court also held that Zumtobel had failed to cast doubt on the official experts' reports such as could disclose a procedural irregularity capable of affecting the decision. In a more general consideration about its jurisdiction and powers in cases like this, the Administrative Court considered:

'The Administrative Court is not allowed, in a case which has been before the respondent administrative authority, to put itself in the place of that authority and take evidence, which the latter may have omitted to take, or to supplement the investigation by itself taking investigative measures to establish the facts. It can, however, take evidence in order to determine whether an essential procedural requirement has been breached, and it is therefore entitled to take investigative measures in order to establish whether a procedural defect is essential or whether the respondent authority could have reached a different decision if that procedural defect had been avoided (…).'[137]

Zumtobel complained before the ECtHR that none of the national authorities before which the case had come in the contested proceedings could be regarded as a 'tribunal' within the meaning of Article 6, first paragraph. This was so, in the first place, with regard to the Office, an organ of the Provincial Government. It was also true of the Constitutional Court, as it was prohibited by law from reconsidering all the facts of a case. The Administrative Court was bound by the findings of the authorities, except in borderline cases – not the position here – in which such findings were material to determining the effect of an alleged procedural defect; and even in those cases, the Administrative Court could not correct or supplement the facts, or rule in the relevant authority's stead, but had always to remit the file to the latter. In short, its review only concerned the question of lawfulness and could not be considered equivalent to a full review, according to the applicant.[138]

The ECtHR did not agree with the applicant. Referring to its earlier jurisprudence, it agreed in principle with the applicant that the Office of the Government did not constitute a tribunal for the purposes of Article 6, first paragraph, and that, as a consequence, there had to be a possibility of appealing to a judicial body having full jurisdiction. The Court also agreed with the applicant that the Constitutional Court did not satisfy the requirement of full jurisdiction, as it could only inquire into the

---

135 *Ibidem*, paras. 6-14.
136 *Ibidem*, para. 14.
137 *Ibidem*, para. 14.
138 *Ibidem*, para. 27.

contested proceedings from the point of view of their conformity with the Constitution. With regard to the review effected by the Austrian Administrative Court, the ECtHR, however, considered:

> 'Regard being had to the respect which must be accorded to decisions taken by the administrative authorities on grounds of expediency and to the nature of the complaints made by the Zumtobel partnership, the review by the Administrative Court accordingly, in this instance, fulfilled the requirements of Article 6(1).'[139]

It is clear from the *Zumtobel* judgment that the national Administrative Court did not have full jurisdiction to re-examine all the relevant facts of the case. In the specific circumstances of the case, the ECtHR, however, did not find this problematic. It is important to note that the Court started its reasoning by referring to its standard jurisprudence that normally in cases like this, where the initial decision had been taken by an administrative body, full judicial review by a national tribunal was required.[140] This was the general rule. The Court then explained why, in this specific case, an exception to this rule was justified:

> 'As regards the review effected by the Administrative Court, its scope must be assessed in the light of the fact that expropriation – the participants in the proceedings all recognise this – is not a matter exclusively within the discretion of the administrative authorities, because Article 44 para. 1 of the Provincial Highways Law makes the lawfulness of such a measure subject to a condition: the impossibility "of constructing or retaining a section of highway which is more suitable from the point of view of traffic requirements, environmental protection and the financial implications" (see paragraph 16 above). It was for the Administrative Court to satisfy itself that this provision had been complied with. In this respect the present dispute may be distinguished from the *Obermeier v. Austria* case (judgment of 28 June 1990, Series A no. 179, p. 23, para. 70).
>
> In addition, it should be stressed that the submissions relied upon before the Administrative Court concerned solely the proceedings before the Government Office. The Administrative Court in fact considered these submissions on their merits, point by point, without ever having to decline jurisdiction in replying to them or in ascertaining various facts. (...) Regard being had to the respect which must be accorded to decisions taken by the administrative authorities on grounds of expediency and to the nature of the complaints made by the Zumtobel partnership, the review by the Administrative Court accordingly, in this instance, fulfilled the requirements of Article 6 para. 1 (art. 6-1).'[141]

Three reasons justifying an exception can be discerned in this consideration. First, the specific nature of the case. The case concerned land planning and expropriation, an area in which the administration had taken decisions on grounds of expediency, in other words, an area which could have been qualified as a classical administrative

---

139 *Ibidem*, para. 32.
140 *Ibidem*, para. 29.
141 *Ibidem*, paras. 31, 32.

task. Second, before the national courts, the applicant had complained mainly about the proceedings before the administrative authority. He had not explicitly requested the national courts to make a fresh factual re-examination. Third, the review effected by the Administrative Court, although it had not included points of fact, had been, nevertheless, rigorous as it had dealt with all the applicant's complaints concerning the proceedings, point by point, and had satisfied itself that a legal condition crucial for the lawfulness of the expropriation had indeed been met.

In the case of *Bryan v. the UK* (1995),[142] the ECtHR followed exactly the same reasoning as in *Zumtobel*. Like the *Zumtobel* case, the case of *Bryan* concerned town and country planning. The Court agreed, in principle, with the applicant that the national High Court did not have full jurisdiction, as its jurisdiction over the facts was limited. The ECtHR considered in *Bryan*, just as in *Zumtobel*, that the litigious decision had been taken by the administration on grounds of expediency. The ECtHR also stressed that there was no dispute as to the primary facts before the national High Court. Next, the Court emphasised that the jurisdiction of the national High Court, as far as the facts were concerned, was indeed limited, but not totally absent, and the High Court had indeed rigorously examined the procedural complaints brought forward by the applicant. Compared to *Zumtobel*, the *Bryan* judgment contains one additional fourth argument supporting the conclusion that no violation of Article 6, first paragraph, had occurred. The Court noted in *Bryan* that the procedure before the administrative inspector – the first instance administrative body – contained many safeguards and could, therefore, be qualified as a 'quasi-judicial procedure governed by many of the safeguards required by Article 6, first paragraph'. The four arguments in conjunction led the ECtHR to the conclusion that no breach of Article 6, first paragraph had occurred.[143]

In addition to *Zumtobel v. Austria* (1993) and *Bryan v. the UK* (1995), the Court accepted in a number of other cases that the national court did not have full jurisdiction on points of fact and points of law. Examples are the cases of *Chapman v. the UK* (2001) and *Jane Smith v. the UK* (2001), which concerned the refusal by the local authorities of an application lodged by Gypsies for permission to occupy land. The ECtHR repeated in those cases the conclusion reached in the *Bryan* judgment, and concluded, in short, that in the specialised area of town-planning, full judicial review of the facts was not required by Article 6, paragraph 1.[144] The case of *Kingsley v. the UK* (2002) concerned a decision by the Gaming Board for Great Britain to declare the applicant, director of casino companies in London, unfit and improper to have this function. The ECtHR noted in this case that the litigious decision concerned the regulation of the gaming industry, which, due to the nature of the industry, called for particular monitoring, which was a decisive factor in accepting limited judicial scrutiny.[145]

---

142 ECtHR, *Bryan v. the UK*, 25 October 1995, Appl. No. 44/1994/491/573.
143 *Ibidem*, paras. 44-48.
144 ECtHR, *Chapman v. the* UK, 18 January 2001, Appl. No. 27238/95, paras. 121-125 and ECtHR, *Jane Smith v. the UK*, 18 January 2001, Appl. No. 25154/94, paras. 131-134.
145 ECtHR, *Kingsley v. the UK*, 28 May 2002, Appl. No. 35605/97, paras. 32-34. Other examples are ECtHR, *Fischer v. Austria*, 26 April 1995, Appl. No. 16922/90, paras. 27-34 (a case concerning re-

→

In *Sigma Radio Television Ltd v. Cyprus* (2011),[146] the ECtHR provided a helpful summary of its full jurisdiction doctrine. The case concerned decisions by the radio and television broadcasting authority of Cyprus, which had imposed fines on a broadcasting company, Sigma Radio Television Ltd, for non-compliance with the National Radio and Television Broadcasting Act. The applicant company complained before the ECtHR that the national judicial scrutiny of the litigious decisions had been insufficient in scope and intensity as the Supreme Court could not look into the merits, did not and was not able to examine the facts of the case, hear evidence or decide on matters afresh.[147]

The ECtHR first made clear that it very much depended on the particular circumstances of the case whether the national judicial review was sufficient for the purposes of Article 6.[148] The Court noted that it was not always necessary for the national court to fully substitute its own opinion for that of the administrative authorities, particularly in cases concerning decisions on grounds of expediency, involving specialised areas. The ECtHR mentioned as concrete examples of such areas land planning, environmental protection and the regulation of gaming:

> 'it is often the case in relation to administrative law appeals in the Member States of the Council of Europe that the scope of judicial review over the facts of a case is limited and that it is the nature of review proceedings that the reviewing authority reviews the previous proceedings rather than taking factual decisions. (…) It is not the role of Article 6 to give access to a level of jurisdiction which can substitute its opinion for that of the administrative authorities. In this regard, particular emphasis has been placed on the respect which must be accorded to decisions taken by the administrative authorities on grounds of "expediency", and which often involve specialised areas of law (for example, planning, environmental protection, regulation of gaming).'[149]

Next, the Court explained what factors determined sufficiency of national court jurisdiction. Here the Court in fact reiterated the factors it had also taken into consideration in the cases of *Zumtobel v. Austria* (1993) and *Bryan v. the UK* (1995). The following factors were mentioned as decisive:
- the powers of the judicial body in question;
- the subject matter of the decision appealed against, in particular whether or not it concerned a specialised issue requiring professional knowledge or experience and whether it involved the exercise of administrative discretion and to what extent;

---

vocation of a refuse tipping license); ECtHR, *Müller and others v. Austria*, admissibility decision, 23 November 1999, Appl. No. 26507/95, under the heading 'the law', point 1 (a case concerning expropriation of land for road construction purposes); ECtHR, *Potocka and others v. Poland*, Appl. No. 33776/96, para. 55 (a case concerning expropriation of land and applications for the return of plots of expropriated land); ECtHR, *Alatullkila and others v. Finland*, 28 July 2005, Appl. No. 33538/96, para. 52 (a case concerning environmental protection).

146 ECtHR, *Sigma Radio Television Ltd v. Cyprus*, 21 July 2011, Appl. Nos. 32181/04 and 35122/05.
147 *Ibidem*, para. 131.
148 *Ibidem*, para. 155.
149 *Ibidem*, para. 153.

- the manner in which the decision was arrived at, in particular, the procedural guarantees available in the proceedings before the administrative body;
- the content of the dispute, including the desired and actual grounds of appeal.[150]

The ECtHR further clarified that it was crucial that the national court was not precluded from determining 'the central issue in dispute'.[151] In the particular case of *Sigma Radio Television Ltd v. Cyprus* (2011) the ECtHR concluded that the intensity of scrutiny in the national judicial review proceedings had been sufficient to comply with Article 6, first paragraph, although the Supreme Court of Cyprus possessed limited jurisdiction over the facts and could not substitute its own decision for that of the radio and television broadcasting authority. The Court noted, first, that the Supreme Court could have annulled the decisions on a number of grounds, including if the decision had been reached on the basis of misconception of fact and of law. Second, as to the subject matter, the ECtHR noted that the litigious decisions had been taken by the radio and television broadcasting authority and concerned the classical exercise of administrative discretion in the specialised area of law concerning broadcasting taken in the context of ensuring standard setting and compliance with the relevant legislation and regulations pursuant to public interest aims (the subject matter of the decision appealed against). Third, the ECtHR noted that a number of procedural guarantees had been available to the applicant in the proceedings before the radio and television broadcasting authority, including an oral hearing before this authority (the procedural guarantees in the proceedings before the administrative body). Finally, the Court took into account the content of the dispute and noted that the applicant's complaints in the national proceedings had centered on points of law and procedure; the applicant's case had not centered on a fundamental question of fact, which the Supreme Court did not have jurisdiction to revisit.[152]

We may draw a number of conclusions from the case law discussed above. The first conclusion is that Article 6, first paragraph, requires, in principle, that a national court has full jurisdiction on points of fact and points of law. In all the cases discussed above, the ECtHR starts out its considerations by reiterating this general rule. A second conclusion is that in the particular circumstances of a given case, a more limited jurisdiction of a national court may, nevertheless, be found to be compatible with Article 6, first paragraph, provided that a number of conditions are met. It seems that the ECtHR has, so far, accepted limited jurisdiction of national courts in a relatively limited number of cases only. In those cases, the ECtHR accepted more limited forms of judicial review because of:

- the fact that the particular subject-matter of the litigious decision belonged to the classical tasks of the administration (the classical exercise of administrative discretion) and/or involved a specialised issue requiring professional knowledge or experience; and
- the thorough safeguards attending the preceding administrative procedure; and

---

150 *Ibidem*, para. 154.
151 *Ibidem*, para. 157.
152 *Ibidem*, paras. 159-169.

- the fact that the national judicial review was, although limited, indeed meaningful as it entailed at least a very thorough examination of the disputed points of law and procedural points; and
- the fact that there was no true dispute on points of fact before the national courts.

The case of *Tsfayo v. the United Kingdom* (2006)[153] illustrates that it may not be assumed too easily that a case concerns a decision in the area of classical tasks of the administration.[154] The dispute between Tsfayo and the local authorities revolved around social benefits, an area which, at first sight, might easily be qualified as a classical administrative task. During the proceedings before the ECtHR, the UK Government tried to explain and justify the limited scope and intensity of the High Court's jurisdiction by referring to the type of case (social benefits). The ECtHR did not follow this argument. It noted that the heart of the case was a simple dispute concerning the credibility of the applicant's statements as to the reasons why she had submitted her benefits renewal form too late. The ECtHR considered:

'(…) the decision-making process in the present case was significantly different. In Bryan (…) the issues to be determined required a measure of professional knowledge or experience and the exercise of administrative discretion pursuant to wider policy aims. In contrast, in the instant case, the Hammersmith and Fulham Council Housing Benefit and Council Tax Benefit Review Board (HBRB) was deciding a simple question of fact, namely whether there was "good cause" for the applicant's delay in making a claim. On this question, the applicant had given evidence to the HBRB that the first moment that she knew that anything was amiss with her claim for housing benefit was the receipt of a notice from her landlord – the housing association – seeking to repossess her flat because her rent was in arrears. The HBRB found her explanation to be unconvincing and rejected her claim for back-payment of benefit essentially on the basis of their assessment of her credibility. No specialist expertise was required to determine this issue (…). Nor, unlike the cases referred to, can the factual findings in the present case be said to be merely incidental to the reaching of broader judgments of policy or expediency which it was for the democratically accountable authority to take.'[155]

The remaining question now is what full jurisdiction on points of fact and points of law precisely entails. The ECtHR has clarified this in a number of judgments. Full jurisdiction means that, when a decision of the administration is based on certain facts that, according to the administration, happened in the past, and the other party

---

153 ECtHR, *Tsfayo v. the UK*, 14 November 2006, Appl. No. 60860/00.
154 See also Van Dijk et al. (2006), p. 561, who present the requirement of full judicial jurisdiction on points of fact and points of law as the main rule, and limited judicial jurisdiction as an exception to the rule, permissible only in specific circumstances.
155 ECtHR, *Tsfayo v. the UK*, 14 November 2006, Appl. No. 60860/00, para. 46. See also ECtHR, *Capital Bank AD v. Bulgaria*, 24 November 2005, Appl. No. 49429/99, for a case in which the Bulgarian Government tried to persuade the ECtHR that the case concerned an area which belonged to the realm of the classical exercise of administrative discretion: supervision over the banking business. The ECtHR was not convinced and concluded that the Bulgarian courts should have exercised full jurisdiction.

denies or challenges these facts, the national court independently determines whether or not the facts indeed took place. The case of *Koskinas v. Greece* (2002)[156] may illustrate this. The case concerned dismissal from employment as a steward by 'Olympic Airways', a company in which the Greek State was the only shareholder. The applicant was dismissed on the basis of a decision taken by the so-called Board of Dismissals, stating that he had sexually intimidated a number of passengers. The applicant lodged an appeal before the First Instance Tribunal of Athens. The Tribunal quashed the decision taken by the Board, basically because no reasons had been given and because it had not been ascertained whether or not the applicant had indeed committed the alleged sexual intimidation. Olympic Airways brought an appeal to the Court of Appeals of Athens, which quashed the First Instance Court's judgment, and after this the applicant applied to the Court of Cassation. Both the Court of Appeals of Athens and the Court of Cassation ruled that the First Instance Court lacked the competence to examine whether the facts mentioned by the Board of Dismissals had or had not taken place. The ECtHR found this to be incompatible with Article 6, first paragraph.[157]

Full jurisdiction also means that the national court has jurisdiction to independently examine the credibility of statements made by a claimant. This appears from *Tsfayo v. the UK* (2006), mentioned above. The central question in this case was the credibility of the applicant's statements that she had never received any correspondence from the local authorities about the need to submit benefit renewal forms for housing benefit and property tax, and that, due to her poor English and her unfamiliarity with the system, she had not herself known about this need. The High Court did not have the power, however, to form its own views as to the credibility of these statements. Instead, it was bound to follow the views of the HBRB, an administrative body. This led the ECtHR to the conclusion that the central issue, the applicant's credibility, had never been determined by a tribunal independent of the administrative body, which constituted a violation of Article 6 first paragraph.[158]

Full jurisdiction also means that a national court does not rely automatically on, and draw automatic inferences from, an advice or opinion given by an organ of the executive. The cases of *Terra Woningen B.V. v. the Netherlands* (1996),[159] *Chevrol v. France* (2003),[160] *Capital Bank AD v. Bulgaria* (2005)[161] and *Druzstevni Zálozna Pria and others v. The Czech Republic* (2008)[162] are illustrative. *Terra Woningen v. the Netherlands* (1996) con-

---

156 ECtHR, *Koskinas v. Greece*, 20 June 2002, Appl. No. 47760/99.

157 *Ibidem*, para. 30.

158 ECtHR, *Tsfayo v. the UK*, 14 November 2006, Appl. No. 60860/00, paras. 48 and 49. In the Netherlands, a very similar situation exists with regard to the credibility of asylum seekers' statements as far as past facts are concerned. It is constant jurisprudence that the courts are not allowed to substitute their own views as to an applicant's credibility. Instead, they are bound by the opinion of the administrative body. Based on the mentioned case law of the ECtHR, it may be held, under Article 47, paragraph 2, of the EU Charter of fundamental rights, that the national courts for this reason do not act as independent tribunals, as is required by Article 6(1).

159 ECtHR, *Terra Woningen B.V. v. the Netherlands*, 28 November 1996, Appl. No. 49/1995/555/64.

160 ECtHR, *Chevrol v. France*, 13 February 2003, Appl. No. 49636/99.

161 ECtHR, *Capital Bank AD v. Bulgaria*, 24 November 2005, Appl. No. 49429/99.

162 ECtHR, *Druzstevni Zálozna Pria and others v. The Czech Republic*, 31 July 2008, Appl. No. 72034/01.

cerned judicial proceedings before the national District Court on a dispute concerning the rent for an apartment between an individual Mr. W. and Terra Woningen B.V., a property development company (hereinafter: the applicant company). In the proceedings before the District Court, Mr. W. argued that there was an undesirable situation that justified reducing the rent to the legal minimum. He submitted to the District Court letters from the Provincial Executive concerning soil cleaning as well as the Provincial Executive's implementation programme for soil cleaning from 1992 onwards. The applicant company argued that the soil pollution should not be taken into account. The company stated that it did not appear that there was pollution of the soil under or in the immediate vicinity of the accommodation such as to cause serious danger to public health or the environment. In addition, in the opinion of the company, the pollution found could not affect the standard of a third-floor flat without a garden. In its decision, the District Court set the rent at the legal minimum. Having regard to the fact that the Provincial Executive had designated the area as one where soil cleaning was required, and had set it down in its annual soil-cleaning programme for 1992 as a site to be dealt with in accordance with that Act, the District Court found it established that there was an 'objectionable situation' that justified reducing the points rating by 20 points and setting the rent at the legal minimum. The District Court explicitly stated that the question of whether the soil-cleaning decision of the Provincial Executive was well-founded fell outside its jurisdiction.

Before the ECtHR, the applicant company complained that it had not had access to a tribunal possessing jurisdiction to make an independent assessment of the relevance of the soil pollution. The applicant company relied on the fact that the District Court had held that the decision of the Provincial Executive to include the Noord-Nieuwlandsepolder-Zuid in its implementation programme for soil cleaning in itself amounted to proof that the legal provision triggering the application of the minimum rent provision had been satisfied. The District Court had not itself examined the report of the further inspection, although, in the applicant company's contention, it did not appear from that report that the pollution found had in any way affected the standard of the flat let to Mr W. The ECtHR ruled as follows:

'The Court recalls that for the determination of civil rights and obligations by a "tribunal" to satisfy Article 6 para. 1 (art. 6-1), it is required that the "tribunal" in question have jurisdiction to examine all questions of fact and law relevant to the dispute before it. (…)

(…) there was uncertainty at the relevant time as to whether district courts should themselves decide whether the "further inspection under the Soil Cleaning (Temporary Provisions) Act" justified the conclusion that "pollution of the soil" was "such as to cause serious danger to public health or the environment", or in the alternative accept without question or examination of their own the determination by the competent authorities that soil-cleaning measures were required. However, the Schiedam District Court, in its judgment in the present case, held that such risk was "necessarily implied" by the Provincial Executive's decision.

In so doing the Schiedam District Court, a "tribunal" satisfying the requirements of Article 6 para. 1 (art. 6-1) (as was not contested), deprived itself of jurisdiction to examine facts which were crucial for the determination of the dispute. In these circumstances the applicant company cannot be considered to have had access to a tribunal invested with sufficient jurisdiction to decide the case before it. There has accordingly been a violation of Article 6 para.1 (art. 6-1).'[163]

Chevrol v. France (2003) concerned permission for an Algerian medical graduate to practise as a doctor in France. From 17 February 1987 onwards, the applicant sought permission to practise as a doctor in France, firstly from the council of the *Ordre des Médecins* and subsequently, on eleven occasions, from the Minister for Health. In these proceedings, she relied on Article 5 of Part 1 of the 1962 'Government Declaration on Cultural Cooperation between France and Algeria', which stipulated that academic diplomas and qualifications obtained in Algeria and France under the same conditions as regards curriculum, attendance and examinations should be automatically valid in both countries. The outcome of these proceedings was unfavourable to the applicant. She then applied to the *Conseil d'Etat*, which gave judgment on 9 April 1999, dismissing her application. In the course of the proceedings before the *Conseil d'Etat*, the Conseil requested the Ministry of Foreign Affairs to submit an opinion on the applicability of the mentioned Article 5 invoked by the applicant. The Ministry thereupon stated that Article 5 could not be applied to the present case, as the reciprocity requirement in Article 55 of the French Constitution could not be regarded as having been satisfied, since Algeria did not recognise French academic diplomas and qualifications as being automatically valid in Algeria. After being apprised of the observations of the Ministry of Foreign Affairs, the applicant produced to the *Conseil d'Etat* declarations from various Algerian authorities certifying that qualifications obtained in France by French practitioners were recognised as being automatically valid in Algeria. In its judgment, the *Conseil d'Etat* did not take these declarations from the Algerian authorities into account. It automatically followed the observations made by the Ministry of Foreign Affairs, ruling that Article 5 of the Declaration on Cultural Cooperation between France and Algeria could not be regarded as having been in force on the date of the decision complained of, as on that date the reciprocity requirement laid down in Article 55 of the Constitution had not been satisfied. The applicant was, accordingly, not entitled to rely on this provision. The applicant complained before the ECtHR that the proceedings before the *Conseil d'Etat* had been unfair. In her opinion, the fact that the Minister for Foreign Affairs' assessment as to whether the international treaty in question was applicable was binding on the *Conseil d'Etat*, which drew automatic inferences from it, was incompatible with judicial independence. The ECtHR agreed with the applicant:

'The Court notes that in the instant case the Conseil d'Etat (...) relied entirely on a representative of the executive for a solution to the problem before it, concerning the applicability of treaties. It dismissed the applicant's application purely on the ground that the Minister for Foreign Affairs had stated that Article 5 of the 1962 Government Declaration could not be regarded as having been in force on the relevant date, as it had not been applied by Algeria. However, even if consultation of the minister by the Conseil d'Etat may appear necessary in order to as-

---

163 ECtHR, *Terra Woningen B.V. v. the Netherlands*, 28 November 1996, Appl. No. 49/1995/555/64, paras. 46 and 51-55.

sess whether the reciprocity requirement has been satisfied, that court's current practice of referring a preliminary question for interpretation, as in the instant case, obliges it to abide by the opinion of the minister – an external authority who is also a representative of the executive – without subjecting that opinion to any criticism or discussion by the parties. The Court observes, in addition, that the minister's involvement, which was decisive for the outcome of the legal proceedings, was not open to challenge by the applicant (…). In fact, when the applicant was apprised of the Minister for Foreign Affairs' observations, she produced to the Conseil d'Etat several pieces of factual evidence to show that the 1962 Government Declaration had indeed been applied by the Algerian government. (…). However, the Conseil d'Etat did not even consider that evidence (…) it based its decision solely on the opinion of the Minister for Foreign Affairs. In so doing, the Conseil d'Etat considered itself to be bound by this opinion, thereby voluntarily depriving itself of the power to examine and take into account factual evidence that could have been crucial for the practical resolution of the dispute before it. That being so, the applicant cannot be considered to have had access to a tribunal which had (…) sufficient jurisdiction to examine all the factual and legal issues relevant to the determination of the dispute (…). There has accordingly been a violation of Article 6(1) of the Convention in that the applicant's case was not heard by a "tribunal" with full jurisdiction.'[164]

Capital Bank AD v. Bulgaria (2005) concerned the liquidation of a private bank due to insolvency. The applicant bank had set up and acquired a banking license in 1993. On 20 November 1997, its license was revoked by the Bulgarian National Bank (BNB) after the BNB established its insolvency. On 6 January 1998, it was put into compulsory liquidation and on 20 April 2005, the bank was wound up and struck off the register of companies. The applicant bank lodged appeals against the decisions taken by the BNB to the Sofia City Court and, subsequently, to a five-member panel of the Supreme Court of Cassation. Both courts, however, considered themselves precluded from conducting their own examination of whether the bank was in fact insolvent after it had been found to be insolvent by the BNB. As a result, the Sofia City Court expressly held that the evidence adduced by the applicant bank and by the prosecutor's office with a view to challenging the BNB's findings should not be taken into account, as it was irrelevant to the dispute before it. The outcome of the case was, thus, in the end determined solely on the basis of the BNB's finding that the applicant bank was insolvent.[165] The ECtHR found that the BNB's determination in the case at hand had not been subject to judicial scrutiny of the scope required by Article 6, first paragraph.[166] It appears from the judgment that in the course of the proceedings before the ECtHR, the Bulgarian Government tried to convince the ECtHR of the need for the national Bulgarian courts to defer to the BNB's findings. It referred to the 'specific character of the banking business', the special position and functions of the BNB as a national supervisor, and, lastly, to the serious banking and financial crisis in Bulgaria which had prompted a quick regulatory response from the authori-

---

164 ECtHR, *Chevrol v. France*, 13 February 2003, Appl. No. 49636/99, paras. 81-84.
165 ECtHR, *Capital Bank AD v. Bulgaria*, 24 November 2005, Appl. No. 49429/99, para. 99.
166 *Ibidem*, paras 100-108.

ties.[167] The ECtHR did not accept these arguments as valid reasons for judicial deference by the national courts towards the BNB. It considered:

'The Court (…) is prepared to accept that the BNB's opinion on this issue carries significant weight because of its special expertise in this area. However, it is not persuaded that the national courts, if need be with the assistance of expert opinion, could not themselves ascertain whether the applicant bank was insolvent or not. The difficulties encountered in this respect could also be overcome through the provision of a right of appeal against the BNB's decision to an adjudicatory body other than a traditional court integrated within the standard judicial machinery of the country, but which otherwise fully complies with all the requirements of Article 6(1), or whose decision is subject to review by a judicial body with full jurisdiction which itself provides the safeguards required by that provision. Indeed, as is apparent from the Court's case-law, similar systems exist in many States Parties in domains in which special expertise is needed.'[168]

Just as in *Capital Bank AD v. Bulgaria* (2005), in the case of *Druzstevni Zálozna Pria and others v. The Czech Republic* (2008),[169] the national court relied heavily on the determination made by the administrative authority – the Office for the Supervision of Credit Unions (OSCU) – that the situation of the applicant credit union called for a receivership. The applicant's national appeal was twofold. Firstly, the applicant contested the legal assessment of the OSCU declaring the transactions entered into by the applicant credit union contrary to national legislation. Secondly, it was asserted in the appeal that the OSCU had imposed on the applicant credit union a disproportionate measure when opting for receivership, although other less strict measures had been available. According to the applicant credit union, that decision had been partly due to an erroneous assessment of the facts, namely of its economic standing, by the OSCU. Due to its jurisdiction being limited to review of legality, the Prague High Court (hereafter: the national court) when dealing with the second limb of the appeal, abstained from conducting its own examination of whether the applicant credit union was in fact in a situation justifying the imposition of receivership. Admitting that receivership was the strictest measure available, the national court held that national legislation reserved for the OSCU acting within its discretionary power the decision as to what measure to adopt in cases of breach of statutory provisions. Instead of ruling on the question of proportionality of the receivership, it confined itself only to verification that the OSCU had not acted beyond its discretionary power reserved by the Act when imposing the receivership. That finding was made on the assumption, not verification, that the economic standing of the applicant credit union as assessed by the OSCU had been accurate.[170] The ECtHR found this limited jurisdiction of the national court incompatible with Article 6, first paragraph. It ruled:

---

167 *Ibidem*, paras. 112, 114.
168 *Ibidem*, para. 113.
169 ECtHR, *Druzstevni Zálozna Pria and others v. The Czech Republic*, 31 July 2008, Appl. No. 72034/01.
170 *Ibidem*, para. 112.

'It ensues that the High Court, prevented from assessing whether there was indeed any factual basis for imposing the receivership, and limited to reviewing whether the impugned decision was adopted within the OSCU's discretionary power instead of examining the lawfulness of that decision, did not exercise full judicial review. The Court therefore finds that the OSCU's determination of the applicant company's civil rights in the case at hand was not subject to judicial scrutiny of the scope required by Article 6 § 1.'[171]

5.4.2   Required national judicial scrutiny under Article 6, first paragraph: interim conclusions

Article 6, first paragraph, requires that administrative decisions can generally be challenged before a tribunal having full judicial jurisdiction on points of fact and points of law. Full jurisdiction implies that the national court is able to make an independent determination of the disputed facts and of the credibility of a claimant. It also implies that the national court subjects to a debate with both parties advisory information invoked and relied on by the administrative decision maker or the applicant. Limited jurisdiction is, exceptionally, permitted, when a number of specific conditions are fulfilled. First, the particular subject-matter of the proceedings is of importance. In cases where the subject-matter belongs to the classical exercise of administrative discretion, such as land planning, environmental protection and the regulation of gaming, and in cases where the subject matter involves a specialised issue requiring professional knowledge or experience, limited judicial scrutiny at national level may be permissible. Other conditions must be met as well. These are that the national proceedings centre upon points of law and not facts, the preceding administrative procedure(s) is governed by many Article 6-safeguards, and the national judicial scrutiny review is, nevertheless, meaningful in the sense that it entails real scrutiny of the points of law and the procedural points raised by the applicant.

5.4.3   The Zumtobel doctrine and national asylum court proceedings

It may be argued that asylum cases do not fit the category of cases in which limited national court jurisdiction, in the form of a restriction on the court's competence as to questions of facts, is acceptable. As Judge Martens sharply clarified in his separate opinion to *Fischer v. Austria* (1995),[172] there are certain obvious areas where it is imperative that administrative courts should be in a position to leave sufficient freedom of manoeuvre to the executive authorities where it concerns issues of expediency. Martens mentioned as obvious examples areas in which highly technical questions or important diplomatic issues are decisive, and also cases where the administrative authorities may legitimately maintain secrecy even towards the courts. Other areas are those which have classically belonged to the exercise of administrative discretion, such as land planning. Land planning is a classical administrative task and the administration will normally be much better positioned than the judiciary to determine the

---

171 *Ibidem*, paras.113, 114.
172 Separate opinion of Judge Martens to the judgment in the case of *Fischer v. Austria*, 26 April 1995, Appl. No. 16922/90.

expediency of its decisions in this area. According to Martens, at the other end of the spectrum we find those cases where the proceedings directly concern rights coming within the ambit of Article 8 (protecting the right to private life and the right to family life), or cases where – more generally – the general interest is clearly much less involved than that of the individual. Martens referred to the case of *W. v. the UK* (1987), discussed above, which concerned parental access to a child in public care. In that case, the ECtHR ruled that both available national judicial remedies were not compliant with Article 6, first paragraph, as they were not competent to examine the merits of the case.[173]

It would seem more logical to place Article 3-cases concerning the expulsion of asylum seekers in the second category of cases which require full judicial scrutiny on points of fact and points of law. As in the Article 8-cases, such as *W. v. the UK* (1987), in asylum cases a very significant, and perhaps even greater, individual interest is at stake. Article 3 contains a fundamental, absolute and non-derogable right.[174] Most Article 3-cases of asylum seekers will not be of a highly technical nature in the sense that complex technical issues are involved, and in only a very limited number of cases will important diplomatic issues be at stake. Taking into account that the requirements of Article 13 reinforce those of Article 6,[175] it may be argued that the requirement of an independent and rigorous scrutiny (Article 13) reinforces the requirement of full jurisdiction on points of fact and points of law (Article 6). Given what Article 13 requires from national courts, it would not be logical to place cases concerning the expulsion of asylum seekers in the category of cases involving the classical exercise of administrative discretion for the purposes of Article 6, first paragraph.

5.5 Article 6, first paragraph: evidentiary issues in national court proceedings

5.5.1 National procedural autonomy

The ECtHR normally regards the determination of the relevant facts of the case – whether criminal, civil or administrative – and the means and rules to determine the relevant facts, as primarily a matter for the national authorities, including the national courts. It will, therefore, generally not substitute its own assessment of the facts for that of the national authorities, including the national courts. The ECtHR is not a fourth instance, but is only called upon to determine whether or not the national proceedings as a whole were fair. A logical consequence of this is that the ECtHR will not generally review the admission, ordering, exclusion and evaluation of evidence by national courts. For example, it will not generally question a national court's

---

173 ECtHR, *W. v. the UK*, 8 July 1987, Appl. No. 9749/82, paras. 81-83.
174 Examples of judgments concerning expulsion in which the absolute nature of Article 3 was stressed by the ECtHR are *Saadi v. Italy* 28 February 2008, Appl. No. 37201/06, paras. 137-141, *A. v. the Netherlands*, 20 July 2010, Appl. No. 4900/06, paras. 142-143, *Charahili v. Turkey*, 13 April 2010, Appl. No. 46605/07, para. 58. See also Harris, O'Boyle, Bates & Buckley 2009, p. 87.
175 ECtHR, *Kudla v. Poland*, 26 October 2000, Appl. No. 30210/96, para. 152. See also Van Dijk et al. 2006, p. 1019.

decision as to the calling of an expert report or witness. This basic principle is reiterated in many judgments and decisions. For example, in the case of *Dombo Beheer B.V. v. the Netherlands* (1993)[176] the Court ruled:

> 'The Court notes at the outset that it is not called upon to rule in general whether it is permissible to exclude the evidence of a person in civil proceedings to which he is a party. Nor is it called upon to examine the Netherlands law of evidence in civil procedure in abstracto. The applicant company does not claim that the law itself was in violation of the Convention; besides, the law under which the decisions complained of were given has since been replaced. In any event, the competence of witnesses is primarily governed by national law. (…). It is not within the province of the Court to substitute its own assessment of the facts for that of the national courts.'[177]

And in *Elsholz v. Germany* (2000),[178] the Court considered:

> 'The Court recalls that the admissibility of evidence is primarily a matter for regulation by national law and that, as a general rule, it is for the national courts to assess the evidence before them. The Court's task under the Convention is rather to ascertain whether the proceedings as a whole, including the way in which evidence was taken, were fair (see (...) the Schenk v. Switzerland judgment (…).'[179]

Under certain circumstances, however, the ECtHR relinquishes this 'hands off' approach and embarks upon answering the question of whether the determination of the facts by the national authorities has been correct and fair. At least two categories of cases can be distinguished in which this happens. The first category comprises cases in which no proper examination of the case by the national court took place, for example because it overlooked submitted evidence or refused to allow serious evidence into the proceedings. The second category comprises cases in which the opportunities to submit evidence to the national court and to react to evidence and statements of the other party were clearly unequal for the parties to the case. Each of these categories is discussed in more detail below.

5.5.2 *The obligation on national courts to conduct a proper examination of submissions, arguments and evidence*

Article 6, first paragraph, places the national court under a duty to conduct a proper examination of the submissions, arguments and evidence adduced by the parties.[180] If the national court fails to conduct such an examination, the ECtHR may conclude that the national proceedings were unfair. Some examples of cases where this was

---

176 ECtHR, *Dombo Beheer B.V. v. the Netherlands*, 27 October 1993, Appl. No. 14448/88.
177 *Ibidem*, para. 31. See also Harris, O'Boyle, Bates & Buckley 2009, pp. 256-259, Ovey & White 2006, pp. 207-209.
178 ECtHR, *Elsholz v. Germany*, 13 July 2000, Appl. No. 25735/94.
179 *Ibidem*, para. 66.
180 See, for example, ECtHR, *Wierzbicki v. Poland*, 18 June 2002, Appl. No. 24541/94, para. 39.

assumed were analysed above, where the doctrine of full jurisdiction was discussed. Another interesting example is the case of *Elsholz v. Germany* (2000).[181] In this case, the ECtHR concluded that no proper examination of the case had taken place by the national court because that court had refused to obtain expert evidence. The case concerned an application to a district court for a decision granting the applicant a right of access to his child C, born out of wedlock. The court had dismissed a previous application for access because it had concluded that contact with the father would not enhance the child's wellbeing. In reaction to the current application, the court referred to this previous decision, without holding an oral hearing and without obtaining a psychological expert opinion on the question of access rights, although the local Youth Office had recommended that the court obtain such advice before taking a decision. The ECtHR concluded on this basis that the court proceedings had been unfair:

> 'The Court recalls that the admissibility of evidence is primarily a matter for regulation by national law and that, as a general rule, it is for the national courts to assess the evidence before them. The Court's task under the Convention is rather to ascertain whether the proceedings as a whole, including the way in which evidence was taken, were fair (see (…) the Schenk v. Switzerland judgment (…).The Court (…) considers that in the present case, because of the lack of psychological expert evidence and the circumstance that the Regional Court did not conduct a further hearing although, in the Court's view, the applicant's appeal raised questions of fact and law which could not adequately be resolved on the basis of the written material at the disposal of the Regional Court, the proceedings, taken as a whole, did not satisfy the requirements of a fair and public hearing within the meaning of Article 6(1). There has thus been a breach of this provision.'[182]

5.5.3   *Equality of arms, adversariality*

As was said above in 5.2.3, 'fair' in Article 6, first paragraph, means, *inter alia*, that the parties to the case have equal arms, meaning that each party is afforded a reasonable opportunity to present his or her case, including his or her evidence, under conditions that do not place him or her at a substantial disadvantage vis-à-vis the other side.[183] 'Fair' also means that proceedings are adversarial: parties must have knowledge of and must be able to comment on the observations filed or evidence adduced by the other party.[184]

A clear example of unequal opportunities to submit evidence to the national court, resulting in a violation of Article 6, first paragraph, is the case of *Dombo Beheer B.V. v. the Netherlands* (1993).[185] The case revolved around a dispute between the applicant company, Dombo Beheer B.V., and a bank concerning an agreement to ex-

---

181 ECtHR, *Elsholz v. Germany*, 13 July 2000, Appl. No. 25735/94.
182 *Ibidem*, para. 66.
183 See, for example, ECtHR, *Dombo Beheer B.V. v. the Netherlands*, 27 October 1993, Appl. No. 14448/88, para. 33.
184 See, for example, *Kress v. France*, 7 June 2001, Appl. No.39594/98, para. 65.
185 ECtHR, *Dombo Beheer B.V. v. the Netherlands*, 27 October 1993, Appl. No. 14448/88.

tend existing credit facilities. In the national judicial proceedings, it was incumbent upon the applicant company to prove that there was an oral agreement between it and the bank to extend the credit facilities. Only two persons had been present at the meeting at which this agreement had allegedly been reached, a manager of Dombo and a representative of the bank. Yet only the bank's representative had been permitted to be heard in court. The ECtHR ruled that this unequal treatment by the Court of Appeal constituted a breach of the principle of equality of arms, and, therefore, a violation of Article 6.[186] Similarly, in the case of *De Haes and Gijsels v. Belgium* (1997),[187] the ECtHR ruled that equality of arms required that a party to national civil proceedings be permitted to have material evidence in support of his or her case admitted in court.[188]

5.5.4   Secret evidence[189]

The requirements of equality of arms and adversarial proceedings are not absolute, though. Non-disclosure of evidentiary materials may be justified if this is strictly necessary to preserve the fundamental rights of another individual or to safeguard an important public interest, such as the protection of national security. A weighing of interests then needs to be made: the interest of the particular party to have knowledge of the evidence must be weighed against the interest of the other party to keep this evidence secret, for example, in order to protect the security of certain other persons, sources of information or to protect national security. If a court allows secret evidence to the proceedings and accepts that this evidence has not been disclosed to the other party, difficulties caused to a party by the non-disclosure of this evidence must be sufficiently counterbalanced by the procedures followed by the judicial authorities.[190]

The ECtHR first developed these principles in the context of criminal cases. *Rowe and Davis v. the UK* (2000) and *Edwards and Lewis v. the UK* (2004) were both criminal cases in which important incriminating evidence had been withheld from the defence. In both cases, the ECtHR found this to be at variance with Article 6, first paragraph, because no counterbalancing measures whatsoever had been taken to protect the interests of the defence. In *Rowe and Davis v. the UK* (2000), the public prosecutor had not even informed the first instance court of the existence of the non-disclosed evidence. It was only at the stage of higher appeal that the public prosecutor had informed the appeal court and requested approval for further non-disclosure. The ECtHR made clear that it had been the task of the first instance national court (not the appellate court) to examine the secret evidence, to determine whether non-dis-

---

186 *Ibidem*, para. 35.
187 ECtHR, *DeHaes and Gijsels v. Belgium*, 27 January 1997, Appl. No. 7/1996/626/809.
188 *Ibidem*, paras. 54 and 58.
189 See for a more extensive analysis of the use of secret information in asylum cases and the principles on this use developed in international and EU asylum law Reneman 2012, pp. 303-377.
190 See, for example, ECtHR, *Rowe and Davis v. the United Kingdom*, 16 February 2000, Appl. No. 29801/95, para. 61; ECtHR, *Edwards and Lewis v. the UK*, 27 October 2004, Appl. Nos. 39647/98 and 40461/98, para. 46.

closure of this evidence to the defence had been strictly necessary, and to take appropriate compensating measures.[191]

The question arises as to whether examination of the secret evidence by the first instance national court always offers a sufficient counterbalancing measure for the non-disclosure of the evidence to the defence, and, thus, sufficient compensation for the lack of adversariality. The case of *A. v. the Netherlands* (2010)[192] concerned a refusal of asylum and an exclusion order resting on information from the Dutch Intelligence Service AIVD that Mr. A. was a danger to national security. The AIVD information underpinning this allegation had not been accessible to the applicant. It had been accessible to the national first instance provisional measures judge (*voorlopige voorzieningenrechter*). This judge had examined the closed evidence at the AIVD premises and had concluded that it constituted a sufficient basis for the conclusion that Mr. A. indeed constituted a danger to the national security of the Netherlands, without disclosing any details in his judgment. The provisional measures judge had also concluded that no Article 3-risk was present.[193] In the proceedings before the ECtHR, the applicant complained that he had not had an effective national remedy for this Article 3-complaint, in that he could not effectively challenge the national authorities' assertion that he posed a threat to national security.[194]

In this case, the ECtHR did not share the applicant's opinion that no effective national remedy had been available. The Court did not find it problematic that the AIVD information had not been disclosed to the applicant. Although it did not explicitly say so, it seems that the Court was satisfied that the national court could examine, and had actually examined, the closed evidence:

> 'Concerning the underlying materials of the AIVD (…) the Court notes that with the parties' consent these materials were disclosed to the provisional measures judge (…) which in the Court's view has not compromised the independence of the national courts involved in the proceedings concerned and neither can it be said that these courts have given less rigorous scrutiny to the applicant's Article 3 claim (...). Furthermore, the Court notes that this report and the underlying materials did not, as such, concern the applicant's fear of being subjected to ill-treatment in Libya but whether he was posing a threat to the Netherlands national security.'[195]

The Court's reasoning on the issue of the use of secret evidence was remarkably short in the light of the more elaborate considerations in the criminal cases mentioned above. This can probably be explained by the fact that the applicant had complained that he had not had an effective national remedy for his Article 3-complaint, whereas the secret evidence underpinned the exclusion order and not the decision that no Article 3-risk was imminent. In other words, the lack of adversariality had oc-

---

191 ECtHR, *Rowe and Davis v. the United Kingdom*, 16 February 2000, Appl. No. 29801/95, para. 65.
192 ECtHR, *A. v. the Netherlands*, 20 July 2010, Appl. No. 4900/06.
193 *Ibidem*, para. 33.
194 *Ibidem*, para. 112.
195 *Ibidem*, para. 160.

curred in the proceedings concerning the exclusion order, and not in the proceedings concerning the alleged Article 3-risk.

It is, so far, not clear whether – in the context of cases concerning migration – examination of closed evidence by the national first instance judge always and under all circumstances offers a sufficient counterbalancing measure. *A. and Others v. the UK* (2009)[196] is an example of a case in which, as well as examination of the closed evidence by the national first instance judge, more counterbalancing measures were taken to compensate the lack of adversariality. These additional counterbalancing measures took the shape of participation in the proceedings of so-called 'special advocates'. The case of *A. and others v. the UK* (2009) revolved around the question of compatibility of detention of alleged foreign terrorists in the UK with Articles 3 and 5 ECHR.[197] One of the main issues before the ECtHR in this case was the compliance of the system of special advocates with Article 5, paragraph 4, ECHR on the right to a speedy court trial in cases of detention, a *lex specialis* of Article 6. The system of special advocates operates in certain cases involving the use of secret evidence, including cases of alleged involvement in terrorist activities. In these cases, a special procedure is applied by the Special Immigration Appeals Commission (SIAC), which enables it to consider not only material which can be made public ('open material') but also material which, for reasons of national security, cannot ('closed material'). Neither the appellant nor his or her legal advisor can see the closed material. Accordingly, one or more security-cleared counsel, referred to as 'special advocates', are appointed by the Solicitor General to act on behalf of each appellant. In the appeals before the SIAC in the case of *A. v. the UK* (2009), the open statements and evidence concerning each appellant had been served first, and the special advocate had been able to discuss this material with the appellant and his legal advisors and to take instructions. The closed material had then been disclosed to the judges and the special advocate, from which point there could be no further contact between the latter and the appellant and/or his representatives, save with the permission of the SIAC. It was the special advocate's role during the closed sessions to make submissions on behalf of the appellant, both as regards procedural matters, such as the need for further disclosure, and the substance of the case.[198]

The ECtHR accepted that the perceived need to protect the population of the United Kingdom from terrorist attacks meant that there was a 'strong public interest' in maintaining the secrecy of sources of information concerning Al-Qaida and its associates.[199] The Court did not find that the system of special advocates was, of itself, non-compliant with Article 5, paragraph 4:

'The Court (…) considers that the special advocate could perform an important role in counterbalancing the lack of full disclosure and the lack of a full, open, adversarial hearing by test-

---

196 ECtHR, *A. and others v. the UK*, 19 February 2009, Appl. No. 3455/05.
197 *Ibidem.*
198 *Ibidem*, paras. 91-93.
199 *Ibidem*, para. 216.

ing the evidence and putting arguments on behalf of the detainee during the closed hearings.'[200]

The Court also noted, however, that the special advocate could not perform this function in any useful way unless the detainee was provided with sufficient information about the allegations against him to enable him to give effective instructions to the special advocate. The Court observed that, where the evidence was disclosed to a large extent and the open material played the predominant role in the determination, it could not be said that the applicant had been denied an opportunity effectively to challenge the Secretary of State's suspicions about him. In other cases, even where all or most of the underlying evidence remained undisclosed, if the allegations contained in the open material were sufficiently specific, it should have been possible for the applicant to provide his representatives and the special advocate with information with which to refute them, if such information existed, without his having to know the detail or sources of the evidence which formed the basis of the allegations.[201] The Court thus made clear that the national court must look at the proportional relationship between the open (or accessible) evidence and the closed (or non-disclosed) evidence, and test the specificity and level of detail of the allegations in the open evidence. The more detailed and specific the open evidence was, the easier it would be for the other party to challenge the allegations and the less problematic the use of the non-disclosed evidence would be. When, to the contrary, all the specific details underpinning the allegations were contained in the closed evidence, whereas the open evidence was in fact no more than a bare accusation, possibilities to challenge the accusation were almost non-existent. In such a situation, the use of secret evidence was problematic.

In the specific case of *A. and Others v. the UK* (2009), the ECtHR concluded that, under the particular circumstances, the system of special advocates did not offer a sufficient counterbalance for the lack of adversariality affecting a number of applicants. The problem was that the open evidence was not specific enough, whereas important and specific details were laid down in the closed evidence:

> 'The principal allegations against the first and tenth applicants were that they had been involved in fund-raising for terrorist groups linked to al 'Qaeda. In the first applicant's case there was open evidence of large sums of money moving through his bank account and in respect of the tenth applicant there was open evidence that he had been involved in raising money through fraud. However, in each case the evidence which allegedly provided the link between the money raised and terrorism was not disclosed to either applicant. In these circumstances, the Court does not consider that these applicants were in a position effectively to challenge the allegations against them. There has therefore been a violation of Article 5 § 4 in respect of the first and tenth applicants.
>
> The open allegations in respect of the third and fifth applicants were of a general nature, principally that they were members of named extremist Islamist groups linked to al 'Qaeda. SIAC

---

200 *Ibidem*, para. 220.
201 *Ibidem*, para. 220.

observed in its judgments dismissing each of these applicants' appeals that the open evidence was insubstantial and that the evidence on which it relied against them was largely to be found in the closed material. Again, the Court does not consider that these applicants were in a position effectively to challenge the allegations against them. There has therefore been a violation of Article 5 § 4 in respect of the third and fifth applicants.'[202]

The ECtHR has dealt with a number of cases concerning the expulsion of migrants (not asylum seekers) on grounds of national security, where the national administration or national prosecutor used secret evidence. Within the framework of Article 8 (containing the right to protection of family life and private life) the ECtHR has stressed the crucial role of the national first instance court in examining the secret evidence and determining whether non-disclosure is justified. Examples are the cases of *Al Nashif v. Bulgaria* (2002)[203] and *Lupsa v. Romania* (2006).[204] In these cases, neither the applicants nor the national judicial authorities had been provided with the information underpinning the allegation that the applicants constituted a threat to the national security of, respectively, Bulgaria and Romania. As a result, the non-disclosure of evidence to the applicants had in no way been counterbalanced by the procedures followed by the national courts. The national courts had not gone beyond the assertions of the public prosecutor's office for the purpose of verifying whether the applicants really represented a danger to national security or public order. The ECtHR found this totally unacceptable and in violation of Article 8.[205] Importantly, in *Lupsa v. Romania* (2006), the Court ruled:

'The existence of adequate and effective safeguards against abuse, including in particular procedures for effective scrutiny by the courts, is all the more important since a system of secret surveillance designed to protect national security entails the risk of undermining or even destroying democracy on the ground of defending it.'[206]

It is clear from this consideration that the ECtHR sees national courts as the primary guardians of adversariality and equality of arms and that national courts must be very careful in accepting secret evidence.

5.5.5 *Evidentiary issues in national proceedings under Article 6: interim conclusions*

To sum up, Article 6, first paragraph, places national courts under a duty to conduct a proper examination of the submissions, arguments and evidence adduced by the parties. Where no proper examination has taken place by the national court, either because that court did not properly examine party evidence or because it did not use

---

202 *Ibidem*, paras. 223, 224.
203 ECtHR, *Al Nashif v. Bulgaria*, 20 June 2002, Appl.No. 50963/99.
204 ECtHR, *Lupsa v. Romania*, 8 June 2006, Appl.No. 10337/04.
205 ECtHR, *Al Nashif v. Bulgaria*, 20 June 2002, Appl. No. 50963/99, paras. 123-128, ECtHR, *Lupsa v. Romania*, 8 June 2006, Appl. No. 50963/99, paras. 38-42.
206 ECtHR, *Lupsa v. Romania*, 8 June 2006, Appl. No. 50963/99, para. 34.

its investigative powers in order to determine disputed facts independently, this may lead the ECtHR to conclude that there have been unfair national proceedings in violation of Article 6, first paragraph.

Article 6, first paragraph, also requires that the parties to the case normally have equal opportunities to bring in evidence, equal knowledge of evidence and equal opportunities to comment on the observations or evidence adduced by the other party. The requirements of adversariality and equality of arms are not absolute, though. Non-disclosure of evidentiary materials may be justified if this is strictly necessary to preserve the fundamental rights of another individual or to safeguard an important public interest, such as the protection of national security. A weighing of interests then needs to be made: the interest of the particular party to have knowledge of the evidence must be weighed against the interest of the other party to keep this evidence secret, for example, in order to protect the security of certain other persons, sources of information or to protect national security. If a national court allows secret evidence into the proceedings and accepts that this evidence has not been disclosed to the other party, it must follow special procedures to counterbalance the lack of adversariality. This means, at least, that the national court itself examines the secret evidence, and, if possible, takes additional counterbalancing measures. An example of such an additional counterbalancing measure is the system of special advocates as it functions in the UK. In taking additional counterbalancing measures, the national court will have to look at the proportional relationship between the open (accessible) evidence and the closed (non-disclosed) evidence, and must test the specificity and level of detail of the allegations in the open evidence. Where all, or most, of the specific details underpinning the allegations are contained in the closed evidence, whereas the open evidence is in fact nothing but a mere accusation or allegation, the possibility to challenge it is almost non-existent. In such situations, the use of secret evidence is problematic under Article 6, first paragraph.

ECHR, Part 2:

The assessment performed by the ECtHR in cases on expulsion of asylum seekers

5.6   Rigorous scrutiny

To describe the assessment it carries out in expulsion cases, the ECtHR uses the term 'rigorous scrutiny'.[207] It is important to note that this criterion is in its terminology identical to the requirement applicable to national court proceedings under Articles 3, 13 and 35, first paragraph – 'independent and rigorous scrutiny' – described in Part 1, section 5.3.

The ECtHR explained the need for it to conduct a rigorous examination or rigorous scrutiny for the first time in *Vilvarajah and others v. the UK* (1991). The Court provided two reasons: the absolute character of Article 3 and the fundamental nature of Article 3, being a right which enshrines one of the fundamental values of the democratic societies making up the Council of Europe.[208] A third reason for a rigorous scrutiny, mentioned by the Court not in considerations about its own test, but in considerations about the rigorous scrutiny to be performed under Article 13 by the national authorities, was the irreversible nature of the harm that might occur if the risk of ill-treatment materialises.[209]

In order to better understand how the ECtHR itself performs its rigorous scrutiny, a step by step analysis is now made of the assessment performed by the ECtHR in cases concerning the expulsion of asylum seekers. The analysis is made with the aid of the eleven aspects of evidence and judicial scrutiny introduced in Chapter 1.

5.6.1   Standard of proof

It is settled case law that substantial grounds have to be shown for believing that upon expulsion there is a real risk of treatment contrary to Article 3.[210]

In *Saadi v. Italy* (2008), a case concerning an asylum seeker suspected of international terrorism, the UK Government, intervening as a third party, tried to persuade the ECtHR to modify this standard of proof by requiring that it 'be proved that sub-

---

207 See, for example, ECtHR, *Chahal v. the United Kingdom*, 15 November 1996, Appl. No. 22414/93, para. 96; ECtHR, *Jabari v. Turkey*, 11 July 2000, Appl. No. 40035/98, para. 39; ECtHR, *Saadi v. Italy*, 28 February 2008, Appl. No. 37201/06, para. 128 and ECtHR, *Sufi and Elmi v. the UK*, 28 June 2008, Appl. Nos. 8319/07 and 11449/07, para. 214: 'the Court's examination of the existence of a real risk must necessarily be a rigorous one'.

208 ECtHR, *Vilvarajah and others v. the UK*, 30 October 1991, Appl. Nos. 13163/87, 13164/87, 13165/87, 13447/87 and 13448/87, para. 108.

209 ECtHR, *Chahal v. the UK*, 15 November 1996, Appl. No. 22414/93, para. 151.

210 We find this standard of proof in all the judgments concerning asylum seekers, from ECtHR, *Cruz Varas v. Sweden*, 20 March 1991, Appl. No. 15576/89, para. 69, up to recent judgments such as ECtHR, *R.C. v. Sweden*, 9 March 2010, Appl. No. 41827/07, para. 48. The standard is also explicitly mentioned in many admissibility decisions.

jection to ill-treatment is more likely than not'.[211] Such a higher standard of proof would make it easier for States to expel persons like Saadi. The Court rejected this and reaffirmed that

'It is necessary – and sufficient – for substantial grounds to have been shown for believing that there is a real risk that the person concerned will be subjected in the receiving country to treatment prohibited by Article 3.'[212]

In another case concerning an asylum seeker suspected of terrorism, *A. v. the Netherlands* (2010), the ECtHR once more reiterated this standard of proof. The Court stressed in this judgment that it was acutely conscious of the difficulties faced by States in protecting their populations from terrorist violence, but that this made it all the more important to underline the important and absolute nature of Article 3 and that given this nature, there was no room for a higher standard of proof.[213]

The level of risk required is a real (not fictional), personal (relating to the individual), and foreseeable risk exceeding the mere possibility of being subjected to proscribed ill-treatment.[214] The risk does not need to be certain or highly probable.[215]

It seems that in Article 3-cases concerning extradition, the ECtHR applies a second standard of proof, as well as the standard that substantial grounds have to be shown for believing that upon expulsion there is a real risk of treatment contrary to Article 3. This second standard is 'beyond reasonable doubt'.[216] The Court has considered in a number of extradition cases that:

'In assessing the evidence on which to base the decision whether there has been a violation of Article 3, the Court adopts the standard of proof "beyond reasonable doubt".'

Immediately added to this was that such proof may follow from the coexistence of sufficiently strong, clear and concordant inferences or of similar unrebutted presumptions of fact.[217]

Spijkerboer (2010) assumes that the inclusion of this second standard must be a slip of the pen.[218] He argues that this standard of proof stems from cases in which it is alleged that a violation of a right occurred in the past; in such cases the facts have

---

211 ECtHR, *Saadi v. Italy*, 28 February 2008, Appl. No. 37201/06, para. 140.
212 *Ibidem*, para. 140.
213 ECtHR, *A. v. the Netherlands*, 20 July 2010, Appl. No. 4900/06, paras. 141-143.
214 ECtHR, *Vilvarajah v. the United Kingdom*, 30 October 1991, Appl. Nos.13163/87, 13164/87, 13165/87, 13447/87 and 13448/87, paras. 108 and 111.
215 Wouters 2009, p. 247.
216 ECtHR, *Shamayev and others v. Georgia and Russia*, 12 April 2005, Appl. No. 36378/02, para. 338; ECtHR, *Garabayev v. Russia*, 7 June 2007, Appl. No. 38411/02, para. 76; ECtHR, *Klein v. Russia*, 1 April 2010, Appl. No. 24268/08, para. 43; ECtHR, *Khodzhayev v. Russia*, 12 May 2010, Appl. No. 52466/08, para. 89; ECtHR, *Khaydarov v. Russia*, 20 May 2010, Appl. No. 21055/09, para. 96.
217 See, for example, ECtHR, *Garabayev v. Russia*, 7 June 2007, Appl. No. 38411/02, para. 76.
218 Spijkerboer 2010, in: *JV* 02-06-2010, afl. 8.

to be ascertained 'beyond reasonable doubt'.[219] In most cases concerning the expulsion of asylum seekers, a violation has not yet occurred, but there is a risk that a violation will occur in the future. According to Spijkerboer and also Wouters (2009), the concepts of real risk and beyond reasonable doubt do not go well together.[220] Spijkerboer refers to *Saadi v. Italy* (2008), mentioned above, in which the Court refused to modify the standard of proof. The standard of proof 'beyond reasonable doubt' does not feature in Article 3-cases concerning the expulsion (not extradition) of asylum seekers. It is, therefore, of no further relevance.

5.6.2 Burden of proof

It is settled case law that the burden of proof rests initially with the applicant. In *Said v. the Netherlands* (2005), the Court expressed this principle as follows:

> 'it is incumbent on persons who allege that their expulsion would amount to a breach of Article 3 to adduce, to the greatest extent practically possible, material and information allowing the authorities of the Contracting State concerned, as well as the Court, to assess the risk a removal may entail'.[221]

In *Saadi v. Italy* (2008), the ECtHR used the following consideration on the burden of proof and the distribution of the burden of proof for the first time:

> 'It is in principle for the applicant to adduce evidence capable of proving that there are substantial grounds to believing that (…) he would be exposed to a real risk of being subjected to treatment contrary to Article 3. Where such evidence is adduced, it is for the Government to dispel any doubts about it.'[222]

This principle is reiterated in many later judgments.[223] It implies that the claimant has to make an arguable claim by submitting statements which can, in general, be considered credible and by providing corroborating evidence which is capable of proving that there are substantial grounds for believing in a real Article 3-risk.[224] This 'arguable claim test' is a threshold below the 'substantial grounds test' (the standard of proof). This follows from the fact that 'evidence capable of proving that there are substantial grounds' is to be submitted, and not 'evidence proving that there are

---

219 Spijkerboer refers to ECtHR, *Ireland v. the UK*, 18 January 1978, Appl. No.5310/71, para. 161, concerning the practice, prohibited by Article 3, of detention in Northern Ireland. See also ECtHR, *Nachova v. Bulgaria*, 6 July 2005, 43577/98, 43579/98, para. 147, concerning killings by the military police.

220 Wouters 2009, p. 269.

221 ECtHR, *Said v. the Netherlands*, 5 July 2005, Appl. No. 2345/02, para. 49.

222 ECtHR, *Saadi v. Italy*, 28 February 2008, Appl. No. 37201/06, para. 129.

223 See, for example, ECtHR, *NA v. the UK*, 17 July 2008, Appl. No. 25904/07, para. 111; ECtHR, *Muminov v. Russia*, 11 December 2008, Appl. No. 42502/06, para. 87; ECtHR, *R.C. v. Sweden* 9 March 2010, Appl. No. 41827/07, para. 50; ECtHR, *Sufi and Elmi v. the UK*, 28 June 2008, Appl. Nos. 8319/07 and 11449/07, para. 214.

224 See Spijkerboer 2009 in: *International Journal of Refugee Law*, Vol. 21, Nr. 1, March 2009.

substantial grounds'. When this initial burden of proof, or arguability test, is met, the burden shifts, as a burden of investigation, towards the State and the conclusions drawn in section 5.3.5 come into play: the State now has to conduct active investigations to establish whether the application is well-founded; the State has to 'dispel any doubts' about the applicability of Article 3. It can do so, for example, by submitting country information which contradicts the applicant's claim, by subjecting documents provided by the asylum seeker to an investigation of authenticity and concluding that the documents are not authentic, by hearing witnesses and concluding on the basis of witness statements that the flight narrative of the applicant is not credible, by obtaining expert (medical) opinions, *et cetera*.[225]

The judgment in *R.C. v. Sweden* (2010)[226] is interesting to mention here once again as it illustrates when a claim may be considered arguable and, as a consequence, a shift of the burden towards the authorities takes place. Reference is made to section 5.3.3 above for the facts of this case and the ECtHR's judgment. The ECtHR clearly found that the applicant had made an arguable claim and that the national administrative and judicial authorities ought to have directed that an expert medical opinion be obtained as to the probable cause of his scars. From this judgment, we may draw the conclusion that, to be arguable, the claim must reach a basic level of substantiation, meaning that the claim must contain a certain number – not necessarily a very high number – of verifiable details and must be supported by some – not necessarily a very large amount of – evidence. Where the applicant has provided this basic level of substantiation, the burden of proof shifts to the national authorities.

Noteworthy to mention in respect of the burden of proof is also a consideration from *Iskandarov v. Russia* (2010).[227] The applicant in this case had been unlawfully extradited from Russia to Tajikistan. Both parties to the case were in strong disagreement in their respective accounts of the circumstances surrounding the applicant's transfer. The applicant stated that he had been abducted and secretly transferred to Tajikistan by law enforcement officials, whereas the respondent State maintained that the applicant had been abducted by unidentified people and had subsequently been arrested in Dushanbe by the Tajik authorities. The ECtHR considered in relation to the burden of proof:

> 'The Court has also recognised that Convention proceedings do not in all cases lend themselves to a rigorous application of the principle *affirmanti incumbit probatio* (he who alleges something must prove that allegation). In certain circumstances, where the events in issue lie wholly, or in large part, within the exclusive knowledge of the authorities, the burden of proof may be regarded as resting on the authorities to provide a satisfactory and convincing explanation (…).'[228]

---

225 See the case of ECtHR, *R.C. v. Sweden*, 9 March 2010, Appl. No. 41827/07, discussed in detail above in section 5.3.3.

226 *Ibidem.*

227 ECtHR, *Iskandarov v. Russia*, 23 September 2010, Appl. No. 17185/05.

228 *Ibidem*, para. 108.

The ECtHR found it established that the applicant had been illegally extradited by Russian officials, based on the clear and coherent description of the events by the applicant, information from the Tajik Ministry of Foreign Affairs to the UNHCR that the applicant had been 'officially extradited', and the fact that the Russian Government had provided no version capable of explaining how the applicant, last seen in the Moscow Region in the evening of 15 April 2005 and admitted to the Tajik prison on 17 April 2005, had arrived in Tajikistan.[229] The consideration of the burden of proof explicated in *Iskandarov* nuances the general principle that it is, in principle, for the applicant to adduce evidence in support of his or her claim. It must be borne in mind that certain aspects of a claim might be extremely difficult for an applicant to prove and that such aspects may probably be rather within the realm of knowledge of the authorities, so that it is more logical to require evidence from the authorities.

Finally, the ECtHR has made clear that there is an inversely proportional relationship between the onus on the claimant and the general human rights situation in the country of origin. The poorer this situation, the sooner it is assumed that the claimant runs a risk, the less he or she has to 'prove' and the sooner the onus shifts to the State party. If the human rights situation is not obviously poor, the onus shifts more towards the claimant, which means that more evidence is expected.[230]

5.6.3   *Relevant facts and circumstances*

The relevant facts and circumstances can be divided into two categories. First, personal circumstances are relevant, such as background, gender, ethnicity, age, sexual orientation, beliefs, activities, personal profile, and experiences. Second, the general human rights situation in the country of origin is relevant. The ECtHR has made clear that personal circumstances and the general situation in the country of origin must always be seen in conjunction: the personal facts must be assessed in the light of the general situation in the country of origin.[231] From the case law, it also becomes clear that it is normally a combination of facts and circumstances, and not a single fact, which establish that there are substantial grounds for assuming a real Article 3-risk.[232]

Some examples of relevant personal facts, and facts and circumstances concerning the country of origin, are provided below, to give an impression of what the ECtHR finds particularly relevant and important. The description is illustrative, but

---

229 *Ibidem*, paras. 109-115.

230 This notion of a gradual scale is expressed in case law. See, for example, ECtHR, *NA v. the United Kingdom*, 17 July 2008, Appl. No. 25904/07, paras.115-117. See also Battjes 2009, p. 82, Cox 2010, p. 392, Van Bennekom & Van der Winden 2011, p. 220.

231 See, for example, ECtHR, *NA v. the United Kingdom*, 17 July 2008, Appl. No. 25904/07, para. 113, in which the Court ruled that: 'this assessment must focus on the foreseeable consequences of the removal of the applicant to the country of destination. This in turn must be considered in the light of the general situation there as well as the applicant's personal circumstances'. See also Battjes 2009, p. 80, Wouters 2009, p. 264.

232 Wouters 2009, p. 255: 'in most cases a single fact will not suffice to show the existence of a real risk, but rather a combination of facts and circumstances must be put forward'.

by no means exhaustive, and I also refer to Wouters (2009) for an extensive discussion of relevant facts and circumstances.[233]

5.6.3.1   Personal facts

Important personal facts and circumstances are engagement in oppositional political or other activities and the level, type and scale of these activities. For example, in *Chahal v. the UK* (1996), the applicant occupied a high-profile position as an advocate of Sikh separatism in India.[234] In *N. v. Finland*, the claimant's special activities as an infiltrator and informant in President Mobutu's special protection force were found to be important.[235] In *Kandomabadi v. the Netherlands* (2004), the minimal role of the Iranian applicant in student demonstrations in 1999 was considered a relevant factor.[236] Political activities in the country of refuge may be a relevant factor.[237] Arrest, criminal charges and detention are, likewise, considered important; in the case of *Hilal v. the United Kingdom* (2001), the applicant had been arrested and detained for being a member of an opposition party.[238]

Past experiences of torture, ill-treatment, persecution or other serious human rights violations, the experiences of either the applicant or his or her relatives, in detention or not, are considered relevant to the extent that they may indicate a risk of future subjection to proscribed ill-treatment.[239] To mention just a few examples: in *Hilal v. the United Kingdom* (2001) the applicant, who had been arrested and detained for membership of an opposition party, was ill-treated in detention and his brother died in detention as a result of torture.[240] And in *Salah Sheekh v. the Netherlands* (2007), the rape of the applicant's sister and the killing of his father were found relevant, in combination with different forms of ill-treatment meted out to the applicant himself, such as beating, kicking, harassment, intimidation and forced labour. These facts were seen in the light of information on violence directed towards the applicant's clan, the Ashraf, in Somalia.[241]

---

233 Wouters 2009, pp. 255-265.
234 ECtHR, *Chahal v. the UK*, 15 November 1996, Appl. No. 22414/93, paras. 98, 105, 106.
235 ECtHR, *N. v. Finland*, 26 July 2005, Appl. No. 38885/01, para. 162.
236 Admissibility decision ECtHR, *Kandomabadi v. the Netherlands*, 29 June 2004, Appl. Nos. 6276/03 and 6122/04.
237 See, for an example of a case in which the Court considered such activities, ECtHR, *A.B. v. Sweden*, admissibility decision, 31 August 2004, Appl. No. 24697/04. In this case the political activities of the applicant in Sweden were not found decisive as they dated back almost ten years and as the book written by the applicant in Sweden was in Swedish, and only 1,000 copies of it had been printed; moreover, the activities described in the book were old and described in a vague and summary manner.
238 ECtHR, *Hilal v. the United Kingdom*, 6 March 2001, Appl. No. 45276/99, para. 64.
239 See, for example, ECtHR, *Salah Sheekh v. the Netherlands*, 11 January 2007, Appl. No. 1948/04. para. 147, in which the ECtHR referred to the ill-treatment of the applicant in the past and considered that it was not persuaded that the situation in the country of origin had changed. See also Wouters 2009, p. 263.
240 ECtHR, *Hilal v. the United Kingdom*, 6 March 2001, Appl. No. 45276/99, para. 64.
241 See, for example, ECtHR, *Salah Sheekh v. the Netherlands*, 11 January 2007, Appl. No. 1948/04, para. 146.

Army desertion may be an important fact. In the case of *Said v. the Netherlands* (2005), the fact that the applicant had deserted from the Eritrean army before demobilisation, seen in combination with the ill-treatment often inflicted upon deserters in the country of origin were found to be decisive.[242]

An example of a case in which the risk of being exposed to corporal punishment after conviction was found a relevant fact is the case of *D. and others v. Turkey* (2006). In that case the risk of twice being subjected to fifty lashes in the execution of a criminal sentence was certain for one of the applicants, who had been convicted of fornication in Iran.[243]

In a number of cases, it is decisive that the applicant has been sentenced to imprisonment in the country of origin and that it is well-known that persons in detention in the particular country are tortured and ill-treated. Examples of such cases are *Saadi v. Italy* (2008),[244] *Ismoilov and others v. Russia* (2008),[245] *Abdulazhon Isakov v. Russia* (2010).[246]

Recognition as a refugee by a State, in combination with (largely) unchanged circumstances in the country of origin, is often a serious indication of a real risk of serious harm under Article 3 ECHR. In *Ahmed v. Austria* (1996), the fact that the applicant had been granted refugee status in Austria was found highly relevant.[247] In a number of cases, the ECtHR has found refugee status determination by the UNHCR a highly relevant factor to which much weight is attached in assuming an Article 3-risk. This happened, for example, in *Jabari v. Turkey* (2000), *Abdolkhani and Karimnia v. Turkey* (2009), *Khaydarov v. Russia* (2010) and *Dbouba v. Turkey* (2010).[248]

Being a failed asylum seeker may be a relevant factor; in *F. v. the UK* (2004) the applicant based his fear on this very fact. The ECtHR referred to documents submitted by the UK that failed asylum seekers were no longer subjected to ill-treatment in Iran.[249]

5.6.3.2   *Facts and circumstances concerning the situation in country of origin*

Relevant circumstances concerning the country of origin are the general human rights situation, the plight of refugees, the level of violence in the country and control thereof by the authorities. Illustrative is the case of *Al Hanchi v. Bosnia and Herzegovina* (2012), in which the ECtHR found it important that a process of democratic transition was going on in Tunisia and that steps had been taken to dismantle the oppres-

---

242 ECtHR, *Said v. the Netherlands*, 5 July 2005, Appl. No. 2345/02, para. 52.
243 ECtHR, *D. and others v. Turkey*, 22 June 2006, Appl. No. 24245/03, para. 47.
244 ECtHR, *Saadi v. Italy*, 28 February 2008, Appl. No. 37201/06, paras. 143-146.
245 ECtHR, *Ismoilov and others v. Russia*, 24 April 2008, Appl. No. 2947/06, paras. 120-121.
246 ECtHR, *Abdulazhon Isakov v. Russia*, 8 July 2010, Appl. No. 14049/08, para. 109.
247 ECtHR, *Ahmed v. Austria*, 17 December 1996, Appl. No. 25964/94, para. 42.
248 ECtHR, *Jabari v. Turkey*, 11 July 2000, Appl. No. 40035/98, paras. 40 and 41; ECtHR, *Abdolkhani and Karimnia v. Turkey*, 22 September 2009, Application No. 30471/08, para. 82; ECtHR, *Khaydarov v. Russia*, 20 May 2010, Appl. No. 21055/09, para. 109; ECtHR, *Dbouba v. Turkey*, 13 July 2010, Appl. No. 15916/09, paras. 42, 43.
249 ECtHR, *F. v. the United Kingdom*, admissibility decision, 31 August 2004, Appl. No. 36812/02.

sive structures of the former regime.[250] In *H.L.R. v. France* (1997) the applicant feared ill-treatment by drug traffickers, for revenge, upon return to Colombia. The ECtHR found it insufficiently demonstrated that the Colombian authorities would not be able to protect the applicant.[251] Other relevant facts are changes in government or policies, the existence of a peace process or an agreed ceasefire, the repatriation of refugees under the supervision of the UNHCR. In *Cruz Varas and others v. Sweden* (1991), the ECtHR noted that 'a democratic evolution was in the process of taking place in Chile which had led to improvements in the political situation and, indeed, to the voluntary return of refugees from Sweden and elsewhere'.[252] And in *Vilvarajah and others v. the UK* (1991), the Court considered it important that there had been an improvement in the situation in the north and east of Sri Lanka and that the UNHCR's voluntary repatriation programme had begun to operate.[253]

Conditions in detention in the country of origin have already been mentioned above as an important factor. Cases such as *Saadi v. Italy* (2008),[254] *Ismoilov and others v. Russia* (2008)[255] and *Abdulazhon Isakov v. Russia* (2010)[256] demonstrate that when a particular country of origin is known to be perpetrating torture and ill-treatment in prisons, and it is likely that the applicant will end up in detention upon expulsion, the ECtHR readily assumes an Article 3-risk.

Diplomatic assurances guaranteeing that the expelled (or extradited) applicant will not be subjected to treatment proscribed by Article 3 have played an important role in a number of cases. To be of serious value, diplomatic assurances must, first, specifically exclude that the applicant would be subjected to treatment contrary to Article 3.[257] In addition, the value of diplomatic assurances will depend on whether it can be established, on the basis of objective information, such as reports from human rights organisations, that the government in question will really be able to prevent torture, and has the sincere intention to fight against it. In *Chahal v. the UK* (1996), the ECtHR did not find the diplomatic assurances provided by the Indian Government convincing. The Court considered that, despite the efforts by that government, the NHRC and the Indian courts to bring about reform, the violation of human rights by certain members of the security forces in Punjab and elsewhere in India was a recalcitrant and enduring problem. Against this background, the Court was not persuaded

---

250 ECtHR, *Al Hanchi v. Bosnia and Herzegovina*, 15 November 2011, Appl. No. 48205/09, para. 43.

251 ECtHR, *H.L.R. v. France*, 29 April 1997, Appl. No. 24573/94, paras. 41-43.

252 ECtHR, *Cruz Varas and others v. Sweden*, 20 March 1991, Appl. No. 15576/89, para. 80.

253 ECtHR, *Vilvarajah and others v. the UK*, 30 October 1991, Appl. Nos. 13163/87, 13164/87, 13165/87, 13447/87 and 13448/87, paras. 109, 110.

254 ECtHR, *Saadi v. Italy*, 28 February 2008, Appl. No. 37201/06, paras. 143-146.

255 ECtHR, *Ismoilov and others v. Russia*, 24 April 2008, Appl. No. 2947/06, paras. 120-121.

256 ECtHR, *Abdulazhon Isakov v. Russia*, 8 July 2010, Appl. No. 14049/08, para. 109.

257 See, for example, ECtHR, *Khaydarov v. Russia*, 20 May 2010, Appl. No. 21055/09, para.113. In *Khaydarov*, the Russian national courts interpreted letters from the Tajik Prosecutor's General Office in such a way as to contain such specific assurances. The ECtHR, however, found decisive that the literal text of the letters did not exclude specifically that the applicant would be subjected to treatment contrary to Article 3.

that the above assurances would provide Mr. Chahal with an adequate guarantee of safety.[258]

However, in some other cases the ECtHR has found diplomatic assurances convincing. An example is *Mamatkulov and Askarov v. Turkey* (2005).[259] In this case, the Court found assurances issued by the Public Prosecutor of Uzbekistan persuasive, first, because they excluded specifically that the applicants would be subjected to treatment contrary to Article 3 or the death penalty. Importantly, the assurances also stressed that 'the Republic of Uzbekistan is a party to the United Nations Convention against Torture and accepts and reaffirms its obligation to comply with the requirements of the provisions of that Convention as regards both Turkey and the international community as a whole'. Finally, the Turkish Government produced medical reports from the doctors of the Uzbek prisons in which the applicants had been held. These reports did not reveal any indication of torture or ill-treatment.[260] For a more detailed study of the role of diplomatic assurances in Article 3 expulsion and extradition cases, I refer to Cox (2010) and to Battjes (2012).[261]

A final example of a relevant circumstance concerning the country of origin is the existence of an internal relocation alternative. It is constant jurisprudence of the ECtHR that as a precondition for relying on an internal relocation alternative, certain guarantees have to be in place: the person to be expelled must be able to travel to the area concerned, gain admittance and settle there, failing which an issue under Article 3 may arise, the more so if in the absence of such guarantees there is a possibility of an applicant ending up in a part of the country where he or she may be subjected to treatment prohibited by Article 3.[262] In *Sufi and Elmi v. the UK* (2011),[263] the ECtHR examined whether certain parts of southern and central Somalia met the mentioned criteria of an internal relocation alternative for people expelled to Mogadishu. It concluded that certain parts of southern and central Somalia were suitable only for those people having close family connections in the area concerned, where they could effectively seek refuge.[264] Another recent example of a case in which the Court examined the question of the availability of a reliable internal relocation alternative is *Izev-*

---

258 ECtHR, *Chahal v. the UK*, 15 November 1996, Appl. No. 22414/93, paras. 92 and 105. See, for the same conclusion that diplomatic assurances could not be relied on: ECtHR, *Kaboulov v. Ukraine*, 19 November 2009, Appl. No. 41015/04, para. 113; ECtHR, *Yuldashev v. Russia*, 8 July 2010, Appl. No. 1248/09, para. 85.

259 ECtHR, *Mamatkulov and Askarov v. Turkey*, 4 February 2005, Appl. Nos. 46827/99, 46951/99.

260 *Ibidem*, para. 76. See also ECtHR, *Chentiev and Ibragimov v. Slovakia*, admissibility decision, 14 September 2010, Appl. Nos. 21022/08, 51946/08, in which case diplomatic assurances were similarly accepted as reliable, and ECtHR, *Othman (Abu Qatada) v. the UK*, 17 January 2012, Appl. No. 8139/09, paras. 190-207. In that case, the ECtHR attached importance to the fact that the diplomatic assurances would be monitored by independent human rights organisations.

261 M. Cox, 'Diplomatieke garanties versus de absolute gelding van artikel 3 EVRM, een stroomschema als praktische handleiding', *NJCM Bulletin* 2010, jrg. 35-4, pp. 388-404; H. Battjes, Comment to ECtHR, *Othman (Abu Qatada) v. the UK*, 17 January 2012, Appl. No. 8139/09, JV 5, 30 March 2012, 16, pp. 670-698.

262 See, for an example of a judgment in which reference was made to earlier judgments: ECtHR, *Sufi and Elmi v. the UK*, 28 June 2011, Appl. Nos. 8319/07 and 11449/07, para. 266.

263 *Ibidem*.

264 *Ibidem*, paras. 265-267.

bekhai and others v. Ireland (2011).[265] The question in this case was whether the daughters of the applicant would run a real risk of subjection to female genital mutilation (FGM) if expelled to Nigeria. The ECtHR followed information from UN organisations as well as NGOs that internal re-location to escape FGM was indeed an option in Nigeria.[266]

5.6.4   Required degree of individual risk

As has been said above, it is normally a combination of personal facts and conditions in the country of origin which constitute substantial grounds for assuming a real Article 3-risk. Since *Vilvarajah v. the UK* (1991),[267] the question to what extent an asylum seeker invoking Article 3 must demonstrate that he or she has been specifically singled out or targeted has, however, been a topic of fierce debate.[268] This is because in *Vilvarajah* the ECtHR used the phrase 'special distinguishing features', which seemed to indicate that, to successfully invoke Article 3, the applicant needed to be really singled out as an individual. Case law from 2007 onwards has brought some clarity to this issue. Three main categories of cases can now be distinguished:
-   Cases in which there is extreme general violence in the country of origin, to such an extent that a real risk of ill-treatment would occur simply by virtue of an individual being exposed to such violence on return. Special distinguishing features, meaning special personal facts and circumstances, are not required. The ECtHR explicitly mentioned this possibility for the first time in *NA v. the UK* (2008). From *NA v. the UK* and subsequent case law it became clear, however, that a general situation of violence would not normally in itself entail a violation of Article 3 in the event of an expulsion and that the Court would only in the most extreme cases of violence adopt the approach that every returnee ran an Article 3-risk.[269] The ECtHR explicitly ruled that such a situation of extreme general violence did not prevail in Sri Lanka in relation to returning Tamils in *NA v. the UK* (2008)[270] and in the subsequent series of judgments on the expulsion of Tamils to Sri Lanka: *T.N. v. Denmark, T.N. and S.N. v. Denmark, S.S. and others v. Denmark, P.K. v. Denmark* and *N.S. v. Denmark* (all 2011),[271] and to Iraq in *F.H. v. Sweden*

---

265 ECtHR, *Izevbekhai and others v. Ireland*, admissibility decision, 17 May 2011, Appl. No. 43408/08.

266 ECtHR, para. 75.

267 ECtHR, *Vilvarajah and others v. the United Kingdom*, 30 October 1991, Appl. Nos. 13163/87, 13164/87, 13165/87, 13447/87 and 13448/87, para. 112.

268 Wouters 2009, pp. 247-255.

269 ECtHR, *NA v. the United Kingdom*, 17 July 2008, Appl. No. 25904/07, paras. 114-115. In 2010 the Court reiterated that it would only assume such a situation of extreme violence in exceptional cases in a series of judgments concerning (like *NA v. the UK*) the (intended) expulsion of Tamils to Sri Lanka: ECtHR, *T.N. v. Denmark*, 20 January 2011, Appl. No. 20594/08, para. 85; ECtHR, *T.N. and S.N. v. Denmark*, 20 January 2011, Appl. No. 36517/08, para. 90; ECtHR, *S.S. and others v. Denmark*, 20 January 2011, Appl. No. 54703/08, para. 86; ECtHR, *P.K. v. Denmark*, 20 January 2011, Appl. No. 54705/08, para. 73; ECtHR, *N.S. v. Denmark*, 20 January 2011, Appl. No. 58359/08, para. 74. See also ECtHR, *Sufi and Elmi v. the UK*, 28 June 2011, Appl. Nos. 8319/07 and 11449/07, para. 218.

270 ECtHR, *NA v. the United Kingdom*, 17 July 2008, Appl. No. 25904/07, para. 125.

271 ECtHR, *T.N. v. Denmark*, 20 January 2011, Appl. No. 20594/08, para. 93; ECtHR, *T.N. and S.N. v. Denmark*, 20 January 2011, Appl. No. 36517/08, para. 98; ECtHR, *S.S. and others v. Denmark*, 20 Jan-

→

(2009).[272] The same conclusion of absence of a situation of extreme general violence was drawn by the Court in relation to the situation in Afghanistan in *Ghulami v. France* (2009),[273] the situation in Kosovo in *Gashi and others v. Sweden*,[274] the situation in the Democratic Republic of the Congo in *Mawaka v. the Netherlands* (2010)[275] and the situation in the West Bank in *Al-Zawatia v. Sweden*.[276] The ECtHR has, so far, assumed the existence of extreme violence resulting in an Article 3-risk for every returnee in only one case, *Sufi and Elmi v. the United Kingdom* (2011).[277] The case concerned the expulsion of two Somali applicants to Mogadishu. The Court considered in this case that the large quantity of objective information overwhelmingly indicated that the level of violence in Mogadishu was of sufficient intensity to pose a real risk of treatment reaching the Article 3 threshold to anyone in the capital, except possibly those who were exceptionally well-connected to 'powerful actors'.[278]

- Cases in which the applicant belongs to a group of persons systematically exposed to ill-treatment. The very fact that an applicant belongs to such a targeted group seems to constitute a special distinguishing feature in itself. It is, so far, not entirely clear whether the Court does or does not require any further special distinguishing features.[279] The reason for this uncertainty is that in *Salah Sheekh v. the Netherlands* (2007)[280] and, one year later, in *NA v. the UK* (2008) the Court said two different things on this. In *Salah Sheekh*, the Somali applicant belonged to the targeted Ashraf minority. In its judgment the Court considered that

'In the present case, on the basis of the applicant's account and the information about the situation in the relatively unsafe areas of Somalia in so far as members of the Ashraf minority are concerned, it is foreseeable that on his return the applicant would be exposed to treatment in breach of Article 3.'[281]

It follows from this consideration that the Court attached importance to the particular personal experiences of the applicant, which included ill-treatment meted out to him and his relatives. This meant that the single fact that the applicant belonged to a targeted group was not sufficient in itself and that (certain) further special distinguishing features were required. In *NA v. the UK* (2008), however,

---

uary 2011, Appl. No. 54703/08, para. 94; ECtHR, *P.K. v. Denmark*, 20 January 2011, Appl. No. 54705/08, para. 81; ECtHR, *N.S. v. Denmark*, 20 January 2011, Appl. No. 58359/08, para. 82.
272 ECtHR, *F.H. v. Sweden*, 20 January 2009, Appl. No. 32621/06, paras. 91-93.
273 ECtHR, *Ghulami v. France*, admissibility decision, 7 April 2009, Appl. No. 45302/05.
274 ECtHR, *Gashi and others v. Sweden*, admissibility decision, 4 May 2010, Appl. No. 61167/08.
275 ECtHR, *Mawaka v. the Netherlands*, 1 June 2010, Appl. No. 29031/04, para. 44.
276 ECtHR, *Al-Zawatia v. Sweden*, admissibility decision, 22 June 2010, Appl. No. 50068/08.
277 ECtHR, *Sufi and Elmi v. the UK*, 28 June 2011, Appl. Nos. 8319/07 and 11449/07.
278 *Ibidem*, paras. 248, 250.
279 See also Van Bennekom & Van der Winden 2011, pp. 218-220; these authors raise the same question and are so far not sure about the answer.
280 ECtHR, *Salah Sheekh v. the Netherlands*, 11 January 2007, Appl. No. 1948/04.
281 *Ibidem*, para. 148.

the Court came back to this consideration from the *Salah Sheekh* judgment and stated:

'The Court's findings in that case (Salah Sheekh) as to the treatment of the Ashraf clan in certain parts of Somalia, and the fact that the applicant's membership of the Ashraf clan was not disputed, were sufficient to conclude that his expulsion would be in violation of Article 3.[282]

This consideration implies that the single fact of belonging to the targeted group was sufficient and no further special distinguishing features were necessary.[283] As the Court clearly deemed it necessary, one year after *Salah Sheekh*, to further explain, in *NA v. the UK*, the line of reasoning followed in *Salah Sheekh*, it is safe to conclude that it accepts certain situations in which a (minority) group is so systematically targeted that merely belonging to such a group results in an Article 3-risk.

- Cases in which there is no extreme general violence in the country of origin and the applicant does not belong to a specially targeted group. In such cases, the general situation in the country of origin does play a more or less important role, but there must also be special personal facts and circumstances (special distinguishing features) which establish that this very applicant runs a risk. A good example of such a case is *Hilal v. the UK* (2001), in which it was a combination of personal facts and circumstances, which against the background of information on the situation in the country of origin, constituted substantial grounds for assuming a real Article 3-risk. The applicant was a member of an opposition party for which he had been arrested and detained, he had been ill-treated during his detention, his brother had also been detained and had died in prison, and the police had gone to his wife's house on a number of occasions looking for him and making threats.[284]

It may sometimes be difficult to place a concrete case in one of the above categories and the boundaries may not always be very clear. What may be helpful to remember is the notion of the gradual scale. The poorer the general human rights situation in the country of origin, the more significant this situation becomes in assessing the risk and the less individual facts and circumstances, including evidence thereof, are required. In line with this principle it may be argued that the more a certain group or category of persons is targeted, the less individual facts and circumstances, including evidence thereof, are required.[285]

---

282 ECtHR, *NA v. the UK*, 17 July 2008, Appl. No. 25904/07, para, 116.
283 See on this question (whether or not further special distinguishing features are required if an applicant belongs to a targeted group) also Van Bennekom & Van der Winden 2011, pp. 217-220.
284 ECtHR, *Hilal v. the UK*, 6 March 2001, Appl. No. 45276/99, paras. 64 to 66.
285 This notion of a gradual scale is expressed in *NA v. the United Kingdom*, 17 July 2008, Appl. No. 25904/07, paras. 115-117, and also in literature. See, for example, Battjes 2009, p. 82, Cox 2010, p. 392, Van Bennekom & Van der Winden 2011, p. 220.

5.6.5   *Credibility assessment*

The ECtHR tries to strike a difficult balance when it comes to assessing the credibility of the claim.[286] On the one hand, it stresses its subsidiary role and considers that the credibility assessment is primarily a matter for the authorities of the Contracting States:

> 'the Court accepts that, as a general principle, the national authorities are best placed to assess not just the facts but, more particularly, the credibility of witnesses since it is they who have had the opportunity to see, hear and assess the demeanour of the individual concerned.'[287]

In line with this general principle, in a number of admissibility decisions the Court has relied on the credibility assessment made by the respondent State.[288] For example, in *Damla and others v. Germany* (2006), the Court considered as follows:

> 'It notes in this regard that the German authorities had due regard to the arguments submitted by the applicants in the administrative court proceedings as well as to the past and current situation in the receiving country. It also observes that the Federal Office for Refugees found that the applicant's recollection of the events which led them to leave Turkey was unreliable and that it had serious reservations about the credibility of the applicants' account in general. Furthermore, the Federal Office for Refugees carefully evaluated the evidence which the applicants submitted in support of their renewed asylum request. Furthermore, the Court observes that altogether three different asylum proceedings have been carried out by the German courts in the applicants' case. They carefully evaluated the evidence which the applicants submitted in support of their asylum requests.'[289]

On the other hand, the ECtHR acknowledges the absolute nature and the fundamental value of Article 3 and considers on that basis that the Court itself must make a thorough (or rigorous) examination of the existence of a real risk:

> 'Its examination of the existence of a real risk of ill-treatment must necessarily be a rigorous one in view of the absolute character of Article 3 (…).'[290]

---

286 For the same conclusion: see Geertsema 2010. See on this also Essakkili & Spijkerboer 2005, p. 44 and Spijkerboer 2009; Essakkili & Spijkerboer use the term 'inconsistency'. With Geertsema, I would rather speak of a difficult search for a balance between avoiding becoming a fourth instance and applying a rigorous scrutiny because Article 3 is a fundamental absolute right.

287 See, for example, ECtHR, *R.C. v. Sweden*, 9 March 2010, Appl. No. 41827/07, para. 52; ECtHR, *A.A. and Others v. Sweden*, 28 June 2012, Appl. Nr. 14499/09. See also admissibility decisions ECtHR, *Damla and others v. Germany* 26 October 2006, Appl. No. 61479/00;ECtHR, *F. v. the UK*, 22 June 2004, Appl. No. 17341/03; ECtHR, *Harutioenyan and others v. the Netherlands*, 1 September 2009, Appl. No. 43700/07.

288 Examples are admissibility decisions ECtHR, *F. v. the UK*, 22 June 2004, Appl. No. 17341/03; ECtHR, *Damla and others v. Germany* 26 October 2006, Appl. No. 61479/00; ECtHR, *Harutioenyan and others v. the Netherlands*, 1 September 2009, Appl. No. 43700/07.

289 ECtHR, *Damla and others v. Germany* 26 October 2006, Appl. No. 61479/00.

290 See, for example, ECtHR, *Chahal v. the United Kingdom*, 15 November 1996, Appl. No. 22414/93, para. 96; ECtHR, *Jabari v. Turkey*,11 July 2000, Appl. No. 40035/98, para. 39; ECtHR, *N. v. Finland*,

$\rightarrow$

Part of this rigorous examination is an independent assessment of credibility when this credibility is in dispute between the parties. The Court has made such an independent credibility assessment in a significant number of final judgments[291] and in some admissibility decisions.[292]

In *Iskandarov v. Russia* (2010),[293] the Court once again, this time in even more precise words, expressed the difficult balancing exercise it makes when it comes to the determination of the facts:

'The Court notes at the outset that it is sensitive to the subsidiary nature of its role and recognises that it must be cautious in taking on the role of a first-instance tribunal of fact, where this is not rendered unavoidable by the circumstances of a particular case (...). Nonetheless, where allegations are made under Article 3 of the Convention the Court must apply a particularly thorough scrutiny even if certain national proceedings and investigations have already taken place (...).'[294]

Finally, the consideration about the intensity of scrutiny used in *A.A. and Others v. Sweden* (2012) is interesting:

'It observes that the applicants' case was thoroughly examined by both the Migration Board and the Migration Court, which included several interviews before the Board. They further appealed against the Migration Court's judgment to the Migration Court of Appeal, which decided to refuse leave to appeal. Before all instances the applicants were assisted by female legal counsel. Furthermore, apart from the ordinary asylum proceedings, which went through three instances, both the Migration Board and the Migration Court have examined the applicants' application for subsequent review of the enforcement order. There are no indications that the proceedings before the domestic authorities lacked effective guarantees to protect the applicants against arbitrary refoulement or were otherwise flawed. Against this background, the Court will continue by examining whether the information presented before this Court would lead it to depart from the domestic authorities' conclusions.'[295]

This consideration reveals two things. First, that the Court, in making up its mind on whether to rely on the respondent State party's determination of the facts or make a

---

26 July 2005, Appl. No. 38885/02, para. 160 (here the Court uses the term 'thorough' instead of the term 'rigorous'); ECtHR, *Saadi v. Italy*, 28 February 2008, Appl. No. 37201/06, para. 128.

291 Geertsema 2010 also states that a rigorous examination implies an independent assessment of the claimant's credibility by the Court. An independent assessment of the claimant's credibility by the Court itself was made in, for example, ECtHR, *Cruz Varas and others v. Sweden*, 20 March 1991, Appl. No. 15576/89; ECtHR, *Hilal v. the UK*, 6 March 2001, Appl. No. 45276/99; ECtHR, *Said v. the Netherlands*, 5 July 2005, Appl. No. 2345/02; ECtHR, *N. v. Finland*, 26 July 2005, Appl. No. 38885/02; ECtHR, *R.C. v. Sweden*, 9 March 2010, Appl. No. 41827/07.

292 See, for example, admissibility decision ECtHR, *Nasimi v. Sweden*, 16 March 2004, Appl. No. 38865/02.

293 ECtHR, *Iskandarov v. Russia*, 23 September 2010, Appl. No. 17185/05.

294 *Ibidem*, para. 106.

295 ECtHR, *A.A. and Others v. Sweden*, 28 June 2012, Appl. No. 14499/09, para. 77. See also ECtHR, *J.H. v. the UK*, 20 December 2011, Appl. No. 48839/09, para. 58.

fresh factual determination of itself, takes a close look at the quality of the national proceedings in the case at hand. If the national proceedings were thorough, the Court will see less room for an independent and fresh determination of the facts. Second, the last sentence of the consideration quoted above reveals that the Court is in principle always free to proceed to a fresh determination of the facts on the basis of all the materials before it and depart from the national authorities' conclusions. The consideration quoted above makes very clear that, also in situations where the national proceedings were adequate, the Court nevertheless has the choice to proceed to an independent, fresh determination of the facts. Like the ComAT (see Chapter 4, section 4.5.5), the ECtHR is, thus, fully free to determine the intensity of its factual scrutiny, depending on the particular circumstances of the case at hand.

The question remains under what circumstances the ECtHR chooses one of these two approaches: reliance on the respondent State's credibility assessment or independent assessment of the credibility on its own account? Unfortunately, so far, it has not developed an elaborate doctrinal position on this issue. From the case law, it may be inferred, however, that at least three circumstances, individually or in combination, may, in particular, trigger the Court to proceed to an independent assessment of the claimant's credibility on its own account. These triggers are the following:

1) Insufficient national proceedings, for example, evidence was overlooked or not taken seriously, or the assessment made at national level was insufficiently supported by relevant country of origin materials;

2) New facts, circumstances and developments, including evidence thereof, or new information which casts doubt on the information relied on by the government; and

3) The absolute nature of Article 3 was disrespected, for example, a weighing of national security considerations against the Article 3-risk took place, or an incorrect application of the standard of proof or another evidentiary standard took place, for example, a too strict standard of proof or a too strict standard on individualisation.[296]

Examples of the first trigger – insufficient national proceedings – are *Jabari v. Turkey* (2000),[297] in which no material assessment at all had been made by the national authorities, and *R.C. v. Sweden* (2010),[298] in which the Court found that no serious investigation at national level had taken place as medical evidence (a report from a physician at a local health care centre) had not been taken seriously. These two cases were discussed above in sections 5.3.2 and 5.3.3. Another illustration of this first trigger is *Salah Sheekh v. the Netherlands* (2007), in which the national authorities relied

---

296 See also Wouters 2009, p. 284: 'it seems that the Court is willing to conduct a full assessment of its own when the national proceedings followed give it reason to so so, for example because the claim was assessed in an accelerated procedure, or because doubts have been cast on the information relied on by the national authorities, in particular because the situation in the country of destination may have changed since the national proceedings ended'.

297 ECtHR, *Jabari v. Turkey*, 11 July 2000, Appl. No. 40035/98.

298 ECtHR, *R.C. v. Sweden*, 9 March 2010, Appl. No. 41827/07.

on information regarding the country of origin from only one single source, being the Dutch Ministry of Foreign Affairs, whereas the ECtHR relied on information from a variety of different sources.[299]

Illustrations of the second trigger – new facts and developments, including new evidence which has not been assessed by the national authorities – are *Hilal v. the UK* (2001) and *N. v. Finland* (2005). In *Hilal*, the Court explicitly considered that it saw fit to proceed to an independent assessment of the claimant's credibility because since the national special adjudicator's decision, which relied, *inter alia*, on a lack of substantiating evidence, the applicant had produced further documentation.[300] In *N. v. Finland*, the ECtHR heard a new witness, K.K., whom the national authorities had not been able to hear. K.K.'s testimony shed new light on the applicant's account.[301] New facts or developments may also concern the situation in the country of origin. The Court is of the opinion that 'a full and ex nunc assessment is called for as the situation in a country of destination may change in the course of time'.[302] Finally, in *J.H. v. the UK* (2011), a case concerning an Afghan applicant who contended that his expulsion to Afghanistan would expose him to a real risk of ill-treatment due to the high and visible profile of his father in Afghanistan, the ECtHR stressed that there was no new evidence before it causing it to depart from the findings arrived at by the national authorities.[303]

An illustration of the third trigger – disrespect for the absolute nature of Article 3 – is *Chahal v. the UK* (1996). Strictly speaking, there were no credibility issues concerning stated past facts in this case; the parties were, instead, mainly divided over the fate that would await the applicant, a well-known supporter of Sikh separatism, if he was expelled to India. Nevertheless, this case does form a good illustration of the third trigger. As the UK had weighed the Article 3-risk against national security considerations, and had, therefore, applied an incorrect standard of proof, the ECtHR deemed it necessary to make a completely new and independent examination of the alleged real risk.[304]

Interestingly, within the ECtHR opinions are sometimes strongly divided over the question of which of the two avenues to choose: reliance on the credibility assessment made by the national authorities or an independent credibility assessment of its own. This appears from a number of dissenting opinions to final judgments.[305]

---

299 ECtHR, *Salah Sheekh v. the Netherlands*, 11 January 2007, Appl. No. 1948/04, paras. 136 and 138-149.

300 ECtHR, *Hilal v. the UK*, 6 March 2001, Appl. No. 45276/99, para. 62.

301 ECtHR, *N. v. Finland*, 26 July 2005, Appl. No. 38885/02, para. 157: 'moreover, the Finnish authorities and courts did not have an opportunity to hear K.K.'s testimony with regard to the applicant's background in the DRC'.

302 ECtHR, *Salah Sheekh v. the Netherlands*, 11 January 2007, Appl. No. 1948/04, para. 136.

303 ECtHR, *J.H. v. the UK*, 20 December 2011, Appl. No. 48839/09, para. 59.

304 ECtHR, *Chahal v. the UK*, 15 November 1996, Appl. No. 22414/93, para. 76.

305 See, for example, the dissenting opinion of Judge Maruste to ECtHR, *N. v. Finland* (2005), stating that 'in essence this is a case of assessment of credibility and risk and I believe that in such situations the national authorities are much better placed than international judges', and the dissenting opinion of Judge Fura to *R.C. v. Sweden* (2010) stating that 'National courts are normally better placed to do this than an international court, since they have had the opportunity to see and hear the parties.'

It is important to mention here that in a number of cases the ECtHR has not determined the facts, and, as part of this, assessed the credibility of the applicant fully independently, but has relied to a large extent on the determination of the facts made by the UNHCR. Examples of such cases are *Jabari v. Turkey* (2000), *Abdolkhani and Karimnia v. Turkey* (2009), *Charahili v. Turkey* (2010), *Ayatollahi and Hosseinzadeh v. Turkey* (2010), *M.B. and others v. Turkey* (2010), *Khaydarov v. Russia* (2010) and *Dbouba v. Turkey* (2010).[306] This does not always mean, however, that the ECtHR fully follows the stance taken by the UNHCR, but it does attach significant weight to the position taken by the UNHCR.[307] An example of a case in which the ECtHR did not follow the assessment made by the UNHCR is *Y. v. Russia* (2010). In that case, which concerned a Chinese Falung Gong practitioner, the ECtHR concluded that there were insufficient grounds for assuming an Article 3-risk whereas the Moscow UNHCR office delivered refugee status. What was important was the fact that the refugee status had been delivered by the UNHCR before the national refugee status determination had begun, that it was not clear whether the same grounds served as a basis for both claims and, finally, that the UNHCR had not intervened in any way during the subsequent appeals or proceedings.[308]

When the ECtHR decides to proceed to an independent assessment of the credibility on its own account, how does it go about this, and which principles does it follow? An important general principle, expressed in a significant number of recent decisions and judgments, is the principle of the benefit of the doubt:

'owing to the special situation in which asylum seekers often find themselves, it is frequently necessary to give them the benefit of the doubt when it comes to assessing the credibility of their statements'.[309]

This general principle, which echoes the principle of the benefit of the doubt expressed in the UNHCR's Handbook,[310] requires that the assessment of the credibility

---

306 ECtHR, *Jabari v. Turkey*, 11 July 2000, Appl. No. 40035/98, para. 41; ECtHR, *Abdolkhani and Karimnia v. Turkey*, 22 September 2009, Appl. No. 30471/08, para. 82; ECtHR, *Ayatollahi and Hosseinzadeh v. Turkey*, admissibility decision, 23 March 2010, Appl. No. 32971/98; ECtHR, *Charahili v. Turkey*, 13 April 2010, Appl. No. 46605/07, para. 59; ECtHR, *Khaydarov v. Russia*, 20 May 2010, Appl. No. 21055/09, para. 109; ECtHR, *M.B. and others v. Turkey*, 15 June 2010, Appl. No. 36009/08, paras. 14 and 33-34; ECtHR, *Dbouba v. Turkey*, 13 July 2010, Appl. No. 15916/09, paras. 42, 43.

307 See on this also Bruin 2011, pp. 244, 245.

308 ECtHR, *Y. v. Russia*, 4 December 2008, Appl. No. 20113/07, para. 90. See for more examples also Bruin 2011, p. 245.

309 See, for example, admissibility decisions ECtHR, *Matsiukhina and Matsiukhin v. Sweden*, 21 June 2005, Appl. No. 31260/04; ECtHR, *Mahin Ayegh v. Sweden*, 7 November 2006, Appl. No. 4701/05; ECtHR, *Collins and Akasiebie v. Sweden* 8 March 2007, Appl.No. 23944/05; ECtHR, *Achmadov and Bagurova v. Sweden*, 10 July 2007, Appl. No. 34081/05; ECtHR, *M. v. Sweden* 6 September 2007, Appl. No. 22556/05; ECtHR, *Elezaj and others v. Sweden*, 20 September 2007, Appl. No. 17654/095; ECtHR, *Limoni and others v. Sweden*, 4 October 2007, Appl. No. 6576/05, and the judgments ECtHR, *F.H. v. Sweden*, 20 January 2009, Appl. No. 32621/06/06, para. 95; ECtHR, *R.C. v. Sweden*, 9 March 2010, Appl. No. 41827/07, para. 50.

310 UNHCR Handbook paras. 197, 204, UNHCR Note on Burden and Standard of Proof in Refugee Claims of 16 December 1998, paras. 11, 12. See Chapter 2 on the RC.

should not be too strict. The ECtHR requires 'general credibility'.[311] General credibility does not mean complete accuracy and consistency of every single aspect and detail of the flight narrative. In the admissibility decision of *Bello v. Sweden* (2006), the Court stated:

'The Court acknowledges that complete accuracy as to dates and events cannot be expected in all circumstances from a person seeking asylum.'[312]

The statements made by the asylum seeker may contain some incredible or not entirely credible aspects, but the core aspects – the 'basic story'[313] – must be credible. The Court decides on a case by case basis when incredible or not entirely credible aspects of a flight narrative undermine the general credibility. Much depends on whether these problematic aspects relate to the core of the flight narrative, the basic story, or may be regarded as more peripheral. The ECtHR regards the journey from the country of origin to the country of refuge as peripheral and, therefore, not very relevant; in *N. v. Finland* (2005), it found that doubts about the journey did not affect the general credibility of the basic story:

'the Court has certain reservations about the applicant's own testimony before the Delegates which it considers to have been evasive on many points and is not prepared to accept every statement of his as fact. In particular, his account of the journey to Finland is not credible. In light of the overall evidence now before it the Court finds however that the applicant's account of his background in the DRC must, on the whole, be considered sufficiently consistent and credible.'[314]

In *Said v. the Netherlands* (2005) and *R.C. v. Sweden* (2010), the Court doubted the credibility of the applicants' statements regarding the escape from armed guards in Eritrea (*Said*) and the escape from a revolutionary court in Iran (*R.C.*), but these uncertainties did not undermine the overall credibility of the basic story.[315]

For the basic story to be credible, it must be consistent with country information.[316] It must also remain consistent throughout the proceedings;[317] numerous

---

311 See, for example, ECtHR, *Said v. the Netherlands*, 5 July 2005, Appl. No. 2345/02, para. 51: '(…) the Court must proceed, as far as possible, to an assessment of the general credibility of the statements made by the applicant before the Netherlands authorities and during the present proceedings'. See also the judgment in ECtHR, *R.C. v. Sweden*, 9 March 2010, Appl. No. 41827/07, para. 52, and admissibility decisions ECtHR, *Nasimi v. Sweden*, 16 March 2004, Appl. No. 38865/02; ECtHR, *M. v. Sweden*, 6 September 2007, Appl. No. 22556/05.

312 ECtHR, *Bello v. Sweden*, admissibility decision, 17 January 2006, Appl. No. 32213/04. In the case of *Bello*, however, the general principle did not help the applicant, as the Court was struck by the large number of major inconsistencies in the applicant's story.

313 The term 'basic story' is used in ECtHR, *R.C. v. Sweden*, 9 March 2010, Appl. No. 41827/07, para. 52.

314 ECtHR, *N. v. Finland* (2005), 26 July 2005, Appl. No. 38885/02, paras. 154 and 155.

315 ECtHR, *Said v. the Netherlands*, 5 July 2005, Appl. No, 2345/02, para.53, ECtHR, *R.C. v. Sweden*, 9 March 2010, Appl. No. 41827/07, para. 52.

316 See, for example, ECtHR, *R.C. v. Sweden*, 9 March 2010, Appl. No. 41827/07, para. 54, in which the Court noted that it was evident from the information available on Iran that the Iranian authorities

→

alterations in statements may make these statements incredible.[318] Numerous major inconsistencies also make the statements incredible.[319] The basic story must be brought forward in a timely manner; late submission of statements may negatively affect the general credibility, particularly when no sound reason is given.[320] The total absence of corroborative evidence may also affect credibility; more will be said on this in the next section below on the admission of evidence. When the ECtHR specifically asks the applicant to submit certain documents and he or she does not fulfill this request, this adversely affects the general credibility of the applicant's basic story.[321] The list of examples provided here is by no means exhaustive, but it does provide an impression of the factors taken into account by the ECtHR when assessing the credibility of the claimant's story.[322]

In the assessment of the facts and circumstances of a case, including the assessment of credibility, the Court actively gathers and checks information. This application of investigative powers for the purpose of independent fact finding will be discussed in detail below in section 5.6.9.

5.6.6 Admission of evidence, means and sources of evidence, minimum quantity and quality of evidence

5.6.6.1 Admission of evidence

The ECtHR demands 'evidence capable of proving' that there is a real Article 3-risk. This is an open and flexible criterion for the admissibility and admission of evidence. It means that, in principle, the Court admits to the proceedings every form of

---

frequently detain and ill-treat persons who participate in peaceful demonstrations in the country, not only the leaders of political organisations or other high profile persons who are detained but anyone who demonstrates or in any way opposes the current regime. As the applicant had maintained that he was arrested with many others when he participated in a demonstration against the regime in July 2001 and that the torture he endured occurred in the months following his arrest, his account was consistent with the information available from independent sources concerning Iran.

317 *Ibidem*, para. 52.

318 See, for example, ECtHR, *B. v. Sweden*, admissibility decision, 26 October 2004, Appl. No. 16578/03, in which decision the Court noted that the applicant had changed his story on many occasions during the national proceedings.

319 See, for example, ECtHR, *Bello v. Sweden*, admissibility decision, 17 January 2006, Appl. No. 32213/04.

320 See ECtHR, *B. v. Sweden*, admissibility decision, 26 October 2004, Appl. No. 16578/03, in which the Court noted that the applicant's allegation that he was tortured during his detention had not been made to the Swedish authorities but only to the ECtHR. In ECtHR, *Tekdemir v. the Netherlands*, 1 October 2002, Appl. No. 49823/99, the Court noted that it was only in the course of national proceedings following a second asylum application that the applicant had raised and relied on his kinship with the brothers A.X. and B.X., one of whom had obtained a residence permit and the other a favourable ruling in the proceedings on his asylum request. It was only in the course of third national proceedings that the applicant claimed that he had been tortured in Turkey, a fact which he had not raised in his previous asylum requests.

321 See, for example, ECtHR, *S.A. v. the Netherlands*, admissibility decision, 12 December 2006, Appl. No. 3049/06.

322 See on the Court's credibility assessment also Geertsema 2010 and Wouters 2009, pp. 283-287.

evidence capable of proving an Article 3-risk. In *Iskandarov v. Russia* (2010), the Court stated literally that

> 'In the proceedings before the Court, there are no procedural barriers to the admissibility of evidence or pre-determined formulae for its assessment. It adopts the conclusions that are, in its view, supported by the free evaluation of all evidence, including such inferences as may flow from the facts and the parties' submissions.'[323]

All materials presented by the parties and, possibly, obtained *proprio motu*, are normally considered materially by the Court. It has reiterated in many judgments and admissibility decisions that:

> 'The Court will assess the issue in light of all the material placed before it (…).'[324]

5.6.6.2   Means and sources of evidence

Examples of evidentiary materials are: documentary evidence from state organs stating that a person is being sought, or is wanted (arrest warrants, police reports);[325] medical reports corroborating statements on past ill-treatment;[326] written or oral statements made by family members or other witnesses (individuals or organisations);[327] and, of course, reports from various sources containing information on the situation in the country of origin, as the individual claim needs to be assessed in the light of the situation in the country of origin.

---

323 ECtHR, *Iskandarov v. Russia*, 23 September 2010, Appl. No. 17185/05, para. 107.

324 This is stated in the first Article 3-judgment concerning asylum ECtHR, *Cruz Varas and others v. Sweden*, 20 March 1991, Appl. No. 15576/89, paras. 75 and 78, and is reiterated in almost all the subsequent judgments concerning asylum seekers, and also in some admissibility decisions. I will mention some older and some more recent examples: ECtHR, *Vilvarajah and others v. the UK*, 30 October 1991, Appl. Nos. 13163/87, 13164/87, 13165/87, 13447/87 and 13448/87, para. 107; ECtHR, *Chahal v. the UK*, 15 November 1996, Appl. No. 22414/93, para. 97; ECtHR, *Mamatkulov and Abdurasulovic v. Turkey*, (2003), para. 67; ECtHR, *Mamatkulov and Askarov v. Turkey*, 4 February 2005, Appl. Nos. 46827/99 and 46951/99, para. 69; ECtHR, *N. v. Finland*, 26 July 2005, Appl. No. 38885/02, paras. 160 and 167; ECtHR, *Saadi v. Italy*, 28 February 2008, Appl. No. 37201/06, para. 128; ECtHR, *Baysakov v. Ukraine*, 18 February 2010, Appl. No. 54131/08, para. 91.

325 See, for example, ECtHR, *Bader and Kanbor v. Sweden*, 8 November 2005, Appl. No. 13284/04, para. 44.

326 Examples of cases in which statements by medical staff were seen as corroboration of statements on past ill-treatment are ECtHR, *T.I. v. the UK*, 7 March 2000, Appl. No. 43844/98, ECtHR, *Hilal v. the UK*, 6 March 2001, Appl. No. 45276/99, and ECtHR, *R.C. v. Sweden*, 9 March 2010, Appl. No. 41827/07.

327 Examples of cases in which the ECtHR accepted statements of family members as evidence supporting the Article 3-claim are ECtHR, *Hilal v. the UK*, 6 March 2001, Appl. No. 45276/99, para. 66, and ECtHR, *N. v. Finland*, 26 July 2005, Appl. No. 38885/02, para. 153. See also ECtHR, *Thampibillai v. the Netherlands*, 17 February 2004, Appl. No. 61350/00, para. 66, in which the Court remarked that 'the applicant submitted that, following his flight and his failure to report to the army, his mother had been arrested and detained for two days. However, the applicant did not keep the letters in which his mother communicated these events to him'. See for an example of a case in which the Court looked at written witness statements by other persons (not relatives): ECtHR, *Shikpohkt and Sholeh v. the Netherlands,* admissibility decision, 27 January 2005, Appl. No. 39349/03.

5.6.6.3   *Minimum quantity and quality of evidence*

How much evidence corroborating the individual claim can reasonably be expected is decided on a case by case basis and depends very much on the particular case. As has been said above, the burden of proof rests initially with the applicant and it is, therefore, incumbent on him or her to adduce, to the greatest extent practically possible, material and information allowing the authorities of the Contracting State concerned, as well as the ECtHR, to assess the risk a removal may entail.[328] In line with this principle, the ECtHR normally demands from the asylum seeker documentary or other evidence corroborating his or her statements. The Court has noted in a number of cases that it must take into account two particularities of asylum cases: the difficulty of substantiating asylum claims with direct documentary evidence[329] and the difficulty of doing this within a short time frame.[330] In spite of these principles, however, the ECtHR normally demands a significant amount of strong evidentiary materials. The Court's case law shows examples of cases where, apart from statements by the asylum seeker, no corroborating evidence whatsoever was submitted and no reasons were provided for the total lack of evidence. This led to the conclusion that the Article 3-claim was manifestly ill-founded and, therefore, inadmissible.[331] We may conclude from these decisions that statements must generally at least be supported by some other corroborating evidence.

In sections 5.6.2 and 5.6.4 above, it was made clear that the graver the general human rights situation in the country of origin, the more significant this situation becomes in assessing the risk and the less individual facts and circumstances, and also evidence corroborating these individual facts and circumstances, are required.[332] Thus, the graver the general human rights situation in the applicant's country of origin, the less individual evidence is required from the applicant.

Although information on conditions in the country of origin is important for the assessment of the situation there, this information alone is generally not sufficient to

---

328 ECtHR, *Said v. the Netherlands*, 5 July 2005, Appl. No. 2345/02, para. 49.

329 *Ibidem*, para. 49: 'direct documentary evidence proving that an applicant is wanted for any reason by the authorities of the country of origin may well be difficult to obtain'; admissibility decision ECtHR, *Shikpohkt and Sholeh v. the Netherlands*, 27 January 2005, Appl. No. 39349/03: 'The Court has recognised that in cases of this nature such evidence may well be difficult to obtain.'

330 See ECtHR, *Cruz Varas and others v. Sweden*, 20 March 1991, Appl. No. 15576/89, para: 78: 'even if allowances are made for (…) the difficulties of substantiating their claims with documentary evidence (…)'; ECtHR, *Bahaddar v. the Netherlands*, 19 February 1998, Appl. No. 25894/94, para. 45: 'in applications for recognition of refugee status it may be difficult, if not impossible, for the person concerned to supply evidence within a short time, especially if (…) such evidence must be obtained from the country from which he or she claims to have fled'.

331 See, for example, the admissibility decisions ECtHR, *Amrollahi v. Denmark,* 28 June 2001, Appl. No. 56811/02; ECtHR, *Ammari v. Sweden*, 22 October 2002, Appl. No. 60959/00; ECtHR, *Fofana Hussein Mossi and others against Sweden*, 8 March 2005, Appl. No. 15017/03; ECtHR, *Gordyeyev v. Poland*, 3 May 2005, Appl. Nos. 43369/98 and 51777/99; ECtHR, *Hukic v. Sweden*, 27 September 2005, Appl. No. 17416/05; ECtHR, *Jeltsujeva v. the Netherlands*, 1 June 2006, Appl. No. 39858/04; ECtHR, *Fazlul Karim v. Sweden*, 4 July 2006, Appl. No. 24171/05; ECtHR, *S.A. v. the Netherlands*, 12 December 2006, Appl. No. 3049/06; ECtHR, *Achmadov and Bagurova v. Sweden*, 10 July 2007, Appl. No. 34081/05.

332 ECtHR, *NA v. the United Kingdom*, 17 July 2008, Appl. No. 25904/07, paras. 115-117. Battjes 2009, p. 82, Cox 2010, p. 392.

assume that an individual runs an Article 3-risk upon expulsion. A possible exception to this would be the situation of extreme general violence mentioned above in the section on individualisation. So far, the ECtHR has assumed such a situation to exist in only one case (see section 5.6.4 above).[333] This means that it tends to demand evidence corroborating the individual flight narrative. To put it differently, the Court normally requires the submitted documentary or other evidence to have a certain direct bearing on the applicant's personal situation. An example of a case in which the Court explicitly ruled that the available country information was insufficient to assume an Article 3-risk is *Mamatkulov and Abdurasulovic* (2003).[334] The evidence submitted by the applicants consisted of general information on the situation (in prisons) in Uzbekistan. The ECtHR ruled:

> 'In the instant case, the Court considers that, in spite of the serious concerns to which they give rise, the reports only describe the general situation in the Republic of Uzbekistan. There is nothing in them to support the specific allegations made by the applicants in the instant case, which require corroboration by other evidence.'

The specific allegations by the applicants were that, before they fled to Turkey, they had been forced by torture to 'confess' to crimes which they had not committed in Uzbekistan, and that, while in detention after extradition to Uzbekistan, they again ran the risk of being subjected to torture. The Grand Chamber of the Court had concluded in the same way that the country information provided had constituted insufficient evidence in *Mamatkulov and Askarov v. Turkey* (2005).[335] Finally, in *Ryabikin v. Russia* (2008), the Court considered that

> 'The evidence from a range of objective sources demonstrates that extremely poor conditions of detention, as well as ill-treatment and torture, remain a great concern for all observers of the situation in Turkmenistan. However, these findings attest to the general situation in Turkmenistan. They should be supported by specific allegations and require corroboration by other evidence.'[336]

It is not necessary for every single detail of the individual account to be supported by evidence. What generally needs to be substantiated by evidentiary materials is the basic story, the core of the individual account. Again, the approach of the ECtHR is strict; it generally requires extensive evidence. It seems that the general principle that account should be taken of the difficulties of substantiating claims with direct documentary evidence is not often applied *in concreto*. For example, in *Cruz Varas v. Sweden* (1991), the ECtHR noted that the applicant had been unable to locate any witnesses or adduce any other evidence which might have corroborated to some degree his

---

333 ECtHR, *Sufi and Elmi v. the UK*, 28 June 2011, Appl. Nos. 8319/07 and 11449/07.
334 ECtHR, *Mamatkulov and Abdurasulovic* 6 February 2003, Appl. Nos. 46827/99 and 46951/99.
335 ECtHR, *Mamatkulov and Askarov v. Turkey*, 4 February 2005, Appl. Nos. 46827/99, 46951/99, para. 73.
336 ECtHR, *Ryabikin v. Russia*, 19 June 2008, Appl. No. 8320/04, paras. 116 and 117.

claims of clandestine political activity.[337] In *Fazlul Karim v. Sweden* (2006), the applicant alleged that he would risk arrest and imprisonment on return to Bangladesh because of a murder charge. The ECtHR reproached the applicant for not submitting documentary proof, such as a formal warrant for his arrest, which he could reasonably have been expected to obtain through his family.[338] In the same way, in *Gomes v. Sweden* (2006), the applicant alleged that he had been sentenced to death by a court in Bangladesh. The Court reprimanded the applicant for not submitting any documents as proof of the alleged death sentence.[339] An extremely strict approach was taken in *Shikpohkt and Sholeh v. the Netherlands* (2005).[340] The basic story of the Iranian applicant was that she came from a family which had always opposed the sitting Iranian regime, that she had taken over oppositional activities from her stepfather, including the distribution of oppositional pamphlets, and that she had received a written threat that had caused her to go into hiding. She had substantiated her claim before the national authorities and the ECtHR with an impressive amount of evidentiary material. The ECtHR found it problematic that she had not, however, submitted the written threat, or the oppositional material she stated she had distributed.

However, not every single detail of the basic story needs to be completely supported by corroborating evidence. In *Hilal v. the UK* (2001), during the second national asylum procedure, the applicant submitted a copy of his brother's death certificate, a medical report about the circumstances of his brother's death, a summons from the police to his parents and a medical report about his treatment in hospital following his detention, during which he had allegedly been tortured.[341] The national authorities found that the death certificate did not have much evidentiary value as it did not indicate that torture or ill-treatment had been a contributory factor in the death of the applicant's brother. The ECtHR considered:

> 'while it is correct that the medical notes and death certificate of his brother do not indicate that torture or ill-treatment was a contributory factor in his death, they did give further corroboration to the applicant's account which the special adjudicator had found so lacking in substantiation. They showed that his brother, who was also a CUF supporter, had been detained in prison and that he had been taken from the prison to hospital, where he died. This is not inconsistent with the applicant's allegation that his brother had been ill-treated in prison.'[342]

It is not only necessary to submit evidence corroborating the individual account. Equally important is evidence about the human rights situation in the country of origin. No judgments or decisions have been found in which the ECtHR has explicitly explained which of the parties – the applicant or the State party's authorities – is responsible for submitting recent information about the general human rights

---

337 ECtHR, *Cruz Varas v. Sweden*, 20 March 1991, Appl. No. 15576/89, para. 79.
338 ECtHR, *Fazlul Karim v. Sweden*, admissibility decision, 4 July 2006, Appl. No. 24171/05.
339 ECtHR, *Gomes v. Sweden*, admissibility decision, 7 February 2006, Appl. No. 34566/04.
340 ECtHR, *Shikpohkt and Sholeh v. the Netherlands*, 27 January 2005, Appl. No. 39349/03.
341 ECtHR, *Hilal v. the UK*, 6 March 2001, Appl. No. 45276/99, paras. 18 and 21.
342 *Ibidem*, para. 65.

situation in the country of origin. It may be argued that, although the burden of proof remains a shared one, in cases where there is an arguable claim particular responsibility for obtaining clarity on the general human rights situation in the country of origin lies with the administrative and judicial authorities of the State. This follows from the fact that where the arguability test has been met, the authorities of the State have to conduct active investigations to establish whether the application is well-founded; the State has to 'dispel any doubts' about the applicability of Article 3.[343] The authorities, thus, have an active role not only in verifying information put forward by the complainant, but also in collecting and presenting evidence regarding the general human rights situation in the country of origin. With regard to the particular responsibility resting on the national authorities for shaping clarity on the situation in the country of origin, reference is also made to chapter 6 on EU asylum law, section 6.4.4.

5.6.7 *Appreciation and weighing of evidence*

In *Iskandarov v. Russia* (2010), the Court stated that

> 'In the proceedings before the Court, there are no (…) pre-determined formulae for its assessment [author: this means the assessment of evidence]. It adopts the conclusions that are, in its view, supported by the free evaluation of all evidence, including such inferences as may flow from the facts and the parties' submissions.'[344]

This means that all the evidence brought forward and gathered in a case is evaluated in a free manner.

5.6.7.1 *Factors determining the probative value and persuasiveness of evidence*

We can, however, distinguish a number of factors determining the exact probative value and persuasiveness of evidence. Important factors are the authenticity of submitted documents, the specificity, comprehensiveness and consistency of the information contained in evidentiary materials or given by witnesses, the independence, and the reliability, objectiveness and authority of the source or author of the evidence.[345] These factors are discussed in more detail below. After that, we will look in more detail at three particular categories of evidence, being witness statements by family members, medical reports, and reports about the situation in the country of origin.

---

343 See, for example, ECtHR, *N.v. the UK*, 17 July 2008, Appl. No. 25904/07, para. 111; ECtHR, *Muminov v. Russia*, 11 December 2008, Appl. No. 42502/06, para. 87; ECtHR, *R.C. v. Sweden*, 9 March 2010, Appl. No. 41827/07, para. 50; ECtHR, *Sufi and Elmi v. the UK*, 28 June 2008, Appl. Nos. 8319/07 and 11449/07, para. 214.

344 ECtHR, *Iskandarov v. Russia*, 23 September 2010, Appl. No. 17185/05, para. 107.

345 See, for example,ECtHR, *Bader and Kanbor v. Sweden*, 8 November 2005, Appl. No. 13284/04, para. 44; ECtHR, *Saadi v. Italy*, 28 February 2008, Appl. No. 37201/06, para. 143; ECtHR, *NA v. the UK*, 17 July 2008, Appl. No. 25904/07, para. 120. See also Wouters 2009, p. 271.

5.6.7.1.a Authenticity of documents

In a number of judgments and decisions, the ECtHR has used a 'benefit of the doubt' consideration concerning, specifically, evaluation of the reliability of documents submitted by claimants:

> 'Owing to the special situation in which asylum seekers often find themselves, it is frequently necessary to give them the benefit of the doubt when it comes to assessing the credibility of (...) documents submitted in support (of statements).'[346]

By virtue of its reiteration in a considerable number of judgments and decisions, this consideration may be regarded as a general principle. It entails that, in principle, the ECtHR holds documents submitted by the claimant to be real and genuine. However, if at national level documents were held to be non-authentic or forged following investigations into their authenticity, the claimant is required to address the specific problematic points found in the documents and to come up with very good reasons as to why the result of the investigation is incorrect. If the applicant does not respond in this way, this undermines the reliability of the claim.[347]

Authentic documents from the authorities of the country of origin containing specific indications of an Article 3-risk may play a decisive role, as the case of *Bader and Kanbor v. Sweden* (2005) illustrates. In that case, the first applicant was convicted *in absentia* of complicity in a murder and sentenced to death by judgment of a Syrian court. The judgment, submitted in the national proceedings, was found to be authentic after an investigation conducted by the Swedish embassy in Syria. Based on this document and the finding that the death penalty is enforced for serious crimes in Syria, the ECtHR concluded that deportation of the applicants to Syria would give rise to a violation of Article 3 (and Article 2, containing the right to life).[348]

If there are doubts about the authenticity of submitted documents, much depends on the quantity and quality of the other available evidentiary materials, and on other circumstances surrounding the submission of the documents. In the case of *Hilal v. the UK* (2001), a summons to appear before the police was discarded as incredible by the national authorities. However, on the basis of other evidence – the medical record of the hospital that had treated the applicant after he was released from

---

346 See, for example, admissibility decisions ECtHR, *Matsiukhina and Matsiukhin v. Sweden*, 21 June 2005, Appl. No. 31260/04; ECtHR, *Mahin Ayegh v. Sweden*, 7 November 2006, Appl. No. 4701/05; ECtHR, *Collins and Akasiebie v. Sweden*, 8 March 2007, Appl. No. 23944/05; ECtHR, *Achmadov and Bagurova v. Sweden*, 10 July 2007, Appl. No. 34081/05; ECtHR, *M. v. Sweden*, 6 September 2007, Appl. No. 22556/05; ECtHR, *Elezaj and others v. Sweden*, 20 September 2007, Appl. No. 17654/05; ECtHR, *Limoni and others v. Sweden*, 4 October 2007, Appl. No. 6576/05; and judgments ECtHR, *F.H. v. Sweden*, 20 January 2009, Appl. No. 32621/06, para. 95 and ECtHR, *R.C.v. Sweden*, 9 March 2010, Appl. No. 41827/07, para. 50.

347 See, for example, the following admissibility decisions: ECtHR, *Matsiukhina and Matsiukhin v. Sweden*, 21 June 2005, Appl. No. 31260/04; ECtHR, *Gomes v. Sweden*, 7 February 2006, Appl. No. 34566/04; ECtHR, *Mahin Ayegh v. Sweden*, 7 November 2006, Appl. No. 4701/05; ECtHR, *Bagheri and Maliki v. the Netherlands*, 15 May 2007, Appl. No. 30164/06; ECtHR, *I.N. v. Sweden*, 15 September 2009, Appl. No. 1334/09; ECtHR, *Izevbekhai and others v. Ireland*, 17 May 2011, Appl. No. 43408/08, paras. 78, 79.

348 ECtHR, *Bader and Kanbor v. Sweden*, 8 November 2005, Appl. No. 13284/04, paras. 44-48.

prison where he had been tortured –the ECtHR accepted that the applicant had been detained and during that detention had indeed been tortured, as he had stated. Unlike the national authorities, the ECtHR did attach weight to the police summons.[349]

In the case of *B. v. Sweden* (2004), the national authorities maintained, on the basis of an unofficial investigation in Tripoli, that a number of Libyan documents adduced to support the asylum request were false. The ECtHR apparently gave the documents the benefit of the doubt, but attached great importance to their late submission:

> 'While there is some uncertainty as to whether some authorities named in the documents had jurisdiction in the matter, their general appearance is not such that they, in and of themselves, can be discounted as falsifications. However, in assessing their authenticity, the circumstances surrounding their submission are of importance. In this respect, the Court notes that they were all submitted to the Swedish authorities and the Court long after their date of issuance. (…) While the Court appreciates the difficulty in obtaining such documents in Libya and to send them abroad, it notes that some of them were purportedly issued when the applicant was still in Libya and generally considers that the delays in submitting the documents are rather remarkable. As an explanation for these delays, the applicant has, *inter alia*, claimed before the Court that he was unable to contact his family while he was in hiding with his friend in Sabrata and that he has had contact with members of his family only on rare occasions even during his stay in Sweden. However, this assertion is difficult to reconcile with the statement given by his counsel to the Migration Board on 16 April 2002 that his friend had visited the applicant's parents a couple of times and had then received information and the applicant's allegedly false passport. The Court further notes that the documents in question have been submitted by the applicant at different stages of the proceedings, following the rejection of his applications by the Migration Board and the Aliens Appeals Board.'[350]

The submission of copies of documents instead of originals diminishes the probative value of such documents. In the case of *S.M. v. Sweden* (2009), the Court concluded that the applicant had not sufficiently substantiated her story and had, therefore, failed to show a real Article 3-risk. This conclusion was based on the fact that only copies of alleged search warrants had been submitted, that the basic story and travel route had been rather vague, and that the applicant had remained in Brazzaville for almost five months following her escape, without any incidents.[351]

5.6.7.1.b Specificity, comprehensiveness and consistency of information contained in evidentiary materials

The more specific and comprehensive the evidentiary materials are about the stated past facts and about the future risk, the more probative value is attached to them. The case of *Bader and Kanbor v. Sweden* (2005) was mentioned above, in which a judgment of a Syrian court stated that the first applicant had been sentenced to death for complicity in a murder. Based on this document and the finding that the death

---

349 ECtHR, *Hilal v. the UK*, 6 March 2001, Appl. No. 45276/99, paras. 63 and 64.
350 ECtHR, *B. v. Sweden*, admissibility decision, 26 October 2004, Appl. No. 16578/03.
351 ECtHR, *S.M. v. Sweden*, admissibility decision, 10 February 2009, Appl. No. 47683/08.

penalty is enforced for serious crimes in Syria, the Court concluded that deportation of the applicants to Syria would give rise to a violation of Article 3 (and Article 2, containing the right to life).[352] In *Garabayev v. Russia* (2007), the applicant submitted in support of his claim several letters written by his lawyer, a member of the Russian State Duma (Parliament) and the Human Rights Centre Memorial, a Russian NGO, addressed to the Russian Public Prosecutor. In these letters, strong fears were expressed that the applicant would be tortured and personally persecuted for political motives. The letters also gave specific information on the general situation in prisons in Turkmenistan. The different letters were consistent with each other, were comprehensive and focused specifically on the applicant's precarious situation and the real personal risk to the applicant.[353]

When the information contained in evidentiary materials is unspecific and vague, little or no evidentiary value is accorded to them. A very strict approach was adopted in *Shikpohkt and Sholeh v. the Netherlands* (2005).[354] In that case, a large amount of evidentiary materials was submitted by the applicants but the ECtHR found these materials lacking in specificity and comprehensiveness and, therefore, insufficient. The basic story of the Iranian applicant was that she came from a family which had always opposed the sitting Iranian regime, that she had taken over from her stepfather oppositional activities, including the distribution of oppositional pamphlets, and that she had received a written threat that had caused her to go into hiding. The ECtHR was not satisfied with this large amount of evidence. It considered as follows:

> 'It would have been helpful had the Court been provided with (…) the written threat that caused her to go into hiding – or at least, plausible information which would enable the Court to assess prima facie the nature and seriousness of the threat which it represented to Ms. Mahkamat Sholeh herself – or if she had been able to provide more detailed information on the written materials which she states she held for Rah-e-Kargar and some of which she states she wrote. It is true that documents have been submitted in support of Ms. Mahkamat Sholeh's allegations. These, in the Court's view, would at most tend to bear out that Ms. Mahkamat Sholeh's stepfather and mother were at one time during the 1980s detained on grounds related to political activities. They contain little of any direct relevance to Ms. Mahkamat Sholeh herself. In so far as they express any fears on her behalf, they are, in the Court's view, vague and speculative.'[355]

Crucial in the Court's reasoning was that the submitted evidence did not focus on the applicant herself, but rather on her stepfather, and that the evidence was unspecific about her political activities.

5.6.7.1.c *Independence, reliability, objectiveness and authority of the source or author*
Another important factor determining the probative value of evidence is the independence, reliability and objectiveness of the source or author of the information. In

---

352 ECtHR, *Bader and Kanbor v. Sweden*, 8 November 2005, Appl. No. 13284/04, para. 44.
353 ECtHR, *Garabayev v. Russia*, 7 June 2007, Appl. No. 38411/02, paras. 11-13, 78.
354 ECtHR, *Shikpohkt and Sholeh v. the Netherlands*, 27 January 2005, Appl. No. 39349/03.
355 *Ibidem.*

particular, when witness statements by family members are submitted as corroborating evidence, the question arises of whether such statements can be seen as independent, reliable and objective. Provided that they are specific, comprehensive and consistent, written and oral statements by family members have considerable evidentiary value in the case law of the ECtHR. I did not come across judgments or decisions in which the Court had ruled that such statements could not be admitted as evidence or were of no evidentiary value because they could not be deemed to be objective sources, given the relationship with the applicant. More will be said about witness statements by family members below in 5.6.7.2.

The issue of the independence, reliability and objectivity of the source is also particularly present when information compiled by scholars, human rights organisations and refugee support organisations is submitted. In the case of *S.H. v. the UK* (2010), the Bhutanese applicant of Nepalese ethnic origin claimed that he would be at risk of imprisonment and ill-treatment in Bhutan, both as an involuntary returnee and as someone who had made representations about the human rights situation there while out of the country. The applicant submitted to the ECtHR a number of expert reports prepared for the purposes of the national proceedings which considered the specific risk to him on return to Bhutan. These included a report prepared by a professor of Nepali and Himalayan studies at the School of Oriental and Asian Studies at the University of London, which stated that it was difficult to predict precisely what would happen to the applicant were he to be returned to Bhutan. However, the fact that the government of Bhutan was willing to facilitate his return by issuing a travel document should not be taken as an indication that he would be able to resume anything resembling his former life. The materials also included two statements made by Amnesty International and a statement by Human Rights Watch on the consequences of deporting the applicant, a more general letter from the UNHCR indicating that no monitoring possibilities for returnees existed, and five reports by Rachel Carnegie, coordinator of the Bhutanese Refugee Support Group (UK), which addressed the plight of southern Bhutanese in general and the situation of the applicant in particular. The Carnegie reports stated that it was not possible to determine exactly what the applicant's fate would be but that it was reasonable to conclude that he would be at significant risk as a failed asylum seeker for whom the Home Office had twice applied for travel documents.

The ECtHR stressed that Bhutan was a closed country, that the UNHCR was unable to monitor returns and that there was a paucity of objective country information which would either confirm or contradict the applicant's allegations. The Court then stated that, nevertheless, all of the expert reports submitted by the applicant had supported his claim that he would be at risk of imprisonment and ill-treatment. Seen in combination with the available general country information reports (mainly reports by the US State Department) the Court found that there were substantial grounds for assuming a real Article 3-risk.[356]

---

356 ECtHR, *S.H. v. the UK*, 15 June 2010, Appl. No. 19956/06, paras. 48-57 (on the expert reports), para. 61 (the basis of the claim of the applicant to the ECtHR), paras. 69-72 (on the evaluation of the evidentiary materials brought in by the applicant).

The expert reports thus played a very important role as corroborating evidence. From the Court's considerations, it became clear that the Court found important that all the expert reports were consistent with each other, consistent with other country information and consistent with the applicant's statements. Although the Court did not specifically mention it, the fact that the expert reports specifically focused on the applicant and were comprehensive must also have contributed to their significant evidentiary value.

A final example worthwhile mentioning here is *N.M. and M.M. v. the United Kingdom* (2011).[357] This case sharply demonstrates the importance of the reliability of a particular source who states in firm and persuasive language that an Article 3-risk is imminent upon the expulsion of an applicant. The applicants in this case alleged that they would be at risk of ill-treatment in Uzbekistan both because their exit visas had expired and because they had claimed asylum in the UK. Among the evidence in the possession of the ECtHR was a letter from Mr. Murray, the former British Ambassador to Uzbekistan, in which he stated that the applicants would almost certainly be at risk of torture if the Uzbek authorities became aware that they had claimed asylum abroad. The Court did not attach substantial evidentiary weight to this statement, however, for two reasons. First, the statement by Mr. Murray was not consistent with all the other evidence available that described that the detention, torture and ill-treatment of forcibly returned Uzbek refugees and asylum seekers related to cases where the Uzbek authorities had a pre-existing interest in the individuals concerned, either because they had been returned pursuant to an extradition request or because they were believed to be connected to the events at Andijan in May 2005. Second, the Court followed the UK Asylum and Immigration Tribunal (AIT) in its conclusion that Mr. Murray's evidence should be approached with some circumspection, given that he had interests of his own, which affected, consciously or otherwise, his interpretation of facts and events.[358]

5.6.7.2   *Witness statements by family members*

Provided that they are specific, comprehensive and consistent, written or oral statements by family members seem to have considerable evidentiary value in the case law of the ECtHR. Statements by family members must normally be supported by other, more objective, evidentiary materials. In *H.L.R. v. France* (1997), a case concerning a Colombian drug smuggler who feared that upon deportation to Colombia he would be exposed to vengeance by the drug traffickers who had recruited him as a smuggler, the Court considered:

'The documents from various sources produced in support of the applicant's memorial provide insight into the tense atmosphere in Colombia, but do not contain any indication of the existence of a situation comparable to his own. Although drug traffickers sometimes take revenge on informers, there is no relevant evidence to show in H.L.R.'s case that the alleged risk

---

357 ECtHR, *N.M. and M.M. v. the UK*, 25 January 2011, Appl. Nos. 38851/09 and 39128/09.
358 *Ibidem*, paras. 62-64.

is real. His aunt's letters cannot by themselves suffice to show that the threat is real. Moreover, there are no documents to support the claim that the applicant's personal situation would be worse than that of other Colombians, were he to be deported.'[359]

Some examples will be given here to illustrate the considerable weight accorded to consistent, specific and comprehensive statements by family members. In *Hilal v. the UK* (2001), part of the applicant's basic story was that the police had gone to his wife's house on a number of occasions looking for him and making threats. This information had been confirmed by statements by the applicant's wife in her own national asylum procedure. The Court compared this information to country information and concluded that it was consistent. Combined with the past detention and torture in detention experienced by the applicant and the death of his brother in detention, this yielded sufficient substantial grounds for a real Article 3-risk:

> 'the Court recalls that the applicant's wife, who has now also claimed asylum in the UK, informed the immigration officer in her interview that the police came to her house on a number of occasions looking for her husband and making threats. This is consistent with the information provided about the situation in Pemba and Zanzibar, where CUF members have in the past suffered serious harassment, arbitrary detention, torture and ill-treatment by the authorities (see paragraphs 38-46 above). This involves ordinary members of the CUF and not only its leaders or high-profile activists. The situation has improved to some extent, but the latest reports cast doubt on the seriousness of reform efforts and refer to continued problems faced by CUF members (see paragraph 46 above). The Court concludes that the applicant would be at risk of being arrested and detained, and of suffering a recurrence of ill-treatment if returned to Zanzibar.'[360]

In the admissibility decision in *Ammari v. Sweden* (2002), the Court noted that

> 'the applicant had submitted no evidence at all – whether (…) or letters from relatives remaining in the country (…) which would have substantiated his allegations that, if returned to Algeria, he would be subjected to treatment contrary to Article 3 on account of activities for the GIA (Groupe Islamique Armé)' (…).[361]

And in *Thampibillai v. the Netherlands* (2004), the Court considered:

> 'the Court notes that the applicant submitted that, following his flight and his failure to report to the army, his mother had been arrested and detained for two days. However, the applicant did not keep the letters in which his mother communicated these events to him.'[362]

---

359 ECtHR, *H.L.R.v. France*, 29 April 1997, Appl. No. 24573/1994, para. 42.
360 ECtHR, *Hilal v. the UK*, 6 March 2001, Appl. No. 45276/99, para. 66.
361 Admissibility decision ECtHR, *Ammari v. Sweden*, 22 October 2002, Appl. No. 60959/00.
362 ECtHR, *Thampibillai v. the Netherlands*, 17 February 2004, Appl. No. 61350/00, para. 66.

Both considerations clearly indicate that the Court would have taken written statements by the mentioned family members into account and seriously assessed them, had they been submitted.

5.6.7.3   Medico-legal reports[363]

In a number of cases before the ECtHR, the applicant has relied on medico-legal reports to corroborate statements that he or she has been subjected to torture in the past. In some cases, medical evidence stating a post-traumatic stress disorder (PTSD) has also been relied on by the applicant to explain the tardy presentation of statements on past torture and evidence of such torture, or to explain inconsistencies in the flight narrative.

5.6.7.3.a Medico-legal reports to explain the tardy presentation of statements and evidence

The ECtHR is generally reluctant to accept medico-legal reports (stating PTSD or other mental disturbance or disorders) as an explanation for the tardy presentation of statements on past torture.[364] In *Cruz Varas v. Sweden* (1991), the applicant stated two years after his initial application for asylum that he had been tortured and sexually abused by the Chilean police on several occasions. He submitted several medical reports which conclusively confirmed his statements and mentioned the presence of PTSD. The Court considered, however, that

> 'Moreover, even if allowances are made for the apprehension that asylum-seekers may have towards the authorities and the difficulties of substantiating their claims with documentary evidence, the first applicant's complete silence as to (...) torture by the Chilean police until more than eighteen months after his first interrogation (…) casts considerable doubt on his credibility in this respect.'[365]

The case of *Nasimi v. Sweden* (2004) is also illustrative of the Court's strict approach. Nasimi went through four asylum application procedures in Sweden. It was more than a year after he had initially applied for asylum that he mentioned past torture. In the second, third and fourth procedure, he had also submitted statements from a psychologist and psychotherapist mentioning PTSD. The Court had to deal with the question of whether the late mention of torture could possibly be explained by the applicant's medical state. However, it did not even mention the presented medical evidence when answering this question. It considered only that:

> 'Moreover, although it recognises that it may be an ordeal to talk about experiences of torture, the Court is struck by the fact that the applicant did not make any specific allegations of tor-

---

363 See on the role of medico-legal reports in the case law of the ECtHR also Bruin & Reneman 2006.
364 Bruin & Reneman 2006 draw the same conclusion.
365 ECtHR, *Cruz Varas and others v. Sweden*, 20 March 1991, Appl. No. 15576/89, para. 78.

ture until (…) more than a year after he applied for asylum, although he must have been aware that such information would be of importance to the immigration authorities.'[366]

However, in *Hilal v. the UK* (2001) the Court did not find the tardy mention of torture problematic. The Court considered in this case that

'In the light of the medical record of the hospital which treated him, the apparent failure of the applicant to mention torture at his first immigration interview becomes less significant and his explanation to the special adjudicator – that he did not think he had to give all the details until the full interview a month later – becomes far less incredible.'[367]

The different approach in *Hilal* may well be explained by the fact that the delay in mentioning past torture was very insignificant in this case. In February 1995, a so-called pro forma asylum interview had been held, during which the applicant had not mentioned his past torture. One month later, in March 1995, a full interview had been held in which the applicant had come forward with his statements on past torture.

5.6.7.3.b Medico-legal reports to explain inconsistencies in the personal account
In its decision in *Hatami v. Sweden* (1998), the European Commission considered that 'complete accuracy is seldom to be expected by victims of torture'.[368] This is the same consideration as the one used by the Committee against Torture in many (mainly early) decisions in cases where the respondent State party pointed out inconsistencies in the personal account and the complainant, in reply, referred to medical evidence to explain the inaccuracies (see Chapter 4, section 4.5.7.4.a).[369] No decisions or judgments of the ECtHR have been found in which this consideration has been used, which suggests that the ECtHR is not willing to accept medical evidence to explain inconsistencies.

5.6.7.3.c Medico-legal reports as corroboration of experiences of torture or ill-treatment in the past
In a number of cases, the ECtHR has attached considerable probative value to medical reports submitted by applicants to corroborate past torture or ill-treatment. In the

---

366 ECtHR, *Nasimi v. Sweden*, admissibility decision, 16 March 2004, Appl. No. 38865/02. The Court considered similarly in its admissibility decisions in *Ovdienko v. Finland*, 31 May 2005, Appl. No. 1383/04 and *Paramsothy v. the Netherlands*, 10 November 2005, Appl. No. 14492/03.
367 ECtHR, *Hilal v. the UK*, 6 March 2001, Appl. No. 45276/99, para. 64.
368 ECtHR, *Hatami v. Sweden*, European Commission, 23 April 1998, Appl. No. 32448/96, para. 106.
369 See, for example, ComAT, *Alan v. Switzerland*, 8 May 1996, No. 021/1995, para. 11.3; ComAT, *Kisoki v. Sweden*, 8 May 1996, No. 041/1996, para. 9.3; ComAT, *Tala v. Sweden*, 15 November 1996, No. 043/1996, para. 10.3; ComAT, *Haydin v. Sweden*, 20 November 1998, No. 101/1997, para. 6.7; ComAT, *E.T.B. v. Denmark*, 30 April 2002, No. 146/1999, para. 10: 'the Committee recalls its jurisprudence that torture victims cannot be expected to recall entirely consistent facts relating to events of extreme trauma. But they must be prepared to advance such evidence as there is in support of a claim'; ComAT, *Karoui v.Sweden*, 8 May 2002, No. 185/2001, para. 10; ComAT, *C.T. and K.M. v. Sweden*, 17 November 2006, No. 279/2005, para. 7.6; ComAT, *Falcon Rios v. Canada*, 23 November 2004, No. 133/1999, para. 8.5 (gaps and vague points are explained away by referring to medical evidence).

evaluation of medical reports, the same requirements play a role as the ones mentioned above in 5.6.7.1: the specificity, comprehensiveness and consistency of the information contained in the medical reports, the independence, reliability and objectiveness of the source and the authority and reputation of the author. Logically, an important factor in determining the probative value is also whether the information contained in the medical reports conclusively identifies a causal link between the individual's bodily or mental injuries and the alleged past ill-treatment.

In *Cruz Varas and others v. Sweden* (1991), the Court assumed on the basis of the available medical evidence, particularly the witness statement of Dr. Jacobsson before the Commission of Human Rights, that the applicant had, at some stage in the past, been subjected to inhuman or degrading treatment. The fact that the Court did not assume an Article 3-risk in this case was due to the absence of direct evidence that the past torture or ill-treatment had been inflicted by the Chilean authorities.[370] In *Hilal v. the UK* (2001), it was accepted by the Court, on the basis of the medical record from the hospital which had treated the applicant after he had been released from the prison where he had been tortured, that he had been detained and during that detention had, indeed, been tortured as he had stated.[371]

In *R.C. v. Sweden* (2010), discussed above in section 5.3.3, the applicant stated in the national proceedings before the Swedish authorities that he suffered from medical and psychiatric problems resulting from torture and ill-treatment in prison. He submitted a medical certificate issued by a physician at a local health care centre. The certificate stated that the applicant had various scars which could, in the physician's opinion, very well have originated from the torture to which the applicant claimed he had been subjected in Iran.[372] The ECtHR requested that the applicant submit a forensic medical report. The applicant submitted a report from a specialist in forensic medicine at the Crisis and Trauma Centre of a Swedish hospital. This report noted that in cases like this, alternative causes for the origins of scars could not be completely excluded, but that experience showed that self-inflicted injuries and injuries resulting from accidents normally had a different distribution to those shown by the applicant. The conclusion of the report was that the findings strongly indicated that the applicant had been tortured.[373] The Court attached great value to this medical report and accepted its general conclusion that the injuries, to a large extent, were consistent with having been inflicted on the applicant by other persons and in the manner described by him, thereby strongly indicating that he had been a victim of torture. Based on this, the very tense human rights situation in Iran and the particular imminent risk for Iranians who could not prove that they had left the country legally, the Court concluded that substantial grounds were present to assume a real Article 3-risk.[374]

---

370 ECtHR, *Cruz Varas and others v. Sweden*, 20 March 1991, Appl. No. 15576/89, para. 77.

371 ECtHR, *Hilal v. the UK*, 6 March 2001, Appl. No. 45276/99, para. 64.

372 ECtHR, *R.C. v. Sweden*, 9 March 2010, Appl. No. 41827/07, para. 11.

373 *Ibidem*, paras. 23-25.

374 ECtHR, *R.C. v. Sweden*, 9 March 2010, Appl. No. 41827/07, paras. 53-56.

5.6.7.4   Reports on the situation in the country of origin

All the judgments of the ECtHR, and many admissibility decisions, in cases concerning the expulsion of asylum seekers demonstrate that information on the situation in the countries of origin plays a very important role. The assessment of whether there are substantial grounds for believing that the applicant faces a real risk inevitably requires the Court to assess the conditions in the receiving country against the standards of Article 3.[375] In assessing the evidentiary value of the country of origin information, the ECtHR gives consideration to its source, in particular its independence, reliability and objectivity. The authority and reputation of the author of the reports, the seriousness of the investigations by means of which the reports were compiled, the consistency of the conclusions, the corroboration by other sources, the presence and the reporting capacities of the author in the country in question are all taken into account.[376]

It seems that four main sources of country of origin information used by the ECtHR can be distinguished, namely:

1. Information compiled by organs, organisations and agencies of the United Nations and the Council of Europe;
2. Information compiled by States (whether respondent in a particular case or any other Contracting or non-Contracting State such as the US);
3. Information from independent international human rights protection organisations such as Amnesty International, Human Rights Watch; and
4. Information from the media and other sources.[377]

The ECtHR has not developed a hierarchy of sources. What is clear, however, is that reports by UN organs, organisations and agencies rank highly and are considered to be important sources.[378] The reasons for this are that United Nations agencies have direct access to the authorities of the country of destination as well as the ability to carry out on-site inspections and assessments in a manner which States and non-governmental organisations may not be able to do. Reports by States also rank highly, because States have the ability to gather information through their diplomatic missions.[379] The precise probative value accorded to country of origin information is not

---

375 See, for example, ECtHR, *Mamatkulov and Askarov v. Turkey*, 4 February 2005, Appl. Nos. 46827/99 and 46951/99, para. 67; ECtHR, *NA v. the* UK, 17 July 2008, Appl. No. 25904/07, para. 110.

376 See, for example, ECtHR, *Saadi v. Italy*, 28 February 2008, Appl. No. 37201/06, para. 143; ECtHR, *NA v. the UK*, 17 July 2008, Appl. No. 25904/07, para. 120; ECtHR, *Sufi and Elmi v. the UK*, 28 June 2011, Appl. Nos. 8319/07 and 11449/07, paras. 230 and 231.

377 See, for example, ECtHR, *NA v. the UK*, 17 July 2008, Appl. No. 2590/07, in which the Court used country of origin information from all these four sources: United Kingdom Government Reports, one US Department of State Report, some information from the Sri Lankan Government, information from the Immigration and Refugee Board of Canada, some information from the British Broadcasting Corporation, United Nations Reports, and reports drawn up by Amnesty International, Human Rights Watch, the International Crisis Group, the Medical Foundation for the Care of Victims of Torture. See also ECtHR, *Sufi and Elmi v. the UK*, 28 June 2011, Appl. Nos. 8319/07 and 11449/ 07, in which also information from the four categories of sources was used by the Court.

378 ECtHR, *NA v. the UK*, 17 July 2008, Appl. No. 25904/07, paras. 121 and 122.

379 ECtHR, *Sufi and Elmi v. the UK*, 28 June 2011, Appl. Nos. 8319/07 and 11449/07, para. 231.

only determined by the source, but, logically, also very much by the specific content of it. The ECtHR distinguishes between more general reports on the socio-economic and humanitarian situation on the one hand, and reports specifically concerning the human rights situation, with a focus on the risk for the particular applicant, on the other hand. The latter category of reports is given greater evidentiary weight:

'While the Court accepts that many reports are, by their very nature, general assessments, greater importance must necessarily be attached to reports which consider the human rights situation in the country of destination and directly address the grounds for the alleged real risk of ill-treatment in the case before the Court. Ultimately, the Court's own assessment of the human rights situation in a country of destination is carried out only to determine whether there would be a violation of Article 3 if the applicant in the case before it were to be returned to that country. Thus the weight to be attached to independent assessments must inevitably depend on the extent to which those assessments are couched in terms similar to Article 3. Thus in respect of the UNHCR, due weight has been given by the Court to the UNHCR's own assessment of an applicant's claims when the Court determined the merits of her complaint under Article 3 (see Jabari v. Turkey, no. 40035/98, § 41, ECHR 2000-VIII). Conversely, where the UNHCR's concerns are focused on general socio-economic and humanitarian considerations, the Court has been inclined to accord less weight to them, since such considerations do not necessarily have a bearing on the question of a real risk to an individual applicant of ill-treatment within the meaning of Article 3 (see Salah Sheekh, cited above, § 141).'[380]

Finally, it is interesting to mention the case of *Sufi and Elmi v. the United Kingdom* (2011),[381] in which the ECtHR developed a rule of evidence concerning State reports based on anonymous sources. In this case, the respondent State submitted a report on a fact-finding mission to Somalia, based on information stemming from sources described as 'international NGO', 'a diplomatic source', 'a security advisor'.[382] The Court stated:

'(...) where a report is wholly reliant on information provided by sources, the authority and reputation of those sources and the extent of their presence in the relevant area will be relevant factors for the Court in assessing the weight to be attributed to their evidence. The Court recognises that where there are legitimate security concerns, sources may wish to remain anonymous. However, in the absence of any information about the nature of the sources' operations in the relevant area, it will be virtually impossible for the Court to assess their reliability. Consequently, the approach taken by the Court will depend on the consistency of the sources' conclusions with the remainder of the available information. Where the sources' conclusions are consistent with other country information, their evidence may be of corroborative weight.

---

380 See, for example, ECtHR, *F.H.v. Sweden*, 20 January 2009, Appl. No. 32621/06, para. 92, where the Court stated that where reports focus on general socio-economic and humanitarian conditions, the Court has been inclined to accord less weight to them, since such conditions do not necessarily have a bearing on the question of a real risk of ill-treatment to an individual applicant within the meaning of Article 3.

381 ECtHR, *Sufi and Elmi v. the UK*, 28 June 2011, Appl. Nos. 8319/07 and 11449/07.

382 *Ibidem*, para. 234.

However, the Court will generally exercise caution when considering reports from anonymous sources which are inconsistent with the remainder of the information before it.'[383]

It may be concluded from this ruling that evidence based on anonymous sources cannot be the only source of evidence but must normally be accompanied by other evidentiary materials.

5.6.8   *Opportunities for presenting evidence and reacting to evidence*

In its proceedings, the ECtHR adheres to the principle of adversarial proceedings. The relevant Rules of Procedure of the Court stipulate that, at both the admissibility stage and the merits stage, both parties to the case are allowed to submit their observations and evidence and to react to the observations and evidence lodged by the other party. For example, under Rule 54, the Chamber or its President gives notice of the application to the respondent Contracting Party and invites that Party to submit written observations on the application. Upon receipt thereof, the Chamber or its President invites the applicant to submit observations in reply. The parties may also be invited to submit further observations in writing. When this happens, a possibility to react is normally provided to the other party.[384]

The structure of the judgments of the Court reflects the principle of adversariality. In the Court's judgments, under the heading 'the parties' submissions' (in most judgments this heading is part of the section THE LAW), the final positions of both parties are reflected.

It seems that the ECtHR does not have a problem with the submission of new evidence which was not presented in the national proceedings. The Court then provides the State party an opportunity to react to this new evidence. This clearly distinguishes the ECtHR from the HRC and the ComAT, which, in principle, do not allow the complainant or the respondent State to submit new statements and evi-

---

383 *Ibidem*, para. 233.

384 Rules of Court, 1 April 2011, to be found at: http://www.echr.coe.int, Rules of Court. Rule 54 stipulates:

'1. The Chamber may at once declare the application inadmissible or strike it out of the Court's list of cases.

2. Alternatively, the Chamber or its President may decide to

(a) request the parties to submit any factual information, documents or other material considered by the Chamber or its President to be relevant;

(b) give notice of the application to the respondent Contracting Party and invite that Party to submit written observations on the application and, upon receipt thereof, invite the applicant to submit observations in reply;

(c) invite the parties to submit further observations in writing.

3. Before taking its decision on the admissibility, the Chamber may decide, either at the request of a party or of its own motion, to hold a hearing if it considers that the discharge of its functions under the Convention so requires. In that event, unless the Chamber shall exceptionally decide otherwise, the parties shall also be invited to address the issues arising in relation to the merits of the application.'

dence which were not presented in the national proceedings.[385] These Committees do not normally take into account such statements and evidence, but will, instead, refer the complainant back to national remedies and conclude that the national remedies have not been exhausted. The ECtHR follows a different approach. In *Cruz Varas v. Sweden* (1991), both the applicant and the Swedish Government submitted large quantities of new evidentiary materials to the ECtHR. The applicant submitted two new medical reports and the Swedish Government also submitted completely new materials which had not been available during the national proceedings: after the applicant's expulsion from Sweden to Chile on 6 October 1989 (the case had been brought to the Commission of Human Rights on 5 October 1989), the Swedish authorities had submitted to the Court a report and a number of affidavits resulting from an inquiry conducted in Chile by the Swedish embassy. The Court examined all this evidence materially and used it in order to assess the alleged Article 3-risk.It is obvious that the Court did not find it problematic that part of the evidence had not been made available earlier, during the national proceedings. From the judgment it also becomes clear that, had the claimant presented additional evidence obtained after his expulsion to Chile, the Court would have taken it into account.[386] *Said v. the Netherlands* (2005) demonstrates the same flexible approach. In this case, crucial evidence was brought in by the applicant after the national proceedings had ended; the ECtHR attached significant value to this evidence.[387]

5.6.9   *Judicial application of investigative powers*

In section 5.6.5 on the credibility assessment, it was noted that the ECtHR tries to strike a difficult balance between an active approach towards determination of the facts and reliance on the facts as presented by the respondent State.[388] On the one hand, the Court stresses its subsidiary role and considers that determination of the facts is primarily a matter for the authorities of the Contracting States:

> 'the Court accepts that, as a general principle, the national authorities are best placed to assess (…) the facts (…).'[389]

---

385 See, for example, ComAT, *M.X. v. Switzerland*, 7 May 2008, No. 311/2007, para. 9.4 (detention and sexual assault were not mentioned before the national Swiss asylum authorities); HRC, *A.Cv. the Netherlands*, 22 July 2008, No. 1494/2006, para. 8.3.

386 ECtHR, *Cruz Varas and others v. Sweden*, 20 March 1991, Appl. No. 15576/89, paras. 26, 27, 29, 30, 41-46, 77, 79.

387 See ECtHR, *Said v. the Netherlands*, 5 July 2005, Appl. No. 2345/02, paras. 28, 29, 51.

388 For the same conclusion: see Geertsema 2010. See on this also Essakkili & Spijkerboer 2005, p. 44 and Spijkerboer 2009. Essakkili & Spijkerboer use the term 'inconsistency'. With Geertsema, I would rather speak of a difficult search for a balance between avoiding becoming a fourth instance and applying a rigorous scrutiny because Article 3 is a fundamental absolute and non-derogable right.

389 ECtHR, *R.C. v. Sweden*, para. 52. See also admissibility decisions ECtHR, *Damla and others v. Germany*, 26 October 2006, Appl. No. 61479/00; ECtHR, *F. v. the UK*, 22 June 2004, Appl. No. 17341/03; ECtHR, *Harutioenyan and others v. the Netherlands*, 1 September 2009, Appl. No. 43700/07.

On the other hand, the Court acknowledges the absolute nature and the fundamental value of Article 3 and considers on that basis that the Court itself must make a thorough (or rigorous) examination of the existence of a real risk:

'Its examination of the existence of a real risk of ill-treatment must necessarily be a rigorous one in view of the absolute character of Article 3 (…).'[390]

Part of this rigorous examination is an independent determination of the facts where these are in dispute between the parties. Within the framework of this rigorous examination, the ECtHR allows itself to gather and verify relevant facts and to conduct a rigorous assessment of them. In order to determine the facts, the ECtHR may apply any investigative measure which it considers capable of clarifying them. The application of investigative measures by the Court is governed by two specific provisions in the Rules of Court. Rule A1 in Annex 1 to the Rules of Court[391] stipulates:

Rule A1 (Investigative measures)

1. The Chamber may, at the request of a party or of its own motion, adopt any investigative measure which it considers capable of clarifying the facts of the case. The Chamber may, *inter alia*, invite the parties to produce documentary evidence and decide to hear as a witness or expert or in any other capacity any person whose evidence or statements seem likely to assist it in carrying out its tasks.

2. The Chamber may also ask any person or institution of its choice to express an opinion or make a written report on any matter considered by it to be relevant to the case.

3. After a case has been declared admissible or, exceptionally, before the decision on admissibility, the Chamber may appoint one or more of its members or of the other judges of the Court, as its delegate or delegates, to conduct an inquiry, carry out an on-site investigation or take evidence in some other manner. The Chamber may also appoint any person or institution of its choice to assist the delegation in such manner as it sees fit.

4. The provisions of this Chapter concerning investigative measures by a delegation shall apply, mutatis mutandis, to any such proceedings conducted by the Chamber itself.

5. Proceedings forming part of any investigation by a Chamber or its delegation shall be held in camera, save in so far as the President of the Chamber or the head of the delegation decides otherwise.

6. The President of the Chamber may, as he or she considers appropriate, invite, or grant leave to, any third party to participate in an investigative measure. The President shall lay down the conditions of any such participation and may limit that participation if those conditions are not complied with.'

---

390 See, for example, ECtHR, *Chahal v. the United Kingdom*, 15 November 1996, Appl. No. 22414/93, para. 96; ECtHR, *Jabari v. Turkey*, 11 July 2000, Appl. No. 40035/98, para. 39; ECtHR, *N. v. Finland*, 26 July 2005, Appl. No. 38885/02, para. 160; ECtHR, *Sufi and Elmi v. the UK*, 28 June 2008, Appl. Nos. 8319/07 and 11449/07, para. 214.

391 Rules of Court, 1 April 2011, to be found at: http://www.echr.coe.int, Rules of Court.

And according to Rule 19, paragraph 2, the ECtHR may decide, at any stage of the examination of an application, that it is necessary that an investigation or any other function be carried out elsewhere by it or one or more of its members. From these provisions it follows that, in order to clarify the facts of the case, the Court may at any stage of the proceedings apply investigative powers, such as hearing witnesses and experts, conducting fact finding missions, and requesting the parties to submit additional information.

In section 5.6.5 above on the credibility assessment, it was noted that there seem to be three triggers which particularly make the ECtHR proceed to an independent determination of the facts and to apply investigative powers to that end. These triggers are the following:

1) Insufficient national proceedings, for example, evidence was overlooked or not taken seriously, or the assessment made at national level was insufficiently supported by relevant country of origin materials;
2) New facts, circumstances and developments, including evidence thereof, or new information which casts doubt on the information relied on by the government; and
3) The absolute nature of Article 3 was disrespected in the national proceedings, for example, a weighing of national security considerations against the Article 3-risk took place; or an incorrect application of the standard of proof or another evidentiary standard took place, for example, a too strict standard of proof or a too strict standard on individualisation.[392]

A good example in which all three triggers came together and pushed the Court to proceed towards an independent determination of the facts is *Salah Sheekh v. the Netherlands* (2007). The national proceedings in this case were insufficient, as a higher appeal to the Council of State would have stood no chance of success. Therefore, this higher appeal did not constitute an effective remedy. At the same time, the administration and the first instance national court had assessed the situation in Somalia mainly on the basis of one source, that being the country of origin reports by the Dutch Ministry of Foreign Affairs, which was, in the ECtHR's opinion, an insufficient basis (trigger 1: insufficient national proceedings). In addition, new developments had taken place while the case was pending in Strasbourg (trigger 2: new developments). Finally, a higher appeal to the Council of State was bound to fail because the Council of State applied a steady jurisprudential line, which incorporated a too strict requirement of individualisation of a claim (trigger 3: an incorrect evidentiary standard, being the standard on individualisation).[393]

---

392 See also Wouters 2009, p. 284: 'it seems that the Court is willing to conduct a full assessment of its own when the national proceedings followed give it reason to so so, for example because the claim was assessed in an accelerated procedure, or because doubts have been cast on the information relied on by the national authorities, in particular because the situation in the country of destination may have changed since the national proceedings ended'.
393 ECtHR, *Salah Sheekh v. the Netherlands*, 11 January 2007, Appl. No. 1948/04, paras. 123, 136, 148 (trigger 1: insufficient national proceedings and trigger 3: a too strict standard of individualisation), paras. 52-84, 94-95, 101, 105-113 (trigger 2: new developments).

In *Salah Sheekh v. the Netherlands* (2007), and many other cases, the ECtHR gathered of its own motion substantial additional information on the conditions in the countries of origin. In *Salah Sheekh*, the Court explained why it did so, and when:

'The establishment of any responsibility of the expelling State under Article 3 inevitably involves an assessment of conditions in the receiving country against the standards of Article 3 of the Convention (…). In determining whether it has been shown that the applicant runs a real risk, if expelled, of suffering treatment proscribed by Article 3, the Court will assess the issue in the light of all the material placed before it, or, if necessary, material obtained *proprio motu*, in particular where the applicant – or a third party within the meaning of Article 36 of the Convention – provides reasoned grounds which cast doubt on the accuracy of the information relied on by the respondent Government. In respect of materials *obtained proprio motu*, the Court considers that, given the absolute nature of the protection afforded by Article 3, it must be satisfied that the assessment made by the authorities of the Contracting State is adequate and sufficiently supported by national materials as well as by materials originating from other reliable and objective sources such as, for instance, other Contracting or non-Contracting States, agencies of the United Nations and reputable non-governmental organisations. In its supervisory task under Article 19 of the Convention, it would be too narrow an approach under Article 3 in cases concerning aliens facing expulsion or extradition if the Court, as an international human rights court, were only to take into account materials made available by the national authorities of the Contracting State concerned, without comparing these with materials from other reliable and objective sources.'[394]

In a number of cases, the Court has reiterated that it will particularly obtain materials on conditions in the country of origin *proprio motu* when the applicant or a third party provides reasoned grounds which cast doubt on the accuracy of the information relied on by the respondent government.[395]

The ECtHR does not always make explicit which reports on conditions in a country of origin have been submitted by a party and which reports have been obtained by the Court *proprio motu*. In a number of recent judgments, however, the Court has explicitly stated that it worked both with the evidence submitted by the parties and the evidence gathered of its own motion.[396]

In a number of cases, the Court has not only obtained information on the country of origin *proprio motu*, but has also used other investigative powers of its own motion. In *N. v. Finland* (2005), after the application had been declared admissible, the Court decided to pursue its examination by taking oral evidence in Finland. Two judges were appointed as Delegates and, together with the Registrar and several

---

394 ECtHR, *Salah Sheekh v. the Netherlands*, 11 January 2007, Appl. No. 1948/04, para. 136.
395 See, for example, ECtHR, *Saadi v. Italy*, 28 February 2008, Appl. No. 37201/06, para. 131; ECtHR, *Ismoilov and others v. Russia*, 24 April 2008, Appl. No. 2947/06, para. 120 and ECtHR, *NA v. the UK*, 17 July 2008, Appl. No. 25904/07, para. 119.
396 See, for example, ECtHR, *Muminov v. Russia*, 11 December 2008, Appl. No. 42502/06, para. 95; ECtHR, *Abdolkhani and Karimnia v. Turkey*, 22 September 2009, Appl. No. 30471/08, para. 90; ECtHR, *Mawaka v. the Netherlands*, 1 June 2010, Appl. No. 29031/04, para. 41: 'the Court observes from the materials in its possession and the materials submitted by the Government (…)'.

members of the Registry, they conducted a fact-finding mission in Finland for two days.[397] The delegation took testimony from the applicant himself, his common-law wife, the Head of the Africa section in the Finnish Directorate of Immigration and an acquaintance of the applicant.[398] Another Article 3-case, concerning extradition, in which a fact-finding mission was conducted, this time to Russia and Georgia, is *Shamayev and others v. Georgia and Russia* (2005).[399] During this mission, Delegates of the Court heard many of the applicants, prison staff and certain administrative officials; the Court also examined prison files.[400]

In other cases, the Court has requested one of the parties to submit (additional) expert information. For example, in *R.C. v. Sweden* (2010), the Court requested the applicant to submit to it an expert medical opinion. In the opinion of the Court, the Swedish authorities should have ordered an expert medical opinion in the national proceedings.[401] In *T.I. v. the United Kingdom* (2000), the Court requested the German authorities to provide information on its asylum law and its enforcement.[402] This case concerned possible indirect *refoulement* from the United Kingdom via Germany to Sri Lanka. In other cases, the ECtHR invited the UNHCR to submit a written intervention as a third party.[403]

In sum, in a significant number of cases concerning the expulsion of asylum seekers the ECtHR has played a very active role in the gathering and verification of facts and circumstances. The Court has been increasingly active in this regard since the abolition of the Commission of Human Rights in 1998.[404]

5.6.10   Time limits for the presentation of statements and evidence

5.6.10.1   Time limits for the presentation of statements

All relevant statements should, in principle, be made as early in the national procedure as possible. Belated statements may cast serious doubt on the credibility of the applicant. Exceptions to this rule can be made where there is very persuasive evidence that a person could not speak about a certain aspect earlier, for example, because of psychological problems as a result of torture or maltreatment in the past; it seems, however, that the ECtHR does not easily assume that this is the case.

For example, in *Cruz Varas v. Sweden* (1991), the ECtHR found it problematic that the applicant had made statements to the national authorities about clandestine political activities and about torture by the Chilean police eighteen months after the first police interrogation following his request for asylum. The Court considered that

---

397 ECtHR, *N. v. Finland*, 26 July 2005, Appl. No. 38885/02, paras. 7, 8, 152.
398 *Ibidem*, paras. 9, 77-116.
399 ECtHR, *Shamayev and others v. Georgia and Russia*, 12 April 2005, Appl. No. 36378/02.
400 *Ibidem*, para. 26, paras. 110-216.
401 ECtHR, *R.C. v. Sweden*, 9 March 2010, Appl. No. 41827/07, paras. 23-25, 53.
402 ECtHR, *T.I. v. the United Kingdom*, admissibility decision, 7 March 2000, Appl. No. 43844/98.
403 See, for example, ECtHR, *Abdolkhani and Karimnia v. Turkey*, 22 September 2009, Appl. No. 30471/08, para. 5. The Submission by UNHCR in the case of *Abdolkhani and Karimnia v. Turkey* (2009) is available at: http://www.unhcr.org/refworld/docid/4991ad9f2.html.
404 Wouters 2009, p. 286.

this tardy presentation cast considerable doubt on his credibility. Importance was attached to the fact that the applicant had been legally represented at all stages during the national proceedings. In reaching its conclusion on the tardy statements, the Court did not (at least not explicitly) pay attention to the information provided in the medical reports and in the witness statements by Dr. Jacobsson, who had stated that victims of sexual torture are often so damaged that they are not prepared to talk about it even to their husbands or wives.[405]

In a number of admissibility decisions, the late submission of statements on past torture has cast such serious doubt on the credibility of these statements that the claim has been considered to be manifestly ill-founded and, therefore, inadmissible. In *Nasimi v. Sweden* (2004), the Court considered:

'Moreover, although it recognises that it may be an ordeal to talk about experiences of torture, the Court is struck by the fact that the applicant did not make any specific allegations of torture until (…) more than a year after he applied for asylum, although he must have been aware that such information would be of importance to the immigration authorities.'[406]

Nasimi had gone through four asylum application procedures in Sweden and in the second, third and fourth procedure he submitted statements from a psychologist and psychotherapist mentioning PTSD. The Court did not refer to this medical evidence when dealing with the question of whether the tardy statement on past torture could have possibly been explained by the applicant's medical state. The Court made a similar consideration as the one quoted from *Nasimi v. Sweden* (2004) in *Ovdienko v. Finland* (2005).[407] Similarly, in *B. v. Sweden* (2004), the Court noted that the applicant's allegation that he had been tortured during his detention had not been made to the Swedish authorities; B. had given this information to the ECtHR. And in *Tekdemir v. the Netherlands* (2002), the Court noted that it had been only in the course of national proceedings following a second asylum application that the applicant had raised and relied on his kinship with the brothers A.X. and B.X., one of whom had obtained a residence permit and the other a favourable ruling in the proceedings on his asylum request. Only in the course of third national proceedings had the applicant claimed that he had been tortured in Turkey, a fact which he had not raised in his previous asylum requests.[408]

In *Hilal v. the UK* (2001), the ECtHR made an exception to the general rule that all the relevant statements should be made as soon as possible. The applicant from Zanzibar had attended a pro forma interview with a UK immigration officer and one month later a full asylum interview had been held. According to the form used, the purpose of the pro forma interview was to take down the initial details of the asylum application. The applicant had failed to mention torture at this pro forma interview and mentioned it only in the second interview. This was held against him in the na-

---

405 ECtHR, *Cruz Varas v. Sweden*, 20 March 1991, Appl. No. 15576/89, para. 78.
406 ECtHR, *Nasimi v. Sweden*, admissibility decision, 16 March 2004, Appl. No. 38865/02.
407 ECtHR, *Ovdienko v. Finland*, 31 May 2005, Appl. No. 1383/04.
408 ECtHR, *B. v. Sweden*, admissibility decision, 26 October 2004, Appl. No. 16578/03; ECtHR, *Tekdemir v. the Netherlands*, 1 October 2002, Appl. No. 49823/99.

tional proceedings. The Court ruled that in the light of the medical record from the hospital which had treated the applicant, submitted in the second national asylum procedure, his apparent failure to mention torture at his first immigration interview became less significant and his explanation to the special adjudicator that he did not think he had to give all the details until the full interview a month later became far less incredible.[409] Taking into account that there had been only a one-month delay in presenting statements, that the pro forma interview in fact had served only to take down initial details of the asylum application and that there was a medical report from the hospital concerning the applicant and indicating past torture, the flexible approach adopted by the Court is very understandable.

5.6.10.2 Time limits for the presentation of corroborating evidence

The approach to evidence submitted to corroborate statements seems to be considerably more flexible. The point in time at which evidentiary materials were submitted by the parties is, seen as a factor alone and in itself, not a relevant consideration, as long as the procedural time limit laid down in Rule 38 of the Rules of Court[410] is observed. Rule 38 stipulates that

> 'No written observations or other documents may be filed after the time-limit set by the President of the Chamber or the Judge Rapporteur, as the case may be, in accordance with these Rules. No written observations or other documents filed outside that time-limit or contrary to any practice direction issued under Rule 32 shall be included in the case file unless the President of the Chamber decides otherwise.'

This rule serves to protect the procedure before the Court in the sense that the judges of the Court and the parties to the case are able to read all the materials in the case file before closure of a certain phase of the proceedings (for example, before a hearing takes place). An example of a case in which the Court excluded from the proceedings materials submitted by the applicant, because of late submission, is *H.L.R. v. France* (1997); the hearing by the Chamber of the Court sitting on the case took place on 25 November 1996. The Chamber decided not to include in the case file the documents lodged by the applicant on 24 October and 12, 20 and 22 November 1996, since they were late and as the government had objected.[411]

It seems that as long as Rule 38 is abided by, the precise moment of presentation of evidence is not, in itself and alone, a decisive factor. In *Bahaddar v. Netherlands* (1998), a case concerning a Bangladeshi asylum seeker, the ECtHR expressed that account must be taken of the fact that it may be difficult for asylum seekers to provide evidence within a short time frame:

> 'It should be borne in mind in this regard that in applications for recognition of refugee status it may be difficult, if not impossible, for the person concerned to supply evidence within a

---

409 ECtHR, *Hilal v. the UK*, 6 June 2001, Appl. No. 45276/99, para. 64.
410 Rules of Court, 1 April 2011, to be found at: http://www.echr.coe.int, Rules of Court.
411 ECtHR, *H.L.R. v. France*, 29 April 1997, Appl. No. 24573/94, para. 7.

short time, especially if – as in the present case – such evidence must be obtained from the country from which he or she claims to have fled. Accordingly, time-limits should not be so short, or applied so inflexibly, as to deny an applicant for recognition of refugee status a realistic opportunity to prove his or her claim.'[412]

In *Cruz Varas v. Sweden* (1991), both the applicant and the Swedish Government submitted large quantities of evidentiary materials to the ECtHR. The Court materially examined all this evidence and used it in order to assess the alleged Article 3-risk. It was obvious that the Court did not find it problematic that part of the evidence had not been made available earlier, during the national proceedings. From the judgment, it also became clear that, had the claimant presented additional evidence obtained after his expulsion to Chile, the Court would have taken it into account.[413]

In *Hilal v. the UK* (2001), crucial evidence corroborating the flight narrative was submitted only in second (repeat) national asylum proceedings. It was only after his national appeal against the negative administrative decision had been rejected by the special adjudicator, in part because of a lack of documentary evidence, that Hilal had obtained and submitted a copy of his brother's death certificate, a medical report about the circumstances of his brother's death, as well as a summons from the police to his parents.[414] Without devoting explicit consideration to the late submission of key corroborating evidence in the national proceedings, the ECtHR assessed the genuineness and evidentiary value of the documents. It attached great value to them as it found the applicant's account credible on their basis and assumed an Article 3-risk.[415]

Said v. the Netherlands (2005) and *Bader and Kanbor* (2005) demonstrate the same flexible approach and reaffirm that the point in time at which evidentiary materials were submitted by the parties is, seen as a factor alone and in itself, not a relevant consideration. In *Said v. the Netherlands* (2005), crucial evidence was brought in by the applicant after the national proceedings had ended.[416] The ECtHR attached significant value to this evidence. In *Bader and Kanbor* (2005),[417] the applicants submitted crucial evidence only after a third application for asylum. In this third procedure, they referred to a judgment delivered by the Regional Court of Aleppo, Syria, which stated that applicant Bader had been convicted *in absentia* of complicity in a murder and sentenced to death. The Aliens Appeals Board requested the applicants to submit the original judgment and other relevant documents in support of their application. The applicants submitted a certified copy of the judgment and also a summons requiring the first applicant to present himself before the court within ten days. An inquiry by the Swedish embassy in Syria showed the judgment to be authentic. The ECtHR attached 'particular weight' to this evidence and nothing was said about the fact that

---

412 ECtHR, *Bahaddar v. the Netherlands*, 19 February 1998, Appl. No. 25894/94, para. 45.
413 ECtHR, *Cruz Varas and others v. Sweden*, 20 March 1991, Appl. No. 15576/89, paras. 26, 27, 29, 30, 41-46, 77, 79.
414 *Ibidem*, para. 18.
415 *Ibidem*, para. 62.
416 See ECtHR, *Said v. the Netherlands*, 5 July 2005, Appl. No. 2345/02, paras. 28, 29, 51.
417 ECtHR, *Bader and Kanbor v. Sweden*, 8 November 2005, Appl. No. 13284/04, paras. 11-23,44.

key corroborating evidence had been submitted by the applicants to the national authorities only in a third asylum procedure.[418]

We may conclude that tardy presentation of evidence, in itself and alone, is, in principle, not seen as problematic *per se* by the ECtHR. Late submission of evidence may, however, become problematic where the procedural conduct of the applicant – whether before the national authorities or before the ECtHR itself – exhibits other problematic aspects as well, such as late statements, numerous inconsistencies and discrepancies, vague statements, escalation of a flight narrative in the different stages of the proceedings, or submission of forged documents. The combination of such features may lead the Court to determine that evidence was produced at a very late moment, and this works to the detriment of the applicant. For example, in the admissibility decision in *Nasimi v. Sweden* (2004), the ECtHR found a combination of the following features problematic:

1. Late statements about torture in the past;
2. Late mention of an important document; and
3. Tardy presentation of this document.

The Court noted the following about this:

> 'The Court is struck by the fact that the applicant did not make any specific allegations of torture until (…) more than a year after he first applied for asylum (…) Similarly, a copy of the purported revolutionary court summons was submitted to the Aliens Appeals Board in June 2002, one year and eight months after its date of issuance. Notwithstanding the difficulties of obtaining a copy of such a document in Iran, the applicant has acknowledged, in his submissions to the Court, that he was aware of the existence of the summons long before he received a copy of it. In these circumstances, the Court finds it remarkable that he apparently failed to even mention the document to the immigration authorities before June 2002. It notes, moreover, that he submitted the summons at a time when he had already had two asylum applications rejected.'[419]

Similarly, in the admissibility decision in *Mahin Ayegh v. Sweden* (2006), the Court found the documentary evidence submitted by the applicant (a summons application and three court summonses) problematic and insufficient to assume an Article 3-risk for three reasons:

1. Its tardy presentation: the applicant had submitted the documents after his asylum claim had been rejected by the administration and had been rejected on appeal;
2. Only copies of the documents were provided;[420] and

---

418 According to Judge Myjer of the ECtHR in an interview (Myjer 2008, p. 490), in asylum cases fundamental rights are at stake and for that reason there is 'less room for a formalistic approach with regard to the acceptance of documents submitted by an applicant at a late moment'.

419 ECtHR, *Nasimi v. Sweden*, admissibility decision, 16 March 2004, Appl. No. 38865/02.

420 See about the question of probative value of copies of documents also however, ECtHR, *Singh and Others v. Belgium*, 2 October 2012, Appl. No 33210/11. In that case, the applicants submitted copies
→

3. The respondent government had established that the forms used for the documents could have been easily obtained in the Iranian courts for a fee.[421]

In the admissibility decision of *Elezaj and others v. Sweden* (2007), the Court found the combination of a tardy production of documentary evidence and a lack of detailed information in the statements (vague statements) problematic.[422]

A final example of a case in which a combination of circumstances, including late presentation of evidence in the national proceedings, were found problematic is *A.A. and Others v. Sweden* (2012). The first applicant in that case feared that she would run an Article 3 ECHR-risk if returned to Yemen because she feared violence from her husband, while nobody would be able to protect her against this. To corroborate this fear, she presented, *inter alia*, a record of a Yemeni court according to which her husband had requested that the applicants be returned home. Paradoxically, the Court concluded in that case that this crucial evidence was presented too early, that is, too soon (within two weeks) after the date of its issuance, and, at the same time, too late in the national proceedings, that is, after the final decision by the Migration Court of Appeal, and was invoked as a new ground in a request for reconsideration of the case. An important factor for the Court was that the applicants had not presented any information about how they obtained this document within a few weeks of its issuance. Finally, the Court made clear that the content of the Yemeni court record did not logically fit with the flight narrative: the applicants had not offered any explanation as to why the first applicant's husband would wait until almost three years after the first and fifth applicant's departure from Yemen before reporting their absence to the court if he was seriously offended by their departure.[423]

5.6.11 Point in time for the risk assessment

In cases where the applicant has not yet been expelled from the respondent State at the moment of examination by the ECtHR, the Court assesses the existence of the alleged Article 3-risk on an *ex nunc* basis, which means that the material point in time is the moment at which the Court examines the case. The assessment of the risk is made on the basis of all the information available at the moment of consideration of the case by the ECtHR.[424]

---

of a number of pages from Afghan passports and copies of UNHCR attestations. The ECtHR concluded that the national Belgian authorities should have made further inquiries with the UNHCR.

421 ECtHR, *Mahin Ayegh v. Sweden*, admissibility decision, 7 November 2006, Appl. No. 4701/05.
422 ECtHR, *Elezaj and others v. Sweden*, 20 September 2007, Appl. No. 17654/05.
423 ECtHR, *A.A. and Others v. Sweden*, 28 June 2012, Appl. No. 14499/09, para. 81.
424 This is a steady consideration reiterated in many judgments and decisions. See, for some examples, ECtHR, *Chahal v. United Kingdom*, 15 November 1996, Appl. No. 22414/93, para. 86; ECtHR, *Ahmed v. Austria*, 17 December 1996, Appl. No. 25964/94, para. 43; ECtHR, *Said v. the Netherlands*, 5 July 2005, Appl. No. 2345/02, para. 48; ECtHR, *Salah Sheekh v. the Netherlands*, 11 January 2007, Appl. No. 1948/04, para. 136; ECtHR, *Saadi v. Italy*, 28 February 2008, Appl. No. 37201/06, para. 133; ECtHR, *NA. v. UK*, 17 July 2008, Appl. No. 25904/07, para. 112; ECtHR, *Sufi and Elmi v. the UK*, 28 June 2008, Appl. Nos. 8319/07 and 11449/07, para. 215.

In cases where deportation from the respondent State has already been effectuated, the point in time for the consideration by the Court remains the moment of that deportation, but the Court may, and actually does, have regard to information that came to light subsequent to the removal. Facts and circumstances which become known after the removal are relevant only in that they may confirm or refute what the State party knew or ought to have known at the time of removal.[425]

5.7   Final concluding remarks

The large number of States parties to the ECHR, the long history and the impressive body of binding case law of the ECtHR make the ECHR a very important human rights treaty in Europe. It is also a very important instrument in international and European asylum law. The ECHR does not contain a right to asylum, but the ECtHR has developed a prohibition on *refoulement* under Article 3. As a result, the (intended) expulsion of a failed asylum seeker is in breach of Article 3 and, therefore, unlawful where substantial grounds have been shown for believing that upon expulsion there is a real risk of treatment contrary to Article 3.

In asylum cases under Article 3 ECHR, the notion of an effective national remedy in the sense of Articles 13 and 35, first paragraph, ECHR requires that national asylum courts undertake independent and rigorous scrutiny. This means a serious, individual, case-specific, factual examination on the merits of the claim, based on a correct standard and burden of proof. In assessing whether national proceedings were adequate, the ECtHR takes into consideration whether an applicant was heard (several times), whether he or she was assisted by appointed counsel, whether the national authorities had the benefit of seeing, hearing and questioning the applicant in person, and of assessing directly the information and documents submitted by him or her, before deciding the case. The ECtHR also takes into account whether the assessment of the national authorities was sufficiently supported by both national materials as well as materials originating from other reliable and objective sources. The cases of *R.C. v. Sweden* (2010) and *Singh and Others v. Belgium* (2012) have clearly illustrated that the national authorities, including the reviewing courts, must carefully and seriously examine evidence submitted by applicants. When and if such evidence leaves questions unanswered, the national authorities, including the reviewing courts, must try to find answers by applying investigative powers in order to further clarify the facts. This is particularly necessary when it is rather easy to make further inquiries, as was the case in *Singh and Others v. Belgium*, where the national authorities could easily have made inquiries with the UNHCR.

---

425 See, for example, the cases of ECtHR, *Cruz Varas and Others v. Sweden*, 20 March 1991, Appl. No. 15576/89, para. 76; ECtHR, *Vilvarajah and others v. United Kingdom*, 30 October 1991, Appl. Nos. 13163/87, 13164/87, 13165/87, 13447/87, 13448/87, para. 107; ECtHR, *Ahmed v. Austria*, 17 December 1996, Appl. No. 25964/94, para. 43; ECtHR, *Mamatkulov and Askarov v. Turkey*, 4 February 2005, Appl. Nos. 46827/99, 46951/99, para. 69; ECtHR, *Abdolkhani and Karimnia v. Turkey*, 22 September 2009, Appl. No. 30471/08, para. 76.

The requirement of an independent and rigorous scrutiny also implies that constant national jurisprudential lines may not normally bar an individual, case-specific and factual examination on the merits by the national authorities.

The requirement of an independent and rigorous scrutiny places direct restrictions on national procedural autonomy. It follows from *Bahaddar v. the Netherlands* (1998) and *Jabari v. Turkey* (2000) that the automatic and mechanical application of procedural rules, for example, rules on times limits, barring an examination of the merits of the asylum claim, is at variance with the requirement to conduct an independent and rigorous scrutiny of the claim. Asylum seekers must normally comply with procedural rules but when these rules are not complied with, regard must be had to the reasons for non-compliance, and the question must be raised whether the particular procedural rule is not too strict, given the difficult evidentiary position of asylum seekers. There should always be room for flexibility in applying national procedural rules.

Finally, independent and rigorous scrutiny also means that the correct evidentiary standards and principles are to be applied by the national court in assessing the Article 3-risk. As was shown above, it follows from *M.S.S. v. Belgium and Greece* (2011) that national courts are not allowed to apply, for example, a stricter standard of proof than the one applied by the ECtHR. For national courts to comply with the requirement of independent and rigorous scrutiny it is, therefore, essential to know exactly what these evidentiary standards are.

Article 6, first paragraph, ECHR is relevant for national asylum courts for two reasons. First, since *Kudla v. Poland* (2000), the ECtHR has held that the requirements of Article 13 should be considered as 'reinforcing' those of Article 6(1), so that the requirements developed under Article 6(1) in fact also form part of Article 13. Second, the case law of the ECtHR under Article 6(1) defines to a large extent the content of Article 47, paragraph 2, of the EU Charter on Fundamental Rights, containing the right to a fair hearing (see Chapter 6); Article 47, paragraph 2, of the EU Charter will almost always be relevant for asylum cases.

Article 6, first paragraph, ECHR requires that administrative decisions can generally be challenged before a tribunal having full jurisdiction on points of law and points of fact. Full jurisdiction includes the power to make an independent determination of the disputed facts and of the credibility of a claimant, and the power to critically question advisory information used by the administrative decision maker or the other party. Article 6, first paragraph, also places national courts under a duty to conduct a proper examination of the submissions, arguments and evidence adduced by the parties. Where no proper examination was carried out by the national court, either because it did not properly examine party evidence or because it did not use its investigative powers in order to determine disputed facts independently, this may lead the ECtHR to conclude that the national proceedings were unfair and in violation of Article 6, first paragraph. In addition, Article 6, first paragraph, requires the parties to be treated equally with regard to the admission, exclusion and evaluation of the evidence. The requirements of adversariality and equality of arms are not absolute, though. Non-disclosure of evidentiary materials may be justified if this is strictly necessary to preserve the fundamental rights of another individual or to safeguard an important public interest, such as the protection of national security. A weighing of interests then needs to be made: the interest of the particular party to have knowledge of the evidence must be weighed against the interest of the other party to keep this evidence secret, for example, in order to protect the security of certain other persons, sources of information or to protect national security. If a national court allows secret evidence into the proceedings and accepts that this evidence has not been disclosed to the other party, it must follow special procedures to counterbalance these difficulties. This means, at least, that the national court itself examines the secret evidence, and that, if possible, takes additional counterbalancing measures.

Limited instead of full jurisdiction of national courts is, exceptionally, permitted under Article 6, first paragraph, when certain specific conditions have been met. First, the particular subject matter of the proceedings is of importance. In cases where the subject-matter came within the classical exercise of administrative discretion, such as land planning, limited judicial scrutiny at national level was found permissible by the ECtHR. One may also think of cases in which complex technical assessments are made and of cases where important diplomatic issues are at stake. In those cases where the ECtHR found limited national court jurisdiction acceptable, other conditions had also been met. For example, the national proceedings had centered on points of law and not facts, the preceding administrative procedure(s) had been governed by many Article 6-safeguards and the national judicial scrutiny review, although limited, had been, nevertheless, meaningful in the sense that it had entailed real scrutiny along the procedural points raised by the applicant.

I have argued that it would seem more logical to place Article 3-cases concerning the expulsion of asylum seekers in the category of cases that require full judicial scrutiny on points of fact and points of law. The reasons are that as opposed to, for example, land planning cases, in asylum cases, the life and safety of the individual is at stake, Article 3 is a fundamental, absolute and non-derogable right, most asylum cases will not be of a highly technical nature, and in only a very limited number of cases will important diplomatic issues be at stake. Taking into account that the requirements of Article 6, first paragraph, reinforce those of Article 13, the requirement of full jurisdiction on points of fact and points of law following from the Zumtobel doctrine may be regarded as reinforcing the requirement from Article 13 that in expulsion cases an individual, case-specific, factual examination on the merits of the claim has to take place.

In part 2 of this chapter, section 5.6, I looked at the assessment performed by the ECtHR in Article 3-cases concerning the expulsion of asylum seekers, with the help of the eleven aspects of evidence and judicial scrutiny. Interestingly, the ECtHR uses the term 'rigorous scrutiny' to describe the assessment it performs. As Articles 3, 13 and 35, first paragraph ECHR require the national asylum court to perform a 'rigorous scrutiny' as well, the conclusion must be that the ECtHR uses identical terms to qualify the assessment it carries out and the assessment to be performed by the national remedy. The investigation has demonstrated that the ECtHR has developed concrete principles with regard to each of the eleven aspects of evidence and judicial scrutiny. The standard of proof is that substantial grounds have to be shown for believing that upon expulsion there is a real risk of treatment contrary to Article 3. The level of risk required is a real, personal, foreseeable risk exceeding the mere possibility of being subjected to proscribed ill-treatment. The risk does not need to be certain or highly probable.

The burden of proof rests initially with the applicant, who has to make an arguable claim. When this arguability test is met, the burden of proof shifts towards the State. At that moment, for national authorities, including the courts, the obligations summed up at the end of Part 1 come into play. These authorities have to conduct active investigations to establish whether the application is well-founded or ill-founded.

Relevant facts and circumstances are all possible personal circumstances, and, in addition to these, the general human rights situation in the country of origin is relevant. Many concrete examples of such circumstances were given above. The personal facts must be assessed in the light of the general situation in the country of origin. From the case law of the ECtHR it becomes clear that it is normally a combination of facts and circumstances, and not a single fact, which establish substantial grounds for assuming a real Article 3-risk.

As to the required level of individualisation, the investigation has demonstrated that, in general, the graver the general human rights situation in the country of origin, the more significant this situation becomes in assessing the risk and the less individual facts and circumstances, and evidence corroborating individual facts and circumstances, are required. In accordance with this principle, we can distinguish three categories of cases:

- Cases in which there is extreme general violence in the country of origin, to such an extent that a real risk of ill-treatment would occur simply by virtue of an individual being exposed to such violence on return;
- Cases in which the applicant belongs to a group of persons systematically exposed to a practice of ill-treatment. This very fact constitutes a special distinguishing feature, so that no further special distinguishing features are required;
- Cases in which there is no extreme general violence in the country of origin and the applicant does not belong to a specially targeted group. In such cases, the general situation in the country of origin does play a more or less important role, but there must also be special personal facts and circumstances (special distinguishing features) which establish that this very applicant runs a risk.

When it comes to determining the facts, and, as part of this, assessing the credibility of the asylum claim, the ECtHR tries to strike a difficult balance. In a number of admissibility decisions, it has relied on the credibility assessment made by the respondent State. However, in a significant number of final judgments, and in some admissibility decisions the Court has made a completely independent determination of the facts, including an assessment of the credibility of the claimant's statements. Three circumstances trigger the Court in particular to proceed to an independent determination of the facts and apply investigative powers to that end. These are: insufficient national proceedings (for example, evidence was overlooked or not taken seriously, or the assessment made at national level was insufficiently supported by relevant country of origin materials); new facts, circumstances and developments, including evidence thereof, or new information which casts doubt on the information relied on by the government; and disrespect for the absolute nature of Article 3, for example, a weighing of national security considerations against the Article 3-risk, or an incorrect application of the standard of proof or another evidentiary standard, for example, a too strict standard of proof or a too strict standard on individualisation.

Once the Court has decided to determine the facts fully independently, it actively gathers and checks information. In assessing the credibility of the claimant's statements, the ECtHR evaluates the 'general credibility'. This means that the statements made by the asylum seeker may contain some incredible or not entirely credible aspects, but that the core aspects – the basic story – must be credible, that is, consistent with country of origin information, consistent throughout the (national and international) proceedings, brought forward in a timely manner and corroborated by (some) evidence.

The ECtHR, in principle, admits to the proceedings every form of evidence capable of proving an Article 3-risk, for example, documentary evidence from State organs stating that a person is being sought, or is wanted (arrest warrants, police reports), medical reports corroborating statements of past-ill treatment, written or oral statements made by family members or other witnesses, and reports from various sources containing the country of origin information. It seems that four main sources of country of origin information used by the ECtHR can be identified: information compiled by agencies of the United Nations and the Council of Europe; information compiled by States; information from independent international human rights protection organisations and information from the media and other sources. All evidentiary materials, whether presented by the parties or obtained *proprio motu*, are considered materially by the Court. The Court normally requires that submitted documentary or other evidence has a certain direct bearing on the applicant's personal situation. What generally needs to be substantiated is the core of the flight narrative, the basic story. The approach of the Court is strict. The general principle that account should be taken of the difficult evidentiary position of asylum seekers is not readily applied *in concreto*.

The value and persuasiveness of evidence is determined by the authenticity of submitted documents, the specificity, comprehensiveness and consistency of the information contained in evidentiary materials or given by witnesses, the independence, reliability and objectiveness of the source and the authority and reputation of the author. In a number of cases, the ECtHR has attached considerable evidentiary weight to medical reports submitted by applicants to corroborate past torture or ill-treatment. In assessing the evidentiary value of the country of origin information, the ECtHR gives consideration to its source, in particular its independence, reliability and objectivity, and the authority and reputation of the author of reports, the seriousness of the investigations by means of which the reports were compiled, the consistency of the conclusions, the corroboration by other sources, the presence and the reporting capacities of the author in the country in question are all taken into account. The precise evidentiary weight accorded to the country of origin information is also determined by its specific content. The more the information contained in it is couched in terms of Article 3, the more value the Court attaches to it. Reports by UN agencies and by States are considered to be important sources, because UN agencies have direct access to the authorities of the country of destination as well as the ability to carry out on-site inspections, and States have the ability to gather information through their diplomatic missions.

In its proceedings, the ECtHR adheres to the principle of adversarial proceedings. The relevant Rules of Procedure stipulate that, at both the admissibility stage and the merits stage, both parties to the case are allowed to submit their observations and evidence and to react to the observations and evidence lodged by the other party. The structure of the judgments reflects the principle of adversariality. The ECtHR does not have a problem with the submission of new evidence which was not presented in the national proceedings, which distinguishes it from the HRC and the ComAT, who do not allow the complainant or the respondent State to submit new statements and evidence which were not presented in the national proceedings.

Statements have to be made as early as possible and their late presentation may cast serious doubts on credibility. To the contrary, the precise moment of presentation of evidence is not, in itself and alone, a decisive factor. Late submission of evidence may, however, become problematic in combination with other problematic features, such as late statements, numerous inconsistencies and discrepancies, vague statements, escalation of a flight narrative in the different stages of the proceedings, or submission of forged documents. With regard to the point in time for the risk assessment, it was concluded that the main rule, applying in cases where the applicant has not yet been expelled at the moment of examination by the ECtHR, is that the Court assesses the existence of the alleged Article 3-risk on an *ex nunc* basis. The assessment of the risk is made on the basis of all the information available at the moment of consideration of the case by the ECtHR. In cases where deportation from the respondent State has already been effectuated, the point in time for the consideration by the Court is the moment of that deportation, but the Court may, and actually does, have regard to information that becomes known subsequent to the deportation.

Chapter 6: European Union[1] asylum law

6.1 Introduction

6.1.1 Brief history of the EU

In 1950, Belgium, France, Germany, Italy, Luxembourg and the Netherlands founded the European Coal and Steel Community (ECSC)[2] in an attempt to unite European countries economically and politically in order to secure lasting peace after the Second World War.

In an attempt to strengthen the economic ties, the Treaty establishing the European Economic Community (TEC, Treaty of Rome) and the Treaty establishing the European Atomic Energy Community (TEAEC) were signed in 1957.[3] On 1 January 1973, Denmark, Ireland and the United Kingdom joined the EEC. In 1981, Greece became the 10th member and Spain and Portugal followed in 1986. In 1987 the Single European Act (SEA)[4] was signed. This treaty provided the basis for a vast six-year programme aimed at creating a Single European Market of 'four freedoms' of movement of goods, services, people and money.

In 1992, the Member States concluded the Treaty on the European Union (TEU, Treaty of Maastricht).[5] This treaty established the European Union (EU) that supplemented the Community and consisted of the same Member States. The EU was a new legal structure consisting of three 'pillars', the first pillar being the European Community as established by the TEC, the two other – intergovernmental – pillars concerning 'security and foreign policy' and 'justice and home affairs'. The Treaty of Maastricht also added, as a new feature, a provision on citizenship of the Union and created a monetary union. Austria, Finland and Sweden became Member States in 1995. On 1 May 1999, the Treaty of Amsterdam,[6] signed on 2 October 1997, entered into force. This treaty radically changed the legal nature of EU asylum law (see section 6.1.4 below on the genesis of EU asylum law.) It moved the area of asylum and immigration from the Union's third pillar – the intergovernmental co-operation among the Member States in the area of justice and home affairs – to the first pillar,

---

1   For consistency and readability throughout, the terms European Union (EU) and EU law will be used, also when referring to provisions and judgments dating from the time when the EU was still the EEC or EC. There is much literature on the EU and EU law; very informative are Craig & De Búrca 2008; much information on the EU can also be found on the internet, for example http://europa.eu/abc/history/index_en.htm, where a detailed description of the history of the EU can be found. Also informative is http://www.minbuza.nl/ecer, the site of the EU Expertise Centre of the Dutch Ministry of Foreign Affairs. It contains frequent updates on important developments in the field of the EU and EU law.
2   Treaty establishing the European Coal and Steel Community (1951), see: http://eur-lex.europa.eu/en/treaties/index.htm.
3   See http://eur-lex.europa.eu/en/treaties/index.htm.
4   Single European Act (1986), *OJ of the EU* L 169 of 29 June 1987.
5   Treaty on European Union (1992), *OJ of the EU* C 191 of 29 July 1992.
6   Treaty of Amsterdam amending the treaty on European Union, the treaties establishing the European Communities and related acts, *OJ of the EU* C 340, 10 November 1997.

hence to the Treaty on European Community. As a result, EU asylum law was no longer intergovernmental, but instead became Union law. This made the issuing of binding EU legislation on asylum possible, together with judicial control asserted by the Court of Justice of the European Union (CJEU or Court, see sections 6.1.2, 6.1.4.4). On 1 May 2004, the Czech Republic, Estonia, Latvia, Lithuania, Hungary, Poland, Slovenia and Slovakia joined the EU and Cyprus and Malta also became members. Bulgaria and Romania joined on 1 January 2007.

On 13 December 2007, the 27 EU Member States signed the Treaty of Lisbon.[7] It entered into force on 1 December 2009 and amended the TEU (Treaty of Maastricht, 1992) and the TEC (Treaty of Rome, 1957). The TEC was renamed the Treaty on the Functioning of the European Union (TFEU). The Treaty of Lisbon abolished the pillar structure and, importantly, made the Charter of Fundamental Rights of the EU legally binding, with the same status as the two treaties. In section 6.1.3 below more will be said on the EU's Charter of Fundamental Rights.

At the time of completion of this research, Croatia, the Former Yugoslav Republic of Macedonia and Turkey were candidates for future membership of the EU.

6.1.2 EU law and its supervisory mechanisms

Although established by a treaty, an intergovernmental instrument of international law, the EU presents a new legal order which is different and independent from international law.[8] To distinguish EU law from common international law, it has been named 'supranational'. A basic tenet of this supranational nature is that EU law has precedence over all national law. This is called the principle of supremacy. It means that EU law applies in the Member States on its own terms, not subject to conditions set out by national law, and that national law contrary to primary or secondary EU law does not apply.[9] This principle of supremacy, developed in the case law of the CJEU, has also been laid down in the Final Act of the Intergovernmental Conference on the Treaty of Lisbon, stating:

> 'The Conference recalls that, in accordance with well settled case law of the CJEU, the Treaties and the law adopted by the Union on the basis of the Treaties have primacy over the law of Member States, under the conditions laid down by the said case law.'[10]

Three main sources of EU law can be distinguished. They are presented below in hierarchical order:
-   Primary EU law: the TEU, the TFEU and the Charter;
-   General principles of EU law, as well as international agreements to which the EU is party;

---

7   Treaty of Lisbon amending the Treaty on European Union and the Treaty establishing the European Community, signed on 13 December 2007, entry into force 1 December 2009, *OJ of the EU* C 306, 17 December 2007.
8   CJEU, *Van Gend en Loos*, 5 February 1963, C-26/62, paras. 1-12.
9   CJEU, *Costa ENEL*, 15 juni 1964, C-6/64.
10 Declaration 17 of the Final Act of the Intergovernmental Conference on the Treaty of Lisbon.

- Secondary EU law, laid down in regulations, directives and decisions.[11]

General principles of EU law are of fundamental importance in the jurisprudence of the CJEU and serve a number of purposes. They may be invoked as an aid to interpretation of EU law, as a means to challenge action by a Member State performed in the context of a right or obligation arising from EU law or to challenge Union action. Many different general principles of EU law can be identified. For this research two of them are of particular importance: the general principle of effective judicial protection and the general principle of respect for human rights.[12]

Most secondary EU law has been laid down in regulations and directives. Both regulations and directives are binding and not addressed at specific individuals. Regulations need not and may not be transposed by the Member States into national legislation and have legal effect independently of any national law.[13] Directives require transposition into national law. They are binding as to the result to be achieved, but leave to the Member States the choice of form and methods.[14]

The EU system of judicial protection is based on the principle that all individuals are entitled to effective judicial protection of the rights they derive from the legal order of the European Union.[15] Judicial protection is provided for by a system of supervision carried out by both the national courts of the EU Member States and the CJEU. Since the entry into force of the Treaty of Lisbon on 1 December 2009, the term 'CJEU' has comprised three institutions: the Court of Justice, the General Court, and the EU Civil Service Tribunal.[16] The CJEU was set up under the ECSC Treaty in 1952. Its job is to make sure that 'in the interpretation and application of the Treaties the law is observed'.[17] On the Court's website a useful brief description of the Court's main tasks can be found. The Court is composed of one judge per Member State, so that all 27 of the EU's national legal systems are represented.[18] For the sake of efficiency, however, the Court rarely sits as the full court of 27. It usually sits as a 'Grand Chamber' of 13 judges or in chambers of five or three judges.[19] The judges have the qualifications or competence needed for appointment to the highest judicial positions in their home countries. They are appointed by joint agreement between the governments of the EU Member States. Each is appointed for a term of

---

11   Article 288 TFEU.
12   See for a more extensive description and analysis of the (development of the) general principles of EU law Bernitz & Nergelius 2000, Tridimas 2006, Steiner & Woods 2009: Chapter 6: The General Principles of Law.
13   See Article 288 TFEU.
14   See Article 288 TFEU.
15   CJEU, *Unión de Pequeños Agricultores v. Council*, 25 July 2002, C-50/00 P, para. 39.
16   Article 19, para. 1, TEU states: 'The Court of Justice of the European Union shall include the Court of Justice, the General Court and specialised courts.'
17   Article 19, para. 1, TEU: 'It shall ensure that in the interpretation and application of the Treaties the law is observed.'
18   Article 19, para. 2, TEU stipulates that the Court shall consist of one judge from each Member State.
19   Article 251 TFEU states: 'The Court of Justice shall sit in chambers or in a Grand Chamber, in accordance with the rules laid down for that purpose in the Statute of the CJEU. When provided for in the Statute, the Court of Justice may also sit as a full Court.'

six years, which may be renewed.[20] The Court is assisted by eight Advocates-General (A-Gs). The task of these A-Gs is to make, in open court, reasoned submissions on cases which, in accordance with the Statute of the Court, require their involvement.[21] Article 19 TEU lists the core tasks of the Court:

a) Rule on actions brought by a Member State, an institution or a natural or legal person;

b) Give preliminary rulings, at the request of courts or tribunals of the Member States, on the interpretation of Union law or the validity of acts adopted by the institutions;

(c) Rule in other cases provided for in the Treaties.[22]

Articles 251-281 TFEU lay down further detailed rules for the performance of these tasks. For the purposes of this study it suffices to describe in some detail the Court's task to give preliminary rulings at the request of national courts of the Member States on the interpretation or validity of Union law. The national courts play a very important role in guaranteeing judicial supervision over the application of EU law. They are obliged to provide the legal protection which individuals derive from the rules of EU law and to ensure that those rules are fully effective.[23] When applying EU law, national courts in fact function as the local branches of the EU judiciary.[24] In national judicial proceedings, questions of interpretation of EU primary or secondary asylum law may arise, as well as questions concerning the validity of secondary EU law. Pursuant to Article 267 TFEU, national lower courts may, and upper courts must, refer those issues for a preliminary ruling to the CJEU.[25] The ruling of the CJEU is 'preliminary', meaning that the Court does not decide in a definitive way on the case itself, but only answers the question of EU law posed by the national court. The refer-

---

20 Article 253 TFEU states: 'The Judges and Advocates-General of the Court of Justice shall be chosen from persons whose independence is beyond doubt and who possess the qualifications required for appointment to the highest judicial offices in their respective countries or who are jurisconsults of recognised competence; they shall be appointed by common accord of the governments of the Member States for a term of six years, after consultation of the panel provided for in Article 255.'

21 Article 252 TFEU.

22 Article 19, para. 3, TEU.

23 See, for example, CJEU, *Pfeiffer and others*, 5 October 2004, joined cases C-397/01 to C-403/1, para. 111, CJEU, *Impact*, 15 April 2008, C-268/06, para. 42, CJEU, *Kücükdeveci*, 19 January 2010, C-555/07, para. 45, CJEU, *Günter Fuss*, 14 October 2010, C-243/09, para. 63.

24 See, for example, CJEU, *Köbler*, 30 September 2003, C-224/01, para. 33: 'In the light of the essential role played by the judiciary in the protection of the rights derived by individuals from Community rules (…).'

25 Article 267 TFEU stipulates: 'The Court of Justice of the Euopean Union shall have jurisdiction to give preliminary rulings concerning: (a) the interpretation of the Treaties; (b) the validity and interpretation of acts of the institutions, bodies, offices or agencies of the Union. Where such a question is raised before any court or tribunal of a Member State, that court or tribunal may, if it considers that a decision on the question is necessary to enable it to give judgment, request the Court to give a ruling thereon. Where any such question is raised in a case pending before a court or tribunal of a Member State against whose decisions there is no judicial remedy under national law, that court or tribunal shall bring the matter before the Court. If such a question is raised in a case pending before a court or tribunal of a Member State with regard to a person in custody, the Court of Justice of the European Union shall act with the minimum of delay.'

ring national court subsequently has to apply the EU rule as interpreted by the CJEU to the case, guided by the preliminary ruling on the matter, and pass judgment.

The CJEU's Rules of Procedure envisage several special procedures under which preliminary questions are answered more rapidly. These are: 1) the simplified procedure of Article 104(3) of the Rules of Procedure, applicable where the question has been answered earlier by the Court and also where the question has not yet been answered by the Court, but there is no doubt about the answer; 2) the urgent procedure of Article 104b, in cases of extraordinary haste.[26] The urgent procedure has already been applied by the CJEU in different cases, including a case concerning migration and the detention of illegal migrants, the case of *Kadzoev* (2009).[27] In that case, the CJEU granted the national court's request to issue a preliminary ruling under the urgent procedure of Article 104b in view of, mainly, the fact that Kadzoev had been detained.[28]

6.1.3   EU human rights law

6.1.3.1   Human rights as general principles

Human rights have gradually obtained a more and more prominent place within the legal order of the EU. For the purposes of this study a brief analysis of this development suffices; for a more comprehensive analysis I refer to Alston (2000), Jacobs (2001), Craig & DeBúrca (2008) and Steiner & Woods (2009). The original three European Community Treaties contained no provisions concerning the protection of human rights. As of 1969, however, the CJEU gradually developed an approach under which general principles of EC law included the protection of fundamental rights. The first case in which this happened was *Stauder v. City of Ulm* (1969).[29] This case was followed in 1970 by *Internationale Handelsgesellschaft* (1970).[30] In both cases the Court considered that

> 'Respect for fundamental rights forms an integral part of the general principles of Community law protected by the Court of Justice.'[31]

In the case of *Nold* (1974),[32] the CJEU further clarified that international human rights agreements are one of the two main sources of inspiration for the general prin-

---

26   The Court's Rules of Procedure may be found at: http://curia.europa.eu/jcms/upload/docs/application/pdf/2011-07/rp_cjue_en.pdf, last visited 21 December 2012; the original version of 19 June 1991 may be found in the *OJ of the EU* L 176 of 4 July 1991, p. 7, and the *OJ of the EU* L 383 of 29 December 1992 (corrigenda). A number of amendments were subsequently made to it. They are all mentioned on the listed site, including their publications.

27   CJEU, *Kadzoev*, 30 November 2009, C-357/09 PPU.

28   CJEU, *Kadzoev*, 30 November 2009, C-357/09 PPU, paras. 31-33.

29   CJEU, *Stauder v. City of Ulm*, 12 November 1969, C-29/69.

30   CJEU, *Internationale Handelsgesellschaft v. Einfuhr und Vorrattstelle für Getreide und Futtermittel*, 17 December 1970, C-11/70.

31   CJEU, *Stauder v. City of Ulm*, 12 November 1969, C-29/69, para. 7, and CJEU, *Internationale Handelsgesellschaft v. Einfuhr und Vorrattstelle für Getreide und Futtermittel*, 17 December 1970, C-11/70, para. 4.

32   CJEU, *Nold v. Commission*, 14 May 1974, C-4/73.

ciples of EU law (the other main source being the common national constitutional traditions).[33] The CJEU has consistently treated the ECHR as a special source of inspiration for the general principles of EU law and has often drawn on it in its case law.[34] In a number of cases, the Court has also drawn explicitly on other human rights instruments, particularly the ICCPR.[35]

This jurisprudence was codified in the Treaty of Maastricht (1992). The binding role of the human rights protected in the ECHR for EU law was now explicitly recognised in the EU Treaty itself, as the new Article F(2) stipulated that

'The Union shall respect fundamental rights as guaranteed by the ECHR and as they result from the constitutional traditions common to the Member States, as general principles of Community Law.'[36]

The inclusion of this provision was deemed necessary as it became clearer, with the expansion of EU powers and tasks to areas in which fundamental rights play an important role,[37] that the originally economic focus of the EU did not exclude fundamental human rights from being affected by EU action.[38] With the Treaty of Amsterdam (1999), a new Article 6, first paragraph, was added to the EU Treaty, which stated that respect for human rights and fundamental freedoms is a founding principle for the Union and a principle common to the Member States.[39]

6.1.3.2   The Charter of Fundamental Rights of the EU

In 2000, the Member States concluded the Treaty of Nice[40] and proclaimed a 'Charter of Fundamental Rights of the European Union' (the EU Charter).[41] In this way the EU created its own set of human rights. Many other authors have commented

---

33   CJEU, *Nold v. Commission*, 14 May 1974, C-4/73, para. 13.
34   Some examples of judgments in which this special position of the ECHR is stressed are: CJEU, *Connolly v. Commission*, 6 March 2001, C-274/99, para. 37 P; CJEU, *Roquette Frères*, 22 October 2002, C-94/00, para. 25; CJEU, *Omega*, 14 October 2004, C-36/02, para. 33.
35   Examples of cases in which the CJEU explicitly ruled that the ICCPR is one of the international instruments for the protection of human rights of which the Court takes account in applying the general principles of Union law are: CJEU, *Dzodzi*, 18 October 1990, C-197/89, para. 68, and *Grant*, 17 February 1998, C-249/96, para.44. In *Grant*, however, the CJEU did not follow the interpretation of the term discrimination given by the HRC for a number of reasons, one of them being that the HRC is not a judicial institution. See for a good example of a judgment in which the CJEU stressed the special character of the ECHR, but at the same time also drew on the ICCPR and the International Convention on the Rights of the Child: CJEU, *European Parliament v. Council*, 27 June 2006, C-540/03, paras. 35-37, 54-57.
36   Article 6(1) Treaty on European Union (1992), *OJ of the EU* C 191 of 29 July 1992.
37   The Treaty of Maastricht added two pillars of intergovernmental co-operation to the EU, concerning 'security and foreign policy' and 'justice and home affairs'. See Barkhuysen & Bos 2011, p. 4.
38   Barkhuysen & Bos 2011, p. 4.
39   Article 6(1) Treaty of Amsterdam amending the treaty on European Union, the treaties establishing the European Communities and related acts, *OJ of the EU* C 340, 10 November 1997.
40   Treaty of Nice, *OJ* C 80, 10 March 2001.
41   *OJ of the EU* 2000, C-364/1. Certain parts of this version were amended subsequently, the version now in force can be found in *OJ of the EU* 2010, C-83/02.

extensively on the history, legal status, scope and content of the Charter, as well as its relationship to the ECHR and its added value. I refer to their works here.[42] For the purposes of this study it will suffice to mention the main stages of the Charter's history and the most important key features before shifting the focus to the significance of the Charter for the asylum context.

As a result of disagreement among the Member States, the Charter was not, in 2000, given legally binding effect within the EU order. It was, subsequently, introduced as a 'bill of rights' into the draft Constitutional Treaty, which was proposed to the Member States for ratification in 2004, but that treaty proposal failed to gather sufficient popular support in two Member States, France and the Netherlands.[43] Although it lacked binding legal force, the A-Gs with the CJEU, and also the Court itself, used the Charter as an important source for the interpretation of human rights.[44]

Under the Treaty of Lisbon, the Charter has become binding primary EU law: Article 6, first paragraph, TEU explicitly states that the Charter will have the same legal value as the TEU and the TFEU.[45] Many of the secondary asylum legislation instruments, about which more below, contain explicit references to the Charter.[46] Also, the CJEU's post-Lisbon case law on the provisions of the Charter is growing steadily.[47] In *Alassini* (2010), the CJEU ruled that the requirement laid down in national law that, before bringing an action to court, an out-of-court settlement should be attempted, is not contrary to the principle of effective judicial protection laid down in Article 47 of the Charter.[48] And in *DEB Deutsche Energiehandels- und Beratungsgesellschaft mbH* (2010) the Court provided a set of very concrete guidelines on how national courts can ascertain whether national conditions for granting legal aid constitute a limitation of the right of access to courts undermining the core of the right to effective judicial protection enshrined in Article 47 of the Charter.[49]

---

42 See, for example, Peers & Ward 2004, Claes 2009, Hailbronner 2010, pp. 18-22, Morijn 2011, Pahladsingh & Van Roosmalen 2011, Barkhuysen & Bos 2011.

43 Guild 2011, p.4.

44 See, for an example of an A-G opinion: A-G Maduro, Opinion of 9 September 2008 in the case of *Elgafaji*, para. 21 (judgment 17 February 2009, C-465/07); see, for some examples of judgments: *Parliament v. Council*, 27 June 2006, C-540/03, commented on by Battjes & Vermeulen in *AB* 2007/ 16 (this judgment was the first one in which the Court referred to the Charter); *Der Grüne Punkt DSD GmbH*, 16 July 2009, C-385/07, para. 179. See also Hailbronner 2010, p. 19. For an extensive discussion of pre-Lisbon references by the CJEU to the Charter, I refer to Mortelmans 2009 and Overkleeft-Verburg 2005.

45 Article 6, para. 1, part 1, TEU reads: 'The Union recognises the rights, freedoms and principles set out in the Charter of Fundamental Rights of the European Union of 7 December 2000, as adapted at Strasbourg, on 12 December 2007, which shall have the same legal value as the Treaties.'

46 See, for example, the Asylum Procedures Directive, Preamble (8), which states: 'This Directive respects the fundamental rights and observes the principles recognised in particular by the Charter of Fundamental Rights of the European Union.' See also the Returns Directive, Preamble (24), which stipulates that 'This Directive respects the fundamental rights and observes the principles recognised in particular by the Charter of Fundamental Rights of the European Union.'

47 For a more extensive discussion of post-Lisbon jurisprudence on provisions of the Charter, see Pahladsingh & Van Roosmalen 2011.

48 CJEU, *Alassini*, 18 March 2010, C-317/08 to C-320/08.

49 CJEU, *DEB Deutsche Energiehandels- und Beratungsgesellschaft mbH*, 22 December 2010, C-279/09.

Two EU countries, Poland and the UK, tried to create a special position in relation to the Charter. According to Protocol 30 to the Treaty of Lisbon relating to the application of the Fundamental Rights Charter in these countries,[50] their national courts and the EU's courts are precluded from finding that national laws, regulations or administrative provisions, practices or action are inconsistent with the Charter.[51] However, in its judgment in the case of *N.S. and Others* (2011, see also Chapter 8), the CJEU made clear that Protocol 30 does not call into question the applicability of the Charter in the UK or Poland. The CJEU interpreted Article 1(1) of Protocol 30 as an explanation of Article 51 of the EU Charter with regard to the scope thereof, and ruled that Article (1) of Protocol 30 does not intend to exempt Poland or the UK from the obligation to comply with the provisions of the EU Charter or to prevent a court of one of those Member States from ensuring compliance with those provisions.[52]

The Charter, in fact, codifies all fundamental rights as we know them from the ECHR, the European Social Charter and the UN treaties like the ICCPR, and brings these rights together in one single document. In most cases, therefore, the rights laid down in the Charter are the same as those explicit and binding rights laid down in other treaties.[53] In some cases, however, the Charter offers innovations, which are mostly related to on-going technological and social developments.[54] For example, Article 8 contains, along with Article 7 on protection of family life and protection of private life, a separately articulated right on the protection of personal data. Another interesting innovation is Article 41 on the right to good administration. This includes the right of every person to be heard before an adverse decision is taken, the right to have access to the file and the obligation of the administration to give reasons for its decisions.

Article 6, first paragraph, TEU and Article 52, seventh paragraph, of the Charter make clear that the Explanations to the Charter, drawn up as a way of providing guidance in the interpretation of this Charter, shall be given due regard by the courts of the Union and of the Member States.[55] Groenendijk (2011) warns, however, against attaching too much weight to the Explanations as they seem to downplay the value of the rights and principles laid down in the Charter itself and because the

---

50 Protocol No. 30 to the Consolidated versions of the Treaty on European Union and the Treaty on the Functioning of the European Union, *Official Journal of the EU*, C 83, 30 March 2010. See for extensive comments on Protocol 30: Claes 2009.

51 Article 1, para. 1, of Protocol No. 30.

52 CJEU, *N.S. and Others*, 21 December 2011, C-411/10 and C-493/10, paras. 119, 120.

53 Barkhuysen & Bos 2011, p. 7.

54 Barkhuysen & Bos 2011, p. 7.

55 Article 6, first paragraph, part 3 TEU states: 'The rights, freedoms and principles in the Charter shall be interpreted in accordance with the general provisions in Title VII of the Charter governing its interpretation and application and with due regard to the explanations referred to in the Charter, that set out the sources of those provisions.' Article 52, seventh paragraph, of the Charter states: 'The explanations drawn up as a way of providing guidance in the interpretation of this Charter shall be given due regard by the courts of the Union and of the Member States.' The Explanations to the Charter of Fundamental Rights of the European Union can be found at http://www.europarl.europa.eu/charter/pdf/04473_en.pdf, visited 22 December 2012. See also Morijn 2011, p. 48, Barkhuysen & Bos 2011, p. 6.

CJEU has, so far, not referred to the Explanations when interpreting provisions of the Charter.[56] Morijn (2011) mentions many unresolved questions concerning the exact purpose and status of the Explanations and calls for an 'explanation to the Explanations'; he points, for example, to the inconsistency that Article 6 TEU gives the Explanations an important status whereas the Explanations themselves set out that they are not legally binding.[57]

It follows from Article 51 and the Explanations to this Article that Member States and, therefore, national courts as State organs are only bound by the provisions of the Charter when they operate within the scope of Union law.[58] Since the entry into force of the Treaty of Amsterdam (1999), asylum has fallen within the scope of powers of the EU.[59] Since then – as will be shown in the next section – extensive secondary legislation on asylum has been adopted. Asylum cases will, therefore, almost always be within the scope of Union law. As a result, the Charter will apply to the implementation and application of this new EU asylum law by the EU Member States.[60]

A provision crucial to understanding the relationship between the Charter and the ECHR is Article 52, third paragraph, which stipulates that:

'In so far as this Charter contains rights which correspond to rights guaranteed by the Convention for the Protection of Human Rights and Fundamental Freedoms, the meaning and scope of those rights shall be the same as those laid down by the said Convention. This provision shall not prevent Union law providing more extensive protection.'

This provision is evidently intended to promote harmony between the provisions of the ECHR and the Charter, while not preventing the EU from developing more extensive protection.[61] The Explanations on Article 52 contain a list of rights 'which may at the present stage, without precluding developments in the law, legislation and the Treaties, be regarded as corresponding both in meaning and scope to rights in the

---

56 Groenendijk 2011.
57 Morijn 2011, pp. 50, 51.
58 Article 51 of the Charter states: 'The provisions of this Charter are addressed to the institutions, bodies, offices and agencies of the Union with due regard for the principle of subsidiarity and to the Member States only when they are implementing Union law.' The Explanations on Article 51 refer to pre-Charter case law of the CJEU and state that 'As regards the Member States, it follows unambiguously from the case-law of the Court of Justice that the requirement to respect fundamental rights defined in the context of the Union is only binding on the Member States when they act in the scope of Union law (…).' See also Hailbronner 2010, p. 18.
59 The Treaty of Amsterdam, which entered into force in 1999, moved the whole area of asylum and immigration from the former so-called third pillar (the intergovernmental co-operation among the Member States) to the first pillar, hence to the former Treaty on European Community. The provisions on asylum and immigration were placed in Title IV of Part III of the TEC. See more extensively on the communautarisation of asylum law De Jong 2000, in: Van Krieken 2000, pp. 22-25, Lavenex 2001, pp. 126-137, Da Lomba 2004, pp. 38-45.
60 An example of cases which would, arguably, fall outside the scope of Union law are cases in which a purely national form of protection – not being refugee protection, subsidiary protection or temporary protection as defined in EU secondary asylum legislation – is invoked and applies.
61 See on the relationship between the Charter and the ECHR Barkhuysen & Bos 2011, pp. 17-25, Pahladsingh & Van Roosmalen 2011, pp. 55-58.

ECHR'.[62] As well as this list, the Explanations contain a second list of rights 'where the meaning is the same as the corresponding Articles of the ECHR, but where the scope is wider'.[63] An example of the first category of rights (corresponding in both meaning and scope with the ECHR-counterpart) is the EU prohibition on *refoulement* contained in Article 19, second paragraph of the Charter, which will be discussed in the next section on EU asylum law. An example of the second category of rights (with a wider scope than the ECHR-counterpart) is the right to an effective remedy and a fair trial contained in Article 47 of the Charter, which will be discussed in section 6.3.

As Barkhuysen & Bos (2011) point out, in addition to these two categories of rights there is a third category, consisting of new rights which do not in any way correspond to the ECHR-rights. Article 41, containing the right to good administration, was mentioned as such an innovation. It is to be expected that the CJEU will develop its own jurisprudential lines with respect to these rights.[64]

Compared to the treaties discussed in the previous chapters of this book, the Charter creates added value is many ways. First, as has been said above, it contains a number of rights which have a wider scope than their corresponding ECHR counterparts; Article 47, which is an example of this category, is discussed below in section 6.3. Second, the Charter contains a number of new rights, such as Articles 8 and 41. Third, as the Charter is now primary binding EU law, human rights can be invoked directly before the national courts and the CJEU, and all national courts have the possibility of referring preliminary questions concerning the interpretation of Charter rights to the CJEU.[65] This possibility has already been used by national courts; the cases are still pending in Luxembourg.[66] In addition to the complaints procedures before the HRC, the ComAT and the ECtHR, the system of judicial supervision of EU human rights law may turn out to have a complementary value. Although they are of great value, the complaints procedures under the ICCPR, the CAT and the ECHR have their weaknesses. The ECtHR, the HRC and the ComAT are overburdened and enter the stage only after the national proceedings (in asylum cases sometimes after the expulsion of the asylum seeker to his or her country of origin). The preliminary procedure before the CJEU offers national first instance and upper courts the possibility of referring questions to the CJEU pending the national judicial proceedings, which may help to prevent or redress violations of human rights at an early stage.[67]

---

62 Explanations on Article 52.
63 Explanations on Article 52.
64 Barkhuysen & Bos 2011, p. 22.
65 Article 267 TFEU stipulates: 'The Court of Justice of the European Union shall have jurisdiction to give preliminary rulings concerning:
    (a) the interpretation of the Treaties;
    (b) the validity and interpretation of acts of the institutions, bodies, offices or agencies of the Union.
    (…).'
    Due to Article 6, para. 1, part 1, TEU, the Charter has the same legal value as the Treaties.
66 An example is *LJN*: BV8942, District Court of Middelburg, the Netherlands, in which the court of Middelburg referred to preliminary questions concerning the interpretation of Articles 8 and 41 of the Charter to the CJEU in a case concerning a request from an asylum seeker to be given insight into the internal administrative note underpinning a negative asylum decision.
67 Barkhuysen & Bos 2011, pp. 28-30, Callewaert 2010.

Fourth, the European Commission can start an infraction procedure against a Member State if it finds that Charter provisions have been violated.[68] In a statement of October 2010, the Commission made clear that it would seriously supervise adherence to the Charter by Member States.[69]

To conclude this section on the development of EU human rights law, it is worth mentioning that human rights have been incorporated into EU law not only via the now binding Charter as stipulated in Article 6, first paragraph, TEU. Human rights enter EU law via two more avenues as well. The second paragraph of Article 6 TEU stipulates that the EU shall in the future accede to the ECHR. At the time of completion of this chapter, negotiations were taking place on the conditions of accession of the EU to the ECHR.[70] And as a result of the third paragraph of Article 6, human rights still constitute general principles of EU law.[71]

6.1.4   EU asylum law[72]

6.1.4.1   Early intergovernmental measures

Before 1993, the Treaty on the European Economic Community (TEC) did not make any mention of asylum. Its main objective was the integration of the economies of the Member States. For this purpose, the Single Market comprising an area without internal frontiers was to be created.[73] This implied shifting control from the

---

68   Article 258 TFEU stipulates: 'If the Commission considers that a Member State has failed to fulfil an obligation under the Treaties, it shall deliver a reasoned opinion on the matter after giving the State concerned the opportunity to submit its observations. If the State concerned does not comply with the opinion within the period laid down by the Commission, the latter may bring the matter before the CJEUropean Union.' Due to Article 6, para. 1, part 1, TEU, the Charter has the same legal value as the treaties.

69   COM (2010) 573, Strategy for the effective implementation of the Charter of Fundamental Rights by the European Union, 19 October 2010. This document is accessible at: http://ec.europa.eu/justice/news/intro/doc/com_2010_573_en.pdf, visited 30 August 2011.

70   Barkhuysen & Bos 2011, p. 5, Callewaert 2010.

71   Article 6, paras. 2 and 3 read:
    '2. The Union shall accede to the European Convention for the Protection of Human Rights and Fundamental Freedoms. Such accession shall not affect the Union's competences as defined in the Treaties.
    3. Fundamental rights, as guaranteed by the European Convention for the Protection of Human Rights and Fundamental Freedoms and as they result from the constitutional traditions common to the Member States, shall constitute general principles of the Union's law.'
    The question why it was deemed necessary to create three different human rights pillars and how they relate to each other is a complex one, which has so far not been answered in a clear way. See, for example, Morijn 2011, p. 50.

72   To trace back and understand the origins and development of EU asylum law, see Battjes 2006, Chapter 1.5, Boeles et al. 2009, Chapter 3.3, Guild 2000, part 1, section 1, Hailbronner 2000, Hailbronner 2010, Chapter 1, De Jong 2000 in: Van Krieken 2000, Chapter 1.2, Lavenex 2001, Chapter 3, Da Lomba 2004, Chapter 1.3 and Chapter 2, Pollet 1994, Van der Klaauw 2000 in: Van Krieken 2000, Chapter 1.1, Van Krieken 2004, Introduction; Van Krieken 2004 contains, in the introduction to the book, a useful chronological overview of the relevant political and legal developments in the field of EU asylum law.

73   Article 7A TEEC (TEC)(old, introduced by the Single European Act of 1986, *Official Journal* (1987) L 169/1, after amendment by the Treaty of Amsterdam Article 14 TEEC (new) stipulated that 'the

→

internal borders (borders between the Member States of the Community) to the external borders of the Community. Policy makers across Europe then realised that the creation of this Single Market would have a profound impact on national asylum policies. It was feared that the abolition of border controls would put incentives in place for asylum seekers to 'shop' for asylum: once inside the territory of the European Community, it would be possible for them to travel unchecked, to apply for asylum in those Members States with the most generous systems and to apply for asylum in more than one Member State. It was for this reason that additional measures dealing with asylum seekers were deemed indispensable.[74] The creation of the internal market was, therefore, perceived as requiring harmonisation of asylum law.[75]

A number of Member States, however, were unwilling to give up control of the entry of third-country nationals. The Member States that did wish to achieve the abolition of internal borders sought the means to do so outside the scope of Community law. In 1985, they concluded the Schengen Agreement.[76] This Agreement offered a framework for adopting measures compensating for the abolition of internal border control.[77] These measures were laid down in the Schengen Implementing Agreement (SIA or, as the CJEU calls it, CISA) that was concluded in 1990.[78] The SIA or CISA contained a mechanism to determine which Member State was responsible for processing asylum applications. Gradually, all Member States acceded to the SIA, except for the United Kingdom and Ireland. The chapter in the SIA on the Member States responsible for asylum requests was subsequently replaced by the Dublin Convention, which entered into force in 1997 in all twelve original Member States of the Community.[79] The new Member States, Austria, Sweden and Finland had followed suit and had all joined the Dublin Convention by 1 January 1998.

In addition to this development, an attempt was made in 1992 to bring asylum matters closer within the ambit of Community law. As was said above, in that year the Member States concluded the Treaty on the European Union (TEU, Treaty of Maastricht), establishing a Union that supplemented the Community and consisted of the same Member States. The European Union was a new legal structure consisting of three pillars. The first pillar was the European Community as established by the Treaty on European Community, with its own powers and its own specific legal order. The two other pillars concerned 'security and foreign policy' and 'justice and home affairs'. The second and third pillars lacked the characteristics of Community

---

Community shall adopt measures with the aim of progressively establishing the internal market over a period expiring on 31 December 1992 (...). The internal market shall comprise an area without internal frontiers in which the free movement of goods, persons, services and capital is ensured in accordance with the provisions of this Treaty.'

74   Boeles 2009, p. 316 and Van der Klaauw 2000 in: Van Krieken 2000, p. 11.

75   White paper on the Completion of the Internal Market (COM (1985) 310def), para. 11.

76   Agreement between the Governments of the States of the Benelux Economic Union, the Federal Republic of Germany and the French Republic on the Gradual Abolition of Checks at their Common Borders of 14 June 1985, *OJ of the EU* 2000 L239/13-18.

77   See Articles 17 and 20 of the Schengen Agreement.

78   Convention applying the Schengen Agreement (CISA) of 14 June 1985 (the Schengen Agreement) of 19 June 1990, *OJ of the EU* 2000 L 239/19.

79   Convention determining the State responsible for examining applications for asylum lodged in one of the Member States of the European Communities, *OJ of the EU* 1997 C/254.

law. According to Article K.1 Treaty of Maastricht, the objective of the third pillar – justice and home affairs – was to achieve the objective of the European Union, 'in particular the free movement of persons'. This Article declared asylum and a number of other immigration matters as 'matters of common interest'. The Council could adopt measures on these matters by unanimity voting. A number of 'joint positions', 'joint actions' and 'decisions' were taken, but they had little binding force.[80]

6.1.4.2   *Intergovernmental co-operation in the field of asylum becomes Union law*

The Treaty of Amsterdam (1999) radically changed the legal nature of EU asylum law. This treaty moved the whole area of asylum and immigration from the Union's third pillar –the intergovernmental co-operation among the Member States in the area of justice and home affairs –to the first pillar, hence to the Treaty on European Community. The provisions on asylum and immigration were placed in Title IV, Part III TEC.[81] EU asylum law was, as a result, no longer intergovernmental, but was, instead, Community law. This made the issuing of binding EU legislation on asylum possible, together with judicial control asserted by the Court of Justice (see more on this below in this section). Article 63 TEC (now Article 78 TFEU) dealt explicitly with asylum and required the adoption of measures on a number of asylum issues within five years after the entry into force of the Treaty of Amsterdam, that is, before 1 May 2004. The United Kingdom and Ireland retained a special position: they can participate in asylum measures at will; and Denmark opted out: secondary EU asylum law does not apply at all to this country.[82] As an attachment to the Treaty of Amsterdam, a special Protocol was adopted on asylum for nationals of the EU Member States (the Aznar Protocol).[83]

---

80   See Hailbronner 2000, p. 49 and Hailbronner 2010, p. 3. See also Van der Klaauw 2000, in: Van Krieken 2000, p. 11, and Boeles et al. 2009, p. 317.

81   Articles 61-69 TEC after consolidation. See more extensively on the communautarisation of asylum law De Jong 2000, in: Van Krieken 2000, pp. 22-25, Lavenex 2001, pp. 126-137, Da Lomba 2004, pp. 38-45.

82   For Title IV measures, Denmark, Ireland and the United Kingdom have secured a special position by means of Protocols to the Treaty of Amsterdam (Protocol on the position of the UK and Ireland and Protocol on the Position of Denmark). See also Article 69 TEC. The UK and Ireland have indicated in the case of each relevant secondary law instrument that they would opt in. The UK has secured that if secondary law measures are accepted by it, these measures bind that country as international law but not as Union law.

83   Protocol on Asylum for nationals of the Member States of the EU (Protocol 29 to the Treaty of Amsterdam, now Protocol 24 to the consolidated version of the TEU and TFEU). In its sole Article, this Protocol stipulates that, given the level of protection of fundamental rights and freedoms by the EU Member States, Member States shall be regarded as constituting safe countries of origin in respect of each other for all legal and practical purposes in relation to asylum matters, and that, accordingly, any application for asylum made by a national of a Member State may only in specific circumstances be taken into consideration. An example of such a specific circumstance is the situation where a Member State takes measures derogating from the ECHR. For more on the Aznar Protocol, see Guild & Garlick (2010).

6.1.4.3   The creation of the Common European Asylum System (CEAS)

The negotiating process on this new legislative programme for asylum and immigration started with the European Council summit in Tampere in 1999. Here, for the first time, the ambition was expressed to create a Common European Asylum System, the CEAS, based on the full and inclusive application of the 1951 Refugee Convention.[84] According to Tampere conclusions 14 and 15, it was decided to construct the CEAS in two phases. During the first phase, to be completed before 1 May 2004, the CEAS would include a clear and workable determination of the State responsible for the examination of an asylum application, common minimum standards for a fair and efficient asylum procedure, common minimum conditions for the reception of asylum seekers, and the approximation of rules on the recognition and content of refugee status. It would be completed with measures on subsidiary forms of protection offering an appropriate status to any person in need of such protection. In this first CEAS stage, on the basis of (old) Article 63 TEC, now Article 78 TFEU, the following secondary legislation on asylum has been brought about:

- The EU Temporary Protection Directive (2001), a measure on the possibility of the Council to decide on temporary protection for mass influxes of asylum seekers and the rights of the beneficiaries of that status;[85]
- The EU Reception Conditions Directive (2003), a measure on the question of which rights and conditions are applicable for asylum seekers pending the asylum procedure;[86]
- The EU Dublin Regulation (2003) on which Member State is responsible for examining an asylum claim;[87]
- The EU Qualification Directive (2004 and 2011), a measure on who is eligible for international protection;[88] and

---

84   Tampere European Council 15 and 16 October 1999 – Presidency Conclusions, SN 200/99, available on http://www.europarl.eu.int/summits/tam_en.htm.
85   Council Directive 2001/55 of 20 July 2001, on minimum standards for giving temporary protection in the event of a mass influx of displaced persons and on measures promoting a balance of efforts between Member States in receiving such persons and bearing the consequences thereof, *OJ of the EU* L 212, 7 August 2001, pp. 12-23.
86   Council Directive 2003/9/EC of 27 January 2003, laying down minimum standards for the reception of asylum seekers, *OJ of the EU* L 031, 6 February 2003, pp.18-25.
87   Regulation 2003/343/EC of 18 February 2003, establishing the criteria and mechanisms for determining the Member State responsible for examining an asylum application lodged in one of the Member States by a third country national, *OJ of the EU* L 50, 25 February 2003, pp. 1-10, last amended by *OJ of the EU* L 304, 14 November 2008, p. 83.
88   Council Directive 2004/83/EC on minimum standards for the qualification and status of third country nationals or stateless persons as refugees or as persons who otherwise need international protection on the content of the protection granted, *OJ of the EU* L 304, 30 September 2004, pp. 12-23, last amended by *OJ* L 204, 5 August 2005, p. 24. On 13 December 2011, the new Qualification Directive was adopted: Directive 2011/95/EU of the European Parliament and of the Council of 13 December 2011 on standards for the qualification of third-country nationals or stateless persons as beneficiaries of international protection, for a uniform status for refugees or for persons eligible for subsidiary protection, and for the content of the protection granted, *OJ of the EU* L 337, 20 December 2011, pp. 9-26. The new directive must be implemented by the EU Member States by 21 December 2013.

- The EU Asylum Procedures Directive (2005), a measure on the rules of procedure for the examination of asylum claims.[89]

Two EU Member States have a special position in relation to the CEAS. Ireland participates in the application of the Dublin Regulation and the EU Qualification Directive, the EU Asylum Procedures Directive and the EU Temporary Protection Directive, but not in the EU Reception Conditions Directive. Denmark is not bound by the four EU Directives mentioned above.[90]

During the second CEAS stage, new measures will lead to a common asylum procedure and a uniform status for those who are granted asylum which is valid throughout the Union. The second stage was set in motion in 2009, when the European Commission presented several proposals to revise the previously adopted measures.[91] As many of these second-stage measures have yet to be decided upon by the Council and the European Parliament, this study focuses mainly on the first-stage instruments. The second EU Qualification Directive 2011/95 is included as this Directive was adopted on 13 December 2011 and must be implemented by the EU Member States by 21 December 2013. Provisions from the EU Qualification Directive mentioned, quoted or referred to in this chapter are from the second EU Qualification Directive 2011/95.

Article 78 TFEU (old Article 63 TEC) stipulates that the secondary EU asylum legislation mentioned above must be in accordance with the 1951 Refugee Convention as well as other relevant treaties.[92] It may safely be argued that 'other relevant treaties' include the treaties dealt with in the previous chapters of this book: the ECHR, the ICCPR and the CAT.

Some provisions of EU asylum law are worded in the same, or in a very similar, way compared to the provisions of these international asylum instruments. In particular, the Qualification Directive is to a large extent aimed at resolving the differences between the EU Member States concerning the application of the existing material international asylum rules, including the refugee definition contained in the RC.[93] In line with this, the secondary asylum legislation often refers to the RC. For example, Preamble (4) to the EU Qualification Directive stipulates that

---

89 Council Directive 2005/85 of 1 December 2005 on minimum standards on procedures in Member States for granting and withdrawing refugee status, *OJ of the EU* L 326, 13 December 2005, pp. 13-34.

90 The Directives mention this special provision. See also CJEU, *N.S. and Others*, 21 December 2011, C-411/10 and C-493/10.

91 See, for example, the proposal for recasting the Dublin regulation 343/2003 EC (COM (2008) 820 final; the proposal for recasting of the Reception Conditions Directive 2003 (COM (2008) 815 final; further proposals are foreseen for recasting the Qualification Directive 2004/83/EC and the Asylum Procedures Directive 2005/85/EC. Recast proposals are included in Hailbronner's book of 2010.

92 Article 78, first paragraph, TFEU, states: 'The Union shall develop a common policy on asylum, subsidiary protection and temporary protection with a view to offering appropriate status to any third-country national requiring international protection and ensuring compliance with the principle of *non-refoulement*. This policy must be in accordance with the Geneva Convention of 28 July 1951 and the Protocol of 31 January 1967 relating to the status of refugees, and other relevant treaties.'

93 See Preambles 3, 4, 5 of this Directive.

'The Geneva Convention and Protocol provide the cornerstone of the international legal regime for the protection of refugees.'[94]

And Preamble (2) to the Dublin Regulation states that

'(2) The European Council, at its special meeting in Tampere on 15 and 16 October 1999, agreed to work towards establishing a Common European Asylum System, based on the full and inclusive application of the Geneva Convention relating to the Status of Refugees of 28 July 1951, as supplemented by the New York Protocol of 31 January 1967, thus ensuring that nobody is sent back to persecution, i.e. maintaining the principle of non-refoulement (...).'

As well as this secondary legislation on asylum, the Charter, which was discussed in more detail in the previous section, contains two provisions on asylum: Article 18 on the right to asylum and Article 19 on the prohibition on *refoulement*. Articles 18 and 19 are discussed in more detail below in section 6.2.

6.1.4.4   Case law of the CJEU in asylum cases[95]

In the past, and for some years, the CJEU had no or only limited jurisdiction as far as EU asylum law was concerned. The Treaty of Maastricht (1993) excluded jurisdiction of the Court in this area; the Treaty of Amsterdam (1999) introduced jurisdiction, with a number of restrictions, in Article 68 TEC. Under this provision, the possibility for national courts to refer questions to the CJEU in cases concerning asylum, migration and visa was limited. National courts of first instance were denied the competence to refer questions on migration and asylum matters. Only the highest national courts could do so. The reason behind this restriction was the fear that the CJEU would not be able to cope with a deluge of questions. This denial of competence was lifted by the Treaty of Lisbon. Under Article 267 TFEU, the CJEU is now fully competent to rule on the validity of secondary asylum law, and on the interpretation of primary and secondary EU asylum law, and all national courts are permitted to refer preliminary questions in pending asylum cases to the CJEU.

So far, in ten cases concerning asylum, preliminary questions referred by national courts of EU Member States have been answered by the CJEU.[96] Most of the ques-

---

94   The CJEU confirmed this in its case law. See, for example, CJEU, *Abdulla*, 2 March 2010, C-175/08, C-176/08, C-178/08 and C-179/08, paras. 52 and 53, where the Court ruled: 'According to points 3, 16 and 17 of the Preamble to the Directive the Geneva Convention is the cornerstone of the international legal regime for the protection of refugees (...). Therefore, the provisions of the Directive must be interpreted in the light of the general system and the purpose of the Directive, taking into account the Geneva Convention and other relevant treaties mentioned in Article 63, para. 1, sub 1, EC.'

95   See for a description and analysis of the development of the Court's jurisdiction over immigration and asylum Guild & Peers 2001. See for a description of the preliminary procedure after Lisbon with a specific focus on migration cases the article 'De prejudiciële procedure na Lissabon' by S. Hubel & M. Stronks in: *Migrantenrecht* 9-10/09. See for a more general description of the impact of the Treaty of Lisbon on the jurisdiction of the Court 'En wat met de rechtsbescherming? Het Verdrag van Lissabon en de Communautaire Rechter', by L. Parret, in: Van Ooijk & Wessel 2009, pp. 49-59.

tions submitted in these cases concerned the interpretation of material provisions contained in the Qualification Directive concerning inclusion and exclusion from protection. Three cases, *Brahim Samba Diouf* (2011), *N.S.* (2011) and *M.M.* (2012) concerned questions pertaining to judicial procedures. In *Brahim Samba Diouf*, the national court asked whether the right to an effective remedy laid down in Article 39 Procedures Directive permits national regulations to deny a right of appeal on a decision to channel an application for international protection into an accelerated procedure. The case of *N.S.* concerned application of the EU Dublin Regulation and the question of whether the referring EU Member State should test the compliance of asylum procedures in the intermediary EU Member State with EU asylum law (See Chapter 8 for more about Dublin cases and this judgment of the CJEU). The case of *M.M.* concerned the requirement of co-operation, laid down in Article 4 of the EU Qualification Directive, between the national authorities and the asylum seeker (see section 6.4.3.2 below). It is interesting to mention here that the UNHCR issued statements in the context of all the cases (see also Chapter 2).[97] Where relevant for the purposes of this research, the asylum case law of the CJEU will be discussed in more detail below.

6.1.5 *Further content and structure of this chapter*

The choice to describe in some detail the development of EU human rights law and EU asylum law was made deliberately. Some knowledge of the genesis of EU human

---

96 The judgments issued up to 31 December 2012 by the CJEU on preliminary questions in asylum cases are: *Petrosian and others*, 29 January 2009, C-19/08, *Elgafaji*,17 February 2009, C-465/07, *Abdulla and others*, 2 March 2010, C-175/08, C-176/08, C-178/08, C-179/08, *Bolbol*, 17 June 2010, C-31/09, *B and D*, 9 November 2010, C-57/09 and C-101/09, and *Brahim Samba Diouf*, 28 July 2011, C-69/10; *N.S. and Others*, 21 December 2011, C-411/10 and C-493/10; *Migrationsverk Sweden v. Nurije, Valdrina and Valdri Kastrati*, 3 May 2012, C-620/10; *Bundesrepublik Deutschland v. Y. and Z.*, 5 September 2012, C-71/11 and C-99/11; *M.M. v. Ireland*, 22 November 2012, C-277/11. In addition, of relevance to the field of asylum are two other judgments, being *Parliament v. Council*, 6 May 2008, C-133/06, concerning an application by the European Parliament for the annulment of Articles 29(1) and (2) and 36(3) of the EU asylum Procedures Directive, concerning safe countries of origin and safe third countries, and *European Commission v. Ireland*, 7 April 2011, C-431/10, concerning an action for failure by Ireland to implement Procedures Directive 2005/85/EC. The CJEU ruled that Ireland had failed to implement the Directive. Relevant judgments are also: CJEU, *Parliament v. Council*, 6 May 2008, C-133/06, concerning an application by the European Parliament for the annulment of Articles 29(1) and (2) and 36(3) of the Procedures Directive, concerning safe countries of origin and safe third countries, and, alternatively, the annulment of that Directive in its entirety; in this case the Court indeed annulled the mentioned provisions due to the fact, in short, that the wrong procedure for decision making had been followed; CJEU, *Kadzoev*, 30 November 2009, C-57/09, in which questions were raised concerning the detention of asylum seekers in the light of Article 15(4) to (6) of Directive 2008/115/EC of 16 December 2008 on common standards and procedures in Member States for returning illegally staying third-country nationals (*OJ of the EU* 2008 L 348, p. 98), and CJEU, *European Commission v. Ireland*, 7 April 2011, C-431/10, a case in which the Commission sought – and obtained – a declaration from the Court that Ireland had failed to implement the Procedures Directive.

97 The UNHCR statements are available at RefWorld. See, for example, the statement issued in the context of the case of *Brahim Samba Diouf* at: http://www.unhcr.org/refworld/docid/4bf67fa12.html.

rights and EU asylum law is indispensable for understanding the position of the Charter of Fundamental Rights of the EU in international human rights law and the position of the secondary asylum legislation in relation to the international treaties discussed in the previous chapters. This knowledge is also necessary for tackling the question of whether EU asylum law offers any additional principles or added value regarding questions of evidence and judicial scrutiny. In the remaining sections of this chapter, the focus will shift to the central theme of this study: evidence, proving and judicial scrutiny in asylum court proceedings. In section 6.2, Articles 18 and 19 of the Charter are analysed, followed by Article 47 of the Charter in section 6.3. Section 6.4 addresses secondary EU asylum law provisions on evidentiary issues. In 6.5, concluding remarks are made.

This chapter deviates from the previous ones as it does not contain a section which meticulously describes the approach of the CJEU to all the eleven aspects of evidence and judicial scrutiny. Such a detailed description is currently impossible as the CJEU has passed judgments in only a limited number of asylum cases and has, as a result, not had an opportunity to express itself on all the aspects. However, in cases concerning other fields, such as, *inter alia*, migration of EU citizens, competition, marketing authorisations, product classification, and taxes, the CJEU has dealt with questions regarding the intensity of national judicial scrutiny, certain questions concerning the admission and evaluation of evidence as well as opportunities to present evidence, and questions concerning time limits. It is difficult to infer from these cases very specific guidelines as to how national judges should do their work in asylum cases, as the subject-matter is quite different. Nevertheless, some general trends and lines can be discerned, and the CJEU may draw on these lines and trends when confronted with similar types of questions in asylum cases. It has done so before with regard to EU migration law in cases concerning the migration of nationals from non-EU countries.[98] It is for that reason that this case law in other fields is analysed in this study.

6.2 Issues of evidence and judicial scrutiny under Articles 18 and 19 of the Charter

6.2.1 *Article 18: respect for the RC, respect for the UNHCR's positions*

Article 18 contains the right to asylum and stipulates:

> 'The right to asylum shall be guaranteed with due respect for the rules of the Geneva Convention of 28 July 1951 and the Protocol of 31 January 1967 relating to the status of refugees and in accordance with the Treaty establishing the European Community.'

The CJEU has not, so far, expressed itself on Article 18 of the Charter. The Court has mentioned Article 18 of the Charter as part of the relevant EU legislation in only one of the seven preliminary procedure judgments given so far in cases concerning

---

98   See, for example, CJEU, *Bozkurt*, 22 December 2012, C-303/08, and CJEU, *Toprak and Oguz*, 9 December 2010, C-300/09.

asylum: *Abdulla and others* (2010).[99] This may be partly explained by the fact that the Charter gained the status of binding primary EU law with the entry into force of the Treaty of Lisbon on 1 December 2009 and two of the judgments in asylum cases (*Petrosian* and *Elgafaji*) were given in the pre-Lisbon period. The fact that the Court referred to Article 18 only in *Abdulla and others*, and not in the three other post-Lisbon judgments, may perhaps also be explained by the fact that *Abdulla* concerned cessation of refugee status and the corresponding secondary rights, in other words, the loss of an earlier gained right to asylum. The Explanations on Article 18 make clear that the text of Article 18 is based on Article 78 TFEU, which stipulates that the common EU policy on asylum must be in accordance with the Refugee Convention and the Refugee Protocol, and other relevant treaties.[100] The right to asylum is to be distinguished from protection from *refoulement*, which is addressed separately by Article 19 of the Charter. The right to asylum is generally assumed to imply a right to durable protection (as opposed to temporary protection) and the appropriate secondary rights (to, for example, housing and employment) as defined in the RC.[101] As opposed to the right to asylum, protection from *refoulement* does not confer secondary rights but only means that the individual concerned may not be expelled or otherwise returned to his or her country of origin. The obligation to guarantee the right to asylum means that Article 18 recognises at least the refugee's claim to asylum. Battjes (2006) and Hailbronner (2010) write that it does not impose an obligation to grant asylum.[102] It may be argued, however, that Article 18 does impose an obligation to grant asylum when the necessary conditions have been fulfilled. Article 14 UDHR envisages the right *to seek and to enjoy* asylum,[103] and not, as Article 18 does, a right to asylum which shall be guaranteed. Next, Article 13 EU Qualification Directive states that Member States shall grant refugee status to a third-country national or a stateless person, who qualifies as a refugee (who meets the criteria laid down in Chapters II and III of the Directive). An interpretation of Article 18 as an obligation to grant asylum where the relevant conditions have been fulfilled is in line with Article 13 EU Qualification Directive and would explain the stronger wording of Article 18, compared to Article 14 UDHR.

The obligation to guarantee the right to asylum is conditioned in Article 18 by the obligation to pay due respect to the RC. According to Battjes (2006) and Hailbronner (2010) the requirement of respect for the RC sets a material standard.[104] Based on the conclusions drawn in Chapter 2 it may be argued that the requirement of respect for the RC also sets concrete procedural standards. The RC contains a number of procedural provisions in Articles 16 (access to courts) and 32 (due process of law in cases of expulsion). In section 2.4, the UNHCR's positions on evidence and judicial scru-

---

99 CJEU, *Abdulla and others*, 2 March 2010, C-175/08, C-176/08, C-178/08, C-179/08.
100 Explanations on Article 18 of the Charter; the Explanations to the Charter of Fundamental Rights of the European Union can be found at http://www.europarl.europa.eu/charter/pdf/04473_en.pdf, last visited 30 August 2011.
101 Battjes 2006, p. 112, Hailbronner 2010, p. 19.
102 Battjes 2006, p. 113, Hailbronner 2010, p. 19.
103 Article 14, first paragraph, UDHR.
104 Battjes 2006, p. 113, Hailbronner 2010, p. 19.

tiny were discussed and it was demonstrated that these positions may serve as a tool for interpreting Articles 16 and 32 RC. By virtue of Article 18 of the Charter, national asylum courts will have to pay due respect to the procedural provisions of the RC, and to the procedural positions taken by the UNHCR, as discussed in Chapter 2. It may be argued that it is no longer possible to set these positions aside as non-binding, as that would amount to non-compliance with Article 18 of the Charter, which is binding primary Union law.

6.2.2 Article 19: incorporation into EU law of the ECtHR's standards

Article 19, second paragraph, contains an explicit prohibition on *refoulement*. It stipulates:

> 'No one may be removed, expelled, or extradited to a State where there is a serious risk that he or she would be subjected to the death penalty, torture or other inhuman or degrading treatment or punishment.'

The Explanations on Article 52, third paragraph, state that 'Article 19(2) corresponds to Article 3 of the ECHR as interpreted by the European Court of Human Rights.' And the Explanations on Article 19 state that 'paragraph 2 incorporates case law from the European Court of Human Rights regarding Article 3 of the ECHR'.[105] In other words, this provision incorporates the ECtHR's case law under Article 3 in expulsion cases.[106]

Battjes (2006) points out the discrepancy between the aim of Article 19 to incorporate the relevant case law of the ECtHR and the wording of Article 19, second paragraph, which suggests a different scope in a number of ways.[107] The most remarkable and for this study most relevant difference is that the ECtHR requires a 'real risk' whereas Article 19, second paragraph, requires a 'serious risk', which seems to be a stricter standard, as it seems to require a higher degree of foreseeability. Battjes also points out, however, that it would be wrong to conclude that Article 19, second paragraph, is indeed different in scope and risk criteria for two reasons.[108] First, Article 52, third paragraph, states that the scope and meaning are the same as the corresponding right under Article 3 ECHR. Second, any person who falls outside the scope of Article 19, second paragraph, will be able to invoke Article 4 of the Charter which states:

> 'No one shall be subjected to torture or to inhuman or degrading treatment or punishment.'

---

105 Explanations on Article 52, paragraph 3, of the Charter and Explanations on Article 19, paragraph 2, of the Charter; the Explanations to the Charter of Fundamental Rights of the European Union can be found at http://www.europarl.europa.eu/charter/pdf/04473_en.pdf, last visited 30 August 2011.
106 Battjes 2006, pp. 114, 115; Hailbronner 2010, p. 20.
107 Battjes 2006, p. 115.
108 Battjes 2006, p. 116.

Scope and meaning of this provision are, according to the Explanations, the same as those of Article 3 ECHR, as interpreted by the ECtHR. Articles 4 and 19 thus overlap.[109]

It follows from the foregoing that Article 19, second paragraph, incorporates into EU asylum law the standards, principles and approaches developed by the ECtHR under Article 3 ECHR in expulsion cases, including the procedural and evidentiary standards set out in Chapter 5. This incorporation has transformed the legal nature of these standards. They have been transformed from intergovernmental international law, which enters national legal orders and works in them via the constitutions of states, into binding primary EU law, which works on its own terms in national legal orders, not subject to conditions set out by national law, and takes precedence over all national law.

Neither the text of Article 19 nor the Explanations refer explicitly to the ICCPR and the CAT. There are, however, three reasons for assuming that Articles 7 ICCPR and 3 CAT, and the corresponding case law of the HRC and the ComAT, must be taken into consideration when applying Article 19 of the Charter. First, the Preamble to the Charter states that

'This Charter reaffirms (…) the rights as they result, in particular, from the constitutional traditions and international obligations common to the Member States, the European Convention for the Protection of Human Rights and Fundamental Freedoms, the Social Charters adopted by the Union and by the Council of Europe and the case-law of the European Union and of the European Court of Human Rights.'

As all the EU Member States are party to both the ICCPR and the CAT (see Chapters 3 and 4), Articles 7 ICCPR and 3 CAT can be qualified as 'international obligations common to the Member States'. Second, Article 78 TFEU requires secondary EU asylum law to be in accordance with the RC and 'other relevant treaties', which must be assumed to include the ECHR, the ICCPR and the CAT. It would be difficult to imagine that it would be acceptable for secondary asylum law to be in conformity with the 'other relevant treaties', whereas primary law, more in particular Article 19 of the Charter, would be at variance with them. In other words, the requirement that secondary Union law is in accordance with international treaties presupposes that primary Union law is also in accordance with these instruments.

Third, Article 53 of the Charter states:

'Nothing in this Charter shall be interpreted as restricting or adversely affecting human rights and fundamental freedoms as recognised, in their respective fields of application, by Union law and international law and by international agreements to which the Union or all the Member States are party, including the European Convention for the Protection of Human Rights and Fundamental Freedoms, and by the Member States' constitutions.'

---

109 The Explanations on Article 4 of the Charter state: 'The right in Article 4 is the right guaranteed by Article 3 of the ECHR, which has the same wording (…).' By virtue of Article 52(3) of the Charter, it therefore has the same meaning and the same scope as the ECHR Article.

Taking all this into account, and bearing in mind that human rights form one of the two main sources of inspiration for the general principles of Union law (see section 6.1.3.1 above), it may safely be assumed that Articles 3 CAT and 7 ICCPR form important additional sources of inspiration for the interpretation of Article 19 of the Charter.[110]

As was demonstrated in Chapters 3 and 4, the Human Rights Committee and the Committee against Torture have developed a number of procedural and evidentiary standards. It follows from the foregoing that these standards must be taken into consideration when applying Article 19, second paragraph, of the Charter.

6.3 Issues of evidence and judicial scrutiny under Article 47 of the Charter

Article 47 of the Charter stipulates:

> 'Everyone whose rights and freedoms guaranteed by the law of the Union are violated has the right to an effective remedy before a tribunal in compliance with the conditions laid down in this Article.
>
> Everyone is entitled to a fair and public hearing within a reasonable time by an independent and impartial tribunal previously established by law. Everyone shall have the possibility of being advised, defended and represented.
>
> (...)'

6.3.1 Article 47: the EU law counterpart of Articles 6 and 13 ECHR

The text of Article 47 of the Charter and the Explanations on Article 47[111] make clear that Article 47 is inspired by Articles 6 and 13 ECHR. In a number of pre-Lisbon judgments, the CJEU explicitly stated that Articles 6 and 13 ECHR apply in Union law as general principles and have been reaffirmed by Article 47 of the Charter.[112] The first paragraph of Article 47 is clearly inspired by Article 13 ECHR.[113] The Explanations make clear, however, that this provision differs in two ways from Article 13 ECHR. First, in EU law the effective remedy requirement is stricter since it guarantees the right to an effective remedy before a genuine judicial body: a court or tribunal, and not an administrative body. Under Article 13 ECHR, the authority before which an effective remedy must be available need not *per se* be a judicial authority.

---

110 See, for the same conclusion, Battjes 2006, p. 116.

111 Explanations on Article 47 of the Charter; the Explanations to the Charter of Fundamental Rights of the European Union can be found at http://www.europarl.europa.eu/charter/pdf/04473_en.pdf.

112 See, for example, CJEU, *Johnston*, 15 May 1986, C-222/84, paras. 18 and 19; CJEU; *Heylens and others*, 15 October 1987, C-222/86, para. 14; CJEU, *Eribrand*, 19 June 2003, C-467/01, para. 61; CJEU, *Unibet*, 13 March 2007, C-432/05, para. 37; CJEU, *Productores de Música de España*, 29 January 2008, C-275/06, para. 62; CJEU, *Der Grüne Punkt DSD GmbH*, 16 July 2009, C-385/07, para. 179.

113 Article 13 ECHR reads: 'Everyone whose rights and freedoms as set forth in the Convention are violated shall have an effective remedy before a national authority notwithstanding that the violation has been committed by persons acting in an official capacity.'

Second, unlike Article 13 ECHR, Article 47, first paragraph, does not impose the requirement for an arguable claim, and, therefore, offers wider protection. The only requirement for applicability is that a case is within the scope of EU law.[114] Thus, the EU right to an effective remedy implies the right to effective judicial scrutiny of the decisions of the EU institutions or national authorities taken pursuant to the applicable provisions of EU law.[115]

The second paragraph of Article 47 is clearly inspired by Article 6, first paragraph, ECHR.[116] Importantly, Article 47 of the Charter offers more extensive protection. The Explanations on Article 47, second paragraph, state explicitly that in EU law, the right to a fair hearing is not confined to disputes relating to civil law rights and obligations and criminal charges, but instead applies to all cases which are within the scope of EU law, that is, cases in which an EU right or freedom is at stake.[117] Since the entry into force of the Treaty of Amsterdam (1999), asylum has fallen within the scope of powers of the EU.[118] Since then (as was shown above) extensive secondary EU legislation on asylum has also been adopted. For these reasons, asylum cases will almost always be within the scope of Union law. Article 47 of the Charter will, therefore, normally apply to asylum cases.

The Explanations on Article 47 make clear that, in all respects other than their scope, the guarantees afforded by the ECHR under Article 6, first paragraph, and Article 13 ECHR apply under Article 47 of the Charter.[119] This also follows logically from Article 52, third paragraph, of the Charter, which stipulates that:

---

114 The Explanations on Article 47, first paragraph, of the Charter state: 'However, in Union law the protection is more extensive since it guarantees the right to an effective remedy before a court. The Court of Justice enshrined that right in its judgment of 15 May 1986 as a general principle of Union law (Case 222/84, CJEU, *Johnston* [1986] ECR 1651; see also judgment of 15 October 1987, Case 222/86, CJEU, *Heylens* [1987] ECR 4097 and judgment of 3 December 1992, Case C-97/91, CJEU, *Borelli* [1992] ECR I-6313). According to the Court, that general principle of Union law also applies to the Member States when they are implementing Union law.'

115 Reneman 2012, p. 92.

116 Article 6, first paragraph, ECHR stipulates: 'In the determination of his civil rights and obligations or of any criminal charge against him, everyone is entitled to a fair and public hearing within a reasonable time by an independent and impartial tribunal established by law. Judgement shall be pronounced publicly but the press and public may be excluded from all or part of the trial in the interest of morals, public order or national security in a democratic society, where the interests of juveniles or the protection of the private life of the parties so require, or to the extent strictly necessary in the opinion of the court in special circumstances where publicity would prejudice the interests of justice.'

117 The Explanations on Article 47, second paragraph, state: 'In Union law, the right to a fair hearing is not confined to disputes relating to civil law rights and obligations. That is one of the consequences of the fact that the Union is a community based on the rule of law as stated by the Court in Case 294/83, *'Les Verts' v. European Parliament* (judgment of 23 April 1986, [1986] ECR 1339).(....).'

118 The Treaty of Amsterdam, which entered into force in 1999, moved the whole area of asylum and immigration from the former so-called third pillar (the intergovernmental co-operation among the Member States) to the first pillar, hence to the former Treaty on European Community. The provisions on asylum and immigration were placed in Title IV of Part III TEC. See more extensively on the communautarisation of asylum law De Jong 2000, in: Van Krieken 2000, pp. 22-25, Lavenex 2001, pp. 126-137, Da Lomba 2004, pp. 38-45.

119 The Explanations on Article 47, second paragraph, state: '(...). Nevertheless, in all respects other than their scope, the guarantees afforded by the ECHR apply in a similar way to the Union.'

'In so far as this Charter contains rights which correspond to rights guaranteed by the Convention for the Protection of Human Rights and Fundamental Freedoms, the meaning and scope of those rights shall be the same as those laid down by the said Convention. This provision shall not prevent Union law providing more extensive protection.'

Article 47 of the Charter, thus, incorporates all the procedural safeguards afforded by Articles 6 and 13 ECHR, set out in Chapter 5.[120] This incorporation into EU law has two important consequences. First, national courts can no longer maintain, with reference to constant case law of the ECtHR, that the safeguards developed under Article 6 ECHR do not apply in asylum cases and that those developed under Article 13 apply only in cases of an arguable asylum claim. Union law has, thus, caused the effect that the procedural safeguards flowing from Articles 6 and 13 will almost always apply in asylum cases. Second, the incorporation means that the procedural safeguards of Articles 6 and 13 ECHR now enter the national legal orders of EU Member States not only as 'intergovernmental' international law, subject to the constitutional conditions set out by national law, but also in their capacity as primary binding Union law which has precedence over all national law and applies in the Member States on its own terms, not subject to conditions set out by national law.[121]

Neither Article 47 nor the Explanations refer explicitly to the ICCPR, the CAT and the RC. For the reasons mentioned above in section 6.2.2, it may be assumed that Articles 2, third paragraph, and 14 ICCPR, Articles 12 and 13 CAT, including the corresponding case law of the Human Rights Committee and the Committee against Torture, and Article 16 RC, must be taken into consideration when applying Article 47 of the Charter. The mentioned provisions on proceedings of the ICCPR, the CAT and the RC thus form important sources for the interpretation of Article 47 of the Charter, along with Articles 6 and 13 ECHR.[122]

6.3.2 Article 47 Charter: codification of the principle of effective judicial protection

6.3.2.1 The principle of effective judicial protection: introduction

Article 47 is not only the mirror of Articles 6 and 13 ECHR. It also constitutes the codification of the Union law principle of effective judicial protection. In *Samba Diouf* (2011), the Court stated that the principle of effective judicial protection:

---

120 See in the same vein Battjes 2006, pp. 325-327, Tridimas 2006, pp. 455-456, and Widdershoven in his comment on CJEU, *Der Grüne Punkt DSD GmbH*, 16 July 2009, C-385/07, in *AB* 2010, 119.

121 Mr Ben Smulders, director at the legal department of the European Commission, expressed the same opinion at the conference for the Dutch judiciary on the Treaty of Lisbon and the Charter, organised by the Training Institute for the Judiciary SSR on 9 June 2010 in Utrecht, the Netherlands. He stated in his presentation that the principles as to how national courts should perform their work, developed by the ECtHR under Articles 6 and 13 ECHR, in fact now form primary EU law as these principles have been incorporated into EU law via Article 47 read in conjunction with Article 52, para. 3, which Articles are primary EU law provisions.

122 The specific obligations flowing from the provisions on national proceedings contained in the RC, ICCPR and the CAT were dealt with in Chapters 2, 3 and 4.

'Is a general principle of EU law to which expression is now given by Article 47 of the Charter of Fundamental Rights of the European Union.'[123]

The leading case in which the CJEU for the first time ruled explicitly that national courts are under a duty to provide effective judicial protection of EU rights is *Johnston v. Chief Constable of the Royal Ulster Constabulary* (1986).[124] This case concerned a female police officer in Northern Ireland who was refused renewal of her contract pursuant to a policy decision that, due to the situation of growing violence, the contracts of female officers would not be renewed. Johnston argued that this policy decision was at variance with the EC Sex Discrimination Directive.[125] The CJEU, referring to Article 6 of the Directive, ruled that

'The requirement of judicial control stipulated in that provision reflects general principle of law which underlies the constitutional traditions common to the Member States. That principle is also laid down in Articles 6 and 13 of the ECHR. By virtue of Article 6 of Directive No. 76/207, interpreted in the light of the general principle stated above, all persons have the rights to obtain an effective remedy in a competent court against measures which they consider to be contrary to the principle of equal treatment of men and women laid down in the Directive.'[126]

The importance of providing effective judicial protection of rights conferred by EU law was subsequently stressed in many other cases.[127]

The principle of effective judicial protection can be further divided into a number of sub-principles. In literature, different stances are taken on how this sub-division can best be made. For example, Jans, De Lange, Prechal & Widdershoven (2007) seem to make a distinction between, on the one hand, the principles of equivalence and effectiveness, and on the other hand, the principle of effective judicial protection; they do not see the first two principles as being part of the latter principle.[128] By contrast, Battjes (2006) discusses in his chapter on judicial supervision a number of

---

123 CJEU, *Samba Diouf*, 28 July 2011, C-69/10, paras. 48-49. See also the judgments in CJEU, *Unibet*, 13 March 2007, C-432/05, para. 37; CJEU, *Der Grüne Punkt DSD GmbH*, 16 July 2009, C-385/07 P, paras. 177-179; CJEU, *Alassini*, 18 March 2010, C-317/08 to C-320/08.

124 CJEU, *Johnston v. Chief Constable of the Royal Ulster Constabulary* 15 May 1986, C-222/84.

125 Council Directive No. 76/207 of 9 February 1976, *Official Journal of the EU* 39 of 14 February 1976, pp. 40-42.

126 CJEU, *Johnston v. Chief Constable of the Royal Ulster Constabulary* 15 May 1986, C-222/84, paras. 18, 19.

127 See, for example, CJEU, *Les Verts v. European Parliament*, 23 April 1986, C-294/83, para. 23; CJEU, *Heylens*, 15 October 1987,C-222/86, paras. 2, 14-17; CJEU, *Oleificio Borelli SpA v. Commission of the EC*, 3 December 1992, C-97/91, para. 14; CJEU, *Van Schijndel* 14 December 1995, C-430/93, para. 19; CJEU, *Siples*, 11 January 2001, C-226-99, paras. 17-19; CJEU, *Union de Pequenos Agricultores v. Council*, 25 July 2002, C-50/00 P, para. 39; CJEU, *Jégo-Quéré et Cie SA v Commission of the European Communities*, 3 May 2002, T-177/01, paras. 41-42; CJEU, *Safalero*, 11 September 2003, C-13/01, para. 50; CJEU, *Ahmed Ali Yusuf*, 21 September 2005, T-306/01, para. 326-327; CJEU, *Unibet*, 13 March 2007, C-432/05, para. 44; CJEU, *PKK and KNK*, 18 January 2007, C-229/05, paras. 109, 110; CJEU, *Kadi & Al Barakaat v. Council of the EU*, 3 September 2008, C-402/05, para. 335; CJEU, *People's Modjahedin Organization of Iran*, 4 December 2008, T-284/08, particularly para. 55; CJEU, *Kücükdeveci*, 19 January 2010, C-555/07, para. 45.

128 Jans, De Lange, Prechal & Widdershoven 2007, pp. 40-56. See also Widdershoven's comment to CJEU, *Pontin* (2009), C-63/08, in: *AB* 2010.

sub-principles, including equivalence, effectiveness, conciliatory interpretation and disapplication of national law contrary to EU provisions having direct effect.[129] Arnull (2011) treats the principles of equivalence and effectiveness as sub-principles of the broader principle of effective judicial protection.[130] This approach is also found in the case law of the CJEU.[131] For the purposes of this study, the principle of effective judicial protection is broken down into four sub-principles[132] and, in addition, into guidelines regarding the required intensity of judicial scrutiny. Below, I will first briefly discuss four sub-principles of the principle of effective judicial protection. These are equivalence, effectiveness, conciliatory interpretation and disapplication of national law contrary to EU law with direct effect. Some knowledge of these sub-principles is needed before addressing the question of the implications of the principle of effective judicial protection for judicial scrutiny in asylum cases. After that, I will discuss case law in which the CJEU – within the framework of the question of whether national procedural rules were compliant with the principle of effective judicial protection – dealt with questions regarding the intensity of judicial scrutiny required by EU law. The CJEU may draw upon this case law when confronted, in the future, with questions regarding the required intensity of judicial scrutiny in asylum cases.

6.3.2.2 *Effective judicial protection: equivalence and effectiveness*

In the absence of EU (harmonisation) rules on legal procedures, it is for the national legal system of each Member State to lay down the detailed procedural rules governing actions at law for safeguarding rights which individuals derive from EU law. This is called the principle of national procedural autonomy. The underlying idea of this principle is that it recognises that national procedural rules may reflect deepseated cultural and ethical values and should, therefore, not be lightly set aside.[133] There are two limitations to national procedural autonomy. First, national procedural rules applied in cases under EU law must be no less favourable than those governing similar national actions. This is called the principle of equivalence. Second, national procedural rules must not, in practice, make it impossible or excessively difficult to exercise rights conferred by EU law. This is called the principle of effectiveness. The CJEU has reiterated and applied this doctrine of national procedural autonomy conditioned by the requirements of equivalence and effectiveness in many different judgments.[134]

---

129 Battjes 2006, Chapter 9: Effective judicial protection, pp. 534-542. A number of other authors make a similar sub-division, see, for example, Craig & De Búrca 2008, Chapter 9, Tridimas 2006, Chapter 9, section 9.7; Steiner & Woods 2009, Chapter 8.

130 Arnull 2011, p. 51, 52.

131 See, for a fairly recent example, CJEU, *Pontin*, 29 October 2009, C-63/08, paras. 43, 44.

132 In making this sub-division, I was inspired by the CJEU, Battjes, and Arnull. It seemed the most appropriate for the purposes of this research.

133 Arnull 2011, p. 52.

134 The first and central judgment in which the CJEU developed this doctrine of national procedural autonomy conditioned by the requirements of equivalence and effectiveness is CJEU, *Rewe*, 16 December 1976, C-33/76, para. 5 and further. Since then the doctrine has been reiterated and applied

→

Craig & De Búrca (2008), Steiner&Woods (2009), Engström (2010) and Arnull (2011) distinguish different stages in the case law of the CJEU.[135] The first stage, from 1958 to the mid-eighties, was dominated by great deference to national procedural autonomy. In this period, the Court was unwilling to rule that national procedural rules were not in conformity with the principle of effective judicial protection. Instead, it urged the Union legislature to take action to harmonise national procedural rules. The second stage, from the mid-eighties to the mid-nineties, was characterised by cases intervening in procedural autonomy. The emphasis yielded a stronger insistence on the effectiveness of EU law and on effective judicial protection as a fundamental right. Examples of judgments where the CJEU adopted a more robust approach after a period of deference to national procedural autonomy are *Factortame* (1990),[136] and *Francovich* (1991).[137] In *Factortame*, the Court ruled, in short, that any provision of a national legal system and any legislative, administrative or judicial practice which might impair the effectiveness of Union law by withholding from the national court the power to do everything necessary to set aside national legislative provisions which might prevent, even temporarily, Union rules from having full force and effect were incompatible with the requirements inherent in the very nature of Union law. The full effectiveness of Union law would be just as much impaired if a rule of national law could prevent a national court seized of a dispute governed by Union law from granting interim relief in order to ensure the full effectiveness of the judgment to be given on the existence of the rights claimed under Union law.[138] In *Francovich*, the Court ruled, in short, that it was inherent in the system of EU law that a State must be liable for loss and damage caused to individuals by breaches of Union law for which the State could be held responsible.[139]

In the third stage, from the mid-nineties up until the present, the case law has been characterised by a careful balancing of interests. The determination of the compatibility of a national procedural rule with the EU requirement of effective judicial protection depends on the character of the specific EU right at stake, the role and purpose of the national procedural rule, and the precise circumstances of each case.[140] In order to answer the question of compatibility, the national court must perform a test consisting of two steps. In the first step, it must look at the question of equivalence: is the specific national procedural rule governing the action involving EU law no less favourable than procedural rules governing similar actions under national law?

---

in numerous other judgments. An example is CJEU, *Alassini*, 18 March 2010, C-317/08 to C-320/08, para. 48.In literature, this jurisprudential line or doctrine is referred to as the Rewe/Comet jurisprudence; see, for example, Barkhuijsen & Bos 2011, p. 11, Steiner & Woods 2009, 8.2, Arnull 2011, p. 52.

135 Craig & De Búrca 2008, pp. 305, p. 328; the Principle of Effective Judicial Protection in EU law, presentation by Johanna Engström, ERA conference on national judicial protection in EU law, Paris, 15 and 16 February 2010; Steiner & Woods 2009, 8.3. and8.3.2; Arnull 2011, p. 52.

136 CJEU, *Factortame*, 19 June 1990, C-213/89.

137 CJEU, *Francovich*, 19 November 1991, C-690 and C-9/90.

138 CJEU, *Factortame*, 19 June 1990, C-213/89, paras. 20 and 21.

139 CJEU, *Francovich*, 19 November 1991, C-690 and C-9/90, paras. 39-41.

140 Craig & De Búrca 2008. p. 322, Battjes 2006, pp. 535-537, Woods & Steiner 2009, 8.2, Arnull 2011, pp. 53-60.

This part of the test can be broken down into two sub-questions: first, are the EU claim and the national claim similar? Regard may be had here to the distinction between public and private law, to the substantive right at stake, and the purpose of the proceedings. Second, is the national procedural rule applicable to the EU law claim less or no less favourable than procedural rules applicable to similar claims based on national law?

In the second step, the national judge must apply a 'procedural rule of reason'.[141] The question of this second step is whether the national procedural rule renders application of EU law impossible or excessively difficult. This question must be answered

'By reference to the role of the procedural rule in the domestic procedure, its progress and its special features, viewed as a whole, before the various national instances. In the light of that analysis, the basic principles of the domestic judicial system, such as the protection of the rights of the defence, the principle of legal certainty and the proper conduct of procedure must, where appropriate, be taken into consideration'.[142]

The second step is in fact a proportionality test, in which the national court weighs the importance of the EU right at stake against the scope and purpose of the national procedural rule – for example, legal certainty, rights of the defence, judicial efficiency and party autonomy – taking into account the specific factual circumstances of the case. Literature points out that there is persistent tension in the case law: in some cases, the CJEU relies heavily on the notion that Union law should be effective, whereas in other cases the procedural autonomy of the Member States is stressed. The balancing approach, and the significance of the specific facts of the case, introduce a large amount of uncertainty and refer the assessment of all the facts back to the national courts.[143]

6.3.2.3   Effective judicial protection: conciliatory interpretation

It is settled case law that national courts are required to interpret national law as much as possible in conformity with EU law. This is inherent in the system of Union law as it permits the national court to ensure the full effectiveness of EU law when it determines the dispute before it.[144] Conciliatory interpretation is not restricted to a specific type of rule of EU law: it applies to directives, but also to EU primary legislation, to provisions having direct effect and provisions having indirect effect.[145] A

---

141 Presentation by Dr. Johanna Engström, ERA conference on domestic judicial protection in EU law, Paris, 15 and 16 February 2010.
142 See, for example, CJEU, *Van Schijndel* (1995), C-430/93, para. 19.
143 See, for example, Battjes 2006, pp. 535-537; Craig & De Búrca 2008, pp. 322, 328, Steiner & Woods 2009, Chapter 8: Remedies in national courts, 8.2, 8.3.2, these authors call the case law on this matter 'uncertain'. See also Arnull 2011, p. 58.
144 See, for example, CJEU, *Santex SpA*, 27 February 2003, C-327/00, CJEU, *Kücükdeveci*, 19 January 2010, C-555/07, para. 48.
145 CJEU, *Von Colson und Kamann*, 10 April 1984, C-14/83, paras. 24-28; see Battjes 2006, p. 538, with references.

good example to mention here is the CJEU's judgment in the asylum case of *Elgafaji* (2009),[146] in which the Dutch Council of State referred questions to the CJEU concerning the interpretation of Article 15(C) of the Qualification Directive. Lower national courts and the Council of State had been wrestling with the question of whether this provision should be seen as offering a new type of international protection or whether it could be seen as the EU asylum law counterpart of the national Dutch Aliens Act Articles 29(1) (b) (corresponding to Article 3 ECHR) or 29(1)(d) (offering temporary national protection to asylum seekers coming from countries where extreme violence prevails). The CJEU stressed in its judgments that national courts were obliged to try to reconcile national law provisions with provisions contained in directives:

> 'In the case of the main proceedings it should be borne in mind that, although Article 15(C) of the Directive was expressly transposed into Netherlands law only after the facts giving rise to the dispute before the referring court, it is for that court to seek to carry out an interpretation of national law, in particular of Article 29(1) (b) and (d) of the national Aliens Act which is consistent with the Directive.
>
> According to settled case law, in applying national law, whether the provisions in question were adopted before or after the directive, the national court called upon to interpret it is required to do so, as far as possible, in the light of the wording and the purpose of the directive in order to achieve the result pursued by the latter and thereby comply with the third paragraph of Article 249 EC (…).'[147]

6.3.2.4 *Effective judicial protection: disapplication of national law contrary to EU law with direct effect*

A rule of EU law has direct effect if it is sufficiently precise, meaning that the wording is unequivocal, and unconditional, meaning that no reservations leaving discretion have been made for implementation. This is also referred to as the 'precision and unconditionality test'.[148] The question of whether a rule of EU law has direct effect depends to a large extent on the type of instrument involved. Provisions of regulations, in principle, have direct effect. Provisions of directives can have direct effect when the transposition term has expired and the provision has not been implemented or has been implemented incorrectly, provided that the provision meets the conditions of being sufficiently precise and unconditional.[149] If the EU rule with direct effect conflicts with a rule of national law, the EU rule has precedence in accordance with the principle of the supremacy of EU law and the national rule cannot apply. The CJEU has ruled in numerous cases that

---

146 CJEU, *Elgafaji*, 17 February 2009, C-465/07.
147 CJEU, *Elgafaji*, 17 February 2009, C-465/07, paras. 41 and 42.
148 See, for example, CJEU, *Becker*, 19 January 1982, C-8/81, para. 25.
149 See, again, CJEU, *Becker*, 19 January 1982, C-8/81, para. 25; see also Battjes 2006, pp. 539-542, with references.

'Where application in accordance with the requirements of Community law is not possible, the national court must fully apply Community law and protect the rights conferred thereunder on individuals, if necessary disapplying any provision in so far as its application would, in the circumstances of the case, lead to a result contrary to Community law.'[150]

6.3.2.5   *Effective judicial protection: required intensity of judicial scrutiny*

As will be shown in more detail below, the intensity of judicial scrutiny applied by the CJEU and the required intensity of judicial scrutiny to be offered by national courts in cases within the scope of EU law, depend on the nature of the right at stake, the discretion of the decision making authority, and the further circumstances of the case. In literature, criticism has been voiced that the CJEU has neither announced nor applied in a consistent way a clear standard of judicial scrutiny even when dealing with similar questions, and that explicit indications of a limited review have been followed by what has seemed to be a comprehensive review, whereas in other cases a limited review has been undertaken without justifying it.[151] Certain lines regarding the intensity of judicial scrutiny can be discerned in the Court's jurisprudence, though.

It is important to note that – just like the ECtHR has ruled in its *Zumtobel* doctrine (full jurisdiction doctrine, see Chapter 5, section 5.4.1) – the CJEU has made clear that

'for a tribunal to be able to determine a dispute concerning rights and obligations arising under EU law in accordance with Article 47 of the Charter, that tribunal must have power to consider all the questions of fact and law that are relevant to the case before it'.[152]

This basic consideration makes clear that a court must be able to look at the relevant facts and the relevant legal rules. It does not, however, specify any further how thorough the factual judicial investigation must be. Below I will describe five main categories of cases for which the CJEU has developed different standards of factual judicial scrutiny. Given the specific asylum focus of this study, the description of these categories is not intended to be comprehensive. The aim is only to give certain insight into the notions the CJEU has developed with regard to the intensity of judicial review in relation to different areas of law. With this insight in mind, I will next raise and try to answer the question of what standard of judicial scrutiny the CJEU is most likely to apply in asylum cases.

6.3.2.5.a *Category 1: complex economic assessments*
Illustrative examples of this category are Commission decisions determining the compatibility of certain State aid regimes with the common market according to Article 107, third paragraph, TFEU, a provision which allows the Commission to declare otherwise forbidden State aid compatible with the common market in order to

---

150 See, for example, CJEU, *Solred*, 5 March 1998, C-347/96, para. 30; CJEU, *Engelbrecht*, 26 September 2000, C-262/97, para. 40; CJEU, *Santex SpA*, 27 February 2003, C-327/00, para. 64.
151 Tridimas 2006, p. 447, Fritzsche 2010, p. 380.
152 CJEU, *EU v. Otis and Others*, 6 November 2012, C-199/11, para. 49.

achieve other Union interests. The Commission has to weigh the interests of undistorted competition in the common market against those interests and to determine whether State aid is necessary to achieve them.

In older case law on the compatibility of State aid with the common market, we find considerations of the Court indicating that the review standard was whether the Commission 'misused its powers or committed a manifest error', which means a very superficial judicial touch. For example, in *Exécutif Régional Wallon and SA Glaverbel v. Commission* (1988), the Court considered as follows:

> 'It should be borne in mind that the Commission enjoys a power of appraisal in applying Article 92(3) (C) as well as in applying Article 92(3) (B). It is, in particular, for the Commission to determine whether trading conditions between the Member States are affected by aid to an extent contrary to the common interest. The applicants have supplied no evidence to suggest that in making that assessment the Commission misused its powers or committed a manifest error.'[153]

In later jurisprudence, however, we find considerations indicating a standard of judicial review which encompasses much more than just the misuse of powers or manifest error test. Under this standard, the CJEU also tests compliance with procedural rules, the duty to state reasons, the accuracy of the facts relied on and whether factual assessments show no manifest error. In *Italy v. Commission* (2004), the Court considered as follows:

> 'In the application of Article 92(3) of the Treaty (now: Article 107, paragraph 3, TFEU), the Commission has a wide discretion the exercise of which involves economic and social assessments which must be made in a Community context (…). Judicial review of the manner in which that discretion is exercised is confined to establishing that the rules of procedure and the rules relating to the duty to give reasons have been complied with and to verifying the accuracy of the facts relied on and that there has been no error of law, manifest error of assessment in regard to the facts or misuse of powers (…).'[154]

The same consideration on the standard of judicial review is found in other judgments as well. A few examples are *Schmitz-Gotha Fahrzeugwerke GmbH v. Commission* (2006)[155] and *Société Régie Networks v. Direction de contrôle fiscal Rhône-Alpes Bourgogne* (2008).[156] In these examples, the Court not only proclaimed a more intense scrutiny standard but also really demonstrated a much greater willingness to go into the factual details of the cases.[157] The manifest error of appraisal standard, therefore, seems

---

153 CJEU, *Exécutif Régional Wallon and SA Glaverbel v. Commission*, 8 March 1988, Joined cases 62/87 and 72/87, para. 34.
154 CJEU, *Italy v. Commission*, 29 April 2004, C-372/97, para. 83.
155 CJEU, *Schmitz-Gotha Fahrzeugwerke GmbH v. Commission*, 6 April 2006, T-17/03, para. 41.
156 CJEU, *Société Régie Networks v. Direction de contrôle fiscal Rhône-Alpes Bourgogne*, 22 December 2008, C-333/07, para. 78.
157 See for the same conclusion Fritzsche 2010, p. 378, with references to other authors.

to have evolved over time towards a standard under which a fuller judicial scrutiny takes place.

This is also what Advocate-General Cosmas observed in his Opinion to *French Republic v. Ladbroke Racing Ltd.* (2000),[158] where he stated:

'A tendency may be observed in the case law of the Court of Justice towards a dynamic broadening of judicial review and a strengthening of jurisdiction even in instances where it is necessary to solve complex legal problems.'[159]

Cases concerning mergers and (possible) cartels form another example of this first category of cases. These cases involve a prospective analysis: a prediction of the effect a planned merger or a cartel will have on the market. Here, too, a standard of judicial scrutiny has evolved which indicates that the CJEU looks closely at the facts and the evidence. *Tetra Laval* (2005) was a case in which the Commission had declared the merger of *Tetra Laval* with another company incompatible with the common market. The CJEU stressed in that case that in cases of a prospective economic analysis of a complex nature, a rigorous judicial scrutiny of the factual accuracy, the reliability and the consistency of the evidence must take place. The Court also had to test whether the evidence was comprehensive and whether it supported the Commission's conclusions.[160] The same considerations can be found in other cases involving complex prospective analyses of an economic nature, for example, *Alrosa Company Ltd v. Commission of the European Communities* (a case concerning the question of whether the Alrosa Company had abused a dominant market position, 2007)[161] and *Qualcomm Wireless Business Solutions Europe BV v. Commission of the European Communities* (a case concerning market concentrations and competition, 2009).[162]

The case of *EU v. Otis and others* (2012) concerned a possible cartel between well-known producers of elevators. It is worthwhile quoting the relevant considerations in this judgment as the CJEU was particularly clear about the intensity of its scrutiny in this type of cases. The CJEU considered as follows:

'The defendants maintain, however, that the review of legality carried out by the EU Courts under Article 263 TFEU in the sphere of competition law is insufficient because of, inter alia, the margin of discretion which those Courts allow the Commission in economic matters. The Court of Justice has stated in this connection that, whilst, in areas giving rise to complex economic assessments, the Commission has a margin of discretion with regard to economic matters, that does not mean that the EU Courts must refrain from reviewing the Commission's interpretation of information of an economic nature. Those Courts must, among other things,

---

158 CJEU, *French Republic v. Ladbroke Racing Ltd*, 16 May 2000, C-83/98.
159 Opinion of A-G Cosmas of 13 November 1999 to *French Republic v. Ladbroke Racing Ltd*, 16 May 2000, C-83/98.
160 CJEU, *Tetra Laval* 15 February 2005, C-12/03, paras. 39-43.
161 CJEU, *Alrosa Company Ltd v. Commission of the European Communities*, 11 July 2007, T-170/06, paras. 108, 109.
162 CJEU, *Qualcomm Wireless Business Solutions Europe BV v. Commission of the European Communities*, 19 June 2009, a case concerning market concentrations and competition, T-48/04.

not only establish whether the evidence relied on is factually accurate, reliable and consistent but also ascertain whether that evidence contains all the information which must be taken into account in order to assess a complex situation and whether it is capable of substantiating the conclusions drawn from it. The EU Courts must also establish of their own motion that the Commission has stated reasons for its decision and, among other things, that it has explained the weighting and assessment of the factors taken into account. The EU Courts must also carry out the review of legality incumbent upon them on the basis of the evidence adduced by the applicant in support of the pleas in law put forward. In carrying out such a review, the Courts cannot use the Commission's margin of discretion – either as regards the choice of factors taken into account in the application of the criteria mentioned in the Commission notice entitled 'Guidelines on the method of setting fines imposed pursuant to Article 23(2)(a) of Regulation (EC) No 1/2003' (OJ 2006 C 210, p. 2) or as regards the assessment of those factors – as a basis for dispensing with the conduct of an in-depth review of the law and of the facts. Finally, the review of legality is supplemented by the unlimited jurisdiction which the EU Courts were afforded (…) which is now recognised by Article 31 of Regulation No 1/2003, in accordance with Article 261 TFEU. That jurisdiction empowers the Courts, in addition to carrying out a mere review of the lawfulness of the penalty, to substitute their own appraisal for the Commission's and, consequently, to cancel, reduce or increase the fine or penalty payment imposed.'[163]

In sum, the CJEU made clear in *EU v. Otis* that the scrutiny provided for by the EU Courts in cases concerning complex economic assessments, involve the law and the facts, and means that the EU Courts have the power to thoroughly assess the evidence, to annul the contested decision and to alter the amount of a fine.

6.3.2.5.b *Category 2: cases requiring expert medical or technical knowledge*

A first group of cases within this category consists of cases where difficult medical questions play an important role. The case of *Upjohn* (1999)[164] is described here as it is illustrative and because the CJEU drew an explicit link between the standard of judicial scrutiny applied by it and the standard of judicial scrutiny required from national courts.

Upjohn concerned the revocation by the national licensing authority of a marketing authorisation for a medicine called Triazolam for the treatment of insomnia. This revocation took place after a woman had killed her mother whilst under the influence of this drug. The national licensing authority based the revocation on an expert medical opinion. In the ensuing proceedings before the High Court and the Court of Appeal of England and Wales, Upjohn pleaded that Directive 65/65[165] and, more generally, Union law, required the Member States to establish a procedure for judicial review of decisions taken by the national authorities responsible for marketing authori-

---

163 CJEU, *EU v. Otis and Others*, 6 November 2012, C-199/11, paras. 58-63.
164 CJEU, *Upjohn Ltd v. The Licensing Authority established by the Medicines Act 1968 and Others*, 21 January 1999, C-120/97.
165 Council Directive 65/65/EEC of 26 January 1965 on the approximation of provisions laid down by law, regulation or administrative action relating to proprietary medicinal products, *Official Journal of the European Union*, English Special Edition 1965-1966, p. 20.

sations, empowering national courts to verify, on the basis of a completely fresh, comprehensive assessment of the issues of fact and of law, whether the decision taken had been correct. The CJEU disagreed with Upjohn. The Court first referred to its doctrine of national procedural autonomy subject to equivalence and effectiveness:

> 'It is settled case-law that in the absence of Community rules governing the matter it is for the domestic legal system of each Member State to (...) lay down the detailed procedural rules governing actions for safeguarding rights which individuals derive from Community law, provided, however, that such rules are not less favourable than those governing similar domestic actions (the principle of equivalence) and do not render virtually impossible or excessively difficult the exercise of rights conferred by Community law (the principle of effectiveness)'.[166]

The CJEU then continued:

> 'As regards decisions revoking marketing authorisations taken by the competent national authorities following complex assessments in the medico-pharmacological field, it does not appear that the only appropriate means of preventing the exercise of rights conferred by Community law from being rendered virtually impossible or excessively difficult would be a procedure for judicial review of national decisions revoking marketing authorisations, empowering the competent national courts and tribunals to substitute their assessment of the facts and, in particular, of the scientific evidence relied on in support of the revocation decision for the assessment made by the national authorities competent to revoke such authorisations.'[167]

Importantly, the Court then drew a parallel with the intensity of its own judicial review in situations where an EU authority had made a complex assessment, and concluded that national courts were not obliged under EU law to perform a more extensive review:

> 'According to the Court's case-law, where a Community authority is called upon, in the performance of its duties, to make complex assessments, it enjoys a wide measure of discretion, the exercise of which is subject to a limited judicial review in the course of which the Community judicature may not substitute its assessment of the facts for the assessment made by the authority concerned. Thus, in such cases, the Community judicature must restrict itself to examining the accuracy of the findings of fact and law made by the authority concerned and to verifying, in particular, that the action taken by that authority is not vitiated by a manifest error or a misuse of powers and that it did not clearly exceed the bounds of its discretion. (...)
> Consequently, Community law does not require the Member States to establish a procedure for judicial review of national decisions revoking marketing authorisations, taken pursuant to Directive 65/65 and in the exercise of complex assessments, which involves a more extensive review than that carried out by the Court in similar cases.'[168]

---

166 CJEU, *Upjohn Ltd v. The Licensing Authority established by the Medicines Act 1968 and Others*, 21 January 1999, C-120/97, para. 32.
167 *Ibidem*, para. 33.
168 *Ibidem*, paras. 34.

Finally, and importantly, the CJEU ruled in *Upjohn* that EU law did not require a national court seized of an application for annulment of a decision revoking a marketing authorisation for a medicinal product to take into account any relevant scientific information coming to light after the adoption of the administrative decision. In other words, the national court was not required to perform an *ex nunc* review.[169] In reaching this conclusion, the CJEU took into account the fact that in the event of new material coming to light, the company concerned would still be able to make a fresh application for a new marketing authorisation.[170]

The standard of judicial scrutiny mentioned in *Upjohn* – an *ex tunc* test of accuracy of findings of fact and law, absence of manifest error and misuse of powers – resembles the standard formulated in State aid cases (see above 6.3.2.5.a) which encompasses the same elements. In the State aid cases, however, two more elements were explicitly mentioned as being part of the judicial test: whether rules of procedure had been adhered to by the administrative authority and whether the administrative authority had adhered to its duty to give reasons for its decision.

The importance of a judicial test on compliance with procedural rules is stressed in a second group of cases coming within the category of 'technical knowledge cases', being customs duty exemption cases. In the case of *Technische Universität München* (1991),[171] the national court asked for a preliminary ruling on the legality of a Commission decision denying customs duty exemption for an electron microscope the university had imported from a third country, on the basis that there were apparatuses of equivalent scientific value in the Union. The national court expressed its doubt as to whether the limited judicial review the Union judicature normally adopted in such cases would be in line with the general principle of effective judicial protection. The CJEU held:

> 'It must be stated first of all that, since an administrative procedure entailing complex technical evaluations is involved, the Commission must have a power of appraisal in order to be able to fulfill its tasks. However, where the Community institutions have such a power of appraisal, respect for the rights guaranteed by the Community legal order in administrative procedures is of even more fundamental importance. Those guarantees include, in particular, the duty of the competent institution to examine carefully and impartially all the relevant aspects of the individual case, the right of the person concerned to make his views known and to have an adequately reasoned decision. Only in this way can the Court verify whether the factual and legal elements upon which the exercise of the power of appraisal depends were present.'[172]

6.3.2.5.c Category 3: complex value judgments in staff matters

In staff cases, the CJEU has demonstrated reluctance to examine in detail the factual findings in reports by superiors on the professional performance of staff members. With regard to the intensity of judicial review the Court has, in a number of judgments, formulated the standard as follows:

---

169 *Ibidem*, paras. 38-42.
170 *Ibidem*, paras. 40-41.
171 CJEU, *Technische Universität München*, 21 November 1991, C-269/90.
172 *Ibidem*, paras. 13, 14.

'The Court considers that, according to settled case-law, it does not have the function of determining whether the assessment by the administration of the occupational ability of an official is well founded when such an assessment involves complex value judgments which, by their very nature, are not capable of objective proof. However, those cases concern only value judgments and the Court is required to carry out a review concerning any irregularities of form or procedure, manifest errors of fact vitiating the assessments made by the administration and any misuse of power.'[173]

In other words, if the assessment of the occupational ability of an official involves a complex value judgment, which will often be so in staff cases, the Court does not see it as its task to examine the facts underpinning this assessment and to examine the question of whether these facts form sufficient basis for the decision. The Court does, however, verify whether the procedural rights guarding the decision-making process were upheld.

6.3.2.5.d   Category 4: protection of consumer rights[174]

The leading case here is *Océano Grupo Editorial and Salvat Editores* (2000)[175] concerning the interpretation of Directive 93/13 on unfair terms in consumer contracts.[176] The referring national court asked the CJEU whether the system of protection which this Directive guaranteed to consumers implied that a national court, in deciding a case concerning alleged non-performance of a contract concluded between a seller or supplier and a consumer, must be able to determine, of its own motion, whether a term inserted into that contract was unfair. The CJEU answered this question in the affirmative, emphasizing the weak position of the consumer vis-à-vis the seller or supplier in the context of the conclusion of consumer contracts as well as in the context of possible legal disputes concerning the performance of those contracts, and the ensuing need to correct this imbalance by positive action. The Court phrased it as follows:

'As to the question of whether a court seized of a dispute concerning a contract between a seller or supplier and a consumer may determine of its own motion whether a term of the contract is unfair, it should be noted that the system of protection introduced by the Directive is based on the idea that the consumer is in a weak position vis-à-vis the seller or supplier, as regards both his bargaining power and his level of knowledge. This leads to the consumer agreeing to terms drawn up in advance by the seller or supplier without being able to influence the content of the terms. The aim of Article 6 of the Directive, which requires Member States to lay down that unfair terms are not binding on the consumer, would not be achieved if the consumer were himself obliged to raise the unfair nature of such terms. In disputes where the

---

173 See, for example, CJEU, *Calvin Williams v. the Court of Auditors of the European Communities*, 10 December 1992, T-33/91, para. 43; CJEU, *Latham v Commission*, 9 February 1994, T-3/92, para. 19.

174 See for a more comprehensive discussion and analysis of case law of the CJEU concerning consumer protection Trstenjak & Beysen 2011.

175 CJEU, *Océano Grupo Editorial and Salvat Editores*, 27 June 2000, Joined Cases C-240-244/98.

176 Council Directive 93/13/EEC of 5 April 1993 on unfair terms in consumer contracts, *OJ of the EU* 1993 L 95, p. 29.

amounts involved are often limited, the lawyers' fees may be higher than the amount at stake, which may deter the consumer from contesting the application of an unfair term. While it is the cases that, in a number of Member States, procedural rules enable individuals to defend themselves in such proceedings, there is a real risk that the consumer, particularly because of ignorance of the law, will not challenge the term pleaded against him on the grounds that it is unfair. It follows that effective protection of the consumer may be attained only if the national court acknowledges that it has power to evaluate terms of this kind of its own motion.

Moreover (…) the system of protection laid down by the Directive is based on the notion that the imbalance between the consumer and the seller or supplier may only be corrected by positive action unconnected with the actual parties to the contract. (…).'[177]

In its case law regarding Directive 93/13, the CJEU has not only ruled that national courts must have the power and are obliged to examine, of their own motion, whether a term of a consumer contract is to be regarded as unfair within the meaning of Article 3 of that Directive, which power may not be subjected to a specific limitation period after which the power would become time-barred.[178] National courts seized of an action for annulment of an arbitration award delivered on the basis of an arbitration agreement in a consumer contract must also have the power to determine whether this arbitration agreement must be regarded as unfair under Directive 93/13, and, in the affirmative, to declare the arbitration agreement void and annul the arbitration award, even though the consumer has omitted to plead that invalidity in the course of the arbitration proceedings.[179]

The CJEU has expanded this line of reasoning to other consumer protection directives as well. As a result of this case law, national courts must have the power to apply, of their own motion, the national law provisions transposing Article 11, paragraph 2, of Directive 87/102 concerning the right of the consumer to pursue remedies against the grantor of credit.[180] The same is true with regard to Article 4 of Directive 85/577 concerning the duty of the trader to give notice of the consumer's right of cancellation of a contract negotiated away from business premises, so that, in the event that the consumer has not been duly informed of this right of cancellation, the national court may then raise, of its own motion, an infringement of this duty of the trader.[181]

In this case law, the CJEU has not fundamentally called into question the principle of procedural autonomy of the Member States, but has resorted to a consumer-oriented interpretation of this principle and raised the effectiveness threshold which national procedural rules for the enforcement of the rights under the consumer protection directives must meet.[182] The CJEU has justified the active role of national courts by referring to the aim of strengthening consumer protection, a measure which

---

177 CJEU, *Océano Grupo Editorial and Salvat Editores*, 27 June 2000, Joined Cases C-240-244/98, paras. 25-27.
178 CJEU, *Codifis* 2002, 21 November 2002, C-473/00.
179 CJEU, *Mostaza Claro*, 26 October 2006, C-168/05.
180 CJEU, *Rampion and Godard*, 4 October 2007, C-429/05.
181 CJEU, *Martín Martín*, 17 December 2009, C-227/08.
182 CJEU, *Mostaza Claro*, 26 October 2006, C-168/05, paras. 24-28.

is essential to the accomplishment of the tasks entrusted to the EU, and to raising the standard of living and the quality of life in its territory.[183] In short, the weak position of the consumer vis-à-vis the seller or supplier and the importance of the public interest underlying consumer protection justifies a firm and active role for national courts.[184]

6.3.2.5.e Category 5: restrictions of fundamental freedoms of EU citizens

The CJEU has dealt with numerous cases concerning the entry of, refusal of a residence permit to, or (planned) expulsion of migrated EU citizens for reasons of public order or public security. In these cases it has gradually developed a specific standard of judicial scrutiny to be applied by national courts. Until April 2006, the Directive regulating the entry of, refusal of a residence permit to, or (planned) expulsion of migrated EU citizens for reasons of public order or public security was Directive 64/221/EC.[185] Article 8 of this Directive provided that the person concerned should have the same legal remedies in respect of any decision concerning entry or refusal of the renewal of a residence permit or expulsion from the territory as were available to nationals of the State concerned in respect of acts of the administration. Article 9 stipulated, in short, that where the national legal system did not provide for a right of appeal to a court or where such appeal would only extend to the legal validity (no appeal on the facts, but only on points of law), the administrative authority had to obtain, prior to the decision, an opinion from an independent competent authority. In a number of judgments the CJEU further explained that, where the national right of appeal was limited only to the legal validity (not factual validity) of the administrative decision, the purpose of the intervention of the authority referred to in Article 9 was to enable an

> 'Exhaustive examination of all the facts and circumstances, including the expediency of the proposed measure, to be carried out before the decision is finally taken.'[186]

In other words, where national law allowed for a judicial review on points of law only, Article 9 of the Directive required an additional national legal remedy allowing for a full review on all the relevant points of law and fact. In the words of the CJEU, the Article 9-procedure was aimed at 'mitigating the effect of deficiencies in the available national legal remedies'.[187] From this qualification – deficiency – it may be

---

183 *Ibidem*, paras. 37, 38.
184 CJEU, *Pannon GSM*, 4 June 2009, C-243/08, para. 31.
185 Council Directive 64/221/EC of 25 February 1964 on the co-ordination of special measures concerning the movement and residence of foreign nationals justified on grounds of public policy, public security of public health, *OJ of the EU* 1963-1964, p.117. This Directive no longer exists; on 30 April 2006, it was replaced by Directive 2004/38/EC of the European Parliament and the Council of 29 April 2004 on the right of citizens of the Union and their family members to move and reside freely within the territory of the Member States, *OJ of the EU*,L 158, 30 April 2004, pp. 77-123.
186 CJEU, *Regina v Secretary of State for Home Affairs*, ex parte *Santillo,* 22 May 1980, Case 131/79, para. 12; CJEU, *Adoui andCornuaille* 18 May 1982, C-115 and 116/81, para. 15; CJEU, *R v Secretary of State for the Home Department*, ex parte *Gallagher* 30 November 1995, Case C-175/94, para. 17; CJEU, *Shingara and Radiom*, 17 June 1997, C-65 and C-111/95, paras. 33-37.
187 CJEU, *Shingara and Radiom*, 17 June 1997, C-65 and C-111/95, para. 35.

inferred that, in cases concerning restrictions on the right of free movement of Union citizens, the CJEU regards a national judicial review on only points of law as deficient and, therefore, inappropriate. In other words, full judicial review on points of fact and points of law is the standard in these cases.[188]

In *Olazabal* (2002), a case which concerned the legality of measures limiting the Spanish citizen Olazabal's rights of residence in France to only a part of French territory, the CJEU clarified that this standard of judicial scrutiny also meant that the national court had to determine whether the measure restricting the right to free movement complied with the principle of proportionality. The proportionality test to be performed by the national court was whether the measure did in fact relate to individual conduct which constituted a genuine and sufficiently serious threat to public order or public security.[189] In *Olazabal*, the Court also shed light on the reason behind this standard of full judicial scrutiny on facts, law and proportionality. The reason why such judicial scrutiny was required was that one of the fundamental freedoms guaranteed by EU law – the freedom of movement of EU citizens – was at stake.[190]

Two years after *Olazabal*, the Court explained in the case of *Orfanopoulos and Oliveiri* (2004)[191] that the standard of full judicial scrutiny on facts, law and proportionality also meant that national courts must take into consideration factual matters which had occurred after the final decision of the administrative authority and which might have pointed to the cessation or substantial diminution of the threat which the conduct of the person constituted to public policy. In other words, *ex nunc* judicial scrutiny was required.[192] In *Orfanopoulos*, a case concerning the expulsion from Germany of a Greek and Italian citizen on grounds of public order, the national court asked whether Article 3 of Directive 64/221 precluded a national practice whereby the courts of a Member State could not take into consideration, in reviewing the lawfulness of the expulsion of a national of another Member State, factual matters and a positive development in that person which had occurred after the final decision of the competent authorities. Under the national German system, the courts could base their decisions on evidence which had become available after the final decision had been taken by the administration only where such evidence would support the administrative decision. Both Orfanopoulos and Oliveri invoked, at the national judicial stage, new facts and circumstances (facts that came up after the administrative decision). Oliveri referred to the fact that he was HIV-infected.

The CJEU first reiterated its standard consideration on national procedural autonomy limited by equality and effectiveness.[193] It then moved on to rule as follows with regard to German judicial practice:

---

188 See also Brouwer 2006, pp. 276-281.
189 CJEU, *Olazabal*, 26 November 2002, C-100/01, para. 44.
190 *Ibidem*, para. 43.
191 CJEU, *Orfanopoulos and Oliveiri*, 29 April 2004, C-482/01 and C-493/01.
192 *Ibidem*, paras. 72-82.
193 *Ibidem*, para. 80.

'A national practice such as that described in the order for reference is liable to adversely affect the right to freedom of movement to which nationals of the Member States are entitled and particularly their right not to be subjected to expulsion measures save in the extreme cases provided for by Directive 64/221. That is especially so if a lengthy period has elapsed between the date of the decision to expel the person concerned and that of the review of that decision by the competent court.

In the light of the foregoing, the reply to the second question must be that Article 3 of Directive 64/221 precludes a national practice whereby the national courts may not take into consideration, in reviewing the lawfulness of the expulsion of a national of another Member State, factual matters which occurred after the final decision of the competent authorities which may point to the cessation or the substantial diminution of the present threat which the conduct of the person concerned constitutes to the requirements of public policy. That is so, above all, if a lengthy period has elapsed between the date of the expulsion order and that of the review of that decision by the competent court.'[194]

For EU citizens and their family members migrating with them, the standard of full judicial scrutiny on facts, law and proportionality has now been codified in Article 31, paragraph 3 of Directive 2004/38, which reads:

'The redress procedures shall allow for an examination of the legality of the decision, as well as of the facts and circumstances on which the proposed measure is based. They shall ensure that the decision is not disproportionate, particularly in view of the requirements laid down in Article 28.'[195]

The CJEU has subsequently extended this standard of full and *ex nunc* judicial scrutiny on facts, law and proportionality to Turkish workers and their family members who enjoy the rights of Decision 1/80 of the Association Council of 19 September 1980 on the development of the Association between the EU and Turkey (Decision 1/80) or the rights or freedoms under the Agreement Creating An Association Between The Republic of Turkey and the European Economic Community of 1963 (The Association Agreement).[196]

6.3.2.5.f Expected standard of judicial scrutiny in asylum cases

The CJEU has so far not had an occasion to express itself extensively on issues relating to the intensity of national judicial review in asylum cases. At this moment in time, I can, therefore, only make a preliminary estimation as to whether it will follow one (or more) of the jurisprudential lines described above and declare one (or more) of the standards described above regarding the intensity of judicial scrutiny applicable to asylum cases. Interestingly, asylum cases are characterised by features which create

---

194 *Ibidem*, paras. 81-82.
195 Article 31(3) of Council Directive 2004/38/EC of 29 April 2004 on the right of citizens of the Union and their family members to move and reside freely within the territory of the Member States.
196 CJEU, *Cetinkaya*, 11 November 2004, C-467/02, para. 64: *ex nunc* review is required; CJEU, *Dörr and Ünal*, 2 June 2005, C-136/03, paras. 47, 67: the procedural guaranteees of Article 9(1) of Directive 64/221 also apply to Turks enjoying the rights of Decision 1/80.

a parallel with each of the categories of cases described above. It is, therefore, not only possible, but also feasible and useful to make such estimation.

First, asylum cases feature a parallel with category 1 cases in which a complex retro-prospective appraisal is made. In asylum cases, too, a complex retro-prospective analysis is made. Based on the flight narrative concerning past events and based on a taxation of the current situation the central question to be answered is whether the asylum seeker runs a risk of persecution or torture or inhuman or degrading treatment upon expulsion to the country of origin. Given this parallel, it would not be surprising if the CJEU drew on the standard that it

> 'must not only (...) establish whether the evidence relied on is factually accurate, reliable and consistent but also whether that evidence contains all the information which must be taken into account in order to assess a complex situation and whether it is capable of substantiating the conclusions drawn from it. Such a review is all the more necessary in the case of a prospective analysis required (...). Thus, the Court (...) was right to find (...) that the [administrative authority's] analysis (...) calls for a close examination of the circumstances which are relevant (...). A prospective analysis (...) must be carried out with great care since it does not entail the examination of past events – for which often many items of evidence are available which make it possible to understand the causes – or of current events, but rather a prediction of events which are more or less likely to occur in future (...).'[197]

And that it is also the CJEU's task

> 'to establish that the rules of procedure and the rules relating to the duty to give reasons have been complied with and to verifying the accuracy of the facts relied on and that there has been no error of law, manifest error of assessment in regard to the facts or misuse of powers (...).'[198]

This would mean an intense scrutiny of the evidence relied on by both parties, the conclusions parties draw from this evidence, the rules of procedure, possible error of law, manifest error of factual assessment and, finally, misuse of powers.

A second parallel can be drawn between asylum cases and category 4 cases concerning consumer rights. In these cases, the CJEU has found that the weak position of the consumer vis-à-vis the seller or supplier and the importance of the public interest underlying consumer protection justify a firm and active role for national courts.[199] It may be argued that asylum seekers are often in a similarly weak position vis-à-vis the administrative decision maker for different reasons. First, because of the difficult evidentiary position in which asylum seekers will often find themselves: it will often be difficult to substantiate asylum claims with direct documentary evidence

---

197 CJEU, *Tetra Laval*, 15 February 2005, C-12/03, paras. 39-43.
198 CJEU, *Italy v. Commission*, 29 April 2004, C-372/97, para. 83.
199 CJEU, *Pannon GSM*, 4 June 2009, C-243/08, para. 31.

and to do this within a short time frame.[200] Second, because asylum seekers are vulnerable: they are foreigners who do not normally speak the language of the country of refuge, who have only recently arrived in that country, who are very much dependent on legal assistance for bringing an asylum claim and who are often also vulnerable in other respects. Given this imbalance between the parties (which is perhaps even greater than the imbalance between consumer and seller or supplier), the CJEU may probably require national courts to take an active role when it comes to fact finding and evidence gathering. It will probably also be inspired by the active role in the gathering and verification of facts played by the ECtHR in a number of asylum cases.[201]

A third parallel can be drawn with category 3-cases concerning complex value judgments in staff matters. It may be argued that especially assessment of the credibility of the statements of asylum seekers in fact involves a complex value judgment with a strong subjective component. The words used by Judge Thomassen in her concurring opinion to the judgment in *Said v. the Netherlands* (2005) spring to mind:

> 'What complicates the examination of the present and similar cases, however, is that the facts – as related by the person concerned – can often not, or can only partially, be established. This cannot always be held against that individual, because one can readily understand that adducing proof of the facts is often a difficult task. At the same time, it is important to recognise that persons who have fabricated the reasons for their flight should not be able to benefit from asylum laws, because this could discredit the very important humanitarian right to asylum. Insufficient facts will often result in the judge having to assess the reliability of the account given by the person concerned. Bearing in mind the subjective elements which are inherent in making such an assessment, judges will to a certain extent, in an area where the most fundamental human rights are at stake, find themselves on thin ice.'[202]

Drawing on this parallel, the CJEU may probably see reasons to rule that it is not the task of the Court itself, and not the task of national courts, to examine the facts underpinning the assessment of credibility and to examine the question of whether these facts form sufficient basis for the decision.

There is a fourth parallel between asylum cases and category 5-cases concerning restrictions of fundamental freedoms of EU citizens. In these category 5-cases, the CJEU has developed the intense standard of full and *ex nunc* judicial scrutiny on facts, law and proportionality by national courts because the EU right at stake in such cases – the freedom of movement of EU citizens – constitutes a 'fundamental freedom of

---

200 See on the difficult evidentiary position of asylum seekers the previous Chapters 2, 3, 4 and 5: sections on admission of evidence, possible types and sources of evidence, minimum quantity and quality of evidence.

201 See Chapter 5, Part 2, the section on judicial application of investigative powers. Examples of cases where the ECtHR played a very active role are ECtHR, *N. v. Finland*, 26 July 2005, Appl. No. 38885/02; ECtHR, *Salah Sheekh v. the Netherlands*, 11 January 2007, Appl. No. 1948/04; ECtHR, *Shamayev and others v. Georgia and Russia*, 12 April 2005, Appl. No. 36378/02.

202 Concurring opinion to the judgment of the ECtHR in the case of *Said v. the Netherlands*, 5 July 2005, Appl. No. 2345/02.

EU law'.[203] Similarly, the right to asylum laid down in Article 18 of the Charter is a fundamental right; in its judgment in *Abdulla* (2010),[204] the CJEU made clear that in asylum cases

'The integrity of human beings and individual freedoms, matters belonging to the *fundamental values of the Union* (italics author) are at stake'.[205]

The similar terminology used – the term 'fundamental freedom' in EU citizen migration cases and the term 'fundamental value' in asylum cases – makes clear that, although the right of free movement of EU citizens and the right to asylum are of a different nature, the CJEU regards both as very important EU rights. Given the fundamental nature of the right at stake, it would not be surprising if the CJEU extended the standard of full and *ex nunc* national judicial scrutiny to asylum cases. There is yet another reason why it seems likely that the CJEU will extend the standard of full and *ex nunc* judicial scrutiny on facts, law and proportionality to asylum cases. This standard comes close to the requirement for full jurisdiction flowing from Article 6, first paragraph, ECHR and the requirement for rigorous scrutiny flowing from Articles 3 and 13 ECHR. As was explained above, the scrutiny performed by the ECtHR under Article 3 has been incorporated into EU asylum law via Article 19, second paragraph, in conjunction with Article 52, third paragraph, of the Charter, and the full jurisdiction and rigorous scrutiny requirements flowing from Articles 6 and 13 ECHR have been incorporated into Union law via Article 47 in conjunction with Article 52, third paragraph, of the Charter.[206] Article 52, third paragraph, stipulates, in short, that Charter rights corresponding to ECHR rights are in meaning and scope the same as their ECHR counterparts, but that Charter rights may provide more extensive protection. It follows that judicial protection offered under EU law may not fall below the standards of judicial protection offered by the ECtHR. A first confirmation for this line of reasoning may be found in the recent judgment, *Samba Diouf* (2011), in which the CJEU ruled that the final decision on an asylum claim must be the subject of a thorough review on the merits of the claim by the national court.[207] It is also interesting to note that in the recast proposal for the new Procedures Directive Article 41, third paragraph, stipulates the following:

'Member States shall ensure that the effective remedy referred to in paragraph 1 provides for a full examination of both facts and points of law, including an *ex nunc* examination of the inter-

---

203 See CJEU, *Olazabal*, 26 November 2002, C-100/01, para. 43.
204 CJEU, *Abdulla*, 2 March 2010, C-175/08, C-176/08, C-178/08 and C-179/08.
205 *Ibidem*, para. 90.
206 See for the same conclusion CJEU, *Elgafaji*, 17 February 2009, C-465/07, para. 28: '(...) the fundamental right guaranteed under Article 3 of the ECHR forms part of the general principles of Community law, observance of which is ensured by the Court, and (...) the case law of the European Court of Human Rights is taken into consideration in interpreting the scope of that right in the Community legal order (...).'
207 CJEU, *Samba Diouf*, 28 July 2011, C-69/10, paras. 56, 61.

national protection needs (…), at least in appeal procedures before a court or tribunal of first instance.'[208]

This recast proposal was, at the time of completion of this chapter, still the subject of negotiations and it is so far unknown whether this text will be included in the new Procedures Directive. The proposed text does, however, indicate that the drafters sought inspiration from both the case law of the ECtHR and the case law of the CJEU in cases concerning the migration of EU and Turkish citizens and deemed it necessary to transpose the standard of judicial scrutiny developed in that case law into the asylum context.

Finally, a small category of asylum cases feature a certain parallel with category 2-cases requiring expert medical and/or technical knowledge. We may think, for example, of cases in which an asylum request has been refused because of doubt as to the asylum seeker's stated minority (age under 18) and in which a medical age test has been performed on the instigation of the administrative decision maker. Another example would be the so-called medical asylum cases – cases in which seriously ill individuals claim asylum abroad because they fear death due to the absence of medical care facilities in their home countries. In such cases, the administrative decision maker often orders medical examinations to be carried out. It is possible that in such special asylum cases the CJEU will resort to the standard developed in category 2 and will regard as appropriate a somewhat more limited factual judicial scrutiny, coupled with close judicial scrutiny of compliance with procedural rules.

6.3.2.5.g *Provisions on judicial scrutiny in secondary EU asylum law*

Secondary EU asylum law contains different provisions on national legal remedies. Three different types of clauses can be distinguished:

- Provisions granting a 'right to mount a legal challenge', for example, Article 29 of the Temporary Protection Directive;[209]
- Provisions granting a 'right to appeal against decisions', for example, Article 21, first paragraph, of the Reception Conditions Directive,[210] and Article 19, second paragraph, of the Dublin Regulation;[211]

---

208 COM (2009) 554 final 21 October 2009, 2009/0165 (COD). The recast proposal can be found integrally in Hailbronner 2010, p. 1311-1350. It can also be found in the EUR-lex database: http://eur-lex.europa.eu, under Preparatory documents, COM documents.

209 Article 29 of Directive 2001/55/EC on Minimum Standards for Temporary Protection stipulates: 'Persons who have been excluded from the benefit of temporary protection by a Member State have the right to mount a legal challenge in this Member State.'

210 Article 21, para. 1, of Directive 2003/9/EC on Minimum Standards for the Reception of Asylum Seekers stipulates: 'Negative decisions relating to the granting of benefits under this Directive or decisions taken under Article 7 (decisions with regard to their residence and freedom of movement) which affect asylum seekers individually may be the subject of an appeal within the procedures laid down in the national law. The Member States must at least in the last instance grant the asylum seeker the right of appeal or review before a judicial body.'

211 Article 19, para. 2, of Regulation 343/2003/EC (Dublin II) stipulates: 'This decision (the decision not to examine an asylum application) may be subject to an appeal or a review. Appeal or review concerning this decision shall not suspend the implementation of the transfer unless the courts or competent bodies so decide on a case by case basis if national legislation allows for this.'

- Provisions granting a 'right to an effective remedy before a court or tribunal', for example, Article 39 of the Procedures Directive.[212]

The directives on migration (regular migration, not asylum) also contain differently worded provisions on national legal protection. The 'right to mount a legal challenge' can be found in Article 18 of Directive 2003/86/EC on the right to family reunification. The 'right to appeal against decisions' can be found in Article 13, third paragraph, of Regulation 562/2006, also known as the Schengen Borders Code. The third type found in the asylum instruments – the 'right to an effective remedy' – is not present in the migration instruments. Instead, we see a different kind of provision in Directive 2004/38 on the right of citizens of the Union and their family members to move and reside freely within the territory of the Member States. Article 31 of this Directive contains a right of access to judicial and administrative redress procedures, which allow for an examination of the legality of the decision, as well as of the facts and circumstances on which the proposed measure is based, and which ensure that the decision is not disproportionate. That standard is the codification of the principle of full judicial scrutiny on facts, law and proportionality discussed above in section 6.3.2.5.e, developed in the case law concerning the migration of EU citizens, their co-migrating third-country family members, and Turkish migrants who enjoy the rights of Decision 1/80 of the EEC-Turkey Association Council.

The legislative history of the provisions on legal remedies in secondary EU asylum law demonstrates that, in the negotiations following the original text proposals, serious attempts were made by representatives of the EU Member States to keep national courts away from negative asylum decisions or to water down the intensity of judicial scrutiny of negative asylum decisions. The original text of Article 29 of the Temporary Protection Directive stated that persons excluded from the benefit of temporary protection were 'entitled to seek redress in the courts' of the Member State concerned.[213] The amended text – persons excluded from temporary protection 'shall be entitled to legal challenge' instead of 'shall be entitled to seek redress in the courts' – occurred for the first time in the Introductory Note from the Council Secretariat to the Permanent Representatives Committee of 18 April 2001, unfortunately without any footnotes explaining the amendment.[214] This Note, however, mentioned that, in between the Council sessions, the Permanent Representatives Committee (COREPER)[215] had been working on the text of the provisions, in order to obtain an

---

212 Article 39, paras. 1 and 2 of Directive 2005/85/EC on Minimum Standards for Asylum Procedures stipulate: 'Member States shall ensure that applicants for asylum have the right to an effective remedy before a court or tribunal, against the following (…) (author: follows a list of all negative decisions on an asylum application). Member States shall provide for time-limits and other necessary rules for the applicant to exercise his/her right to an effective remedy pursuant to paragraph 1.'

213 COM(2000)0303.

214 In many of these reports, text amendments are indicated in bold and explanations are provided in footnotes. Unfortunately, not all amendments are made explicit and explained in this way.

215 Article 240 TFEU lays down the legal basis of COREPER, the Committee of Permanent Representatives in the EU, made up of the head or deputy head of missions from the EU member states in Brussels. The functioning of COREPER is very well explained at http://www.europa-nu.nl/id/vga3ex9vr2z9/comite_van_permanente_vertegenwoordigers.

agreement. This leads to the conclusion that the amendment was brought about by the Permanent Representatives of the Member States, obviously in an attempt to maintain the option of remedies other than judicial control, as a 'legal challenge' includes both administrative and judicial remedies.[216] It is interesting to mention here that a similar development occurred in the history of the provisions granting a 'right to mount a legal challenge' in the migration directives. Article 18 of Directive 2003/86/EC on the right to family reunification, which, just like Article 29 of the Temporary Protection Directive, contains the 'right to mount a legal challenge' (against a decision rejecting family reunification), has a similar drafting history. The first two proposals granted a 'right to apply to the courts of the Member State concerned'[217] and the third proposal even granted a 'de facto and de jure right to apply to the courts'.[218] Here, too, the text was amended in the course of the negotiations. It was obviously thought that a 'right to mount a legal challenge' would make it allowable to have (only) administrative remedies and keep national courts away from refusals of family reunification. Guèvremont (2009) makes clear in her dissertation that in the process of negotiations on the Family Reunification Directive it became clear that in Austria, Ireland and Sweden no judicial remedies existed against refusals of family reunification.[219] By amending the text to the vague 'right to mount a legal challenge', the negotiators clearly attempted to restrict the impact of the Directive on existing national remedies.

The legislative history of Article 19, second paragraph, of the Dublin Regulation demonstrates the same transformation. The initial text in the initial legislative proposal from the Commission was different and stipulated that 'appeal from the decision shall lie to the courts'.[220] The amended text 'the decision may be subject to an appeal or a review' instead of 'appeal from the decision shall lie at the courts' appeared for the first time in the Report on the outcome of the proceedings of the Asylum Working Party[221] of 8, 9 and 17 May 2002.[222] The Report contained no clarifications explaining the amendment.[223] The amendment had obviously been brought about by the members of the Asylum Working Party of the Council of the EU in an attempt to maintain the option of remedies other than judicial control. As Asylum

---

216 Hailbronner 2010, p. 868.
217 COM (1999) 638 final, Article 16; COM (2000) 624 final, Article 16.
218 COM (2002) 225 final, Article 18.
219 Guèvremont 2009, pp. 231-235.
220 COM(2001)0447, Article 20(2), the legislative observatory.
221 The Asylum Working Party of the Council of the EU deals with the proposed legal instruments aimed at creating a common European system of asylum. The Working Party prepares all asylum issues before they go to COREPER and then on to ministerial level. The Working Party comprises senior officials, either from the Member States' permanent representations in Brussels or from national ministries.
    See: http://www.europa-nu.nl/id/vga3ex9vr2z9/comite_van_permanente_vertegenwoordigers.
222 Outcome of proceedings of the Asylum Working Party, Report of 8, 9 and 17 May 2002, No. 8752/02. This report was found in the following way on the internet: Radboud Universiteit Nijmegen, European Documentation Centre, Institutions, Council of the EU, Documents, Advanced Search, interinstitutional number CNS 2001/0182.
223 In many of these reports, text amendments are indicated in bold and explanations are provided in footnotes. Unfortunately, not all amendments are made explicit and explained in this way.

Working Party deliberations and reports thereof are not open to the public, it cannot be traced any further whether there were any other or additional reasons behind the amendment.

In contrast to the Temporary Protection Directive and the Dublin Regulation, where amendments were made to provisions on national legal remedies in an attempt to maintain the option of remedies other than judicial control, the text of Article 39, first paragraph, of the Asylum Procedures Directive was not amended in the same way. What did occur, however, was a different type of amendment. The initial Commission proposal was based on the notion of a two-tier review/judicial appeal system. The first paragraph of Article 38 stated that 'Member States shall ensure that in all cases applicants for asylum have a right to further appeal to the Appellate Court'. It stipulated, in Article 38, second paragraph, that 'if the reviewing body is an administrative or quasi-judicial body, Member States shall ensure that the Appellate Court has the power to examine decisions on both facts and points of law. If the reviewing body is a judicial body, Member States may decide that the Appellate Court has to limit its examination of decisions to points of law'. According to the explanation by the Commission, the idea behind this text was that there should be at least one judicial examination on both facts and points of law.[224] The first legislative stage after this modified proposal by the Commission in which the addition 'examination on both facts and points of law' no longer formed part of the text was the so-called Council Re-consultation, the result of which was laid down in a report of 9 November 2004.[225] In this report, the text of Article 38 spoke of the right to an effective remedy before a court, without specifying that the judicial scrutiny should encompass both points of fact and points of law. The report did not explain the reasons behind the amendment but it follows that the intention of the amendment must have been to create room for forms of judicial scrutiny not encompassing review of the facts.

It may be argued that the described attempts to keep national courts away from negative asylum decisions or to water down the intensity of judicial scrutiny over negative asylum decisions were made in vain.[226] Secondary EU law provisions have to be interpreted in accordance with higher ranking EU law provisions.[227] Article 47 of the Charter is such a higher ranking EU law provision as since the entry into force of the Treaty of Lisbon the Charter has been binding primary Union law.[228] As was explained above in section 6.1.3.2, the legal status of the Charter was very different at

---

224 COM 2000/0578.

225 Council Re-consultation No. 14203/2004.

226 See for the same conclusion Brouwer 2007.

227 See, for example, CJEU, *Deticek*, 23 December 2009, C-403/09, paras. 53-55. The reference for a preliminary ruling in this case concerned the interpretation of Article 20 of Council Regulation (EC) No 2201/2003 of 27 November 2003 concerning jurisdiction and the recognition and enforcement of judgments in matrimonial matters and the matters of parental responsibility, repealing Regulation (EC) No. 1347/2000 (OJ 2003 L 338, p. 1). The CJEU ruled, in paras. 53-55, that Article 20 of Regulation No. 2201/2003 must be interpreted in such a way that respect is paid to the fundamental right of the child set out in Article 24(3) of the Charter, to maintain on a regular basis a personal relationship and direct contact with both parents.

228 Article 6, para. 1, part 1, TEU reads: 'The Union recognises the rights, freedoms and principles set out in the Charter of Fundamental Rights of the European Union of 7 December 2000, as adapted at Strasbourg, on 12 December 2007, which shall have the same legal value as the Treaties.'

the time of the negotiations on the secondary asylum instruments. In that period the Charter was no more than a non-binding solemn declaration of principles. Obviously, at that time, the negotiators who drafted the texts of the secondary EU law asylum instruments did not foresee that the Charter's legal status would change so drastically in the near future. Article 47 of the Charter guarantees the right to an effective remedy before a judicial body: a court or tribunal, and not an administrative body, and requires an intense form of judicial scrutiny when fundamental rights are at stake. When interpreting secondary law provisions, it must also be ensured that there is harmony with the higher ranking general principle of effective judicial protection, which principle is now codified in Article 47 of the Charter.[229]

6.4 Provisions on evidentiary issues in secondary EU asylum law

6.4.1 Preliminary remarks

When interpreting secondary Union law provisions on evidentiary issues, the standards and principles developed by the UNHCR, the HRC, the ComAT and the ECtHR must constantly be kept in mind for two reasons. First, EU secondary law must be interpreted in such a way that there is harmony with the relevant primary law provisions, being Articles 18, 19 and 47 of the Charter.[230] Above it has been explained that Articles 18, 19 and 47 of the Charter encompass the standards on judicial scrutiny and evidence developed by the UNHCR, the HRC, the ComAT and the ECtHR.

Second, Article 78 TFEU (old Article 63 TEC) stipulates that the secondary EU asylum legislation mentioned above must be in accordance with the RC as well as the other relevant treaties, including the ECHR, the ICCPR and the CAT.[231] It must also be kept in mind that EU secondary asylum law does not provide an exhaustive regulation for all possible issues of evidence. It does not regulate, for example, the appreciation and evaluation of evidence.[232] Also unregulated is the point in time for the assessment of the risk. With regard to the issues that are not regulated, national courts, and the CJEU as well, will have to fall back on the standards and principles de-

---

229 CJEU, *Siples Srl, in liquidation*, 11 January 2001, C-226/99, paras. 16-20.
230 See, for example, CJEU, *Deticek*, 23 December 2009, C-403/09, paras. 53-55. The reference for a preliminary ruling in this case concerned the interpretation of Article 20 of Council Regulation (EC) No. 2201/2003 of 27 November 2003 concerning jurisdiction and the recognition and enforcement of judgments in matrimonial matters and the matters of parental responsibility, repealing Regulation (EC) No. 1347/2000 (OJ 2003 L 338, p. 1). The CJEU ruled, in paras. 53-55, that Article 20 of Regulation No. 2201/2003 must be interpreted in such a way that respect is paid to the fundamental right of the child set out in Article 24(3) of the Charter, to maintain on a regular basis a personal relationship and direct contact with both parents.
231 Article 78, first paragraph, TFEU, states: 'The Union shall develop a common policy on asylum, subsidiary protection and temporary protection with a view to offering appropriate status to any third-country national requiring international protection and ensuring compliance with the principle of *non-refoulement*. This policy must be in accordance with the Geneva Convention of 28 July 1951 and the Protocol of 31 January 1967 relating to the status of refugees, and other relevant treaties.'
232 See for the same conclusion Noll 2005.

veloped under the RC, the ICCPR, the CAT and the ECHR, and, in addition, may draw inspiration from the CJEU's case law in other areas, as long as no asylum case law is available on such issues. The relevant secondary EU law provisions are ana-lysed below, with the aid of the aspects of evidence and judicial scrutiny introduced in Chapter 1. Where possible, the jurisprudence of the CJEU in both asylum cases and other areas is used as a source of interpretation.

6.4.2   Standard of proof

Article 2, sub paragraph d, of the EU Qualification Directive defines a refugee as a third-country national who, owing to a well-founded fear of being persecuted for reasons of race, religion, nationality, political opinion or membership of a particular social group, is outside the country of nationality and is unable or, owing to such fear, unwilling to avail himself or herself of the protection of that country, or a stateless person, who, being outside of the country of former habitual residence for the same reasons, is unable or, owing to such fear, unwilling to return to it.[233] The term 'well-founded fear' in the definition corresponds to the wording of the refugee definition in the RC.

Article 2, sub paragraph f, of the EU Qualification Directive qualifies a person eligible for subsidiary protection as an individual in respect of whom substantial grounds have been shown for believing that the person concerned would face a real risk of suffering serious harm.[234] This phrase is taken from the ECtHR's constant case law under Article 3, in which that Court developed the standard that 'substantial grounds have been shown for believing that the individual concerned, if expelled, faces a real risk of being subjected to torture or to inhuman or degrading treatment or punishment'.[235]

In the Commission Proposal the standard of proof was further elaborated: the necessary level of risk was defined as a 'reasonable possibility'. The applicant's fear of being persecuted or exposed to serious harm had to be objectively established by determining whether there was a 'reasonable possibility' that he or she would be per-secuted or otherwise subjected to serious harm if returned to the country of origin. However, this standard was deleted during the negotiation process as Member States could not agree on it. For this reason, the Directive does not further elaborate on the standard 'well-founded fear', or on the standard of 'real risk'.[236]

Article 78 TFEU (old Article 63 TEC) stipulates that the secondary EU asylum legislation mentioned above must be in accordance with the RC as well as other rele-vant treaties (ECHR, ICCPR, CAT).[237] This implies that the standards of proof laid

---

233 Article 2, sub d, of the Qualification Directive (Directive 2011/95/EU of 13 December 2011).
234 Article 2, sub f, of the Qualification Directive (Directive 2011/95/EU of 13 December 2011).
235 We find this standard of proof in all the judgments of the ECtHR concerning the expulsion of asy-lum seekers, from the first case of ECtHR, *Cruz Varas v. Sweden*, 20 March 1991, Appl. No. 15576/89, para. 69, up to later judgments such as ECtHR, *R.C. v. Sweden*, 9 March 2010, Appl. No. 41827/07, para. 48. This standard also explicitly features in many admissibility decisions.
236 Council doc. No. 12199/02, p. 8. See also Battjes 2006, pp. 224, 225, and Hailbronner 2010, p. 1026.
237 Article 78, first paragraph, TFEU, states: 'The Union shall develop a common policy on asylum, subsidiary protection and temporary protection with a view to offering appropriate status to any

$\rightarrow$

down in Article 2, sub d and sub f, must be interpreted in such a way that they do not fall below the standards developed under these treaties, while EU law may offer more protection by creating a lower threshold. As was made clear in Chapter 2, the standard of proof under the RC as developed by the UNHCR is that it must be established, *to a reasonable degree* that, upon expulsion, the claimant's life or freedom would be threatened.[238] In its Note on Burden and Standard of Proof in Refugee Claims,[239] the UNHCR has made clear that the determination of refugee status does not purport to identify refugees as a matter of certainty, but as a matter of likelihood. It is not required to prove well-foundedness conclusively beyond doubt, or even that persecution is more probable than not. To establish 'well-foundedness', persecution must be proved to be *reasonably possible*.[240] It was exactly this standard of proof – reasonably possible – that was deleted from the Commission Proposal text in the process of the negotiations on the Qualification Directive. The negotiators obviously did not realise, at the time of deleting the 'reasonably possible standard', that this very standard would enter EU asylum law anyway via Article 78 TFEU in conjunction with the standard developed by the UNHCR under the RC.

As the standard in Article 2, sub paragraph f, is taken literally from the ECtHR's case law under Article 3, it is only logical, in the light of Article 78 TFEU, to resort to the standard of proof developed by the ECtHR. That standard is that the risk is real and not fictional, that it is personal (relates to the individual), and that it is foreseeable. The risk does not need to be certain or highly probable,[241] but it must exceed the mere possibility of being subjected to proscribed ill-treatment.[242]

6.4.3   Burden of proof

Article 4 of the EU Qualification Directive contains a number of paragraphs on the burden of proof. These paragraphs read as follows:

> '1. Member States may consider it the duty of the applicant to submit as soon as possible all elements needed to substantiate the application for international protection. In co-operation with the applicant it is the duty of the Member State to assess the relevant elements of the application.'

---

third-country national requiring international protection and ensuring compliance with the principle of *non-refoulement*. This policy must be in accordance with the Geneva Convention of 28 July 1951 and the Protocol of 31 January 1967 relating to the status of refugees, and other relevant treaties.'

238 UNHCR Handbook paras. 42 and 51. Wouters 2009, p. 93, p. 549: there must be a 'serious possibility' that the claimant's life or freedom would be threatened because of one of the persecution grounds.

239 Note on Burden and Standard of Proof in Refugee Claims of 16 December 1998, available at: http://www.unhcr.org/refworld/docid/3ae6b3338.html, visited on 23 August 2011.

240 Note on Burden and Standard of Proof in Refugee Claims of 16 December 1998, paras. 2 and 17.

241 Wouters 2009, p. 247.

242 ECtHR, *Vilvarajah v. the United Kingdom*, 30 October 1991, Appl. Nos.13163/87, 13164/87, 13165/87, 13447/87 and 13448/87, paras. 108 and 111.

'3. The assessment of an application for international protection is to be carried out on an individual basis and includes taking into account: (…).'

'4. The fact that an applicant has already been subject to persecution or serious harm or to direct threats of such persecution or such harm, is a serious indication of the applicant's well-founded fear of persecution or real risk of suffering serious harm, unless there are good reasons to consider that such persecution or serious harm will not be repeated.'

'5. Where Member States apply the principle according to which it is the duty of the applicant to substantiate the application for international protection and where aspects of the applicant's statements are not supported by documentary or other evidence, those aspects shall not need confirmation, when the following conditions are met:
(a) The applicant has made a genuine effort to substantiate his application;
(b) All relevant elements, at the applicant's disposal, have been submitted, and a satisfactory explanation has been given regarding any lack of other relevant elements;
(c) The applicant's statements are found to be coherent and plausible and do not run counter to available specific and general information relevant to the applicant's case;
(d) The applicant has applied for international protection at the earliest possible time, unless the applicant can demonstrate good reason for not having done so; and
(e) The general credibility of the applicant has been established.'

6.4.3.1   *Burden of assertion on the applicant*

Under Article 4 of the Qualification Directive, the applicant is enjoined with a burden of assertion.[243] This means that he or she needs to provide elements to substantiate his or her claim for international protection. These elements consist of: a) statements; and b) corroborating documentation at the applicant's disposal. The burden of assertion comprises the issues listed in the second paragraph (see 6.4.4 below on the relevant facts and circumstances). The burden on the applicant in paragraph 1 is facultative: 'Member States *may* (italics author) consider it the duty of the applicant …'. The facultative nature is further emphasised by paragraph 5: 'Where Member States apply the principle according to which it is the duty of the applicant to substantiate the application for international protection.' Hence, the burden of assertion is placed on the applicant when the Member State chooses to do so.[244] The facultative formulation in the first and fifth paragraphs makes clear that it would be allowable under the Qualification Directive to operate a system in which the authorities alone bear the information burden and the investigative burden.[245] As far as I have been able to establish, no such system exists in the EU.[246]

---

243 Noll 2005, pp. 3, 5.
244 Noll 2005, p. 6, Hailbronner 2010, p. 1028. See on this also Battjes 2006, p. 226, who reads this facultative formulation in a different way: according to him, the terms 'may consider' give the Member State discretion not as to the burden of proof, but rather as to the duty to submit grounds 'as soon as possible'. That reading seems less convincing as it does not take account of paragraph 5.
245 Noll 2005, p. 6.
246 A questionnaire to my colleagues in other EU Member States, judge-members of the International Association of Refugee Law Judges (IARLJ) to respond to the question of who carries the initial

→

The burden of assertion on the applicant seems to be a rather low threshold. It does not embrace the formulation of a legal claim and the identification of its basis in law. This rather low threshold follows from the fact that the elements listed in the second paragraph are limited to identity data, such as age, nationality, previous places of residence, travel route, background, possible previous asylum applications, and the flight reasons (see below 6.4.4 on the relevant facts and circumstances). The low threshold also follows from the formulation that the applicant needs to state 'the reasons for applying for international protection' and not 'the reasons for being granted international protection'.[247] It, finally, also follows from paragraph 5, which makes clear that not all the aspects of the applicant's account need to be corroborated by evidence other than statements, provided that the claim was made as early as possible and is, in short, coherent, plausible, generally credible and the applicant has made a genuine effort to substantiate his or her claim.[248] What is required from the applicant is that he or she submits the statements and the documentary evidence at his or her disposal, in other words, discloses all relevant facts and provides all the relevant documentation at his or her disposal, so that the authorities are able to assess the claim for protection in co-operation with the applicant.[249] This strongly resembles the burden of proof on the applicant developed by the ECtHR:

> 'it is incumbent on persons who allege that their expulsion would amount to a breach of Article 3 to adduce, to the greatest extent practically possible, material and information allowing the authorities of the Contracting State concerned, as well as the Court, to assess the risk a removal may entail'.[250]

The fourth paragraph of Article 4 of the Qualification Directive envisages an alleviated burden of proof for cases of earlier persecution. Persecution, serious harm or direct threats thereof in the past are a serious indication of the applicant's well-founded fear of persecution or real risk of suffering serious harm. In other words: previous persecution or serious harm or threats give rise to a refutable presumption that the applicant qualifies for refugee or subsidiary protection.[251] The alleviation of the burden of proof echoes paragraph 8, sub b and sub c, of General Comment No. 1 of the Committee against Torture, which indicates that pertinent information to be taken into account is the fact that the claimant has been tortured or maltreated in the (recent) past, as well as evidence of such (recent) torture or maltreatment.[252] The rule

---

burden of assertion and proof in national asylum proceedings and how such proceedings are initiated, yielded 21 responses from the same number of EU Member States. They revealed that the starting point of national asylum proceedings is an application for asylum lodged by the applicant and that the application must, as much as possible, be supported by statements and evidence.

247 Noll 2005, p. 8.
248 Hailbronner 2010, p. 1027.
249 Hailbronner 2010, p. 1030.
250 See, for example the judgment of the ECtHR in *Said v. the Netherlands*, 5 July 2005, Appl. No. 2345/02, para. 49.
251 Battjes 2006, p. 227, Boeles 2009, p. 263, Hailbronner 2010, p. 1037.
252 General Comment No. 1, adopted on 21-11-1997, A/53/44, Annex XI., para. 8.

also reflects the principle laid down in paragraph 45 of the UNHCR Handbook on procedures and criteria for determining refugee status, which states that

> 'It may be assumed that a person has well-founded fear of being persecuted if he has already been the victim of persecution for one of the reasons enumerated in the 1951 Convention.'[253]

There is an exception where there are 'good reasons' for assuming non-repetition of persecution or serious harm or threats. The onus for these 'good reasons' lies with the authorities of the Member State; they must show, on an individual basis, why past persecution or harm will not entail renewed persecution or harm.[254] The original text in the Commission Proposal read: 'unless a radical change of conditions has taken place since then in the applicant's country of origin or in his or her relation with this country'.[255] A good reason to assume non-repetition of persecution, serious harm or threats may, thus, be a regime change leading to a less oppressive regime. In its judgment in the case of *Abdulla and others* (2010), the CJEU made clear that, for the lower burden of proof to be activated, the earlier acts of persecution, serious harm or threats needed to be connected with the reason for persecution relied on by the applicant.[256]

6.4.3.2 *Investigative burden on the authorities, the co-operation requirement*

Where the elements have been submitted by the applicant, the authorities need to perform an assessment of them. The authorities have an investigative burden with regard to the issues mentioned in the third paragraph of Article 4 of the Qualification Directive, in short: the situation in the country of origin, the relevant statements and documentation presented by the applicant, the individual position and personal circumstances of the applicant, possible *sur place* activities of the applicant and possible protection of another country where the applicant could assert citizenship (see below 6.4.4 on the relevant facts and circumstances). It follows from the wording of paragraph 3 – 'the assessment includes taking into account' – that the list is not exhaustive.[257]

It follows from the second sentence of Article 4, first paragraph that the assessment of the elements needs to be done in co-operation with the applicant. The requirement of co-operation is new compared to the instruments studied in the previous chapters, although it may be assumed that there is a certain link with the notion of the shared burden of proof developed under Articles 3 ECHR, 7 ICCPR, 3 CAT, and paragraphs 195-196 and 192, sub ii, of the UNHCR Handbook.[258] Because of the

---

253 *UNHCR Handbook*, para. 45.
254 Hailbronner 2010, p. 1038.
255 Council doc. no. 12199/02, p. 9.
256 CJEU, *Abdulla and others*, 2 March 2010, joined cases C-175/08, C-176/08, C-178/08 and C-179/08, para. 94.
257 Battjes 2006, p. 226, Hailbronner 2010, p. 1031.
258 Paras. 195 and 196 of the *UNHCR Handbook*; Note on Burden and Standard of Proof in Refugee Claims of 16 December 1998, para. 6. See also para. 19 in the Submission in the case of *Mir Isfahani v. the Netherlands*, available at: http://www.unhcr.org/refworld/docid/454f5e484.html, visited on 23

→

explicit use of the term co-operation, Article 4 of the Qualification Directive seems to be attempting to bring out more clearly that the applicant and the authorities need to work together in assessing the elements of the international protection claim. In the case of *M.M. v. Minister for Justice, Equality and Law Reform, Ireland* (2012)[259] the CJEU has explained in a detailed way what the requirement of co-operation entails. The reference for a preliminary ruling in that case was made by the High Court of Ireland in proceedings between M. and the Minister concerning the lawfulness of the proce dure followed in processing an application for subsidiary protection which Mr M. had lodged following rejection of his application for refugee status. In Ireland an application for asylum and an application for subsidiary protection are dealt with in distinct procedures, with one procedure following the other.[260] Mr M. submitted an application for subsidiary protection following rejection of his application for refugee status which was upheld by the Refugee Appeals Tribunal. His application for subsidiary protection was also rejected and Mr M. brought proceedings before the High Court seeking annulment of this refusal. In those proceedings he disputed the legality of the rejection on the ground that the procedure did not comply with EU law. Mr M. submitted, *inter alia*, that the co-operation requirement laid down in Article 4 of the Qualification Directive means that the Minister is obliged to supply the applicant for asylum with the results of his assessment before taking a final decision. This would enable the applicant to address those matters which suggest a negative result by putting forward all documents which are then available or any argument capable of challenging the position of the competent national authority. It would also enable him to draw the authority's attention to any relevant matters of which due account has not, in the applicant's view, been taken. Mr M. also submitted that he was at no time heard in the course of the examination of his application for subsidiary protection. Furthermore, at no point in time was he informed of the matters which the Minister regarded as relevant to the decision to refuse him subsidiary protection.[261]

Referring to the procedure in the Netherlands where the intention to reject an asylum application is communicated with the applicant before a decision is taken, the High Court of Ireland referred to the CJEU the question whether the requirement to co-operate requires the administrative authorities to supply to the applicant the results of the assessment before a decision is finally made, as to enable him or her to address those aspects of the proposed decision which suggest a negative result.[262] The CJEU did not follow the applicant in his proposition that the co-operation requirement requires the national authority to supply the applicant, before adoption of a negative decision on the application for subsidiary protection after refusal of an asylum application, with the elements on which it intends to base its decision and to

---

December 2012. The case of *Mir Isfahani v. the Netherlands* brought to the European Court of Human Rights ended in a decision of 31 January 2008, Appl. No. 31252/03, to strike the application out of the list as pending the proceedings on her asylum application she was allowed to stay in the Netherlands.

259 CJEU, *M.M. v. Minister for Justice, Equality and Law Reform, Ireland*, 22 November 2012, C-277/11.
260 *Ibidem*, paras. 28, 29.
261 *Ibidem*, paras. 50, 51.
262 *Ibidem*, paras. 55, 56.

seek the applicant's observations in that regard.[263] In addition to this, the CJEU gave the following interpretation of the requirement of co-operation:

'As is clear from its title, Article 4 of Directive 2004/83 relates to the 'assessment of facts and circumstances'. In actual fact, that 'assessment' takes place in two separate stages. The first stage concerns the establishment of factual circumstances which may constitute evidence that supports the application, while the second stage relates to the legal appraisal of that evidence, which entails deciding whether, in the light of the specific facts of a given case, the substantive conditions laid down by Articles 9 and 10 or Article 15 of Directive 2004/83 for the grant of international protection are met. Under Article 4(1) of Directive 2004/83, although it is generally for the applicant to submit all elements needed to substantiate the application, the fact remains that it is the duty of the Member State to cooperate with the applicant at the stage of determining the relevant elements of that application. This requirement that the Member State cooperate therefore means, in practical terms, that if, for any reason whatsoever, the elements provided by an applicant for international protection are not complete, up to date or relevant, it is necessary for the Member State concerned to cooperate actively with the applicant, at that stage of the procedure, so that all the elements needed to substantiate the application may be assembled. A Member State may also be better placed than an applicant to gain access to certain types of documents. Moreover, the interpretation set out in the previous paragraph finds support in Article 8(2)(b) of Directive 2005/85, pursuant to which Member States are to ensure that precise and up-to-date information is obtained on the general situation prevailing in the countries of origin of applicants for asylum and, where necessary, in countries through which they have transited. It is thus clear that Article 4(1) of Directive 2004/83 relates only to the first stage mentioned in paragraph 64 of this judgment, concerning the determination of the facts and circumstances *qua* evidence which may substantiate the asylum application.'[264]

The CJEU has so far not explained any further what is meant by 'active co-operation with the applicant so that all the elements needed to substantiate the application may be assembled.' One may probably think here of situations in which the applicant informs the authority that he or she is trying to obtain certain documentation from the country of origin and the authority offers him or her a certain (additional) period for submitting this documentation. Also coming to mind are situations in which the applicant proposes that the authority hear certain witnesses and the authority in response to that arranges hearing sessions, or situations in which the applicant submits certain documents and the national administrative or judicial authority orders an expert authenticity examination, etc.

What is clear from the judgment in *M.M.* is that, in principle, the applicant remains responsible for submitting the elements substantiating his or her claim: the CJEU states clearly that 'it is generally for the applicant to submit all elements needed to substantiate the application'. At the same time, the CJEU has made clear that if the elements provided by an applicant are not complete, up to date or relevant, it is necessary for the national authorities to cooperate actively with the applicant so that

---

263 *Ibidem*, para. 60.
264 *Ibidem*, para. 63.

all the elements needed to substantiate the application may be assembled. Moreover, the CJEU has made clear that there may be specific circumstances in which the administrative or judicial authority is better placed than the applicant to get hold of certain types of documents. This consideration of the CJEU strongly mirrors the ECtHR's consideration in the case of *Iskandarov v. Russia* (2010) that

> 'The Court has also recognized that Convention proceedings do not in all cases lend them selves to a rigorous application of the principle *affirmanti incumbit probatio* (he who alleges something must prove that allegation). In certain circumstances, where the events in issue lie wholly, or in large part, within the exclusive knowledge of the authorities, the burden of proof may be regarded as resting on the authorities to provide a satisfactory and convincing explanation (...).'[265]

It seems safe to conclude, with Noll (2005), that the requirement of co-operation entails at least two things: communication by both parties as regards the elements relevant to the claim and guidance from the Member State to the applicant on exactly what is needed to corroborate the claim.[266] In addition to that, there may be situations in which it is up to the administrative or judicial authority to attempt to obtain certain evidence. An example would probably be the situation in which the applicant asserts and substantiates that he himself or herself tried to obtain certain documents from the authorities of his country of origin, but was refused access to these documents. In such a situation it would then be up to the administration or the judiciary to make a request to obtain such documents.

6.4.3.3   *Certain substantiation of the claim is also required in other areas*

Abdulla and others (2010) has so far been the only case in which the CJEU has shed some light on a question concerning the burden of proof in asylum cases.[267] The CJEU has, however, dealt with burden of proof issues in other fields. As the CJEU is likely to draw on this jurisprudence – next to the positions of the UNHCR and the case law of the ECtHR, the HRC and the ComAT – it is interesting to take a brief look at a leading case.

The case of *Nölle* (1990)[268] concerned anti-dumping duties imposed on Nölle's imports of paintbrushes from China. The qualification of the import as 'dumping' had resulted from a comparison of the value of these Chinese paintbrushes with the value of a similar product from Sri Lanka. Nölle claimed that the normal value had not been determined in an appropriate manner since Sri Lanka, the country chosen as the reference country, satisfied none of the conditions of which the Commission had always taken account, namely the existence in the country concerned of a like product

---

265 ECtHR, *Iskandarov v. Russia*, 23 September 2010, Appl. No. 17185/05, para. 108.

266 Noll 2005, p. 4. See on assessment in co-operation with the applicant also Hailbronner 2010, pp. 1028-1030.

267 See for the same conclusion Van Bennekom & Van der Winden 2011, p. 287, who state that so far there is no guiding jurisprudence from the CJEU.

268 CJEU, *Detlef Nölle*, 22 October 1991, C-16/90.

of like volume and production methods, of conditions of access to raw materials comparable to those of the exporting country concerned and of prices resulting from the operation of the rules of the market economy.[269] Based on the available material, the CJEU could not answer the question of whether or not the Chinese and Sri Lankan brushes were similar.[270]

The Commission was of the opinion that production methods of this product in China and Sri Lanka were similar as in both these countries the firms were small or medium-sized with labour-intensive production in small-scale units with low wage rates. Nölle contested this by stating that in Sri Lanka there were only two major producers, one of whom manufactured practically none of the products in question, whereas in China there were at least 150 small and medium-sized businesses and the production volume there was, accordingly, at least 200 times greater than that in Sri Lanka.[271] The CJEU did not follow the Commission in its opinion that production methods in both countries were similar, because the Commission had not substantiated its statements in any way:

'It must also be noted that the Commission and the Council did not produce during either the written or the oral procedure any figures or details capable of showing that, as they stated, production methods in Sri Lanka consisted in labour-intensive production in small-scale units with low wage rates, so that they were comparable to production methods in China.'[272]

Nölle claimed finally that the prices charged in Sri Lanka were not the result of the rules of a market economy since there was no natural competition there. In support of this statement, Nölle produced two documents from the Sri Lankan firms in question, showing that they could supply the Union only to a very limited extent as the production of brushes adapted to the needs of the domestic market and that there was no price advantage in comparison with the prices which the parent company was able to offer in Europe.[273] The Court found that Nölle in this way sufficiently substantiated the statement:

'It appears from the foregoing that Nölle has produced sufficient factors, already known to the Commission and the Council during the anti-dumping proceeding, to raise doubts as to whether the choice of Sri Lanka as a reference country was appropriate and not unreasonable.'[274]

Finally, as to the question of why Taiwan had not been considered as a possible reference country by the Commission while the relevant rules had considered Taiwan as a possibility, the Court ruled that the Commission had not corroborated in any way its statement that the physical characteristics and the production costs of the products were different and that the Taiwanese producers who had been approached refused

---

269 *Ibidem*, para. 4.
270 *Ibidem*, paras. 15-17.
271 *Ibidem*, paras. 18-19.
272 *Ibidem*, para. 23.
273 *Ibidem*, paras. 27-29.
274 *Ibidem*, para. 30.

to co-operate.[275] It follows from the case of *Nölle* that claims and statements must normally be supported by some substantiation, in the form of certain substantiating facts, details or figures, laid down in documentation.

6.4.4　*Relevant facts and circumstances*

Article 4, second paragraph, of the EU Qualification Directive stipulates:

> '2. The elements referred to in paragraph 1 consist of the applicant's statements and all documentation at the applicants disposal regarding the applicant's age, background, including that of relevant relatives, identity, nationality(ies), country(ies) and place(s) of previous residence, previous asylum applications, travel routes, identity and travel documents and the reasons for applying for international protection.'

Article 4, third paragraph, of the EU Qualification Directive stipulates:

> '3. The assessment of an application for international protection is to be carried out on an individual basis and includes taking into account: (…)
> (a) all relevant facts as they relate to the country of origin at the time of taking a decision on the application; including laws and regulations of the country of origin and the manner in which they are applied;
> (b) The relevant statements and documentation presented by the applicant including information on whether the applicant has been or may be subject to persecution or serious harm;
> (c) the individual position and personal circumstances of the applicant, including factors such as background, gender and age, so as to assess whether, on the basis of the applicant's personal circumstances, the acts to which the applicant has been or could be exposed would amount to persecution or serious harm;
> (d) whether the applicant's activities since leaving the country of origin were engaged in for the sole or main purpose of creating the necessary conditions for applying for international protection, so as to assess whether these activities will expose the applicant to persecution or serious harm if returned to that country;
> (e) Whether the applicant could reasonably be expected to avail himself of the protection of another country where he could assert citizenship.'

And Article 4, fourth paragraph, of the EU Qualification Directive stipulates:

> '4. The fact that an applicant has already been subject to persecution or serious harm or to direct threats of such persecution or such harm, is a serious indication of the applicant's well-founded fear of persecution or real risk of suffering serious harm, unless there are good reasons to consider that such persecution or serious harm will not be repeated.'

It becomes clear from these provisions that, just as under the international instruments discussed in the previous chapters, the relevant facts and circumstances can be

---

275　*Ibidem*, paras. 33, 34.

divided into two categories: a) personal circumstances such as background, gender, ethnicity, age, sexual orientation, beliefs, activities, personal profile, personal experiences and experiences of relatives; and b) facts and circumstances relating to the situation in the country of origin.

Article 4, fourth paragraph, makes clear that, within the category of personal circumstances, past persecution, past serious harm or threats thereof are highly relevant facts. As was said above in the section on the burden of proof, previous persecution or serious harm or threats thereof give rise to a refutable presumption that the applicant qualifies for refugee or subsidiary protection.[276]

The lists of facts and circumstances provided in paragraphs 2 and 3 of Article 4 are not exhaustive. In the light of Article 78 TFEU,[277] we may safely assume that all the facts and circumstances mentioned in Chapters 2, 3, 4 and 5 are also relevant under Article 4 of the Qualification Directive.

The investigation of the situation in the country of origin must include its laws and regulations and the manner in which they are applied. Laws and regulations may be of particular importance when they authorise or condone the persecution of the applicant or the infliction upon him or her of serious harm.[278] The requirement for the authorities to investigate the situation in the country of origin is reaffirmed in Article 8, second paragraph, of the Procedures Directive, which stipulates that Member States shall ensure that precise and up-to-date information is obtained from various sources, such as the UNHCR, as to the general situation prevailing in the countries of origin of applicants for asylum, and, where necessary, in countries through which they have transited, and that such information is made available to the personnel responsible for examining applications and taking decisions.[279] For national courts it is important that Article 8, third paragraph, stipulates that courts shall have access to this country of origin information through the administrative decision maker or via the applicant or otherwise.[280] The obligations on the national authorities flowing from Article 8, second and third paragraph, of the Procedures Directive mirror the notion developed under the ICCPR, the CAT and the ECHR that particular responsibility for shaping clarity on the general human rights situation in the country of origin lies with the administrative and judicial authorities of the State (see Chapter 3, section 3.5.6, Chapter 4, section 4.5.6, and Chapter 5, section 5.6.6).

When assessing *sur place* activities under Article 4, third paragraph, sub d, it must be borne in mind that the RC does not deny protection to persons whose reasons for

---

276 Battjes 2006, p. 227, Boeles 2009, p. 263, Hailbronner 2010, p. 1037.

277 Article 78, first paragraph, TFEU, states: 'The Union shall develop a common policy on asylum, subsidiary protection and temporary protection with a view to offering appropriate status to any third-country national requiring international protection and ensuring compliance with the principle of *non-refoulement*. This policy must be in accordance with the Geneva Convention of 28 July 1951 and the Protocol of 31 January 1967 relating to the status of refugees, and other relevant treaties.'

278 Hailbronner 2010, p. 1032; he refers to the draft text in which this was explicitly clarified.

279 Article 8, second paragraph, sub b of the Procedures Directive (Council Directive 2005/85/EC of 1 December 2005).

280 Article 8, third paragraph, of the Procedures Directive (Council Directive 2005/85/EC of 1 December 2005).

flight have resulted from *sur place* activities, irrespective of intent.[281] In line with this, Hailbronner (2010) makes clear that Article 4, third paragraph, sub d does not automatically exclude recognition in cases of post-flight activities engaged in an abusive way, but that the element of abuse has to be taken into consideration in assessing whether these activities will expose the applicant to persecution or serious harm, in other words, whether the activities will be taken seriously by the country of origin and may, therefore, create a risk.[282]

As regards the possible protection of another country where the applicant could assert citizenship (Article 4, third paragraph, sub e), it has been pointed out by the UNHCR that this element does not reflect the requirements emanating from the RC. In its comments on the Qualification Directive, the UNHCR stated:

'The factor outlined in Paragraph (3)(e) should not form part of the refugee status determination assessment. There is no obligation on the part of an applicant under international law to avail him- or herself of the protection of another country where s/he could "assert" nationality. The issue was explicitly discussed by the drafters of the Convention. It is regulated in Article 1A(2) (last sentence), which deals with applicants of dual nationality, and in Article 1E of the 1951 Convention. There is no margin beyond the limits of these provisions. For Article 1E to apply, a person otherwise included in the refugee definition would need to fulfil the requirement of having taken residence in the country and having been recognized by the competent authorities in that country "as having the rights and obligations which are attached to the possession of the nationality of that country". Since Article 1E is already reflected in Article 12(1)(b) of the Directive, Article 4 (3)(e) should not be incorporated into national legislation and practice if full compatibility with Article 1 of the 1951 Convention is to be ensured.'[283]

It is problematic that Article 4, third paragraph, sub e, of the Qualification Directive has no predecessor in international asylum law and contains two factors of uncertainty: availability of protection in the other country and assertion of citizenship of that other country.[284] However, based upon the rationale of the provision– no need for international protection when protection can be offered by a State –it may be interpreted to mean that an applicant who is entitled to citizenship in another country is not in need of international protection.[285]

6.4.5   *Required degree of individual risk*

Article 2, sub f, of the EU Qualification Directive qualifies a person eligible for subsidiary protection as an individual in respect of whom substantial grounds have been shown for believing that the person concerned would face a real risk of suffering se-

---

281 Noll 2005, p. 10.
282 Hailbronner 2010, p. 1034.
283 UNHCR Annotated Comments on the EC Council Directive 2004/83/EC of 29 April 2004 on Minimum Standards for the Qualification and Status of Third Country Nationals or Stateless Persons as Refugees or as Persons who otherwise need International Protection and the Content of the Protection granted, Geneva, January 2005, p. 15.
284 Hailbronner 2010, p. 1036.
285 Hailbronner 2010, p. 1036.

rious harm.[286] This phrase is taken from the ECtHR's constant case law under Article 3, in which that Court developed the standard that 'substantial grounds have been shown for believing that the individual concerned, if expelled, faces a real risk of being subjected to torture or to inhuman or degrading treatment or punishment'.[287] Under the heading 'Serious harm', Article 15 of the Qualification Directive stipulates that serious harm consists of:

a) Death penalty or execution; or
b) Torture or inhuman or degrading treatment or punishment of an applicant in the country of origin; or
c) Serious and individual threat to a civilian's life or person by reason of indiscriminate violence in situations of international or internal armed conflict.'[288]

In Chapter 5 it was demonstrated that in the ECtHR's case law concerning the expulsion of asylum seekers three different types of situations can be distinguished:
- Situations of extreme general violence; in those cases no individual risk is required as everyone returned to such a situation automatically runs an Article 3-risk;
- Situations of violence against a particular group; in these cases membership of that group forms sufficient individual Article 3-risk; and
- Other cases; in these cases special personal facts and circumstances indicating that this very applicant runs an Article 3-risk must be established.

Based on the judgment of the CJEU in the case of *Elgafaji* (2009),[289] it may be argued that this distinction is also workable for subsidiary protection under Union asylum law. The CJEU made clear in its judgment that Article 15(b) of the Directive corresponds to Article 3 ECHR and that, by contrast, the content of Article 15(c) is different from that of Article 3 ECHR and must, therefore, be interpreted independently, although with due regard for fundamental rights, as they are guaranteed by Article 3 ECHR.[290] Second, the Court clarified that Article 15(c) does not require that an applicant is specifically targeted or singled out. Referring to the fact that in Article 15(c) the term 'threat' is used instead of specific acts of violence, such as mentioned in Articles 15(a) and 15(b), the fact that the threat is inherent in a general situation of international or internal armed conflict, and, finally, the fact that the violence is described as indiscriminate, the Court ruled that, to assume the existence of an Article 15(c)threat, it is not necessary that the applicant adduces evidence that he or she has been specifically targeted or singled out by reason of factors particular to his or her personal circumstances.[291] The Court also made clear that it would only be in excep-

---

286 Article 2, sub f, of the EU Qualification Directive (Directive 2011/95 of 13 December 2011).
287 We find this standard of proof in all the judgments of the ECtHR concerning the expulsion of asylum seekers, from the first case of ECtHR, *Cruz Varas v. Sweden*, 20 March 1991, Appl. No. 15576/89, para. 69, up to later judgments such as ECtHR, *R.C. v. Sweden*, 9 March 2010, Appl. No. 41827/07, para. 48. This standard also explicitly features in many admissibility decisions.
288 Article 15 of the EU Qualification Directive (Directive 2011/95 of 13 December 2011).
289 CJEU, *Elgafaji*, 17 February 2009, C-465/07.
290 *Ibidem*, para. 28.
291 *Ibidem*, paras. 31-34, para. 43.

tional situations that the existence of such an Article 15(c)-threat could be considered to have been established. These were situations where the degree of indiscriminate violence characterising the armed conflict taking place reached such a high level that any person returned to the relevant country or region, would, solely on account of his or her presence there, faced a real risk of being subjected to that threat.[292] The typical Article 15(c) situation as defined by the CJEU thus strongly resembles the situation described by the ECtHR as the exceptional situation of extreme general violence, where no individual risk is required as everyone returned to such a situation would automatically run an Article 3 ECHR-risk.[293] The CJEU has acknowledged this by stating explicitly that the given interpretation of Article 15(c) is 'fully compatible' with Article 3 ECHR.[294] As the Court also made clear in *Elgafaji* that Article 15(b) of the Qualification Directive corresponds in essence to Article 3 ECHR, it must be assumed that Article 15(b) covers the other two categories of cases mentioned above – the category of group violence, where belonging to the targeted group forms sufficient singling out, and the rest (third) category where the individual needs to demonstrate that he or she as a person has been specifically targeted or singled out. Finally, the CJEU's finding in paragraph 39 of the *Elgafaji* judgment is important for assessing the required degree of individual risk in subsidiary protection cases:

> 'the more the applicant is able to show that he is specifically affected by reason of factors particular to his personal circumstances, the lower the level of indiscriminate violence required for him to be eligible for subsidiary protection.'[295]

This approach echoes the notion of the gradual scale developed in the case law of the ECtHR and (less explicitly) the Committee against Torture that, the graver the general human rights situation in the country of origin, the less individual facts and circumstances, including evidence corroborating these individual facts and circumstances, are required.[296]

The CJEU has so far not dealt with the question of what the required degree of individual risk is in cases concerning refugee protection (not subsidiary protection). Given that Article 2, sub paragrah d, of the Qualification Directive defines the refugee in the same way as the RC, and that Article 78 TFEU requires an interpretation harmonising with the RC, it is likely that the Court will look at the guidelines developed by the UNHCR on this aspect. In Chapter 2 it was made clear, in short, that the RC does not impose a requirement of being singled out.

---

292 *Ibidem*, paras. 35, 37, 38, 43.
293 See, for example, ECtHR, *Sufi and Elmi v. the UK*, 28 June 2011, Appl. No. 8319/07, 11449/07, paras. 241-250.
294 CJEU, *Elgafaji*, 17 February 2009, C-465/07, para. 44.
295 *Ibidem*, para. 39.
296 See Chapter 4 on the CAT, section 4.5.4, and Chapter 5 on the ECHR, section 5.6.4.

6.4.6   Admission of evidence, appreciation of evidence

6.4.6.1   *Admission of evidence, possible types and sources of evidence*

Article 4, first paragraph, of the Qualification Directive uses the terms 'all elements needed to substantiate the application for international protection'. The neutrality of the terms 'element' and 'substantiate' indicates that, in principle, every form of evidence capable of proving the risk can be admitted to the procedure, whether oral or written or evidence in another form.

The first paragraph specifically mentions documentation corroborating the applicant's identity (including age, nationality, name, country and place of former residence), travel documents and documents regarding travel routes, documentation concerning previous asylum applications, and, finally, documents corroborating the reasons for applying for international protection. Examples of documents corroborating the material claim are arrest warrants, police reports, medical reports corroborating statements on past ill-treatment, written or oral statements made by family members or other witnesses relating to harm inflicted upon the applicant or threats of such harm. Reports containing country of origin information from various organisations are an important source of evidence, as follows from the second paragraph of Article 4 of the Qualification Directive, which mentions all relevant facts as they relate to the country of origin, and Article 8, second paragraph, of the Procedures Directive, which stipulates that Member States shall ensure that precise and up-to-date information is obtained from various sources, such as the UNHCR, as to the general situation prevailing in the countries of origin of the applicants for asylum.

6.4.6.2   *Minimum quantity and quality of evidence*

Secondary EU asylum law does not contain provisions making clear exactly how much evidence is required to sufficiently corroborate a claim for international protection, and of what quality that evidence should be. Nor does it contain any provisions regarding the evaluation of evidence. The fifth paragraph of Article 4 of the Qualification Directive gives some guidance on the required quantity of evidence, as it makes clear that in the case of a timely claim (a claim made as early as possible) which is, in short, coherent, plausible, and generally credible, and provided that the applicant has made a genuine effort to substantiate this claim, not all the aspects of the applicant's account need to be corroborated by evidence other than statements. This echoes the approach of the ECtHR and the ComAT that not all the aspects of the claim need corroboration as long as the very core of the flight narrative is corroborated with specific evidence relating personally to the applicant.

6.4.7   Opportunities for presenting evidence and reacting to evidence; secret evidence

It follows from Article 4, first paragraph, of the EU Qualification Directive, that asylum applicants must be given the opportunity to present and submit all the elements substantiating the claim. Elements consist of statements and evidence, so there must always be an opportunity for asylum applicants to hand over to the authorities the evidence in their possession. The duty to co-operate in the assessment of the relevant elements of the asylum claim flowing from Article 4, first paragraph, of the EU Qualification Directive, implies that the applicant must be given access to information and assessments the authorities have considered relevant in the case. It may be argued that this implies that secret investigative material which cannot be shared with the applicant must be excluded from the basis for a decision, otherwise he or she would not be part of the assessment process, which would arguably conflict with the requirement of co-operation laid down in Article 4, paragraph 1.[297] In other words: it may be argued that Article 4, first paragraph, of the Qualification Directive contains a prohibition on the use of secret information. Such a prohibition would go much further than the principle flowing from the RC – information and its sources may only be withheld where disclosure of sources would seriously jeopardize national security or the security of the organizations or persons providing information.[298] It also goes much further than the principle developed by the ECtHR that non-disclosure of evidence may be justified if this is strictly necessary to preserve the fundamental rights of another individual or to safeguard an important public interest, such as the protection of national security,[299] and that non-disclosure of evidence to one of the parties must be counterbalanced in the judicial proceedings, at least by disclosure of the evidence to the national court.[300] A prohibition on the use of secret information would, however, echo the prohibition on the use of secret evidence in expulsion proceedings formulated by the HRC in the case of *Mansour Ahani* (2004)[301] and the ComAT in the case of *Sogi* (2007).[302] Both the HRC and the ComAT concluded that there had been unfairness in national expulsion proceedings because of non-disclosure to the applicants of secret evidence underpinning the decisions on expulsion based on national security considerations. From *Sogi v. Canada* (2007), it follows explicitly that the secret evidence was disclosed to the national court, but that the ComAT did not see this as a sufficient counterbalance for the non-disclosure of evidence to the claimant.[303]

At this point in time we cannot be entirely sure whether the co-operation requirement laid down in Article 4, first paragraph, of the Qualification Directive indeed carries an absolute prohibition on the use of secret evidence. When confronted with this question, it is likely that the CJEU will look at Article 16 of the Procedures Directive as well, which stipulates that the legal adviser to the applicant shall enjoy access to such information in the applicant's file as is liable to be examined by the judicial authorities, but that an exception may be made where disclosure of information

---

297 Noll 2005, p. 7.
298 Fair and Efficient Asylum Procedures: A Non-Exhaustive Overview of Applicable International Standards, 2 September 2005, available at: www.unhcr.org/refworld/docid/432ae9204.html, p. 5 and 6.
299 See ECtHR, *Edwards and Lewis*, 27 October 2004, para. 46.
300 ECtHR, *Al-Nashif v. Bulgaria*, 20 June 2002, Appl. No. 50963/99, paras. 123-128; ECtHR, *Lupsa v. Romania*, 8 June 2006, Appl. No. 50963/99, paras. 38-42.
301 HRC, *Mansour Ahani v. Canada*, 15 June 2004, Communication No. 1051/2002.
302 ComAT, *Sogi v. Canada*, 16 November 2007, No. 297/2006.
303 *Ibidem*, para. 2.6.

or sources would jeopardise national security, the security of organisations or person(s) providing the information or the security of the person(s) to whom the information relates, or where the investigative interests relating to the examination of applications for asylum by the competent authorities of the Member States or the international relations of the Member States would be compromised. In such cases, the judicial authorities need to be given access to such information or sources, except where such access is precluded in cases of national security.[304]

When confronted with questions concerning the equality of arms, adversarial proceedings and the use of secret evidence, the CJEU is also likely to draw on its case law in other areas, such as food control and competition. It is, therefore, worthwhile taking a brief look at the CJEU's case law in other fields.

Secret evidence[305]

The CJEU has not yet ruled on the use of secret evidence in asylum cases. It has addressed the legality of the non-disclosure of evidence in in cases concerning other fields of EU law, for example competition law and EU anti-terrorism measures such as freezing of funds of suspected terrorists. In competition cases the EU Commission's decision to impose a fine on one or more companies is often based on evidence provided by other companies which is considered business secret. In cases concerning anti-terrorism measures evidence is often withheld to the party concerned for national security reasons.

The general principles developed by the CJEU to answer the question of legality of non-disclosure of evidence strongly resemble the principles developed by the ECtHR, discussed in Chapter 5, section 5.5.4. These general principles include the following notions:
- The use of secret evidence is permitted provided that it has a legitimate aim and that it is necessary;[306]
- The interest of the State to keep the evidence secret must be balanced against the individual's right to have knowledge of this evidence and his procedural rights of adversarial proceedings and equality of arms;[307]
- The court examining the appeal should be able to effectively review the confidential evidence on which the impugned decision is based;[308]
- Limitations to a party's procedural rights as a consequence of the use of secret evidence should be compensated by taking counterbalancing measures (compensation techniques).[309]

---

304 See Article 16, first paragraph, of the Procedures Directive (Council Directive 2005/85/EC of 1 December 2005).

305 See for a more extensive analysis of the use of secret information in asylum cases and the principles on this use developed in international and EU asylum law Reneman 2012, pp. 303-377.

306 See, for example, CJEU, *Aalborg Portland and others v. Commission*, 7 January 2004, Joined Cases C-204/00 P etc, para 68; CJEU, *Kadi and Al Barakaat v. Council and Commission*, 3 September 2008, Joined Cases C-402/05 P and C-415/05 P, para. 342.

307 See, for example, CJEU, *Varec*, 2008, C-450/06, para 51; CJEU, *Kadi and Al Barakaat v. Council and Commission*, 3 September 2008, Joined Cases C-402/05 P and C-415/05 P, para. 344.

308 See, for example, CJEU, *Mobistar*, 13 July 2006, C-438/04, para 40; CJEU, *Organisation des Modjahedines du peuple d'Iran v. Council*, 12 December 2006, T-228/02, para. 155.

It seems that the CJEU has set stricter requirements for the use of confidential evidence in competition cases than in anti-terrorism cases. In a number of competition cases the CJEU has stressed that, for the adversarial process to work effectively and fairly, it is important that relevant material is available to both parties and that a company charged with infringing competition rules needs to have full access to the file prepared by the Commission so that it is familiar with all the evidence and may produce counter-evidence.[310] In competition cases the CJEU seems to distinguish between 'relevant evidence' and 'irrelevant evidence', the latter category comprising evidence which is not relied on, that is, evidence which does not form part of the material underpinning the impugned decision. The CJEU has ruled in a number of cases that there is no need to disclose documents which are not relevant for the decision.[311]

Unlike in competition cases, in cases concerning anti-terrorism measures the CJEU seems to place somewhat less emphasis on the right to adversarial proceedings and equality of arms. An important aspect of proceedings concerning anti-terrorism measures is that the right to be heard and the right to be notified of the evidence do not need to be complied with during the administrative procedure; these rights may be exercised only during the appeal procedure before the EU Courts. The reason for this is that the party concerned can take advantage of the time period allowed to it to submit its comments to transfer funds out of the Union.[312] However, in order for the parties concerned to be able to defend their rights effectively, particularly in legal proceedings which might be brought before the CJEU, it is necessary that the evidence adduced against them be notified to them, *in so far as reasonably possible*, either concomitantly with or as soon as possible after the adoption of the initial decision to freeze funds.[313]

The differences have so far not been explained explicitly by the CJEU in its judgments. They may probably be explained by the nature of the interests involved; probably the CJEU considers the national security of the EU and its Member States and their relations with third countries worthy of more protection than the interests of businesses in protecting their secrets.

National courts as the guardians of adversariality and equality of arms
The case of Steffensen (2003)[314] is interesting to discuss in some more detail here as it makes clear that the CJEU gives the national court an active role as guardian of the principles of adversariality and equality of arms. Steffensen concerned food control by the German administrative authorities at the Böklunder Plumrose Company, a

---

309 See, for example, CJEU, *Kadi and Al Barakaat v. Council and Commission*, 3 September 2008, Joined Cases C-402/05 P and C-415/05 P, para. 344.
310 See, for example, CJEU, *Cimenteries CBR*, 18 December 1992, joined cases T-10/92 to T-12/92 and T-15/92, para. 38; CJEU, *Imperial Chemical Industries*, 29 June 1995, T-37/91, para. 49; CJEU, *Solvay*, 29 June 1995, T-30/91, para. 59.
311 See, for example, CJEU, *Knauf Gips v. Commission*, 1 July 2010, C-407/08 P, paras. 13, 23; CJEU, *Aalborg Portland and Others v. Commission*, Joined Cases C-204/00 P etc, 7 January 2004, paras. 71-73.
312 CJEU, *Organisation des Modjahedines du peuple d'Iran v. Council*, 12 December 2006, T-228/02, para. 128.
313 *Ibidem*, para. 129.
314 CJEU, *Steffensen*, 10 April 2003, C-276/01.

manufacturer of sausages. The administrative authorities took retail outlet samples and, based on the results of an analysis of the samples, imposed a fine on the company for marketing products without adequate labelling. The company lodged an appeal against this decision before the national court. Article 7(1) of the applicable Council Directive 89/397EEC[315] stipulated that Member States should take the necessary steps to ensure that those subject to inspection might apply for a second opinion. In this case, no second opinion was forthcoming – the only evidence available before the national court was the analysis of the samples taken by the administrative authorities. The reasons behind the absence of a second opinion remain unclear: the CJEU mentioned explicitly that

> 'the national court states that it does not know whether the retail traders concerned informed Plumrose or Mr Steffensen that samples had been taken and that it has not been possible to ascertain whether the results of the analyses of those samples were in each case notified to Mr Steffensen or Plumrose in time to enable them to apply for a second opinion'.[316]

However, the national court obviously assumed the 'worst case scenario' – a situation in which the company had not been informed and had, therefore, not been able to produce counter evidence in the form of a second opinion. It referred to Luxembourg the question of whether a national court is prohibited from using the results of the analysis of samples of a manufacturer's products as evidence that the manufacturer has infringed the national rules of a Member State on foodstuffs where the manufacturer has been unable to exercise his or her right of a second opinion under Article 7(1) of the Directive. In the procedure before the CJEU, the German Government made clear that national German administrative procedural law did not impose a general prohibition on the admission of evidence obtained in an improper administrative procedure. The CJEU ruled as follows:

> 'It is for the national court to assess whether, in the light of all the factual and legal evidence available to it, the admission as evidence of the results of the analyses at issue in the main proceedings entails a risk of an infringement of the adversarial principle and, thus, of the right to a fair hearing. In the context of that assessment, the national court will have to examine, more specifically, whether the evidence at issue in the main proceedings pertains to a technical field of which the judges have no knowledge and is likely to have a preponderant influence on its assessment of the facts and, should this be the case, whether Mr Steffensen still has a real opportunity to comment effectively on that evidence. If the national court decides that the admission as evidence of the results of the analyses at issue in the main proceedings is likely to give rise to an infringement of the adversarial principle and, thus, of the right to a fair hearing, it must exclude those results as evidence in order to avoid such an infringement.'[317]

---

315 Council Directive 89/397EEC of 14 June 1989 on the official control of foodstuffs, *Official Journal of the EU* 1989 L 186, p. 23.
316 CJEU, *Steffensen*, 10 April 2003, C-276/01, para. 18.
317 *Ibidem*, paras. 78, 79.

It may be inferred from *Steffensen* that, in a situation where a company, during the administrative procedure, has not had a real opportunity to obtain a second opinion, the national court should arrange a real opportunity for the company to comment effectively on the evidence relied on by the administration, for example, in the form of staying the court proceedings so that a second opinion can still be obtained.

6.4.8 *Time limits for the presentation of statements and evidence*

It follows from Article 4, first paragraph, of the EU Qualification Directive that it is the applicant's duty to submit all elements as soon as possible.[318] The Qualification Directive does not further specify what is meant by this. The terms 'as soon as possible' must be read in conjunction with Article 8, first paragraph, of the Procedures Directive, which stipulates that Member States shall ensure that applications for asylum are neither rejected nor excluded from examination on the sole ground that they have not been made as soon as possible.[319] They must also be read in accordance with Article 4, fifth paragraph, sub paragraph d, of the Qualification Directive, which states – as a condition that aspects of the applicant's claim do not need confirmation – that the applicant 'has applied (…) at the earliest possible time, unless he can demonstrate good reasons for not having done so'.[320]

Both Noll (2005) and Hailbronner (2010) infer from the fact that the assessment needs to take place in co-operation with the applicant, that the expression 'as soon as possible' must be understood to mean that the applicant is required to present information as soon as the need for this information has been established, which can happen at any time during the process.[321]

There is extensive CJEU case law in other areas on the compatibility with Union law of national limitation periods and time limits. To answer the question of whether national time limits and limitation periods are compatible with EU law, the CJEU generally applies the principle of national procedural autonomy, provided that the requirements of equality and effectiveness have been met (see above section 6.3.2.2).[322] The general rule is that reasonable national time limits are compatible with EU law, as they are an application of the fundamental principle of legal certainty.[323] As time limits and limitation periods may vary greatly among the EU Member States, the Court generally grants considerable latitude in determining what is reasonable.[324]

---

318 Article 4, first paragraph, of the EU Qualification Directive 2011/95 stipulates, *inter alia*: 'Member States may consider it the duty of the applicant to submit as soon as possible all elements needed to substantiate the application for international protection.'

319 Article 8, first paragraph, of the Procedures Directive (Council Directive 2005/85/EC of 1 December 2005).

320 Article 4, fifth paragraph, sub d, of the EU Qualification Directive 2011/95.

321 Noll 2005, p. 6; Hailbronner 2010, p. 1028.

322 See, for example, CJEU, *Fisscher*, 28 September 1994, C-128/93, paras. 39-40; CJEU, *Santex*, 27 February 2003, C-327/00, paras. 51, 52; CJEU, *Manfredi*, 13 July 2006, Joined Cases C-295/04 to C-298/04, para. 77; CJEU, *Pontin*, 29 October 2009, C-63/08, paras. 43-49.

323 See, for example, CJEU, *Universale Bau*, 12 December 2002, C-470/99, para. 76 ; CJEU, *Santex*, 27 February 2003, C-327/00, para. 52.

324 Craig & De Búrca 2008, p. 323-324.

The principle of national procedural autonomy is reflected in Article 39, second paragraph, of the Procedures Directive, which states, *inter alia*, that the Member States shall provide for time-limits for the applicant to exercise his or her right to an effective remedy.[325] The text of the Recast Proposal of the Procedures Directive adds that national time limits must be reasonable: Article 41, fourth paragraph, stipulates that Member States shall provide for reasonable time-limits for the applicant to exercise his or her right to an effective remedy.[326]

The CJEU often leaves the determination of the question of whether a national time limit or limitation period is (in)compatible with the principle of effective judicial protection to the national courts. The Court does, however, provide the national courts with tools to answer this question. In a number of cases, tools have been provided in the form of imagined situations in which, due to particular circumstances, the effect of the national time limit at issue is particularly harmful for one of the parties. A clear example of this approach is *Manfredi and others v. Lloyd Adriatico Assicurazioni SpA and Others* (2006).[327] This case concerned a dispute between a number of individuals and a number of insurance companies. The judicial proceedings before the domestic Italian court were based on Article 81 of the former EC Treaty (currently Article 101 TFEU on the prohibition on contracts which negatively affect trade and competition within the single market) and were aimed at obtaining damages against insurance companies related to the increase in the cost of premiums paid under an agreement declared unlawful by the national Italian competition authority (AGCM). In the national proceedings, the insurance companies pleaded that the right to compensation in damages was out of time; according to them, the limitation period for bringing proceedings started to run from the day on which the agreement, which was subsequently declared unlawful, had been adopted. The national judge referred to the CJEU the question of whether Article 81 EC precludes a national rule which provides that the limitation period for seeking compensation for harm caused by an agreement or practice prohibited under Article 81 EC begins to run from the day on which that prohibited agreement or practice had been adopted. The CJEU did not find this national rule problematic. The Court did, however, indicate that, in combination with a short appeal limitation period (for example, fourteen days), and in combination with the absence of a possibility of suspension, the national rule in question might become problematic. The Court considered that it was for the national court to determine whether a national rule which provided that the limitation period for seeking compensation for harm caused by an agreement or practice prohibited under Article 81 EC began to run from the day on which that prohibited agreement or practice had been adopted, particularly where it also imposed a short limitation

---

325   Article 39, second paragraph, of the Procedures Directive (Council Directive 2005/85/EC of 1 December 2005).

326   COM (2009) 554 final 21 October 2009, 2009/0165 (COD). The recast proposal can be found integrally in Hailbronner 2010, p. 1311-1350. It can also be found in the EUR-lex database: http://eur-lex.europa.eu, under Preparatory documents, COM documents.

327   CJEU, *Manfredi and others v. Lloyd Adriatico Assicurazioni SpA and Others*, 13 July 2006, Joined Cases C-295/04 to C-298/04.

period that could not be suspended, rendered it practically impossible or excessively difficult to exercise the right to seek compensation for the harm suffered.[328]

In *Pontin* (2009),[329] the CJEU clearly found the national time limit problematic. *Pontin* was dismissed by her employer with immediate effect on grounds of unauthorised absence. The day following her dismissal, Pontin informed her employer that she was pregnant and that her dismissal was null and void by virtue of the legal protection enjoyed by pregnant workers. Her employers did not respond. She then brought proceedings before the Employment Tribunal of Esch-sur-Alzette, Luxembourg. The problem was that the Luxembourg Labour Code stipulated that the dismissed female employee might, within 15 days of the termination of the contract, request the president of the court exercising jurisdiction in employment matters, to declare the dismissal null and void and order her continued employment. Ms Pontin had waited for three months before initiating proceedings. She had also addressed the wrong instance: the court and not the president of the court. The Employment Tribunal asked the CJEU, *inter alia*, whether EU law precludes national legislation which makes legal action brought by a pregnant employee who has been dismissed during her pregnancy subject to a 15-day time limit.

In its judgment, the CJEU noted that short time limits for actions of this type were, in principle, legitimate in the interests of legal certainty. The Court then considered that the 15-day time limit in this case was particularly short in view, *inter alia*, of the situation in which a pregnant woman found herself at the start of her pregnancy, and for obtaining proper advice. The Court took into account that some of the days included in that period might have expired before the pregnant woman received the letter notifying her of the dismissal, since it would seem that this period began to run, according to the case law of the CJEU, from the time the letter of dismissal was posted and not from the time it was received. The Court concluded that the combination of the short time limit and the requirement to address specifically the president of the court, appeared to give rise to procedural problems and, therefore, made the exercise of the rights that pregnant women derived from Article 10 excessively difficult. This seemed to be non-compliant with the principle of effectiveness, although this was for the national court to determine.[330]

In its judgment in *Samba Diouf* (2011),[331] a case concerning asylum, the CJEU ruled that a national time limit of 15 days for bringing an appeal against rejection of an application for asylum did not generally seem to be insufficient, but that particular circumstances might give rise to decide otherwise, and that it was up to the national court to do so in such circumstances:

'As regards the fact that the time-limit for bringing an action is 15 days in the case of an accelerated procedure, whilst it is 1 month in the case of a decision adopted under the ordinary procedure, the important point, as the Advocate General has stated in point 63 of his Opinion,

---

328 *Ibidem*, paras. 73-82.
329 CJEU, *Pontin*, 29 October 2009, C-63/08. See also the comment on this case by R.J.G.M. Widdershoven in *AB* 2010, 1.
330 *Ibidem*, paras. 60-69.
331 CJEU, *Samba Diouf*, 28 July 2011, C-69/10.

is that the period prescribed must be sufficient in practical terms to enable the applicant to prepare and bring an effective action. With regard to abbreviated procedures, a 15-day time limit for bringing an action does not seem, generally, to be insufficient in practical terms to prepare and bring an effective action and appears reasonable and proportionate in relation to the rights and interests involved. It is, however, for the national court to determine – should that time-limit prove, in a given situation, to be insufficient in view of the circumstances – whether that element is such as to justify, on its own, upholding the action brought indirectly against the decision to examine the application for asylum under an accelerated procedure, so that, in upholding the action, the national court would order that the application be examined under the ordinary procedure.'[332]

So far, the CJEU has not been able to express itself on national time limits for submitting statements and presenting evidence in asylum cases. However, there have been cases concerning other areas of law in which the Court did rule on questions concerning time limits for submitting evidence. An example is the case of *Laub* (2007),[333] which concerned the recovery of export refunds unduly paid by national authorities. The CJEU ruled in this case that the time limit for submitting evidence must be reasonable:

'As there are no specific Community law rules prescribing the time-limits for the presentation of supplementary evidence in the context of a recovery procedure, it is a matter for the competent national authorities, in accordance with national law, and subject to the limits imposed by Community law, to grant a supplementary period on the basis of the specific circumstances of each case. The period allowed must be reasonable in order to allow the exporter to obtain and produce the required documentation and must take account of, in particular, any effect of the actions of the competent authority on the exporter.'[334]

When confronted with issues regarding time limits for presenting statements and evidence in asylum cases, it is likely that the CJEU will draw on this case law and will rule that reasonable national time limits are in conformity with EU law, provided that the principles of equivalence and effectiveness are met and that the party invoking the EU right is not affected in a particularly adverse way by the time limit in question, due to additional circumstances. It may also be expected that the CJEU will draw upon the principles concerning time limits developed by the ECtHR.[335] It will possibly also look at the principles developed by the HRC and the ComAT.[336] In sum, reasonable national time limits will normally not be problematic, but there must be room for national courts to be flexible when the circumstances of the case so require.

---

332 *Ibidem*, paras. 66-68.
333 CJEU, *Laub*, 21 June 2007, C-428/05.
334 *Ibidem*, para. 27.
335 See Chapter 5, section 5.6.10.
336 See Chapter 3, section 3.5.10, and Chapter 4, section 4.5.10.

6.5   Final concluding remarks

Since the Treaty of Lisbon (1 December 2009), the EU has had its own legally bind-ing bill of human rights, the Charter of Fundamental Rights of the EU, with the status of primary binding EU law. Asylum cases will almost always be within the scope of Union law, so the Charter will normally apply to asylum cases. The Treaty of Lisbon has made the CJEU fully competent to rule on the validity of secondary asy-lum law, and on the interpretation of primary and secondary EU asylum law. All na-tional courts are permitted to refer preliminary questions in pending asylum cases to the CJEU. It has so far issued only a limited number of judgments concerning asy-lum, so that at this point in time we can only describe this Court's position on a limit-ed number of aspects of evidence and judicial scrutiny and not on all the eleven as-pects.

Article 18 of the Charter stipulates that the right to asylum shall be guaranteed with due respect for the rules of the RC. By virtue of this provision, national asylum courts will have to pay due respect to the procedural provisions of the RC, and to the procedural positions taken by the UNHCR, discussed in Chapter 2. It may be argued that it is no longer possible to set these positions aside as non-binding as this would amount to non-compliance with Article 18 of the Charter, which is binding primary Union law.

The standards and principles on proceedings, evidence and judicial scrutiny flowing from the ECHR (discussed in Chapter 5) are incorporated into EU law via Articles 19, 47 and 52, third paragraph, of the Charter. They transform from inter-governmental international law into supranational EU law, which takes precedence over all national law. Finally, by virtue of the Charter Preamble, Article 78 TFEU and Article 53 of the Charter, the standards and principles on proceedings, evidence and judicial scrutiny flowing from the ICCPR and the CAT (discussed in Chapters 3 and 4) form important additional sources of interpretation of Articles 19, second para-graph, and 47 of the Charter.

Article 47 of the Charter is – as well as the mirror of Articles 6 and 13 ECHR – also the codification of the Union law principle of effective judicial protection. Within the framework of the principle of effective judicial protection, five different standards of intensity of judicial scrutiny for different categories of cases have been developed, varying from a very light judicial touch with no factual review (cases about staff matters) to an intense full and *ex nunc* judicial scrutiny on facts, law and propor-tionality (cases concerning restrictions on the fundamental freedoms of EU citizens, their third-country national family members and Turkish workers and their family members who enjoy the rights of Decision 1/80 or under the Association Agree-ment).It has been estimated that the CJEU will apply the most intense standard of judicial scrutiny in asylum cases. First, due to the strong parallel between asylum cases and cases concerning restrictions on the fundamental freedoms of EU citizens, which are both about fundamental freedoms or rights. Second, because that standard comes very close to the type of judicial scrutiny performed by the ECtHR under Article 3 ECHR in a significant number of asylum cases, and to the full jurisdiction require-ment and the rigorous scrutiny requirement flowing from, respectively, Articles 6 and 13 ECHR. The judgment in the case of *Samba Diouf* (2011), in which the CJEU ruled that the final decision on an asylum claim must be the subject of a *thorough* review on the merits by the national court, shows that this expectation is not imaginary.

The provisions regarding judicial review in secondary EU asylum law must be interpreted in accordance with the higher ranking Article 47 of the Charter and the higher ranking general principle of effective judicial protection. The attempts to keep national courts away from asylum refusals or to water down the intensity of judicial scrutiny over such decisions, which are reflected in the texts of these provisions, have, therefore, been made in vain.

The standard of proof laid down in Article 2, sub d, of the EU Qualification Directive 2011/95 is that it must be established, *to a reasonable degree* that, upon expulsion, the claimant's life or freedom would be threatened. The standard in Article 2, sub f, is taken literally from the ECtHR's case law under Article 3 ECHR and is that the risk is real and not fictional, that it is personal (relates to the individual), and that it is foreseeable. The risk does not need to be certain or highly probable, but must exceed the mere possibility of the claimant being subjected to proscribed ill-treatment. As to the burden of proof, under the first and second paragraphs of Article 4 of the Qualification Directive, the applicant is enjoined with a burden of assertion, which seems to be a rather low threshold. It entails that he or she submit the statements and the documentary evidence at his or her disposal. The authorities have an investigative burden with regard to the issues mentioned in the third paragraph of Article 4 of the Qualification Directive in particular the situation in the country of origin. In its judgment in *M.M. v. Minister for Justice, Equality and Law Reform, Ireland* (2012) the CJEU has ruled that this requirement of co-operation contained in Article 4 of the Qualification Directive means that if, for any reason whatsoever, the elements provided by an applicant for international protection are not complete, up to date or relevant, it is necessary for the Member State concerned to cooperate actively with the applicant, at that stage of the procedure, so that all the elements needed to substantiate the application may be assembled. A Member State may also be better placed than an applicant to gain access to certain types of documents. The CJEU has so far not explained any further what is meant by 'active co-operation with the applicant so that all the elements needed to substantiate the application may be assembled.' One may probably think of situations in which the authority offers the applicant a certain (additional) period for submitting new relevant documentation, of situations in which the applicant proposes that the authority hears witnesses and the authority in response to that arranges hearing sessions, and situations in which the applicant submits certain documents and the national administrative or judicial authority orders an expert authenticity examination. Like the ECtHR did in 2010 in *Iskandarov v. Russia*, the CJEU makes clear in *M.M.* that there may be specific circumstances in which the administrative or judicial authority is better placed than the applicant to get hold of certain types of documents.

Under Article 4 of the Qualification Directive the relevant facts and circumstances can be divided into two categories: a) personal circumstances, and b) facts and circumstances relating to the situation in the country of origin. Article 4, fourth paragraph, makes clear that past persecution, past serious harm or threats thereof are highly relevant facts which give rise to a refutable presumption that the applicant qualifies for refugee or subsidiary protection. The lists of facts and circumstances provided in paragraphs 2 and 3 of Article 4 are not exhaustive. In the light of Article 78 TFEU, we may safely assume that all the facts and circumstances mentioned in the previous chapters are equally relevant under Article 4 of the Qualification Directive.

As to the required degree of individual risk, it was concluded, with reference to the *Elgafaji* judgment (2009) that the division into three types of situations developed in the ECtHR's case law is also workable for subsidiary protection under Union asylum law. The three categories are: situations of extreme general violence, situations of group violence and other cases. In situations of extreme general violence no individual risk is required; in situations of group violence membership of that group forms sufficient individual Article 3-risk and in all other cases special personal facts and circumstances are required to establish that this very applicant runs a risk. In paragraph 39 of *Elgafaji*, the CJEU ruled that 'the more the applicant is able to show that he is specifically affected by reason of factors particular to his personal circumstances, the lower the level of indiscriminate violence required for him to be eligible for subsidiary protection.' This is the mirror of the gradual scale notion emerging from the case law of the ECtHR and the ComAT that, the graver the general human rights situation in the country of origin, the less individual facts and circumstances, including evidence corroborating these individual facts and circumstances, are required. Finally, it was concluded that, for refugee protection under EU asylum law, no requirement of being singled out may be imposed.

The neutrality of the terms 'element' and 'substantiate' in Article 4, first paragraph, of the Qualification Directive indicates that, in principle, every form of evidence capable of proving the risk can be admitted to the procedure, whether oral or written or evidence in another form. Secondary EU asylum law does not contain provisions making clear exactly how much evidence is required to sufficiently corroborate a claim for international protection, and of what quality that evidence should be. Nor does it contain any provisions regarding the evaluation of the evidence.

Secondary EU asylum law does not address in a detailed way the aspect of opportunities for presenting evidence and reacting to evidence and the CJEU has so far not been able to express itself on this aspect in asylum cases. There is much case law on the right to *inter partes* or adversarial judicial proceedings in other areas, such as marketing and competition. It appears from this jurisprudence that adversariality and equality of arms are considered to be important safeguards. The general principles developed by the CJEU concerning the use of secret evidence strongly resemble those developed by the ECtHR (see 5.5.4). These general principles include the notions that the use of secret evidence is permitted provided that it has a legitimate aim and that it is necessary; that the interest of the State to keep the evidence secret must be balanced against the individual's right to have knowledge of this evidence and his procedural rights of adversarial proceedings and equality of arms; that the court examining the appeal should be able to effectively review the confidential evidence on which the impugned decision is based and that limitations to a party's procedural rights as a consequence of the use of secret evidence should be compensated by taking counterbalancing measures (compensation techniques).

The case of *Steffensen* (2003) clearly demonstrates that the CJEU regards national courts as guardians of the safeguards of adversarial proceedings and equality of arms.

Article 4, first paragraph, of the EU Qualification Directive 2011/95 requires the applicant to submit as soon as possible all elements underpinning his or her claim for international protection. The general rule established in the constant case law of the CJEU is that reasonable national time limits are compatible with EU law. In *Samba Diouf* (2011), an asylum case, the CJEU reiterated the rule that reasonable national time limits are compatible with EU law. In this judgment, the Court also made clear that national courts must have room for flexibility when the circumstances of the case require this.

It may be concluded that EU law offers added value in three ways. First, it causes a transformation in the legal status of existing standards on evidence and judicial scrutiny contained in or flowing from international asylum law. These existing standards transform from non-binding principles into more important rules which must be respected (the standards developed by the UNHRC via Article 18 of the Charter), from intergovernmental international law into binding primary supranational EU law (the standards developed by the ECtHR via Articles 19 and 47 of the Charter) and from intergovernmental international law into important sources of inspiration for binding EU law (the standards and principles developed by the HRC and the ComAT via Articles 19 and 47 of the Charter). This incorporation into EU law makes the obligations and standards from the ECHR, the ICCPR and the CAT more important. The reason for this is that not only the treaties themselves, but also primary binding supranational EU law requires that the obligations and standards from the treaties are taken into account, with the CJEU as the international monitoring court.

Second, the standards and principles developed under Article 6 ECHR are now applicable to asylum cases, as they form part of Article 47 of the EU Charter.

Third, the system of judicial supervision over EU asylum law has a strong complementary value. The preliminary procedure before the CJEU offers national courts the possibility to refer questions to the CJEU pending the national judicial proceedings. In this way, violations of human rights may be prevented or redressed at a much earlier stage.

Chapter 7: National courts and the independent and rigorous scrutiny

7.1 Towards a coherent set of standards for use by national courts

The previous chapters were aimed at discovering standards on judicial scrutiny and evidence in international and European asylum law. To find such standards, treaty and EU law provisions on or relevant to national (judicial) proceedings were analysed. In addition, the assessment in expulsion cases as performed by the HRC, the ComAT and the ECtHR was analysed in order to discover the standards on judicial scrutiny and evidence applied by these international treaty monitoring bodies and court.

From the discovered standards on national judicial scrutiny, a common denominator appeared. A national judicial remedy in cases concerning the expulsion of asylum seekers is ECHR-compliant if it performs an 'independent and rigorous scrutiny' of the protection claim.[1] It is ICCPR-compliant if it considers the claim for protection 'thoroughly and fairly'.[2] CAT-compliance is ensured when a national judicial remedy offers an 'effective, independent and impartial review' of the decision on expulsion.[3] On many occasions the UNHCR has expressed its opinion that national judges dealing with asylum cases should be able to 'obtain a personal impression of the applicant' and that 'appeal or review proceedings should involve points of fact, including credibility, and points of law'.[4] Finally, in *Samba Diouf* (2011), the CJEU ruled that the final decision on an asylum claim must be the subject of a 'thorough review on the merits of the claim' by the national court.[5] Thus, the common denominator following from international and EU asylum law is that national courts are required to offer an independent and rigorous (thorough) scrutiny of the asylum refusal.

The central question in this chapter is how national asylum courts can live up to this requirement. In order to find an answer to this question, the results of the analysis conducted in the previous chapters are now brought together with the aim of defining more exactly what a 'rigorous and independent national judicial scrutiny' is about.

The first question looked at in this chapter, in section 7.2, is how the treaties studied in this book and EU asylum law relate to each other. This question is address-

---

1   See, for some recent examples, ECtHR, *Muminov v. Russia*, 11 December 2008, Appl. No. 42502/06, para. 101; *Abdolkhani and Karimnia v. Turkey*, 22 September 2009, Appl. No. 30471/08, para. 108; ECtHR, *Hirsi Jamaa and others v. Italy*, 23 February 2012, Appl. No. 27765/09, para. 198.

2   See, for example, HRC, *Dawood Khan v. Canada*, 10 August 2006, No. 1302/2004, para. 5.3.

3   See, for example, ComAT, *Agiza v. Sweden*, 20 May 2005, No. 233/2003, paras. 13.6 and 13.7.

4   See, for example, submission of the UNHCR in the case of *Mir Isfahani v. the Netherlands*. Appl. No. 31252/03, May 2005, www.unhcr.org/refworld/docid/454f5e484.html, last visited 23 December 2012, paras. 31-42.

5   CJEU, *Samba Diouf*, 28 July 2011, C-69/10, paras. 56, 61.

ed in order to make clear how national asylum courts are bound by the procedural obligations flowing from the treaties and EU asylum law.

After that, in sections 7.3 and 7.4, an attempt is made to integrate into a coherent whole the standards on judicial scrutiny and evidence flowing from international and EU asylum law, with the objective of arriving at a coherent set of standards ready for use by national asylum courts.

One question that will be looked at in this exercise is whether the standards on judicial scrutiny and evidence featuring in the assessment in expulsion cases as performed by the HRC, the ComAT and the ECtHR, are binding on national asylum courts, in the sense that national courts must work in exactly the same way. Other questions that will be looked at are whether a hierarchy of international sources and supervisors exists, what to do in case of conflicting standards, and whether cross-references are acceptable.

A basic presumption underpinning the analysis in this chapter is that in many asylum cases coming before national asylum courts within the EU, both refugee protection (Articles 1 and 33 RC, Article 18 of the EU Charter) and subsidiary protection (Articles 7 ICCPR, 3 CAT, 3 ECHR, Articles 4 and 19 of the EU Charter) will be invoked in parallel, as in many EU countries both types of protection are dealt with in the same single procedure. Such a 'one-stop shop' procedure exists, for example, in Belgium, the Netherlands, the UK, Poland, Spain and Italy.[6] As a result, all the treaties and instruments covered by this study are relevant to and applicable in such cases. (A two-step procedure exists in Ireland, where separate applications for asylum and for subsidiary protection are required and these applications are dealt with in separate subsequent procedures.[7])

7.2 National courts are 'double bound' by treaty obligations

The transfer by the EU Member States to the EU of the competence to make binding rules on asylum has not affected the obligations flowing from the RC, the ICCPR, the CAT and the ECHR. This follows from Articles 26 and 34 VTC, read in conjunction. Article 26 VTC states:

'Every treaty in force is binding upon the parties to it and must be performed by them in good faith'.[8]

The Member States of the EU constitute a minority of the States parties to the RC, the ECHR, the ICCPR and the CAT. Article 34 VTC stipulates:

---

6 See for a description of different national procedures in the countries mentioned here Zwaan 2008, pp. 57-161.
7 See CJEU, *M.M. v. Minister for Justice, Equality and Law Reform*, 22 November 2012, C-277/11, paras. 28, 29.
8 Article 26 VTC.

'A treaty does not create either obligations or rights for a third State without its consent.'[9]

It follows from these provisions, read in conjunction, that national asylum courts within the EU Member States must comply with the procedural obligations flowing from the RC, the ICCPR, the CAT and the ECHR, analysed in the previous Chapters 2-5. The transfer of powers on asylum to the EU in 1999 has not changed this.[10]

The case law of both the ECtHR and the CJEU lends support to this conclusion. In *T.I. v. the UK* (2000), *K.R.S. v. the UK* (2008) and *M.S.S. v. Belgium and Greece* (2011), the ECtHR ruled that States remain responsible under the ECHR for the consequences of removing asylum seekers from their territory, notwithstanding the fact that removal is carried out under the EU Dublin mechanism.[11] In *M.S.S. v. Belgium and Greece* (2011), the ECtHR ruled that the 'equivalent protection' doctrine developed in its *Bosphorus* judgment[12] did not apply.[13] In its judgment in *ERT v. DEP* (1991),[14] the CJEU made clear that fundamental rights form an integral part of the general principles of EU law and that the ECHR has special significance in this respect.[15] To conclude, the procedural obligations on national asylum courts flowing from the RC, the ICCPR, the CAT and the ECHR, set out in Chapters 2-5, exist *alongside* EU asylum law, as separate obligations flowing from international law.

National asylum courts are also bound by the procedural obligations flowing from the treaties *via* EU law. In Chapter 6, it was demonstrated how the procedural obligations from the treaties are incorporated into EU asylum law. Reference is made to sections 6.1.3.1, 6.1.4, 6.2 and 6.3. This incorporation into EU law makes the obligations and standards from the treaties more important. The reason for this is that compliance with the obligations and standards from the treaties is now also required by primary binding supranational EU law, with the CJEU as the international monitoring court. In Chapter 6 it was also made clear that the procedural obligations and

---

9   Article 34 VTC.
10   See for the same conclusion Battjes 2006, pp. 59-77.
11   ECtHR, *T.I. v. the UK*, admissibility decision, 7 March 2000, Appl. No. 43844/98; ECtHR, *K.R.S. v. the UK*, admissibility decision, 2 December 2008, Appl.No. 32733/08; ECtHR, *M.S.S. v. Belgium and Greece*, 21 January 2011, Appl. No. 30696/09, paras. 342, 343.
12   ECtHR, *Bosphorus Hava Yollari Turizm ve Ticet Anonim Serketi v. Ireland*, 30 June 2005, Appl. No. 45036/98. This case was about a seizure by the Irish Government in 1993 of an aircraft owned by Yugoslav airlines, but leased to Bosphorus Airways, a Turkish company, based on an EC regulation, which gave effect to UN Security Council Resolutions imposing sanctions against the Federal Republic of Yugoslavia. Before the ECtHR two issues were raised, being Ireland's responsibility under the ECHR and the interference with the right to property under Article 1, Protocol 1 ECHR. In its judgment, the ECtHR developed the 'equivalent protection' doctrine. It held that Ireland was acting as required under EU law and that this was in itself a legitimate general interest of considerable weight capable of serving as a justification for breaches of property rights. *Bosphorus* seems to have no implications for asylum. It is relevant in only two situations, namely where actions of the EU itself are being challenged or where national implementing measures are challenged and the Member States have no discretion whatsoever. In asylum cases the EU Member States will always have some discretion. See Battjes 2006, p. 75, Costello 2006, p. 107.
13   ECtHR, *M.S.S. v. Belgium and Greece*, 21 January 2011, Appl. No. 30696/09,para. 340. See also Costello 2006, pp. 109, 121-123, Battjes 2006, p. 75.
14   CJEU, *ERT v. DEP*, 18 June 1991, C-260/89.
15   CJEU *ERT v. DEP*, 18 June 1991, C-260/89, paras.41 and 42.

standards from the ECHR form 'bottom norms' and that EU asylum law may offer more protection.[16]

National asylum courts in the EU Member States are, thus, 'double bound' by the procedural obligations and standards flowing from the treaties investigated in this study as they are bound by the treaties and by EU law which incorporates the treaty obligations.

7.3 The 'independent and rigorous national judicial scrutiny': sources of interpretation

7.3.1 Origins

The requirement of an 'independent and rigorous national judicial scrutiny' follows primarily from the effective remedy provisions and the procedural limbs of the *refoulement* prohibitions contained in the international treaties studied in this book. A national judicial remedy in cases concerning the expulsion of asylum seekers is compliant with Articles 7, 2, third paragraph, ICCPR and Article 5, second paragraph, sub b Optional Protocol to the ICCPR if it considers the claim for protection 'thoroughly and fairly'.[17] Article 3 and Article 22, fifth paragraph, CAT require an opportunity for 'effective, independent and impartial review' of the decision on expulsion.[18] A national judicial remedy in cases concerning the expulsion of asylum seekers is compliant with Articles 3, 13 and 35, first paragraph, ECHR if it is able to comprise both substantive and procedural points and is able to quash the administrative asylum refusal.[19] Asylum courts at national level will, thus, need to perform an 'independent and rigorous scrutiny' of the protection claim.[20] Two common elements appear from these standards developed by the HRC, the ComAT and the ECtHR. National judicial review must be: 1) thorough (rigorous, effective); and 2) independent (impartial). The question is whether we can define in a more precise way what these two elements mean.

---

16 Article 52, third paragraph, of the EU Charter stipulates that: 'In so far as this Charter contains rights which correspond to rights guaranteed by the Convention for the Protection of Human Rights and Fundamental Freedoms, the meaning and scope of those rights shall be the same as those laid down by the said Convention. This provision shall not prevent Union law providing more extensive protection.'

17 See, for example, HRC, *Dawood Khan v. Canada*, 10 August 2006, No. 1302/2004, para. 5.3.

18 See, for example, ComAT, *Agiza v. Sweden*, 20 May 2005, No. 233/2003.

19 ECtHR, *Baysakov v. Ukraine*, 1 June 2010, Appl. No. 29031/04, para. 75; ECtHR, *Abdulazhon Isakov v. Russia*, 8 July 2010, Appl. No. 14049/08, para. 137; ECtHR, *A. v. the Netherlands*, 20 July 2010, Appl. No. 4900/06, para. 158.

20 For example, ECtHR, *Muminov v. Russia*, 11 December 2008, Appl. No. 42502/06, para. 101; ECtHR, *Abdolkhani and Karimnia v. Turkey*, 22 September 2009, Appl. No. 30471/08, para. 108.

7.3.2 Articles 19 and 47 EU Charter: standards on national judicial proceedings come together

Based on the results of the analysis conducted in the previous chapters, we may distinguish the following categories of provisions on or relevant to national court proceedings:

- *Non-refoulement* provisions hosting a procedural limb;
- Provisions guaranteeing an effective remedy at national level;
- Provisions requiring exhaustion of effective national remedies;
- Provisions guaranteeing access to court at national level and provisions requiring a fair court hearing;
- Provisions guaranteeing due process of law at national level in cases of expulsion;
- Other procedural provisions.

Table 1 below provides an overview of these provisions. Provisions not explicitly covered due to lack of jurisprudence and literature are put in brackets. Table 1 below illustrates the phenomenon of the incorporation of existing treaty provisions into EU law described in Chapter 6. It illustrates that Article 18 of the EU Charter – by stating that respect is required for the rules of the RC – incorporates into EU law the provisions on proceedings from the RC and incorporates into EU law the UNHCR's positions on evidence and judicial scrutiny, as the UNHCR is the RC's supervisor. Table 1 also illustrates that Article 19, second paragraph, of the EU Charter incorporates into EU law, via Articles 52, third paragraph, and 53, of the EU Charter:

- The procedural limb of the *refoulement* prohibition from the ICCPR (Article 7 ICCPR);
- The procedural limb of the *refoulement* prohibition from the CAT (Article 3 CAT);
- The procedural limb of the *refoulement* prohibition from the ECHR (Article 3 ECHR).

Table 1, finally, illustrates that Article 47, first and second paragraph, of the EU Charter incorporates into EU law, via Articles 52, third paragraph, and 53, of the EU Charter:

- The effective remedy provision from the ICCPR (Article 2, paragraph 3 ICCPR);
- The effective remedy provisions from the CAT (Articles 12 and 13 CAT);
- The effective remedy provision from the ECHR (Article 13);
- The fair court hearing provision from the ICCPR (Article 14);
- The fair court hearing provision from the ECHR (Article 6);
- The access to court provision from the RC (Article 16).

It follows from the foregoing that the requirement of an independent and rigorous national judicial scrutiny – originally developed within the context of the effective remedy provisions and *refoulement* prohibitions of the ICCPR, the CAT and the ECHR – also forms part of Articles 19 and 47 of the EU Charter.

Table 1: The provisions relevant to national judicial proceedings in the treaties and EU law

Treaty or instrument ▶ Type of provision ▼	RC	ICCPR	CAT	ECHR	EU law
1. *Refoulement* prohibitions with procedural limb	(Article 33)	Article 7	Article 3	Article 3	Article 4 Charter Article 18 Charter Article 19(2) Charter
2. Effective remedy		Article 2(3)	Articles 12, 13	Article 13	Article 47(1) Charter Article 39 PD Article 29 TPD (right to mount a legal challenge) Article 21(1) RCD (right to appeal) Article 19(2) DR (right to appeal)
3. Exhaustion rules		Article 5(2)(b) First Optional Protocol	Article 22(5)	Article 35(1)	
4. Access to court, fair court hearing	Article 16	Article 14		Article 6	Article 47(2) Charter Article 18 Charter
5. Due process of law	Article 32	Article 13		(Article 1 Protocol 7)	
6. Other provisions	Article 35 on co-operation UNHCR – national authorities		Article 15 on the prohibition on using statements resulting from torture as evidence		Provisions on evidentiary issues in secondary asylum law: Article 2, sub c and sub e, QD on the standard of proof; Article 4 QD on the assessment of facts and circumstances; Article 8 PD on requirements for the examination of applications

It also follows from the foregoing that for the purpose of defining the requirement of an independent and rigorous national judicial scrutiny in a more precise way, we may turn to a variety of sources. These are:
-   The case law of the HRC, the ComAT and the ECtHR under the procedural limb of the *refoulement* prohibitions (Article 7 ICCPR, Article 3 CAT, Article 3 ECHR);

- The case law of the HRC, the ComAT and the ECtHR under the effective remedy provisions (Article 2, paragraph 3 ICCPR, Articles 12 and 13 CAT, Article 13 ECHR);
- The case law of the HRC and the ECtHR under the fair court hearing provisions (Article 14 ICCPR, Article 6 ECHR);
- The positions of the UNHCR concerning national judicial scrutiny and evidence as these positions form part of Article 16 RC on access to courts;
- The CJEU's case law on the principle of effective judicial protection as Article 47 also constitutes the codification of this EU law principle (see section 6.3.2).

For the purpose of defining the requirement of an independent and rigorous national judicial scrutiny, we may also turn to another important source of interpretation. This is the assessment as it is performed by the international supervisors and court, analysed in the second parts of chapters 3, 4 and 5. The standards on judicial scrutiny and evidence featuring in the assessment as applied by the international supervisors and court may help to further define what an independent and rigorous national judicial scrutiny is about.

7.3.3 Hierarchy of sources (1)?

The question arises of whether the sources of interpretation mentioned above can be classified into a hierarchy. The CJEU is the international court responsible for the interpretation and application of EU law, which is supranational.[21] It has consistently treated the ECHR as a special source of inspiration for EU law human rights and has often drawn on the ECHR in its case law.[22] This special status of the ECHR and the ECtHR's case law is also reflected in Article 52, third paragraph, of the EU Charter (see section 6.1.3.2). It would, therefore, be logical for national asylum courts to treat the case law of the CJEU and the ECtHR as the first and most important sources of interpretation. At this point in time there is only limited CJEU jurisprudence on evidence and judicial scrutiny in asylum cases, so the case law of the ECtHR must so far be seen as the leading source of interpretation.

The next source to turn to would be the UNHCR. Article 18 of the EU Charter requires that national courts pay due respect to the procedural provisions of the RC. One of these provisions is Article 35, the provision on co-operation between the UNHCR and national authorities. Respect for Article 35 RC as required by Article 18 of the EU Charter carries an obligation to pay respect to the positions on judicial scrutiny and evidence taken by the UNHCR, discussed in Chapter 2 (see Chapter 6, section 6.2.1.)

The case law of the HRC and the ComAT may be used as subsidiary or additional sources of interpretation. This follows from Article 53 of the EU Charter (see

---

21   Article 19, para. 1, TEU: 'It shall ensure that in the interpretation and application of the Treaties the law is observed.'

22   Some examples of judgments in which this special position of the ECHR is stressed are: CJEU, *Connolly v. Commission*, 6 March 2001, C-274/99, para. 37 P; CJEU, *Roquette Frères*, 22 October 2002, C-94/00, para. 25; CJEU, *Omega*, 14 October 2004, C-36/02, para. 33.

sections 6.2.2, 6.3.1) and also from the case law of the CJEU. In a number of cases, the CJEU has drawn explicitly on other human rights instruments, in addition to the ECHR, particularly the ICCPR.[23]

7.3.4   *Hierarchy of sources (2): the ECtHR's assessment as 'role model'?*

In the second part of Chapter 5, the assessment performed by the ECtHR in cases concerning the expulsion of asylum seekers was analysed with the aid of the eleven aspects of evidence and judicial scrutiny introduced in Chapter 1. It was concluded that, pertaining to those, the ECtHR has developed a set of precise and detailed standards. The question we will look at below is whether these standards are binding on national asylum courts.

There are many reasons for national asylum courts to ensure that they offer at least the same level of judicial protection as the level offered by the ECtHR by working with at least the same standards as the ones applied by the ECtHR.[24] First, Article 52, third paragraph, of the EU Charter stipulates that the rights contained in the Charter which correspond to rights in the ECHR, must be interpreted in conformity with their counterpart ECHR-rights as elucidated by the ECtHR. The standards on judicial scrutiny and evidence featuring in the assessment performed by the ECtHR in expulsion cases may be seen as standards elucidating Article 3 ECHR. In other words, these standards form part of Article 3. Article 19 of the EU Charter is the counterpart of Article 3 ECHR. Due to Article 52, third paragraph of the EU Charter, Article 19 of the EU Charter must be interpreted in conformity with Article 3 ECHR. It would amount to non-compliance with Article 19 of the Charter, which is binding primary Union law, if national asylum courts applied standards deviating significantly from those applied by the ECtHR under Article 3 ECHR.

Second, applying stricter standards at national court level may result in violations of Article 13 and may lead the ECtHR to declare cases admissible, in spite of the non-exhaustion of national remedies. In Chapter 5, examples were given in which this had happened: in *M.S.S. v. Belgium and Greece* (2011), a violation of Article 13 ECHR occurred because the Aliens Appeals Board applied a standard of proof which was much stricter than the one applied by the ECtHR.[25] In *Salah Sheekh v. the Netherlands* (2007), the ECtHR did not hold non-exhaustion of national remedies against the applicant as the national Council of State applied a constant jurisprudential line which incorporated a stricter requirement of individualisation than the one applied by the ECtHR.[26]

Third, the ECtHR has given more or less explicit messages under Article 13 ECHR that there should not be significant differences between the judicial scrutiny

---

23   See, for example, CJEU, *Dzodzi*, 18 October 1990, C-197/89, para. 68; CJEU, *Grant*, 17 February 1998, C-249/96, para. 44; CJEU, *European Parliament v. Council*, 27 June 2006, C-540/03, paras. 35-37, 54-57.

24   See, for the same conclusion, Battjes 2006, p. 322, Bruin 2003, Corstens (President of the Supreme Court of the Netherlands) 2010, pp. 166, 167, p. 386, Damen 2008, Wouters 2009, pp. 338, 339, 574.

25   ECtHR, *M...S.S. v. Belgium and Greece*, 21 January 2011, Appl. No. 30696/09, paras. 389, 390.

26   ECtHR, *Salah Sheekh v. the Netherlands*, 11 January 2007, Appl. No. 1948/04, paras. 123, 136, 148.

applied at national level and the judicial scrutiny offered by the ECtHR. The judgments of *Vilvarajah v. the UK* (1991)[27] and *Hilal v. the UK* (2001)[28] at first glance give the impression that the ECtHR accepted a national judicial investigation which was, at least in name and form, not a very rigorous one. However, closer examination of these two judgments reveals that the ECtHR considers its own 'rigorous scrutiny' in Article 3-cases as guidance for national courts, and that it is no coincidence that the ECtHR uses identical terminology for both the scrutiny exercised by the Court itself under Article 3 ('rigorous scrutiny') and the scrutiny required from the national authorities under Article 13 ('independent and rigorous scrutiny'). In both *Vilvarajah* and *Hilal*, the ECtHR concluded that the UK judicial review did provide an effective degree of control over the decisions of the administrative authorities in asylum cases and was sufficient to satisfy the requirements of Article 13.[29] The ECtHR noted in this connection that the UK courts examine whether the Home Secretary has correctly interpreted the law in relation to the grant or refusal of asylum and that, if the national courts are satisfied that he has made no error of law, they may, nevertheless, review the refusal of asylum in the light of the 'Wednesbury principles ' – an examination of the exercise of discretion by the Secretary of State to determine whether he or she left out of account a factor that should have been taken into account or took into account a factor that he or she should have ignored, or whether he or she came to a conclusion so unreasonable that no reasonable authority could have reached it. In *Vilvarajah*, the ECtHR took into account that the English courts had emphasised, in a number of judgments, their special responsibility to subject administrative decisions in the area of asylum to 'the most anxious scrutiny'.[30]

In *Smith and Grady v. the UK* (1999)[31] – a case in which the two applicants complained that investigations into their homosexuality and their discharge from the Royal Air Force on the ground of their homosexuality constituted violations of Article 8 ECHR alone and in conjunction with Article 14 ECHR – the ECtHR dealt with the applicants' complaint under Article 13 ECHR about the limited national judicial review by contrasting the case with the cases of *Soering v. the UK* (1989)[32] and *Vilvarajah v. the UK* (1991, author's emphasis):

'The present applications can be contrasted with the cases of *Soering* and *Vilvarajah* (…). In those cases, the Court found that the test applied by the national courts in applications for

---

27 ECtHR, *Vilvarajah and others v. the UK*, 30 October 1991, Appl. Nos. 13163/87, 13164/87, 13165/87, 13447/87 and 13448/87.

28 ECtHR, *Hilal v. the UK*, 6 March 2001, Appl. No. 45276/99.

29 ECtHR, *Vilvarajah and others v. the UK*, 30 October 1991, Appl. Nos. 13163/87, 13164/87, 13165/87, 13447/87 and 13448/87, paras. 117-127, ECtHR, *Hilal v. the UK*, 6 March 2001, Appl. No. 45276/99, paras. 75-79. See also Essakkili & Spijkerboer 2005, pp. 47-51, and Simon 1992 in his article 'Tamils and persecution of a group' in *NJCM Bulletin* 17-5 (1992), pp. 563-572.

30 ECtHR, *Vilvarajah and others v. the UK*, 30 October 1991, Appl. Nos. 13163/87, 13164/87, 13165/87, 13447/87 and 13448/87, paras. 90-91.

31 ECtHR, *Smith and Grady*, 27 September 1999, Appl. No. 33985/96; 33986/96.

32 ECtHR, *Soering v. the UK*, 7 July 1989, Appl. No. 1403/88.

judicial review of decisions by the Secretary of State in extradition and expulsion matters *coincided with the Court's own approach* under Article 3 of the Convention.'[33]

In *Hilal v. the UK* (2001), the Court considered:

'While the applicant argued that in judicial review applications, the courts will not reach findings of fact for themselves on disputed issues, the Court is satisfied that the national courts give careful scrutiny to claims that an expulsion would expose an applicant to the risk of inhuman or degrading treatment. The Court is not convinced that the fact that this scrutiny takes place against the background of the criteria applied in judicial review of administrative decisions, namely, rationality and perverseness, deprives the procedure of its effectiveness. The substance of the applicant's complaint was examined by the Court of Appeal, and it had the power to afford him the relief he sought.'[34]

And in *Hatton and others v. the UK* (2003) – a case concerning the acceptability under Article 8 ECHR of the noise and disturbance caused by night flights at Heathrow airport[35] – the ECtHR explained once again why in *Vilvarajah* compliance with the procedural limb of Article 3 ECHR was assumed:

'The scope of the national review in Vilvarajah (…) was relatively broad because of the importance national law attached to the matter of physical integrity. It was on this basis that judicial review was held to comply with the requirements of Article 3.'[36]

It follows from this case law that the ECtHR found the national judicial examination Articles 3- and 13-proof because, in essence, it did not differ significantly from the assessment performed by the ECtHR itself. In *Salah Sheekh v. the Netherlands* (2007), the ECtHR was particularly clear that in cases concerning expulsion or extradition involving an Article 3-claim rigorous scrutiny is needed. As the considerations in the judgment were so elaborate on this point, the judgment gave the impression that the ECtHR had specifically and critically reacted to the (partially) marginal judicial review applied by the asylum courts in the Netherlands.[37]

Fourth, protection of the subsidiary nature of the ECHR is a sound legal argument for national courts to apply the same standards as those applied by the ECtHR.[38] If national judicial proceedings offer fewer safeguards compared to the proceedings in Strasbourg, it will always make sense for individuals to apply to the ECtHR. This runs counter to the subsidiary nature of the Convention system. Subsidiarity means that citizens should be able to vindicate their rights in the national courts and that, however well organised, international protection of human rights can

---

33   ECtHR, *Smith and Grady*, 27 September 1999, Appl. No. 33985/96; 33986/96, para. 138.
34   ECtHR, *Hilal v. the UK*, 6 March 2001, Appl. No. 45276/99, para. 78.
35   ECtHR, *Hatton and others v. the UK*, 8 July 2003, Appl. No. 36022/97.
36   *Ibidem*, para. 140.
37   ECtHR, *Salah Sheekh v. the Netherlands*, 11 January 2007, Appl. No. 1948/04, para. 136; Wouters 2009, p. 339.
38   Battjes 2006, p. 322.

never be as effective as a well-functioning national system of protection.[39] Subsidiarity of the ECHR is already under serious threat as a result of the ever-increasing number of applications to the ECtHR. Asylum cases are heavily responsible for this. ECtHR Judge Myjer estimated that, in 2006, 80 per cent of all the cases against the Netherlands concerned migration and a large part of this category concerned asylum cases.[40] This sharp rise in asylum cases has continued up to the present; in their speeches on the occasion of the opening of the judicial year on 28 January 2011, both Jean-Paul Costa, President of the ECtHR, and António Guterres, United Nations High Commissioner for Refugees, stressed that a large proportion of the ECtHR's workload concerned asylum issues.[41]

When this study was embarked upon (early 2007), the highest national asylum court in the Netherlands, the Council of State, took the position that different standards at national and international judicial level were acceptable (as far as the credibility assessment was concerned).[42] In support of this position, it was argued that the position of national courts was different as they operated within a framework of checks and balances with the national executive and legislative powers and was, therefore, different from that of the ECtHR as international supervisor. Although this is true, this does not constitute a valid reason for national courts and the ECtHR to assess asylum cases under Article 3 ECHR in significantly different ways, as this argument does not rebut the above-mentioned reasons for working in a congruent way.

Another argument voiced at national level in the Netherlands was that, when it came to the credibility assessment, the national judiciary should be careful and pay deference to the national executive, as the executive processed more cases and, therefore, had much broader experience and expertise. It would, therefore, be unwise if national courts always actively determined the facts independently and on their own account.[43] This argument makes some sense, at least for the situation in the Netherlands and other countries where asylum claims are first examined by an administrative decision maker and appeals against refusals are dealt with by courts. It cannot be denied that in such a situation the administrative decision maker assesses all the asylum cases and also sees the (obviously) deserving cases, whereas the national courts deal only with those cases where asylum was initially refused. However, the ECtHR's approach to the credibility assessment and the application of investigative powers offers a very reasonable solution here, which also ensures respect for the experience and expertise of administrative decision makers. As was explained in the second part of Chapter 5, the ECtHR actively proceeds towards an independent determination of the facts, including credibility, and applies investigative powers to that end, in cases where (one of the following) triggers occur(s): insufficient national proceedings (for

---

39 Barkhuysen 1998, pp. 12 and 13. See also the annual report for 2006 of the ECtHR, p. 30.

40 Speech by ECtHR Judge Myjer held on 21 June 2007 on the occasion of the retirement and emeritus status of Professor P. Boeles.

41 'Chroniques Strasbourgeoises', *NJCM Bulletin* 36 (2011), 2, p. 258.

42 See the judgment of the Council of State of 5 June 2006, 200602132/1and 200602135/1, para. 2.6; it was stated that the immigration judge in the Netherlands is not obliged to review the administrative stance on flight narrative credibility in the same way as the ECtHR investigates whether or not the Netherlands have violated their treaty obligation under Article 3.

43 See, for example, Lubberdink 2009.

example, evidence was overlooked or not taken seriously, or the assessment made at national level was insufficiently supported by relevant country of origin materials); new facts, circumstances and developments, including evidence thereof, or new information which casts doubt on the information relied on by the government; and disrespect for the absolute nature of Article 3, for example, a weighing of national security considerations against the Article 3-risk, or an incorrect application of the standard of proof or another evidentiary standard, for example, a too strict standard of proof or a too strict standard on individualization. National courts can easily follow this approach without heavily disturbing national systems of checks and balances. This would mean that national asylum courts would actively and independently make a fresh factual determination in cases of insufficient administrative proceedings (for example, evidence had not been properly examined by the administrative decision maker), in cases where at the judicial stage new facts or circumstances were invoked or new evidence was submitted and in cases where the national court established that the administrative decision maker had disrespected the absolute nature of Article 3 ECHR by weighing national security or public order arguments against the risk, or had applied an incorrect evidentiary standard under Article 3. In other circumstances, national courts would rely on the determination of the facts made by the administrative decision maker.

It may be argued that, like the ECtHR, national courts should at least always have the fully free choice to determine, in each particular case at hand, whether full judicial scrutiny or a somewhat less intense form of judicial review is appropriate. National courts are the last national instances looking at cases and are as such best positioned to see all the relevant circumstances conditioning this choice. As Judge Martens stated in his separate opinion to *Fischer v. Austria* (1995):

> 'The balancing operation is far too subtle and too dependent on the specific type of subject-matter of each case to be left to the legislature; the rule of law implies that it should be left to the judiciary, which should have the last word. (...) Only if the national tribunal is in principle competent to review completely the original decision, be it that it should be empowered to exercise restraint with regard to such decisions and assessments by the executive authorities which, in its opinion, should properly be left to their discretion.'[44]

Finally, the workload argument is not very convincing either. There is no reason to fear that working in the same way as the ECtHR would mean that national courts would have to organise, in all pending asylum cases, fact-finding missions and hear witnesses, as the ECtHR did in the case of *N. v. Finland* (2005).[45] Just like criminal and civil cases, some asylum cases are truly difficult and require extensive investigations, whereas other asylum cases are easy to decide and do not require much research. It all depends on the individual flight narrative, the particular situation in the country of origin, the quantity and quality of the available evidence and the quality of the administrative decision.

---

44   ECtHR, *Fischer v. Austria*, 26 April 1995, Appl. No. 16922/90, separate opinion of Judge Martens.
45   ECtHR, *N. v. Finland*, 27 July 2005, Appl. No. 38885/02.

All the arguments discussed above lead me to conclude that the standards on judicial scrutiny and evidence as applied by the ECtHR are, as minimum norms, binding on national asylum courts.

7.3.5 Hierarchy of sources (3): UNHCR, HRC and ComAT as 'role models'?

In section 7.3.4, it was made clear that the ECtHR's standards are the first source for national asylum courts when defining the standard of an independent and rigorous national judicial scrutiny. The standards developed by the UNHCR were mentioned as a second source, and the standards developed and applied in the case law of the HRC and the ComAT were mentioned as subsidiary sources of interpretation.

It follows from the conclusions arrived at in Chapters 2, 3, 4 and 5 that the standards on evidence and judicial scrutiny developed and applied by the ECtHR, the UNHCR, the HRC and the ComAT often coincide. At the same time, there are a number of major differences concerning, mainly, adversariality (a relatively stricter stance by the HRC and the ComAT), the standard of proof (a relatively stricter standard applied by the HRC), the credibility assessment and the application of investigative powers (a relatively more active role by the ECtHR and a clear standard developed by the UNHCR on the required intensity of national judicial scrutiny, being full and independent scrutiny on facts, including credibility, and law), the evaluation of evidence (concrete standards developed by the ECtHR versus the less concrete standards of the other international supervisors), and the weight attached to medico-legal reports (special position of the ComAT). When confronted with diverging standards, the international preference rules laid down in the VTC and in the treaties themselves may be of assistance to national courts. Article 30, second paragraph, VTC stipulates:

'when a treaty specifies that it is subject to, or that it is not to be considered as incompatible with, an earlier or later treaty, the provisions of that other treaty prevail'.

Article 5 RC states:

'Nothing in this Convention shall be deemed to impair any rights and benefits granted by a Contracting State to refugees apart from this Convention'.

Similarly, Article 53 ECHR stipulates:

'nothing in this Convention shall be construed as limiting or derogating from any of the human rights and fundamental freedoms which may be ensured under the laws of any High Contracting Party or under any other agreement to which it is a Party'.

Article 5, second paragraph, ICCPR reads:

'there shall be no restriction upon or derogation from any of the fundamental human rights recognized or existing in any State Party to the present Covenant pursuant to law, conventions, regulations or custom on the pretext that the present Covenant does not recognize such rights or that it recognizes them to a lesser extent'.

Article 16, second paragraph, CAT stipulates:

'the provisions of this Convention are without prejudice to the provisions of any other international instrument or national law which prohibit cruel, inhuman or degrading treatment or punishment or which relate to extradition or expulsion'.

Finally, Article 351 TFEU reads:

'the rights and obligations arising from agreements concluded before 1 January 1958 or, for acceding States, before the date of their accession, between one or more Member States on the one hand, and one or more third countries on the other, shall not be affected by the provisions of the Treaties. To the extent that such agreements are not compatible with the Treaties, the Member State or States concerned shall take all appropriate steps to eliminate the incompatibilities established. Member States shall, where necessary, assist each other to this end and shall, where appropriate, adopt a common attitude'.

As Battjes has persuasively argued, 'anterior treaties ' must be understood as treaties in force before 1 May 1999, the date of the entry into force of the Treaty of Amsterdam by which powers on asylum were transferred to the EU, and include all the treaties investigated.[46] Thus, in the case of conflict between obligations under EU asylum law and obligations flowing from the RC, the ECHR, the ICCPR and the CAT, which cannot be solved by conciliatory interpretation, the obligations of the latter treaties prevail. This preference rule is also laid down in Article 53 of the Charter, which stipulates, *inter alia*:

'nothing in the Charter shall be interpreted as restricting or adversely affecting human rights and fundamental freedoms as recognised by international agreements to which the Member States are party'.

When we read the preference rules contained in the treaties and in EU law in conjunction, the emerging solution for national courts is that the provision offering the broadest human rights protection in a specific case must prevail.[47] In other words, in cases of diverging standards, national courts must apply those standards which offer the highest protection to the claimant in the particular case at hand. Such an approach would be fully in line with the notion laid down in Article 52, third paragraph, of the EU Charter that Union law may provide more extensive protection than the ECtHR.

---

46   See Battjes 2006, pp. 64-66.
47   Horbach et al. 2007, p. 493.

7.3.6   *Cross-references: problematic or not?*

Is it allowed for national asylum courts to refer, at the same time, to different sources of interpretation when defining the requirement of an independent and effective national remedy? Cross-references are references to other human rights treaties or instruments covering the same or a similar right, and to the corresponding case law. Article 31, third paragraph, sub c VTC states, in short, that any relevant rules of international law applicable in the relations between the parties may be taken into account when clarifying a treaty.[48] This provision makes cross-references possible as long as references are made to provisions (case law) applicable in the relations between the parties. Cross-references may become problematic when a regional treaty such as the ECHR is used for the interpretation of provisions from universal treaties such as the RC, the ICCPR and the CAT. Such cross-references may cause situations in which States that are not party to the regional treaty (as they are outside the region) nevertheless are, through case law, *de facto* bound by that regional treaty. In the context of this study, such problems are practically non-existent. This study is targeted at national asylum courts within the EU and all the EU Member States are parties to all the treaties covered by this study. The international supervisors often make cross-references in their case law. To mention two examples: in *Kindler v. Canada* (1993)[49] the HRC referred to the judgment of the ECtHR in *Soering v. the UK* (1989).[50] And in *Maslov v. Austria* (2008)[51] – a case concerning an exclusion order for a Bulgarian national living in Austria in which one of the central questions before the ECtHR was whether in national judicial review proceedings against the exclusion order account must be taken of factual matters which occurred after the final decision of the competent authorities – the ECtHR referred to the judgment of the CJEU in *Orfano-poulos and Oliveri* (2004), in which the CJEU ruled, in short, that an *ex nunc* assessment by the national judicial authorities was called for.[52]

7.4   The independent and rigorous national judicial scrutiny defined

The results of the analysis conducted in the previous chapters are now brought together with the aim of defining more exactly the requirement of an 'independent and rigorous national judicial scrutiny'. The hierarchy as defined above is applied, which means that the case law of the CJEU and ECtHR are treated as the prime sources of interpretation, followed by the position of the UNHCR and the case law of the HRC and the ComAT, unless one of these secondary sources offers a higher standard of

---

48   Article 31(3) VTC stipulates: 'There shall be taken into account, together with the context: a) any subsequent agreement between the parties regarding the interpretation of the treaty or the application of its provisions; b) any subsequent practice in the application of the treaty which establishes the agreements of the parties regarding its interpretation; c) any relevant rule of international law applicable in the relations between the parties.'

49   HRC, *Kindler v. Canada*, 18 November 1993, No. 470/1991.

50   ECtHR, *Soering v. the UK*, 7 July 1989, Appl. No. 14038/88.

51   ECtHR, *Maslov v. Austria*, 23 June 2008, Appl. No. 1638/03, paras. 42-44 and 82.

52   CJEU, *Orfanopoulos and Oliveri*, 29 April 2004, C-482/01 and C-493/01, paras. 90-100.

protection. The exercise of defining the 'independent and rigorous national judicial scrutiny' is undertaken with the assistance of the eleven aspects of evidence and judicial scrutiny.

7.4.1 Standard of proof

The standard of proof under EU asylum law, the ECHR, the RC and the CAT is the same: the level of risk required is a real, personal, and foreseeable risk exceeding the mere possibility of being subjected to proscribed ill-treatment,[53] but the risk does not need to be certain (necessary), highly probable or beyond reasonable doubt.[54] The case law of the HRC is stricter as a real risk means that it is a necessary and foreseeable consequence of the expulsion that Article 7 ICCPR will be violated.[55] National courts must stick to the first mentioned standard and not use the standard developed in the HRC's case law as it is stricter.

7.4.2 Burden of proof

The burden of proof is shared: there is an initial burden of assertion, and, preferably, some corroboration, on the applicant, after which an investigative burden on the authorities of the State party, including the national courts, emerges.[56] It is important to see that the applicant only bears a burden of presenting an arguable claim, not of proving the feared risk. The CJEU and the ECtHR, and – albeit less explicitly – also the ComAT have developed the notion of a gradual scale: the poorer the general human rights situation is, the less individual circumstances and corroborating individual evidence are required and the sooner the onus shifts to the State party.[57] The EU Qualification Directive, the ECHR, the RC and the CAT envisage an alleviated burden of proof for cases in which previous persecution or ill-treatment took place.[58]

---

53 See Article 2, sub paragraphs d and f of the EU Qualification Directive; ECtHR, *Vilvarajah v. the United Kingdom*, 30 October 1991, Appl. Nos. 13163/87, 13164/87, 13165/87, 13447/87 and 13448/87, paras. 108 and 111; ComAT, *Haydin v. Sweden*, 20 November 1998, No. 101/1997, para. 6.5.

54 Wouters 2009, p. 247.

55 HRC, *A.R.J. v. Australia*, 11 August 1997, No. 692/1996, para. 6.8.

56 See Article 4 of the EU Qualification Directive; for the position of the ECtHR, see for example, *Saadi v. Italy*, 28 February 2008, Appl. No. 37201/06, para. 129; for the position of UNHCR see for example, paras. 195 and 196 of the UNHCR Handbook; for an example in the case law of the HRC see *Irene Bleier Lewenhoff and Rosa Valino de Bleier v. Uruguay*, 29 March 1982, No. 30/1978, para. 13.3; for an example from the case law of the ComAT see *A.S. v. Sweden*, 24 November 2000, No. 149/1999, paras. 8.6, 8.7.

57 CJEU, *Elgafaji*, 17 February 2009, C-465/07, para. 39; ECtHR, *NA v. the United Kingdom*, 17 July 2008, Appl. No. 25904/07, paras.115-117; see also Ingelse 1999, p. 252, Nowak & McArthur 2008, p. 164, p. 224, Wouters 2009, p. 473, Battjes 2009, p. 82, Cox 2010, p. 392, Van Bennekom & Van der Winden 2011, p. 220.

58 Article 4, fourth paragraph, EU Qualification Directive; ECtHR, *Salah Sheekh v. the Netherlands*, 11 January 2007, Appl. No. 1948/04. para. 147; UNHCR Handbook, para. 45; ComAT, General Comment No. 1, paragraph 8, sub b and sub c, adopted on 21-11-1997, A/53/44, Annex XI. See also Battjes 2006, p. 227, Boeles 2009, p. 263, Wouters 2009, p. 263, Hailbronner 2010, p. 1037.

The notion of a shared burden of proof, developed in international asylum law, is also clearly present in EU asylum law in the form of the co-operation requirement laid down in Article 4 of the Qualification Directive. In its judgment in *M.M. v. Minister for Justice, Equality and Law Reform, Ireland* (2012) the CJEU has ruled that this requirement of co-operation means that if, for any reason whatsoever, the elements provided by an applicant for international protection are not complete, up to date or relevant, it is necessary for the Member State concerned to cooperate actively with the applicant, at that stage of the procedure, so that all the elements needed to sub-stantiate the application may be assembled. A Member State may also be better placed than an applicant to gain access to certain types of documents. The CJEU has so far not explained any further what is meant by 'active co-operation with the applicant so that all the elements needed to substantiate the application may be as-sembled.' National courts may probably think of situations in which it is necessary to offer the applicant a certain (additional) period for submitting new relevant documen-tation, of situations in which the applicant proposes that the court hears certain wit-nesses, and situations in which the applicant submits certain documents and the court orders an expert authenticity examination or orders the administrative authority to do that. Like the ECtHR did in 2010 in *Iskandarov v. Russia*, the CJEU makes clear in *M.M.* that there may be specific circumstances in which the administrative or judicial authority is better placed than the applicant to get hold of certain types of docu-ments. Thus, when it is much easier for the national administrative or judicial authori-ty than for the applicant to gain access to certain relevant documentation, the burden of obtaining such evidence rests primarily with that authority.

7.4.3 Relevant facts and circumstances

Personal circumstances, such as background, gender, age, beliefs, activities, and cir-cumstances concerning the general (human rights) situation in the country of origin, such as the general human rights situation, conditions in detention, the level of vio-lence in the country and control thereof by the authorities, changes in government or policies, are relevant.

It follows from the treaties and EU asylum law that a holistic and integrated ap-proach must be taken towards the personal facts and the situation in the country of origin.[59]

7.4.4 Required degree of individual risk

Under EU asylum law and the ECHR, three categories of cases may be distinguished: 1) cases of extreme general violence, where an Article 3-risk is assumed for everyone returning to the particular country; 2) cases of group violence; and 3) individual risk-cases. In the third category of cases it is required that an individual risk is established,

---

59   Article 4, third paragraph, of the EU Qualification Directive; see for an example from the ECtHR's case law *NA v. the United Kingdom*, 17 July 2008, Appl. No. 25904/07, para. 113; *UNHCR Handbook*, paras. 43 and 55; ComAT General Comment No. 1, para. 8; see also Battjes 2009, p. 80, Wouters 2009, p. 264.

in other words, that the individual concerned has been singled out. Reference is made to sections 5.6.4 and 6.4.5. The HRC and ComAT have taken significant steps towards incorporating the lines of theory developed by the ECtHR on situations of group violence.[60] In classifying cases into one of these categories and determining, accordingly, the required amount of individual facts and evidence, national courts must also take into consideration that under the RC, no singling out is required. The UNHCR Handbook distinguishes two main kinds of status determination: the normal situation in which refugee status is determined on an individual basis and the exceptional situation in which group determination takes place whereby each member of the group is *prima facie* regarded as a refugee.[61] Neither of these two situations imposes a strict requirement of being singled out as the risk does not necessarily need to be based on the personal experiences of the applicant.[62]

The notion of the gradual scale as developed by the CJEU, the ECtHR and the ComAT is important for this aspect as well. The poorer the general human rights situation is, the less individual circumstances and corroborating individual evidence are required and the sooner the onus shifts to the State party.[63]

7.4.5   Credibility assessment

7.4.5.1   Intensity of scrutiny by national courts

On the required intensity of scrutiny to be provided by national courts, the stances of the international supervisors are highly similar. The CJEU ruled in *Samba Diouf* (2011) that a thorough national judicial review on the merits of the claim is required. As previously stated, the ECtHR's Zumtobel-doctrine under Article 6 ECHR requires that national administrative decisions can normally be challenged before a tribunal having full judicial jurisdiction on points of fact and points of law.[64] Full jurisdiction also implies that the national court is able to make an independent determination of the disputed facts[65] and of the credibility of a claimant.[66] The UNHCR's position is very much the same: national judges should be able to obtain a personal impression of the applicant, appeal or review proceedings should involve points of fact and points of law and national courts should be able to independently assess the credi-

---

60   HRC, *Kaba v. Canada*, 25 March 2010, No. 1465/2006, paras. 10.1 and 10.2; ComAT, *Njamba v. Sweden*, 14 May 2010, No. 322/2007, paras. 9.5 and 9.6.
61   *UNHCR Handbook*, paras. 44 and 45.
62   See Battjes 2011, p. 20.
63   CJEU, *Elgafaji*, 17 February 2009, C-465/07, para. 39; ECtHR, *NA v. the United Kingdom*, 17 July 2008, Appl. No. 25904/07, paras.115-117; see also Ingelse 1999, p. 252, Nowak & McArthur 2008, p. 164, p. 224, Wouters 2009, p. 473, Battjes 2009, p. 82, Cox 2010, p. 392, Van Bennekom & Van der Winden 2011, p. 220.
64   See, for example, ECtHR, *Terra Woningen B.V. v. the Netherlands*, 28 November 1996, Appl. No. 49/1995/555/64, paras. 46 and 51-55; ECtHR, *Druzstevni Zálozna Pria and others v. The Czech Republic*, 31 July 2008, Appl. No. 72034/01, para. 107; ECtHR, *Koskinas v. Greece*, 20 June 2002, Appl. No. 47760/99, para. 29, ECtHR, *Veeber v. Estonia*, 8 November 2002, Appl. No. 37571/97, para. 70, ECtHR, *Chevrol v. France*, 13 February 2003, Appl. No. 49636/99, para. 76.
65   See, for example, ECtHR, *Koskinas v. Greece*, 20 June 2002, Appl. No. 47760/99, para. 30.
66   See, for example, ECtHR, *Tsfayo v. the UK*, 14 November 2006, Appl. No. 60860/00, para. 46.

bility of the statements of the asylum seeker (see section 2.4.5). The ComAT ruled in *Nirmal Singh v. Canada* (2011) that States parties to the CAT are obliged to provide for judicial review of the merits, rather than merely of the reasonableness, of decisions on expulsion.[67] It is also useful to look at the interpretation of the term 'impartiality' by the ComAT. Impartiality as enshrined in Articles 12 and 13 CAT obliges the national judge to reconstruct as meticulously as possible what happened and to use his or her investigative powers to that end.[68] Impartiality under Article 3 CAT should be interpreted as meaning the same thing.

The ECtHR's approach to credibility offers additional guidelines to national courts. As was said above in section 7.3.4, these guidelines constitute a reasonable solution which ensures respect for national systems of checks and balances, and for the experience and expertise of national administrative decision makers. The ECtHR actively proceeds towards an independent and fresh determination of the facts, including credibility, in cases of insufficient national proceedings, new facts, circumstances and developments, including evidence thereof, and an incorrect application of evidentiary standards (for example, the standard or proof) at national level. National courts can easily follow this approach without heavily disturbing national systems of checks and balances. This would mean that national asylum courts would actively and independently make a fresh factual determination, including an assessment of credibility, in cases of one or more of the mentioned circumstances. If such circumstances do not occur, national courts can rely on the determination of the facts, including the assessment of credibility, as made by the administrative decision maker.

7.4.5.2   *How to assess credibility?*

The ECtHR, the UNHCR, and the ComAT (and to a lesser extent the HRC) have developed clear standards for credibility assessment which national courts need to follow to live up to Articles 18 and 19 of the EU Charter. These three international supervisors require 'general credibility' ('general veracity'), not complete accuracy and consistency of every single detail of the claim. The basic story – the very core aspects of the flight reasons – must be credible.[69] The ECtHR has made clear that doubts about more peripheral aspects of the claim, such as statements concerning the journey to the country where asylum has been requested or statements concerning escape from prison or from guards do not necessarily undermine general credibility.[70] The ECtHR and the ComAT have, furthermore, made clear that the basic story should normally meet a number of requirements in order to be credible:

---

67   ComAT, *Nirmal Singh v. Canada*, 30 May 2011, No. 319/2007, paras. 8.8, 8.9, 9.
68   ComAT, *M'Barek v. Tunisia*, 10 November 1999, No. 060/1996, paras. 11.9, 11.10, 12, ComAT, *Ristic v. Yugoslavia*, 11 May 2001, No. 113/1998, paras. 9.4-9.8.
69   See for an example from the case law of the ECtHR *Said v. the Netherlands*, 5 July 2005, Appl. No. 2345/02, para. 51; *UNHCR Handbook,*paras. 197, 204 and UNHCR, *Note on Burden and Standard of Proof in Refugee Claims* of 16 December 1998, paras. 11, 12; see for an example from the case law of the ComAT *Kisoki v. Sweden*, 8 May 1996, No. 041/1996, para. 9.3.
70   ECtHR, *N. v. Finland* (2005), 26 July 2005, Appl. No. 38885/02, paras. 154 and 155; ECtHR, *Said v. the Netherlands*, 5 July 2005, Appl. No. 2345/02, para. 53, ECtHR, *R.C. v. Sweden*, 9 March 2010, Appl. No. 41827/07, para. 52.

- It must be sufficiently detailed;[71]
- It must be internally consistent throughout the proceedings;[72] numerous major inconsistencies[73] and numerous alterations in statements may make these statements incredible;[74]
- It must be consistent with country information;[75]
- It must be brought forward in a timely manner: late submission of statements may negatively affect the general credibility, particularly when no sound reason for it is given;[76]
- The core of the flight narrative must – as much as possible – be corroborated with evidence.[77]

Compared to the other supervisors, the UNHCR takes a more lenient stance on corroboration with evidence as a requirement for credibility. It takes the stance that the absence of corroborative documents should not prevent the claim from being accepted if the statements are consistent with known facts and the general credibility of the applicant is good.[78] The UNHCR has also made clear that there is no justification for imposing a stricter credibility standard – stricter than the standard of general credibility – in cases where corroborating evidence is totally absent.[79] As the preference rules require that, in the case of diverging standards, national courts apply those standards offering the highest level of protection, national courts must pay due respect to this UNHCR position.

7.4.6   Admission of evidence

7.4.6.1   Admission of evidence, means and sources of evidence

Under the treaties and under EU asylum law the approach to admission and admissibility of evidence is liberal. There are no procedural barriers to the admissibility of evidence or pre-determined formulae for its assessment.[80] National courts must apply the same liberal approach to live up to their EU Charter obligations. In Chapters 2-5 different examples of evidentiary materials were provided. Reference is made to sections 2.4.6.1, 3.5.6.1, 4.5.6.2, 5.6.6.2 and 6.4.6.1.

---

71 See, for example, ComAT, *A.S. v. Sweden*, 15 February 2001, No. 149/1999, para. 8.6.

72 ECtHR, *R.C. v. Sweden*, 9 March 2010, Appl. No. 41827/07, para. 52.

73 See, for example *Bello v. Sweden*, admissibility decision, 17 January 2006, Appl. No. 32213/04.

74 See, for example, *B. v. Sweden*, admissibility decision, 26 October 2004, Appl. No. 16578/03; ComAT, General Comment No. 1, para. 8, sub f and sub g.

75 See, for example, ECtHR, *R.C. v. Sweden*, 9 March 2010, Appl. No. 41827/07, para. 54; HRC, *Mehrez Ben Abde Hamida v. Canada*, 18 March 2010, No. 1544/2007, para. 8.7; ComAT, *Chahin v. Sweden*, 30 May 2011, No. 310/2007, para. 9.4.

76 See, for example, ECtHR, *B. v. Sweden*, admissibility decision, 26 October 2004, Appl. No. 16578/03; ComAT, *X.Y. v. Switzerland*, 15 May 2001, No. 128/1999, para.8.5.

77 See, for example, ECtHR, *Fazlul Karim v. Sweden*, admissibility decision, 4 July 2006, Appl. No. 24171/05; ComAT, *G.T. v. Switzerland*, 2 May 2000, No. 137/1999, paras. 6.5-6.8.

78 *Note on Burden and Standard of Proof in Refugee Claims* of 16 December 1998, para. 10.

79 Submission in the case of *Mir Isfahani v. the Netherlands,* paras. 25-27.

80 See, for example, ECtHR, *Iskandarov v. Russia*, 23 September 2010, Appl. No. 17185/05, para. 107.

7.4.6.2   Minimum quantity and quality of evidence

The ECtHR, the HRC and the ComAT require a significant amount of evidence with a direct personal bearing corroborating the core of the flight narrative, the 'basic story'.[81]

As opposed to this, the UNHCR has often underlined that, due to the special and difficult evidentiary position of the applicant for asylum, the requirement of evidence should not be applied too strictly.[82] It has also taken the stance that complete absence of supportive evidence does not automatically mean that the claim is unmeritorious.[83] The UNHCR's position is echoed in the fifth paragraph of Article 4 of the EU Qualification Directive, which makes clear that under certain circumstances, including a genuine effort to corroborate the claim, not all the aspects of the applicant's account need to be corroborated by evidence other than statements (see section 6.4.6.2). As the preference rules require that, in cases of diverging standards, national courts apply those standards offering the highest level of protection, national courts must pay due respect to the more lenient standards laid down in Article 4, fifth paragraph, of the EU Qualification Directive and to the UNHCR's position.

7.4.7   Appreciation and weighing of evidence

EU asylum law and the RC do not regulate this aspect and the case law of the HRC and the ComAT are not very explicit and transparent on the evaluation of evidence (with the exception of the evaluation of medico-legal reports by the ComAT, which will be discussed below). The ECtHR's case law is much more explicit and transparent and offers national asylum courts concrete guidelines for the evaluation of evidence. The authenticity of submitted documents, the specificity, comprehensiveness and consistency of the information contained in evidentiary materials or given by witnesses, and the independence, reliability, objectiveness and authority of the source or author of the evidence determine how much probative value or weight is attached.[84] In Chapters 3, 4 and 5, a number of categories of evidence were discussed in detail and it was demonstrated that specific and comprehensive witness statements by family members played an important role in the case law of the ECtHR[85] and both

---

81 See, for example, ECtHR, *Cruz Varas v. Sweden*, 20 March 1991, Appl. No. 15576/89, para. 79; ECtHR, *Shikpohkt and Sholeh v. the Netherlands*, 27 January 2005, Appl. No. 39349/03; HRC, *Mehrez Ben Abde Hamida v. Canada*, 18 March 2010, No. 1544/2007; ComAT, *G.T. v. Switzerland*, 2 May 2000, No. 137/1999, paras. 6.5-6.8.

82 *UNHCR Handbook*, para. 202.

83 *UNHCR Handbook*, paras. 196, 197, 203; Report of July 2003 'Implementation of the Aliens Act 2000 in the Netherlands, UNHCR's Observations and Recommendations'; *Note on Burden and Standard of Proof in Refugee Claims* of 16 December 1998, paras. 10, 20, 22; paras. 25-27 in the Submission in the case of *Mir Isfahani v. the Netherlands*.

84 See, for example, ECtHR, *Bader and Kanbor v. Sweden*, 8 November 2005, Appl. No. 13284/04, para. 44.

85 See, for example, ECtHR, *Hilal v. the UK*, 6 March 2001, Appl. No. 45276/99, para. 66.

Committees.[86] The ECtHR has made clear that statements by family members must normally be supported by other, more objective, evidentiary materials.[87]

Medico-legal reports form another important category of evidence, particularly in the case law of the ComAT. The ECtHR is generally reluctant to accept medical evidence (stating PTSD or other mental disturbance or disorders) as an explanation for tardy presentation of statements on past torture[88] and inconsistencies,[89] but it has accepted medical reports as evidence corroborating statements on past torture in a number of cases.[90] The same goes for the HRC.[91] Medico-legal reports play a particularly prominent role in the case law of the ComAT. The ComAT requires such reports to be drawn up by medical specialists and to conclusively identify a causal link between the individual's bodily or mental injuries and the alleged past torture.[92]

In a significant number of – mostly early – cases medico-legal reports were accepted as corroboration of statements on past torture,[93] as an explanation for inconsistencies,[94] gaps or vague points,[95] major changes in the flight narrative[96] and late presentation of crucial statements and evidence.[97] In the ComAT's later jurisprudence, medical evidence has been downgraded from decisive to supportive, but it still remains important and the ComAT has shown dissatisfaction over the fact that in national proceedings in the Netherlands, medical reports are not normally taken into account as evidence.[98] Compared to the other supervisors, this case law of the ComAT clearly offers a higher degree of protection as it attaches more consequences to medico-legal reports in assessing the claimant's credibility. The preference rules require that national courts pay due respect to this approach by the ComAT.

---

86 See, for example, HRC, *Mehrez Ben Abde Hamida v. Canada*, 18 March 2010, No. 1544/2007, paras. 5.1, 8.3; ComAT, *A.S. v. Sweden*, 15 February 2001, No 149/1999, paras. 7.7, 8.4, ComAT, *T.A. v. Sweden*, 6 May 2005, No. 226/2003, paras. 5.5, 7.3, 7.4.

87 ECtHR, *H.L.R. v. France*, 29 April 1997, Appl. No. 24573/1994, para. 42.

88 See, for example, ECtHR, *Cruz Varas and others v. Sweden*, 20 March 1991, Appl. No. 15576/89, para. 78; ECtHR, *Nasimi v. Sweden*, admissibility decision, 16 March 2004, Appl. No. 38865/02.

89 In *Hatami v. Sweden*, European Commission, 23 April 1998, Appl. No. 32448/96, para. 106, the Commission considered that 'complete accuracy is seldom to be expected from victims of torture'. No decisions or judgments of the ECtHR have been found in which this consideration was used, which suggests that the ECtHR is not willing to accept medical evidence to explain inconsistencies.

90 See, for example, ECtHR, *Hilal v. the UK*, 6 March 2001, Appl. No. 45276/99, para. 64, *R.C. v. Sweden*, 9 March 2010, Appl. No. 41827/07, paras. 11, 23-25, paras. 53-56.

91 See, for example, HRC, *Ernest Sigman Pillai and Laetecia Swenthi Joachimpilla v. Canada*, 25 March 2010, No. 1763/2008, para. 11.4.

92 See, for example, ComAT, *El Rgeig v. Switzerland*, 15 November 2006, No. 280/2005, para. 7.4.

93 *Ibidem.*

94 See, for example, ComAT, *Kisoki v. Sweden*, 8 May 1996, No. 041/1996, para. 9.3, ComAT, *Haydin v. Sweden*, 20 November 1998, No. 101/1997, para. 6.7, ComAT, *C.T. and K.M. v. Sweden*, 17 November 2006, No. 279/2005, para. 7.6.

95 See, for example, ComAT, *Falcon Rios v. Canada*, 23 November 2004, No. 133/1999, para. 8.5.

96 ComAT, *Ayas v. Sweden*, 12 November 1998, No. 097/1997, para. 6.5, ComAT, *A. v. Netherlands*, 13 November 1998, No. 91/1997.

97 ComAT, *A.F. v. Sweden*, 8 May 1998, No. 089/1997, paras. 2.6 and 6.5. In this case crucial evidence was submitted in support of a fourth asylum application at national level.

98 ComAT, Conclusions and Recommendations regarding the Netherlands, 3 August 2007, CAT/C/NET/CO/4, para. 8.

In the case law of the HRC and the ComAT, significant weight is normally attached to reports containing the result of inquiries conducted by embassies or missions in the countries of origin.[99]

Reports on the situation in the country of origin logically play an important role in the case law of the international supervisors. Unlike the HRC and the ComAT, the ECtHR has developed a number of concrete guidelines for the evaluation of country reports. Reports by UN agencies and States rank highly.[100] This is because United Nations agencies have direct access to the authorities of the country of destination as well as the ability to carry out on-site inspections and assessments in a manner which States and non-governmental organisations may not be able to do, and States have the ability to gather information through their diplomatic missions.[101] The precise probative value accorded to country of origin information is not only determined by the source, but also very much by its specific content. The ECtHR distinguishes between more general reports on the socio-economic and humanitarian situation, on the one hand, and reports specifically concerning the human rights situation, with a focus on the risk for the particular applicant, on the other hand. The latter category of reports is given greater evidentiary weight.[102]

7.4.8   *Opportunities for presenting evidence*

All the international supervisors regard adversarial proceedings and equality of arms as crucial safeguards for a fair hearing at both the international level and the national level. The position of the HRC and the ComAT seem to be stricter compared to the other international supervisors, as they require that in cases concerning the expulsion of asylum seekers, both parties to the case must have equal access to all the documents in the case file, including documents underpinning allegations that the individual concerned constitutes a danger to the national security of the country.[103]

As opposed to this, the ECtHR has ruled in a number of cases that the use of secret evidence may be justified if this is strictly necessary to preserve the fundamental rights of another individual or to safeguard an important public interest, such as the protection of national security.[104] In the same vein, the UNHCR takes the position that non-disclosure of evidence is allowed when disclosure of sources would seriously jeopardize national security or the security of the organisations or persons providing information.[105] The principles concerning the use of secret evidence devel-

---

99   See, for example, HRC, *A.R.J. v. Australia*, 11 August 1997, No. 692/1996, para. 4.6, 4.7; ComAT, *Y.S. v. Switzerland*, 14 November 2000, No. 147/1999, para. 6.6.

100   ECtHR, *NA v. the UK*, 17 July 2008, Appl. No. 25904/07, paras. 121 and 122.

101   ECtHR, *Sufi and Elmi v. the UK*, 28 June 2011, Appl. No. 8319/07 and 11449/07, para. 231.

102   See, for example, ECtHR, *F.H. v. Sweden*, 20 January 2009, Appl. No. 32621/06, para. 92.

103   ComAT, *Sogi v. Canada*, 16 November 2007, No. 297/2006; HRC, *Mansour Ahani v. Canada*, 15 June 2004, No. 1051/2002.

104   See, for example, *Rowe and Davis v. the United Kingdom*, 16 February 2000, Appl. No. 29801/95, para. 61; *Edwards and Lewis v. the UK*, 27 October 2004, Appl. Nos. 39647/98 and 40461/98, para. 46.

105   *Fair and Efficient Asylum Procedures: A Non-Exhaustive Overview of Applicable International Standards*, 2 September 2005, www.unhcr.org/refworld/docid/432ae9204.html, last visited 18 December 2012, pp. 5 and 6.

oped by the CJEU strongly resemble the ECtHR's principles. They include the notions that the use of secret evidence is permitted provided that it has a legitimate aim and that it is necessary;[106] that the interest of the State to keep the evidence secret must be balanced against the individual's right to have knowledge of this evidence and his procedural rights of adversarial proceedings and equality of arms;[107] that the court examining the appeal should be able to effectively review the confidential evidence on which the impugned decision is based;[108] and that limitations to a party's procedural rights as a consequence of the use of secret evidence should be compensated by taking counterbalancing measures (compensation techniques).[109]

The prohibition on the use of secret evidence in national court proceedings on expulsion developed by the HRC and the ComAT has so far not been reiterated in other cases, so that we cannot speak of a constant line in their case law. As the prohibition as developed in *Ahani* (HRC, 2004) and *Sogi* (ComAT, 2007) offers a higher degree of protection than the standards of the CJEU, the ECtHR and the UNHCR, national courts must take due notice of them because the preference rules in the treaties so require. As a consequence, national courts must normally not allow the use of secret evidence and must limit its use to an absolute minimum of cases where very strong reasons justify non-disclosure of evidence.

7.4.9   *Judicial application of investigative powers*

Reference is made to section 7.4.5.1 on the required intensity of scrutiny by national courts regarding the determination of the facts. It was pointed out here that on the required intensity of scrutiny to be provided by national courts, the stances of the international supervisors are highly similar: they require a thorough national judicial review on the merits of the claim (CJEU, *Samba Diouf* 2011, ComAT, *Nirmal Singh v. Canada* 2011), full judicial jurisdiction on points of fact and points of law (the ECtHR's Zumtobel doctrine) and appeal or review proceedings on points of fact and points of law (UNHCR). Reference was also made to the interpretation of the term 'impartiality' by the ComAT under Articles 12 and 13 CAT, which obliges the national judge to reconstruct as meticulously as possible what happened and to use his or her investigative powers to that end.[110]

The ECtHR is the most active when it comes to the determination of the facts. In a significant number of cases concerning the expulsion of asylum seekers, it has played a very active role in the gathering and verification of facts and circum-

---

106 See, for example, CJEU, *Aalborg Portland and others v Commission*, 7 January 2004, Joined Cases C-204/00 P etc, para 68; CJEU, *Kadi and Al Barakaat v Council and Commission*, 3 September 2008, Joined Cases C-402/05 P and C-415/05 P, para. 342.

107 See, for example, CJEU, *Varec*, 2008, C-450/06, para 51; CJEU, *Kadi and Al Barakaat v. Council and Commission*, 3 September 2008, Joined Cases C-402/05 P and C-415/05 P, para. 344.

108 See, for example, CJEU, *Mobistar*, 13 July 2006, C-438/04, para 40; CJEU, *Organisation des Modjahedines du peuple d'Iran v. Council*, 12 December 2006, T-228/02, para. 155.

109 See, for example, CJEU, *Kadi and Al Barakaat v. Council and Commission*, 3 September 2008, Joined Cases C-402/05 P and C-415/05 P, para. 344.

110 ComAT, *M'Barek v. Tunisia*, 10 November 1999, No. 060/1996, paras. 11.9, 11.10, 12, ComAT, *Ristic v. Yugoslavia*, 11 May 2001, No. 113/1998, paras. 9.4-9.8.

stances.[111] The preference rules dictate that national courts take the ECtHR as their role model as a more active role in the determination of the facts offers a higher degree of protection than a more deferential approach (taken generally by the HRC): a more active role by the Court implies more intense judicial scrutiny. In order to determine the facts, the ECtHR may apply at any stage in the proceedings any investigative measure which it considers capable of clarifying the facts, including inviting a party or parties to submit additional evidence, hear witnesses and experts, order expert opinions, hold fact-finding missions and on-site investigations.[112] The ECtHR has clarified that it will particularly obtain materials on conditions in the country of origin *proprio motu* when the applicant or a third party provides reasoned grounds which cast doubt on the accuracy of the information relied on by the respondent government.[113]

In this section, special attention must also be drawn to the UNHCR's role as expert or witness in court proceedings. In Chapter 2 it was demonstrated that, on the basis of Article 35 RC and Article 21, first paragraph, sub c of the EU Procedures Directive, national courts may invite the UNHCR to participate in national court proceedings as an expert or witness who can advise the court on a particular aspect of a pending asylum case, or advise the court on the question of whether or not the claimant is a refugee. In sections 2.5.2 and 2.5.3 it was shown that the UNHCR has made submissions to the ECtHR in a significant number of cases and also issued statements (positions) in the context of cases pending before the CJEU. The ECtHR gives considerable weight to information submitted by the UNHCR and national courts should do the same. An independent and rigorous national judicial scrutiny may in some cases imply that national courts involve the UNHCR as an expert.

7.4.10   Time limits for the presentation of statements and evidence

The CJEU, the ECtHR, the UNHCR and the HRC take similar positions. The core of these positions is that national procedural rules must be reasonable, or applied by the national court in a reasonable and flexible manner if the circumstances of the case so require.[114]

---

111 Examples of cases in which the ECtHR played a very active role in the determination of the facts are ECtHR, *N. v. Finland*, 26 July 2005, Appl. No. 38885/02, paras. 9, 77-116 (the Court held a fact-finding mission), ECtHR, *Shamayev and others v. Georgia and Russia*, 12 April 2005, Appl. No. 36378/02, para. 26, paras. 110-216 (extradition, the Court held a fact-finding mission), ECtHR, *R.C. v. Sweden*, 9 March 2010, Appl. No. 41827/07, paras. 23-25, 53 (the Court requested the applicant to submit to it an expert medical opinion), ECtHR, *Abdolkhani and Karimnia v. Turkey*, 22 September 2009, Application No. 30471/08, para. 5 (the Court requested the UNHCR to make a submission.

112 Rules of Court, Rule A1 in Annex 1, Rule 19, second paragraph, 1 April 2011, to be found at: http://www.echr.coe.int, Rules of Court.

113 See, for example, ECtHR, *Saadi v. Italy*, 28 February 2008, Appl. No. 37201/06, para. 131, ECtHR, *Ismoilov and others v. Russia*, 24 April 2008, Appl. No. 2947/06, para. 120, and ECtHR, *NA v. the UK*, 17 July 2008, Appl. No. 25904/07, para. 119.

114 CJEU, *Universale Bau*, 12 December 2002, C-470/99, para. 76; CJEU, *Santex*, 27 February 2003, C-327/00, para. 52; ECtHR, *Bahaddar v. the Netherlands*, 19 February 1998, Appl. No. 25894/94, paras. 45-49, ECtHR, *Jabari v. Turkey*, 11 July 2000, Appl. No. 40035/98, para. 40; UNHCR Submission in

→

It follows from EU asylum law and the case law of the ECtHR, the position of the UNHCR and the case law of the ComAT that all relevant statements should, in principle, be made as early in the national procedure as possible and that belated statements may cast doubt on the credibility of the applicant.[115] The approach to evidence submitted to corroborate statements is generally more flexible. In the case law of the ECtHR and the HRC, the point in time at which evidentiary materials were submitted in national proceedings by the parties is, seen as a factor alone and in itself, not a relevant consideration.[116]

The UNHCR has stressed that no case should be rejected solely on the basis that the relevant information was not presented or documents were not submitted earlier.[117] In the same vein, in a significant number of cases the ComAT did not see the tardy presentation of relevant statements and evidence as problematic and easily accepted that good reasons had been brought forward for their belated presentation.[118] Based on the preference rules, national asylum courts must pay respect to these positions of the UNHCR and the ComAT as they offer a higher degree of protection, compared to the ECtHR and the HRC. In line with this, it follows from Article 8, first paragraph, of the Procedures Directive, that Member States shall ensure that applications for asylum are neither rejected nor excluded from examination on the sole ground that they have not been made as soon as possible.[119]

7.4.11   Point in time for the risk assessment

The positions of the international supervisors on this issue are by and large identical. They all take the position that, in principle, an assessment *ex nunc* is required. The assessment of the risk is made on the basis of all the information available at the moment of consideration. In cases where deportation from the respondent State has already been effectuated, the point in time for consideration by the ECtHR remains the moment of that deportation, but the Court may, and actually does, have regard to in-

---

the case of *Mir Isfahani v. the Netherlands*, para. 41, http://www.unhcr.org/refworld/docid/454f5e484.html. HRC, *Jagjit Singh Bhullar v. Canada*, 13 November 2006, No. 982/2001, para. 7.3.

115 Article 4, first paragraph, of the Qualification Directive stipulates, *inter alia*: 'Member States may consider it the duty of the applicant to submit as soon as possible all elements needed to substantiate the application for international protection.' See for an example from the ECtHR's case law *Nasimi v. Sweden*, admissibility decision, 16 March 2004, Appl. No. 38865/02; Submission by the UNHCR in the case of *Mir Isfahani v. the Netherlands*, Appl. No. 31252/03, May 2005, www.unhcr.org/refworld/docid/454f5e484.html, para. 41. See an example from the ComAT's case law ComAT, *X.Y. v. Switzerland*, 15 May 2001, No. 128/1999, para.8.5.

116 See, for example, ECtHR, *Cruz Varas and others v. Sweden*, 20 March 1991, Appl. No. 15576/89, paras. 26, 27, 29, 30, 41-46, 77, 79, ECtHR, *Hilal v. the UK*, 6 March 2001, Appl. No. 45276/99, paras. 14, 18, 21, 22, 62, 63, ECtHR, *Said v. the Netherlands*, 5 July 2005, Appl. No. 2345/02, paras. 28, 29, 51; HRC, *Byahuranga v. Denmark*, 9 December 2004, No. 1222/2003, *Mehrez Ben Abde Hamida v. Canada*, 18 March 2010, No. 1544/2007.

117 See para. 41 in the Submission in the case of *Mir Isfahani v. the Netherlands*.

118 See ComAT, *V.L. v. Switzerland*, 22 January 2007, 262/2005, para. 8.8, ComAT, *Iya v. Switzerland*, 16 November 2007, No. 299/2006, paras. 2.6, 2.7, 2.8, 6.5, ComAT, *Chahin v. Sweden*, 30 May 2011, No. 310/2007, paras. 5.5, 95.

119 Article 8, first paragraph, of the Procedures Directive (Council Directive 2005/85/EC of 1 December 2005).

formation that came to light subsequent to the removal so that in fact again an *ex nunc* assessment takes place.[120] The HRC has so far adopted no guidelines for situations where the removal has already taken place and the ComAT's case law is not entirely consistent. In *T.P.S. v. Canada* (2000), however, the ComAT explicitly took subsequent facts and circumstances into consideration without any reservation.[121]

7.5   Concluding remarks

The central question in this chapter was what the findings arrived at in the previous chapters mean exactly for national asylum courts. The first question looked at in this connection was how the treaties studied in this book and EU asylum law relate to each other. It was concluded that national asylum courts in the EU Member States are 'double bound' by the procedural obligations and standards flowing from the treaties investigated in this study as they are bound by the treaties, and by the EU law which incorporates these treaty obligations.

It was established that international and EU asylum require an independent and rigorous national judicial scrutiny. An attempt was made to define in a more precise way what this requirement means.

Sources of interpretation were identified and a hierarchy of sources was created. It was concluded that national asylum courts must first and foremost turn to the case law of the CJEU and the ECtHR, next, to the UNHCR and then to the HRC and the ComAT as subsidiary means of interpretation. National asylum courts within the EU may cross-refer to these different sources of interpretation as all the EU Member States are parties to the RC, the ICCPR, the CAT and the ECHR. It was also concluded that, when confronted with conflicting or diverging standards, national courts should abandon the mentioned hierarchy and opt for those standards offering the highest degree of protection. This is justified because the standards developed by the international courts and supervisors covered in this study all form part of EU asylum law and Article 52, third paragraph, of the EU Charter allows EU law to provide more extensive protection than the protection offered under the ECHR.

The requirement of an independent and rigorous national judicial scrutiny was, finally, defined with the assistance of the eleven aspects of evidence and judicial scrutiny, introduced in Chapter 1. This resulted in a set of evidentiary and scrutiny standards ready for use by national courts.

---

120 See, for example, ECtHR, *Cruz Varas and Others v. Sweden*, 20 March 1991, Appl. No. 15576/89, para. 76; ECtHR, *Vilvarajah and others v. United Kingdom*, 30 October 1991, Appl. Nos. 13163/87, 13164/87, 13165/87, 13447/87, 13448/87, para. 107; ECtHR, *Ahmed v. Austria*, 17 December 1996, Appl. No. 25964/94, para. 43, ECtHR, *Mamatkulov and Askarov v. Turkey*, 4 February 2005, Appl. Nos. 46827/99, 46951/99, para. 69.
121 ComAT, *T.P.S. v. Canada*, 4 September 2000, No. 99/1997, paras. 15.4 and 15.5.

Chapter 8: Repeat cases, Dublin cases, fast-track national proceedings

This chapter pays separate attention to three special types of national asylum court proceedings and the positions of the international supervisors regarding such proceedings.

These three special types are briefly referred to as 'repeat cases', 'Dublin cases' and 'fast-track proceedings.'

Repeat cases are cases in which a claimant lodges a second (or third, or fourth *et cetera*) asylum application after a negative decision on a first application, often with the aim of submitting new evidence corroborating the claim for protection.

In Dublin cases, an asylum application is decided upon on the basis of the EU Dublin Regulation 2003/343/EC.[1] The EU Dublin Regulation provides criteria for establishing which EU Member State is responsible for the examination of an asylum application submitted in one of the EU Member States. The Regulation is based on the 'single application' principle, aimed at discouraging individuals from applying for asylum in more than one EU Member State. Based on the criteria laid down in the Regulation, EU Member States may decide not to examine an asylum application and to refer the asylum applicant to the authorities of another EU Member State.

In fast-track proceedings, shorter than normal time limits (and sometimes also other special rules) apply, created with the aim of faster and more efficient processing of asylum claims and appeals.

Based on my experience as a national asylum judge, I can say without any doubt that the most difficult and urgent questions concerning evidence and judicial scrutiny arise within the framework of these special types of cases. In repeat cases, asylum seekers often present new evidence. Sometimes, this evidence has been obtained as a result of long and intensive searches for witnesses, documents, and information about events and the situation in the country of origin. I vividly remember a repeat case in which an 18-year-old Iranian woman presented a significant amount of evidentiary materials in corroboration of a second application for asylum. During the proceedings following her first asylum application she had not presented any evidence corroborating her claim for protection. She had fled her country of origin in great haste, as a minor, and had not realised at the time that it would be asked of her to present evidence in corroboration of her statements. It was only after the dismissal of her first request for asylum that she realised that she really needed evidentiary materials to support her claim. A difficult and long search followed, resulting in witness statements from both individuals who had known her father – a well-known opponent of the Iranian regime – witness statements from different organisations and country information. Following the constant jurisprudence of the highest Dutch

---

1   Council Regulation 2003/343/EC of 18 February 2003, establishing the criteria and mechanisms for determining the Member State responsible for examining an asylum application lodged in one of the Member States by a third country national, *Official Journal of the EU* L 50, 25 February 2003, pp. 1-10, last amended by *Official Journal of the EU* L 304, 14 November 2008, p. 83.

asylum court, the administration took the stance that this evidence could and should have been presented during the proceedings following the first application for protection. It is not only in the Netherlands that judges wrestle with the problem of evidence presented in repeat cases. From *Hilal v. the UK* (ECtHR, 2001), it appears that the applicant presented crucial evidence in second national asylum proceedings and that neither the administrative nor the national courts attached weight to this evidence because of its late presentation.[2]

In Dublin cases, other evidentiary problems occur. The file of a Dublin case normally contains a so-called 'claim approval', which means that the intermediary EU Member State (the first EU State where the applicant applied for asylum, or the first EU State which was transited), approves referral of the asylum seeker back to it. The administrative and judicial authorities of the referring EU Member State tend to decide in a very speedy manner. By way of illustration: first instance asylum courts in the Netherlands are normally allowed a time slot of 20 court hearing minutes per Dublin case. It is normally assumed that the intermediary EU Member State will live up to its obligations under international and EU asylum law. In other words, it is assumed that the asylum procedure and living conditions of (failed) asylum seekers in the intermediary EU country are in conformity with international and EU asylum law. It is very difficult for asylum seekers to prove the opposite. The case of *M.S.S. v. Belgium and Greece* (2011),[3] in which the ECtHR ruled that the asylum procedure and living conditions of (failed) asylum seekers in Greece were not compliant with international and EU asylum law and that Belgium, by referring asylum seekers to Greece, had violated its obligations under Articles 3 and 13 ECHR, has a long history. In many cases before *M.S.S.*, asylum seekers in different EU Member States tried to prove, without success, that Greece was violating its obligations under international and EU asylum law. They invoked alarming reports from many different sources, but the national authorities and the (upper) courts did not want to conclude that asylum seekers could not be sent back to Greece.[4]

In fast-track court proceedings, particular evidentiary and investigative problems may occur as a result of tight time limits for filing an appeal in combination with tight time limits for the different stages of the court proceedings themselves, including limited time for reading the file and doing research, for the court hearing, and for preparing the judgment.

Combinations of the types of cases discussed here may occur frequently when, for example, Dublin cases are processed in fast-track proceedings. This reinforces the mentioned evidentiary and investigative difficulties. Enough reason to explore the positions of the international supervisors and courts with regard to the mentioned

---

2   *Hilal v. the UK*, 6 March 2001, Appl. No. 45276/99, paras. 18, 21, 22, 62, 63
3   See ECtHR, *M.S.S. v. Belgium and Greece*, 21 January 2011, Appl. No. 30696/09, paras. 352, 358.
4   See, for the situation in Belgium, ECtHR, *M.S.S. v. Belgium and Greece*, 21 January 2011, Appl. No. 30696/09, paras.143-157. In the Netherlands, before *M.S.S.*, the first instance court of Zwolle assumed in a large number of Dublin cases that Greece was violating its obligations under Articles 3 and 13 ECHR and that, for that reason, asylum seekers could not be transferred to Greece. For a long time, the judicial division of the Council of State quashed these judgments and ruled that Greece was living up to its obligations under international and EU asylum law.

three types of cases, and raise and answer the question of what these positions imply for national asylum courts.

8.1 Repeat asylum cases

8.1.1 Nova-test

The RC, the ICCPR, the CAT, the ECHR and EU asylum law do not contain explicit prohibitions on a so called *nova* test: a national system in which subsequent asylum applications are subjected to a preliminary examination to assess whether new elements have arisen or new evidence has emerged which would warrant examination of the substance of the claim. The UNHCR has taken this stance explicitly on a number of occasions,[5] albeit with the warning that a preliminary *nova*-test is only justified if the previous claim was considered fully on the merits.[6] According to the UNHCR, the determination of whether new elements have arisen shall not be limited to changes which have occurred in the country of origin, but will also include examination of whether new evidence has emerged or whether there have been changes in the situation of the individual concerned that give rise to a *sur place* claim.[7]

Both the ECtHR and the HRC have made clear that national procedural rules, such as time limits, must normally be complied with.[8] Similarly, the ComAT has made clear in its case law that States parties have national procedural autonomy.[9] The HRC has so far not explicitly expressed a position on special national procedural rules applying in repeat asylum cases.[10] It has made clear – in other contexts (not asylum) – that national procedural rules must be reasonable, and that, in cases of non-

---

5   UNHCR International standards relating to refugee law, Checklist to review draft legislation of March 2009, section 5, UNHCR Research Project on the Application of Key Provisions of the Asylum Procedures Directive in selected Member States of March 2010, p. 72;

6   UNHCR International standards relating to refugee law, Checklist to review draft legislation of March 2009, section 5.

7   UNHCR International standards relating to refugee law, Checklist to review draft legislation of March 2009, section 5.

8   ECtHR, *Bahaddar v. the Netherlands*, 19 February 1998, Appl. No. 258/94, para. 45; ECtHR, *Jabari v. Turkey*, 2000, Appl. No. 40035/98, paras. 49, 50; HRC, *Ngoc Si Truong v. Canada*, 5 May 2003, No. 743/1997, para. 7.6; *Jagjit Singh Bhullar v. Canada*, 13 November 2006, No. 982/2001, para. 7.3.

9   See, for example, ComAT, *Rios v. Canada*, 23 November 2004, No. 133/1999. See also ComAT, *S.P.A. v. Canada*, 7 November 2006, No. 282/2005.

10   In HRC, *Hamid Reza Taghi Khadje v. the Netherlands*, 15 November 2006, No. 1438/2005, the author had gone through a second asylum procedure in the Netherlands after his first asylum claim had been found incredible and had therefore been rejected. In support of his second asylum application, the author submitted identity documents, which he had not done during the first procedure. Before the HRC, the author complained about unfair national court proceedings as the court had not done anything with these identity documents and the decision on incredibility remained unchanged. The HRC did not see reason to express itself about this complaint. It noted that no order had been made for the forcible return of the author to Iran, and that it was not an inevitable consequence of a failed application for asylum that a deportation would take place (para. 6.3.)

compliance with those rules, the reasons for non-compliance and the other particular circumstances of the case must be taken into account.[11]

The EU Asylum Procedures Directive contains specific provisions on repeat asylum cases in Article 32. These provisions give Member States the possibility to operate, in cases of repeat asylum claims, a special preliminary procedure aimed at establishing whether there are new elements or findings (a *nova*-test).[12] Member States also have the possibility to further process a repeat asylum claim in which new elements or findings are submitted only if it is established that the applicant was, through no fault of his or her own, incapable of asserting the new elements or findings in the previous procedure, in particular by exercising his or her right to an effective remedy.[13]

8.1.2 *Presentation of new evidence: no full and formal exclusion of evidence because of its late moment of presentation*

The positions taken by the UNHCR, the ECtHR and the ComAT all have in common that the presentation of new corroborating evidence within the framework of a repeat asylum claim is, in principle, not perceived to be problematic and detrimental to the claim and the claimant. The UNHCR has made clear that there may be many reasons why an applicant may wish to submit further evidence following the examination of a previous asylum application, and has stressed that Member States should not automatically refuse to examine a subsequent application on the ground that new elements or findings could have been raised in the previous procedure or on appeal.[14]

The ECtHR's case law features a significant number of cases in which crucial evidence corroborating the claim for protection was submitted only in repeat asylum proceedings. Examples are *Hilal v. the UK* (2001)[15] and *Bader and Kanbor* (2005).[16] In both cases, the ECtHR attached great value to this evidence without paying attention to the question of why it had not been submitted earlier, and concluded that an Article 3-risk existed. This is in line with the principle developed in *Bahaddar v. the*

---

11   See HRC, *Ngoc Si Truong v. Canada*, 5 May 2003, No. 743/1997 and *Jagjit Singh Bhullar v. Canada*, 13 November 2006, No. 982/2001.

12   Article 32, second paragraph, of the PD, stipulates: 'Member States may apply a specific procedure as referred to in paragraph 3, where a person makes a subsequent application for asylum.'
The third paragraph stipulates: 'A subsequent application for asylum shall be subject first to a preliminary examination as to whether, after the withdrawal of the previous application or after the decision referred to in paragraph 2(b) of this Article on this application has been reached, new elements or findings relating to the examination of whether he/she qualifies as a refugee by virtue of Directive 2004/83/EC have arisen or have been presented by the applicant.'

13   Article 32, sixth paragraph, stipulates: 'Member States may decide to further examine the application only if the applicant concerned was, through no fault of his/her own, incapable of asserting the situations set forth in paragraphs 3, 4 and 5 of this Article in the previous procedure, in particular by exercising his/her right to an effective remedy pursuant to Article 39.'

14   UNHCR Research Project on the Application of Key Provisions of the Asylum Procedures Directive in selected Member States of March 2010, p. 74.

15   ECtHR, *Hilal v. the UK*, 6 March 2001, Appl. No. 45276/99, paras. 18, 21, 22, 62, 63.

16   ECtHR, *Bader and Kanbor v. Sweden*, 8 November 2005, Appl. No. 13284/04.

Netherlands (1998) that regard must always be had to the difficult evidentiary position of asylum seekers.[17]

We find the same flexible approach in the jurisprudence of the ComAT. In a significant number of early and also later cases, the ComAT accepted tardy presentation of evidence, including presentation of new evidence corroborating a repeat asylum application, without further ado and proceeded to examine whether the evidence sufficiently corroborated the claim.[18] The ComAT seems to have become somewhat stricter over the years though, in the sense that in the more recent jurisprudence a more explicit requirement has been imposed that there must be convincing explanations for tardy production of statements and evidence. Nevertheless, a significant number of cases demonstrate that the ComAT readily accepts explanations for tardy presentation of evidence as convincing.[19]

The HRC requires under Article 14 ICCPR that evidence regarding the substance of the claim, which is submitted to national courts, must be taken into account, even when such evidence was presented at a late stage in national proceedings.[20]

The CJEU has ruled that reasonable national time limits will normally not be problematic, but that there must be room for national courts to be flexible when the circumstances of the case so require.[21]

In sum, a *nova*-test in repeat asylum cases is in itself not problematic from the viewpoint of international and EU asylum law. Given the positions of the international supervisors and courts, national courts should not fully or formally exclude evidence just because it should have been presented at an earlier moment in the asylum procedure.

8.2   Dublin cases

The CJEU, the ECtHR and the UNHCR have taken clear and highly similar positions concerning Dublin cases. The HRC and the ComAT have so far not expressed themselves on the question of what kind of judicial scrutiny is required in this particular category of cases.

The CJEU made clear in its judgment in *N.S. and others* (2011) that it must, in general, be assumed that the treatment of asylum seekers in all EU Member States complies with the requirements of the EU Charter, the RC and the ECHR.[22] This

---

17   ECtHR, *Bahaddar v. the Netherlands*, 19 February 1998, Appl. No. 258/94, para. 45.

18   ComAT, *Khan v. Canada*, 15 November 1994, No. 15/1994; ComAT, *Kisoki v. Sweden*, 8 May 1996, No. 041/1996; ComAT, *V.L. v. Switzerland*, 20 November 2006, 262/2005; ComAT, *Iya v. Switzerland*, 16 November 2007, No. 299/2006; ComAT, *Chahin v. Sweden*, 30 May 2011, No. 310/2007.

19   See, for example, ComAT, *X.Y. v. Switzerland*, 15 May 2001, No. 128/1999, para. 7.3; ComAT, *H.B. and others. v. Switzerland*, 16 May 2003, No. 192/2001, para. 6.8; ComAT, *Zubair Elahi v. Switzerland*, 20 May 2005, No. 222/2002, para.6.7; ComAT, *Z.K. v. Sweden*, 16 May 2008, No. 301/2006, para. 8.4.

20   HRC, *Jansen-Gielen v. the Netherlands*, 14 May 2001, No. 846/1999, para. 8.2.

21   CJEU, *Laub*, 21 June 2007, C-428/05, para. 27; CJEU, *Samba Diouf*, 28 July 2011, C-69/10, paras. 66-68.

22   CJEU, *N.S. and Others*, 21 December 2011, C-411/10 and C-493/10, paras. 78-80, para. 99.

presumption is rebuttable.[23] If, however, there are substantial grounds for believing that there are systemic flaws in the asylum procedure and reception conditions for asylum applicants in the EU Member State responsible, resulting in inhuman or degrading treatment within the meaning of Article 4 of the EU Charter, of asylum seekers transferred to the territory of that Member State, the transfer will be incompatible with that provision.[24] EU Member States, including the national courts, may not transfer an asylum seeker to the EU Member State responsible within the meaning of the EU Dublin Regulation where they are aware that systemic deficiencies in the asylum procedure and in the reception conditions of asylum seekers in that EU Member State amount to substantial grounds for believing that the asylum seeker would face a real risk of being subjected to inhuman or degrading treatment within the meaning of Article 4 of the EU Charter.[25]

The UNHCR and the ECtHR take the position that the Dublin system does not absolve the EU Member States from upholding their obligations under international refugee and human rights law, including, in particular, Article 33 RC and Article 3 ECHR. The national administrative and judicial authorities of the EU Member State intending to transfer an asylum seeker to another EU Member State under the Dublin Regulation cannot solely refer to this regulation without conducting any investigation into an alleged risk of indirect *refoulement* to the country of origin and conducting an investigation into an alleged threat of a violation of Article 3 ECHR, due to the extremely bad living conditions of the asylum seekers.[26]

In its Submission in the case of *M.S.S. v. Belgium and Greece*, the UNHCR pointed to a number of situations in which EU Member States should consider themselves responsible for taking a material decision on the protection claim instead of sending the asylum seeker to another Dublin State:

> 'In UNHCR's view, Dublin II transfers should not take place when there is evidence showing: (1) A real risk of return/expulsion to a territory where there may be a risk of persecution or serious harm; (2) obstacles limiting access to asylum procedures, to a fair and effective examination of claims or to an effective remedy; or (3) conditions of reception, including detention, which may lead to violations of Article 3 ECHR. In these cases, UNHCR considers a State should apply Article 3(2) of the Dublin II Regulation, even if it does not bear responsibility under the criteria laid down in Articles 5-14 of the Regulation.'[27]

---

23 CJEU, *N.S. and Others*, 21 December 2011, C-411/10 and C-493/10, para. 104.
24 CJEU, *N.S. and Others*, 21 December 2011, C-411/10 and C-493/10, para. 86.
25 CJEU, *N.S. and Others*, 21 December 2011, C-411/10 and C-493/10, para. 94.
26 See, for the UNHCR's position, UNHCR Submission in *M.S.S. v. Belgium and Greece*, para. 5.1. The UNHCR Submission can be found at: http://www.unhcr.org/refworld/docid/4c19e7512.html. See for the position of the ECtHR for example *K.R.S. v. the UK*, 2 December 2008, Appl. No. 32733/08, under "B. The responsibility of the United Kingdom."; ECtHR, *T.I. v. the UK*, admissibility decision, 7 March 2000, Appl. No. 43844/98; ECtHR, *M.S.S. v. Belgium and Greece*, 21 January 2011, Appl. No. 30696/09. See for a more detailed analysis of this case Van Bennekom and Van der Winden 2011, pp. 99-103, and Battjes 2011.
27 UNHCR Submission in *M.S.S. v. Belgium and Greece*, para. 5.2.

In *M.S.S.*, the ECtHR clarified what kind of investigation is required from the authorities of the EU Member State intending to expel an asylum seeker under the Dublin Regulation. The ECtHR explained that the investigation should follow two steps. The first step is a presumption that the authorities of the intermediary EU Member State will respect their international obligations in asylum matters:

> 'The Court must therefore now consider whether the Belgian authorities should have regarded as rebutted the presumption that the Greek authorities would respect their international obligations in asylum matters, in spite of the K.R.S. case-law, which the Government claimed the administrative and judicial authorities had wanted to follow in the instant case.'[28]

The second step entails an investigation into the quality of the asylum procedure in the intermediary EU Member State. This second step is to be undertaken where there is an arguable claim and materials have become available which contain certain indications that the intermediary EU Member State may, in practice, not respect its international obligations:

> 'When they apply the Dublin Regulation, therefore, the States must make sure that the intermediary country's asylum procedure affords sufficient guarantees to avoid an asylum seeker being removed, directly or indirectly, to his country of origin without any evaluation of the risks he faces from the standpoint of Article 3 of the Convention.'[29]

In addition to this, the second step entails an investigation into the living conditions of (failed) asylum seekers in the intermediary country when materials have become available pointing out problems in that respect.[30] In the case of *M.S.S*, the applicant alleged that because of the conditions of detention and existence to which asylum seekers were subjected in Greece, by returning him to that country in application of the Dublin Regulation the Belgian authorities had exposed him to treatment prohibited by Article 3 ECHR.[31]

The applicant does not bear the entire burden of proof. Situations may arise in which the national authorities of the EU Member State intending to transfer, including national courts, are aware or could have been aware of deficiencies in the intermediary EU Member State:

> 'In these conditions the Court considers that the general situation was known to the Belgian authorities and that the applicant should not be expected to bear the entire burden of proof. (...) The Court considers that at the time of the applicant's expulsion the Belgian authorities knew or ought to have known that he had no guarantee that his asylum application would be seriously examined by the Greek authorities.'[32]

---

28   ECtHR, *M.S.S. v. Belgium and Greece*, 21 January 2011, Appl. No. 30696/09, para. 345.
29   *Ibidem*, para. 342.
30   *Ibidem*, paras. 342-358.
31   *Ibidem*, para. 362.
32   *Ibidem*, paras. 352, 358. See also Battjes 2011: in his extensive comments to the judgment he stresses this notion of a shared burden in 6.2.1, calling this a 'spectacular turn' as in other (not Dublin) cases

→

This resembles the CJEU's approach that EU Member States' authorities, including the national courts, may not transfer an asylum seeker to the responsible EU Member State when they are aware of systemic deficiencies in the asylum procedure and in the reception conditions of asylum seekers in that EU Member State.[33] This, too, implies that the applicant should not be expected to bear the entire burden of proof and that the national authorities, including national courts, have a responsibility of their own to investigate the quality of living conditions and the asylum procedure in the intermediary EU Member State.

We may conclude that, in cases of the expulsion of asylum seekers under the Dublin Regulation, the expelling EU Member State's authorities, including the national courts, are, to a certain extent, allowed to presume that the authorities of the intermediary EU Member State will respect their international obligations. With Van Bennekom and Van der Winden (2011), I infer from *M.S.S.* that, at the same time, the ECtHR has clearly put a firm restriction on the presumption of treaty compliance.[34] As soon as (some) information to the contrary becomes available – either because the applicant has submitted this information or because the authorities are familiar with it or should be familiar with it – the national authorities must assess whether the asylum procedure in the intermediary EU Member State affords 'sufficient guarantees' and whether living conditions violate Article 3 ECHR.

8.3 Fast-track proceedings

On the issue of fast-track national proceedings, the stances of the international supervisors and courts are, in fact, identical. The UNHCR, the ECtHR and the CJEU have pointed out that they are not opposed to fast-track proceedings as it is in the interests of both the asylum seeker and the State that a decision is taken as soon as possible.[35] The CJEU has emphasised that under the EU Asylum Procedures Directive, EU Member States enjoy national procedural autonomy and are, therefore, free to accelerate the processing of asylum applications, as long as they live up to their obligations flowing from the Directive:

> 'Thus, the organisation of the processing of applications for asylum is, as stated in recital 11 to Directive 2005/85, left to the discretion of Member States, which may, in accordance with their national needs, prioritise or accelerate the processing of any application, taking into account the standards provided for by the directive, without prejudice, in the words of Article 23(2) of the directive, to an adequate and complete examination.'[36]

---

it is required that the applicant adduces evidence capable of proving that there are substantial grounds to believe that a real risk exists.

33 CJEU, *N.S. and Others*, 21 December 2011, C-411/10 and C-493/10, para. 94.

34 Van Bennekom & Van der Winden 2011, p. 103.

35 UNHCR Statement on the right to an effective remedy in relation to accelerated asylum procedures, paras. 5, 6 and 7, http://www.unhcr.org/refworld/pdfid/4bf67fa12.pdf; ECtHR, *I.M. v. France*, 2 February 2012, Appl. No. 9152/09, para. 142; CJEU, *Samba Diouf*, 28 July 2011, C-69/10, para. 30.

36 CJEU, *Samba Diouf*, 28 July 2011, C-69/10, para. 30.

The HRC has stressed in its case law under Article 14 ICCPR that the procedural practice applied by national courts to determine the facts and to admit, exclude, and evaluate evidence is a matter for those courts to determine, in the interests of justice.[37] The ComAT has also stressed national procedural autonomy when it comes to the determination of the facts.[38]

At the same time, the UNHCR, the ECtHR, the HRC and the ComAT have all seriously warned that setting short time limits for the examination of asylum claims and sacrificing key procedural safeguards for the sake of speed may not allow asylum seekers the opportunity to adequately substantiate their claims and may result in a more cursory review of relevant facts, leading to flawed decisions.[39]

Both the UNHCR and the ECtHR have emphasised that fast-track proceedings are generally only suitable for certain categories of cases. The UNHCR mentions as suitable 'clearly abusive' and 'manifestly unfounded' cases, and also 'obviously well-founded cases'.[40] The ECtHR speaks of 'clearly unreasonable' and 'manifestly ill-founded' cases, as well as repeat asylum applications after a first asylum application has been processed under normal proceedings.[41] The ECtHR has also made clear that it is opposed to a practice of automatic registration of claims under a fast-track national procedure on procedural grounds, without taking into consideration the nature or merits of the claim.[42]

The CJEU has, furthermore, warned in its judgment in *Petrosian* (2009) that the safeguards of national judicial protection should never be sacrificed to speed:

> '(...) it is clear that the Community legislature did not intend that the judicial protection guaranteed by the Member States (...) should be sacrificed to the requirement of expedition in processing asylum applications'.[43]

In line with this, the CJEU stressed in *Samba Diouf* (2011) that, where fast-track proceedings are applied, the national court must at all times remain able to perform a thorough review on the merits of the claim.[44]

---

37   For example, HRC, *Anni Äärelä and Jouni Näkkäläjärvi v. Finland*, 7 November 2001, No. 779/1997, para. 7.3.

38   See, for example, ComAT, *A.R. v. Netherlands*, 14 November 2003, No. 203/2002; ComAT, *Rios v. Canada*, 23 November 2004, No. 133/1999.

39   UNHCR Statement on the right to an effective remedy in relation to accelerated asylum procedures, para. 6; ECtHR, *I.M. v. France*, 2 February 2012, Application. No. 9152/09, paras. 144-160; HRC, Concluding Observations on the Netherlands, 25 August 2009, UN doc. CCPR/C/NLD/CO/4, para. 9; HRC, Concluding Observations and Recommendations on Latvia of 6 November 2003, CCPR/CO/79/LVA; ComAT, Conclusions and Recommendations regarding Finland, 21 June 2005, CAT/C/CR/34/FIN, para. 4.b, ComAT, Conclusions and Recommendations regarding France, 3 April 2006, CAT/C/FRA/CO/3, para. 6; ComAT, Conclusions and Recommendations regarding the Netherlands, 3 August 2007, CAT/C/NET/CO/4, para. 7; ComAT, Conclusions and Recommendations regarding Norway of 5 February 2008, CAT/C/NOR/CO/5; ComAT, Conclusions and Recommendations regarding Latvia, 19 February 2008, CAT/C/LVA/CO/2, para. 8.

40   UNHCR Statement on the right to an effective remedy in relation to accelerated asylum procedures, paras. 5, 6 and 7.

41   ECtHR, *I.M. v. France*, 2 February 2012, Appl. No. 9152/09, para. 142.

42   *Ibidem*, para. 141.

43   CJEU, *Petrosian*, 29 January 2009, C-19/08, para. 48.

It may be concluded that fast-track asylum court proceedings are not problematic *per se*. What is important is that, when operating such proceedings, national courts remain able to perform a thorough review on the merits of the asylum claim. It must also be remembered that fast-track court proceedings may deprive asylum seekers of the opportunity to substantiate the claim for protection. If a national court estimates that, as a result of operating fast-track proceedings, a thorough review on the merits cannot take place or that the asylum seeker is deprived of the opportunity to substantiate his or her claim, that court must have possibilities to reroute the case into normal or prolonged proceedings which offer more room for further judicial investigations or further substantiation of the claim by the asylum seeker.

---

44   CJEU, *Samba Diouf*, 28 July 2011, C-69/10, paras. 56, 61.

Epilogue: Open letter to my colleagues in national courts in the EU

When I embarked upon this research project, some people within and outside my District Court of Amsterdam were highly surprised by the subject. They commented that I was surely not going to find in international and EU asylum law any standards on judicial scrutiny and evidence. The results of this research demonstrate that the opposite is true: international and EU asylum law contain many specific standards on the intensity of judicial scrutiny to be applied by national courts, as well as standards on evidence. In this epilogue, I wish to highlight the main discoveries resulting from this research and, based on these research results, provide a number of guidelines for the future.

For me, a very important discovery was the added value of EU asylum law. This added value is first of all the transformation in legal status of existing standards on evidence and judicial scrutiny contained in international asylum law by virtue of their incorporation into EU law, via Articles 18, 19, 47 and 52(3) of the EU Charter. This is a transformation from non-binding principles into more important rules which must be respected (the standards developed by the UNHCR), from intergovernmental international law into binding primary supranational EU law (the standards developed by the ECtHR) and from intergovernmental international law into important sources of inspiration for binding EU law (the standards and principles developed by the HRC and the ComAT). As a result of this incorporation of existing international law standards on evidence and judicial scrutiny into EU law, national asylum courts can no longer ignore, disregard or discard these standards, as that would amount to a violation of the EU Charter, which is binding primary supranational EU law.

The added value of EU asylum law is also that Article 6 ECHR on a fair hearing is – via Article 47 of the Charter – now fully applicable to national asylum court proceedings. This study has demonstrated that Article 6 ECHR contains important specific standards on the intensity of judicial scrutiny to be applied by national courts. Article 6 ECHR also contains important specific standards on handling evidence.

This study has revealed that international and EU asylum law require national asylum courts to perform an 'independent and rigorous scrutiny' of the protection claim (ECtHR), a 'thorough and fair examination of the claim' (HRC), an 'effective, independent and impartial review on the merits of the claim' (ComAT), 'appeal or review proceedings on points of fact, including credibility, and points of law' (UNHCR) and a 'thorough review on the merits of the claim' (CJEU). Article 6 ECHR and Article 47 of the EU Charter require that asylum refusals can be challenged before a tribunal having full judicial jurisdiction on points of fact and points of law. This full jurisdiction under Articles 6 ECHR and 47 of the EU Charter means, *inter alia*, that the national court is able to make an independent determination of the disputed facts and of the credibility of a claimant (e.g. ECtHR, *Tsfayo v. the UK*). Full jurisdiction also means that the national court examining the case is not precluded from determining 'the central issue in dispute' (ECtHR, *Sigma Radio Television Ltd v. Cyprus*).

Thus, the common denominator emerging from international and EU asylum law is independent, impartial, full and rigorous national judicial scrutiny. This standard requires national courts to examine evidence submitted by applicants in a careful and serious manner. Second, independent, impartial, full and rigorous national judicial scrutiny requires that national courts are able to make an independent and fresh determination of the facts and that, if necessary in order to clarify the facts, these courts undertake judicial investigations. Below, I will highlight both aspects by discussing those research findings which were true eye-openers for me.

Evidence presented by the applicant

The HRC, the ComAT, the ECtHR and the CJEU have all made clear that evidence presented by the applicant for asylum must be taken seriously and examined carefully by the national authorities. The recent ECtHR judgment in *Singh v. Belgium* (2012) forms the perfect illustration: the applicants provided copies of pages from Afghan passports and copies of UNHCR documents, but the national authorities did not make any effort to investigate these documents as they found it incredible anyway that the applicants were of Afghan nationality.

The national authorities must also seriously and carefully examine medical evidence (medico-legal reports, but also short notes from first line doctors). If such reports leave doubts, national authorities, including national courts, must take additional investigative measures to further clarify the facts. Medico-legal reports play a particularly prominent role in the case law of the ComAT. Provided that such reports are drawn up by medical specialists and conclusively identify a causal link between the individual's bodily or mental injuries and the alleged past torture, such reports may serve as corroboration of statements on past torture, and as an explanation for inconsistencies, gaps or vague points, major changes in the flight narrative and the late presentation of crucial statements and evidence. The approach of the international supervisors towards medical evidence stands in sharp contrast to practice in the Netherlands where generally medico-legal reports presented to corroborate past torture are not given probative value.

The ECtHR, the HRC and the ComAT have, in a significant number of cases, attached serious probative value to witness statements by family members of asylum claimants. This stands in sharp contrast with the national approach practised in the Netherlands that such statements do not stem from objective sources and, therefore, cannot have probative value.

In the case law of the ECtHR, the HRC, and the ComAT, and in the positions of the UNHCR, the point in time at which evidentiary materials are submitted in proceedings by the parties is – seen as a factor alone and in itself – not a relevant consideration. In a significant number of cases dealt with by the ECtHR and the ComAT, crucial evidence was submitted for the first time in the context of repeat national asylum proceedings. The international supervisors did not see this as problematic *per se*. This flexible approach to the moment of presentation of evidence stands in sharp contrast with national judicial practice in a number of EU countries, among them the Netherlands, to discard evidence on the ground that it was not submitted earlier. This practice is no longer tenable as it is at odds with the far more flex-ible international standard.

Another important finding arrived at in this study concerns the required quantity of evidence. It is clear that, in order to win a case before the HRC, the ComAT and the ECtHR, the core aspects of the flight narrative need to be corroborated with substantial evidentiary materials. However, these international supervisors do not require evidence in support of the travel route, which is seen as a more peripheral, and not central, aspect. Similarly, they do not, as a hard and fast rule, require evidence of the stated identity and nationality. Given the position of these three international supervisors, and given the emphasis the UNHCR has constantly placed on the diffi-cult evidentiary position of asylum seekers, the question rises whether it is tenable to require evidence in corroboration of more than the core of the flight narrative. In the Netherlands, evidence is required in corroboration of identity, nationality, travel route and flight narrative. Like the UNHCR stated in its Submission in *Mir Isfahani v. the Netherlands*, I would conclude that this practice is not tenable.

Independent fresh determination of the facts, judicial investigations

As has been said above, Article 6 ECHR and Article 47 of the EU Charter require that asylum refusals can be challenged before a tribunal having full judicial jurisdic-tion on points of fact and points of law. This full jurisdiction means, *inter alia*, that the national court is able to make an independent determination of the disputed facts and of the credibility of a claimant (e.g. ECtHR, *Tsfayo v. the UK*). It also means that the national court examining the case is not precluded from determining 'the central issue in dispute' (ECtHR, *Sigma Radio Television Ltd v. Cyprus*).

Marginal national judicial review of the credibility of asylum seekers' accounts will, in many cases, be at variance with the full jurisdiction requirement flowing from Articles 6 ECHR and 47 of the EU Charter, as it will preclude the national court from determining 'the central issue in dispute'. In many asylum cases, the fear to be persecuted or ill-treated upon expulsion to the country of origin is fully based on the flight narrative: facts that allegedly took place in the country of origin in the past which the applicant fears to be repeated if he or she returns to the country of origin, given the situation there. If the national court is allowed to only marginally assess the credibility of the alleged past facts, and the fear for the future risk is fully based on these past facts, how can that court truly independently determine the central issue in dispute: the feared future risk? Marginal judicial review of the credibility of the flight account will arguably be less problematic in those asylum cases where, next to the flight narrative, there are also so called *sur place* activities in the country of refuge. Pro-vided that the national court is able to fully and independently assess the risk which may emanate from such *sur place* activities, it will arguably be less problematic that that court does not fully independently assess the credibility of the stated past facts (the flight narrative). Not all asylum cases contain such a *sur place* component, though.

Independent, impartial, full and rigorous national judicial scrutiny requires an active judicial approach towards fact finding and evidence. The interpretation of im-partiality by the ComAT under Articles 12 and 13 is very helpful in this respect. In cases of allegations or suspicions of internal torture, the requirement of impartiality enshrined in Articles 12 and 13 obliges the national judge to reconstruct as meticulously as possible what actually happened and to use his or her investigative powers if that may help to come as close as possible to the truth. Impartiality of national asylum courts may be interpreted as meaning the same thing as impartiality under Articles 12 and 13. That would mean that national asylum courts must act impartially and must, therefore, make their own independent, thorough search for the truth and apply investigative powers to that end. Compared to internal torture cases, it may indeed be much more difficult for national asylum courts to find the truth. Unlike in internal torture cases, courts will not readily be able to conduct on site investigations, to check prison records and hear witnesses in prisons, etc. That does not mean, however, that it not possible to use other investigative powers, such as searching for additional information on the situation in the country of origin, seeking expert opinions, hearing individuals from the same country of origin as witnesses.

The interpretation of impartiality by ComAT is in line with the ECtHR's *Zumtobel*-doctrine under Article 6 ECHR, which requires that national administrative courts are able to make an independent determination of the disputed facts and of the credibility of a claimant; it also fits well with the active fact finding and evidence gathering role played by the ECtHR in a significant number of cases concerning expulsion of asylum seekers, and with the position of UNHCR that national judges should be able to obtain a personal impression of the applicant, that court proceedings should involve points of fact and points of law and national courts should be able to independently assess the credibility of the statements of the asylum seeker.

This interpretation of impartiality stands in sharp contrast to the notion sometimes expressed in national Dutch jurisprudence, that first instance judges are not allowed to use the investigative powers they possess under the General Administrative Law Act, as it is held to be the task of the asylum seeker to present the facts and the evidence and it is not up to the judge to 'help' him or her in fulfilling this task. The ComAT's interpretation of impartiality makes clear that active judicial investigations have nothing to do with helping one of the parties, but are a matter of independence and impartiality.

A clear expression of the requirement of impartiality is that under Article 8, second and third paragraph, of the EU Asylum Procedures Directive and under the ICCPR, the CAT and the ECHR particular responsibility for shaping clarity on the general human rights situation in the country of origin lies with the national authorities, including the judicial authorities.

I cannot conceal that some findings I arrived at in this study disappointed me. The HRC, the ComAT and the ECtHR have, so far, not developed elaborate and coherent doctrinal positions on the intensity of the scrutiny with which they themselves determine the facts in expulsion cases concerning asylum seekers. The case law of these three supervisors demonstrates that, in certain cases, they rely on the respondent State party's determination of the facts, including the credibility assessment, whereas in other cases they make a fully independent determination of the facts of their own account. It is not always clear why a certain choice for one or other intensity of scrutiny is made. The case law of the ECtHR is the clearest in this respect as we may at least infer from it that there seem to be three triggers which make that the ECtHR actively proceeds towards an independent determination of the facts, including credibility, and applies investigative powers to that end. These triggers are, in short: (1) insufficient national proceedings (evidence was overlooked or not taken seriously); (2) new facts, circumstances and developments, including evidence thereof; and (3) disrespect for the absolute nature of Article 3 (or an incorrect application of another evidentiary standard such as a too strict requirement of individualization). To be honest, I had expected more elaborate doctrinal positions on the intensity of scrutiny applied by the HRC, the ComAT, and the ECtHR.

At the same time, an important discovery was that the HRC, the ComAT and the ECtHR at least always have the free choice to apply an intense and full factual scrutiny or, instead, rely on the facts as presented by the respondent State. I have argued – with reference to ECtHR-judge Martens' opinion – that national asylum courts should similarly at least have this free choice to apply, in the specific cases coming before them, either full factual scrutiny or a somewhat more deferent approach towards the determination of the facts. National first instance asylum courts should not be under an absolute obligation to apply a marginal judicial review regarding credibility assessments. Such an obligation forces national asylum courts into a position which is very far from the judicial discretion, determined by and available to the HRC, the ComAT and the ECtHR to apply either a very intense scrutiny or a somewhat more deferential type of review. Such an inflexible obligation threatens the independence and impartiality of the national judiciary and the subsidiary nature of the international human rights systems.

It was equally disappointing to discover that the conclusions in the views of the HRC and the ComAT are in many cases ultra-brief and offer no clear linkage between facts and conclusions. Many views offer little to no guidance to national courts on the burden of proof, the requirement of individualisation, the assessment of credibility, and the admission and evaluation of evidence. I discovered a number of reasons which may explain this. Especially the HRC and the ComAT have limited meeting time and are multidisciplinary and are not composed of lawyers only. On top of that, the HRC has only a limited body of asylum case law on which to draw. Although these reasons created understanding, I found it difficult and disappointing to see that these important international treaty supervisors did not provide clearer guidance to national courts. Given this result, I would like to make a plea to the HRC and the ComAT to try and come up with more elaborate considerations on the mentioned issues of evidence and on the intensity of judicial scrutiny they themselves apply. It is crucial for national asylum courts to receive clearer guidance from the HRC and the ComAT on the mentioned aspects of evidence. Only then will they be able to live up to their treaty obligations.

It is my strong conviction that independent, impartial and thorough national judicial scrutiny, including thorough judicial investigations aimed at finding the truth, are of utmost importance in national asylum court proceedings, as most fundamental human rights are at stake there and the determination of the facts and the credibility assessment in such proceedings is a very difficult task. It is also my strong belief that thorough judicial investigations aimed at finding the truth have nothing to do with helping one of the parties to the case, but have to do with independence and impartiality of the judiciary. International and EU asylum law provide support for these personal convictions.

Samenvatting (Summary in Dutch)

GRONDIG ONDERZOEK VERSUS MARGINALE TOETSING

STANDAARDEN VOOR RECHTERLIJKE TOETSING EN BEWIJSSTANDAARDEN IN
INTERNATIONAAL EN EUROPEES ASIELRECHT

Twee arresten van het Europees Hof voor de Rechten van de Mens (EHRM) vorm-
den de directe aanleiding om dit onderzoek te starten. Het betrof de zaken *Said tegen
Nederland* (2005) en *Salah Sheekh tegen Nederland* (2007). Uit deze arresten sprak duidelijk dat het EHRM ontevreden was over het onderzoek door de nationale rechter in
Nederland in zaken betreffende de uitzetting van asielzoekers. Deze ontevredenheid
baarde mij als nationale rechter zorgen. Samen met mijn collega Willem van Bennekom van de Rechtbank Amsterdam, waar ik net begonnen was te werken als vreemdelingenrechter na voltooiing van de RAIO-opleiding, heb ik toen een aantal bekende
arresten van het EHRM inzake de uitzetting van asielzoekers geanalyseerd om pre-
ciezer te kunnen zien hoe dit internationale hof de risicotaxatie maakt. Ik ontdekte
significante verschillen tussen de rechterlijke praktijk op internationaal niveau en onze
eigen nationale werkwijze. Ten eerste leek de intensiteit of de grondigheid van het
rechterlijk onderzoek te verschillen. Het leek erop dat het EHRM volledig onafhankelijk en zelfstandig de feiten vaststelde en het risico taxeerde. De Nederlandse nationale vreemdelingenrechters daarentegen dienden het standpunt van verweerder (de
IND) met betrekking tot de geloofwaardigheid van de door de asielzoeker gepresen-
teerde feiten in het verleden terughoudend oftewel marginaal te toetsen. Ten tweede
werden bewijsvraagstukken, zoals de toelating van bewijs en de waardering daarvan,
op geheel verschillende wijze benaderd en opgelost op internationaal en nationaal
niveau. Ik raakte geïntrigeerd door de resultaten van dit kleinschalige onderzoek. Ik
wilde graag in nog meer detail onderzoeken welke lessen getrokken zouden kunnen
en moeten worden uit het EVRM waar het gaat om de intensiteit van de rechterlijke
toetsing en bewijskwesties. Daarnaast wilde ik graag uitzoeken of andere relevante
internationale verdragen en EU (asiel)recht concrete instructies bevatten omtrent bewijsvraagstukken en omtrent de intensiteit van rechterlijk onderzoek die geboden
hoort te worden op nationaal niveau. Mijn wens om onderzoek hiernaar te doen werd
sterk gevoed door het feit dat in het nationale debat uiteenlopend werd gedacht over
de vraag of verschillen in toetsing door de nationale en de internationale rechter
aanvaardbaar waren, terwijl de argumentatie voor de uiteenlopende posities (althans
voor mij) niet geheel overtuigend was. Mijn wens om onderzoek te doen werd nog
groter toen ik de resultaten van mijn kleinschalige onderzoek deelde met een aantal
collega-rechters binnen de Internationale Associatie van Asielrechters. Hierdoor
ontdekte ik dat niet alleen nationale rechtbanken in Nederland tegen de vraagstukken
zoals hierboven beschreven aanliepen. Ook in een aantal andere EU lidstaten
(bijvoorbeeld Polen en Griekenland) bleken problemen te bestaan met betrekking tot
de intensiteit van het rechterlijk onderzoek en bewijs in asielzaken.

Het hoofddoel van deze studie is te onderzoeken wat internationaal en Europees
asielrecht eisen van de nationale rechter op het gebied van:

1) de vereiste intensiteit van het rechterlijk onderzoek, en
2) bewijsvraagstukken, zoals bijvoorbeeld de bewijsstandaard en de bewijslast, de toelating en waardering van bewijs, termijnen voor het indienen van bewijsmateriaal.

De onderzoeksvragen luiden als volgt:
- Welke bepalingen van internationaal en EU asielrecht reguleren de nationale asielberoepsprocedure bij de rechter?
- Bevatten deze bepalingen concrete normen omtrent de vereiste intensiteit van het rechterlijk onderzoek op nationaal niveau?
- Bevatten deze bepalingen concrete normen voor bewijsvraagstukken, zoals de bewijsstandaard en de bewijslast, de toelating en waardering van bewijs, termijnen voor het indienen van bewijsmateriaal?
- Welke standaarden en beginselen passen de internationale hoven en verdragstoezichthouders zelf toe waar het gaat om de intensiteit van hun onderzoek, en hoe benaderen deze hoven en verdragstoezichthouders bewijsvraagstukken?
- Zijn deze standaarden en beginselen maatgevend of bindend voor nationale asielrechters?
- Hoe verhouden de gevonden normen zich tot elkaar en welke norm moet worden gekozen in geval van uiteenlopende of conflicterende normen?

Om te onderzoeken welke maatstaven worden toegepast door de internationale hoven en toezichthouders worden in deze studie elf aspecten (vraagstukken) van bewijs en rechterlijk onderzoek gebruikt. Het gaat om de volgende aspecten:
- Bewijsstandaard: wat is de maatstaf of het criterium voor het beoordelen van een mogelijk risico van *refoulement*?
- Bewijslast: wie moet bewijzen dat aan dit criterium is voldaan?
- Relevante feiten en omstandigheden: welk soort feiten en omstandigheden zijn nodig om tot het bestaan van een risico te concluderen?
- Vereiste mate van individueel risico: in welke mate moet een asielzoeker individueel risico aannemelijk maken?
- Beoordeling van geloofwaardigheid: analyseert het internationale hof of de toezichthouder de geloofwaardigheid op onafhankelijke en zelfstandige wijze? Hoe analyseert het internationale hof of de toezichthouder de geloofwaardigheid van de verklaringen van verzoeker?
- Toelating van bewijs, soorten bewijsmateriaal, minimale hoeveelheid en kwaliteit van bewijs: welke middelen en bronnen van bewijs kunnen worden ingebracht om het relaas te onderbouwen of ontkrachten? Hoeveel bewijs is vereist om de verklaringen van de asielzoeker te onderbouwen? Hoe hoog moet de kwaliteit van het bewijsmateriaal zijn?
- Waardering en weging van bewijs: hoe worden verschillende soorten bewijs gewogen en gewaardeerd? Bestaat er een zekere hiërarchie in de waardering van bewijs in de zin dat aan bepaalde bronnen een sterkere bewijswaarde wordt toegekend dan aan andere?

- Mogelijkheden of kansen voor het aandragen van bewijs: hebben beide partijen dezelfde mogelijkheden om bewijs te presenteren en om te reageren op bewijs aangevoerd door de andere partij?
- Toepassing van rechterlijke onderzoeksbevoegdheden: gebruikt het internationale hof of de toezichthouder onderzoeksbevoegdheden (uit eigen beweging of anderszins)? Zo ja, in welke situaties?
- Termijnen voor het aanvoeren van verklaringen en het indienen van bewijsstukken: op welk moment in de procedure moet de asielzoeker de relevante verklaringen aanvoeren en het stavende bewijs overleggen?
- Moment van risicotaxatie: van welk moment gaat het internationale hof of de toezichthouder uit bij de inschatting van het risico?

Deze studie omvat het Verdrag betreffende de Status van Vluchtelingen en het Protocol betreffende de Status van Vluchtelingen (Vluchtelingenverdrag, 1951, en het Vluchtelingenprotocol, 1967), het Internationale Verdrag inzake Burger en Politieke Rechten (IVBPR, 1966), het Anti-Folterverdrag (AFV, 1984), het Europees Verdrag voor de Rechten van de Mens en de Fundamentele Vrijheden (EVRM, 1950), primaire wetgeving van de Europese Unie relevant voor asiel, alsmede een aantal secundaire instrumenten van de EU zoals de EU Kwalificatierichtlijn en de EU Procedurerichtlijn.

UNHCR documentatie en literatuur zijn de belangrijkste bronnen voor de interpretatie van de bepalingen in het Vluchtelingenverdrag. De jurisprudentie van het Mensenrechtencomité, het Comité tegen Foltering, het EHRM en het HvJEU, alsmede literatuur, vormen de belangrijkste bronnen voor respectievelijk hoofdstuk 3 (IVBPR), hoofdstuk 4 (AFV), hoofdstuk 5 (EVRM) en hoofdstuk 6 (EU asielrecht).

Na de introductie in hoofdstuk 1 behandelt hoofdstuk 2 het Vluchtelingenverdrag, gevolgd door het IVBPR in hoofdstuk 3 en het AFV in hoofdstuk 4. Hoofdstuk 5 spitst zich toe op het EVRM en hoofdstuk 6 is gewijd aan EU asielrecht. Hoofdstuk 7 bespreekt de consequenties van de gevonden normen en maatstaven voor nationale asielrechters. Dit hoofdstuk poogt de verschillende internationale en EU-rechtelijke maatstaven voor de intensiteit van rechterlijk onderzoek en bewijs te integreren tot een samenhangend geheel. Het probeert ook een antwoord te vinden op de vraag of de maatstaven inzake rechterlijk onderzoek en bewijs zoals toegepast door de internationale hoven en toezichthouders bindend zijn voor nationale asielrechters en of nationale asielrechters een rolmodel kunnen kiezen uit de verschillende internationale hoven en toezichthouders. Een andere vraag waarop in hoofdstuk 7 wordt ingegaan is wat moet gebeuren in gevallen van uiteenlopende of conflicterende normen. Hoofdstuk 8 besteedt afzonderlijk aandacht aan de positie van de internationale toezichthouders en hoven ten aanzien van drie specifieke soorten zaken en procedures: Dublinzaken, herhaalde asielaanvragen en versnelde nationale procedures. In de epiloog aan het einde van dit boek worden de belangrijksteresultaten van het onderzoek belicht en worden concluderende opmerkingen gemaakt.

Bepalingen in internationaal en EU asielrecht over, of relevant voor, nationale gerechtelijke asielprocedures

Het Vluchtelingenverdrag (VLV)

Het Vluchtelingenverdrag bevat een aantal bepalingen die relevant zijn voor nationale gerechtelijke procedures. Dit zijn artikel 16 over toegang tot de rechter, artikel 32 over uitzetting op grond van nationale veiligheid en openbare orde, alsmede de te volgen procedure in geval van uitzetting, en artikel 35 over samenwerking van nationale autoriteiten met de UNHCR. In hoofdstuk 2 stond de vraag centraal wat deze artikelen betekenen voor de onderzoeksvragen. Artikel 16 Vluchtelingenverdrag vereist dat vluchtelingen vrije toegang hebben tot de nationale rechter. Artikel 32 vereist dat de beslissing om een vluchteling uit te zetten voldoet aan de regels van een behoorlijk proces. In de literatuur wordt verschillend gedacht over de vraag of deze twee bepalingen van toepassing zijn op procedures omtrent het vaststellen van de vluchtelingenstatus en *refoulement*. In deze studie is om verschillende, in hoofdstuk 2 uiteengezette, redenen gekozen voor een dynamische interpretatie van deze bepalingen, wat leidt tot de conclusie dat beide bepalingen inderdaad van toepassing zijn op zulke gerechtelijke procedures.

Artikel 16 Vluchtelingenverdrag is allereerst een non-discriminatiebepaling. Het houdt in dat van vluchtelingen niet mag worden geëist dat zij aan meer of strengere ontvankelijkheidsvereisten voldoen dan eigen onderdanen. De artikelen 16 en 32 Vluchtelingenverdrag kunnen worden geïnterpreteerd met behulp van de standpunten van de UNHCR over bewijsvraagstukken en rechterlijk onderzoek in nationale gerechtelijke asielprocedures. De UNHCR heeft concrete normen en beginselen ontwikkeld ten aanzien van tien van de in dit onderzoek centraal staande elf aspecten van bewijs en rechterlijk onderzoek. Deze zijn hieronder genoemd in de rubriek 'Standpunten van de internationale hoven en toezichthouders over de elf aspecten van bewijs en rechterlijk onderzoek'. Bezien in samenhang met artikel 21, paragraaf 1, sub e van de EU Procedurerichtlijn houdt artikel 35 Vluchtelingenverdrag in dat de UNHCR bevoegd is om zijn standpunt kenbaar te maken in bij de rechter aanhangige asielberoepszaken. De standpunten van de UNHCR kunnen langs verschillende wegen de nationale gerechtelijke procedure binnen komen: de UNHCR kan op eigen initiatief zijn standpunt aan de nationale rechtbank kenbaar maken, het initiatief om de UNHCR naar zijn mening te vragen kan van een partij uitgaan, of de nationale rechter kan de UNHCR uitnodigen om deel te nemen aan de procedure. Op grond van de artikelen 16 en 35 Vluchtelingenverdrag, gelezen in samenhang, kunnen nationale rechters de UNHCR uitnodigen deel te nemen aan de nationale gerechtelijke procedure als deskundige of getuige die de rechter kan adviseren over een specifiek aspect van een zaak of die een standpunt kan geven over de vraag of een verzoeker al dan niet als vluchteling moet worden aangemerkt.

Het Internationaal Verdrag voor de Burgerlijke en Politieke Rechten (IVBPR)

Uit de bepalingen van het IVBPR over nationale (gerechtelijke) procedures vloeien een aantal concrete verplichtingen voort voor nationale asielrechters. Op grond van

410

artikel 2 lid 3 en artikel 7 IVBPR moeten de nationale autoriteiten, en dus ook nationale rechters, een verzoek om bescherming grondig en eerlijk overwegen. Het Mensenrechtencomité is echter in het algemeen terughoudend met het toetsen van nationale (gerechtelijke) asielprocedures aan dit vereiste. Het Mensenrechtencomité verzuimt vaak om daadwerkelijk in te gaan op de specifieke procedurele problemen die worden aangedragen door individuele klagers. Deze passieve houding heeft te maken met het feit dat het Mensenrechtencomité de vaststelling en beoordeling van feiten en bewijsmateriaal primair ziet als een verantwoordelijkheid van de nationale autoriteiten. Het Mensenrechtencomité mengt zich daar normaal gesproken niet in. Als gevolg hiervan zal het Mensenrechtencomité de nationale rechtsgang niet snel als onvoldoende bestempelen op grond van argumenten die te maken hebben met de vaststelling van de feiten. De voorzichtige aanpak van het Mensenrechtencomité kan ook verklaard worden vanuit de beperkte onderzoeksmogelijkheden en de beperkte tijd voor de behandeling van zaken. De zaak *Pillai en Joachimpillai t. Canada* (2011) vormt mogelijk een keerpunt in de richting van strenger toezicht op de naleving van procedurele eisen die uit het IVBPR voortvloeien. In die zaak concludeerde het Mensenrechtencomité dat door nationale autoriteiten meer aandacht had moeten worden besteed aan de stellingen van de klagers dat zij in hun land van herkomst waren gemarteld. Het Mensenrechtencomité concludeerde op grond van dit gebrek aan aandacht dat de nationale (gerechtelijke) procedure onvoldoende waarborgen bood. Verdere jurisprudentie moet worden afgewacht om daadwerkelijk te kunnen concluderen dat het Mensenrechtencomité voortaan strikter toeziet op de naleving van de procedurele IVBPR-eisen. De zaak *Mansour Ahani t. Canada* (2004) heeft laten zien dat het Mensenrechtencomité in sommige gevallen zijn terughoudende aanpak laat varen. In die zaak schonden de nationale rechters de fundamentele beginselen van gelijke wapens van partijen en een procedure op tegenspraak. Het Mensenrechtencomité vond dat de nationale uitzettingsprocedure, waaronder de gerechtelijke procedure, in *Ahani* met onvoldoende waarborgen was omkleed aangezien de minister niet alle stukken waarop de uitzettingsbeslissing was gebaseerd aan Ahani ter beschikking had gesteld. De geheim gehouden stukken bevatten informatie waarin Ahani als een gevaar voor de Canadese nationale veiligheid werd bestempeld. De nationale rechter had dit gebrek vervolgens niet hersteld in de gerechtelijke procedure waarin de beslissing tot uitzetting werd aangevochten.

Nationale gerechtelijke procedures zullen normaal gesproken niet op basis van nationale procedurele regels onverenigbaar zijn met het vereiste van grondig en eerlijk onderzoek naar het verzoek om bescherming, mits deze procedurele regels redelijk zijn en niet automatisch en op mechanische wijze worden toegepast. Nationale rechters mogen daarnaast niet zonder meer hun oordeel vormen op basis van precedentwerking.

Het Mensenrechtencomité heeft in het kader van artikel 14 IVBPR geoordeeld dat de door de nationale rechter toegepaste procedurele praktijk met betrekking tot de vaststelling van de feiten en de toelating, uitsluiting, weging en waardering van bewijs een aangelegenheid is van de nationale rechter. Anders dan het EHRM, heeft het Mensenrechtencomité in het kader van artikel 14 IVBPR tot op heden (nog) geen doctrine ontwikkeld over de vereiste intensiteit van toetsing door de rechter in bestuursrechtelijke zaken. In een aantal zaken die niet gingen over uitzetting van asielzoekers, heeft het Mensenrechtencomité in het kader van artikel 14 IVBPR geoordeeld dat de nationale rechter de beginselen van gelijke wapens voor partijen en tegensprakelijkheid had geschonden. In die zaken liet het Mensenrechtencomité haar terughoudendheid ten aanzien van het beoordelen van nationale procedures varen en oordeelde het dat de nationale gerechtelijke procedure niet eerlijk was geweest. Uit deze zaken blijkt duidelijk dat het Mensenrechtencomité het beginsel van gelijke wapens voor partijen en het beginsel van tegensprakelijkheid ziet als de ware essentie van een eerlijke procedure. De principes die het Mensenrechtencomité heeft ontwikkeld in het kader van artikel 14 IVPRB lijken sterk op de besproken beginselen die zijn ontwikkeld in het kader van artikel 2, paragraaf 3, artikel 7 en artikel 13 IVBPR.

Het Anti Folterverdrag (AFV)

De artikelen 3 en 22 lid 5, tweede deel AFV vereisen de mogelijkheid tot een doeltreffende, onafhankelijke en onpartijdige beoordeling van de uitzettingsbeslissing, voorafgaand aan de daadwerkelijke uitzetting. Het Comité tegen Foltering is, vergelijkbaar met het Mensenrechtencomité, doorgaans terughoudend geweest met het onderwerpen van nationale (gerechtelijke) procedures aan grondig onderzoek naar de naleving van de procedurele vereisten van het AFV. In meer recente jurisprudentie heeft het Comité tegen Foltering echter duidelijk gemaakt dat het voor een doeltreffende, onafhankelijke en onpartijdige nationale procedure zoals vereist door artikel 3 AFV noodzakelijk is dat gerechtelijke procedures de mogelijkheid bieden tot onderzoek naar de essentie van de zaak en de garantie bieden van gelijkheid van wapens voor partijen en een proces op tegenspraak. In de zaak *Sogi t. Canada* (2007) oordeelde het Comité tegen Foltering dat alle documenten in het dossier aan verzoeker ter beschikking gesteld hadden moeten worden, ook de documenten die ten grondslag lagen aan de aantijging dat Sogi een gevaar vormde voor de nationale veiligheid van Canada. Anders gezegd zag het Comité tegen Foltering tegenspraak en gelijkheid van partijen in *Sogi* als absolute rechten en accepteerde het niet dat nationale veiligheidsbelangen het achterhouden van bepaald bewijsmateriaal rechtvaardigden.

In zaken waarin het gaat om aantijgingen of vermoedens van interne foltering (foltering in het verleden in het land van de klager zelf) verplicht het vereiste van onpartijdigheid uit de artikelen 12 en 13 AFV de nationale rechter tot grondige waarheidsvinding, zo nodig door middel van toepassing van onderzoeksbevoegdheden. Voor de duiding van de term onpartijdigheid in de zin van artikel 3 AFV kan aansluiting worden gezocht bij deze interpretatie van de term onpartijdigheid. Dat zou betekenen dat nationale asielrechters onpartijdig moeten optreden en daartoe op onafhankelijke en diepgaande wijze aan waarheidsvinding moeten doen met behulp van hun onderzoeksbevoegdheden.

Artikel 15 AFV verbiedt het gebruik van verklaringen ingegeven door foltering als bewijsmateriaal in elke procedure, behalve in strafzaken tegen personen die beschuldigd worden van foltering, bewijs voor deze beschuldiging. Het Comité tegen Foltering heeft zich nog niet uitgesproken over de betekenis van artikel 15 in asielzaken.

Het Europees Verdrag voor de Rechten van de Mens en de Fundamentele Vrijheden (EVRM)

In zaken over de uitzetting van asielzoekers voldoet een nationale beroepsprocedure bij de rechter aan de vereisten van de artikelen 3, 13 en 35, paragraaf 1, als in deze procedure materiële en procedurele punten aan de orde kunnen komen en als de rechter in staat is om de weigering van het bestuursorgaan om bescherming te verlenen te vernietigen.

De procedurele tak van artikel 3, bezien in samenhang met artikel 13 en artikel 35, eerste lid EVRM vereisen dat de nationale autoriteiten, waaronder nationale rechtbanken, een adequate beoordeling verrichten van het verzoek om bescherming. Bij de beoordeling van de vraag of de nationale procedure(s) inderdaad adequaat was (waren), neemt het EHRM in aanmerking of de asielzoeker is gehoord (meermaals), of hij of zij is bijgestaan door professionele rechtshulp, of de nationale autoriteiten daadwerkelijk in staat zijn geweest om de asielzoeker te zien, horen en bevragen, en om de door hem of haar verstrekte informatie en bewijs te beoordelen alvorens een beslissing te nemen. Het EHRM neemt hierbij ook in aanmerking of de nationale autoriteiten in voldoende mate gebruik hebben gemaakt van zowel nationale landeninformatie als landeninformatie uit andere betrouwbare en objectieve bronnen.

De zaken *R.C. tegen Zweden* (2010) en *Singh en anderen tegen België* (2012) hebben duidelijk laten zien dat de nationale authoriteiten, inclusief de nationale rechter, zorgvuldig en serieus moeten kijken naar bewijs dat is ingediend door de asielzoeker. Wanneer dat bewijs vragen onbeantwoord laat, dan moeten de nationale autoriteiten, waaronder de rechtbanken, proberen om antwoorden te vinden door onderzoeksbevoegdheden in te zetten. Dit dient vooral te gebeuren wanneer nader onderzoek op eenvoudige wijze kan worden verricht, zoals het geval was in de zaak *Singh en anderen tegen België*. In die zaak hadden de nationale autoriteiten eenvoudig bij de UNHCR navraag kunnen doen naar de betekenis van de door de verzoekers ingebrachte kopieën van documenten van de UNHCR waarbij verzoekers waren erkend als vluchteling. De nationale autoriteiten lieten dit echter na. Om te voldoen aan het criterium van een onafhankelijk en grondig onderzoek moet er dus daadwerkelijk diepgaand onderzoek worden verricht door de nationale autoriteiten, inclusief de nationale rechtbanken.

Bestendige lijnen in nationale jurisprudentie mogen niet doorkruisen dat een individuele, op de zaak toegesneden, feitelijke beoordeling van de essentie van de zaak plaatsvindt. Uit *Bahaddar tegen Nederland* (1998) en *Jabari tegenTurkije* (2000) volgt bovendien dat in de nationale regelgeving neergelegde termijnen en andere procedurele regels normaal gesproken moeten worden nageleefd, maar dat deze niet zo kort mogen zijn en niet zo star mogen worden toegepast dat een asielzoeker in feite geen reële mogelijkheid meer heeft om zijn verzoek te onderbouwen.

Tot slot betekent een onafhankelijk en grondig onderzoek ook dat de nationale autoriteiten de juiste bewijsstandaarden hanteren in het onderzoek naar het gevreesde risico in de zin van artikel 3 EVRM. Zo volgt bijvoorbeeld uit het arrest *M.S.S. tegen België en Griekenland* (2011) dat het de nationale rechtbank niet is toegestaan om, bijvoorbeeld, een strengere bewijsstandaard te hanteren dan de standaard die het EHRM zelf toepast. Om te kunnen voldoen aan het vereiste van onafhankelijk en grondig onderzoek is het daarom voor nationale rechtbanken van groot belang om te weten hoe de bewijsstandaarden die het EHRM hanteert er exact uitzien. In deel 2 van hoofdstuk 5 zijn die bewijsstandaarden nader onderzocht.

Uit vaste jurisprudentie van het EHRM volgt dat artikel 6 lid 1 EVRM niet van toepassing is in uitzettingszaken. Toch is artikel 6 EVRM om twee redenen wel degelijk relevant voor nationale gerechtelijke asielprocedures. Ten eerste heeft het EHRM sinds de uitspraak in *Kudla t. Polen* (2000) geoordeeld dat de vereisten van artikel 13 EVRM gezien moeten worden als een versterking van de vereisten van artikel 6 lid 1 EVRM, zodat de vereisten ontwikkeld in het kader van artikel 6 lid 1 EVRM in feite ook deel uitmaken van artikel 13 EVRM. Ten tweede bepaalt de jurisprudentie van het EHRM in het kader van artikel 6 lid 1 in grote mate de inhoud van artikel 47 lid 2 EU Handvest, dat het recht op een eerlijk proces vastlegt. Artikel 47 lid 2 EU Handvest is in het algemeen van toepassing in asielzaken.

Artikel 6 lid 1 EVRM vereist dat beslissingen van bestuursorganen in beginsel aangevochten kunnen worden bij een rechtbank met volledige bevoegdheid op het gebied van de feiten en het recht. Volledige bevoegdheid omvat ook de bevoegdheid om onafhankelijk en zelfstandig de betwiste feiten en de geloofwaardigheid van een verzoeker vast te stellen, en de bevoegdheid om informatie gebruikt door de bestuurlijke autoriteiten of door de andere partij kritisch te bejegenen. Artikel 6 lid 1 EVRM verplicht nationale rechters er ook toe om een betekenisvol onderzoek te verrichten naar de stellingen, argumenten en bewijsstukken aangevoerd door partijen. Als blijkt dat dit niet gebeurd is, ofwel vanwege gebrekkig onderzoek naar door partijen aangevoerd bewijs ofwel doordat geen gebruik is gemaakt van onderzoeksbevoegdheden teneinde betwiste feiten op onafhankelijke wijze vast te stellen, dan kan dit bij het EHRM leiden tot de conclusie dat de gerechtelijke procedure in strijd met artikel 6 lid 1 EVRM niet eerlijk was. Gedeeltelijke in plaats van volledige bevoegdheid van de nationale rechter is in uitzonderingsgevallen toegestaan onder artikel 6 lid 1 EVRM. Allereerst is de specifieke inhoud van de zaak hierbij van belang. In een aantal zaken waarbij de inhoud raakte aan de klassieke uitoefening van bestuurlijke discretionaire bevoegdheden, zoals ruimtelijke ordening, werd een meer beperkte bevoegdheid van de nationale rechter geaccepteerd door het EHRM. Gedacht kan ook worden aan zaken waarin complexe technische analyses zijn uitgevoerd of waarin belangrijke diplomatieke vraagstukken centraal staan. In die zaken waarin het EHRM gedeeltelijke (beperkte) bevoegdheid van de nationale rechter accepteerde, werd daarnaast voldaan aan een aantal andere criteria: het ging in de nationale gerechtelijke procedure hoofdzakelijk om vragen van recht en niet zozeer om feitelijke zaken, de administratiefrechtelijke procedure die voorafging aan de procedure bij de nationale rechter was omgeven met veel artikel 6-waarborgen, en het onderzoek bij de nationale rechter was ondanks de beperkingen wel doeltreffend, in die zin dat het daadwerkelijk kritisch onderzoek omvatte naar de procedurele kwesties die verzoeker naar voren bracht.

Ik heb om de volgende redenen beargumenteerd dat het logisch zou zijn om artikel 3-zaken betreffende de uitzetting van asielzoekers in de categorie zaken te plaatsen die volledig rechterlijk onderzoek op nationaal niveau behoeven. Allereerst staat in asielzaken, in tegenstelling tot bijvoorbeeld zaken over ruimtelijke ordening, het le-

ven en de veiligheid van het individu op het spel. Artikel 3 is een fundamenteel, absoluut recht waarvan niet kan worden afgeweken in bijzondere situaties zoals oorlog.
Ten tweede zullen de meeste asielzaken niet van complexe technische aard zijn, en
slechts in enkele gevallen zullen belangrijke diplomatieke zaken op het spel staan. Ten
derde versterken de vereisten van artikel 13 EVRM die van artikel 6 EVRM. Het vereiste uit artikel 13 EVRM dat in uitzettingszaken een individueel, zaakspecifiek en fei-
telijk onderzoek naar de inhoud moet worden verricht, kan dus als een versterking
worden gezien van het uit artikel 6 EVRM volgende vereiste dat de nationale rechter
volledig bevoegd is te oordelen over feiten en recht.

Artikel 6 lid 1 EVRM vergt verder dat partijen gelijk behandeld worden ten aanzien van de toelating, uitsluiting en beoordeling van bewijs. De vereisten van een procedure op tegenspraak en gelijkheid van wapens van partijen zijn echter niet absoluut.
Het niet openbaren van bewijsmateriaal kan gerechtvaardigd zijn waar dit strikt noodzakelijk is voor het beschermen van de fundamentele rechten van een ander of een
belangrijk algemeen belang zoals nationale veiligheid. Als een nationale rechter toestaat dat bepaald bewijs niet aan een partij wordt geopenbaard, moet deze wel speciale handelingen verrichten ter compensatie. Dit betekent dat de nationale rechter op
zijn minst zelf het geheim gehouden bewijs bestudeert en dat, waar mogelijk, aanvullende compenserende maatregelen worden getroffen.

Het asielrecht van de Europese Unie (EU)

Sinds het Verdrag van Lissabon (1 december 2009) heeft de EU een eigen, bindend
mensenrechtendocument met de status van primair EU recht in de vorm van het
Handvest van de Grondrechten van de Europese Unie. Nu de EU bevoegd is bindende regelgeving over asiel uit te vaardigen en deze regelgeving ook daadwerkelijk
tot stand is gekomen, zullen asielzaken vrijwel altijd binnen de reikwijdte van het EU
recht vallen. Het gevolg hiervan is dat het Handvest normaliter van toepassing zal
zijn. Op grond van artikel 18 Handvest moeten nationale asielrechters de procedurele
voorschriften van het Vluchtelingenverdrag en de in hoofdstuk 2 besproken standpunten van de verdragstoezichthouder, de UNHCR, over bewijs en toetsing door de
nationale rechter in acht nemen. Het is niet langer mogelijk de standpunten van de
UNHCR af te doen als niet bindend, nu dit een schending oplevert van artikel 18
Handvest, dat primair bindend EU recht is.

De standaarden over procedures, bewijs en rechterlijk onderzoek die voortvloei-
en uit het EVRM – besproken in hoofdstuk 5 – komen via de artikelen 19, 47 en 52
lid 3 EU Handvest het EU recht binnen en worden daarvan onderdeel. Deze integra-
tie in het EU recht brengt met zich dat normen van intergouvernementeel internationaal recht transformeren tot supranationaal EU recht dat voorrang heeft op al het nationale recht van EU lidstaten. Op basis van de preambule van het Handvest, artikel
78 VWEU en artikel 53 Handvest vormen de standaarden over procedures, bewijs en
rechterlijk onderzoek die voortvloeien uit het IVBPR en het AFV – besproken in de
hoofdstukken 3 en 4 – belangrijke aanvullende bronnen bij de interpretatie van artikel
19 lid 2 en artikel 47 Handvest.

Artikel 47 Handvest is – naast evenkniebepaling van de artikelen 6 en 13 EVRM
– ook de codificatie van het binnen het EU recht ontwikkelde beginsel van effectieve

rechtsbescherming. In het kader van het beginsel van effectieve rechtsbescherming zijn vijf verschillende standaarden ontwikkeld voor de intensiteit van rechterlijk onderzoek, die corresponderen met vijf verschillende categorieën van zaken. Deze standaarden variëren van marginaal rechterlijk toezicht zonder feitenonderzoek (procedures over personeelszaken) tot een grondig, integraal en *ex nunc* rechterlijk onderzoek naar feiten, recht en proportionaliteit (zaken betreffende inperkingen van fundamentele vrijheden van EU burgers, hun familieleden-derdelanders en Turkse werknemers en hun familie die rechten hebben onder Besluit 1/80 of rechten voortvloeiend uit de Associatieovereenkomst zelf). Vooralsnog weten we niet welke standaard het HvJEU zal hanteren ten aanzien van asielzaken. Mijn inschatting is dat het HvJEU de meest indringende standaard voor rechterlijk onderzoek van toepassing zal achten op asielzaken. Ten eerste vanwege de sterke gelijkenis tussen asielzaken en zaken omtrent inperkingen van fundamentele vrijheden van EU burgers. Beide soorten zaken gaan over fundamentele rechten of vrijheden. Ten tweede lijkt de meest indringende standaard op het soort rechterlijk onderzoek dat door het EHRM is uitgevoerd in een aanzienlijk aantal zaken over uitzetting van asielzoekers in het kader van artikel 3 EVRM. De meest indringende standaard lijkt daarnaast ook op het vereiste van volledige bevoegdheid ten aanzien van feiten en recht, en het vereiste van onafhankelijk en grondig rechterlijk onderzoek, die volgen uit de artikelen 6 en 13 EVRM. In het recente arrest in de zaak *Samba Diouf* (2011) oordeelde het HvJEU dat de finale beslissing op een asielverzoek onderworpen moet kunnen worden aan een grondige inhoudelijke beoordeling door de nationale rechter. Dit arrest laat dus zien dat de uitgesproken verwachting niet enkel denkbeeldig is.

De bepalingen in secundair EU recht over rechtsmiddelen moeten geïnterpreteerd worden in samenhang met de hogere regeling van artikel 47 Handvest en het daarin vervatte hogere algemene beginsel van effectieve rechtsbescherming. Uit de wetsgeschiedenis van de bepalingen in secundair EU recht over rechtsmiddelen volgt dat er verschillende pogingen zijn gedaan om nationale rechters weg te houden van negatieve beslissingen dan wel de intensiteit van de rechterlijke toetsing te verminderen. Door de noodzaak van interpretatie conform hogere regelgeving moet echter vastgesteld worden dat die pogingen tevergeefs zijn ondernomen.

Secundair EU asielrecht geeft geen uitputtende regeling voor alle mogelijke bewijsvraagstukken. Het bevat echter wel specifieke bepalingen over een aantal van de elf aspecten van bewijs en rechterlijk onderzoek, zoals de bewijsstandaard en de bewijslast. In hoofdstuk 6 werden deze bepalingen geïnterpreteerd met behulp van jurisprudentie van het HvJEU in zowel asielzaken als andere zaken, en met behulp van de standaarden ontwikkeld door de UNHCR, het Mensenrechtencomité, het Comité tegen Foltering en het EHRM, aangezien artikel 78 VWEU vereist dat secundair EU recht in overeenstemming is met het Vluchtelingenverdrag alsmede de andere relevante verdragen (zijnde het IVBPR, het AFV en het EVRM).

In hoofdstuk 6 werd geconcludeerd dat het EU asielrecht op drie manieren toegevoegde waarde heeft. Ten eerste zorgt het EU asielrecht voor een transformatie van bestaande standaarden over bewijs en rechterlijk onderzoek die voortvloeien uit internationaal asielrecht. Deze bestaande standaarden transformeren van niet bindende beginselen tot belangrijkere regels die gevolgd moeten worden (dit geldt voor de normen ontwikkeld door de UNHCR via artikel 18 Handvest), van intergouvernementeel internationaal recht tot supranationaal primair EU recht (de standaarden ontwikkeld door het EHRM via de artikelen 19 en 47 Handvest) en van intergouvernementeel internationaal recht tot belangrijke inspiratiebronnen voor de uitlegging van bindend EU recht (de standaarden ontwikkeld door het Mensenrechtencomité en het Comité tegen Foltering via artikelen 19 en 47 Handvest).

Ten tweede zijn de standaarden ontwikkeld door het EHRM in het kader van artikel 6 EVRM nu van toepassing in asielzaken, aangezien zij deel uitmaken van artikel 47 Handvest.

Ten derde heeft het systeem van rechterlijk toezicht op de naleving van EU asielrecht een sterke aanvullende werking ten opzichte van de individuele klachtenprocedures van het IVBPR, het AFV en het EVRM. De preliminaire procedure voor het HvJEU biedt nationale rechters de mogelijkheid vragen te stellen aan het HvJEU gedurende de nationale gerechtelijke procedure. Op deze wijze kunnen mensenrechtenschendingen in een veel vroeger stadium voorkomen worden.

Standpunten van de twee internationale hoven en de verdragstoezichthouders over de elf aspecten van bewijs en rechterlijk onderzoek

Bewijsstandaard

De bewijsstandaard onder het EU asielrecht, het EVRM, het Vluchtelingenverdrag en het AFV is dezelfde: het vereiste risico is een daadwerkelijk, persoonlijk en voorzienbaar risico dat verder gaat dan alleen de mogelijkheid tot onmenselijke behandeling. Het risico hoeft echter niet zeker of onvermijdelijk, hoogst waarschijnlijk of zonder gerede twijfel te zijn. De jurisprudentie van het Mensenrechtencomité is strikter aangezien een daadwerkelijk risico daar betekent dat schending van artikel 7 een onvermijdelijk en voorzienbaar gevolg is van de uitzetting.

Bewijslast en de verplichting tot samenwerking

Zowel de in dit boek besproken verdragen als het EU asielrecht voorzien in een gedeelde bewijslast. Op de asielzoeker rust allereerst de last om zijn relaas naar voren te brengen en om met enig onderbouwend bewijs te komen. Vervolgens rust op de nationale autoriteiten, inclusief de nationale rechter, een onderzoeksplicht. Het HvJEU en het EHRM hebben, net als op minder expliciete wijze het Comité tegen Foltering, hierbij de notie van de glijdende schaal ontwikkeld: hoe slechter de algemene mensenrechtensituatie in een land, des te minder individuele omstandigheden en stavend bewijsmateriaal nodig zal zijn en hoe eerder de bewijslast verschuift van de aanvrager naar de nationale autoriteiten. De EU Kwalificatierichtlijn, het EVRM, het Vluchtelingenverdrag en het AFV voorzien daarnaast ook in een lichtere bewijslast in zaken waar al eerder vervolging of onmenselijke behandeling plaatsvond.

De notie van de gedeelde bewijslast heeft in het EU asielrecht een bijzondere vorm gekregen. Dit is het vereiste van samenwerking dat is neergelegd in artikel 4 van de EU Kwalificatierichtlijn. In het arrest *M.M. tegen de Minister voor Justitie, gelijkheid en rechtshervorming van Ierland* (2012) heeft het HvJEU geoordeeld dat dit vereiste van samenwerking het volgende betekent. Indien, om welke reden dan ook, de door de aanvrager verstrekte elementen niet volledig zijn, of niet up-to-date of relevant, dan dienen de nationale autoriteiten actief samen te werken met de aanvrager in die betreffende fase van de procedure, opdat alle elementen die noodzakelijk zijn om de aanvraag te onderbouwen kunnen worden vergaard. De nationale autoriteiten kunnen soms in een betere positie zijn dan de aanvrager om toegang te krijgen tot bepaalde soorten documenten. Het HvJEU heeft tot op heden niet verder uitgelegd wat wordt bedoeld met 'actieve samenwerking met de aanvrager opdat alle elementen die benodigd zijn om de aanvraag te onderbouwen kunnen worden vergaard'. Nationale rechtbanken kunnen hierbij wellicht denken aan situaties waarin het nodig is om de aanvrager een extra termijn te gunnen voor het inbrengen van nieuwe relevante documenten, aan situaties waarin de aanvrager voorstelt dat de rechtbank getuigen hoort en aan situaties waarin de aanvrager documenten heeft overgelegd en de rechtbank een onderzoek naar de authenticiteit daarvan gelast of verweerder opdraagt om een dergelijk onderzoek uit te voeren. Net zoals het EHRM deed in het arrest *Iskandarov tegen Rusland* (2010), heeft het HvJEU in *M.M.* uitgelegd dat zich specifieke omstandigheden kunnen voordoen waarin de administratieve autoriteiten of de rechtbank in een betere positie is dan de aanvrager om toegang te krijgen tot bepaalde documenten. Dit betekent dat wanneer het voor verweerder of voor de rechtbank veel eenvoudiger is dan voor de aanvrager om aan bepaalde relevante documenten te komen, de last om die documenten te verkrijgen en in te brengen ook op die autoriteit rust.

Relevante feiten en omstandigheden

Wat dit punt betreft komen de onderzochte verdragen en het EU asielrecht sterk overeen. Relevant zijn zowel persoonlijke omstandigheden zoals bijvoorbeeld achtergrond, geslacht, overtuigingen en activiteiten als omstandigheden die zien op de algemene (mensenrechten-)situatie in het land van herkomst, zoals detentieomstandigheden, de mate van geweld in het land en de controle van de overheid daarover en veranderingen in regering of beleid. Uit de onderzochte verdragen en het EU asielrecht volgt dat de persoonlijke feiten en de situatie in het land van herkomst zoveel mogelijk holistisch moeten worden benaderd: ze moeten worden bezien in elkaars licht, als een geheel.

Vereiste mate van individueel risico

Onder het EVRM en het EU asielrecht kan onderscheid worden gemaakt naar drie soorten situaties en daarmee zaken: 1) situaties van extreem algemeen geweld, waarin een artikel 3-risico wordt aangenomen voor iedereen die terugkeert naar het betreffende land; 2) situaties van groepsgeweld en 3) situaties waarin het gaat om een individueel risico. In zaken uit de derde categorie is het vaststellen van een individueel risico vereist. Dit betekent dat het betreffende individu aannemelijk dient te maken dat alleen hij of zij risico loopt. Uit de jurisprudentie van zowel het Mensenrechtencomité (*Kaba v. Canada*, 2010 en *Joachimpillai v. Canada*, 2011) alsook het Comité tegen Foltering (*Njamba tegen Zweden*, 2010, en *Bakatu-Bia tegen Zweden*, 2011) volgt dat deze beide verdragstoezichthouders in belangrijke mate de door het EHRM ontwikkelde doctrine over groepsgeweld hebben overgenomen.

Bij het onderbrengen van zaken in één van de drie genoemde categorieën en het in overeenstemming daarmee vaststellen van de vereiste hoeveelheid persoonlijke feiten en bewijs moeten nationale rechters ook in aanmerking nemen dat het Vluchtelingenverdrag geen individualisering vereist. Het UNHCR-handboek onderscheidt in hoofdzaak twee manieren om de vluchtelingenstatus vast te stellen: de normale situatie waarin vluchtelingenstatus wordt vastgesteld op individuele gronden, en de uitzonderlijke situatie waarin de vluchtelingenstatus wordt vastgesteld voor een groep, waarbij elk lid van die groep *prima facie* als vluchteling wordt gezien. Geen van deze situaties stelt een strikte individualiseringseis aangezien het risico niet *per se* gebaseerd hoeft te zijn op persoonlijke ervaringen van de verzoeker.

Beoordeling van de geloofwaardigheid: intensiteit van (rechterlijk) onderzoek uitgevoerd door het EHRM en de andere verdragstoezichthouders, standpunten van het HvJEU en de UNHCR

Het Mensenrechtencomité en het Comité tegen Foltering benadrukken vaak hun subsidiaire rol als het gaat om het vaststellen van de feiten, daarbij inbegrepen de beoordeling van de geloofwaardigheid van de asielzoeker. Dit is een logisch gevolg van het feit dat deze verdragstoezichthouders de vaststelling van de feiten primair als een verantwoordelijkheid zien van de autoriteiten van de staat en zij zelf – met name het Mensenrechtencomité – slechts beperkte onderzoeksbevoegdheden hebben ten aanzien van de feiten. Het lijkt erop dat twee situaties in het bijzonder zorgen voor een meer onafhankelijke vaststelling van de feiten door het Comité tegen Foltering. Dit is allereerst de situatie waarin in de nationale (gerechtelijke) procedure het absolute karakter van het refoulementverbod is miskend en er een weging heeft plaatsgevonden van het risico enerzijds en nationale veiligheids- of openbare orde-aspecten anderzijds. Daarnaast de situatie waarin de autoriteiten van de staat bepaalde belangrijke feiten of bewijsstukken niet meegenomen hebben in de beoordeling. In vergelijking met beide Comités is het EHRM actiever waar het gaat om het vaststellen van de feiten. In een aanzienlijk aantal zaken over de uitzetting van asielzoekers was het EHRM zeer actief in het verzamelen en verifiëren van feiten en omstandigheden en maakte het EHRM ook een eigen zelfstandige beoordeling van de geloofwaardigheid van de verklaringen van de asielzoeker. Het EHRM stelt onafhankelijk en zelfstandig de feiten, geloofwaardigheid inbegrepen, vast in zaken waarin de procedure op nationaal niveau niet adequaat is geweest, in zaken waarin nieuwe feiten, omstandigheden of ontwikkelingen aan het licht zijn gekomen, inclusief bewijs daarvan, en in zaken waarin in de nationale procedure het absolute karakter van het refoulementverbod is miskend en er een weging heeft plaatsgevonden van het risico enerzijds en nationale veiligheids- of openbare ordeaspecten anderzijds, dan wel dat anderszins een of meerdere bewijsstandaarden onjuist zijn toegepast (bijvoorbeeld de bewijsstandaard of de vereiste mate van individualisering).

In tegenstelling tot de Comités en het EHRM ontvangen het HvJEU en de UNHCR geen individuele klachten. Het HvJEU en de UNHCR hebben echter wel duidelijke standpunten ingenomen betreffende de intensiteit van het rechterlijk onderzoek dat uitgevoerd moet worden door de nationale asielrechter. Het HvJEU oordeelde in *Sambia Diouf* (2011) dat een grondige beoordeling van de inhoud van het verzoek vereist is. De UNHCR is de mening toegedaan dat de beoordeling door de nationale asielrechter zowel kwesties van feiten als kwesties van recht dient te omvatten en dat de nationale rechter onafhankelijk de geloofwaardigheid van de verklaringen van de asielzoeker moet kunnen vaststellen.

Beoordeling van de geloofwaardigheid: hoe beoordelen het EHRM en de andere internationale verdragstoezichthouders de geloofwaardigheid?

Het EHRM, de UNHCR en het Comité tegen Foltering (en in mindere mate het Mensenrechtencomité) hebben duidelijke criteria ontwikkeld voor het vaststellen van de geloofwaardigheid. Deze internationale toezichthouders eisen 'algemene geloofwaardigheid' ('algemene waarheidsgetrouwheid'), geen complete nauwkeurigheid en consistentie ten aanzien van ieder detail van het gestelde. Dit betekent dat het basisverhaal – de kern van de vluchtredenen – geloofwaardig dient te zijn. Het EHRM heeft duidelijk gemaakt dat twijfels over marginale onderdelen van het verhaal, zoals verklaringen over de reis naar het land waar asiel is aangevraagd of verklaringen over ontsnappingen uit de gevangenis of aan bewakers, niet direct afdoen aan de algemene geloofwaardigheid. Het EHRM en het Comité tegen Foltering hebben verder duidelijk gemaakt dat het basisverhaal aan een aantal vereisten moet voldoen om geloofwaardig te zijn:
- Het moet voldoende gedetailleerd zijn;
- Het moet innerlijk consistent zijn tijdens de gehele procedure; talrijke relevante inconsistenties en vele wijzigingen in verklaringen kunnen die verklaringen ongeloofwaardig maken;
- Het moet aansluiten bij informatie over het land van herkomst;
- Het moet tijdig naar voren worden gebracht: laat met nieuwe verklaringen komen kan van negatieve invloed zijn op de algemene geloofwaardigheid, vooral wanneer hiervoor geen goede reden wordt gegeven;
- De kern van het vluchtverhaal moet – zoveel mogelijk – gestaafd worden met bewijs.

In vergelijking met de andere toezichthouders neemt de UNHCR een flexibeler standpunt in waar het gaat om onderbouwend bewijs als eis voor geloofwaardigheid. De UNHCR stelt zich op het standpunt dat de afwezigheid van stavend bewijsmateriaal niet in de weg mag staan aan toewijzing van het verzoek als de verklaringen overeenkomen met bekende feiten en de aanvrager algemeen geloofwaardig is. De UNHCR heeft ook duidelijk gemaakt dat er geen rechtvaardiging te bedenken valt voor het hanteren van een strengere geloofwaardigheidsmaatstaf die uitstijgt boven de standaard van de 'algemene geloofwaardigheid' in zaken waarin stavend bewijs geheel ontbreekt.

Toelating van bewijs: middelen en bronnen

De onderzochte verdragen en het EU asielrecht voorzien in een flexibel regime waar het gaat om de toelating van bewijs. Er zijn in feite geen procedurele drempels voor de toelating van bewijs. Wat betreft de weging van bewijs zijn er evenmin vooraf vastgestelde formules. In de hoofdstukken 2 tot en met 5 zijn verschillende voorbeelden van bewijsmateriaal gegeven.

Minimale hoeveelheid en kwaliteit van bewijs

Het Mensenrechtencomité, het Comité tegen Foltering en het EHRM vereisen een aanzienlijke hoeveelheid persoonlijk bewijs ter onderbouwing van de kern van het vluchtverhaal.

Hiertegenover staat de UNHCR, die vaak heeft benadrukt dat het vereiste van bewijs niet te strikt moet worden toegepast, gezien de bijzondere en lastige bewijspositie van de asielzoeker. De UNHCR heeft ook het standpunt ingenomen dat een algeheel gebrek aan stavend bewijs nog niet meteen betekent dat het verzoek om bescherming kansloos is. Het standpunt van de UNHCR heeft zijn weerslag gevonden in artikel 4 lid 5 van de EU Kwalificatierichtlijn. Deze bepaling maakt duidelijk dat onder bepaalde omstandigheden, onder meer bij een reële poging van de asielzoeker om zijn verzoek om bescherming te staven, niet alle aspecten van het verhaal onderbouwd hoeven te worden met bewijsmateriaal anders dan de eigen verklaringen.

Waardering en weging van bewijs

Het Vluchtelingenverdrag en het EU asielrecht reguleren dit aspect niet en de jurisprudentie van het Mensenrechtencomité en het Comité tegen Foltering is niet erg expliciet en eenduidig over de waardering van bewijs (met als uitzondering het Comité tegen Foltering over de waardering van medisch-juridische rapporten). De jurisprudentie van het EHRM is veel explicieter en duidelijker en biedt nationale asielrechters concrete richtlijnen voor de waardering en weging van bewijs. De authenticiteit van de overgelegde documenten, de precisie, de begrijpelijkheid en de consistentie van de informatie in het bewijsmateriaal en de onafhankelijkheid, betrouwbaarheid, objectiviteit en het gezag van de bron of de auteur van het bewijs bepalen hoeveel bewijskracht of gewicht er wordt toegekend.

In de hoofdstukken 3, 4 en 5 werd een aantal categorieën bewijsmateriaal in meer detail besproken en werd duidelijk gemaakt dat specifieke en begrijpelijke getuigenverklaringen van familieleden een belangrijke rol spelen in de jurisprudentie van het EHRM en de beide Comités. Het EHRM heeft duidelijk gemaakt dat verklaringen van familieleden in beginsel gesteund moeten worden door ander, meer objectief bewijsmateriaal.

Medisch-juridische rapporten vormen een andere belangrijke categorie bewijsmateriaal, met name in de jurisprudentie van het Comité tegen Foltering. Het EHRM lijkt in het algemeen niet bereid om medisch bewijs, waarin staat dat sprake is van PTSS of een andere psychische stoornis, te accepteren als een reden voor inconsistenties en het laat inbrengen van verklaringen over marteling in het verleden. Wel heeft het EHRM, evenals het Mensenrechtencomité en het Comité tegen Foltering, medische rapporten in een aanzienlijk aantal zaken geaccepteerd als bewijs van marteling in het verleden. Het Comité tegen Foltering vereist dat medisch-juridische rapporten opgesteld zijn door medisch specialisten en dat daarin geconcludeerd wordt dat een causaal verband bestaat tussen de fysieke of mentale verwondingen van het individu en de gestelde marteling. In veel – vooral wat oudere – zaken heeft het Comité tegen Foltering medisch-juridische rapporten geaccepteerd als onderbouwing voor marteling in het verleden en daarnaast ook als verklaring voor inconsistenties, hiaten, vaagheden en ongerijmde wendingen in het vluchtverhaal, alsmede voor het laat inbrengen van cruciale verklaringen en bewijsstukken. Het lijkt erop dat in de meer recente jurisprudentie van het Comité tegen Foltering medisch bewijs is gedegradeerd van beslissend naar ondersteunend. Niettemin blijft medisch bewijs belangrijk en het het Comité tegen Foltering heeft in dit verband haar onvrede geuit over het feit dat medische rapporten in Nederlandse nationale gerechtelijke procedures in beginsel niet meegenomen worden als bewijs.

In de jurisprudentie van het Mensenrechtencomité en het Comité tegen Foltering wordt in het algemeen veel bewijskracht toegekend aan rapporten die het resultaat bevatten van onderzoek uitgevoerd door ambassades of missies in herkomstlanden.

Rapporten over de situatie in het land van herkomst spelen logischerwijs een belangrijke rol in de jurisprudentie van alle internationale toezichthouders. Het EHRM heeft een aantal concrete richtlijnen ontwikkeld voor het evalueren van landenrapportages. Rapporten van organisaties, organen en agentschappen die onderdeel uitmaken van de VN, almede rapporten van staten, staan hoog aangeschreven. De reden hiervoor is dat VN-organen, organisaties en agentschappen vaak directe toegang hebben tot de autoriteiten van het land van herkomst, alsmede mogelijkheden om ter plaatse inspecties en analyses uit te voeren. Staten hebben de mogelijkheid om informatie te verzamelen via diplomatieke posten. De precieze bewijskracht die wordt toegekend aan informatie over het land van herkomst wordt niet alleen bepaald door de bron, maar uiteraard ook door de specifieke inhoud ervan.

Mogelijkheden voor het presenteren van bewijs

Alle internationale toezichthouders zien een proces op tegenspraak en gelijke wapens voor partijen zowel op internationaal niveau als op nationaal niveau als cruciale waarborg voor een eerlijk proces. De houding van het Mensenrechtencomité en het Comité tegen Foltering lijkt op dit punt strikter te zijn dan die van de andere internationale toezichthouders, aangezien de beide Comités hebben geëist dat waar het gaat om de uitzetting van asielzoekers beide partijen gelijke toegang moeten hebben tot alle documenten uit het dossier, inclusief documenten die een aantijging onderbouwen dat het betreffende individu een gevaar vormt voor de nationale veiligheid. Het verbod van het Mensenrechtencomité en het Comité tegen Foltering op het gebruik van geheim bewijsmateriaal in nationale gerechtelijke uitzettingsprocedures is nog niet herhaald in andere zaken, dus we kunnen nog niet spreken van vaste jurisprudentie.

Hier tegenover staat het EHRM dat in meerdere zaken geoordeeld heeft dat het gebruik van geheim bewijsmateriaal gerechtvaardigd kan zijn als dit strikt noodzakelijk is ter bescherming van de fundamentele rechten van een ander of ter bescherming van een belangrijk algemeen belang zoals de nationale veiligheid. De UNHCR neemt een vergelijkbaar standpunt in door te stellen dat het niet openbaren van bewijs toegestaan is als de openbaring van bronnen een ernstig gevaar zou opleveren voor de nationale veiligheid of de veiligheid van organisaties of personen die de informatie leveren. Het EHRM vereist dat de nationale rechter compenserende maatregelen treft als hij of zij accepteert dat bepaald bewijs niet wordt geopenbaard aan de andere partij. De principes voor het gebruik van geheim bewijs ontwikkeld door het HvJEU lijken in sterke mate op de principes ontwikkeld door het EHRM.

Toepassing van (rechterlijke) onderzoeksbevoegdheden

Het Mensenrechtencomité en het Comité tegen Foltering benadrukken vaak hun subsidiaire rol in het vaststellen van de feiten van de zaak. Beide Comités, in het bijzonder het Mensenrechtencomité, hebben en gebruiken slechts enkele onderzoeksbevoegdheden. Het EHRM, een volwaardig internationaal gerechtshof, heeft een groot aantal onderzoeksbevoegdheden tot zijn beschikking. In een aanzienlijk aantal zaken heeft het EHRM zeer actief bijgedragen aan het verzamelen en verifiëren van feiten en omstandigheden. Het EHRM kan in elke fase van de procedure elke onderzoeksmaatregel instellen die het nodig acht ter verduidelijking van de feiten. Het EHRM gaat er met name toe over uit eigen beweging materiaal te verkrijgen over de omstandigheden in het land van herkomst als de klager of een derde partij gegronde redenen aanvoert om te twijfelen aan de juistheid van de informatie waar de staat zich op beroept.

Wat betreft de vereiste intensiteit van het onderzoek door nationale rechters zijn de standpunten van alle in dit onderzoek betrokken internationale toezichthouders in grote mate gelijk aan elkaar: ze vereisen een volledig nationaal rechterlijk onderzoek naar de inhoud van het verzoek (zie bijvoorbeeld HvJEU, *Samba Diouf* 2011; Comité tegen Foltering, *Nirnal Singh t. Canada* 2011). Een dergelijk rechterlijk onderzoek betekent dat de rechter volledig bevoegd is om te beslissen over feitelijke kwesties en rechtsvragen (de Zumtobel-doctrine van het EHRM). Verwezen werd in dit verband naar de interpretatie van de term 'onpartijdigheid' door het Comité tegen Foltering onder de artikelen 12 en 13 AFV. Het vereiste van onpartijdigheid brengt met zich mee dat de nationale rechter zo nauwkeurig mogelijk probeert te reconstrueren wat er is gebeurd en hiertoe zijn of haar onderzoeksbevoegdheden inzet.

Termijnen voor het inbrengen van verklaringen en bewijs

Het HvJEU, het EHRM, de UNHCR en het Mensenrechtencomité nemen vergelijkbare posities in. De kern hiervan is dat nationale procedureregels redelijk moeten zijn, of op een redelijke en flexibele wijze toegepast moeten worden als de omstandigheden van de zaak hiertoe nopen. Uit het EU asielrecht en de jurisprudentie van het EHRM, het standpunt van de UNHCR en de jurisprudentie van het Comité tegen Foltering blijkt dat alle relevante verklaringen in beginsel zo snel mogelijk in de nationale procedure moeten worden ingebracht en dat verlate verklaringen afbreuk kunnen doen aan de geloofwaardigheid van de verklaringen van de asielzoeker. De benadering ten aanzien van ondersteunend bewijs is in het algemeen flexibeler. In de jurisprudentie van het EHRM, het Mensenrechtencomité en het Comité tegen Foltering is het moment waarop bewijs in de nationale gerechtelijke procedure werd ingebracht door partijen als op zichzelf staande factor niet van groot belang.

De UNHCR heeft benadrukt dat een zaak niet mag worden afgewezen op de enkele grond dat de relevante verklaringen of documenten niet eerder zijn ingebracht. Ook het Comité tegen Foltering vond het in een aanzienlijk aantal zaken niet problematisch dat verklaringen en bewijs pas op een laat moment in de nationale procedure werden ingebracht. In die zaken accepteerde het Comité tegen Foltering vrij gemakkelijk dat gegronde redenen waren aangevoerd voor het op een laat moment inbrengen van verklaringen en bewijs. De mildere aanpak van de UNHCR en het Comité tegen Foltering heeft zijn weerslag gevonden in artikel 8 lid 1 EU Procedurerichtlijn, dat van lidstaten vergt dat asielaanvragen niet verworpen worden of uitgesloten van onderzoek enkel vanwege het feit dat deze niet zo snel mogelijk zijn ingediend.

Moment van risicobeoordeling

De standpunten van alle in deze studie onderzochte internationale toezichthouders hieromtrent zijn grotendeels identiek. Allemaal vergen ze in beginsel een *ex nunc* beoordeling: de beoordeling van het risico vindt plaats op basis van alle beschikbare informatie op het moment dat de risicotaxatie wordt gemaakt. In zaken waarin uitzetting uit de betrokken staat al heeft plaatsgevonden, blijft het moment voor de beoordeling volgens het EHRM het moment van die uitzetting, maar het EHRM kan wel informatie in aanmerking nemen die pas na de uitzetting aan het licht is gekomen en doet dit ook geregeld, waardoor het in feite alsnog neerkomt op een *ex nunc* beoordeling. Het Mensenrechtencomité heeft vooralsnog geen richtlijnen ontwikkeld voor situaties waarin de uitzetting al heeft plaatsgevonden en de jurisprudentie van het Comité tegen Foltering is niet geheel consistent. Echter, in *T.P.S. t. Canada* (2000) nam het Comité tegen Foltering expliciet en zonder voorbehoud nieuwe feiten en omstandigheden mee in de afweging. De benadering lijkt daarmee op die van het EHRM.

Integratie van de onderzoeksresultaten: nationale rechtbanken en het onafhankelijke grondige onderzoek

Waar de hoofdstukken 2 tot en met 6 erop gericht waren te ontdekken welke verplichtingen volgen uit internationaal en EU asielrecht met betrekking tot de intensiteit van rechterlijk onderzoek en bewijs, spitste hoofdstuk 7 zich toe op de onderlinge verhouding van de verdragen en EU asielrecht. Geconcludeerd werd dat het overdragen van de bevoegdheid om bindende regels omtrent asiel op te stellen van de lidstaten aan de EU geen effect heeft gehad op de verplichtingen voortvloeiend uit het Vluchtelingenverdrag, het IVBPR, het AFV en het EVRM. Nationale asielrechters in EU lidstaten zijn in feite 'dubbel gebonden' door de verplichtingen die volgen uit de in deze studie onderzochte verdragen. Zoals hoofdstuk 6 heeft laten zien, zijn nationale rechters namelijk gebonden aan de verdragen op zich enerzijds, en aan EU recht dat dezelfde verdragsverplichtingen incorporeert anderzijds, zoals hoofdstuk 6 liet zien.

In hoofdstuk 7 is vervolgens geprobeerd om de verplichtingen en standaarden die volgen uit internationaal en EU asielrecht te integreren tot een samenhangend geheel. Het doel van deze exercitie was om tot een gebruiksklaar en coherent stelsel van standaarden voor bewijs en rechterlijk onderzoek te komen dat eenvoudig zou kunnen worden gebruikt door nationale asielrechters. Uitgangspunt bij deze integratiepoging was dat in veel asielzaken die voor de nationale rechter komen zowel vluchtelingrechtelijke bescherming (de artikelen 1 en 33 Vluchtelingenverdrag, artikel 18 EU Handvest) als subsidiaire bescherming (de artikelen 7 IVBPR, 3 AFV, 3 EVRM en artikelen 4 en 19 EU Handvest) worden ingeroepen. Daardoor zijn alle verdragen en instrumenten behandeld in dit onderzoek relevant en van toepassing op zulke zaken. De integratiepoging resulteerde in een gemene deler: geconcludeerd werd dat internationaal en EU asielrecht een 'onafhankelijk en grondig nationaal rechterlijk onderzoek' vereisen. Dit vereiste van een onafhankelijk en grondig nationaal rechterlijk onderzoek werd vervolgens verder uitgewerkt met behulp van de volgende bronnen:

- de jurisprudentie van het Mensenrechtencomité, het Comité tegen Foltering en het EHRM onder de bepalingen inzake doeltreffende rechtsmiddelen en de procedurele tak van de *refoulement*-verboden;
- de standpunten van de UNHCR over nationaal rechterlijk onderzoek en bewijs;
- de jurisprudentie van het HvJEU over effectieve rechtsbescherming;
- de beoordeling zoals uitgevoerd door het Mensenrechtencomité, het Comité tegen Foltering en het EHRM in zaken over uitzetting van asielzoekers; deze beoordeling werd in het tweede deel van de hoofdstukken 3, 4 en 5 onderzocht.

Er is een hiërarchie in deze bronnen aangebracht: geconcludeerd werd dat nationale asielrechters allereerst de jurisprudentie van het HvJEU en het EHRM dienen te raadplegen, vervolgens de standpunten van de UNHCR en tenslotte de jurisprudentie van het Mensenrechtencomité en het Comité tegen Foltering als subsidiaire interpretatiebronnen. Ook werd geconcludeerd dat kruisverwijzingen niet problematisch zijn: nationale asielrechters binnen de EU kunnen verwijzen naar de verschillende hierboven genoemde interpretatiebronnen aangezien alle lidstaten partij zijn bij het Vluchtelingenverdrag, het IVBPR, het AFV en het EVRM. Ook werd de vraag behandeld wat te doen in geval van uiteenlopende of zelfs conflicterende standaarden. Onder verwijzing naar de voorrangsregels in de verschillende verdragen en het EU recht is betoogd dat wanneer nationale asielrechters geconfronteerd worden met uiteenlopende of conflicterende standaarden, zij de vastgestelde hiërarchie moeten laten varen en moeten kiezen voor die standaard die de aanvrager de meeste bescherming biedt. Om deze aanpak te verdedigen werd ook verwezen naar artikel 52 lid 3 EU Handvest, dat toestaat dat EU recht verdergaande bescherming biedt dan die geboden door het EVRM.

Het vereiste van een onafhankelijk en grondig nationaal rechterlijk onderzoek werd uiteindelijk nader gedefinieerd aan de hand van de elf aspecten van bewijs en rechterlijk onderzoek zoals geïntroduceerd in hoofdstuk 1. Dit resulteerde in een set standaarden voor bewijs en rechterlijk onderzoek dat door nationale rechters gebruikt kan worden.

Herhaalde asielaanvragen, Dublinzaken en versnelde nationale procedures

In hoofdstuk 8 werd onderzoek gedaan naar de standpunten van de internationale hoven en toezichthouders ten aanzien van drie bijzondere categorieën van zaken en procedures: herhaalde asielaanvragen (zaken waarin een verzoeker een tweede, derde of volgende asielaanvraag ingediend heeft na een negatieve beslissing op een eerste aanvraag), Dublinzaken (zaken waarin op een asielaanvraag is beslist op grond van EU verordening 2003/343/EC) en versnelde nationale procedures (procedures waar in kortere termijnen en soms ook andere speciale regels gehanteerd worden om asielaanvragen en beroepen tegen afwijzingen sneller en efficiënter af te kunnen doen).

Ten aanzien van herhaalde asielaanvragen werd geconcludeerd dat, bezien vanuit internationaal en EU asielrecht, een novumtoets op zichzelf niet problematisch is. Een tweede conclusie ten aanzien van herhaalde asielaanvragen was dat, gezien de standpunten van de internationale toezichthouders en hoven, nationale rechtbanken bewijs niet formeel of volledig mogen uitsluiten enkel omdat het op een eerder moment in de nationale procedure had moeten worden ingebracht.

In zaken waarin asielzoekers op basis van de Dublinverordening worden overgedragen aan een andere EU lidstaat mogen de autoriteiten van de overdragende lidstaat, inclusief de nationale rechtbanken, tot op zekere hoogte uitgaan van het interstatelijk vertrouwensbeginsel en op grond daarvan aannemen dat de autoriteiten van de andere lidstaat hun internationale verplichtingen zullen naleven. Tegelijkertijd hebben zowel het EHRM als het HvJEU dit beginsel expliciet en stevig aan banden gelegd. Zodra (enige) informatie wijzend in de richting van het tegendeel beschikbaar is gekomen – omdat de verzoeker deze informatie heeft aangedragen, ofwel omdat de autoriteiten ermee bekend zijn of behoren te zijn – moeten de nationale autoriteiten van de overdragende lidstaat beoordelen of de asielprocedure van de overnemende of terugnemende lidstaat voldoende waarborgen biedt en of de leefomstandigheden aldaar (g)een schending opleveren van artikel 3 EVRM.

Wat betreft versnelde nationale procedures werd vastgesteld dat de standpunten van de internationale toezichthouders en hoven identiek zijn. Versnelde (gerechtelijke) asielprocedures zijn op zichzelf geoorloofd. Het is echter belangrijk dat nationale rechtbanken bij het behandelen van zulke zaken de mogelijkheid behouden om de inhoud van het asielverzoek grondig te beoordelen. Versnelde procedures kunnen asielzoekers de mogelijkheid ontnemen hun verzoek om bescherming te onderbouwen. Als een nationale rechtbank tot het oordeel komt dat als gevolg van de toepassing van de versnelde procedure een grondige beoordeling van de inhoud niet langer kan plaatsvinden, of dat de asielzoeker geen kans heeft gekregen zijn of haar verzoek te onderbouwen, dan dient de rechtbank de mogelijkheid te hebben om de zaak te verwijzen naar de gewone of uitgebreide(re) procedure die meer ruimte biedt voor verder rechterlijk onderzoek of voor een nader onderbouwing van het verzoek door de asielzoeker.

Epiloog

In de epiloog ben ik teruggekomen op de belangrijkste onderzoeksresultaten en lichtte ik hun relevantie toe, waarbij ik een aantal malen heb verwezen naar het contrast met de vaste nationale rechterlijke praktijk in Nederland.

Ik heb daarnaast ook mijn teleurstelling geuit over het feit dat het Mensenrechtencomité, het Comité tegen Foltering en het EHRM tot nu toe geen uitgebreide en coherente doctrinaire standpunten hebben ontwikkeld over de intensiteit van het rechterlijk onderzoek waarmee zij zelf de feiten vaststellen in zaken over de uitzetting van asielzoekers. Daar komt bij dat de conclusies in de beslissingen van het Mensenrechtencomité en het Comité tegen Foltering vaak zeer kort zijn en geen duidelijke koppeling bevatten tussen feiten en conclusies. Deze beslissingen bevatten dikwijls geen duidelijke richtlijnen voor nationale rechters ten aanzien van een aantal bewijsvraagstukken, zoals de bewijslast, het vereiste van individualisering, het waarderen van bewijs (beide Comités) en het beoordelen van de geloofwaardigheid (met name het Mensenrechtencomité). Op grond van deze bevinding heb ik een pleidooi gericht aan het Mensenrechtencomité en het Comité tegen Foltering om te komen tot uitgebreidere overwegingen over de genoemde bewijsvraagstukken en ook expliciter uit te leggen welke intensiteit van onderzoek zij zelf toepassen en op grond waarvan. Hierdoor zouden deze internationale toezichthouders betere gidsen voor nationale rechters worden. Nationale rechters zouden hierdoor beter toegerust zijn om hun verdragsverplichtingen na te leven.

Ik heb tot slot geconcludeerd dat internationaal en EU asielrecht steun bieden voor mijn persoonlijke overtuiging dat een onafhankelijk en grondig nationaal rechterlijk onderzoek, waaronder grondige rechterlijke waarheidsvinding, van groot belang is in nationale asielprocedures. Grondig rechterlijk onderzoek heeft niets te maken met het willen helpen van een van de partijen. Het heeft wel te maken met de onafhankelijkheid en onpartijdigheid van de rechterlijke macht.

Summary

RIGOROUS SCRUTINY VERSUS MARGINAL REVIEW

STANDARDS ON JUDICIAL SCRUTINY AND EVIDENCE IN INTERNATIONAL AND EUROPEAN ASYLUM LAW

Introduction

Two judgments of the European Court of Human Rights (ECtHR) formed the immediate reason for embarking upon this research project. These were *Said v. the Netherlands* (2005) and *Salah Sheekh v. the Netherlands* (2007). It appeared from these judgments that the ECtHR was dissatisfied with the level of judicial scrutiny offered at national level in the Netherlands in cases concerning the expulsion of asylum seekers. This dissatisfaction troubled me as a national asylum judge. Together with a colleague from the Amsterdam Court where I worked, I analysed a number of well-known judgments of the ECtHR in expulsion cases concerning asylum seekers to find out in a more precise way how this international Court assessed the risk. I discovered significant differences between the judicial practice applied at international level and our own national judicial practice. First, the intensity or thoroughness of the judicial scrutiny applied seemed to be different. It seemed that the ECtHR fully independently and on its own account determined the facts of the case and assessed the risk, whereas national asylum courts in the Netherlands had to pay deference to the position of the administration concerning the credibility of the past facts as stated by the asylum seeker. Second, issues of evidence, such as the admission and evaluation of evidence, were approached and resolved in very different ways at international and national level. This small-scale investigation, conducted in 2006 and early 2007, made me anxious to find out in a more precise way what lessons on both aspects – intensity of judicial scrutiny and evidence – could and should be drawn from the ECHR. I also became anxious to find out whether other relevant international treaties and EU asylum law contained concrete instructions on evidentiary issues and on the level of judicial scrutiny to be offered at national level. My wish to do research into these questions was strongly fed by the fact that in the national debate in the Netherlands at the time, different positions were voiced on the question of whether differences between the scrutiny offered by national judges and the scrutiny applied at the international level were acceptable or not, while the arguments underpinning these positions were not fully convincing (to me at least). This anxiety became stronger when I shared the results of my small-scale investigation with some of my colleagues, first instance court judges, in the International Association of Refugee Law Judges (IARLJ) and found out that it was not only in the Netherlands that national courts encountered the issues described above, but that similar issues with regard to the intensity of judicial scrutiny and evidence also existed in a number of other EU countries (for example, Belgium and Poland). That is how this research project was born.

The main objective of this study is to explore what international and EU asylum law require from the national asylum judge as to: 1) the required intensity of the judicial scrutiny to be applied; and 2) evidentiary issues, such as the standard and burden of proof, the admission and evaluation of evidence and time limits for submitting evidence. The research questions are as follows:

- Which provisions of international and EU asylum law regulate national judicial asylum proceedings?
- do the provisions regulating national judicial asylum proceedings contain concrete norms about the required intensity of judicial scrutiny to be offered at national level?
- do these provisions contain concrete norms on evidentiary issues, such as the standard and burden of proof, the admission and evaluation of evidence and time limits for submitting evidence?
- What standards and principles do the international courts and treaty monitoring bodies apply concerning their own judicial scrutiny, and how do they approach evidentiary issues?
- are the standards and principles as applied by the international courts and treaty monitoring bodies normative or binding on national asylum courts?
- How do the found norms (inter)relate, and what should be done in cases of divergence or conflict?

In this study eleven aspects (or issues) of evidence and judicial scrutiny are used as a research tool to discover the standards applied by the international courts and treaty monitoring bodies. These are:

- Standard of proof: what is the standard or criterion used to measure whether there is a risk of *refoulement*?
- Burden of proof: who has to prove that the standard has been met?
- Relevant facts and circumstances: what kinds of facts and circumstances are necessary to conclude that a risk exists?
- Required degree of individual risk: to what degree must an applicant be singled out?
- Credibility assessment: does the international court or supervisor independently and on its own account assess credibility? How does the international court or supervisor assess the credibility of the claimant's statements?
- Admission of evidence, sources of evidence, minimum quantity and quality of evidence: what means and sources of evidence can be brought in to substantiate a claim or to refute a claim? How much evidence is required to corroborate the applicant's statements? What quality of evidence is required?
- Appreciation and weighing of evidence: how are different types of evidence weighed and appreciated? Is there a certain hierarchy in the appreciation of evidence, in the sense that certain sources are given more value than others?
- Opportunities for presenting evidence: do both parties have the same opportunities and chances to present evidence and to react to the evidence presented to the other party?
- Judicial application of investigative powers: does the international court or supervisor apply investigative powers (of its own motion or otherwise)? If so, in which situations does this happen?

- Time limits for the presentation of statements and evidence: at what moment in the proceedings must the claimant submit the relevant statements and corroborating evidence?
- Point in time for the risk assessment: at what point in time does the international court or supervisor assess the risk?

This study covers the Convention relating to the Status of Refugees and the Protocol relating to the Status of Refugees (the Refugee Convention or RC, 1951, and the Refugee Protocol or RP, 1967), the International Covenant on Civil and Political Rights (ICCPR, 1966), the Convention against Torture (CAT, 1984), the European Convention for the Protection of Human Rights and Fundamental Freedoms (ECHR, 1950), European Union primary legislation on asylum and a number of secondary EU law instruments such as the EU Qualification Directive and the EU Procedures Directive.

UNHCR documentation and literature formed the main source of interpretation of the provisions contained in the RC. The case law of the HRC, the ComAT, the ECtHR and the CJEU, as well as literature, formed the main source for respectively Chapters 3 (ICCPR), 4 (CAT), 5 (ECHR) and 6 (EU asylum law). After the introduction in Chapter 1, Chapter 2 covers the RC, followed by the ICCPR in Chapter 3 and the CAT in Chapter 4. Chapter 5 is dedicated to the ECHR. Chapter 6 deals with EU asylum law. Chapter 7 discusses the consequences of the found norms and standards for national asylum courts. It attempts to integrate the different international and EU law standards on national judicial scrutiny and on evidence into a coherent whole. It also raises and tries to answer the question of whether the standards on evidence and judicial scrutiny as applied by the international supervisors and courts are binding on national asylum courts, whether national asylum courts can choose, from among the international supervisors, a 'best role model', and what to do in cases of conflicting or diverging standards. Chapter 8 pays separate attention to the positions of the international supervisors with regard to three special types of cases and the corresponding national asylum court proceedings: Dublin cases, repeat cases and fast-track national court proceedings.In the Epilogue at the end of this book, the highlights of this study are revisited and some concluding remarks are made.

Provisions in international and EU asylum law governing national asylum court proceedings

The RC

The RC contains a number of provisions relevant to national asylum court proceedings. These are Article 16 on access to courts, Article 32 on expulsion on grounds of national security and public order and the procedure to be followed in cases of expulsion, and Article 35 on co-operation of national authorities with the UNHCR. In Chapter 2 the content of these provisions was explored in relation to the research questions. Article 16 RC requires that refugees have free access to national courts. Article 32 requires that the decision to expel a refugee is taken in accordance with due process of law. In literature, different positions are taken on the question of whether these two provisions apply to contemporary judicial proceedings concerning the determination of refugee status and *refoulement*. In this study, a dynamic interpretation of these provisions was adopted, which led to the conclusion that both provisions do apply to such judicial proceedings. Article 16 RC is primarily a non-discrimination provision. It entails that refugees should not be required to meet extra, or more stringent, admissibility conditions which do not apply to nationals in similar court proceedings. Articles 16 and 32 RC may be interpreted with the aid of the UNHCR's position on issues of evidence and on judicial scrutiny in national judicial asylum proceedings. The UNHCR has developed concrete standards and principles with regard to ten of the eleven aspects of evidence and judicial scrutiny. They are listed below under the heading 'Positions of the international courts and treaty monitoring bodies on the eleven aspects of evidence and judicial scrutiny'.

Article 35 RC, in conjunction with Article 21, first paragraph, sub c, of the EU Procedures Directive, entails that the UNHCR is entitled to make submissions to national courts in individual asylum appeal cases. The UNHCR's submissions may enter the national court proceedings via different avenues: on its initiative, on the initiative of a party to the case or by invitation of the national court. On the basis of Articles 16 and 35 RC, seen in conjunction, national courts may invite the UNHCR to participate in national court proceedings as an expert or witness who can advise the court on a particular aspect of a case or submit its opinion on the question of whether or not the claimant is a refugee.

The ICCPR

The ICCPR's provisions on national proceedings impose a number of obligations on national asylum courts. Under Articles 2, third paragraph, 7, and 13 ICCPR national authorities, including national courts, are required to consider the claim thoroughly and fairly. However, the HRC is generally reluctant to put national asylum court proceedings to a rigorous test of compliance with this requirement. It often fails to respond in a meaningful way to the specific procedural problems raised by authors of individual communications. This passive position is linked to the fact that the HRC regards the determination and evaluation of facts and evidence as matters for the national courts. The HRC itself will normally not engage in that. As a consequence of this, the HRC will not easily find national judicial remedies ineffective for reasons having to do with the determination of the facts. The HRC's hands-off approach may also be explained by its limited investigative possibilities and limited meeting time. The case of *Pillai and Joachimpillai v. Canada* (2011) may mark a turning point towards firmer monitoring of procedural ICCPR compliance. In that case the HRC concluded that more attention should have been paid to the authors' allegations of past torture, and that the failure of the national authorities to do so made the national proceedings defective. However, more jurisprudence must be awaited before firmly drawing the conclusion that the HRC has begun to monitor procedural ICCPR compliance in a stricter way. The case of *Mansour Ahani v. Canada* (2004) has shown that the HRC is incidentally prepared to give up its hands-off approach if national authorities breach the key principles of equality of arms and adversarial proceedings. The HRC found the national expulsion proceedings in *Ahani* to be defective under Article 13 ICCPR as the Minister did not provide Ahani with all the materials – including secret information that Ahani was a danger to Canada's national security – on which the expulsion decision was based and the national courts did not correct this unfairness in the procedure. National procedural rules will normally not render national proceedings incompliant with the requirement of a thorough and fair examination of the claim, provided that such rules are reasonable and provided that they are not applied in an automatic and mechanical way. National courts must also be careful in automatically relying on steady jurisprudential lines.

Within the framework of Article 14 ICCPR, the HRC has ruled that the procedural practice applied by national courts to determine the facts and to admit, exclude, weigh and evaluate evidence is a matter for those courts to determine. Unlike the ECtHR, the HRC has (so far) not developed a doctrine regarding the required intensity of national judicial scrutiny in administrative law cases. In a number of cases not concerning the expulsion of asylum seekers, the HRC concluded that there had been a breach by national courts of the principles of equality of arms and adversarial proceedings. In those cases, the HRC relinquished its deference to national procedural autonomy and overtly criticised the national court proceedings for being unfair. It is obvious from these cases that the HRC regards equality of arms and adversarial proceedings as the very essence of fair proceedings. The principles developed by the HRC within the framework of Article 14 ICCPR strongly mirror those developed within the context of Articles 2, third paragraph, 7 and 13 ICCPR.

The CAT

Articles 3 and 22, fifth paragraph, second part, CAT require an opportunity for effective, independent and impartial review of the decision on expulsion, prior to the expulsion itself. Just like the HRC, the ComAT has generally been reluctant to submit national remedies, including court proceedings, to a rigorous procedural CAT compliance test. However, in more recent jurisprudence the ComAT has made clear that in order to qualify as an effective, independent and impartial national remedy, as required by Article 3 CAT, national judicial remedies must make it possible to look at the substance, the merits, of the case, and must guarantee equality of arms and adversarial proceedings. In the case of *Sogi v. Canada* (2007), the ComAT required that all the documents in the file be disclosed to the claimant, including those underpinning the allegation that Sogi constituted a threat to Canada's national security. In other words, in *Sogi* the ComAT treated adversariality and equality of arms as an absolute right and did not tolerate that national security interests justified non-disclosure of part of the evidentiary materials.

In cases where there are allegations or suspicions of internal torture, the requirement of impartiality enshrined in Articles 12 and 13 CAT obliges the national judge to reconstruct as meticulously as possible what actually happened and to use his or her investigative powers to that end. Impartiality under Article 3 CAT may be interpreted as meaning the same thing as impartiality under Articles 12 and 13 CAT. That would mean that national asylum courts must act impartially and must, therefore, make their own independent, thorough search for the truth and apply investigative powers to that end. Article 15 CAT prohibits the use of statements made as a re-

433

sult of torture as evidence in any proceedings, except in criminal proceedings against a person accused of torture as evidence of the very fact that this statement was made. The Committee has so far not dealt with Article 15 in the context of asylum.

The ECHR

In cases concerning the expulsion of asylum seekers, a national judicial remedy is compliant with Articles 3, 13 and 35, first paragraph, if it is able to comprise both substantive and procedural points and is able to quash the administrative decision upholding refusal of a protection claim. The procedural limb of Article 3, Article 13, and Article 35, first paragraph, ECHR require the national authorities, including the national courts, to conduct an adequate examination claim for protection. In assessing whether national proceedings are adequate, the ECtHR takes into consideration whether an applicant was heard (several times), whether he or she was assisted by appointed counsel, whether the national authorities had the benefit of seeing, hearing and questioning the applicant in person, and of assessing directly the information and documents submitted by him or her, before deciding the case. The ECtHR also takes into account whether the assessment of the national authorities was sufficiently supported by both national materials as well as materials originating from other reliable and objective sources. The cases of *R.C. v. Sweden* (2010) and *Singh and Others v. Belgium* (2012) have clearly illustrated that the national authorities, including the reviewing courts, must carefully and seriously examine evidence submitted by the applicant. When and if such evidence leaves questions unresolved, the national authorities, including the reviewing courts (or reviewing authorities) must apply investigative powers in order to further clarify facts. This is particularly necessary when it is rather easy to make further inquiries, as was the case in *Singh and Others v. Belgium*, where the national authorities could easily have made inquiries with the UNHCR. Decisive is the thoroughness of the investigations undertaken at national level, including the investigations of the involved national court(s).

Constant national jurisprudential lines may not normally bar an individual, case-specific and factual examination on the merits. It follows from *Bahaddar v. the Netherlands* (1998) and *Jabari v. Turkey* (2000) that time limits and other procedural rules laid down in national law – although they must normally be adhered to – should not be so short, or applied so mechanically or inflexibly, as to deny an applicant for asylum a realistic opportunity of proving his or her claim.

Finally, independent and rigorous scrutiny also means that the correct evidentiary standards and principles are to be applied by the national court in assessing the Article 3-risk. As was shown above, it follows from *M.S.S. v. Belgium and Greece* (2011) that the national court is not allowed to apply, for example, a stricter standard of proof than the one applied by the ECtHR. For national courts to comply with the requirement of independent and rigorous scrutiny it is, therefore, essential to know exactly what these evidentiary standards are. Part 2 of this chapter explores the evidentiary standards applied by the ECtHR.

It has been constant case law of the ECtHR that Article 6, first paragraph, ECHR does not apply to expulsion. Article 6 ECHR is, nevertheless, relevant for national asylum court proceedings for two reasons. First, since its judgment in *Kudla v. Poland*

(2000), the ECtHR has held that the requirements of Article 13 ECHR should be considered as 'reinforcing' those of Article 6, first paragraph, ECHR, so that the requirements developed under Article 6, first paragraph, ECHR in fact also form part of Article 13 ECHR. Second, the case law of the ECtHR under Article 6, first paragraph, defines to a large extent the content of Article 47, second paragraph, of the EU Charter, containing the right to a fair hearing. Article 47, second paragraph, of the EU Charter will normally apply in asylum cases.

Article 6, first paragraph, ECHR requires that administrative decisions can generally be challenged before a tribunal having full jurisdiction on points of law and points of fact. Full jurisdiction includes the power to make an independent determination of the disputed facts and of the credibility of a claimant, and the power to critically question advisory information used by the administrative decision maker or the other party. Article 6, first paragraph, ECHR also places national courts under a duty to conduct a proper examination of the submissions, arguments and evidence adduced by the parties. If no proper examination was conducted by the national court, either because it did not properly examine party evidence or because it did not use its investigative powers in order to determine disputed facts independently, this may lead the ECtHR to conclude that the national proceedings were unfair and in violation of Article 6, first paragraph, ECHR. Limited instead of full jurisdiction of national courts is exceptionally permitted under Article 6, first paragraph, ECHR. First, the particular subject-matter of the proceedings is of importance. In a number of cases where the subject-matter came within the classical exercise of administrative discretion, such as land planning, limited judicial scrutiny at national level was accepted by the ECtHR. One may also think of cases in which complex technical assessments are made and cases where important diplomatic issues are at stake. In those cases where the ECtHR found limited national court jurisdiction acceptable, other conditions were met as well: the national proceedings centered around points of law and not around factual issues, the preceding administrative procedure(s) was governed by many Article 6-safeguards and the national judicial scrutiny review was, although limited, nevertheless meaningful in the sense that it entailed real scrutiny of the procedural points raised by the applicant. I have argued that it would seem logical to place Article 3-cases concerning the expulsion of asylum seekers in the category of cases which require full national judicial scrutiny on points of fact and points of law, for the following reasons. First, as opposed to, for example, land planning cases, in asylum cases the life and safety of the individual are at stake. Article 3 ECHR is a fundamental, absolute and non-derogable right. Second, most asylum cases will not be of a highly technical nature, and in only a very limited number of cases will important diplomatic issues be at stake. Third, the requirements of Article 13 ECHR reinforce those of Article 6 ECHR. The requirement flowing from Article 13 ECHR that in expulsion cases an individual, case-specific, factual examination on the merits of the claim has to take place, can be seen as reinforcing the requirement for full jurisdiction on points of fact and points of law following from the Zumtobel doctrine under Article 6 ECHR.

In addition to this, Article 6, first paragraph, ECHR requires that the parties are treated equally with regard to the admission, exclusion and evaluation of evidence. The requirements of adversariality and equality of arms are not absolute, though.

Non-disclosure of evidentiary materials may be justified if this is strictly necessary to preserve the fundamental rights of another individual or to safeguard an important public interest, such as the protection of national security. If a national court allows that certain evidence is not disclosed to a party, it must follow special proceedings to counterbalance these difficulties. This means, at least, that the national court itself examines the secret evidence, and that, if possible, additional counterbalancing measures are taken.

EU asylum law

Since the Treaty of Lisbon (1 December 2009) the EU has had its own legally binding bill of human rights, the Charter of Fundamental Rights of the EU, with the status of primary binding EU law. Asylum cases will almost always be within the scope of Union law, so the Charter will normally apply to them. By virtue of Article 18 of the EU Charter, national asylum courts must pay due respect to the procedural provisions of the RC and the positions taken by the UNHCR, the RC's supervisor, discussed in Chapter 2. It may be argued that it is no longer possible to set the positions taken by UNHCR aside as non-binding as that would amount to non-compliance with Article 18 of the Charter which is binding primary Union law. The standards on procedures, on evidence and on judicial scrutiny flowing from the ECHR – discussed in Chapter 5 – have been incorporated into EU law via Articles 19, 47 and 52, third paragraph, of the EU Charter. This incorporation into EU law entails that these standards transform from intergovernmental international law into supranational EU law which takes precedence over all national law. By virtue of the Charter's Preamble, Article 78 TFEU and Article 53 of the EU Charter, the standards on procedures, on evidence and on judicial scrutiny flowing from the ICCPR and CAT – discussed in Chapters 3 and 4 – form important additional sources of interpretation of Articles 19, second paragraph, and 47 of the Charter.

Article 47 of the EU Charter is – as well as being the mirror of Articles 6 and 13 ECHR – also the codification of the EU law principle of effective judicial protection. Within the framework of the principle of effective judicial protection, five different standards of intensity of judicial scrutiny for different categories of cases have been developed, varying from a very light judicial touch with no factual review (cases about staff matters) to an intense, full and *ex nunc* judicial scrutiny on facts, law and proportionality (cases concerning restrictions of fundamental freedoms of EU citizens, their third-country national family members and Turkish workers and their family members who enjoy the rights of Decision 1/80 or rights flowing from the Association Agreement). As yet we do not know which of these standards will be applied by the CJEU in cases concerning asylum. It is my estimation that the CJEU will apply the most intense standard of judicial scrutiny. First, due to the strong parallel between asylum cases and cases concerning restrictions of fundamental freedoms of EU citizens. Both categories of cases concern fundamental freedoms or rights. Second, the most intense standard comes very close to the type of judicial scrutiny performed by the ECtHR under Article 3 ECHR in a significant number of asylum cases, and also to the full jurisdiction requirement and the rigorous scrutiny requirement flowing from, respectively, Articles 6 and 13 ECHR. The recent judgment in the case of

Samba Diouf (2011), in which the CJEU ruled that the final decision on an asylum claim must be the subject of a *thorough* review on the merits by the national court, shows that this expectation is not entirely imaginary. The provisions regarding judicial review in secondary EU asylum law must be interpreted in accordance with the higher ranking Article 47 of the Charter and the higher ranking general principle of effective judicial protection. The attempts to keep national courts away from asylum refusals or to water down the intensity of judicial scrutiny over such decisions, which are reflected in the texts of these provisions, were therefore made in vain.

Secondary EU asylum law does not provide an exhaustive regulation for all possible issues of evidence. It does, however, contain specific provisions regarding a number of the eleven aspects of evidence, such as the standard and burden of proof. In Chapter 6, these provisions were interpreted with the aid of the jurisprudence of the CJEU in both asylum cases and other areas, and with the aid of the standards developed by the UNHCR, the HRC, the ComAT and the ECtHR, as Article 78 TFEU stipulates that secondary EU asylum legislation must be in accordance with the RC as well as the other relevant treaties.

It was concluded in Chapter 6 that EU procedural asylum law offers added value in three ways. First, it causes a transformation in legal status of existing standards on evidence and judicial scrutiny contained in or flowing from international asylum law. These existing standards transform from non-binding principles into more important rules which must be respected (the standards developed by the UNHRC via Article 18 of the Charter), from intergovernmental international law into binding primary supranational EU law (the standards developed by the ECtHR via Articles 19 and 47 of the Charter) and from intergovernmental international law into important sources of inspiration for binding EU law (the standards and principles developed by the HRC and the ComAT via Articles 19 and 47 of the Charter).Second, the standards developed by the ECtHR under Article 6 ECHR are now applicable to asylum cases as they form part of Article 47 of the EU Charter. Third, the system of judicial supervision over EU asylum law has a strong complementary value. The preliminary procedure before the CJEU offers national courts the possibility to refer questions to the CJEU pending the national judicial proceedings. In this way, violations of human rights may be prevented or redressed at a much earlier stage.

Positions of the international courts and treaty monitoring bodies on the eleven aspects of evidence and judicial scrutiny

Standard of proof

The standard of proof under EU asylum law, the ECHR, the RC and the CAT is the same: the level of risk required is a real, personal, and foreseeable risk exceeding the mere possibility of being subjected to proscribed ill-treatment, but the risk does not need to be certain or necessary, highly probable or beyond reasonable doubt. The case law of the HRC is stricter as a real risk means that it is a necessary and foreseeable consequence of the expulsion that Article 7 ICCPR will be violated.

Burden of proof, the notion of co-operation

Under EU asylum law and the treaties included in this study the burden of proof is shared: there is an initial burden of assertion, and, preferably, some corroboration, on the applicant; after which an investigative burden on the authorities of the State party, including the national courts, emerges. The CJEU and the ECtHR, and – albeit less explicitly – also the ComAT have developed a notion of a gradual scale: the poorer the general human rights situation is, the less individual circumstances and corroborating individual evidence are required and the sooner the onus shifts to the State party. The EU Qualification Directive, the ECHR, the RC and the CAT envisage an alleviated burden of proof for cases in which previous persecution or ill-treatment took place.

The notion of a shared burden of proof, developed in international asylum law, is also clearly present in EU asylum law in the form of the co-operation requirement laid down in Article 4 of the Qualification Directive. In its judgment in *M.M. v. Minister for Justice, Equality and Law Reform, Ireland* (2012) the CJEU has ruled that this requirement of co-operation means that if, for any reason whatsoever, the elements provided by an applicant for international protection are not complete, up to date or relevant, it is necessary for the Member State concerned to cooperate actively with the applicant, at that stage of the procedure, so that all the elements needed to substantiate the application may be assembled. A Member State may also be better placed than an applicant to gain access to certain types of documents. The CJEU has so far not explained any further what is meant by 'active co-operation with the applicant so that all the elements needed to substantiate the application may be assembled'. National courts may probably think of situations in which it is necessary to offer the applicant a certain (additional) period for submitting new relevant documentation, of situations in which the applicant proposes that the court hears certain witnesses, and situations in which the applicant submits certain documents and the court orders an expert authenticity examination or orders the administrative authority to do that. Like the ECtHR did in 2010 in *Iskandarov v. Russia*, the CJEU makes clear in *M.M.* that there may be specific circumstances in which the administrative or judicial authority is better placed than the applicant to get hold of certain types of documents. Thus, when it is much easier for the national administrative or authority than for the applicant to gain access to certain relevant documentation, the burden of obtaining such evidence rests primarily with that authority.

Relevant facts and circumstances

The positions on this aspect are highly similar under the different treaties and EU asylum law. Personal circumstances, such as background, gender, age, beliefs, activities, and circumstances concerning the general (human rights) situation in the country of origin, such as conditions in detention, the level of violence in the country and control thereof by the authorities, changes in government or policies, are relevant. It follows from the treaties and EU asylum law that a holistic and integrated approach must be taken towards the personal facts and the situation in the country of origin:

the personal facts must be seen in the light of the general situation in the country of origin; all the facts and circumstances must be seen as a whole.

Required degree of individual risk

Under EU asylum law and the ECHR, three categories of cases may be distinguished: 1) cases of extreme general violence, where an Article 3risk is assumed for everyone returning to the particular country; 2) cases of group violence and 3) individual risk cases. In the third category of cases it is required that an individual risk is established, in other words, that the individual concerned has been singled out. The HRC and ComAT have taken significant steps towards incorporating the lines of theory developed by the ECtHR on situations of group violence. In classifying cases into one of these categories and determining, accordingly, the required amount of individual facts and evidence, national courts must also take into consideration that under the RC, no singling out is required. The UNHCR Handbook distinguishes two main kinds of status determination: the normal situation in which refugee status is determined on an individual basis and the exceptional situation in which group determination takes place whereby each member of the group is *prima facie* regarded as a refugee. Neither of these two situations poses a strict requirement of being singled out as the risk does not necessarily need to be based on the personal experiences of the applicant.

Credibility assessment: intensity of scrutiny applied by the ECtHR and the international supervisors, positions of the UNHCR and the CJEU

The HRC and the ComAT often stress their subsidiary role when it comes to the determination of the facts of the case, including assessment of the credibility of the claimant. This is a logical consequence of the fact that these bodies consider the determination of the facts as primarily a matter for the authorities of the States parties and that they (particularly the HRC) have limited fact finding instruments. It seems that two triggers in particular make the ComAT proceed towards an independent determination of the facts. A first trigger is that in the national proceedings the absolute nature of Article 3 CAT was not respected and a weighing took place of, on the one hand, the risk and, on the other hand, aspects of national security or public order. A second trigger is that the State party's authorities have not taken into consideration important facts or evidence. Compared to both Committees the ECtHR is more active: in a significant number of cases concerning the expulsion of asylum seekers, the ECtHR played a very active role in the gathering and verification of facts and circumstances, including the assessment of the credibility of the claimant. The ECtHR actively proceeds towards an independent and fresh determination of the facts, including credibility, in cases of insufficient national proceedings, new facts, circumstances and developments, including evidence thereof, and an incorrect application of evidentiary standards (for example, the standard or proof, the required level of individualisation) at national level.

Unlike the Committees and the ECtHR, the CJEU and the UNHCR do not receive individual claims, but both supervisors have taken clear positions on the intensity of the scrutiny to be applied by national asylum courts. The CJEU ruled in *Samba*

Diouf (2011) that a thorough national judicial review on the merits of the claim is required; the UNHCR has taken the position that appeal or review proceedings should involve points of fact and points of law and national courts should be able to independently assess the credibility of statements by the asylum seeker.

Credibility assessment: how do the ECtHR and the international supervisors assess credibility?

The ECtHR, the UNHCR, and the ComAT (and to a lesser extent the HRC) have developed clear standards for credibility assessment. These international supervisors require 'general credibility' ('general veracity'), not complete accuracy and consistency of every single detail of the claim. The basic story – the very core aspects of the flight reasons – must be credible. The ECtHR has made clear that doubts about more peripheral aspects of the claim, such as statements concerning the journey to the country where asylum is requested or statements concerning escape from prison or from guards do not necessarily undermine the general credibility. The ECtHR and the ComAT have, furthermore, made clear that the basic story must meet a number of requirements in order to be credible:
- It must be sufficiently detailed;
- It must be internally consistent throughout the proceedings; numerous major inconsistencies and numerous alterations in statements may make these statements incredible;
- It must be consistent with country information;
- It must be brought forward in a timely manner: late submission of statements may negatively affect the general credibility, particularly when no sound reason for it is given;
- The core of the flight narrative must – as much as possible – be corroborated with evidence.

Compared to the other supervisors, the UNHCR takes a more lenient stance with regard to corroboration with evidence as a requirement for credibility. It takes the stance that the absence of corroborative documents should not prevent the claim from being accepted if the statements are consistent with known facts and the general credibility of the applicant is good. It has also made clear that there is no justification for imposing a stricter credibility standard – stricter than the standard of general credibility – in cases where corroborating evidence is totally absent.

Admission of evidence: means and sources

Under the studied treaties and under EU asylum law the approach towards the admission and admissibility of evidence is liberal. There are no procedural barriers to the admissibility of evidence or pre-determined formulae for its assessment. In Chapters 2-5 different examples of evidentiary materials were provided.

Minimum quantity and quality of evidence

The HRC, the ComAT and the ECtHR require a significant amount of evidence with a direct personal bearing corroborating the core of the flight narrative, the 'basic story'.

As opposed to this, the UNHCR has often underlined that due to the special and difficult evidentiary position of the applicant for asylum, the requirement of evidence should not be applied too strictly. It has also taken the stance that complete absence of supportive evidence does not automatically mean that the claim is unmeritorious. The UNHCR's position is echoed in the fifth paragraph of Article 4 of the EU Qualification Directive, which makes clear that under certain circumstances, including a genuine effort to corroborate the claim, not all aspects of the applicant's account need to be corroborated by evidence other than statements.

Appreciation and weighing of evidence

EU asylum law and the RC do not regulate this aspect and the case law of the HRC and the ComAT are not very explicit and transparent on the evaluation of evidence (with the exception of the evaluation of medico-legal reports by the ComAT). The ECtHR's case law is much more explicit and transparent and offers national asylum courts concrete guidelines for the evaluation of evidence. The authenticity of submitted documents, the specificity, comprehensiveness and consistency of the information contained in evidentiary materials, and the independence, reliability, objectiveness and authority of the source or author of the evidence determine how much probative value or weight is attached.

In Chapters 3, 4 and 5, a number of categories of evidence were discussed in more detail and it was demonstrated that specific and comprehensive witness statements by family members played an important role in the case law of the ECtHR and both Committees. The ECtHR has made clear that statements by family members must normally be supported by other, more objective, evidentiary materials.

Medico-legal reports form another important category of evidence, particularly in the case law of the ComAT. The ECtHR is generally reluctant to accept medical evidence (stating PTSD or other mental disturbance or disorder) as an explanation for tardy presentation of statements on past torture and inconsistencies. The ECtHR, the HRC and the ComAT have accepted medical reports as evidence corroborating statements on past torture in a significant number of cases. The ComAT requires that medico-legal reports are drawn up by medical specialists and conclusively identify a causal link between the individual's bodily or mental injuries and the alleged past torture. In a significant number of – mostly early – cases the ComAT accepted medico-legal reports as corroboration of statements on past torture, and as an explanation for inconsistencies, gaps or vague points, major changes in the flight narrative and late presentation of crucial statements and evidence. In the ComAT's later jurisprudence, medical evidence has been downgraded from decisive to supportive, but still remains important and the ComAT has shown dissatisfaction over the fact that in national proceedings in the Netherlands, medical reports are not normally taken into account as evidence.

In the case law of the HRC and the ComAT, much probative weight is normally attached to reports containing the result of inquiries conducted by embassies or missions in countries of origin.

Reports on the situation in the country of origin logically play an important role in the case law of all the international supervisors. The ECtHR has developed a number of concrete guidelines for the evaluation of country reports. Reports by UN organs, organisations and agencies and reports by States rank highly because United Nations agencies have direct access to the authorities of the country of destination as well as the ability to carry out on-site inspections and assessments. States have the ability to gather information through their diplomatic missions. The precise probative value accorded to country of origin information is not only determined by the source, but also by its specific content.

Opportunities for presenting evidence

All the international supervisors regard adversarial proceedings and equality of arms as crucial safeguards for a fair hearing at international level and at the level of national court proceedings. The positions of the HRC and the ComAT seem to be stricter compared to the other international supervisors, as the HRC and the ComAT have required that in cases concerning the expulsion of asylum seekers, both parties to the case must have equal access to all the documents in the case file, including documents underpinning allegations that the individual concerned constitutes a danger to the national security of the country. The prohibition on the use of secret evidence in national court proceedings on expulsion developed by the HRC and the ComAT has so far not been reiterated in other cases, so we cannot speak of a constant line in their case law. As opposed to this, the ECtHR has ruled in a number of cases that the use of secret evidence may be justified if this is strictly necessary to preserve the fundamental rights of another individual or to safeguard an important public interest, such as the protection of national security. In the same vein, the UNHCR takes the position that non-disclosure of evidence is allowed when disclosure of sources would seriously jeopardize national security or the security of the organisations or persons providing the information. The ECtHR requires that national courts, when accepting that evidence is not disclosed to the other party, must take counterbalancing measures. The principles developed by the CJEU concerning secret evidence strongly mirror the ECtHR's principles.

Judicial application of investigative powers

The HRC and the ComAT often stress their subsidiary role when it comes to the determination of the facts of the case. Both Committees, but particularly the HRC, have at their disposal and apply only a limited number of investigative powers. The ECtHR, a fully-fledged international court, has a wide array of investigative powers at its disposal. In a significant number of cases concerning the expulsion of asylum seekers it has played a very active role in the gathering and verification of facts and circumstances. The ECtHR may apply at any stage in the proceedings any investigative measure which it considers capable of clarifying the facts. It will particularly obtain materials on conditions in the country of origin *proprio motu* when the applicant or a third party provides reasoned grounds which cast doubt on the accuracy of the information relied on by the respondent government.

As regards the required intensity of scrutiny to be provided by national courts, the stances of the international supervisors are highly similar: they require a thorough national judicial review on the merits of the claim (see, for example, CJEU, *Samba Diouf* 2011, ComAT, *Nirmal Singh v. Canada* 2011), full judicial jurisdiction on points of fact and points of law (the ECtHR's Zumtobel doctrine) appeal or review proceedings on points of fact and points of law (UNHCR). Reference was also made to the interpretation of the term 'impartiality' by the ComAT under Articles 12 and 13 CAT, which obliges the national judge to reconstruct as meticulously as possible what happened and to use his or her investigative powers to that end.

Time limits for the presentation of statements and evidence

The CJEU, the ECtHR, the UNHCR and the HRC take similar positions. The core of these positions is that national procedural rules must be reasonable or applied by the national court in a reasonable and flexible manner if the circumstances of the case so require.

It follows from EU asylum law and the case law of the ECtHR, the position of the UNHCR and the case law of the ComAT that all relevant statements should, in principle, be made as early in the national procedure as possible and that belated statements may cast doubt on the credibility of the applicant. The approach towards evidence submitted to corroborate statements is generally more flexible. In the case law of the ECtHR, the HRC and the ComAT, the point in time at which evidentiary materials were submitted in national proceedings by the parties is, seen as a factor alone and in itself, not a relevant consideration.

The UNHCR has stressed that no case should be rejected solely on the basis that the relevant information was not presented or documents were not submitted earlier. In the same vein, in a significant number of cases the ComAT did not see the tardy presentation of relevant statements and evidence as problematic and rather easily accepted that good reasons had been brought forward for the belated presentation of statements and evidence. The more lenient positions of the UNHCR and the ComAT are echoed in Article 8, first paragraph, of the EU Procedures Directive, under which Member States must ensure that applications for asylum are neither rejected nor excluded from examination on the sole ground that they have not been made as soon as possible.

Point in time for the risk assessment

The positions of the international supervisors on this issue are by and large identical. They all take the position that, in principle, an assessment *ex nunc* is required. The assessment of the risk is made on the basis of all the information available at the moment of consideration. In cases where deportation from the respondent State has already been effectuated, the point in time for the consideration by the ECtHR remains the moment of that deportation, but the Court may, and actually does, have regard to information that came to light subsequent to the removal so that in fact again an *ex nunc* assessment takes place. The HRC has so far adopted no guidelines for situations where the removal has already taken place and the ComAT's case law is not entirely consistent. In *T.P.S. v. Canada* (2000), however, the ComAT explicitly took subsequent facts and circumstances into consideration without any reservation. This resembles the ECtHR's approach.

Integrating the results: national courts and the independent and rigorous scrutiny

Whereas Chapters 2-6 were aimed at discovering the procedural obligations and standards flowing from international asylum law and EU asylum law, Chapter 7 focused on their implications for national asylum courts. The first question looked at in Chapter 7 was how the treaties and EU asylum law related to each other. It was concluded that the transfer to the EU by the EU Member States of the competence to make binding rules on asylum had not affected the obligations flowing from the RC, the ICCPR, the CAT and the ECHR. National asylum courts in the EU Member States were in fact 'double bound' by the procedural obligations and standards flowing from the treaties investigated in this study as they were bound by the treaties as such on the one hand, and, on the other hand, bound by EU law which incorporated the treaty obligations, as was demonstrated in Chapter 6.

Next, an attempt was made to integrate into a coherent whole the procedural obligations and standards flowing from international and EU asylum law, with the objective of arriving at a coherent set of standards ready for use by national asylum courts. A basic presumption underpinning this integration exercise was that in most asylum cases coming before national asylum courts, both refugee protection (Articles 1 and 33 RC, Article 18 of the EU Charter) and subsidiary protection (Articles 7 ICCPR, 3 CAT, 3 ECHR, Articles 4 and 19 of the EU Charter) were invoked. As a result, all the treaties and instruments covered by this study were relevant and applicable in such cases. The integration exercise resulted in a common denominator: it was concluded that international and EU applications for asylum required an 'independent and rigorous national judicial scrutiny'. The requirement for independent and rigorous national judicial scrutiny was then further defined with the aid of the following sources:

- The case law of the HRC, the ComAT and the ECtHR under the respective effective remedy provisions and the procedural limbs of the non-*refoulement* provisions;
- The position of the UNHCR concerning national judicial scrutiny;
- The CJEU's case law on the principle of effective judicial protection;
- The assessment as performed by the HRC, the ComAT and the ECtHR, analysed in the second part of Chapters 3, 4 and 5.

A hierarchy of these sources was created: it was concluded that national asylum courts must first and foremost turn to the case law of the CJEU and the ECtHR, next, to the UNHCR and then to the HRC and the ComAT as subsidiary means of interpretation. It was also concluded that cross-references were not problematic: national asylum courts within the EU could cross-refer to these different sources of interpretation as all the EU Member States were parties to the RC, the ICCPR, the CAT and the ECHR. Finally, the question of conflicting or diverging standards was addressed. With reference to the preference rules contained in the different treaties and EU asylum law, it was argued that when confronted with the problem of conflicting or diverging standards, national asylum courts should abandon the established hierarchy and opt for those standards offering the highest degree of protection. To justify this approach, reference was also made to Article 52, third paragraph, of the EU Charter which allows EU law to provide more extensive protection than the protection offered under the ECHR.

The requirement of an independent and rigorous national judicial scrutiny was, finally, defined with the assistance of the eleven aspects of evidence and judicial scrutiny, introduced in Chapter 1. This resulted in a set of evidentiary and scrutiny standards ready for use by national courts.

Repeat cases, Dublin cases and fast-track national proceedings

Chapter 8 explored the stances of the international courts and treaty monitoring bodies on three special categories of cases: repeat cases (cases in which a claimant had lodged a second or third *et cetera* asylum application after a negative decision on a first application), Dublin cases (cases in which an asylum application was decided upon on the basis of the EU Dublin Regulation 2003/343/EC), and fast-track national proceedings (proceedings in which shorter than normal time limits and sometimes also other special rules applied, created with the aim of faster and more efficient processing of asylum claims and appeals). With regard to repeat cases it was concluded that a *nova* test was, in itself, not problematic from the viewpoint of international and EU asylum law. A second conclusion concerning repeat cases was that, given the positions of the international treaty monitoring bodies and courts, national courts should not fully or formally exclude evidence only because it should have been presented at an earlier moment in national asylum proceedings.

In cases of the expulsion of asylum seekers under the Dublin Regulation, the expelling EU Member State's authorities, including the national courts, were, to a certain extent, allowed to presume that the authorities of the intermediary EU Member State would respect their international obligations. At the same time, the ECtHR and the CJEU had clearly put a firm restriction on this presumption of treaty compliance. As soon as (some) information to the contrary became available – either because the applicant had submitted this information or because the authorities were familiar with it or should have been familiar with it – the national authorities of the referring EU Member State had to assess whether the asylum procedure in the intermediary EU Member State afforded sufficient guarantees and whether living conditions violated Article 3 ECHR.

It was, finally, established that, on the issue of fast-track national proceedings, the stances of the international treaty monitoring bodies and courts were identical. Fast-track asylum court proceedings were not problematic as such. What was important was that, when operating such proceedings, national courts remained able to perform a thorough review on the merits of the asylum claim. Fast-track proceedings could deprive asylum seekers of the opportunity to substantiate their claim for protection. If a national court estimated that, as a result of operating fast-track proceedings, a thorough review on the merits could not take place or that the asylum seeker had been deprived of the opportunity to substantiate his or her claim, that court needed to have the possibility to reroute the case into normal or prolonged proceedings which offered more room for further judicial investigations or further substantiation of the claim by the asylum seeker.

Epilogue

In the Epilogue, I revisited the main research findings and explained their importance, sometimes by referring to their contrast with standing national jurisprudential practice in the Netherlands. I also expressed my disappointment at the fact that the HRC, the ComAT and the ECtHR had so far not developed elaborate and coherent doctrinal positions on the intensity of the scrutiny with which they themselves determined the facts in expulsion cases concerning asylum seekers, and at the fact that the conclusions in the views of the HRC and the ComAT were often *ultra*-brief and offered no clear guidelines to national courts on a number of evidentiary issues, such as the evaluation of evidence (both HRC and ComAT) and the credibility assessment (particularly the HRC). Based on this I made a plea to the HRC and the ComAT to try to come up with more elaborate considerations on the mentioned issues of evidence and on the intensity of judicial scrutiny they themselves applied, so that national courts would receive clearer guidance and would be better equipped to live up to their treaty obligations.

I concluded by arguing that international and EU asylum law provide support for my personal conviction that an independent and thorough national judicial scrutiny, including thorough judicial investigations aimed at finding the truth, is of utmost importance in national asylum court proceedings, and that thorough judicial investigations aimed at finding the truth have nothing to do with helping one of the parties to the case, but have to do with independence and impartiality of the judiciary.

Bibliography

Ackers 2005

D. Ackers, 'The negotiations on the Asylum Procedures Directive', *European Journal of Migration and Law* (7), 2005, pp. 1-33.

Alston 2000

P. Alston, *The EU and Human Rights*, Oxford: Oxford University Press 2000.

Arnull 2011

A. Arnull, 'The principle of effective judicial protection in EU law: an unruly horse?', *European Law Review* 2011, 36(1), pp. 51-70.

Aust 2004

A. Aust, *Modern Treaty Law and Practice*, Cambridge: CambridgeUniversity Press 2004.

Barkhuysen 1998

T. Barkhuysen, *Artikel 13 EVRM, effectieve nationale rechtsbescherming bij schending van mensenrechten [Article 13 ECHR, effective domestic remedies against violations of human rights]*, diss. Leiden, Lelystad: Koninklijke Vermande 1998.

Barkhuysen & Bos 2011

T. Barkhuysen & A.W. Bos, 'De Betekenis van het Handvest van de Grondrechten van de Europese Unie voor het bestuursrecht', *JB Plus* 2011, pp. 3-34.

Battjes 2005

H. Battjes, 'Kroniek Asieljurisprudentie EHRM, 2004-2005', *NJCM-Bulletin* 2005, jrg. 30-8, pp. 1124-1137.

Battjes 2006

H. Battjes, *European asylum law and international law*, Leiden-Boston: Martinus Nijhoff Publishers 2006.

Battjes 2007

H. Battjes, 'Straatsburg en het Migratierecht, Recente Ontwikkelingen in de EHRM-jurisprudentie over Asiel en Gezinshereniging', *NJCM-Bulletin* 2007, jrg. 32-3, pp. 274-298.

Battjes 2009-I

H. Battjes, 'De algemene mensenrechtensituatie en andere risicofactoren in uitzettingszaken', *NJCM-Bulletin 2009*, jrg. 34-1, pp. 71-86.

Battjes 2009-II

H. Battjes, 'Geschonden vertrouwen? Dublin-overdrachten aan Griekenland en artikel 3 EVRM', *NJCM-Bulletin* 2009, jrg. 24-7, pp. 722-746.

Battjes 2011

H. Battjes, 'Subsidiaire bescherming', *A&MR* 2011, nr. 5/6, pp. 208-212.

Battjes 2012

H. Battjes, 'Comment to ECtHR, *Othman (Abu Qatada) v. the UK*, 17 January 2012, Appl. No. 8139/09, *JV* 5, 30 March 2012, 16, pp. 670 – 698.

Bem 2007

K. Bem, *Defining the Refugee, American and Dutch asylum case law 1975-2005*, Amsterdam: Vrije Universiteit Amsterdam 2007.

Van Bennekom 2005

W. van Bennekom,'EHRM verbiedt uitzetting Eritrese asielzoeker', *NJCM Bulletin* 2005, jrg. 30-6, pp. 831-843.

Van Bennekom & Van der Winden 2011

W.J. van Bennekom & J.H. van der Winden, *Asielrecht*, Den Haag: Boom Juridische Uitgevers 2011.

Van Bennekom 2011

W.J. van Bennekom, 'Het verhaal van het vluchtelingenverdrag: kanttekeningen bij 60 jaar Verdrag van Genève', *A&MR* 2011, nr. 5/6, pp. 202-207.

Bernitz & Nergelius 2000

U. Bernitz & J. Nergelius (ed), *General Principles of Community Law*, The Hague-London-Boston: Kluwer Law International 2000.

Blake & Husain 2003

N. Blake & R. Husain, *Immigration, Asylum and Human Rights*, Oxford-New York: Oxford University Press 2003.

Blake 2004

N. Blake, 'Developments in the Case Law of the European Court of Human Rights', in: B. Bogusz & R. Cholewinski et al. (eds), *Irregular Immigration and Human Rights, Theoretical, European and International Perspectives*, Leiden-Boston: Martinus Nijhoff Publishers 2003, p. 431.

Boeles 1997

P. Boeles, *Fair Immigration Proceedings in Europe*, The Hague-Boston-London: Martinus Nijhoff Publishers 1997.

Boeles 2005

P. Boeles, 'Fair and Effective Immigration Procedures in Europe?', *European Journal of Migration and Law* 7, 2005, pp. 213-218.

Boeles 2008

P. Boeles, 'Case reports of the European Court of Human Rights, the Human Rights Committee, and the Committee against Torture', *European Journal of Migration and Law* 10(1) (2008), pp. 105-118.

Boeles 2009

P. Boeles, M. den Heijer, G. Lodder & K. Wouters, *European Migration Law*, Antwerp: Intersentia 2009.

Bogusz & Cholewinsky 2004

B. Bogusz, R. Cholewinski et al. (eds), *Irregular Immigration and Human Rights, Theoretical, European and International Perspectives*, Leiden/Boston, Martinus Nijhoff Publishers 2003.

Bossuyt 1987

M.J.B.Bossuyt, *Guide to the Travaux Preparatoires of the ICCPR*, Dordrecht: Nijhoff 1987.

Bossuyt 2012

M.J.B.Bossuyt, 'The Court of Strasbourg Acting as an Asylum Court', *European Constitutional Law Review* 2012, 8(2), pp. 203-245.

Boulesbaa 1999

A. Boulesbaa, *The UN Convention against Torture and its Prospects for Enforcement*, The Hague:Martinus Nijhoff Publishers 1999.

Brouwer 2006

E. Brouwer, *Digital Borders and Real Rights, Effective Remedies for Third-Country Nationals in the Schengen Information System*, diss. Nijmegen, Nijmegen: Wolf Legal Publishers 2006.

Brouwer 2007

E. Brouwer, 'Effective Remedies in Immigration and Asylum Law Procedures: A Matter of General Principles of EU Law', in: A. Baldaccini, E. Guild & H. Toner (eds), *Whose Freedom, Security and Justice? EU Immigration and Asylum Law and Policy*, Oxford-Portland-Oregon: Hart Publishing 2007, pp. 57-83.

Bruin 1998

R.Bruin, 'More than a mere possibility; risicogroepen, het Comité tegen foltering en de bewijslast', *Nieuwsbrief Asiel en Vluchtelingenrecht (NAV)* 1998, pp. 145-150.

Bruin 2003

R. Bruin, 'Geen lijdelijke rechter', *Nieuwsbrief Asiel- en Vluchtelingenrecht* 08/2003, pp. 572-576.

Bruin & Reneman 2006

R. Bruin & A.M. Reneman, 'Supervising bodies and medical reports', in: R. Bruin, A.M. Reneman & E. Bloemen (eds), *Care Full. Medico-legal Reports and the Istanbul Protocol in Asylum Procedures*, Utrecht: Pharos/Amnesty International/Vluchtelingenwerk (Dutch Council for Refugees)2006, pp. 86-109.

Bruin & Reneman 2009

R. Bruin & M. Reneman, 'Commentaar bij de zaak Abdolkhani & Karimnia tegen Turkije', *Nieuwsbrief Asiel- en Vluchtelingenrecht* 06/2009, pp. 424-427.

Bruin 2011

R. Bruin, 'UNHCR's mandaatverklaringen: de rol van UNHCR in de Nederlandse asielprocedure', *A&MR* 2011, nr. 5/6, pp. 242-248.

Burgers & Danelius 1988

J.H. Burgers & H. Danelius, *The United Nations Convention against Torture, a Handbook on the Convention against Torture and Other Cruel, Inhuman or Degrading Treatment and Punishment*, Dordrecht: Martinus Nijhoff Publishers1988.

Burns 2001

P. Burns, 'The UN Committee against Torture and its role in refugee protection', *Georgetown Immigration Law Journal* 2001, 15, pp. 403-413.

Byrne 2005

R. Byrne, 'Remedies of Limited Effect: Appeals under the forthcoming Directive on EU Minimum Standards on Procedures', *European Journal of Migration and Law* (7), 2005, pp. 71-86.

Byrnes 1992

A. Byrnes, 'The Committee against Torture', in: P. Alston (ed.), *The United Nations and Human Rights, a critical appraisal*, Oxford: Clarendon Press 1992.

Callewaert 2010

J. Callewaert, 'Het EVRM en de EU: van Bosphorus naar Lissabon', *NtER*, april 2010, nr. 3, pp. 101-107.

Carlson & Gisvold 2003

S.N. Carlson & G. Gisvold, *Practical Guide to the International Covenant on Civil and Political Rights*, New YorkArdsley 2003.

Cholewinski 2004

R. Cholewinsky, 'The Need for Effective Remedies in Matters of Immigration and Border Control', *Migrantenrecht* 2004, pp. 259-262.

Cholewinski 2005

R. Cholewinski, 'The Need for Effective Individual Legal Protection in Immigration Matters', *European Journal of Migration and Law*, 2005, nr. 7, pp. 237-262.

Claes 2009

M.Claes, 'Het Verdrag van Lissabon en de Europese Grondrechtenmozaiek', in: R.H. van Ooik & R.A. Wessel (red.), *De Europese Unie na het Verdrag van Lissabon,* Europa in Beeld 6, Deventer: Kluwer 2009.

Clark & Aiken 1997

T. Clark & S. Aiken, 'International Human Rights Law and Legal Remedies in Expulsion', *Netherlands Quarterly of Human Rights*, 1997, nr. 4, pp. 429-455.

Conte, Davidson & Burchill 2004

A. Conte, S. Davidson & R. Burchill, *Defining Civil and Political Rights*, Aldershot: Ashgate 2004.

Corstens 2010

G. Corstens, 'Het Europees Hof voor de Rechten van de Mens en de Verdragsstaten: over subsidiariteit', *NJCM Bulletin* 2010, jrg. 35-2, pp. 165-172.

Costello 2007

C. Costello, 'The Asylum Procedures Directive in Context', in: A. Baldaccini, E. Guild & H. Toner (eds), *Whose Freedom, Security and Justice? EU Immigration and Asylum Law and Policy*, Oxford-Portland-Oregon: Hart Publishing 2007.

Cox 2010

M. Cox, 'Diplomatieke garanties versus de absolute gelding van artikel 3 EVRM, een stroomschema als praktische handleiding', *NJCM Bulletin* 2010, jrg. 35-4, pp. 388-404.

Craig 2006

P. Craig, *EU administrative law*, New York: Oxford University Press 2006.

Craig & De Búrca 2008

P. Craig & G. de Búrca, *EU law – text, cases and materials*, New York: Oxford University Press 2008.

Craig & De Burca 2011

P. Craig & G. de Búrca, *EU law – text, cases and materials*, New York: Oxford University Press 2011.

Da Lomba 2004

S. da Lomba, *The Right to Seek Refugee Status in the EU*, Antwerp-Oxford-New York: Intersentia 2004.

Damen 2008

L.J.A.Damen, 'Lees eerst het arrest Salah Sheekh!',*Ars Aequi*, January 2008, pp. 53-66.

Delicostopoulos 2003

J.S.Delicostopoulos, Towards European Procedural Primacy in National Legal Systems, *European Law Journal* 2003, Vol. 9, no. 5.

Dembour 2006

M. Dembour, *Who believes in Human Rights? Reflections on the European Convention*, Cambridge: Cambridge University Press 2006.

Van Dijk 1987

P. van Dijk, *Het internationale verdrag inzake burgerlijke en politieke rechten en zijn betekenis voor Nederland*, Nijmegen: Ars Aequi Libri – Rechten van de Mens 1987.

Van Dijk et al. 1998

P. van Dijk, C. Flinterman & P.E.L. Janssen, *International Law, Human Rights*, Lelystad: Koninklijke Vermande 1998.

Van Dijk 2006

P. van Dijk, P. et al., *Theory and Practice of the European Convention on Human Rights*, Antwerpen-Ofxord: Intersentia, 2006.

Dougan 2008

M. Dougan, 'The Treaty of Lisbon: Winning Minds, Not Hearts', *CML Review* 2008, p. 45.

Edwards 2009

A. Edwards, 'The Optional Protocol against Torture and the Detention of Refugees', *International and Comparative Law Quarterly* 2009, pp. 789-825.

Engström 2010,

J. Engström, *The Principle of Effective Judicial Protection in EU Law*, presentation at ERA conference on national judicial protection in EU law, Paris, 15 and 16 February 2010.

Essakkili & Spijkerboer 2005

S. Essakkili & T. Spijkerboer, *Marginal Judicial Review in the Dutch Asylum Procedure*, Amsterdam: Vrije Universiteit 2005.

Fernhout 1990

R. Fernhout, *Erkenning en toelating als vluchteling in Nederland*, Deventer: Kluwer 1990.

Fitzpatrick & Szyszczak 1994

B. Fitzpatrick & E. Szyszczak, 'Remedies and Effective Judicial Protection in Community Law', *The Modern Law Review*, no. 3, 1994, pp. 434-441.

Franssen 2011

K.A.E. Franssen, *Tijdelijke bescherming van asielzoekers in de EU. Recht en praktijk in Duitsland, Nederland en het Verenigd Koninkrijk en richtlijn 2001/55/EG*, Den Haag: Boom Juridische uitgevers 2011.

Fritzsche 2010

A. Fritzche, 'Discretion, Scope of Judicial Review and Institutional Balance in European Law', *CMLR* 2010, 47, pp. 361-403.

Geertsema 2010

K.E. Geertsema, 'Het EHRM en de geloofwaardigheid van een asielrelaas: de zaak R.C. tegen Zweden', *Asiel- en Migrantenrecht* 2010, nr. 3, pp. 133-136.

Gerards et al. 2008

J.H. Gerards, A.W. Heringa, H.L. Janssen & J. van der Velde, *EVRM, Rechtspraak en Commentaar*, Den Haag: Sdu Uitgevers 2008.

Ghandi 1998

P.R. Ghandi, *The Human Rights Committeee and the Right of Individual Communication*, Dartmouth: Ashgate 1998.

Goodwin-Gill 1998

G. Goodwin-Gill, *The Refugee in International Law*, Clarendon: Oxford University Press 1998.

Goodwin-Gill& McAdam 2007

G. Goodwin Gill& J. McAdam, *The Refugee in International Law*, Oxford: Oxford University Press, 2007.

Gorlick 1999

B. Gorlick, 'The Convention and Committee against Torture: a complementary protection regime for refugees', *International Journal of Refugee Law* 1999, Vol. 11, nr. 3, pp. 479-495.

Grahl-Madsen 1963

A. Grahl-Madsen, *Commentary on the Refugee Convention 1951. Articles 2-11, 13-23, 24-30 & Schedule 31-37*, Geneva: UNHCR, Division of International Protection 1963.

Grahl-Madsen 1966-1972

A. Grahl-Madsen, *The Status of Refugees in International Law*, Volume I. *Refugee Character*, and Volume II. *Asylum, Entry and Sojourn*, Leiden: Sijthof 1972.

Groenendijk & Terlouw 2009

C.A. Groenendijk & A.B. Terlouw, *Tussen onafhankelijkheid en hiërarchie, de relatie tussen vreemdelingenrechters en de Raad van State, 2001-2007*, Den Haag: Sdu Uitgevers 2009.

Groenendijk 2011

C.A. Groenendijk, *The Charter of Fundamental Rights of the European Union,* Presentation at the Court of Amsterdam, 18 July 2011.

Guèvremont 2009

S.R.M.C.Guèvremont, *Vers un traitement equitable des étrangers extracommunautaires en séjour régulier*, Zutphen: Wöhrmann Print Service 2009.

Guild 2000

E. Guild, *European Community Law from a Migrant's Perspective*, The Hague-London-Boston: Kluwer Law International2000.

Guild & Harlow 2001

E. Guild & C. Harlow, *Implementing Amsterdam. Immigration and Asylum Rights in EC Law*, Oxford-Portland: Hart Publishing 2001.

Guild & Peers 2001

E. Guild & S. Peers, 'Deference or Defiance? The Court of Justice's Jurisdiction over Immigration and Asylum', in: E. Guild & C. Harlow, *Implementing Amsterdam. Immigration and Asylum Rights in EC Law*, Oxford-Portland: Hart Publishing 2001, pp. 267-289.

Guild & Garlick 2010

E. Guild & M. Garlick, 'Refugee Protection, Counter-terrorism and Exclusion in the European Union', *Refugee Survey Quarterly. Country reports, documentation, literature survey, reviews*, 2010, 29(4), pp. 63-82.

Guild 2011

E. Guild, *Asylum Seeker's Right to Free Legal Assistance and/or Representation in EU Law*, presentation for the 9th Conference of the International Association of Refugee Law Judges, Bled, 7-9 September 2011.

Hailbronner 2000

K. Hailbronner, *Immigration and Asylum Law and Policy of the EU*, The Hague: Kluwer Law International 2000.

Hailbronner 2010

K. Hailbronner, *EU Immigration and Asylum law, Commentary on EU Regulations and Directives*, München-Oxford: C.H. Beck-Hart-Nomos 2010.

Hammarberg 2008

T. Hammarberg, *Report by the Commissioner for Human Rights on his visit to the Netherlands21-25 September 2008*, CommDH(2009)2.

Hanski & Scheinin 2003

R. Hanski & M. Scheinin, *Leading cases of the Human Rights Committee*, Turku/Abo: Institute for Human Rights, Abo Akademi University 2003.

Hanski & Scheinin 2007

R. Hanski & M. Scheinin, *Leading cases of the Human Rights Committee*, Turku/Abo: Institute for Human Rights, Abo Akademi University 2007.

Harris, O' Boyle, Bates & Buckley 2009

D.J. Harris, M. O'Boyle, E.P. Bates & C.M. Buckley, *Law of the European Convention on Human Rights*, Oxford: Oxford University Press, 2009.

Hathaway 2005

J.C. Hathaway, *The Rights of Refugees under International Law*, Cambridge: Cambridge University Press 2005.

Hoeksma 1990

J.A. Hoeksma, *De menselijke maat, zienswijzen in asielzaken*, Nijmegen: Ars Aequi Libri 1990.

Horbach, Lefeber & Ribbelink 2007

N. Horbach, R. Lefeber & O. Ribbelink, *Handboek Internationaal Recht*, Den Haag: T.M.C. Asser Press 2007.

Ingelse 1999

C. Ingelse, *De rol van het Comité in de ontwikkeling van het VN-Verdrag tegen Foltering*, Maastricht: Thela Thesis 1999.

Ingelse 2000

C. Ingelse, 'The Committee against Torture: One Step Forward, One Step Back', *Netherlands Quarterly of Human Rights* 2000, 18, pp. 307-327.

Jacobs 2001

F.G. Jacobs, 'Human Rights in the European Union: the Role of the Court of Justice', *European Law Review*, 2001, p. 339 ff.

Jacobs Ovey & White 2006

F.G. Jacobs, C. Ovey & R. White, *The European Convention on Human Rights,* Oxford: Oxford University Press 2006.

Jans, De Lange, Prechal & Widdershoven 2007

    J. Jans, R. de Lange, S. Prechal & R. Widdershoven, *Europeanisation of Public Law (study on the influence of European law on national administrative law)*, Groningen: Europa Law Publishing 2007.

De Jong 2000

    C.D.de Jong,'Harmonisation of Asylum and Immigration Policies; the long and winding road from Amsterdam via Vienna to Tampere', in: P.J. van Krieken (ed.), *The Asylum Acquis Handbook, the foundation for a common European Asylum Policy*, The Hague: Asser Press 2000, pp. 21-37.

Joseph, Schultz & Castan 2005

    S. Joseph, J. Schultz & M. Castan, *The International Covenant on Civil and Political Rights, cases, material and commentary*, second edition, Oxford: Oxford University Press 2005.

Joseph, Mitchell, Gyorki & Benninger-Budel 2006

    S. Joseph, K. Mitchell, L. Gyorki & C. Benninger-Budel, *A Handbook on the Individual Complaints Procedures of the UN Treaty Bodies*, World Organisation against Torture 2006.

Julien-Lafierre, Labayle & Edström 2005

    F. Julien-Lafierre, H. Labayle & O. Edström (eds), *The European Immigration and Asylum Policy: Critical Assessment five years after the Amsterdam Treaty*, Brussels: Bruylant 2005.

Kempees 1996

    P. Kempees, *A Systematic Guide to the Case Law of the European Convention on Human Rights 1960-1994, Vol. I*, The Hague: Martinus Nijhoff Publishers 1996.

Kempees 1996

    P. Kempees, *A Systematic Guide to the Case Law of the European Convention on Human Rights 1960-1994, Vol. II*, The Hague: Martinus Nijhoff Publishers 1996.

Kempees 1998

    P. Kempees, *A Systematic Guide to the Case Law of the European Convention on Human Rights 1995-1996, Vol. III*, The Hague: Martinus Nijhoff Publishers 1998.

Kempees 2000

    P. Kempees, *A Systematic Guide to the Case Law of the European Convention on Human Rights 1995-1996, Vol. IV*, The Hague: Martinus Nijhoff Publishers1998.

Kjaerum 2010

    A. Kjaerum, 'The Treaty Body Complaint System, Expanding Protection against refoulement. A Survey of Recent Views by Treaty Bodies on Individual Complaints', *Human Rights Monitor Quarterly*, October 2010, pp. 27-32.

Van der Klaauw 2000

    J. van der Klaauw, 'The EU Asylum Acquis, history and context', in: P.J. van Krieken (ed.), *The Asylum Acquis Handbook, the foundation for a common European Asylum Policy*, The Hague: Asser Press 2000, pp. 9-21.

Kooijmans et al. 1987,

    P.H. Kooijmans e.a., *Asielzoekers en mensenrechten*, Leiden: Stichting NJCM boekerij 1987.

Van Krieken 2004

P.J. van Krieken, *The Consolidated Asylum and Migration Acquis, the EU Directives in an Expanded Europe*, The Hague: Asser Press 2004.

Lavenex 2001

S. Lavenex, *The Europeanisation of Refugee Policies; between human rights and internal security*, Burlington USA: Ashgate Publishing Company 2001.

Lawson 1999

R. Lawson, *Het EVRM en de Europese Gemeenschappen*, Europese Monografieën no. 61, The Hague: Kluwer 1999.

Lawson 2006,

R. Lawson, 'Terugblik op Straatsburg, Interview met mr. W.M.E. Thomassen', *NJCM-Bulletin*, jrg. 31, (2006), nr. 1, pp. 6-28.

Lubberdink 2009

H.G. Lubberdink, 'Toetsing van de feitenvaststelling door de vreemdelingenrechter' (Judicial review of the determination of the facts), *Migrantenrecht* 2, 2009, 53, pp. 53-55.

Malanczuk 1997

P. Malanczuk, *Akehurst's Modern Introduction to International Law*, New York: Routledge 1997.

Martens 2000

S.K. Martens, 'Het EHRM en de nationale rechter', *NJCM Bulletin* 25-2, 2000, pp. 753-760.

McAdam 2007

J. McAdam, *Complementary Protection in International Refugee Law*, Oxford: Oxford University Press, 2007.

McGoldrick 1996

D. McGoldrick, *The Human Rights Committee, its Role in the Development of the International Covenant on Civil and Political Rights*, Oxford: Clarendon Press 1996.

Mole 2007

N. Mole, *Asylum and the European Convention on Human Rights*, Council of Europe Publishing 2007.

Morijn 2011

J. Morijn, 'Het juridisch bindende handvest van de grondrechten van de Europese Unie: eerste ervaringen en openstaande vragen', *NJCM Bulletin* 2011, jrg. 36, nr. 1, pp. 45-62.

Mortelmans 2009

K. Mortelmans, 'Het Handvest van de grondrechten van de EU in de Europese en Nederlandse rechtspraak', in: T. Barkhuijsen et al. (red.), *Geschakeld recht*, Deventer: Kluwer 2009, pp. 379-397.

Myjer & Lawson 2000

E. Myjer & R. Lawson, *Vijftig jaar EVRM*, Leiden: Stichting NJCM Boekerij 2000.

Myjer 2008

E. Myjer, 'De dodelijke waarheid in vreemdelingenzaken', *Trema* 2008, nr. 10, pp. 487-492.

NJCM 1985

NJCM, *Rechter en mensenrechtenbeleid, 10 jaar NJCM, Verslag van het symposium ter gelegenheid van het tienjarig bestaan van het Nederlands Juristen Comite voor de Mensenrechten*, Leiden 1985.

Noll 2005

G. Noll, *Evidentiary assessment and the EU Qualification Directive, New Issues in Refugee Research*, Working Paper No. 117, UNHCR June 2005.

Nowak 1993

M. Nowak, *The UN Covenant on Civil and Political Rights, CCPR Commentary*, Kehl am Rhein: Engel 1993.

Nowak 1996

M. Nowak, 'UNCAT and the Prohibition of Refoulement', *Netherlands Quartely of Human Rights* 1996, nr. 4, pp. 435-437.

Nowak 2005

M. Nowak, *The UN Covenant on Civil and Political Rights, CCPR Commentary*, Kehl am Rhein: Engel 2005.

Nowak & McArthur 2008

M. Nowak & E. McArthur, *The United Nations Convention against Torture, A Commentary*, Oxford: Oxford University Press 2008.

Office of the United Nations High Commissioner for Human Rights 2005

Human Rights Fact Sheet No. 15 (rev 1): Civil and Political Rights: the Human Rights Committee, UNHCR 2005.

Office of the United Nations High Commissioner for Human Rights 2002

Human Rights Fact Sheet No. 4 (rev 1): Combating Torture, New York and Geneva: United Nations.

Office of the United Nations High Commissioner for Human Rights 2002

Human Rights Fact Sheet No. 17: The Committee against Torture, New York and Geneva: United Nations.

Office of the United Nations High Commissioner for Human Rights 2006

Human Rights Fact Sheet No. 20: Human Rights and Refugees, New York and Geneva: United Nations.

Office of the United Nations High Commissioner for Human Rights 2006

The Core International Human Rights Treaties, New York and Geneva: United Nations 2006.

Okafor & Okoronkwo 2003

O.C. Okafor & P.L.Okoronkwo, 'Reconfiguring Non-refoulement? The Suresh Decision, "Security Relativism", and the International Human Rights Imperative', *International Journal of Refugee Law*, 2003, vol. 15 no 1, pp. 30-67.

O'Keeffe 2000

D. O'Keeffe, *Judicial Review in European Union Law*, The Hague: Kluwer Law International 2000.

Van Ooik & Wessel 2009

R.H. van Ooik & R.A. Wessel (red.), *De Europese Unie na het Verdrag van Lissabon*, Europa in Beeld 6, Deventer: Kluwer 2009.

Orakhelashvili 2003

A. Orakhelashvili, 'Restrictive interpretation of Human Rights Treaties in the Recent Jurisprudence of the European Court of Human Rights', *EJIL* 2003, pp. 529-568.

Overkleeft-Verburg 2005

G. Overkleeft-Verburg, *Het Handvest van de Grondrechten in de rechtspraak van het Hof van Justitie*, 2005, at: www.overkleeft-verburg.nl.

Pahladsingh & Van Roosmalen 2011

A. Pahladsingh & H.J.Th.M. van Roosmalen, 'Het Handvest van de Grondrechten van de Europese Unie één jaar juridisch bindend: rechtspraak in kaart', *NtEr*, maart 2011, nr. 2, pp. 54-61.

Peers 2001

S. Peers, 'Immigration, Asylum and the European Union Charter of Fundamental Rights', *European Journal of Migration and Law* 2001, 141, p. 141-169.

Peers & Ward 2004

S. Peers & A. Ward, *The EU Charter of Fundamental Rights*, Oxford and Portland Oregon: Hart Publishing 2004.

Peers 2005-I

S. Peers, 'Key Legislative Developments on Migration in the European Union', *European Journal of Migration and Law* (7), 2005, pp. 87-118.

Peers 2005-II

S. Peers, 'The Future of the EU judicial system and EC immigration and asylum law', *European Journal of Migration and Law*(3), 2005, pp. 263-274.

Peers & Rogers 2006

S. Peers & N. Rogers (eds), *EU Immigration and Asylum Law: Text and Commentary*, Leiden-Boston: Martinus Nijhoff Publishers 2006.

Van der Poel 1998

M. van der Poel, 'Uitzetting van Vreemdelingen, Straatsburg en de artikelen 3 en 8 EVRM (*Dalia v. France)*', *NJCM Bulletin* 1998, nr. 23-5, pp. 611-621.

Pollet 1994

K. Pollet, *Asielrecht in de Europese Unie, ontwikkeling van een harmonisatieproces*, Antwerpen: Maklu Uitgevers 1994.

Pollet 2011

K. Pollet, 'De Definitierichtlijn en het Vluchtelingenverdrag, bedenkingen bij een Europees Experiment', *A&MR* 2011, nr. 5/6, pp. 216-224.

Reneman 2007

M. Reneman, 'Effectieve rechtsbescherming, schorsende werking, artikel 13 EVRM, comment on the ECtHR Judgment in the case of *Gebremedhin vs France*', *NAV*, Nr. 4 September 2007, pp. 288-296.

Reneman 2007

A.M.Reneman, 'Procedurerichtlijn biedt kansen, over effectieve rechtsbescherming in asielprocedures', *NAV*, nr. 5, October 2007, pp. 328-341.

Reneman 2008

A.M. Reneman, *Access to an effective remedy in European asylum procedures*, on Amsterdam Law Forum, Vrije Universiteit Amsterdam. Available at: <http://ojs.ubvu.vu.nl/ alf/article/view/42/50.

Reneman 2012

A.M. Reneman, *EU asylum procedures and the right to an effective remedy*, Oegstgeest: Proefschriftmaken.nl – Uitgeverij BOXPress.

Rieter 2010

E. Rieter, *Preventing Irreparable Harm: Provisional Measures in International Human Rights Adjudication*, Antwerpen: Intersentia 2010.

Rietiker 2010

D. Rietiker, 'The Principle of "Effectiveness" in the Recent Jurisprudence of the European Court of Human Rights: Its Different Dimensions and Its Consistency with Public International Law – No Need for the Concept of Treaty Sui Generis', *Nordic Journal of International Law*, 79, 2010, pp. 245-277.

Robertson 1975-1985

A.H. Robertson, *Collected edition of the 'travaux préparatoires' of the European Convention on Human Rights*, The Hague: Martinus Nijhoff 1975-1985.

Van Rooij 2004

J. van Rooij, *Asylum Procedure versus Human Rights*, Amsterdam: Vrije Universiteit 2004.

Schokkenbroek 2006

J. Schokkenbroek, 'The Supervisory Function of the Secretary General of the Council of Europe', in: P. van Dijk & F. van Hoof et al. (eds), *Theory and Practice of the European Convention on Human Rights*, Antwerpen: Intersentia 2006, pp. 323-332.

Schuurmans 2007

Y.E. Schuurmans, 'De toetsing van de feitenvaststelling in Europees perspectief', in: T. Barkhuysen, W. Den Ouden, E. Steyger, *Europees recht effectueren: Algemeen bestuursrecht als instrument voor de effectieve uitvoering van EU recht*, Alphen aan den Rijn: Kluwer 2007.

Shah 2005

P. Shah (ed.), *The Challenge of Asylum to Legal Systems*, London: Routledge Cavendish 2005.

Simon 1992

H.J. Simon, 'Tamils en groepsvervolging (*Vilvarajah vs. UK*)', *NJCM Bulletin* 1992, 17-5, pp. 567-572.

Sitaropoulos 2008

N. Sitaropoulos, *Supervising execution of the European Court of Human Rights' judgments concerning minorities – the Committee of Ministers' potentials and constraints*, paper at ssrn.com, id. 1968186, code 1153.

Slingenberg 2006

L. Slingenberg, *Dutch Accelerated Asylum Procedure in Light of the European Convention on Human Rights*, Amsterdam: Vrije Universiteit 2006.

Spijkerboer 2003

T. Spijkerboer, 'De mensenrechtentoets door de vreemdelingenrechter, het trechtermodel in asielzaken', *NJCM Bulletin* 2003, 28-5, pp. 549-562.

Spijkerboer & Vermeulen 1995

T.P. Spijkerboer & B.P. Vermeulen, *Vluchtelingenrecht*, Utrecht: Nederlands Centrum Buitenlanders 1995.

Spijkerboer & Vermeulen 2005

T.P. Spijkerboer & B.P. Vermeulen, *Vluchtelingenrecht*, Nijmegen: Ars Aequi Libri 2005.

Spijkerboer 2008

T. Spijkerboer, 'Chahal bevestigd: uitzettingsverbod artikel 3 EVRM fundamenteel en absoluut (*Saadi vs. Italy*)', *NJCM Bulletin* 2008, 33-7, pp. 1005-1017.

Spijkerboer 2009

T. Spijkerboer, 'Subsidiarity and Arguability: the European Court of Human Rights' Case Law on Judicial Review in Asylum Cases', *International Journal of Refugee Law*, Vol. 21, no. 1, March 2009, pp. 48-74.

Spijkerboer 2010

T. Spijkerboer, comment to the judgment of the ECtHR in the case of Klein v. Russia, *JV* 02-06-2010, afl. 8.

Spronken 2010

T.N.B.M. Spronken, 'De Weg naar Rome gaat ook via Lissabon, een essay over Europese rechtsbecherming in strafzaken', *Strafblad* 2010, pp. 63-69.

Steiner, Alston & Goodman 2008

H.J. Steiner, P. Alston & R. Goodman, *International Human Rights in Context, law, politics and morals*, Oxford: Oxford University Press 2008.

Steiner & Woods 2009

J. Steiner & L. Woods, *EU Law*, Oxford: Oxford University Press 2009.

Steenbergen 2000

H. Steenbergen, '50 jaar EVRM en het Nederlandse Immigratierecht', *NJCM Bulletin* 2000, 25-I, pp. 452-459.

Swart 1987

A.H.J. Swart, 'Mensenrechten en de Nederlandse asielprocedure', in: Th. van Boven, *Asielzoekers en mensenrechten*, Leiden: NJCM-boekerij 1987, pp. 20-47.

Strik 2011

T. Strik, 'Overnameovereenkomsten met transitlanden: een bedreiging voor de mensenrechten?', *A&MR* 2011, nr. 5/6, pp. 248-255.

Tahbaz & Takkenberg 1989

C.C. Tahbaz & A. Takkenberg, *The Collected Travaux Préparatoires of the 1951 Geneva Convention relating to the Status of Refugees*, Amsterdam:Dutch Refugee Council under auspices of the European Legal Network on Asylum 1989.

Takahashi 2001

S. Takahashi, *Effective monitoring of the Refugee Convention*, paper 2001, http://www.isanet.org/archive/takahashi.html.

Terlouw 2011

A. Terlouw, 'Alles is tijdelijk: tijdelijkheid en de ontkenning van artikel 34 Vluchtelingenverdrag', *A&MR* 2011, nr. 5/6, pp. 224-232.

Tiemersma 2006

H. Tiemersma, 'De rol van medische informatie, medische informatie in de asielprocedure: de discussie beweegt, de praktijk is weerbarstig', in: *Nieuwsbrief Asiel en Vluchtelingenrecht (NAV)*, nr. 1, februari 2006, pp. 4-17.

Tomuschat 2003

C. Tomuschat, *Human Rights, between Idealism and Realism*, Oxford: Oxford University Press 2003.

Toner 2007

H. Toner, 'Article 8 ECHR – Full judicial scrutiny?', *Migrantenrecht* 1+2, 2007, pp. 177-182.

Tridimas 2006

T. Tridimas, *The General Principles of Community Law*, Oxford: Oxford University Press 2006.

Trstenjak & Beysen 2011

V. Trstenjak & E. Beysen, 'European Consumer Protection Law: Curia Semper Dabit Remedium?', *Common Market Law Review* 2011, 48, pp. 95-124.

Türk 2002

V. Türk, *UNHCR's supervisory responsibility, New Issues in Refugee Research*, Working Paper No. 67, UNHCR 2002; http://www.unhcr.org/3dae74b74.pdf.

UNHCR 1979

UNHCR, *Handbook on procedures and criteria for determining refugee status*, Geneva 1979.

UNHCR 1998

UNHCR, *Note on Burden and Standard of Proof in Refugee Claims*, 16 December 1998, available at: http://www.unhcr.org/refworld/docid/3ae6b3338.html.

UNHCR 1999

UNHCR, *Towards common standards on asylum procedures: Reflections by UNHCR on some of the issues raised in the Working Document prepared by the European Commission*, Geneva: UNHCR 1999.

UNHCR 2000

UNHCR, *Submission to the Strasbourg Court in the Case of T.I. v. the UK*, Geneva: UNHCR 2000, at: http://www.unhcr.org/refworld/pdfid/42f7737c4.pdf.

UNHCR 2001

UNHCR, *Global Consultations on International Protection/Third Track: Asylum Processes (Fair and Efficient Asylum Procedures)*, 31 May 2001, EC/GC/01/12, available at: www.unhcr.org/refworld/docid/3b36f2fca.html.

UNHCR 2002

UNHCR, Submission to the Strasbourg Court in the case of K.K.C. v. the Netherlands, Geneva: UNHCR, November 2002, available at: http://www.unhcr.org/refworld/pdfid/42f774674.pdf.

UNHCR 2003

UNHCR, *Implementation of the Aliens Act 2000 in the Netherlands, UNHCR's Observations and Recommendations*, available at: http://www.unhcr.org/refworld/docid/410f83f44.html.

UNHCR 2003

UNHCR, *Guidelines on International Protection No. 5: Application of the Exclusion Clauses: Article 1F of the 1951 Convention relating to the Status of Refugees* (HCR/GIP/03/05) 4 September 2003

UNHCR 2005-I
UNHCR, *Annotated Comments on the EC Council Directive 2004/83/EC of 29 April 2004 on Minimum Standards for the Qualification and Status of Third Country Nationals or Stateless Persons as Refugees or as Persons who otherwise need International Protection and the Content of the Protection granted*, Geneva: UNHCR, January 2005.

UNHCR 2005-II
UNHCR, *Provisional Comments on the Proposal for a Council Directive on Minimum Standards on Procedures in Member States for Granting and Withdrawing Refugee Status, 10 February 2005*, available at: www.unhcr.org/refworld/docid/42492b302.html.

UNHCR 2005-III
UNHCR, *Statement on Fair and Efficient Asylum Procedures: A Non-Exhaustive Overview of Applicable International Standards, 2 September 2005*, available at: www.unhcr.org/refworld/docid/432ae9204.html.

UNHCR 2005-IV
UNHCR, *Submission in the Case of Mir Isfahani v. the Netherlands*, Geneva: UNHCR 2005, available at: http://www.unhcr.org/refworld/docid/454f5e484.html.

UNHCR 2007
UNHCR, *Eligibility Guidelines for Assessing the International Protection Needs of Iraqi Asylum-seekers*, Geneva: UNHCR 2007, available at: www.unhcr.org/refworld/docid/46deb05557.html, visited 23 August 2011.

UNHCR 2007-II
UNHCR, *Submission to the Strasbourg Court in the case of Saadi v. the UK*, March 2007, available at: http://www.unhcr.org/refworld/pdfid/47c520722.pdf.

UNHCR 2001-2009
UNHCR,*Manual on Refugee Protection and the ECHR*, available at: http://www.unhcr.org.

UNHCR 2009-I
UNHCR, *Comments on the European Commission's proposal for a Directive of the European Parliament and of the Council on minimum standards on procedures in Member States for granting and withdrawing international protection* (COM(2009)554), 21 October 2009, available at: http://www.unhcr.org/refworld/pdfid/4c63ebd32.pdf.

UNHCR 2009-II
UNHCR, *Submission to the Strasbourg Court in the case of Abdolkhani and Karimnia v. Turkey*, January 2009, available at:
http://www.unhcr.org/refworld/docid/4991ad9f2.html, visited 23 August 2011.

UNHCR 2010-I
UNHCR, *Improving Asylum Procedures, Comparative Analysis and Recommendations for Law and Practice, a UNHCR research project on the application of key provisions of the Asylum Procedures Directive in selected Member States*, Brussels, March 2010, at: http://www.unhcr.org/cgi-bin/texis/vtx/refworld/rwmain?docid=4bab55752.

UNHCR 2010-II
UNHCR, *Statement on the right to an effective remedy in relation to accelerated asylum procedures, issued in the context of the preliminary ruling reference to the Court of Justice of the European Union from the Luxembourg Administrative Tribunal regarding the interpretation of Article 39, Asylum Procedures Directive, and Articles 6 and 13 ECHR*, available at: http://www.unhcr.org/refworld/docid/4bf67fa12.html.

UNHCR 2010-III

UNHCR, *The Eligibility Guidelines for Assessing the International Protection Needs of Asylum-seekers from Somalia*, 2010, available at:
http://www.unhcr.org/refworld/pdfid/4be3b9142.pdf.

UNHCR 2010-IV

UNHCR, *Submission to the Strasbourg Court in the case of M.S.S. v. Belgium and Greece*, June 2010, available at: http://www.unhcr.org/refworld/docid/4c19e7512.html.

UNHCR 2011

UNHCR, *Submission to the Strasbourg Court in the case of Hirsi and others v. Italy*, Geneva March 2011, available at:
http://www.unhcr.org/refworld/docid/4d92d2c22.html.

Vermeulen 1990

B.P. Vermeulen, 'Artikel 3 EVRM in verband met asielzoekers en vluchtelingen', *NAV* 1990, pp. 186-199.

Vermeulen 2000

B.P. Vermeulen, 'Uitputtende uitputting van rechtsmiddelen in asielzaken? (Bahaddar vs. Netherlands)', *NJCM Bulletin* 2000, 25-1, pp. 245.

Wakefield 2007

J. Wakefield, *The right to good administration*, Alphen aan de Rijn: Kluwer Law International 2007 (chapter on Charter, pp. 50 onwards)

Ward 2007

A. Ward, *Judicial Review and the Rights of Private Parties in EU Law*, Oxford: Oxford University Press 2007 (particularly pp. 150-210).

Weis 1995

P. Weis, *The Refugee Convention 1951, The Travaux Préparatoires Analysed*, Cambridge: Cambridge University Press, 1995.

Weissbrodt 2001

D. Weissbrodt, *The right to a fair trial under the Universal Declaration of human rights and the International Covenant on Civil and Political Rights*, Den Haag: Nijhoff 2001.

Werd 2003

M. Werd, 'Dilemma's van Mensenrechtenbescherming', *NJCM Bulletin*2003, 28-5, pp. 563-573.

Westerveen 2011

G. Westerveen, 'Vluchtelingenverdrag en EVRM', *A&MR* 2011, nr. 5/6, pp. 212-216.

Wijnkoop 2011

M. Wijnkoop, 'External processing: de deur uit! Delen, niet afschuiven van verantwoordelijkheid voor vluchtelingenbescherming', *A&MR* 2011, nr. 5/6, pp. 232-242.

Wouters 2009

C.W.Wouters, *International Legal Standards for the Protection from Refoulement, a legal analysis of the prohibitions on refoulement contained in the Refugee Convention, the European Convention on Human Rights, the International Covenant on Civil and Political Rights and the Convention against Torture*, Antwerp-Oxford-Portland: Intersentia 2009.

Zwaan 2003

  K. Zwaan, *Veilig derde land. De exceptie van het veilig derde land in het Nederlands asiel-recht,* Nijmegen: GNI 2003.

Zwaan 2005

  K. Zwaan, *UNHCR and the European Asylum Law*, Nijmegen: Wolf Legal Publishers 2005.

Zwaan 2007

  K. Zwaan (ed.), *The Qualification Directive; Central Themes, Problem Issues and Implementation in Selected Member States*, Nijmegen: Wolf Legal Publishers 2007.

  Zwaan 2008

K. Zwaan (ed.), *The Procedures Directive; Central Themes, Problem Issues and Implementation in Selected Member States*, Nijmegen: Wolf Legal Publishers 2008.

International case law

International Court of Justice

- ICJ, Legal Consequences for States of the Continued Practice of South Africa in Namibia (South West Africa) Notwithstanding Security Council Resolution 276 (1970) (Advisory Opinion), 21 June 1971, ICJ Reports 1971, p.16.

ECtHR, judgments

title	date	Apl. no.
Neumeister v. Austria	27 June 1968	1936/63
Golder v. the UK	21 February 1975	4451/70
Engel and others v. the Netherlands	8 June1976	5100/71
		5101/71
		5102/71
		5354/72
		5370/72
Ireland v. the United Kingdom	18 January 1978	5310/71
Albert and Le Compte v. Belgium	10 February 1983	7299/75
		7496/76
W. v. the UK	8 July 1987	9749/82
Klass v. Germany	6 September 1987	5029/71
Schenk v. Switzerland	12 July 1988	10862/84
Soering v. the UK	7 July 1989	14038/88
Obermeier v. Austria	28 June 1990	11761/85
Cruz Varas and others v. Sweden	20 March 1991	15576/89
Vilvarajah and others v. the UK	30 October 1991	13163/87
		13164/87
		13165/87
		13447/87
		13448/87
Oerlemans v. the Netherlands	27 November 1991	12565/86
Ruiz-Mateos v. Spain	23 June 1993	12952/87
Zumtobel v. Austria	21 September 1993	12235/86
Kremzow v. Austria	21 September 1993	12350/86
Dombo Beheer B.V. v. the Netherlands	27 October 1993	14448/88
Van de Hurk v. the Netherlands	19 April 1994	16034/90
McMichael v. the United Kingdom	24 February 1995	16424/90
Fischer v. Austria	26 April 1995	16922/90
Schmautzer v. Austria	28 September 1995	15523/89
Procola v. Luxembourg	28 September 1995	14570/89
Bryan v. the United Kingdom	25 October 1995	19178/91
Vermeulen v. Belgium	20 February 1996	19075/91

Chahal v. the UK	15 November 1996	22414/93
Terra Woningen B.V. v. the Netherlands	28 November 1996	20641/92
Nsona v. the Netherlands	28 November 1996	23366/94
Ahmed v. Austria	17 December 1996	25964/94
De Haes and Gijsels v. Belgium	17 December 1996	20641/92
H.L.R. v. France	29 April 1997	24573/94
Paez v. Sweden	30 October 1997	29482/95
Bahaddar v. the Netherlands	19 February 1998	25894/94
Garcia Ruiz v. Spain	21 January 1999	30544/96
T. and V. v. the UK	16 December 1999	24724/94
Rowe and Davis v. the UK	16 February 2000	28901/95
Jabari v. Turkey	11 July 2000	40035/98
Elsholz v. Germany	13 July 2000	25735/94
Kudla v. Poland	26 October 2000	30210/96
Jane Smith v. the UK	18 January 2001	25154/94
Chapman v. the UK	18 January 2001	27238/95
Hilal v. the UK	6 March 2001	45276/99
Kress v. France	7 June 2001	39594/98
Morris v. the UK	26 February 2002	38784/97
Kingsley v. the United Kingdom	28 May 2002	35605/97
Wierzbicki v. Poland	18 June 2002	24541/94
Koskinas v. Greece	20 June 2002	47760/99
Al Nashif v. Bulgaria	20 June 2002	50963/99
Veeber v. Estonia	8 November 2002	37571/97
Salomonsson v. Sweden	12 November 2002	38978/97
Mamatkulov and Abdurasulovic	6 February 2003	46827/99
		46951/99
Chevrol v. France	13 February 2003	49636/99
Sommerfeld v. Germany	8 July 2003	31871/96
Slivenko v. Latvia	9 October 2003	48321/99
Thampibillai v. the Netherlands	17 February 2004	61350/00
Venkadajalasarma v. the Netherlands	17 February 2004	58510/00
Slimani v. France	27 July 2004	57671/00
Edwards and Lewis v. the United Kingdom	27 October 2004	39647/98
		40461/98
Mamatkulov and Askarov v. Turkey	4 February 2005	46827/99
		46951/99
Steel and Morris v. the UK	15 February 2005	68416/01
Shamayev and others v. Georgia and Russia	12 April 2005	36378/02
Muslim v. Turkey	26 April 2005	53566/99
Bosphorus Hava Yollari Turizm Ticaret Anonim Sirketi v. Ireland	30 June 2005	45036/98
Said v. Netherlands	5 July 2005	2345/02
N. v. Finland	26 July 2005	38885/02
Bader and Kanbor v. Sweden	8 November 2005	13284/04

Capital Bank AD v. Bulgaria	24 November 2005	49429/99
Lupsa v. Romania	8 June 2006	10337/04
D. and others v. Turkey	22 June 2006	24245/03
Jalloh v. Germany	11 July 2006	54810/00
Olaechea Cahuas v. Spain	10 August 2006	24668/03
Mayeka and Mitunga v. Belgium	12 October 2006	13178/03
Tsfayo v. the UK	14 November 2006	60860/00
Salah Sheekh v. the Netherlands	11 January 2007	1948/04
Gebremedhin v. France	26 April 2007	25389/05
Garabayev v. Russia	7 June 2007	38411/02
Sultani v. France	20 September 2007	45223/05
Stoll v. Switzerland	10 December 2007	69698/01
Mir Isfahani v. the Netherlands	31 January 2008	31252/03 (decision to strike the case out of the list)
Hussain v. Romania	14 February 2008	12338/02
Saadi v. Italy	28 February 2008	37201/06
Nnyanzi v. the UK	8 April 2008	21878/06
Ismoilov and others v. Russia	24 April 2008	2947/06
Ryabikin v. Russia	19 June 2008	8320/04
NA v. the UK	17 July 2008	25904/07
Soldatenko v. Ukraine	23 October 2008	2440/07
Muminov v. Russia	11 December 2008	42502/06
Y. v. Russia	4 December 2008	20113/07
F.H. v. Sweden	20 January 2009	32621/06
A. and others v. the UK	19 February 2009	3455/05
Svetlorusov v. Ukraine	12 March 2009	2929/05
Hamraoui v. Italy	24 March 2009	16201/07
Bouyahia v. Italy	24 March 2009	46792/06
Darraji v. Italy	24 March 2009	11549/05
Soltana v. Italy	24 March 2009	37336/06
Sellem v. Italy	5 May 2009	12584/08
Opuz v. Turkey	9 June 2009	33401/02
Abdolkhani and Karimnia v. Turkey	22 September 2009	30471/08
Kaboulov v. Ukraine	19 November 2009	41015/04
Daoudi v. France	3 December 2009	19576/08
Gurguchiani v. Spain	15 December 2009	16012/06
Z.S.N. v. Turkey	19 January 2010	21896/08
Baysakov v. Ukraine	18 February 2010	54131/08
Al-Saadoon and Mufdhi v. the United Kingdom	2 March 2010	61498/08
R.C. v. Sweden	9 March 2010	41827/07
Ayatollahi and Hosseinzadeh v. Turkey	23 March 2010	32971/98
Klein v. Russia	1 April 2010	24268/08
Tehrani and others v. Turkey	13 April 2010	32940/08

		41626/08
		43616/08
Charahili v. Turkey	13 April 2010	46605/07
Khodzhayev v. Russia	12 May 2010	52466/08
Khaydarov v. Russia	20 May 2010	21055/09
Mawaka v. the Netherlands	1 June 2010	29031/04
M.B. and others v. Turkey	15 June 2010	36009/08
S.H. v. the UK	15 June 2010	19956/06
Abdulazhon Isakov v. Russia	8 July 2010	14049/08
Yuldashev v. Russia	8 July 2010	1248/09
Dbouba v. Turkey	13 July 2010	15916/09
N. v. Sweden	20 July 2010	23505/09
A. v. the Netherlands	20 July 2010	4900/06
Ramzy v. the Netherlands	20 July 2010	25424/05
A.A. v. Greece	22 July 2010	12186/08
Shchukin and others v. Cyprus	29 July 2010	14030/03
Y.P. and L.P. v. France	2 September 2010	32476/06
Iskandarov v. Russia	23 September 2010	17185/05
Gaforov v. Russia	21 October 2010	25404/09
B.A. v. France	2 December 2010	14951/09
T.N. v. Denmark	20 January 2011	20594/08
T.N. and S.N. v. Denmark	20 January 2011	36517/08
S.S. and others v. Denmark	20 January 2011	54703/08
P.K. v. Denmark	20 January 2011	54705/08
N.S. v. Denmark	20 January 2011	58359/08
M.S.S. v. Belgium and Greece	21 January 2011	30696/09
Diallo v. the Czech Republic	23 June 2011	20493/07
Sufi and Elmi v. the United Kingdom	28 June 2011	8319/07
		11449/07
Auad v. Bulgaria	11 October 2011	46390/10
Husseini v. Sweden	13 October 2011	10611/09
-	-	48205/09
-	-	48839/09
-	-	8139/09
Bajsultanov v. Austria	12 June 2012	54131/10
		14499/09
Singh and Others v. Belgium	2 October 2012	33210/11

ECtHR, decisions

title	*date*	*Apl. no.*
Waldberg v. Turkey	6 September 1995	22909/93
Paez v. Sweden	18 April 1996	29482/95
M.A.R. v. the UK	17 January 1997	28038/95
Hatami v. Sweden	23 January 1997	32448/96
S.N. v. the Netherlands	4 May 1999	38088/97
T.I. v. the United Kingdom	7 March 2000	43844/98
Damla and others v. Germany	26 October 2000	61479/00
Solhan v. the Netherlands	16 January 2001	48784/99
Katani and others v. Germany	31 May 2001	67679/01
Amrollahi v. Denmark	28 June 2001	56811/00
Tekdemir v. the Netherlands	1 October 2002	49823/99
Ammari v. Sweden	22 October 2002	60959/00
Milovan Tomic v. UK	14 October 2003	17837/03
Florencia Alfonso and Maria Janete Antonio v. the Netherlands	8 July 2003	11005/03
Hida v. Denmark	19 February 2004	38025/02
Nasimi v. Sweden	16 March 2004	38865/02
F. v. the UK	22 June 2004	17341/03
Said v. the Netherlands	5 October 2004	2345/02
B. v. Sweden	26 October 2004	16578/03
M.H. Mawajedi Shikpohkt and A. Mahkamat Sholeh v. the Netherlands	27 January 2005	39349/03
Hussein Mossie v. Sweden	8 March 2005	15017/03
Gordyeyev v. Poland	3 May 2005	43369/98 51777/99
Ovdienko v. Finland	31 May 2005	1383/04
Matsiukhina and Matsiukhin v. Sweden	21 June 2005	31260/04
Bonger v. Netherlands	15 September 2005	10154/04
Hukic v. Sweden	27 September 2005	17416/05
Bello v. Sweden	17 January 2006	32213/04
Gomes v. Sweden	7 February 2006	34566/04
Jeltsujeva v. the Netherlands	1 June 2006	39858/04
Karim v. Sweden	4 July 2006	24171/05
Gebremedhin v. France	10 October 2006	25389/05
Ayegh v. Sweden	7 November 2006	4701/05
S.A. v. the Netherlands	12 December 2006	3049/06
Collins and Akaziebie v. Sweden	8 March 2007	23944/05
Novik v. Ukraine	3 March 2007	48068/06
Ryabikin v. Russia	10 April 2007	8320/04
Goncharova and Alekseytsev v. Sweden	3 May 2007	31246/06
Bagheri and Maliki v. the Netherlands	15 May 2007	30164/06
Achmadov and Bagurova v. Sweden	10 July 2007	34081/05
Mohammadi v. Turkey	30 August 2007	3373/06

M. v. Sweden	6 September 2007	22556/05
Elezaj and Others v. Sweden	20 September 2007	17654/05
Limoni and Others v. Sweden	4 October 2007	6576/05
Hakazimana v. Sweden	27 March 2008	37913/05
Ramzy v. the Netherlands	27 May 2008	25424/05
A.J. v. Sweden	8 July 2008	13508/07
K.R.S. v. UK	2 December 2008	32733/08
S.M. v. Sweden	10 February 2009	47683/08
Ghulami v. France	7 April 2009	45302/05
Quraishi v. Belgium	12 May 2009	6130/08
A.M. and others v. Sweden	16 June 2009	38813/08
Harutioenyan v. the Netherlands	1 September 2009	43700/07
I.N. v. Sweden	15 September 2009	1334/09
Panjeheighalelei v. Denmark	13 October 2009	11230/07
O. v. the Netherlands	17 November 2009	37755/06
Hokic and Hrustic v. Italy	1 December 2009	3449/05
E.N. v. Sweden	8 December 2009	15009/09
Ayatollahi and Hosseinzadeh v. Turkey	23 March 2010	32971/98
Miah v. the United Kingdom	27 April 2010	53080/07
Gashi and others v. Sweden	4 May 2010	61167/08
Al-Zawatia v. Sweden	22 June 2010	50068/08
Chentiev v. Slovakia	14 September 2010	51946/08
Joesoebov v. the Netherlands	2 November 2010	44719/06
N.M. and M.M. v. the United Kingdom	25 January 2011	38851/09
		39128/09
Izevbekhai and others v. Ireland	17 May 2011	43408/08
Afif v. the Netherlands	24 May 2011	60915/09

HRC, views

title	*date*	*no.*
Alberto Grille Motta v. Uruguay	29 July 1980	11/1977
Maroufidou v. Sweden	9 April 1981	8/1979
Delia Saldias de Lopez v. Uruguay	29 July 1981	52/1979
Violeta Setelich on behalf of her husband Raul Sendic Antonaccio v. Uruguay	28 October 1981	63/1979
Irene Bleier Lewenhoff and Rosa Valino de Bleier v. Uruguay	29 March 1982	30/1978
Miguel Angel Estrella v. Uruguay	23 March 1983	74/1980
J.R.T. and the W.G. Party v. Canada	6 April 1983	104/1981
Almeida de Quinteros v. Uruguay	21 July 1983	107/1981
Nina Muteba on behalf of Tshitenge Muteba v. Zaire	24 July 1984	124/1982
Ilda Thomas on behalf of her brother Hiber Conteris v. Uruguay	17 July 1985	139/1983

Felicia Gilboa de Reverdito on behalf of her niece Lucia Arzuada Gilboa v. Uruguay	1 November 1985	147/1983
Y.L. v. Canada	8 April 1986	112/1981
J. and others v. Canada	18 July 1986	118/1982
Lilo Miango v. Zaire	27 October 1987	194/1985
Joaquin Herrera Rubio v. Colombia	2 November 1987	161/1983
Portorreal v. Dominican Republic	5 November 1987	188/1984
V.M.R.B. v. Canada	18 July 1988	236/1987
Avellanal v. Peru	28 October 1988	202/1986
Muñoz Hermoza v. Peru	4 November 1988	203/1986
R.M. v. Finland	27 March 1989	301/1988
R.T. v. France	30 March 1989	162/1987
Morael v. France	28 July 1989	207/1986
Mario Inés Torres v. Finland	5 April 1990	291/1988
John Campbell v. Jamaica	30 March 1992	307/1988
Carlton Linton v. Jamaica	22 October 1992	255/1987
Michael Bailey v. Jamaica	12 May 1993	334/1988
Maurice Thomas v. Jamaica	19 October 1993	321/1988
Oló Bahamonde v. Equatorial Guinea	20 October 1993	468/1991
Isidore Kanana Tshiongo a Minanga v. Zaire	8 November 1993	366/1989
Kindler v. Canada	18 November 1993	470/1991
Chitat Ng v. Canada	7 January 1994	469/1991
Garcia Pons v. Spain	30 June 1994	454/1991
Hugo Rodriguez v. Uruguay	19 July 1994	322/1988
Casanovas v. France	19 July 1994	441/1090
Dwayne Hylton v. Jamaica	21 July 1994	407/1990
Mukong v. Cameroon	10 August 1994	458/1991
Länsman et al v. Finland	26 October 1994	511/1992
Cox v. Canada	9 December 1994	539/1993
Errol Sims v. Jamaica	3 April 1995	541/1993
Fei v. Colombia	4 April 1995	514/1992
Griffin v. Spain	4 April 1995	493/1992
Bautista v. Colombia	27 October 1995	563/1993
Agnès N'Goya v. Zaire	16 April 1996	542/1993
Basilio Laureano Atachahua v. Peru	16 April 1996	540/1993
Fuenzalida v. Ecuador	15 August 1996	480/1991
Stewart v. Canada	1 November 1996	538/1993
Faurisson v. France	8 November 1996	550/1993
Dwayne Hylton v. Canada	18 November 1996	600/1994
Williams Adu v. Canada	18 July 1997	654/1995
A.R.J. v. Australia	11 August 1997	692/1996
Vicente et al v. Colombia	19 August 1997	612/1995
G.T. v. Australia	4 December 1997	706/1996
Polay v. Peru	9 January 1998	577/1994

Johannes Vos v. the Netherlands	26 July 1999	786/1997
Gridin v. the Russian Federation	20 July 2000	770/1997
Carolina Teillier Arredondo, on behalf of her mother María Sybila Arredondo v. Peru	28 July 2000	688/1996
Jansen-Gielen v. the Netherlands	3 April 2001	846/1999
Anni Äärelä and Jouni Näkkäläjärvi v. Finland	7 November 2001	779/1997
C. v. Australia	13 November 2002	900/1999
Ngoc Si Truong v. Canada	5 May 2003	743/1997
Pastukhov v. Belarus	5 August 2003	814/1998
Judge v. Canada	13 August 2003	829/1998
Bakhtiyari and Bakhtiyari v. Australia	6 November 2003	1069/2002
Mansour Ahani v. Canada	15 June 2004	1051/2002
Everett v. Spain	9 July 2004	961/2000
Singarasa v. Sri Lanka	21 July 2004	1033/2001
Borzov v. Estonia	26 July 2004	1135/2002
Byahuranga v. Denmark	9 December 2004	1222/2003
Czernin v. Czech Republic	29 March 2005	823/1998
Daljit Singh v. Canada	30 March 2006	1315/2004
Dawood Khan v. Canada	10 August 2006	1302/2004
Alzery v. Sweden	10 November 2006	1416/2005
Jagjit Singh Bhullar v. Canada	13 November 2006	982/2001
Hamid Reza Taghi Khadje v. the Netherlands	15 November 2006	1438/2005
Taghi Khadje v. Netherlands	15 November 2006	1438/2005
Dranichnikov v. Australia	16 January 2007	1291/2004
P.K. v. Canada	3 April 2007	1234/2003
Dudko v. Australia	23 July 2007	1347/2005
Bianca Lilia Londoño Soto and others v. Australia	14 April 2008	1429/2005
A.C. acting on her own behalf and on behalf of her children v. the Netherlands	22 July 2008	1494/2006
Mahmoud Walid Nakrash and Liu Qifen v. Sweden	30 October 2008	1540/2007
Moses Solo Tarlue v. Canada	27 March 2009	1551/2007
Mehrez Ben Abde Hamida v. Canada	18 March 2010	1544/2007
Diene Kaba acting on her own behalf and on behalf of her children v. Canada	25 March 2010	1465/2006
Ernest Sigman Pillai and Laetecia Swenthi Joachimpillai on their own behalf and on behalf of their children v. Canada	25 March 2011	1763/2008

HRC, General Comments

- General Comment of the HRC No. 15 (1986)
- General Comment of the HRC No. 20 (1992)
- General Comment of the HRC No. 24 (1994)
- General Comment of the HRC No. 31 (2004)
- General Comment of the HRC No. 32 (2007)

HRC, Concluding Observations

- HRC, Concluding Observations on the Netherlands, 25 August 2009, UN doc. CCPR/C/NLD/CO/4

ComAT, decisions

title	date	no.
Halimi-Nedyibi v. Austria	30 November 1993	9/1991
Mutombo v. Switzerland	27 April 1994	13/1993
Khan v. Canada	15 November 1994	15/1994
Irene Ursoa Parot, on behalf of her brother, Henri Unai Parot, v. Spain	2 May 1995	006/1990
M.A. v. Canada	3 May 1995	22/1995
X. v. Spain	15 November 1995	23/1995
K.K.H. v. Canada	22 November 1995	35/1995
Alan v. Switzerland	8 May 1996	021/1995
Kisoki v. Sweden	8 May 1996	041/1996
X. v. the Netherlands	8 May 1996	036/1995
Muzonzo v. Sweden	8 May 1996	41/1996
Tala v. Sweden	15 November 1996	043/1996
Omer v. Greece	28 April 1997	040/1996
Paez v. Sweden	28 April 1997	039/1996
X. v. Switzerland	28 April 1997	27/1995
Mohamed v. Greece	28 April 1997	No. 40/1996
X. v. Switzerland	9 May 1997	38/1995
Aemei v. Switzerland	29 May 1997	34/1995
E.A. v. Switzerland	10 November 1997	028/1995
P.Q.L. v. Canada	17 November 1997	57/1996
R.K. v. Canada	20 November 1997	42/1996
X.Y. and Z. v. Sweden	6 May 1998	61/1996
I.A.O. v. Sweden	6 May 1998	065/1997
A.F. v. Sweden	8 May 1998	089/1997
Encarnación Blanco Abad v. Spain	14 May 1998	059/1996
G.R.B. v. Sweden	15 May 1998	83/1997
A.L.N. v. Switzerland	19 May 1998	90/1997

K.N. v. Switzerland	19 May 1998	94/1997
H.W.A. v. Switzerland	20 May 1998	48/1996
J.U.A. v. Switzerland	10 November 1998	100/1997
Ayas v. Sweden	12 November 1998	097/1997
A. v. Netherlands	13 November 1998	91/1997
Korban v. Sweden	16 November 1998	088/1997
Haydin v. Sweden	20 November 1998	101/1997
H.D. v. Switzerland	30 April 1999	112/1998
S.M.R. and M.M.R. v. Sweden	5 May 1999	103/1998
M.B.B. v. Sweden	5 May 1999	104/1998
N.P. v. Australia	6 May 1999	106/1998
A. v. the Netherlands	12 May 1999	124/1999
Elmi v. Australia	14 May 1999	120/1998
Arkauz v. France	9 November 1999	63/1997
M'Barek v. Tunisia	10 November 1999	060/1996
A.D. v. the Netherlands	12 November 1999	96/1997
K.M. v. Switzerland	16 November 1999	107/1998
G.T. v. Switzerland	16 November 1999	137/1999
P.S. v. Canada	18 November 1999	86/1997
Z.T. v. Norway	19 November 1999	127/1999
S.H. v. Norway	19 November 1999	121/1998
K.T. v. Switzerland	19 November 1999	118/1998
A.D. v. Netherlands	24 January 2000	96/1997
G.T. v. Switzerland	2 May 2000	137/1999
N.M. v. Switzerland	9 May 2000	116/1998
H.A.D. v. Switzerland	10 May 2000	126/1999
S.C. v. Denmark	10 May 2000	143/1999
L.O. v. Canada	19 May 2000	95/1997
T.P.S. v. Canada	4 September 2000	99/1997
V.X.N. and H.N. v. Sweden	2 September 2000	130/1999
		131/1999
A.M. v. Switzerland	14 November 2000	144/1999
Y.S. v. Switzerland	14 November 2000	147/1999
M.R.P. v. Switzerland	24 November 2000	122/1998
A.S. v. Sweden	15 February 2001	149/1999
M.K.O. v. the Netherlands	9 May 2001	134/1999
S.S. and S.A. v. the Netherlands	11 May 2001	142/1999
S.L. v. Sweden	11 May 2001	150/1999
Ristic v. Yugoslavia	11 May 2001	113/1998
S.V. v. Canada	15 May 2001	49/1996
Z.Z. v. Canada	15 May 2001	123/1998
X.Y. v. Switzerland	15 May 2001	128/1999
Y.S. v. Switzerland	15 May 2001	147/1999
M.S. v. Switzerland	13 November 2001	156/2000
H.O. v. Sweden	13 November 2001	178/2001
B.S. v. Canada	14 November 2001	166/2000

Dragan Dimitrijevic v. Serbia and Montenegro	24 November 2004	207/2002
Danilo Dimitrijevic v. Serbia and Montenegro	24 November 2004	172/2000
Falcon Rios v. Canada	17 December 2004	133/1999
Jovica Dimitrov v. Serbia and Montenegro	3 May 2005	171/2000
Ruben David v. Sweden	17 May 2005	220/2002
M.M.K. v. Sweden	18 May 2005	221/2002
Agiza v. Sweden	24 May 2005	233/2003
Zubair Elahi v. Switzerland	20 May 2005	222/2002
Brada v. France	24 May 2005	195/2002
T.A. v. Sweden	27 May 2005	226/2003
S.S.H. v. Switzerland	15 November 2005	254/2004
Slobodan and Ljiljana Nikolic, on their own behalf and on behalf of their son, N.N., v. Serbia and Montenegro	24 November 2005	174/2000
S.N.A.W. v. Switzerland	29 November 2005	231/2003
R.T. v. Switzerland	30 November 2005	242/2003
Dadar v. Canada	5 December 2005	258/2004
S.S.S. v. Canada	5 December 2005	245/2004
M.C.M.V.F. v. Sweden	12 December 2005	237/2003
M.S.H. v. Sweden	14 December 2005	235/2003
Aung v. Canada	15 May 2006	273/2005
Mehdi Zare v. Sweden	17 May 2006	256/2004
A.A.C. v. Sweden	16 November 2006	227/2003
M.N. v. Switzerland	22 November 2006	259/2004
V.L. v. Switzerland	20 November 2006	262/2005
N.Z.S. v. Sweden	29 November 2006	277/2005
S.P.A. v. Canada	6 December 2006	282/2005
A.A.C. v. Sweden 14 December 2006	227/2003	
El Rgeig v. Switzerland	22 January 2007	280/2005
C.T. and K.M. v. Sweden	22 January 2007	279/2005
E.V.I. v. Sweden	1 May 2007	296/2006
A.A. v. Switzerland	11 May 2007	268/2005
Tebourski v. France	11 May 2007	300/2006
E.R.K. and Y.K. v. Sweden	2 May 2007	270/2005 271/2005
Nadeem Ahmad Dar v. Norway	16 May 2007	149/2004
C.A.R.M. v. Canada	18 May 2007	298/2006
Pelit v. Azerbaijan	29 May 2007	281/2005
Ali Ben Salem v. Tunisia	7 November 2007	269/2005
Iya v. Switzerland	16 November 2007	299/2006
Sogi v. Canada	16 November 2007	297/2006
K.A., on her own behalf and on behalf of her husband, R.A., and their children,	21 November 2007	308/2006

ComAT, General Comments

- General Comment No. 1, 21 November 1997, A/53/44, Annex XI
- General Comment No. 2, 23 November 2007, CAT/C/GC/2

ComAT, Conclusions and Recommendations

- Conclusions and Recommendations regarding Finland, 21 June 2005, CAT/C/CR/34/FIN
- Conclusions and Recommendations regarding France, 3 April 2006, CAT/C/FRA/CO/3
- Conclusions and Recommendations regarding the Netherlands, 3 August 2007, CAT/C/NET/CO/4
- Conclusions and Recommendations regarding Norway of 5 February 2008, CAT/C/NOR/CO/5
- Conclusions and Recommendations regarding Latvia, 19 February 2008, CAT/C/LVA/CO/2,

CJEU, judgments

Van Gend en Loos	5 February 1963	C-26/62
Costa ENEL	15 juni 1964	C-6/64
Consten and Grundig v Commission	13 July 1966	C-56/64
		C-58/64
Stauder v. City of Ulm	12 November 1969	C-29/69
Internationale Handelsgesellschaft	17 December 1970	C-11/70
Nold	14 May 1974	C-4/73
Rutili	28 October 1975	C-36/75
Balkan Import/Export	22 January 1976	C-55/75
Rewe	16 December 1976	C-33/76
Pecastaing	5 March 1980	C-98/79
Santillo	22 May 1980	C-131/79
Express Dairy Foods	12 June 1980	C-130/79
Becker	19 January 1982	C-8/81
Øhrgaard and Delvaux v Commission	14 July 1983	C-9/82
Adoui and Cornuaille	18 May 1982	C-115/81
		C-116/81
Johnston	15 May 1986	C-222/84
Les Verts v. European Parliament	23 April 1986	C-294/83
Heylens	15 October 1987	C-222/86
Exécutif Régional Wallon and SA	8 March 1988	C-62/87
Glaverbel v. Commission		C-72/87
Factortame	19 June 1990	C-213/89
Dzodzi	18 October 1990	C-197/89
Vlassopoulou	7 May 1991	C-340/89
ERT v. DEP	18 June 1991	C-260/89
Emmott	25 July 1991	C-208/90
Detlef Nölle	22 October 1991	C-16/90
Oleificio Borelli SpA v. Commission of the EC	3 December 1992	C-97/91

Cimenteries CBR	18 December 1992	T-10/92
		T-12/92
		T-15/92
Matra v. Commission	15 June 1993	C-225/91
Fisscher	28 September 1994	C-128/93
Solvay SA v Commission	29 June 1995	T-30/91
Imperial Chemical Industries plc v Commission	29 June 1995	T-37/91
R v Secretary of State for the Home Department ex parte Gallagher	30 November 1995	C-175/94
Van Schijndel	14 December 1995	C-430/93
Peterbroeck	14 December 1995	C-312/93
FMC	8 February 1996	C-212/94
Dietz	24 October 1996	C-435/93
Radiom and Shingara	17 June 1997	C-65/95
		C-111/95
Dorsch Consult Ingenieurgesellschaft mbH	17 September 1997	C54/96
Grant	17 February 1998	C-249/96
Solred	5 March 1998	C-347/96
National Farmers' Union and Others	5 May 1998	C-157/96
Ministero Delle Finanze	15 September 1998	C-260/96
Edis v. Ministero Delle Finanze	15 September 1998	C-231/96
Levez	1 December 1998	C-326/96
Upjohn	21 January 1999	C-120/97
Gencor v Commission	25 March 1999	T 102/96
Kharalambos Dounias and Ipourgos Ikonomikon	3 February 2000	C-228/98
Océano Grupo Editorial and Salvat Editores	27 June 2000	C-240/98
		C-241/98
		C-242/98
		C-243/98
		C-244/98
Roquette Frères	28 November 2000	C-88/99
Siples	11 January 2001	C-226-99
Connolly v. Commission	6 March 2001	C-274/99
Commission v. Austria	27 November 2001	C-424/99
De Coster	29 November 2001	C-17/00
Max. mobil Telekommunikation Service GmbH	30 January 2002	T-54/99
MRAX	25 July 2002	C-459/99
Union de Pequenos Agricultores v. Council	25 July 2002	C-50/00 P
Jégo-Quéré et Cie SA v Commission of the European Communities	3 May 2002	T-177/01
Pfizer Animal Health SA	11 September 2002	T-13/99

Roquette Frères	22 October 2002	C-94/00
Codifis 2002	21 November 2002	C-473/00
Olazabal	26 November 2002	C-100/01
Universale Bau	12 December 2002	C-470/99
Santex	27 February 2003	C-327/00
Steffensen	10 April 2003	C-276/01
Eribrand	19 June 2003	C-467/01
P&O European Ferries (Vizcaya) SA	5 August 2003	T-116/01
and Diputacion Foral de Vizcaya v.		T-118/01
Commission		
Safalero	11 September 2003	C-13/01
Köbler	30 September 2003	C-224/01
Evans	4 December 2003	C-63/01
Orfanopoulos and Oliveiri	29 April 2004	C-482/01
		C-493/01
Italy v. Commission	29 April 2004	C-372/97
Omega	14 October 2004	C-36/02
Cetinkaya	11 November 2004	C-467/02
Panayotova	16 November 2004	C-327/02
Tetra Laval v. Commission	15 February 2005	C-12/03
Dörr and Unal	2 June 2005	C-136/03
HLH Warenvertrieb	9 June 2005	C-299/03
		C-316/03
		C-318/03
Pupino	16 June 2005	C-105/03
Ahmed Ali Yusuf	21 September 2005	T-306/01
Schmitz-Gotha Fahrzeugwerke GmbH	6 April 2006	T-17/03
v. Commission		
European Parliament v. Council	27 June 2006	C-540/03
Manfredi and others	13 July 2006	C-295/04
		C-298/04
Laboratoires Boiron SA	7 September 2006	C-526/04
Graham J. Wilson	19 September 2006	C-506/04
Mostaza Claro	26 October 2006	C-168/05
City Motors Group	18 January 2007	C-421/05
PKK and KNK v Council	18 January 2007	C-229/05
BVBA Management Training and	15 February 2007	C-239/05
Consultancy		
Unibet	13 March 2007	C-432/05
Commission v. Greece	7 June 2007	C-156/04
Alrosa Company Ltd v Commission of	11 July 2007	T-170/06
the European Communities		
Rampion and Godard	4 October 2007	C-429/05
Spain v. Lenzing	22 November 2007	C-525/04
Productores de Música de Espana	29 January 2008	C-275/06
(Promusicae)		

Tele2 Telecommunication	21 February 2008	C-426/05
Impact	15 April 2008	C-268/06
Arcor AG & Co. KG	24 April 2008	C-55/06
Parliament v. Council	6 May 2008	C-133/06
Metock and others	28 July 2008	C-127/08
Kadi & Al Barakaat v. Council of the EU	3 September 2008	C-402/05
György Katz	9 October 2008	C-404/07
People's Modjahedin Organization of Iran	4 December 2008	T-284/08
Altun	18 December 2008	C-337/07
Société Régie Networks v. Direction de contrôle fiscal Rhône-Alpes Bourgogne	22 December 2008	C-333/07
Petrosian and others	29 January 2009	C-19/08
Elgafaji	17 February 2009	C-465/07
Pannon GSM	4 June 2009	C-243/08
Qualcomm Wireless Business Solutions Europe BV v Commission	19 June 2009	T-48/04
Der Grüne Punkt DSD GmbH	16 July 2009	C-385/07
Pontin	29 October 2009	C-63/08
Rodriguez Mayor	10 December 2009	C-323/08
Martín Martín	17 December 2009	C-227/08
Kücükdeveci	19 January 2010	C-555/07
Abdulla and others	2 March 2010	C-175/08
		C-176/08
		C 178/08
		C 179/08
Rottmann	2 March 2010	C-135/08
Chakroun	4 March 2010	C-578/08
Alassini	18 March 2010	C 317/08
		C 318/08
		C 319/08
		C 320/08
Bolbol	17 June 2010	C-31/09
Knauf Gips v. Commission	1 July 2010	C-407/08
J. McB	5 October 2010	C-400/10 PPU
Fuss	14 October 2010	C-243/09
Volker	9 November 2010	C-92/09
		C-93/09
Schecke	9 November 2010	C-92/09
		C-93/09
B and D	9 November 2010	C-57/09
		C-101/09
Tsakouridis	23 November 2010	C-145/09
Toprak and Oguz	9 December 2010	C-300/09
		C-301/09

Index

Curriculum Vitae

Dana Baldinger was born on 7 January 1969 in Amsterdam. She attended the Copernicus College in Hoorn between 1981 and 1987. She obtained a master's degree in Russian and English in 1992 and a master's degree in Law in 1999 at the University of Amsterdam. While studying Law she worked as an interpreter, protocol officer and, subsequently, legal officer at the European Headquarters of American Telephone and Telegraph (AT&T), since 1996 Lucent Technologies, a multinational company manufacturing and supplying telecommunications equipment throughout the world.

Between 2001 and 2005 she attended the vocational training scheme for the judiciary, a specialised programme in the Netherlands which prepares Law graduates for the job of a judge or public prosecutor through a combination of courses and practical work. As a judge-trainee she was stationed at the District Court of Alkmaar and the District Court of The Hague. She was appointed as a judge at the District Court of Amsterdam in 2006, where she has worked as a judge ever since, in the field of administrative law, including asylum law, and criminal law. Between 2007 and 2010 she combined her judicial work with teaching at the Dutch Training Institute for the Judiciary and with membership of the board of editors of *Jurisprudentie Vreemdelingenrecht* (Journal for migration and asylum law). Between 2007 and 2013, she worked on this PhD research next to her judicial work. She is a member of the International Association of Refugee Law Judges (IARLJ). Dana is married and has two sons.

13W09550/ T3/ 9789058509529